W9-AVB-401

# Contents

# List of Tables

# About the Author

**Bernice Simone Elger** is Professor at the Center of Legal Medicine (Unit for Health Law and Medical Ethics), University of Geneva, Switzerland.

# Foreword

There are numerous biobanks all over the world. They have been created and are maintained by government agencies, individual researchers and private concerns. They hold biological materials, data derived from these materials, as well as scans and images of the parts and tissues of individuals. These materials were collected for a variety of purposes.

Individual researchers interested in a particular disease or condition who have solicited their subjects to donate tissues or biological samples with varying degrees of informed consent have built some banks. Some biobanks were built decades ago by researchers who realized or, perhaps more accurately, hoped that a tissue bank of biological samples would one day prove of great value to future generations of scientists and patients. They collected samples of tumours and other materials under the presumption that these were waste materials for which no consent was required. For example, a search through decades-old frozen infant stool samples for which no valid consent was obtained recently yielded rich dividends for scientists from the National Institute of Allergy and Infectious Diseases (NIAID) helping to devise a test for the norovirus, a major cause of acute gastroenteritis outbreaks in people of all ages.

Other biobanks have been built up by public health agencies routinely sampling the blood of newborns for genetic testing at birth. Still others consist of banks collected for one specific purpose – forensic identification or to conduct research on a particular disease using a specific research protocol. Private entities have collected various forms of biological materials for study, to assist in facilitating various forms of organ, tissue and cell transplantation or to better understand pathological disease processes.

All of these biobanks have, in recent years, come to be seen as hugely valuable in the investigation of diseases, disorders, behavioural differences, anthropological and genealogical history and for many other purposes. While some rules have emerged to govern the collection and use of tissues, genetic information, biological samples and data linked to biological samples to create new biobanks the huge number of existing biobanks poses an enormous ethical challenge for researchers and society.

No policies exist to regulate the circumstances and conditions under which historical biobanks may be used for important retrospective research in situations where the data/specimens were collected in the past for clinical research or other purposes but, for which consent and authorization were not given to use in current and future studies. And even new tissue banks tend to be constructed using local rules and values.

The emergence of biobanks at a time when consent was rare and little thought given to who owns biological samples and any products made from them create a host of ethical and legal challenges, which form the core of this important book.

Bernice Elger understands the importance of having both rules and policies in place to govern prospective and retrospective biobanking. She stresses the need to have international consensus on both terminology and rules in order to insure that the true value of biobanks is captured. The benefit to society of allowing researchers access to existing biobanks despite problems with the ethics that governed their original formulation to conduct research in the emerging era of personalized medicine and the identification of genetic markers for risk factors for disease and disability rightly attracts her sharp analysis and insight.

If biobanking is to truly benefit humanity then we must insure that humanity has faith in how it is being conducted. To gain that trust far more clarity and consensus must be generated about issues such as the need for consent, the power of anonymization, the duty to warn contributors to biobanks of risks they may face or cures from which they may benefit, how to handle the collection and storage of materials from children and newborns, and the claims that persons, institutions and society may make upon the profits garnered by a fast approaching wave of new diagnostic tests and safer, more effective therapies aimed at specific genotypes and markers. There is much ethics, law and policy to be done and this book is the place to begin that work.

Arthur L. Caplan
University of Pennsylvania, USA

# Acknowledgements

I thank the Swiss National Science Foundation, as well as the Geneva International Academic Network, for their financial support for this work.

# Chapter 1
# Introduction

## General Background

In 2003, the human genome project was completed. The human genome was entirely sequenced (Little et al. 2003). A consortium of universities and pharmaceutical companies has been analysing genetic variations related to susceptibility to diseases (Greenhalgh 2005; Knudsen 2005). The challenge has not changed since 2003: it is to match genotypes against phenotype and survival in the real world (Radford 2003). Indeed, many common diseases are believed to result from a combination of defects in multiple genes and lifestyle, biographical or other environmental factors (Sensen 2005; Mikail 2008, 71–9). Environmental factors comprise lifestyle-related issues such as exercise, diet and smoking, reproductive and demographic aspects, as well as exposure to infectious agents, pollution or other environmental hazards. The technical possibilities of automated data analysis of DNA samples and their bioinformatic processing have developed dramatically over the last few years and are constantly being improved (Allore 2007). They provide important new possibilities for this type of medical research. The combination of health and genetic data on large populations promises to deliver new insights about interactions between genes and environmental factors (Burton et al. 2009). In addition, the new discipline of pharmacogenetics explores the genetic idiosyncrasies of drug metabolism in individual patients that explain why some develop severe side effects to useful medications and others do not (Ashcroft and Hedgecoe 2006). Advanced knowledge in these areas becomes a prerequisite for a preventive and curative 'personalized' medicine providing maximum efficacy with minimal side effects (Gurwitz, Lunshof and Altman 2006; Lunshof, Pirmohamed and Gurwitz 2006).

Scientists and the pharmaceutical industry place great hopes in prospective population-based genetic studies (Breithaupt 2001; Brand and Probst-Hensch 2007). These hopes explain the population databases 'boom' observed during the past years (Kaiser 2002a, 1158–61).[1] Various databases have been established or are planned, some on a national basis in Iceland, Estonia, Spain (Bosch 2004; Nys and Fobelets 2008), Croatia (Rudan et al. 2009), Taiwan (Fan, Lin and Lee 2008) and the UK (Barbour 2003; Elliott and Peakman 2008), others so far only including a county or region in Sweden (Austin, Harding and McElroy 2003a), the United States and Canada (Kaiser 2002a and 2002b). An example of a Swiss genetic

---

1 For a definition of the terms 'genetic database' and 'biobank', see below under the heading 'The Scope and Definitions'.

database that has been approved by the cantonal ethics commissions of Zurich, Bern, Lucerne and Basel in 2002 and 2003 is the Swiss Pediatric Oncology Group (SPOG) Tumor Bank (Grotzer et al. 2003, 180–84).

In its summary of the most pressing issues raised by advances in genetic research, the 2002 Report of the World Health Organization's (WHO) Advisory Committee on Health Research (ACHR) on *Genomics and World Health* states: 'The planned development of large-scale genetic [...] databases offers a series of hazards and ethical issues which have not been encountered before' (The Advisory Committee on Health Research [ACHR] 2002, 26).

Iceland's Act on a Health Sector Database (no. 139/1998) marks the beginning of a sustained and intense international debate about genetic databases. The political processes preceding these databases, as well as their particular legal and ethical arrangements, have stirred considerable controversies.[2] In particular, it is the protection of genetic data collected in databases which has emerged as a highly complex ethical issue that has still not been addressed in an internationally satisfying way (Arnason, Nordal and Arnason 2004; Monsour 2007).

Ethical issues become even more acute when genetic data are combined with information on individuals' health, lifestyle or genealogy, as is the case in major biobanks, for example, in the UK Biobank and the Icelandic Health Sector Database. The first combines genetic data with medical records and lifestyle information, and the second contains genetic data combined with medical records and genealogical information.

Ethical issues are sharpened in the international context (Benatar 2007; Capron et al. 2009), in particular when researchers and the populations being studied come from different cultural and socioeconomic backgrounds, such as in the Human Genome Diversity Project:

> The HGD Project is an international effort to collect, preserve, analyze, and make available genetic and ethnographic information from people all around the world. The Project expects that its work will lead to advances in understanding the biological development and the history of our species and, ultimately, in understanding and treating many diseases with genetic components. The Project will collect DNA samples and ethnographic information from communities throughout the world, thus correcting the current bias in research in human

---

2   The literature that deals with ethical, as well as anthropological (Pálsson 2007, 91–122), issues of biobanks started about 10 years ago (Greely 1999; Hauksson 1999, 707–8), and is still increasing steadily (Anderlik 2003; Austin, Harding and McElroy 2003b; Bauer, Taub and Parsi 2004; Cambon-Thomsen 2003 and 2004; Caulfied 2004b; Deschênes 2004; Maschke and Murray 2004; Deschênes and Sallee 2005; Martin Uranga et al. 2005; Lipworth 2005; Maschke 2005 and 2006; Elger 2006; Etzioni 2006; Hansson 2004, 2006 and 2009; Joly and Knoppers 2006; Abascal Alonso et al. 2007; Davis and Khoury 2007; Greely 2007; Zika et al. 2008; Gibbons 2009; Karlsen and Strand 2009; Skrikerud and Grov 2009; Solbakk, Holm and Hofmann 2009).

genetics toward people of European descent. The Project expects that the samples will be preserved in repositories where they will be available to all qualified researchers. The samples will be analyzed, and the results of these analyses will be widely available through computerized databases. The Project is currently in its early stages and is still largely being planned (NARC 1997).

The boom of population databases (Kaiser 2002a) has been followed by a boom of different guidelines. Several national and international organizations and committees have recently published guidelines and statements concerning genetic databases and population biobanks. These guidelines differ considerably in their recommendations as regards some ethical problems.[3]

The following are the most important issues of controversy in the ethical debate and need further attention:

- *Consent*
  Is the 'opt-out' model (which presumes consent to enter an individual's data into a database unless the individual has explicitly refused) a morally acceptable solution?

  Is individual consent a meaningful or sufficient concept when research will provide information on a family, group or population (including those who may have refused their consent, but are 'indirect' subjects of research)?

  Can individuals give a 'blanket consent' concerning the future use of their samples, or do they have to be recontacted and asked for their consent each time a new research project is planned or the nature of an ongoing research project is changed?
- *Confidentiality and access to the genetic databank*
  To what extent should databases be made secure enough to guarantee participants' privacy, for example, should the government/the police or other third parties have access?[4]

  Does society/the researcher/the company have a responsibility to avoid discriminatory effects (with regard to health insurance, employment, and so on) and to what extent?

  Should access to repositories/databases be universal for all researchers or should some researchers have privileged access?

---

3  For a list of different guidelines, see Table 3.1.

4  Data in the UK Biobank will be treated in accordance with the UK Data Protection Act 1998. This allows the government and/or the police access to the data 'for safeguarding national security', 'if requested by a Minister of the Crown', 'for the prevention or detection of a crime', and so on. The Human Genetics Commission (HGC) did not endorse the option to give an explicit statement to participants when consent is sought that police might have access to research data. HGC considered that it 'would seriously discourage participation' (Parliamentary Office of Science and Technology 2002, 4). See also the discussion in the scientific literature (Laurie 2002; Anonymous 2006).

Should databases and resulting research findings be commercially exploited?
- *Feedback to study participants*
Should participants be informed about the results of the genetic tests performed on their data, and under what conditions should such feedback take place (for example, availability of genetic counselling)?
Should test results be transmitted to a participant if they indicate risks for diseases of which the participant was not aware?
- *Benefit sharing*
Should benefits be shared and what is to be considered a fair way of sharing?

More and more countries in Europe and North America, as well as in other continents (Sleeboom-Faulkner 2009), are addressing the problems presented by genetic databases: some countries have passed laws specifically regulating biobanks, as is the case, for example, in Iceland (Act on a Health Sector Database 1998) or Estonia (Eesti geenivaramu 2004c),[5] and the list of countries considering and passing laws that contain sections explicitly addressing biobanks is steadily growing (Lindgren 2003; Elger 2006; Seoane and Da Rocha 2008); in others, like France (CCNE 2003),[6] Germany (Nationaler Ethikrat 2004),[7] Canada (CEST 2003),[8] the UK (HGC 2002) and the US (National Bioethics Advisory Commission [NBAC] 1999), major national bioethics advisory committees have issued reports and position statements. However, the Steering Committee for Bioethics' (CDBI) statement is still true today: '[L]egislative action in the field of research with human biological materials is still in its infancy both on a national and on an international level' (CDBI 2002b).[9]

On the international level a few relevant documents already exist, while others are currently in preparation. The Declaration of Helsinki, until its revision in 2008, was relevant only in a general sense, laying out the ethical basis for research using human subjects. In 2008, under the influence of the boom of new guidelines, Helsinki added a new paragraph (para. 25) on 'medical research using identifiable human material or data' (WMA 2008).

In its International Ethical Guidelines for Biomedical Research Involving Human Subjects (CIOMS 2002), which addresses general topics of research ethics,

---

5   The Human Genes Research Act 2001.

6   Comité Consultatif National d'Ethique pour les Sciences de la Vie et de la Santé. Avis No 77 2003.

7   Biobanken für die Forschung. Stellungnahme 2004.

8   Commission de l'Ethique de la Science et de la Technologie: Avis. Les enjeux éthiques des banques d'information génétique: pour un encadrement démocratique et responsable.

9   The CDBI draft explanatory report (CDBI 2002b) to the precursor version (CDBI 2002a) of the final recommendation of the Council of Europe (COE 2006) is mentioned occasionally because no explanatory report for the final recommendation exists for the time being and the report contains interesting detailed considerations that illuminate the reasoning that preceded the final text (COE 2006).

the Council for International Organizations of Medical Sciences provides some guidance on issues of confidentiality in genetic research (for example, guideline 18: Safeguarding confidentiality), but does not give a full account of the ethically problematic aspects of genetic databases.

The Council of Europe has issued an instrument on the use of human biological materials in biomedical research. This instrument contains general guidelines and more specific recommendations. It points out the necessity of practice guidelines, but the current document does not provide any.

Directive 95/46/EC of the European Parliament and the Council provides guidance on the protection of individuals with regard to the processing of personal data and on the free movement of such data, but it is not targeted towards genetic databases (European Parliament and the Council 1995). Its scope is limited to Europe.

Following a 2000 symposium, jointly sponsored with WHO in response to the debate on the Icelandic database, the World Medical Association (WMA) adopted in 2002 a Declaration on Ethical Considerations regarding Health Databases (WMA 2002). This document focuses on general principles of health databases and does not contain specific guidance for biobanks.

The UNESCO International Bioethics Committee has published an International Declaration on Human Genetic Data in 2003 (UNESCO 16 October 2003). The document provides a general normative framework in line with the human rights approach of UNESCO (Abbing 2004; Adalsteinsson 2004; Ten Have 2007), but does not elaborate on ethical problems arising at the technical and practical level.

The Proposed International Guidelines on Ethical Issues in Medical Genetics and Genetic Services of the WHO Human Genetics programme contains only a short chapter on genetic databases (WHO 1998). The WHO Handbook for Good Clinical Research Practice (WHO 2005) provides ethical background rather than targeted information on genetic databases and refers to future guidance: 'Due consideration should be given to obtaining consent for the collection and/or use of biological specimens, including future purposes. Guidance is developing in this area' (WHO 2005, 64). The WHO Handbook refers in this context to future guidance from CIOMS and the Council of Europe.

In comparison to the multitude of existing recommendations and guidelines, thorough ethical discussion in the literature is rather scarce, although the number of publications on selected issues concerning biobanks is growing steadily. As justification for their recommendations, many guidelines list a number of principles, including the 'classical' *prima facie* principles of autonomy, beneficence and justice (National Bioethics Advisory Commission [NBAC] 1999; UNESCO 16 October 2003), some very general principles that are used in different meanings, such as 'human dignity', and therefore judged useless by many ethicists,[10] and

---

10  See Macklin (2003, 1419–20, and 2004). See also other opinions (Brownsword 2003; Caulfield and Brownsword 2006) and the huge number of rapid responses to Macklin's article, especially Caplan (2003) and Capron (2003).

new principles believed to be particular to the era of genetics, such as 'genetic solidarity and altruism' (HGC 2002, 37).

In the guidelines, the reasons for the different balancing of principles and its underlying values are in general not explicitly discussed. Several endeavours to present an ethically argued position on some of the issues have formulated the ethical issues in terms of *morally legitimate interests* (Buchanan 1999; Hansson 2001; Elger and Mauron 2003). The underlying reasoning is that principles and values reflect (and rights serve to protect) morally legitimate interests which need to be balanced in a way acceptable to the individuals and groups concerned. Defending a proper balance of the chief legitimate interests seems to be more promising than balancing principles, because, first, it can be shown that not all interests involved are of equal weight[11] and, second, it becomes clear that it is not possible to satisfy and maximize all interests.

In conclusion, ethical problems concerning genetic databases have not so far been sufficiently discussed or resolved. Although the published recommendations mentioned above provide some guidance, no regulatory framework has been developed to date that (a) discusses in detail the controversial issues and the underlying ethical positions and argumentation, (b) is specific enough to provide practical guidance, and (c) is internationally accepted. There is a large national and international interest in resolving ethical problems related to biobanks.

In spite of the ethical controversy, new genetic databases continue to be established on a national and international level (Mitchell and Waldby 2009). They have different ethical frameworks and continue to capture political and ethical attention. The efforts of those who establish biobanks are important because promising research projects involve more and more cross-border flows of data and samples. The efficiency of the research, as well as the extent of potential risks to those who contribute their DNA to this type of biobank (Baumann 2001; Wichmann and Gieger 2007), will greatly depend on the development and implementation, first, of a global ethical framework and, second, of concrete practice guidelines that adapt the global framework to the needs of local research and health care institutions.

**The Scope and Definitions**

Many researchers, entrepreneurs who start to establish a biobank, as well as patients and active members of the community, continue to be perplexed by the highly controversial debate surrounding the ethical and legal issues concerning biobanks (Cavusoglu et al. 2008; Stege and Hummel 2008; Gibbons 2009). Given the rapid advances of biobanks and related biotechnology (Ennis et al. 2009), their promises and their risks, it is timely to present in more detail the controversial ethical issues related to research involving genetic databases. After more than 50

---

11   See Buchanan (1999), B-28.

years of classical research ethics that are widely accepted in all parts of the world, one might be surprised as to why human genetic databases stir such tremendous debate. Is research involving biobanks indeed so different from classical research? One would like to look at existing biobanks to understand better the practical and theoretical issues and to try to compare the new area of biobanking with the long tradition of ethically accepted classical research. It is also timely to examine and discuss critically existing guidelines and the different ethical and regulatory positions they take, as well as the arguments they use to defend their positions.

To understand the debate about biobanks and the related ethical controversies, several steps are necessary. First, it is helpful to show what are the distinctive features of selected existing genetic databases,[12] and what are the issues about which the public and opponents are concerned. This is done in Chapter 2 through a review of the literature on specific features of selected databases. This review will also permit the resumption of the controversial discussion concerning ethical or legal frameworks of biobanks.

The second step is to identify the detailed aspects of consensus and controversy. Indeed, it is important to direct attention not only to existing biobanks, but also to existing guidelines, be they local, national or international, and to analyse the ethical foundation of the different guidelines. Do guidelines use the same ethical approach, for example, the widely employed approach based on principles? If yes, do guidelines agree about the principles that are important for medical research and especially research involving genetic databases? Is the principle-based approach used in guidelines an efficient way to deal convincingly with the ethical conflicts?

Consensus and controversy in guidelines is also of interest as regards the specific practical recommendations that they offer concerning genetic databases. A review and comparison of classical guidelines on research ethics and the most widely accessible national and international guidelines that are relevant for the regulation of genetic databases will be helpful for university scholars in ethics, but will be of even greater use to biobankers, policy makers and researchers themselves. The review will permit better understanding of why, and the extent to which, genetic databases are a challenge to classical health research ethics. It will also permit identification of the points on which differences exist and analysis of the reasons why guidelines differ, for example, disagreement about facts versus disagreement about ethical principles, versus disagreement about balancing or trade-offs. In Chapter 3, we will resume the analysis concerning ethical foundations and in Chapter 4 we will summarize consensus and controversy concerning specific recommendations as regards genetic databases.

---

12    Concerning the databases as well as the guidelines, we focus on Europe and North America and well-known international guidelines. Indeed, we are not aware of any biobank guidelines from Africa, and those from other continents have been examined in detail in recent publications (Chung et al. 2009; Sleeboom-Faulkner 2009).

To make the scope and definitions more clear, it should be noted that the terms 'genetic databanks'[13] and 'biobanks' are in general used with similar meaning. We include in the definition of biobanks or genetic databases collections of human samples containing DNA or collections composed of the information contained in DNA. The term biobank or genetic database as it is used in this volume implies further that the DNA or the information contained in the DNA is in some form linked to other data or information about the donors of the samples or can be linked to such data or information. We believe that it is not possible to distinguish completely between DNA samples and data.[14] The reason for this is that new methods permit the sequencing of the entire genome contained in a human cell. These data about the sequences are not completely equivalent to the DNA samples, but might contain sufficient amounts of information to conduct the studies of gene–environment interactions for which many biobanks are established. The ethical issues related to biobanks will therefore not depend necessarily on the presence of DNA, but to an important extent on the presence of the information about the sequences contained in the DNA.

We will focus on genetic databases or biobanks used for *medical research*, funded publicly or privately. This means that we do not consider ethical questions related to forensic databases that are only used for purposes other than medical research.

It has to be noted that the existing guidelines do not always advise this restriction to medical research.[15] Several guidelines are not explicit as to whether their recommendations also concern, besides biobanks established for medical research, other types of human genetic databases, or human genetic databases used for purposes other than medical research. The UNESCO international declaration on human genetic data does not make it sufficiently clear whether some ethical aspects of forensic databases are included or not.[16] These guidelines define the scope of their recommendations in a broad fashion, including the 'collection, processing, use and storage of human genetic data, human proteomic data and of the biological samples from which they are derived, referred to hereinafter as "biological samples"' (UNESCO 2003, 3). Another relatively broad definition of genetic databases is given in the Canadian guidelines. These guidelines define

---

13    'Database' is understood as 'any methodical or systematic collection of data, structured in a fashion that allows accessibility to individual or collective elements of that database by electronic, manual or any other means' (WHO May 2001, 6).

14    However, this does not mean that no difference exists between data and samples. 'Human biological materials have to be processed and analyzed before they generate data, these data cannot be read from them as they can be from a medical file' (Trouet and Sprumont 2002, 16). See also Ummel et al. (2002, 63–5).

15    However, the German guidelines of the Nationaler Ethikrat also restrict the scope of their guidelines to biobanks 'die der medizinischen Forschung dienen' (Nationaler Ethikrat. Pressemitteilung 03/2004, Berlin 17.3.2004).

16    See UNESCO (2003) Art. 1c, which seems to indicate the exclusion of these databases, although forensic databases are mentioned and discussed in other articles (Art. 5 iii, Art. 12, Art. 17b and Art. 21c).

biobanks as a 'structured or non-structured collection of human specimens (DNA, cells, and tissues) or personal information of a genetic or proteomic nature from a variety of sources – including medical and other health files, and genealogical, socioeconomic, and environmental information – which is stored electronically as a single entity or as part of a larger database' (CEST 2003, 3).[17]

It should also be noted that genetic databanks vary widely in size. Large-scale genetic databanks pose some particular challenges that are of less importance to smaller databanks. We do not think that it is useful to limit the discussion to databanks of a particular size since it is not possible to draw a clear line between ethical problems according to the size of the database. Any attempt to differentiate on the basis of scale would therefore be difficult to justify. A useful resolution of issues should not be restricted to particular problems of large-scale databases, but should include the concerns raised by smaller-scale genetic databases.

A detailed discussion of all ethical aspects concerning biobanks would fill several bookshelves. Here we will address those ethical issues that are the most controversial (Elger 2008a and 2008b) and the most relevant for an ethical discussion. Some issues are not discussed in a separate chapter, such as, for example, the risks of genetic discrimination resulting from biobanks (Halldenius 2007). This issue appears, however, as one important aspect concerning confidentiality. We do not explicitly discuss the question of ownership of data or samples. The reason for this is that we believe that the underlying legal definitions (Knoppers et al. 1998; Nwabueze 2007, 24) are not of primary importance for our ethical reflections. From an ethical point of view, the question is not so much what the legal status of samples or data is, that is, whether property rights or personality rights of a given country apply. Instead, it is generally agreed that DNA and the information contained in the DNA has a special status ('*sui generis*') that lies somewhere between property rights and personal rights (Pullman and Latus 2003c).[18] A view held by the Canadian scholar Moe Litman (1997) is that human DNA does not belong to any of the established legal categories such as private property, public property, person or information. Instead, it is a separate category on its own that possesses some, but never all, aspects of each of the categories cited. Knoppers is concerned about the increasing commodification of parts of the human body, including DNA. She proposes using the term 'conditional gift' when describing the contribution of DNA by individuals. This term implies that individuals are not paid for their DNA, but that some conditions are attached to the gift, for example, benefit sharing (Knoppers 1996). Also noteworthy is the statement by the College of American Pathologists (CAP):

> In fact, the Uniform Anatomical Gift Act specifically permits the gift of tissue even at death. Pathologists, in the course of ordinary medical practice,

---

17  See also the English version (CEST February 2003).

18  See Pullman and Latus (2003c, 557) and other discussions of property models and their alternatives (Harmon 2009; O'Brien 2009).

substantially transform specimens from their original state. The durable materials thus produced (slides and blocks) can fairly be claimed as the property of the entity that produced them. Even within this framework, the hospital or pathologist may be reasonably considered to hold the tissue in trust, primarily for the patient, but also for society at large (Grizzle et al. 1999).

The ethical endeavour is therefore not to settle the legal debate, but to argue from an ethical point of view how samples and data should be treated and protected. The issues dealing with consent, confidentiality, feedback of results and benefit sharing are concrete forms of such ethically argued 'treatments' and 'protections'.

In research involving genetic databases, it is not clear how the individuals whose tissue is used should be referred to. The possibilities vary between 'research subjects', 'research participants', 'tissue sources' and 'donors'. We have decided to use predominantly the term 'donor', although it is somewhat controversial.[19] We use this term not in order to express a particular opinion on ownership, but only because it describes patients or research subjects who provide tissue in a less 'instrumental' way than the term 'sources', while expressing the difference between subjects or participants who are directly involved in research and those individuals of whom 'only' the tissue 'participates' in the research.[20]

Finally, it should be noted that the terminology concerning the degree of identification of data differs largely in the literature and the guidelines. In Chapter 4 we explain the different terms used and define in detail our terminology concerning different types of storage. We try to make sure that the meaning of the terms we use is always sufficiently explained. Readers should refer to Chapter 4 for any doubt concerning the terms used throughout this book with regard to anonymization and identification of data.

---

19   See '*Who Owns the DNA in a Bank?* Banked DNA is the property of the depositor unless otherwise stipulated. Therefore, the word "donor", which implies a gift (Busby 2004 and 2006; Tutton 2004), is inappropriate' (ASHG 1988). The NBAC report (1999) used the term 'sources' to avoid any reference to the ownership issue.

20   See also Trouet and Sprumont (2002, 10). They suggest making a distinction between: '(1) research with human subjects (clinical research), namely research done "at the bed side", implying direct contact between the research subjects (healthy volunteers or patients) and the investigator; (2) epidemiological research which is based on medical data usually collected for other purposes than the research itself; and (3) research on biological materials of human origin.'

# Chapter 2
# Selected Existing Genetic Databases: Distinctive Features, Ethical Problems and the Public Debate

In this chapter we examine the distinctive features of selected existing genetic databases and provide a summary of the ethical problems and the public debate about them that accompanied their establishment. We have limited our analysis to genetic databases of which the details have been most widely analysed in the available scientific literature, that is, the Health Sector Database in Iceland, the UK Biobank and the biobank established in Estonia. In addition, we review more briefly the known features of a Swiss example of a genetic database, the Swiss Pediatric Oncology Group (SPOG) Tumor Bank.

## The Icelandic Health Sector Database

*Introduction*

Iceland was the first country to pass legislation on health sector databases (1998) and on biobanks (2000). The specific choices of solutions to the ethical problems of genetic databases reflected in these laws have raised an important national and international debate. As stated by Ragnhei Haraldsdottir, 'the ethical and legal issues under consideration are not unique to Iceland' (1999a, 487). It is important to understand the Icelandic situation in order to comprehend the international discussion of ethical problems related to other forms of biobanks and genetic research using stored samples. All clinicians and researchers who are in contact with human subjects and human samples or data used for medical research are concerned by the debate over the legislation in Iceland because their medical, ethical and scientific responsibilities are challenged (McInnis 1999, 238) and need to be clarified in an internationally acceptable way. Many declarations have provided general answers to the ethical problems of genetic databases. But since many ethical questions, if judged from a consequentialist perspective of benefits and risks, can only be answered by considering the details of a biobank in its particular context, it becomes of crucial importance to study a concrete situation. Iceland is one of the examples which have been evaluated by a great number of specialists from the relevant domains such as data protection, genetics, law and ethics. Furthermore, it is among the 'oldest' projects to construct a genetic population database and therefore permits judgement of medical, scientific and social benefits resulting from the biobank project over a certain time.

In addition, it is important to look at details of the Icelandic 'experience' because they illustrate not only ethical and legal, but also practical, problems that biobank regulations should address. Such practical problems are often detected only after a 'real history' trial.

*The History of the Icelandic Health Sector Database*

In 1996, the US (Delaware) corporation deCode received US$12 million from US venture capital companies and opened laboratories in Reykjavik (Winickoff 2001, 11f). Kari Stefansson, a native Icelander and former professor of neuropathology at Harvard University, who founded the company deCode Genetics, explained the project in several articles in scientific journals (Gulcher and Stefansson 1998, 1999a, 1999b and 2000). Modern information technology 'offers the possibility of mining large data sets for knowledge without a priori hypotheses, by systematically juxtaposing various data in the search for the best fit. This kind of pure combinatorial analysis may be particularly powerful in the case of common diseases' (Gulcher and Stefansson 2000, 1827). DeCode therefore proposed the construction of a centralized database, the Icelandic Health Sector Database. Phenotypic information, such as data from the entire Icelandic health care system, would be combined with genealogic and genetic information from biological samples. For several reasons, Iceland was thought to be a unique location for this type of research. In the first place, due to several bottleneck effects (Potts 2002, 5) such as diseases that led to population thinning (Lewis 1999, 10) and to the absence of immigration for a thousand years (Chadwick 1999, 442), Iceland's gene pool was judged to be relatively homogenous, a hypothesis which has, however, been questioned recently.[1] The assumption was that detecting disease-causing mutations would be easier in a homogenous gene pool and in a population exposed to similar environmental factors (the population's standard of living is uniformly good).[2] Second, the universal and effective national health coverage in place since 1915 is able to provide detailed health care records. Third, extensive genealogical records exist for Icelanders. Fourth, Iceland's population size of about 280,000 is large enough to make research valuable, but still small enough to be manageable. Fifth, it was perceived (Rose 2001) that Icelanders are generally enthusiastic as regards science and technology and that they trust the medical system (Rose 2001, 12). Compared to the United States, the percentage of people agreeing to participate in research seems to be higher (Greely 2000, 7).

According to a poll, the great majority (75 per cent) of Icelanders were in favour of the database (Gulcher and Stefansson 1999b, 620) and of the role of deCode. They thought that the database would bring important benefits to the community.

---

1   See Abbot (2003, 678), Helgason et al. (2003a and 2003b) and Arnason (2003).
2   See Chadwick (1999, 442).

In a public relations campaign, deCode promised to provide, for free, Icelanders with drugs and diagnostic tests based on their genes during the patent period. These promises were called unrealistic by scientists who opposed the database project (Enserink 1998a and 1998b).

The project was supported by the Icelandic government, led by Prime Minister David Oddsson, who is said to have known Stefansson from childhood.[3] In 1998, the Icelandic parliament discussed a first, and later a second, version of the Health Sector Database Bill. The final version of the 'Act on a Health Sector Database no. 139/1998'[4] was accepted at the end of 1998. The Act regulates the operation of clinical medical information about Icelanders, obtained from their medical records. The law states explicitly that it does not apply to 'the storage or handling of, or access to biological samples' (Act I, Art. 2). It describes the conditions under which a licensee is authorized to create and operate the health information database. The database must be located in Iceland, and requirements of the Icelandic Data Protection Commission must be met. The licence 'shall not be granted for more than 12 years at a time' (Art. 5). During the 12 years, the licensee controls access to the database as regards uses for commercial purposes (Annas 2000). A three-person committee, composed of a health professional experienced in epidemiology, a person with expertise in information technology and a lawyer, oversees the manipulations of the data (Enserink 1998b) and ensures that the licensee complies with the conditions of the Act. Health care organizations and independent health care workers have to give their consent to the transfer of information from medical records. They are authorized to do so without the individual informed consent of the patients. All personally identifying information is supposed to be coded in a way so as to make the data not personally identifiable. Patients have the right to opt out by filling out particular forms and sending them to the Director General of Public Health. Information entered into the database before the arrival of the opt-out forms will not be retrieved from the database. Any person in contact with the data, such as employees and any contractors of the licensee, are bound to respect confidentiality. The database may be used for a wide range of purposes: 'to develop new or improved methods of achieving better health, prediction, diagnosis and treatment of disease, to seek the most economic ways of operating health services, and for making reports in the health sector' (Art. 10).

> The licensee shall develop methods and protocols that meet the requirements of the Data Protection Commission to ensure confidentiality in connecting data from the health-sector database, from a database of genealogical data, and from a database of genetic data [...] the licensee is authorized during the period of the license to use the database for purposes of financial profit (Art. 10).

---

3   This was reported in *Der Standard* on 12 April 2003 (*Der Standard* 2003).
4   See Act on a Health Sector Database no. 139/1998.

The legislation describes the financial obligations of the licensee as payment for the costs of data entry and of fees to compensate the government for the costs of overseeing the database and issuing the licence. In case of a violation of the Act, civil liability and other penalties including imprisonment are stipulated.

In January 2000, the licence was awarded to deCode. The US company Hoffmann-La Roche was said to have paid US$200 million in order to obtain the rights to develop and market drugs resulting from genes that deCode hoped to find for a dozen disorders (Enserink 1998b; Durham and Hall 1999; Schwartz 1999; Nutley 2002; Lemonick 2006).[5] This promise of US$200 million was unique in the brief history of the 'genomic economy' (Fortun 2008, 3).

In May 2000, the Icelandic parliament passed legislation dealing more specifically with the storage of human tissue, the Biobanks Act. Notes to the bill, prepared by the Ministry of Health and Social Security, and the legislative history of the parliamentary discussions in Iceland seem to suggest that 'the passage of the Icelandic Biobanks Act was rushed and that the legislative process was marked by a surprising lack of community consultation and public debate' (Winickoff 2001, 13f). Article 2 of the Act states that 'this Act applies to the collection of biological samples, and their keeping, handling, utilization and storage in biobanks' (Act on Biobanks 2000). It does not apply to tissue stored temporarily for up to five years. The wording seems to indicate that the Act does not apply to already existing genetic databases, but only to collections established in the future. Article 7 mandates the 'free, informed consent of the person giving the biological sample' (Act on Biobanks 2000). Consent should be given 'in writing after the donor of a biological sample has been informed of the objective of the sample collection, the benefits, risks associated with its collection, and that the biological sample will be permanently stored at a biobank for use as provided in Art. 9'. Article 9 allows that the samples be used for future research without the donor's consent. The board overseeing the biobank 'grants access to biological samples for further diagnosis of diseases'. The conditions for authorizing the use of samples for 'other purposes than those for which the samples were originally collected' are the approval of the Data Protection Commission and the National Bioethics Committee, the fact that 'important interests are at stake' and 'that the potential benefits outweigh any potential inconvenience to the donor of a biological sample or other parties'. The Act announces that the 'Minister shall […] issue regulations defining more precisely the use of biological samples'. In the Act, levels of coding and anonymization are not specified and no distinction is made between commercial and non-commercial research.

Article 7 states that a 'donor of a biological sample may at any time withdraw his/her consent […], and the biological sample shall then be destroyed'. It has to be noticed that '[m]aterial that has been produced from a biological sample by performance of a study or the results of studies already carried out shall, however, not be destroyed'. This could mean that, although the sample will be destroyed,

---

5    See Durham and Hall (1999, 196) and Enserink (1998b, 890).

sensitive information – including all data derived from the sample – would not be destroyed (Winickoff 2001).[6]

Article 7 also describes a form of so-called 'assumed consent' for biological samples collected outside a research context, that is, during clinical testing and treatment. This is a form of opt-out provision. If the donor does not withdraw his/her assumed consent by informing the Director General of Public Health, the samples can be stored in a biobank and used for other purposes. If the donor withdraws this consent, the sample 'shall thereafter only be used in the interest of the donor [...] or by his/her specific permission, but see also para. 4 art. 9'. The 'but'-clause seems to imply that the samples can be used for future research although the donor has withdrawn the assumed consent, if the conditions of Article 9 are fulfilled: as stated above, these conditions are the approval of the Data Protection Commission and of the National Bioethics Committee, the fact that 'important interests are at stake', and 'that the potential benefits outweigh any potential inconvenience to the donor of a biological sample or other parties'.

The Act on Biobanks makes it theoretically possible for the oversight committee to allow samples taken in other contexts, and even samples of people who have withdrawn their assumed consent, to be included in any of deCode's databases, if the benefits outweigh the inconveniences. Since the stated aim of the Health Sector Database is to improve health care, the law could be interpreted in the sense that this basic aim fulfils the condition about 'important interests' at stake.

The Icelandic Health Sector Database has provoked national and international opposition (Abbott 2000). Richard Lewontin, a geneticist at Harvard University, suggested that a scientific boycott of Iceland may be called for 'but only provided our Icelandic colleagues agree'.[7] In March 2003, according to Sigurdsson (2003, 3), about 20,000 Icelanders had opted out of the Health Sector Database. About 90,000 had consented to give samples for genetic analysis. The value of deCode shares fell from US$60 to US$2 in April 2003 on the stock market (Meek 2002; *Der Standard* 2003).

An 18-year-old student, Ragnhildur Gudmundsdottir, filed a law suit because she wanted to protect her right to privacy which could be infringed if her deceased father's medical records went into the deCode health database. In 2003 Iceland's Supreme Court ruled in her favour (Abbott 2004). The court based its decision on the fact that the daughter might be identified as being at risk of any genetic disease that is confirmed through the analysis of data and samples of her father once they are part of the database. This risk persisted because anonymity could not be entirely guaranteed through anonymization and encrypting of the data (Law Review 2004).

DeCode reacted to the opposition of the public and the lost law case by approaching patients and research participants individually to obtain consent. The company 'turned into a more traditional biotech company' (Gross 2006)

---

6 See Winickoff (2001, 16f).
7 Lewontin is quoted by Enserink (1998a, 859).

and focused in particular on several disease-related studies where samples and information were collected with the explicit consent of research participants. The actual Health Sector Database, consisting of the information from medical records, has so far not been constructed because the Icelandic Data Protection Commission and deCode did not reach agreement on the adequacy of security measures for the database (Sigurdsson 2003). In addition, the national university hospital in Reykjavik, which serves more than half of the population, did not consent to the transfer of information (Sigurdsson 2003). Among Iceland's 800 physicians, in 2003, 171 had not consented to reveal health record information to deCode (*Der Standard* 2003).

Kari Stefansson is the co-author of numerous articles involving genetic studies published in Medline since 1998.[8] Many of the publications resulted from collaborations with Icelandic scientists. DeCode was recently involved in the identification of three new schizophrenia-associated mutations (Stefansson et al. 2008). Overall, the company is said to have 'isolated 15 gene variants for 12 diseases, including stroke, schizophrenia, osteoarthritis and, most recently, diabetes' (Lemonick 2006). In November 2007, deCode attracted media attention when it launched its personal-genomics division (Wadman 2008). However, investors are disappointed because therapeutics and diagnostics have not yet produced the promised serious returns. Not surprisingly, deCode was affected by the worldwide banking crisis. In 2008, it was trading at 53 cents a share and had to face the risk of being delisted and losing access to NASDAQ investors (Wadman 2008). In April 2009 deCode announced that it had received a letter from NASDAQ that effectively stayed delisting of the firm's stock from the NASDAQ Capital Market (GenomeWeb staff reporter, 29 April 2009). It is now being discussed whether deCode will survive. Since deCode does not have enough financial resources on its own, it would need to find a pharmaceutical company partner to pay for clinical trials concerning its drugs on heart attack and thrombosis and, put generally, it would need to regain the trust of investors (Wadman 2008). According to the most recent press reports, in January 2010, deCode was purchased from its former parent company by Saga Investments LLC and a 'new' deCode Genetics ehf emerged as a newly financed, private company which intends to continue all of its operations and product lines in its previous field (Anonymous 2010).

*Ethical and Legal Objections to the Icelandic Health Sector Database*

The debate about the Icelandic Health Sector Database included 'over 700 newspaper articles, more than 100 radio and television programs and several town

---

8   A few examples are cited here: Stefansson et al. (2001); Bjornsson et al. (2003); Blondal et al. (2003); Gretarsdottir et al. (2003); Jonasdottir et al. (2003); Reynisdottir et al. (2003); Stefansson et al. (2003a); Stefansson et al. (2003b); Styrkarsdottir et al. (2003); Thorgeirsson et al. (2003); Hallgrimsson et al. (2004); Reynisdottir et al. (2004); Stefansson et al. (2008); Thorgeirsson et al. (2008); Stefansson et al. (2009).

meetings all across Iceland' (Traulsen, Bjornsdottir and Almarsdottir 2008, 3). Criticism has not been limited to the ethical and legal problems of the Icelandic genetic database. Scientists also expressed doubts about the scientific value of the project (Lewis 1999). In the first place, geneticists have contested the idea that the Icelandic gene pool is as uniform as claimed by deCode, permitting easy detection of disease-causing gene variants, especially concerning multifactorial diseases (Edwards 1999). In addition, opponents have expressed concern that the database will be biased because healthy individuals are less motivated to participate, and families suffering from diseases suspected to be inherited will avoid participation because of fear of discrimination.[9] Although many geneticists think that it is of value to study the Icelandic population, many think that it could be sufficient to use smaller databases of disease-based patient groups (Pálsson and Thorgeirsson 1999). The advantage would be that errors could be more easily detected and corrected and changes in diagnosis noted. Several small high-quality databases could be linked.

Criticism of ethical and legal aspects of the database came from Icelanders, especially from the Icelandic Medical Organization and from Mannvernd, the Association of Icelanders for Ethics in Medicine and Science, but also from international organizations and sources. Among the international opponents was the World Medical Association (WMA) (Duncan 1999). It stated that the legislation 'violates the WMA's commitment to confidentiality, the principles of real and valid consent and the freedom of scientific research' (English et al. 2000, 216).

*Confidentiality and privacy*
Opponents claimed that safeguards to protect patients' confidentiality and privacy are inadequate (Andersen and Arnason 1999; Hauksson 1999; Zoëga and Andersen 2000; Garfinkel 2001; Wei 2002): the Data Protection Commission, similarly to the Supreme Court later (Abbott 2004), came to the conclusion that 'the Bill's assertion that the database will contain non-personally identifiable health data does not hold'.[10] The Commission recommended that the definition be dropped from the Bill (Arnason 2002). The question whether confidentiality is truly respected is, firstly, an empirical problem: are individuals identifiable? It is, secondly, a problem of defining what counts truly as non-personally identifiable, because in databases which contain genetic data, individuals might always be identifiable because the information contained in the DNA of each individual is unique.

The Icelandic Medical Association tried to evaluate the empirical question whether it will be possible, from the data contained in the Health Sector Database, to identify individuals or not. The Association therefore asked Ross Anderson, a computer safety expert from the University of Cambridge, to study whether the privacy provisions in Icelandic law are respected in the health database. According to his conclusions, the 'lack of competence at computer security is quite evident'

---

9    See E. Arnason, cited by Lewis (1999).
10   Quoted in Arnason (2002, 3.4). See also Wei (2002, 77).

(Anderson 1998; Enserink 1998a; Anderson 1999; Berger 1999; Anderson 2001). The problems of confidentiality in the Icelandic database come from the existence of a key that permits future adding of new information from the health care system to the database. According to Greely,[11] the Act is inconsistent because the idea of adding future information to the database means that a key exists at least for the licensee. According to the definition of the Act, the data are therefore identifiable, in contrast to what the Act promises about the database. The possibility that such a key will be disclosed or misused cannot be reduced to zero (Greely 2000, 34). Even if the key were completely secure, any employee who is adding new information would have the possibility of searching in the database for particular combinations of information (height, particular disease, and so on). In relation to the frequency of the particular disease or the height, it will take a smaller number (for rare data – that is, unusual height together with a particularly high number of siblings in the family) or a larger number of variables to find the matching record. This might lead to the identification of a person. The Act has anticipated this risk and requires employees of the database to be bound by an obligation of confidentiality. In addition, the Act states that the licensee must compensate an individual who suffers from violation of confidentiality of his/her information included in the database (Art. 17). Other penalties are provided for, if the licensee violates the conditions described in the Act. Such provisions may discourage violations, but the protection is not absolute (Greely 2000, 35).

The problems of privacy in the Icelandic databases are, independently from the existence of a key and the plan to add data in the future, linked to the relatively small size of the country. According to the evaluation of Ross Anderson, in a country of the size of Iceland, it is not sufficient to take off direct personal identifiers such as name, address and birth date, because other pieces of data, such as profession and family relations, especially together with information from the genealogy database, permit indirect identification of individuals through the unique combinations of demographic or medical variables. It is therefore possible to discover the identity of individuals independently from the delicate process of adding new information where a code is used which links the information to the name of the person. Employees will be reviewing the records of individual patients to see the health backgrounds of Icelanders who have a particular genotype and the diagnosis of a particular disease. The risk of identifying individuals from socio-demographic characteristics and of learning about sensitive health care data is substantial.[12] It has been admitted by Kari Stefansson that no database could be 100 per cent secure.[13] The answer to the empirical question 'is it possible to identify individuals?' seems clear: yes, it is theoretically possible.

The next question is: what are the consequences of this fact? Legal experts, including several of Europe's national data protection commissioners responsible

---

11    See Greely (2000, 34); see also Garfinkel (2001, 193–6).
12    See Enserink (1998b, 890–91) and Greely (2000, 35).
13    See Stefansson quoted according to Enserink (1998b, 890).

for overseeing data-privacy laws, examined the legal consequences (Anonymous 2002; EPIC 2002). They informed Iceland's Minister of Justice that the Bill might violate European treaties, in particular the European Convention on Human Rights and Fundamental Freedoms. This implied that a conviction by the European Court in Strasbourg was one of the possible consequences (Enserink 1998a, 859). Iceland is a member of the Council of Europe and has ratified the European Convention on Human Rights. European human rights law and recommendations stipulate the requirement for informed consent for the collection and handling of personally identifiable data. Concerning other European laws, it is not completely clear whether they apply to Iceland which is part of the European Economic Area (EEA), consisting of all the European Union (EU) member states and some European states that have not yet joined the EU but agree to respect certain joint rules (Greely 2000, 32). Whether European treaties are violated by biobanks such as the Icelandic Health Sector Database depends on the definition of non-personally identifiable data (Arnason 2002). Different definitions exist: never identifiable, or needing 'considerable amount of time and manpower' as a criterion of defining personal 'identifiability'. The latter definition is found in Recommendation R(97)5 of the Committee of Ministers of the Council of Europe on Medical Data (COE 1997a). After criticism, this definition has been replaced by definitions from Directive 95/46/EC of the European Parliament and of the Council of 24 October 1995 (European Parliament and the Council 1995) on the Protection of Individuals with Regard to the Processing of Personal Data and on the Free Movement of Such Data. The Icelandic Data Protection Commission overturned an earlier version of the Bill in order to make it compatible with Directive 95/46/EC of the European Parliament and of the Council of 24 October 1995. This Directive states that data on individuals are personal data, if a decoding key exists for the coded data. It is of no importance whether this identification would require considerable time and manpower (European Parliament and the Council 1995; Data Protection Commission 1998).[14] Independently from the legal questions, physicians and the WMA opposed the database, because they feared negative consequences for the health care system due to the lack of safeguards in confidentiality.

The importance of confidentiality comes from a consequentialist argument: if patients cannot be sure that their confidentiality is safeguarded, they will not reveal important facts, for example, that they suffer from sexually transmitted diseases. This will not only undermine the care of the individual patients, but also affect public health. It has therefore been claimed that data collection for the Health Sector Database 'would undermine the trust of patients in their health care providers, which could negatively affect their care; indeed the primary purpose of medical confidentiality is precisely to promote trust and openness' (Merz, McGee and Sankar 2004a).[15]

---

14   See Arnason (2002, 8), and Data Protection Commission (1998), cited by Arnason (2002, iv).

15   Merz, McGee and Sankar (2004a, 1206); see also Zoëga and Anderson (2000).

Another important aspect of confidentiality is to protect against discrimination or stigmatization. Concerning the Health Sector Database, patients might face stigmatization secondary to the lack of confidentiality concerning 'embarrassing' diseases. More importantly, since genetic data were involved, public fear focused specifically on discrimination in the work place and in regard to insurance companies. The two main Icelandic trade unions feared that employers could try to obtain data concerning their workers. Whether the fears of the Icelandic Medical Association and the Icelandic trade unions are justified is an empirical question. The fears might be exaggerated: it could turn out that the Health Sector Database will not erode the trust of Icelandic patients and will not lead to stigmatization or discrimination.

A third aspect of confidentiality and privacy is independent from such empirical evaluations. The question is whether confidentiality or privacy, justified by the respect for individual autonomy (Räikkä 2007), are values by themselves (Greely 2000, 34) or not (Harris 1999, 77), independently from the question whether a risk of harm exists through discrimination and stigmatization. Those who think that the answer is yes, that is, that confidentiality is a value by itself, will object to the Health Sector Database, because confidentiality for these particularly complete and sensitive data is not assured.

One answer to the debate used by deCode was a publication in the *European Journal of Human Genetics* (Gulcher et al. 2000). Gulcher et al. explain that complete anonymity of the data is not the way that should be chosen to protect confidentiality because 'the future cannot be predicted [...] future benefits may be lost when the links to these benevolent volunteers [who have agreed to provide samples and health care information] are gone forever'. They propose to use 'a reversible third-party encryption system' in genetic research in Iceland. This strategy implies strong barriers between the laboratories such as those of deCode and the origin of samples and data. An independent third party assures encryption of the data in direct collaboration with the Data Protection Commission. This method might minimize the risks of uncovering the encryption key. It does not, however, eliminate the risk of indirect identification of individuals due to the small population size in Iceland.

*Informed consent*

Opponents have argued that patients' rights were violated by the use of presumed consent instead of informed consent for transferring data from medical records to the Health Sector Database (Annas 2000; Zoëga and Andersen 2000; Merz, McGee and Sankar 2004a).[16] According to international guidelines (CIOMS 2002; WMA 2008), it is ethically justified not to require any consent of the research subject for empirical studies using anonymous data. Such anonymous data are often used in epidemiological studies without consent. However, as stated by Merz, McGee and Sankar (2004a), the Health Sector Database is not a public health project for

---

16   See also Enserink (1998a, 859).

which no consent at all would have been justified. They argue that, because of the commercial interests involved, relying on presumed consent of the Icelanders is not enough.

Annas (2000) acknowledges that medical-records research is frequently done without informed consent, 'as long as confidentiality is properly protected'. For Annas, this exemption of consent does not apply to the Icelandic population database. The main difference between medical-records research and the Health Sector Database is that in the latter case information from medical records will be linked with genetic information. Unlike information contained in medical records, genetic information is not restricted to the past, but will provide probabilistic information about the future. In addition, according to Annas, genetic information has a particular status because of the history of eugenic and euthanasia programmes during the past century. This creates the obligation to be particularly cautious with respect to risks.

The requirement for informed consent can be waived in the case of research for which it is impossible or particularly difficult to obtain consent. No special reason existed to believe that this would be particularly difficult in Iceland (Greely 2000, 29). Creating the Health Sector Database required enormous resources in the form of money and time. It is unlikely that the additional requirement for individual informed consent would have represented a substantial barrier (Greely 2000, 30). Retrospectively, deCode have probably incurred more costs resulting from the delays due to the objections to presumed consent and the debate about it than they would have from the informed consent procedure.

Arguments against presumed consent in Iceland that have been mentioned by opponents were:

- The opt-out model violated individuals' autonomy. Presumed consent cannot sufficiently grant decisional autonomy to Icelanders, compared to written informed consent, because, according to Sigurdsson (1999), Icelanders have not been informed widely enough about the procedure to opt out. In addition the procedure is complex.
- The absence of informed consent violates European law (European Parliament and the Council 1995) if the data are considered to be identifiable, as well as international guidelines such as the Declaration of Helsinki (Greely 2000, 29). This Declaration, in its 2000 version, requires the informed consent of research subjects to all research. Medical research involving human subjects includes research on identifiable human material or identifiable data (WMA 2000, para. A.1).[17]
- Previously expressed wishes of the dead are not considered. Therefore, in May 2001, Icelandic student Ragnhildur Gudmundsdottir filed a lawsuit (Law Review 2004) against the Director General of Public Health, to

---

17 As explained later, the 2008 version of the Declaration somewhat softened its position on consent to research using identifiable data and samples (WMA 2008, para. 25).

overturn the Director General's refusal to honour her request that the health records of her deceased father should not be transferred to the Health Sector Database (Greely 2000, 30).

- Presumed consent in Iceland does not require a face-to-face discussion that gives the participants whose data are to be used the possibility to ask questions (Greely 2000, 30).
- Incompetent persons cannot decide for themselves. They depend on whether their legal guardian will opt out for them.
- The opt-out model says that any information already processed cannot be retrieved. Only new information will not be added and the remaining tissue samples in the biobank will be destroyed (Winickoff 2001). This is not in line with the right of research subjects to meaningful withdrawal from research, a right upheld since the Code of Nuremberg (Annas 2000).
- The opting-out is general. Since the Health Sector Database can be used for research on all kinds of human health questions, it is not possible to opt out specifically for research concerning particular disorders, such as alcoholism or sexually transmitted disease, while opting in for others (Greely 2000, 30).
- Community consultation cannot replace individual consent (Annas 2000; Sigurdsson 2003).[18] Gulcher and Stefansson write that the international bioethics community recommends community consent for research on populations (Weijer, Goldsand and Emanuel 1999; Weijer 2000; Weijer and Emanuel 2000). 'It is, however, not easy to find definitions of what community consent is. We believe the way in which Icelanders handled the database idea provides a reasonable definition of the concept of community consent' (Gulcher and Stefansson 1999a, 620). According to Annas (Annas and Grodin 1992; Annas 2000), community approval of a research project that concerns a group or the whole community is important. However, 'it cannot legally or ethically require individual members of the community to participate [...] without their voluntary, competent, informed and understanding consent' (Annas 2000, 1831–2).

Some opponents argued, in addition, that even informed consent might not be sufficient to protect vulnerable populations. Informed consent is used by deCode, in line with the requirements of the Icelandic Biobank Act, when obtaining tissue samples for genetic studies. Sigurdsson (2003) argues that 'atomized' informed consent takes advantage of vulnerable groups, such as the elderly. He mentions that up until early 2003, deCode obtained DNA samples and detailed disease data from 80,000 volunteer participants in more than 50 disease projects (Sigurdsson 2003, 3). 'Approximately one-third (28%) of the adult population in Iceland is participating in one or more of deCode's research projects, as are more than 90% of Icelanders over the age of 65' (Sigurdsson 2003, 8).

---

18   See Sigurdsson (2003, 8).

*Freedom of scientific research*

Before being voted on in the Icelandic parliament, the Bill was revised several times. One reason for the revisions was that academics from Iceland feared that the licence monopoly would interfere with their own studies[19] and threaten academic freedom (Andersen 1998). In order to promote academic freedom, Icelandic scientists were granted access to the database for non-commercial research. Ragnhei Haraldsdottir, the Deputy Permanent Secretary of the Ministry of Health and Social Sciences of Iceland, explained in a letter to the *British Medical Journal* that the 'central database will be privately owned and run, but Icelandic health authorities will have access to the information provided that they comply with specific regulations. Other scientists will also have access unless commercial interests are affected' (Haraldsdottir 1999b). Indeed, the Act states (Art. 9) that the 'Ministry of Health and Director General of Public Health shall always be entitled to statistical data from the health sector so that it may be used in statistical processing for the making of health reports and planning, policy making and other projects of these bodies. This information to the specific parties shall be provided free of charge' (Act on a Health Sector Database 1998). According to Greely (2000, 36), health institutions and self-employed health workers may 'negotiate for "payments in the form of access [...] to information from the database for specific research" as part of their compensation for coding and entering information into the database. There is no general exception for non-commercial research.' Otherwise, it is possible for deCode to sell access to the databases, which can be used as a research tool for studies in epidemiology, in genetics, and for studies examining how to maintain health systems (Arnason 2002, 2).

Opponents have criticized this final version of the Act, claiming that it is unfair to grant one company use of the data while denying it to outside researchers whose studies might harm that company's commercial interests (Enserink 1998a, 859). According to the opponents, this provision not only is unfair to other researchers, but also harms the interests of patients because it interferes with the advances of science. It is not ethically justifiable to prohibit free access to the data because this will deprive the Icelandic community and patients from all over the world of potential benefits resulting from additional research using the data.

*Commercialization*

It has been said that Icelanders 'sell' their genes (Hacking 2001–2002; Kahn 22 February 1999). As a matter of fact, the licence states that all information contained in the database remains the 'common property of the Icelandic nation'[20] under the protection and rule of the Minister of Health and Social Security. However, it was not the question of ownership of the data or the samples which was of concern to the WMA and other opponents. Instead, they argued that medical records become a commodity, because the government's legislation provides a company with the

---

19  See Enserink (1998b, 890).
20  Licence quoted by Arnason (2002, 3).

exclusive right to make money from the use of the information contained in the records (Hodgson 1998; Sullivan 1999).[21] Anthropologists complained about the 'contrast between commercial and communitarian perspectives' (Pálsson and Rabinow 2001).

Those who defend commercialization (Greely 2000, 27–8) have argued that most health care research will ultimately be used commercially (Lewis 2004). The difference is not whether commercialization is acceptable, but only from which point on. Gulcher, Stefansson and others[22] who are in favour of commercialization have in addition claimed that this commercialization of biomedical research benefits not only Iceland's economy, but also science, because useful results are obtained more quickly by commercial organizations which are motivated to capitalize on their inventions (Hirshhorn and Langford 2001).

*Financial fairness*
It has also been argued that deCode benefits unduly from public resources such as health information in Iceland without adequately redistributing benefits to the community. The Act on a Health Sector Database (1998) stipulates only that the licensee pays fees to cover the costs incurred by the government from the issuing of the licence, from the processing of the data, and from the monitoring of the database, for example, by the Data Protection Commission.[23] The government and the population of Iceland will not benefit if deCode profits from the database. The only benefit that has been promised to Icelanders has not been disclosed in a fully open manner. It is not a commitment of deCode, and has not been negotiated with the Icelandic population. Promises have so far not been fulfilled. Hoffmann-La Roche announced that it had agreed with deCode to provide Icelanders with drugs developed from the work with deCode (Lemonick 2006). These drugs were promised to be provided free of charge during the patent period (Greely 2000, 16), but the drugs announced to be in the pipeline have so far not been successfully tested (Wadman 2008).

*Other concerns of opponents*
Icelandic physicians have expressed their concern that the database 'will be used to examine physicians' practices (physicians have not been ensured anonymity) and whether physicians will alter their record keeping practices to protect their patients and, potentially, themselves' (Merz, McGee and Sankar 2004a, 1206).

Merz, McGee and Sankar[24] have argued that the government made insufficiently informed decisions: '[W]e do not believe that full information about all of the

---

21    See Sullivan (1999); and Hodgson (1998).

22    See Gulcher and Stefansson (2000, 1827f): 'private enterprise has increased, not decreased, the pace of scientific discovery'.

23    See Act on a Health Sector Database no. 139/1998 II, Art. 4; see also Greely (2000, 37).

24    See Merz, McGee and Sankar (2004b, 1213).

potential ramifications of the project could have been available when initial political decisions were made, or that reasonable alternatives were considered' (Merz, McGee and Sankar 2004b, 1213). In addition, the Icelandic government has been criticized for acting against international convention, because in 1999 it dissolved the existing Icelandic National Bioethics Committee. In 1997, the seven members were selected by the Ministry from candidates that had been nominated by the academic and medical communities. The Health Minister announced that members of the new five-member committee would be selected by the Ministry without taking into account previous nominations. Since the legislation stipulates an important role for the committee in the approval of research protocols involving biobanks (Abbott 1999), opponents interpreted the changes as undue government influence on medical research. This influence contravenes the Declaration of Helsinki. It states that all research ethics committees need to be independent of the researchers or institutions who initiate or finance the research and of the relevant authorities (WMA 2000; WMA 2008). The government is in charge of granting the licence for the Health Sector Database and thus represents a relevant authority.

## The UK National Biobank

*Introduction*

The UK Biobank project implies the creation of a genetic databank. The debate about this project has been influenced by the Icelandic experience. It is important to have a closer look at the UK Biobank because this project is another well-documented tentative attempt, not only to advance research in the UK, but to do so while respecting ethical requirements. John Newton, chief executive of the UK Biobank project, said that the sponsors have 'clearly defined the purpose of biobank, which will be to undertake biomedical research in the public interest'. He acknowledged that the project needs 'a strict mechanism for making sure that all the uses we allow of the data comply with that purpose' (Radford 2003).[25] In addition he hoped that the UK 'biobank will set a new standard for ethics and governance'.[26] The project caused considerable discussion (Giles 2006) and started several years later than originally planned, because it took time to find convincing solutions not only for the technical problems (Elliott and Peakman 2008), but also for the ethical and legal issues which were similar to those raised by the Icelandic database. In some aspects, the UK Biobank has 'learned' from Iceland. What has been learned from the Icelandic experience is, according to Fears and Poste (1999, 268),[27] that it 'is important to understand the concerns expressed about privacy

---

25  Cited in Radford (2003).
26  Cited in Barbour (2003, 1738).
27  The authors, Fears and Poste, acknowledged their affiliation with SmithKline Beecham, UK (Fears and Poste 1999).

and informed consent, and the apprehension that a commercial company, put into a monopoly position, might impede academic research or propagate commercial abuses'. On the other hand, the critics of the UK Biobank project show that some of the 'mistakes' have been perpetuated (Fortun 2003, 4) and that the concerns about privacy and informed consent have not been completely eradicated (Fortun 2003; Fortun 2008).

*The History of the UK Biobank and its Database*

'UK Biobank' is a prospective cohort study (Wright, Carothers and Campbell 2002; Ollier, Sprosen and Peakman 2005). The protocol specifies that the aim is to collect health data and blood samples from 500,000 individuals aged between 44 and 69 (UK Biobank Coordinating Centre 2006). When entering the study, participants will fill in a questionnaire and will be screened by a limited number of routine measures. Blood will be used for some baseline tests, for example, a full blood count, and then blood and urine will be stored for future use, including genetic testing. Participants will be recruited from different regions and socioeconomic environments in about six centres distributed around the UK. Patients are contacted by mail and receive a brochure which explains the project (UK Biobank 2009d). At the recruitment centre, they will also receive a consent form, and if they agree, they will have an interview with a research nurse and fill in a questionnaire (Parliamentary Office of Science and Technology 2002, 1). Participants will then be followed for up to 30 years or until they die, in order to add new data (Barbour 2003; Revill 2003; Staff and agencies 2003; MRC 2009). The expectation is that, 10 years from the beginning of the study, over 11,000 of the study participants will have developed diabetes mellitus; 8,000 myocardial infarction; and almost 15,000 either breast, colorectal or prostate cancer (Anonymous 2003, 325). The UK Biobank, like other biobanks in the United Kingdom, does not offer feedback of results to participants. Feedback is judged to be of questionable value (UK Biobank 2007, 7) or even 'dangerous' (Staley 2001) because results are likely to be preliminary and could cause harmful reactions, especially if it is not possible to provide genetic counselling. By signing the consent form, participants agree to the fact that their genetic data can be linked to the information contained in their full medical record, past and ongoing (UK Biobank 2007, 5). Participation in the UK Biobank is voluntary. Participants have the right to withdraw at any time. They can choose between different options of withdrawal. Complete withdrawal means that the samples and the link to the medical record will be destroyed, but not data derived by research projects and included in anonymized datasets.[28] Participants will be informed that

---

28   The term used is 'anonymized', without explanation about the degree of anonymization and whether anonymization is truly irreversible. In many places, the term anonymized is used when reversibly anonymized data is referred to, that is, data that can be linked to the participant through a code. 'Information is encrypted. We do need to be able to identify your samples and information so that we can track your medical records, contact

it might not be possible to trace and destroy all sample remnants given away for research studies. Discontinued participation, a weaker withdrawal option, means that the information in the database and the samples will be anonymized,[29] but not destroyed. The link with the medical record will be destroyed and participants will not be contacted again to update information (UK Biobank 2007, 9).

In 1998, the British government promised additional funds to establish nationally available DNA collections (Currie 1998). The UK Biobank is a project commonly funded by the British Department of Health, the Medical Research Council and the charity, the Wellcome Trust, a large funder of biomedical research in the UK. The original budget of £45m has lately been increased to £61m (Barbour 2003; Coghlan 2006; Hall Tuesday 22 August 2006).

It took some time to develop the final protocol, as well as the ethical governance framework, of the biobank (Kaye 2001b; Watson and Cyranoski 2005; UK Biobank Coordinating Centre 2006). In 1999, an expert working panel examined the project and published a report in 2000. The panel recommended two prospective population cohort studies. One consisted of following half a million middle-aged individuals, the other in following 20,000–50,000 individuals from birth on. Since the first was supposed to provide results more rapidly, it was favoured over the second. A protocol development committee worked on the details of the protocol. The committee was divided on the degree of accuracy needed at the baseline examination of participants in order to establish the phenotype. In addition, the commission disagreed about the exact composition of the cohort. This controversy concerned the question whether stratifying for ethnic minorities or using family cohorts would be of greater scientific value than the 'whole' population project. According to Barbour (2003), dissenting members of the committee wrote a second project and described the scientific justification to do more detailed phenotyping of a smaller cohort (40,000 participants). The existence of such a 'supplementary report' is contested by Tom Meade who chaired both the expert working panel and the protocol development committee (Meade 2003, 492). According to Radda et al., both proposals were sent for peer review to international reviewers and received mostly positive evaluation (Radda, Dexter and Meade 2002, 2282). According to Barbour (2003, 1735), most members of the protocol development committee did not see the reviewer comments. The smaller proposal was abandoned because it would have cost an additional £8–10m. According to Meade, establishment of a separate familial cohort 'would be prohibitively expensive'. Concerning the inclusion of minority groups, he stated that in the main project there 'is likely to be a sufficiently large Asian group for useful analysis' (Meade 2003, 492).

Pilot studies were carried out to test the storage procedures (Jackson, Best and Elliott 2008) and feasibility, the comprehension and acceptability of the questionnaire,

---

you again or destroy your samples if you withdraw. We do this by using a code. Only those UK Biobank staff with access to the code will be able to connect you with your information and samples' (UK Biobank 2009a).

29   See note 28 above.

and the distribution of responses to the questions in order to finalize the questionnaire and methodology (UK Biobank Coordinating Centre 2006; Palmer 2007).

A biobank company was set up as a charitable company limited by guarantee. It is owned by the project's funders, that is, the British Department of Health, the Medical Research Council and the Wellcome Trust (Opinion Leader Research 2003, 35). The board of the biobank company, together with a scientific committee and an independent oversight committee, will conduct the project. The company will be based in Manchester (Opinion Leader Research 2003, 35) where data and samples will be stored. The recruitment of participants and of samples was originally planned to be done in collaboration with general practitioners (GPs) by six different consortia of 21 universities called Collaborating Centres (Opinion Leader Research 2003). Application to become a spoke required 'a prequalification questionnaire that ran to several hundred pages, and then a formal application of a similar size' (Barbour 2003, 1735). The aim was to be sure that institutions applying had the necessary infrastructure, organization and experience and were not in financial difficulties. Participating scientists argued that it would not be possible for spokes to retain biological samples or to undertake additional data collection, as has been the case for another study collecting samples, the European Prospective Investigation into Cancer and Nutrition. The final protocol promises patients that recruiting is independent from their GP and that their physicians will only be informed that patients from their practices have been enrolled, without revealing the names (UK Biobank 2009a). Indeed, public consultation showed that future participants did not want their GPs to have detailed information about lifestyle and other data collected as part of the biobank project (see next section).

In 2002, applications to participate in the UK Biobank project as spokes were invited. During the same year, the protocol development committee issued a report and ethics workshops on relevant issues took place.

One important Ethics Consultation Workshop was held in April 2002 (Wellcome Trust, Medical Research Council and Department of Health 2002). At the end of 2002, the Human Genetics Commission issued a memorandum concerning the biobank to the House of Commons Science and Technology Committee. In February 2003, an Ethics and Governance Interim Advisory Group was appointed (Interim Advisory Group on Ethics and Governance 2003). In autumn 2003, the UK Biobank funders published the first public draft Ethics and Governance Framework with the advice of the Interim Advisory Group (version 1). This version was revised several times and the final version (version 3) was established in 2007 (Godfrey 2003; UK Biobank 2007).

After 'eight years of planning, criticism, and debate' (Watts 2007) and after finally having achieved full funding (£59m) for the main study, UK Biobank was launched 'to mixed reception' (Senior 2006, 390). It started recruitment in February 2007 and is likely to be finished in 2010: in January 2009, half of the 500,000 participants had been successfully included in the biobank (Press release 2009). An average of 10 per cent of the contacted volunteers have agreed to participate (Watts 2007).

As required under the Human Tissue Act 2004 (Ironside 2006; Lucassen and Kaye 2006), the UK Biobank also needed to be licensed by the Human Tissue Authority to store biological samples for research (UK Biobank 2007, 17).

*Public Attitudes to Participating in the UK Biobank*

In order to address the controversial aspects of the biobank, consultations were held in 2000 with practitioners involved in primary care. They thought that participation in the project would depend on marketing and on the image of the UK Biobank in the media (Barbour 2003, 1738). Some expressed the opinion that too much discussion of the project would unnecessarily alarm participants and interfere with recruitment. It was also feared that ongoing discussion could be deleterious to the project if large numbers of the public withdrew their consent later in the course of the project.

However, in general, the UK public had more positive attitudes to genetic research and the biobank project than the public in other countries (Traulsen, Bjornsdottir and Almarsdottir 2008). Trust in the health system and the welfare state seems to have been among the reasons for the rather optimistic attitudes (Tutton and Corrigan 2004; Tutton, Kaye and Hoeyer 2004).

Shickle et al. (2003) have conducted two surveys, in each of which almost 2,000 interviews were held with adults from different areas in the United Kingdom. One question was what the research nurse should do if an illness was found during the initial interview. The aim of this interview is to gather lifestyle and morbidity data which will be included in the biobank database. The public thought that feedback should occur, with a slight preference for telling the patient first rather than the general practitioner (Shickle et al. 2003). Most of the participants indicated that they would like to be asked once whether they consented to the access of biobank researchers to their medical records, although many thought that permission should be sought annually. No consensus existed on what should happen to the DNA and other information if donors decided that they no longer wanted to participate in the study.

The participants thought that public sector researchers and the police should have access to the DNA bank (Shickle et al. 2003). The use of the databank and the samples by the drug or biotechnology industry was a controversial issue. The public strongly opposed access by insurance companies. Close to 40 per cent said that they would agree to participate in the biobank project and almost the same percentage would not; 23 per cent were unsure. Participants who were 45–65 years old and those from higher social classes were more willing to participate in the UK Biobank project than other groups of participants.

The Wellcome Trust charged People Science & Policy Ltd with conducting a public consultation about the public's perceptions as regards the collection of human biological samples for the UK Biobank project. In January 2002, three sessions with about 20 members of the public were held in three different locations in the United Kingdom (People Science & Policy Ltd 2002). The participants were from the age group to be included in the UK Biobank. The consultations revealed that confidentiality was a main concern of participants:

> Many did not want their GPs to have access to the lifestyle data and everyone was clear that employers and insurance companies should not have access to the individual data. However, many realized that the general findings will be published and therefore accessible to anyone and that this might indirectly affect insurance premiums (People Science & Policy Ltd 2002, 3).

Participants at the consultations were ambivalent about whether the police should be allowed to have access to the data. After more detailed discussions, members of the consultation groups seemed to agree with police access if a court order was obtained. The public was sceptical about the security of data in general, as expressed in one quote (People Science & Policy Ltd 2002, 3): 'You don't have to wait for Biobank to exist for people to hack into data about you.' One example was of a hacker who described himself as an 'ethical whistle blower'. In 1999, he succeeded in accessing patient files at a hospital in Seattle. His aim was to prove that the security of computer systems could not be taken for granted (Songini 2000).[30]

Participants were interested to know whether certain diseases would be given priority among the biobank research projects. However, they seemed not to be particularly concerned about research on behavioural genetics and about the risk of stigmatizing a 'genetic underclass' (People Science & Policy Ltd 2002, 4).

In 2003, People Science & Policy Ltd again invited a panel of 64 lay people aged between 45 and 69 years to comment on the UK Biobank Ethical and Governance Framework (People Science & Policy Ltd 2003). Between 42 and 47 of the invited individuals attended the sessions. According to People Science & Policy Ltd, the panel members mostly agreed to the Ethical and Governance Framework. They appreciated the necessity to grant biobank researchers access to full past and present medical records. However, they were concerned that information in the records might not be accurate and complete. The panel members found it to be important that participants in the biobank were asked about their wishes at the time of recruitment. They should especially have the opportunity to decide what should happen to their data and samples in case of death or mental incapacity. The participants thought that these wishes should be respected. They insisted on confidentiality, insisting that researchers should not know the identity of participants. Use of the samples by academics and the pharmaceutical industry was accepted, but access to the data by tobacco or alcohol companies was judged controversial.

*Ethical and Legal Objections to the UK Biobank Database*

Long before the UK Biobank project started to recruit participants, it raised 'extraordinary passions' (Barbour 2003, 1734) among scientists and consumer

---

30   See also Staley (2001, 19).

protection associations. Opponents stated that they were 'not against genetic research', but that they 'want open debate and proper consultation before any decisions are taken' (McGrath 2002).

*Unclear benefits*

The organization GeneWatch argued that the UK Biobank provides 'unclear benefits to individuals and society' (Wallace 2002, 2282). Indeed, the scientific debate about the benefits and the best way to obtain them is still ongoing (Corrigan 2006). Scientific objections continue to be raised about whether the actual study design will produce the benefit intended at justifiable costs (Anonymous 2009). Scientists claim that the actual study design will permit the detection of moderate risk factors concerning only the most common cancers and that case control studies would be cheaper and more powerful (Clayton and McKeigue 2001). If it is true that many rare genetic variants each contribute to a very small part of disease susceptibility, the project encounters a methodological problem: even when including 500,000 participants, it will be difficult to identify and describe the effects of the genetic variants. By contrast, a cohort study enriched in family members would provide more valuable information, because phenotypes observed in familial cases are often due to mutations that provide more insight into the biological pathway interrupted.

Criticism also includes the question whether the project is technologically feasible. Although information technology used by the National Health Service has been modernized, multiple different computer systems are used. It is not clear whether the soft data of variable quality, entered from medical records (as compared to hard endpoints such as death) will accurately reflect the patients' phenotypes. A reliable way to detect whether patients suffer from a condition is still to be found, be it general practice codes, hospital diagnosis for a condition, or the prescription of a drug specific to the condition (Barbour 2003, 1736).

GeneWatch has argued that the peer-review process has been managed solely by the funding agencies. According to Wallace, this has allowed them to 'select their own reviewers and potentially to sideline any scientific criticisms when making their decisions' (Wallace 2002).

*Informed consent and future use of the samples and information*

It has been argued that the biobank funders favour 'general consent' or 'open consent' (Fortun 2003, 4). This implies that when they enter the study participants consent to the fact that their samples can be used for further studies, the aims and details of which are not yet known. The biobank funders argue that this form of consent will permit maximization of the usefulness and benefits expected from the biobank. They plan to provide sufficient ethical safeguards in the form of ethical review committees (UK Biobank 2007, 15) and regulations drawn up by the oversight committee (Parliamentary Office of Science and Technology 2002, 3). However, John Newton, the chief executive officer of the biobank project, acknowledged that 'once data had been given out under licence for one research project, it could be difficult to control the further uses of the data' (Godfrey 2003). GeneWatch, the Consumer's Association and Human Genetics Alert prefer more specific consent. They consider that general consent is not 'fully informed' and thus ethically questionable. Diseases to be studied should be specified, while excluding studies on behavioural genetics. Specific consent should be given concerning the use of samples for commercial research. Participants should have the possibility of receiving information on the studies for which their samples are used. Any use that is not explicitly mentioned during the original informed consent procedure should require the re-contacting of the participants for new informed consent.

The Human Genetics Commission, in their consultation paper (HGC 2000) and report (HGC 2002), recommended that thorough information should be given to the participants on the purpose and nature of the research, on details of storage, about the control of access to the data, on the involvement of commercial interests, and on any implications and risks for the participants.

Critics are concerned that the Ethics and Governance Framework of the biobank does not give participants the possibility of consenting separately to specific uses and of withdrawing consent for any specific use of the data. Critics prefer to have the option of excluding specific users of the biobank, such as the tobacco industry, or specific uses, such as studies on behavioural genetics (Staley 2001; Godfrey 2003).

*Confidentiality and privacy*

The confidentiality problems of the UK Biobank are similar to those of the Icelandic Health Sector Database. Since the project includes the plan to add new data during follow-up, it must be possible to link the new data to the original person who provided the DNA sample. It has been recommended that more research about encryption of the data should be done, that legal safeguards should be created to protect participants against potential harm before data collection is started, and that volunteers have the right to be informed adequately on the risks to confidentiality (Spinney 2003, 491). In the UK, the provisions of the Data Protection Act (1998) apply to genetic information. The Act states that data must be: 'fairly and lawfully processed'; 'processed in accordance with the data subject's rights'; used 'for limited purposes'; 'not kept longer than necessary'; and must be 'adequate, relevant and not excessive; accurate; [...] secure; and not transferred to countries without adequate protection'. Exemptions from these principles exist 'for safeguarding national security', 'if requested by a Minister of the Crown', 'for the prevention or detection of crime', 'for apprehending or prosecuting an offender', and 'for assessing or collecting tax or duty'.[31] The Human Genetics Commission (2002, 19) has recommended that 'rigorous steps' should be undertaken by operators of all genetic research databases 'to ensure that unauthorized access or disclosure are prevented'. Similarly, Liberty (the National Council for Civil Liberties) is convinced that the current framework of law against the unauthorized

---

31    See also Parliamentary Office of Science and Technology Postnote (2002, 2).

disclosure of medical information does not provide adequate protection against the unauthorized disclosure and use of genetic information. Liberty is not only concerned about disclosure of information to insurance companies and employers, but also about direct or indirect disclosure to family members (Liberty 2001).[32] GeneWatch reminds us that the Human Genome Organization's (HUGO) guidelines suggest that immediate family members should be allowed access to samples (HUGO 1998).[33] If knowing information derived from the DNA of a participant is of potential benefit to the family, but the participant is unwilling to share the information, the health professionals or researchers will 'be left in a very uncertain position' (Staley 2001, 21). They would be bound by a duty of confidence to the participant. On the other hand, disclosure to family members could be justified in order to prevent serious harm. GeneWatch recommends further legal clarification of this issue. In the final protocol, the UK Biobank does not allow access by family members to data or samples, and after the death of a participant, family members do not have any right to ask for withdrawal of samples or data of their dead relative (UK Biobank 2009b).

Among the security measures described on the UK Biobank website are hacker-safe computers, and encryption and coding of data and samples. The Consumer's Association and Human Genetics Alert have recommended that the persons or bodies responsible for encryption and reversing encryption should be independent from the biobank users and owners (Parliamentary Office of Science and Technology 2002, 3). The UK Biobank mentions only that 'access is kept to a minimum. Very few staff have access to the key code' (UK Biobank 2009a).

The Human Genetics Committee and other critical NGOs recommended that the government create specific legislation in order to prevent genetic discrimination by insurance companies and employers in the UK. However, this legislation will not protect individuals who move outside the UK. In addition, the exemptions of the Data Protection Act apply. Critics have therefore proposed that participants receive explicit information, before they give consent, about the possibility that the police and other authorities may have lawful access to the data.[34] The Human Genetics Commission judged that this type of information 'would seriously discourage participation'. Instead, it recommended that legal means should be sought to prevent the police and other law enforcement agencies from access to database information (HGC 2002, 23). GeneWatch is concerned about police access to the data, too. They remind us that this access is authorized according to the Data Protection Act and ask for further legal clarification of this issue, especially referring to the case of Stephen Kelly. This prisoner had agreed to donate blood to a study about an HIV outbreak in prison. Although all participants

---

32  See in particular Liberty (2001, 6.3).

33  See also Staley (2001, 21).

34  'Will the police have access to the information? We will not grant access to the police, the security services or to lawyers unless forced to do so by the courts (and, in some circumstances, we would oppose such access vigorously)' (UK Biobank 2009a).

in the study had been assured of strict confidentiality, Kelly's sample was later used to provide important evidence in a criminal trial to prove his participation in a criminal act. GeneWatch believes that if this practice is condoned in the interest of seeing justice prevail, 'many people will refuse to take part in research because they do not believe their confidentiality will be respected' (Dyer 2001).[35]

The debate about confidentiality has been somewhat less animated than in Iceland because informed consent and not presumed consent is used in the UK project to obtain access to the participants' health care records. One of the participants in an ethics workshop, a member of the public aged between 45 and 69 years old, explained a frequent opinion concerning confidentiality: '[Y]ou have to accept that there is a risk, [but] this is for the greater good then surely that's a good enough reason to say all right I'll go with this ... [as] this is gonna help us over the longer period of time' (Opinion Leader Research 2003, 11).

*Commercialization, ownership and financial fairness*
Although no single company, such as deCode in Iceland, will have exclusive rights to the UK Biobank, the project is under criticism because pharmaceutical companies will be able to have access to the information. Those in favour of this access claim that this will speed up the development of diagnostic tests and therapies (Revill 2003). Critics are concerned about the 'unruly amalgamation of state agencies, private philanthropies, universities, and commercial entities' (Fortun 2003, 4). They question the balance between public and commercial interests. Companies could 'influence the research agenda to promote profits over public interest' (Staley 2001, 20). The research agenda will not give priority to research which is most beneficial for health, but to research which promises the greatest profit. An example of concern is research into beauty products. Giving participants the option to decide whether their samples will or will not be used for commercial research might not be a solution. The boundaries between academic and industrial activities are not clear cut because of the inevitable collaboration of both.

Participants consent to the fact that the UK Biobank will be 'the legal owner of the database and the sample collection' (UK Biobank 2007, 5). This means that participants will have no property rights in the samples. It is not yet clear what kind of payment will be decided for granting access to the data to other researchers or companies from the private and public sector. Although future financial benefit will be reinvested for further research (UK Biobank 2007, 18), critics are concerned about whether and how participants, the community and the public good will benefit from the biobank. GeneWatch sees a need for new legislation to regulate the commercial use of biobank collections. They claim that patenting of genes should be ended because it is not compatible with scientific freedom and the public good. Since companies could impede further research by others, patenting will actually hinder the progress of medical research.[36]

---

35   See also Staley (2001, 21).
36   See Staley (2001, 27 and 33).

*Costs of the project*

Researchers from outside the genetic epidemiology community have complained that the UK Biobank project receives inadequate amounts of funding. In 2003, the House of Commons Science and Technology Committee issued a report in which it criticized the British Medical Research Council (MRC). It found evidence for financial 'mismanagement'. According to the committee's chairman, 'something has gone badly wrong with the MRC, which has left Britain's best medical research groups starved of funds. Our report shows why scrutiny of British science is so badly needed' (MacLeod 2003). The report noted as part of the discriminating funding that the UK Biobank project had not been peer-reviewed on the same basis as any other proposals. The authors of the report stated that their 'impression is that a scientific case for Biobank has been put together by the funders to support a politically driven project'. They argued that the MRC had funded the UK Biobank initiative with a £45m grant 'without the full confidence of the public and the research community'. 'It has been a top-down initiative the merits of which have not been adequately balanced by other funding options' (MacLeod 2003; BBC News 25 March, 2003a and 2003b).[37] The MRC defended its funding strategies, saying that the 'report does not give adequate recognition of the fact that our mission is to promote medical research with a view to improving human health'.[38] The MRC had previously been criticized for funding research in molecular biology because the relevance to health of this research was questioned. According to the MRC, the subsequent mapping of the human genome demonstrated the importance of this investment.

> A similar issue arises with UK Biobank today. We strongly refute the committee's suggestion that UK Biobank is a 'politically-driven project' […] It is being established to use information generated by the human genome project to improve the health of the public and meet the research needs of the scientific community in their efforts to develop better healthcare (BBC News 25 March 2003b).

*Over-emphasis on genetic factors*

Opponents are concerned that the UK Biobank project may reinforce over-emphasis on genetic factors. They remind us that this could lead to an under-emphasis on other, perhaps cheaper and more causal, treatments, such as changing environmental factors. Critics point out that the commercial industry reinforces this over-emphasis because they are interested in selling drugs and other treatments to prevent or treat genetically caused diseases; genetic research promises more profit than convincing people to change lifestyle or environmental factors.[39]

---

37  Quotations from the report according to MacLeod (2003).
38  For the MRC response, see BBC News (25 March 2003b).
39  See also Parliamentary Office of Science and Technology Postnote (2002, 2).

## The Estonian Gene Bank

*Introduction*

When interviewed about the Estonian Genome Project (EGP), Andres Metspalu, professor of biotechnology and co-founder of the project in 1999, summarized its goal as carrying out 'good basic research' that 'can also lead to good economic benefits' (Tzortzis 2003b). Estonia became independent in 1991. It is another small and ambitious country (Parfitt 2004) that, like Iceland, hoped to gain international recognition and to attract biotechnology industry and researchers (Frank 2001, 514). Like the UK Biobank project, the Estonian project tried to avoid 'mistakes' made in Iceland. As in Iceland, the project has received large support from the government. Although the Gene Bank can build on wide public trust, critics claim that there has not been enough public debate on the project and that several aspects are not ethically sound.

*The History of the Estonian Gene Bank*

The non-profit Estonian Genome Project Foundation started with the support of US$4.5 million from private investment (Tzortzis 2003b). The main project was planned to involve one million Estonians over a five-year period. This represents about 70 per cent of Estonia's 1.4 million population. The project began with a pilot project in 2002 (Eesti geenivaramu 2003). The idea was to include 10,000 volunteers to test the data handling procedures and general logistics in order to prepare for the project (Frank 2001). In 2002–2003, 1,000 samples out of the planned 10,000 had been collected (Sutrop 2003). Blood sampling for the main project began in October 2002 (Tzortzis 2003a and 2003b). By the end of 2003, about 10,000 donors had been recruited. Two thirds of the donors were women. Individuals aged between 30 and 50 represented 40 per cent of all gene donors (Eesti geenivaramu 2004a).

    The project is regulated by a law voted by the parliament in 2000 (and amended in 2007, see below), the Human Genes Research Act. This law stipulates the necessity of written informed consent of each participant before contributing his/her DNA (Human Genes Research Act 2000; Tzortzis 2003b) and prohibits the collection of data or samples using coercion or financial inducement. Scientists who carry out research without the informed consent of the subjects can be punished by imprisonment for three years (Schimmek 2003). The founders of the project emphasize that the legal and ethical framework of the Gene Bank has been developed with the help of international specialists such as Bartha Knoppers, based on international guidelines such as the Convention on Human Rights and Biomedicine of the Council of Europe, the Declaration of Helsinki and the UNESCO Universal Declaration on the Human Genome and Human Rights (Rannamäe 2003, 23).

    Family physicians received training organized by the Gene Bank project to collect blood samples and to gather health data of their patients through a questionnaire (Tzortzis 2003b). For the original size of the database (samples from one million Estonians), the collaboration of about 800 physicians would have been needed to carry out the nationwide collection of the data (MacWilliams 2003). The objective was to combine detailed information about the lifestyle, nutrition, work habits, genealogy, family history and health of each individual with high density single nucleotide polymorphism (SNP) maps of DNA derived from the blood samples, through the testing of about 100,000 SNPs per individual. This data can permit whole-genome association studies based on linkage disequilibria (Lahteenmaki 2000, 1135). The Estonian Gene Bank project advertised its usefulness in the opposite way to Iceland. It is not the homogenous gene pool which is said to be advantageous, but the genetic diversity of the population. As a consequence of a long history of occupation by Danes, Russians, Germans and Swedes, Estonia's population reflects the diverse genetic make-up prevalent in Europe (Frank 1999; Tzortzis 2003b). The Gene Bank aims to study genes that have an influence on diseases found in Europe, among others asthma, diabetes and different types of cancer (Lahteenmaki 2000).

When the Gene Bank was started, the EGP website stated that data from the Gene Bank belonged to the Estonian Genome Project Foundation (EGPF). The Gene Donor Consent Form was described (the donor receives a copy and the original stays with the Gene Bank), and donors were informed that tissue samples and uncoded data cannot be sold, presented or otherwise transferred (Eesti geenivaramu 2004d). Since 2001, the EGP worked on the development of its quality management system and received an ISO 9001:2000 certificate in 2003 (Eesti geenivaramu 2009f).

A scientific advisory board was founded in 2002 (Eesti geenivaramu 2009e). The government also financed the Ethics Committee: the costs for this committee were estimated to be about US$15,000 per year (Koik 2003). When the law was changed in 2007, the genetic database became a structural unit of the University of Tartu and the Ethics Committee on Human Research of the University of Tartu is now responsible for ethical review (Kattel and Suurna 2008).

An interesting difference to the UK Biobank is that participants in Estonia were told in the beginning that they had the possibility of learning about their own risks of developing diseases (Lahteenmaki 2000). It was planned to communicate the findings of the research back to participants. The underlying idea was that this communication would be beneficial for the Estonian health care system which remained underdeveloped as a consequence of the Soviet regime period. For this reason the Gene Bank was advertised as 'a "medical care" model' (Public Population Project in Genomics P3G 2003). The only genetic information Estonians are not entitled to obtain from the Gene Bank data is that about genetic genealogy, for example, about paternity (Eesti geenivaramu 2009c).

The EGP was built originally with private funding. It can be called a public–private partnership in R&D (Kattel and Suurna 2008). This type of organizational structure implies 'loss of coherence and adequate control over the respective service implementation by the government' due to the 'fragmented coordination mechanism' (Kattel and Suurna 2008, 4). In the following this caused 'serious discontinuities' (Kattel and Suurna 2008, 4) between what the concrete public programme expected from the database and the market-oriented interests of the private investors. In January 2004, EGeen, the organization representing the international investors financing most of the project, requested a change in direction. EGeen proposed that the EGP should focus more on collecting data from specific disease groups and should invest less workforce on the collection of data from the entire population (Eesti geenivaramu 2004b). The database should give priority to research concerning particular diseases because of 'economic realities' (Burgermeister 2004). This type of research was hoped to lead to drug development more quickly than the original plan to collect general health data on the majority of the population. Since no agreement was reached during 2004 between the private and public stakeholders, EGeen stopped its funding in 2004. Between 2004 and 2007, the project stagnated. Researchers involved in the EGP did not give up and were able to convince the Estonian government to provide public funding for a smaller biobank. In 2007, the government financed the EGP with around 1.15 million euros (Kattel and Suurna 2008, 10) and the EGP was reorganized. After an amendment of the law (Human Genes Research Act 2000), the EGP was affiliated to the University of Tartu (O'Neill 2007). The aim became less ambitious: instead of one million, only samples from some 100,000 participants will be included, about one tenth of Estonia's population (Eesti geenivaramu 2009f). In 2008 the Gene Bank had included data and samples from close to 20,000 donors. It is planned to expand the database to contain 100,000 donors by 2010.

*Public Attitudes to the Estonian Gene Bank Project*

Similar to the funding institutions of the UK Biobank project, the founders of the Estonian project were concerned about public opinion and asked a company to study the attitudes and knowledge of the Estonian population about the Gene Bank project. In 2003, 500 citizens of the Republic of Estonia aged 15 to 74 years were approached (Koik 2003). According to Koik (2003), the survey showed that about two thirds of Estonians were well informed about the project. However, outside the counties in which the pilot project was carried out, the percentage of Estonians who knew about the project was low. In the participating counties, only a small minority seemed not to agree with the project. More than three quarters of participants in the survey agreed with the statement that the Estonian Genome Project is carried out in the interests both of the state and of the people of Estonia.

A sociological survey, commissioned by the Ethics Centre at the University of Tartu, was carried out in December 2002 (Sutrop 2003). It was part of the international European project ELSAGEN about the ethical, legal and social aspects of human genetic databases (Häyry et al. 2007). Sutrop reported that according to this survey, 62 per cent of the Estonians who participated claimed to have heard of the Estonian Genome Project, but only 7 per cent considered themselves to be well informed; 24 per cent planned to participate, 37 per cent had not made up their mind, and 39 per cent said that they would not participate in the project. Participants in the survey thought that researchers and employees of the EGP were more trustworthy information sources than politicians and journalists (Sutrop 2003).[40]

## Ethical and Legal Objections to the Estonian Gene Bank Project

In spite of the relatively high acceptance of the project amongst the population, some ethical and legal objections to the Estonian Gene Bank project have been expressed.

### Inducement

Critics say that Estonians have undergone some form of inducement. The population has been extensively informed by the media. Some believe that the Estonian population is vulnerable because Estonians, used to socialist propaganda, are not as critical as western European populations.[41] Others think that too many unrealistic promises have been made, some of which are similar to those made to Icelanders. The founders of the project announced that Estonian participants in the project would have the opportunity to receive medications developed through the Gene Bank research. The promise was that new medication might be developed which would be adapted to the genes of the individual patients (Schimmek 2003). Another benefit promised to donors when the project started was the opportunity to obtain a personal gene card in order to have access to individualized medicine based on pharmacogenetic knowledge. A great majority (83 per cent) of participants in a sociological survey said that they planned to ask for such a card. Relying on (at least in the short term) unrealistic promises, the project was declared important for the country's economy and international reputation. Estonians, therefore, were said to have been misled when they were told that contributing DNA might be considered beneficial for oneself and even become a patriotic duty.

The EGP has also been criticized for using undue inducement: for gathering data and blood samples for the Gene Bank project, the participating family physicians received 12 times the payment provided by the state health care system for equivalent work (Tzortzis 2003b). The physicians, motivated by the payment, might be tempted to persuade their patients to take part in the project. According to Tzortzis (2003b), physicians who participated admitted that few of their patients refused (about 7 per cent).

### Absence of sufficient debate before taking a political decision

Opponents argued that the project was presented to the government before any public debate took place (Frank 1999). Critics were also concerned about the fact

---

40   More details of the opinion survey in Estonia have been published recently (Korts 2007).

41   See Tasmuth, cited in MacWilliams (2003).

that the EGP started without having been approved by the Faculty of Medicine at the University of Tartu, nor by the board of the Estonian Academy of Sciences (Tasmuth 2003).

*Unclear benefits, costs of the project and over-emphasis on genetic factors*
It has been argued that the benefits of the Estonian Gene Bank project are not clear.[42] The EGP could be said to play with the hopes of the country's inhabitants because neither the promised scientific progress, nor the economic benefits, were visible in the short term. Critics continue to believe that the influence of genetics on disease is greatly overestimated compared to the influence of environment. For this reason, the biobank is a 'tremendous waste of public financing' and a 'scientific imagination'.[43] The gene card which was promised to participants at the beginning, and which was supposed to contain all information about their genes and to be useful to their health care, has been called a 'myth' and will not be available in the near future, although the EGP website still promises donors the right to access their genetic data stored in the Gene Bank free of charge (Eesti geenivaramu 2009c). Tasmuth (2003) has so far been correct that it is unlikely that such a card will be of any clinical use in the foreseeable future. The pharmaceutical industry has also expressed doubts: the health information collected using a questionnaire in the Estonian project might not be sufficiently accurate. Detailed and valid information about the phenotype is the prerequisite for obtaining valuable research results. The pharmaceutical companies 'would be interested in paying for the Estonian records only if they are exhaustive and detailed' (Uehling 2003).

The overall costs of the original ambitious Estonian Genome Project were estimated to amount to US$150 million over five years (Frank 2001, 514). Although most of the financial support was supposed to come from private sources, predominantly venture capital from abroad, the Estonian government had to provide several million dollars even before the private investors backed out. Critics have drawn attention to the fact that the important amount of government finances invested in the Gene Bank project at present would be better invested in other aspects of the 'chronically underfunded' (Tasmuth 2003) health care system. Estonians would benefit far more from interventions focused on lifestyle factors, such as alcoholism, drug abuse and smoking (Frank 1999). The government and the founders of the project defended their financial investment in the EGP by saying that the project would attract resources to Estonia which would help the country to raise funds in order to improve their health care system in the long run. Furthermore, the founders of the project argued that the taxes which the EGPF has paid to the State of Estonia outweigh the amount of money invested by the government into the project (Koik 2003).

---

42   The Estonian Genome Project 'is a gamble; there is no guarantee at all' (A. Caplan, cited by Tzortzis 2003b).

43   M.-W. Ho, director of the Institute of Science in Society (London), cited in MacWilliams (2003).

*Participation of minors*

The Human Genes Research Act, the Estonian law regulating the Genome Project, allows in principle the participation of children aged 7 to 15 in the database. This has been criticized on the grounds that it is not in line with international guidelines on human research, including the Declaration of Helsinki (Tasmuth 2003). The founders of the project deny plans to include children. According to them, the Ethics Committee of the Estonian Genome Project began to examine the issue of including minors because of requests from adolescents to allow their participation (Koik 2003). On the 2004 website of the EGP, the 'introduction of the Estonian Gene Bank's Questionnaire of the State of Health and Genealogy' seemed to imply the participation of children older than seven years, because it gives explicit information how the questionnaire should be filled in for these and how the children should be informed about their participation (Eesti geenivaramu 2004e). On the new website, these explanations have not been maintained (Eesti geenivaramu 2009a).

*Lack of an independent Ethics Committee*

Critics have directed attention to the fact that the members of the original project-specific Ethics Committee supervising the Estonian Genome Project were appointed by the Supervisory Board of the project. The Supervisory Board also had the right to remove members. This gave the Supervisory Board the possibility of controlling the activities of the Ethics Committee and did not permit complete independence of ethical advice. Defenders of the project argued that the members of the Supervisory Board would not have any interest in choosing 'irresponsible' individuals as members of the Ethics Committee, because the Supervisory Board itself is composed of members appointed by respectable institutions such as the Estonian parliament, the government and the Estonian Academy of Sciences. Critics did not accept this defence since the government, which was known to favour the project, as well as scientists from the Estonian Academy, might be biased towards uncritical support of the project.

Critics believed that an independent Ethics Committee should have been consulted before starting the project (Tasmuth 2003). In 2007 the EGP responded to the critics by transferring the project to the University of Tartu where the university's Ethics Committee on Human Research is now appointed to examine the ethical questions related to scientific studies involving the Estonian biobank.

*Confidentiality and privacy*

The founders promised that the privacy of all information contained in the database would be assured through coding. Although for the time being no concrete plans exist to systematically update the health information, this is part of the project. The consent form (Eesti geenivaramu 2009c) mentions that donors 'may submit additional information [...] to the Estonian Genome Project Foundation' and that this foundation 'has the right to receive information about my [the donor's] state of health from other databases', for example, from tumour registries. In order to add information and to provide feedback to the donor, anonymization must be reversible: the code must be broken. Critics question whether data protection can be guaranteed when it is allowed to decode data for renewal, supplementation of information and feedback to the donors (Sutrop 2003). They fear that scientists might later repeatedly try to contact certain donors in order to know whether they have now developed the symptoms of a predicted disease (Schimmek 2003). The founders of the Gene Bank denied such projects. They explained that gene donors decide themselves when to visit their family physicians. The donor has the option to provide future health information to the Gene Bank or not. Only with the permission of the Ethics Committee might donors be invited by their physicians to participate in further research (Eesti geenivaramu 2002).

The Estonian law passed in 2000 states that misuse of gene donor information will entail criminal prosecution (Tzortzis 2003b).[44] In order to prevent misuse, it is not allowed to take any information about donors and their samples out of Estonia. The problem persists that Estonians are protected against such discrimination only in Estonia. If Estonians move to live in another country, insurance companies or employers in these countries are only bound by the laws of the new country. If these laws do not forbid discrimination, Estonians who have received information about genetic predispositions might be required to disclose this information.

The code which permits the identification of a person in the Estonian Gene Bank Project is stored in a separate computer, not connected to any other source. Three people have access to the computer (Schimmek 2003) but, according to the head of the Genome Project laboratory, no single person holds the key to the code (Boyes 2003; Tzortzis 2003b). Critics claim that the coding does not provide enough security. In the context of the illegal trade of transplant organs, criminals could try to find out which Estonian has genetic compatibility with some wealthy individuals all over the world. People might be killed because they have suitable organs.[45] Those in favour of the Gene Bank have answered that these fears are exaggerated. Moreover, the risk described is not specific to the Gene Bank. Any other blood samples, such as those obtained from newborns, could be used to test for histocompatibility in the search for a suitable organ.

The data collected by family physicians are encrypted and sent electronically to the databank centre. Blood samples, together with consent forms, are transported in armoured trucks to the laboratory (MacWilliams 2003). In addition, computers and the offices of participating physicians have been inspected to ensure that they are sufficiently secure concerning burglary (Schimmek 2003). Critics fear that these security measures are not enough in a country where the Mafia is known to be omnipresent.[46] The supporters of the project hold that protection is higher than in other countries that are building a national biobank. In contrast to the UK Biobank project, 'courts, police authorities, insurance companies, banks, the

---

44   See Human Genes Research Act (2000, §16).
45   Professor M. Sutrop, cited in Schimmek (2003).
46   Professor M. Sutrop, cited in Schimmek (2003).

health insurance fund, or employers' will 'certainly not' receive genetic or health data (Eesti geenivaramu 2009b), since this is regulated by a law, the Human Genes Research Act.

*Informed consent and future use of the samples*
Participation is voluntary (Eesti geenivaramu 2009c). All donors need to give individual informed consent before participation. The donors have the option of presenting additional data about themselves or prohibiting the adjustment of their data. They have the right to opt out at any time later in the process. This means that their data will be unlinked, to the extent that identification becomes impossible.

According to the Estonian Human Genes Research Act (2000, amended in 2007), a gene donor has the right to withdraw his or her consent only 'until his or her tissue sample or the description of his or her state of health is coded' (§12, 7). Critics of the Estonian Human Genes Research Act pointed out that the text implies a limited right to withdraw consent which is not in accordance with international ethical recommendations, for example, guidelines from UNESCO (Tasmuth 2003).

The 2009 version of the consent form contains a different wording than in the Estonian Human Genes Research Act. Donors have the right to demand the destruction of identifiable, and even all, data stored in the bank:

> If a gene donor does not want to participate in the Genome Project anymore, he or she shall have the right to demand deletion of the data that enable identification of his or her person or, in certain cases, of all the information stored in the Gene Bank about him or her. After deletion of the given data, it will not be possible to associate a blood sample and a gene donor and the donor shall never receive any information about him or her (Eesti geenivaramu 2009d).

The informed consent procedure has been criticized infrequently in journal articles, although it represents, as in the United Kingdom, a form of general consent to all future research projects. Critics mentioned the problem that this form of open consent cannot be informed because the research projects cannot be specified ahead of time. Another criticism is that the information related to genetic databases is too complex and exceeds what individuals can grasp or interpret (Sutrop 2003). Tasmuth argued that family members of donors are not required to consent to the project, although information about them will figure in the questionnaire (Tasmuth 2003).

*Access to data*
The founders of the Estonian project claim to have learned from problematic issues in the Icelandic project. One such issue is that Icelanders, and participants in the UK Biobank, do not have access to their own information. Estonians will have the opportunity to learn the results concerning their own DNA (Frank 1999). According to the information posted on its website in 2004, the Gene Bank 'will notify gene donors through the media of its readiness to issue data' (Eesti geenivaramu 2004f). At present, the right of donors to learn about their own

genetic results is maintained (Eesti geenivaramu 2009c). Those in favour of the database claim that this information might be useful for the participants and their families to prevent disease and to plan their life. Critics warn that this knowledge might put Estonians at risk of at least some form of stigmatization, because the risks of violations of confidentiality and privacy are never reduced to zero.

The Donor Consent Form attests to the donor's 'right to genetic counseling upon accessing my [the donor's] data stored in the Gene Bank'.[47] Eugenijus Gefenas of Vilnius University, chair of the Lithuanian National Committee on Biomedical Ethics, sees a problem in the fact that, due to the paternalistic tradition of the post-communist Baltic states, it will not be possible to assure non-directive counselling.[48] An argument that does not depend on the local context is added by Tiina Tasmuth, professor of medical education at the University of Tallinn: given that the interactions between genes and environment are still poorly understood, it will be 'irresponsible' to provide genetic information to individuals which may have 'profound implications' for themselves, family members and unborn children.[49] Critics point out that, on the practice level, no consideration has been given so far to details of how the disclosure of research results to the participants will be managed (Sutrop 2003).

*Commercialization, ownership and financial fairness*
Although the Estonian database was owned from the beginning by a non-profit foundation set up by the Estonian government,[50] a problematic issue in respect to commercialization existed in the early years which was somewhat similar to Iceland. Before 2005, only one single company held the rights to commercialize and license out the data of the database. This was the Estonian-led start-up company, named EGeen, based in the United States.[51] The Estonian government gave the company exclusive access to all DNA samples and the health and family data collected through the project (Habeck 2003). The company declared that it planned to work with many biotechnology companies on multiple projects concerning different diseases. The founders of the project argued at the time that, in contrast to Iceland, commercial companies were not in control of the samples because Estonia would not give DNA to any company (MacWilliams 2003). The original interdiction to export data or material out of Estonia was intended to force foreign companies and researchers to realize their projects within the country (Frank 2001, 514).

Those who defended the original project said that adequate benefit-sharing agreements were in place: EGeen was supposed to return a percentage of its profits to the Estonian Genome Project to permit the running of the database (MacWilliams 2003). By contrast, gene donors themselves would not receive a share of the profit

---

47   See Eesti geenivaramu, General information: Gene donor consent form.
48   E. Gefenas, cited in Frank (1999, 1263).
49   T. Tasmuth, cited in Frank (1999, 1263).
50   See Lahteenmaki (2000, 1135).
51   See Frank (2001, 514).

and this clause remained unchanged after the reconfiguration of the project in 2007 (Eesti geenivaramu 2009c). Supporters of the original project also claimed that freedom of scientific research was assured, since local researchers would have free or low-fee access to the biobank data (Frank 2001, 514).

Critics mentioned that, at the beginning of the project, it had not been disclosed that the Gene Bank had a commercial plan. They criticized the fact that only after the publication of the commercial projects in a foreign country had the Estonian informed consent form been changed to include the information that the tissue donated has a commercial value and that the data could be commercially exploited (Tasmuth 2003).

Several of the objections led to changes when the project was transformed in 2007: since the private funders quit the project, concerns about commercial interests have decreased. However, at present the Gene Bank maintains the commercial use of data and donors are informed of this: 'I am aware of the fact that the tissue sample I provide may have some commercial value and that anonymized data from the Gene Bank may be released to commercial entities' (Eesti geenivaramu 2009c). The Gene Bank also maintains the sharing of data with research institutions and declares on its website that: '[f]irst batches of anonymized data contributed by gene donors were released to our partners in 2004' (Eesti geenivaramu 2009f).

## A Genetic Database from Switzerland: The Swiss Pediatric Oncology Group (SPOG) Tumor Bank

*Introduction*

In Switzerland, for the time being, no population genetics gene bank has been established.[52] However, as in other countries, large human genetic databases are created, most often related to specific diseases. In order to understand how the international debate related to biobanks has influenced ethical and legal frameworks in countries other than those with a large debate about their own biobanks (Iceland, Estonia, the UK in particular), we describe here an example of a large Swiss genetic database.

A characteristic of many pediatric tumours is their morphologic similarity to embryologic precursor cells. The early manifestation of these tumours suggests that few genetic changes are necessary to lead to the malignant phenotype. Tumour

---

52    The Foundation biobank-suisse is not a national biobank. It was established as 'a network of human biobanks across Switzerland; it also provides various services for the biobanks'. 'The samples will continue to be stored decentrally in individual biobanks. Only a few personal data will be merged into a central database. The biobank-suisse website enables researchers to simply and quickly determine whether the samples they need for their research are available. In a next step the researchers can then order these samples along with the corresponding personal data' (see: <http://www.biobank-suisse.ch/>).

banks have already been established in the United States, Japan and Germany. The aim of the SPOG Tumor Bank (Grotzer 2002; Grotzer et al. 2003) is to provide a basis for advances in molecular genetic cancer research in Switzerland. The Tumor Bank assures the central conservation of tissue samples of the greatest possible number of malignant child tumours; the development and preservation of primary cell cultures and permanent cell lines derived from these tumours; the documentation of the preservation and associated phenotypic information, as well as the updating of this information; and the use of the material and data for research studies by SPOG-associated research groups (Grotzer et al. 2003, 180).

*The History of the SPOG Tumor Bank*

The SPOG Tumor Bank project was initiated in 2000 by Professor Michael Grotzer. In June 2001 it received the unanimous approval of the scientific committee (Forschungsrat) of the Swiss Pediatric Oncology Group. The project was approved by the cantonal ethics commissions of Zurich (August 2002), Bern (January 2003), Lucerne (February 2003) and Basel (May 2003).

 The research goals of the Tumor Bank are to investigate whether genetic particularities represent relevant steps in the development of these tumours or are only secondary changes, and whether these genetic particularities are useful as diagnostic or prognostic criteria (Grotzer 2002, 5). In addition, tumour cell cultures can be used to test the potential of new substances to inhibit the growth of the tumour cells in vitro (Grotzer 2002, 20).

*Public Attitudes to the Tumor Bank Project*

So far, there has been no public debate on the project or evaluation of public attitudes. According to Grotzer, no refusal by parents or their children to donate samples has so far been recorded.[53]

*Ethical and Legal Details of the Project and Discussion of Possible Ethically Problematic Issues*

*Commercialization, ownership and financial fairness*
The logistic resources, including laboratory material and project staff, are financed jointly by the University Children's Hospital of Zurich and SPOG.

 Commercial use of the tissue samples, or the products developed from the samples, such as RNA, DNA, cDNA, primary cell cultures and permanent cell lines, is forbidden. Exempt from this regulation are tests or treatments which will be developed based on the results of the research carried out while using the samples. These tests and treatments can be commercially exploited (Grotzer 2002, 7). The

---

 53 Grotzer, personal communications (e-mails of 13 February 2003 and 29 August 2009).

issue of possible commercialization has stirred some controversy among members of the local ethics committees. Since child tumours are rare diseases, it has been judged that the material is of almost no interest to pharmaceutical companies or to the biotechnological industry in general. The possibility of commercialization has therefore been evaluated as rather remote. If the question arose, the local ethics committee in charge of the evaluation of a research study, the results of which might be commercially exploited, would have to decide on this issue.[54]

The tissue or derived products will be provided free of charge to research groups which are composed of at least one active member of SPOG. The material transmitted is anonymized. The scientific committee of SPOG decides which projects are accepted. Approval of the research group by the local ethics committee is also required. The research groups carry out the research without knowledge of any data related to treatment or follow up. After the completion of the project, the groups' results are transmitted to the Tumor Bank, which correlates them with the clinical data.

*Inducement*
The consent form specifies explicitly that the donor will not receive any remuneration for providing his or her tissue, even if, based on the research results, new tests or treatments (which might be commercially exploited) will be developed. The treating institution receives a compensation of 50 Swiss francs per patient for the preparation and sending of the tissue, the consent form and the patient information to the Tumor Bank.

The consent form also specifies that future research results will not influence the present treatment decisions of the tumour patient who provides the tissue (Grotzer 2002, 20–21).

In the absence of any direct clinical benefit and of any future benefit sharing, participation relies only on altruistic reasons. No indication of any form of inducement to participation exists.

*Informed consent and future use of the samples*
The legal representative of the minor child gives written informed consent, separately, (a) to the storage of the tissue and its use for cancer research, and (b) to the transmission and processing of health data. The consent form specifies the following future uses: research about the molecular, genetic, immunological and other disease-related characteristics of child tumours.[55] The possibility of opting out at any moment is specified in the consent form. The child's treating physician needs

---

54  Grotzer, personal communication (e-mail of 13 February 2003).

55  'Wir fragen Sie um die Erlaubnis [...] Tumorgewebe [...] und Blutproben Ihres Kindes in einer speziellen Tumorbank zu lagern, und Wissenschaftlern zur Erforschung der kindlichen Krebserkrankung in ihren molekularen, genetischen, immunologischen und anderen, mit der Krankheit zusammenhängenden Merkmalen zur Verfügung zu stellen' (Grotzer 2002, 20).

to be informed of the desire to opt out. The consequence will be the destruction of the tissue samples. The document can be criticized because it does not indicate what will happen to the data already used in research studies or the data stored in the tumour databank. Will all data be destroyed or unlinked? Clearly, data already used in a research project or published cannot be destroyed retrospectively. In addition, it is not clear what will happen to the tissue that has already been given to research groups. Although the organization of the Tumor Bank will make it possible to know which research group uses the tissue, it seems problematic to the ongoing research studies to destroy material that has already been included in the study.

According to Grotzer,[56] in the case of withdrawal of consent, the destruction of material that has already been given to the researchers of an accepted project is not planned. All sample remnants, that is, all material that the researchers did not use for their project, must be sent back to the Tumor Bank, where it will then be destroyed if the donor of the sample or his or her legal representative has manifested the wish to opt out.

Concerning the transmission of clinical data, the second consent form describes in general terms how the patient's personal data (age, gender, tumour staging, diagnosis, treatment type and outcome) will be processed and transmitted to the central Tumor Bank (Grotzer 2002, 22). It is not explicitly explained that this transmission includes not only present, but also future information. No possibility is mentioned of opting out of the information transmission, except for the adolescent who will be asked for his or her consent at the age of 16. If the patient was a minor child at the moment of storage of his or her tissue, he or she will be contacted by his or her family physician after his or her 16th birthday in order to give his or her informed consent about the storage and uses of his or her tissue.

Research projects which have different goals than those explained in the consent form, and specified in more scientific detail in the documents of the SPOG Tumor Bank,[57] will only be realized after approval by the local ethics committee in charge, and with new informed consent (Grotzer 2002, 19). However, in another publication, the authors admit that, according to Article 321bis of the Swiss Criminal Code, permission to use the data will be granted if the research cannot be executed with anonymized data, the permission of the data subject cannot be obtained or can only be obtained with unreasonable effort, and the research interests outweigh the secrecy interests (Grotzer et al. 2003, 182). Although the authors state that '[i]n practice, this procedure is rather complicated and has not achieved the expected significance', the possibility of further use of the Tumor Bank data for research projects not specified in the consent form exists as a legal alternative. The consent form does not inform about this possibility. In practice, Grotzer thinks that such a case would be rare and would then be decided by SPOG, together with the local ethics committee.[58]

---

56    Grotzer, personal communication (e-mail of 13 February 2003).
57    See above, 'Informed consent and future use of the samples'.
58    Grotzer, personal communication (e-mail of 14 February 2003).

In Switzerland, access by the police or legal authorities to the data is possible under current legislation.[59] This creates a similar ethical issue as for the UK Biobank. Should donors or their legal representatives be informed about this fact, or should new laws be created, such as in Estonia, to prohibit access to research material by the police or legal authorities, as well as by other third parties such as insurance companies or employers? The Swiss law regulating genetic testing stipulates in Article 4 that any discrimination towards an individual because of his genetic make-up is prohibited (Swiss federal law 8.10.2004). However, although the preparatory commission proposed that the law should also forbid employers and all types of insurance companies[60] to require an individual to disclose results of genetic tests, the national parliament did not follow these propositions recently. According to the present text of the law, life insurance companies will be authorized to have access to results of genetic tests of an individual carried out in the past (Swiss federal law 8.10.2004, Article 27).[61] Although the law came into force on 1 April 2007, the consequences of possible misuse of genetic information are not yet clear. The donor should be informed about possible risks even if they might be remote.

*Confidentiality and privacy*

After the collection of tissue, the institution in charge of the patient anonymizes the sample: a code is attributed which is composed of the two letters of the canton in which the institution is located (for example, ZH for Zurich) and a four-digit number. Decoding the number and linking it to the identity of the patient is only possible for the oncologists from the institution treating the patient. This coding system is referred to as 'linked anonymization' (MRC 2000 and 2001), based on the recommendations and terminology of the Medical Research Council in the UK (Grotzer 2002, 13). The institution treating the patient sends the anonymized sample to the Tumor Bank. In addition, the reports of the local pathologist or of another reference pathologist are sent immediately after reception in anonymized form, that is, containing the same patient code as the tissue, to the SPOG Tumor Bank, addressed directly to Professor Grotzer (Grotzer 2002, 11).

The Tumor Bank stores the following patient-related data: patient's age when the tumour was diagnosed, staging, type of treatment, treatment outcome. These data are periodically updated by recontacting the treating institution. A SPOG document announces that linkage of the Tumor Bank data with other genetic databases, allowing identification, is forbidden (Grotzer et al. 2003, 183).

---

59   See Code Pénal Suisse Article 321 Alinea 3: 'Demeurent réservées les dispositions de la législation fédérale et cantonale statuant une obligation de renseigner une autorité ou de témoigner en justice.'

60   See above in this chapter the discussion about discrimination risks in Estonia.

61   'Le Conseil national a suivi jeudi le Conseil fédéral contre la volonté de sa commission préparatoire.' See *Le Temps* 19 March 2004: Les députés autorisent les assureurs vie à accéder aux tests génétiques déjà effectués.

The research groups receive anonymized material marked by a second code, which differs from the previous code. Different codes are assigned to different types of material derived from the same patient. Other information transmitted to the research groups is the type of tissue and the type of tumour.

The coding system can be criticized for permitting identification of the canton where the tissue has been obtained and the patient treated. In the case of relatively rare tumours, identification of the patient, based on the canton where treatment took place, might be possible. However, as research groups receive material with a second, different code, they are not able to identify the canton. Only personnel handling the data in the central databank, and individuals in contact with the information sent to the Tumor Bank, might be able to identify the patient according to the canton and specific information such as the tumour type or treatment outcome. The practice of the Tumor Bank can be defended and it could be argued that confidentiality is sufficiently guaranteed on the following grounds: if these persons are health care workers or their auxiliaries, they are bound by Swiss confidentiality laws. Moreover, the handling of the information is comparable and does not imply more risks than the handling of other, non-coded information in the health care system, when such information is routinely transmitted between different treating institutions of a patient.

*Access to data*

The consent form explains that future research results will not be transmitted either to the tissue donor or to his or her family physician. One exception is specified: unless the donor has not specifically objected, results obtained incidentally which influence the health or life of the donor can be transmitted to the treating physicians, requesting that these physicians give the information to the donor.[62]

In contrast to the Estonian Genome Project, the consent form does not mention any right to genetic counselling with respect to the transmission of possible genetic information. However, according to Swiss law (Swiss federal law 8.10.2004), genetic counselling is obligatory if the results of a gene test are transmitted to a patient. Moreover, the definition of the type of results that will be given to the treating physicians is rather large. It is not clear who will decide which type of information should be transmitted and which should not. Will an ethics committee and/or the SPOG scientific committee be involved in the decision? Has the family physician the right or the duty to inform living family members if the donor is dead, and who is supposed to update addresses to make sure that the donor or his/her family can be traced?

---

62   'Ausgenommen davon sind Zufallsbefunde, die Auswirkungen haben auf Rettung/ Erhaltung von Gesundheit und/oder Leben. Solche Befunde werden ohne Ihren [the donor's] ausdrücklichen Widerspruch den behandelnden Ärzten weitergeleitet mit der Aufforderung, sie an den Patienten weiterzuleiten' (Grotzer 2002, 21).

## Four Biobanks – Four Situations – Four Ethical and Legal Solutions?

The biobanks in Iceland, Estonia and the UK are all running behind schedule because they have encountered ethical and legal problems and opposition from the public (Arnason and Hjörleifsson 2007). All three of them have had to adapt and change important ethical and legal aspects of the biobanks. Both in Iceland and Estonia, the original plans of the biobanks have had to be abandoned. The UK Biobank, which started most recently, was able to avoid repeating the mistakes of the previously established biobanks. The present reorganized biobank in Estonia, the UK biobanks and the SPOG Tumor Bank have avoided private funding and rely instead exclusively on public funding. This seems to be advantageous because it increases trust (Kaiser 2002b) and independence concerning decision making of the public authorities in line with public health arguments (Anderlik 2003; Kattel and Suurna 2008).

It is also interesting to compare the ethical and legal frameworks used by the four biobanks with regard to whether solutions are the same or different for a particular ethical or legal problem (Andorno 2006). In summary, although the four biobanks have developed in different settings and with different solutions, over time the solutions have become closer to each other than they were at the beginning of the 'biobank era': presumed consent has been abandoned in favour of general consent; withdrawal includes the right to destruction of the samples and not just the right to anonymization; private funding has been abandoned in favour of public funding; in all four biobanks samples are given out to researchers in reversibly (linked) anonymized form, that is, the researchers themselves do not have access to the code (MRC 2001). Regulated differently is, first, the issue of whether general practitioners or clinical institutions are involved in the banking. This is the case in Estonia and the SPOG Tumor Bank, but not in the UK and was controversial in Iceland since many GPs refused to participate. The second issue is the feedback of results to individual sample and data donors: this is not possible in the UK Biobank, in contrast to the Estonian Genome Project, while the SPOG Tumor Bank adopts a unique way for sample donors to opt out of future feedback of health and life-relevant information to the patient's treating physician.

The history of the debate and the examples of existing biobanks is a mirror of the ethical and legal challenges of biobanks, especially in comparison with guidelines about classical research ethics. In the following chapters, the ethical debate that emerged as a reaction to the existing biobanks will be analysed in more detail, firstly with respect to the theoretical foundation of research ethics, and, secondly, examining more closely the most controversial ethical and legal issues related to research involving biobanks.

# Chapter 3

# The Ethical Debate: Principles, Values and Interests – The Ethical Foundations of Guidelines

## Value and Limits of Ethical Principles

*The Challenge of Biobanks: Old and New Guidelines*

The ethical questions raised by the establishment and the possible uses of human genetic databases have caused a debate about whether traditional frameworks of health research ethics provide the necessary guidance to distinguish in an internationally acceptable way between ethically justified and unjustified uses of samples and data. Those who propose to substitute or complement the existing framework of research ethics would need to defend their position and bear the burden of proof that the classical framework is insufficient and that the new framework(s) are necessary and/or are superior to the former.

Do we need new guidelines for research involving biobanks, and if yes, why? To answer this question it is necessary, first, to analyse the ethical framework of the most important 'classical' international guidelines on health research ethics. Second, in comparison, the 'new' ethical framework needs to be examined in detail as it is proposed in the various guidelines that regulate more specifically human genetic databases. The guidelines that have been included in the analysis are summarized in Table 3.1 (at the end of the chapter).[1] These guidelines were examined with respect to the following questions:

- Do ethical frameworks proposed for human genetic databases differ from the classical framework of medical research ethics?
- Looking only at guidelines relevant for research involving human genetic databases, do these guidelines contain similar ethical frameworks or can important differences between these guidelines be shown?

---

1  For the analysis of principles and interests, we have restricted our analysis to the CIOMS guidelines from 2002 for simplification. Indeed, the guidelines on epidemiological research (CIOMS 2009) refer to a similar ethical framework and particular passages are quoted from these guidelines if they contain noteworthy aspects that have not been covered by analysis of the more general guidelines (CIOMS 2002); see, for example, the section on the feedback of research results.

- If new frameworks are proposed to guide the establishment and use of human genetic databases as compared to the traditional ethical approach for health research, are the reasons to substitute or complement the classical framework sufficiently strong and convincing?
- Do the new framework(s) provide more appropriate guidance and resolve the controversies more efficiently than the classical guidelines?
- Do guideline frameworks for biobanks or classical health research guidelines that are based on ethical principles, values or interests give sufficiently concrete guidance on how to deal with conflicts between different principles, values or interests with regard to biobank research?
- Do different ethical frameworks or different guidance to resolve conflicts lead to different recommendations concerning the controversial aspects of human databases, such as, for example, the use of informed consent or the feedback of research results?

We will first look closely at the most influential international guidelines on medical research ethics. We will then analyse whether the guidelines contain a general part which describes their ethical foundations. Since health research ethics has traditionally been dominated by a principle-based approach, it is not surprising that the most common way in which ethical foundations are explained in the guidelines is by reference to ethical principles. The different principles and their explanations are summarized in Table 3.2 (at the end of the chapter). If the guidelines give any explanation how to balance conflicting principles or how to deal with conflicts between principles, this explanation is quoted.

Among guidelines dealing with human genetic databases, we have included all international (with the exception of Asia)[2] and national statements on human DNA sampling and human genetic databases that were available to us through publication in Medline and/or the internet (see Table 3.1 at the end of the chapter). We did not take into account the entire range of guidelines from professional organizations in the United States, the United Kingdom and Europe, but included only the most important of those available through the internet.[3] Some aspects of the whole range of US professional guidelines are summarized elsewhere.[4] Not

---

2    The guidelines about genetic databases in Asia have been recently analysed in much detail (Porter 2009; Sleeboom-Faulkner 2009). We have not included classical guidelines which address predominantly clinical trials (ICH 2002; WHO 2005). They are cited sporadically where appropriate.

3    This analysis does not include in detail the German guidelines (German National Ethics Council 2004). These guidelines are, however, mentioned in the discussions of the issues in Chapter 4, if they contain specific recommendations that are unique to the German position. Some other guidelines that do not contain important contributions to the ethical problems posed by genetic databases are mentioned occasionally, for example, The Advisory Committee on Health Research (ACHR) (2002).

4    See National Bioethics Advisory Commission (1999, appendix C, 103).

all of the included guidelines are written to guide specifically the establishment, maintenance and use of human genetic databases. However, the ethical questions underlying these activities have been more or less explicitly addressed by various guidelines about research involving human tissue and about genetic research. All the guidelines that we have included are still valuable and are used by the professional groups who have produced them.

In the same way as for the classical research ethics guidelines, we will analyse first whether the guidelines concerning genetic databases contain a general part in which they describe their ethical foundations. Similar to the classical research ethics guidelines, in the guidelines relevant for biobanks the most common way in which ethical foundations are explained is by making reference to ethical principles. We therefore searched all guidelines for use of the term 'principle' (referring to an ethical principle) and for explanations as to how conflicting principles should be balanced (see Table 3.3 at the end of the chapter). In addition, we also noted other approaches, mainly those referring to 'rights', 'values' and 'interests'.

*Ethical Principles and Human Rights: The Ethical Framework of Classical Health Research Ethics*

The field of health research ethics has been governed traditionally by a principle-based ethical framework, as documented by the Belmont Report, a visible milestone in research ethics in the 1970s (Belmont Report 1979).[5] The Belmont Report 'attempts to summarize the basic ethical principles identified by the Commission in the course of its deliberations' (1979, 1). The principles used reflect those of the so called 'Georgetown Mantra', referring to the influential work of Beauchamp and Childress (2008), the 'principles of biomedical ethics'. The four classical mid-level principles of the 'Georgetown Mantra' are respect for autonomy, beneficence, non-maleficence and justice. These principles and derived 'mezzanine rules' (Häyry and Takala 2007) have not only influenced the field of medical research ethics, but can be called the most widely used framework of modern bioethics in the US and Europe.

Principlism is a mixture of more or less absolute values (Bruce and Tait 2004) such as respect for autonomy, respect for persons or for human rights and a consequentialist approach introduced through the principles of beneficence and non-maleficence.

As Table 3.2 shows, the Belmont Report (1979) and the Council for International Organizations of Medical Sciences' 'International ethical guidelines' (2002),

---

5   In all guidelines listed in Table 3.1, we searched for explanations of the ethical framework. We also used the computer search function to search the electronic documents (most of the documents were available in this form) for the terms and principles listed in Tables 3.4–3.6 and 3.9–3.12. In the tables on benefit, 3.7 and 3.8, only the most frequent or most important formulations concerning benefit are cited. Above the double lines are listed the classical international guidelines for medical research ethics (on human beings), and below the double lines are resumed the positions of specific guidelines concerning biobanks/genetic databanks.

called hereafter CIOMS guidelines, provide a similar approach based on the three principles of respect for persons, beneficence (complemented by non-maleficence) and justice. Both note two fundamental ethical considerations that follow from the principle of respect for persons, namely the 'respect for autonomy, which requires that those who are capable of deliberation about their personal choices should be treated with respect for their capacity of self-determination; and [...] protection of persons with impaired or diminished autonomy, which requires that those who are dependent or vulnerable be afforded security against harm or abuse'.[6] The classical 'Georgetown Mantra' has been praised, and sometimes criticized, for giving prominent weight to the principle of autonomy. Autonomous persons are allowed to make choices that are against their best interest defined according to the criteria of medical benefit. They are allowed to refuse life-saving interventions for religious reasons (Kleinman 1994; Wilson 1994; Muramoto 2001) or even to have mutilating surgery, if they find a surgeon who is willing to act according to the patient's desire (Dyer 2000). Interfering with the choices of a competent person is condemned as unjustified paternalism (Beauchamp 1978; Veatch and Spicer 1994, 410). Interestingly, the CIOMS guidelines (CIOMS 2002) state at the beginning ('General ethical principles', 8) that, at least in the abstract, the three principles have 'equal moral force'. This reflects an important difference in the scope of the 'principle of autonomy' as it is used in research ethics, compared to its use outside research. The choice of the autonomous agent, that is, his or her informed consent, is necessary, but not sufficient: 'Informed consent protects the individual's freedom of choice and guarantees respect for the research subject's autonomy' (CIOMS 2002, commentary on guideline 4, 16). The principle of autonomy is overriding in the case of an individual's refusal to participate in research, even if this research were of great benefit to him or her. However, the principle of beneficence has more weight overall than the principle of autonomy as regards the range of research participants' possible choices (CIOMS 2002, 8). They will not be allowed to participate in research that a research ethics committee finds too dangerous, or for which the benefit–harm ratio is evaluated as not being sufficiently favourable. Informed consent must be complemented by the 'safeguard of independent review' of research proposals. This 'is particularly important as many individuals are limited in their capacity to give adequate consent; they include [...] persons who are unfamiliar with medical concepts and technology' (CIOMS 2002, 16, commentary on guideline 4).

In the therapeutic context, the principles of beneficence and non-maleficence were clearly defined as relating to the individual patient. In the research setting, the risk–benefit ratio is not necessarily calculated for each research subject, but takes account of benefits to future patients, to society, to patients from other populations and societies and to science. Therefore the principles of beneficence and non-maleficence cannot be discussed outside considerations of justice.

---

6    Council for International Organizations of Medical Sciences (2002, General ethical principles, 8).

The most recent version of the CIOMS guidelines (2002) reflects 'the rapid advances in medicine and biotechnology' (CIOMS 2002, 5, 'Background'), especially the growing practice of cross-country research involving rich and poor countries. In general, researchers from a rich country propose projects involving vulnerable populations from poorer countries. This raises the problem of 'paternalism on the part of the richer countries towards poorer countries' (CIOMS 2002, 5). Should poorer countries be allowed to make local decisions, that is, to accept risks and trial conditions which have some advantages to them but which would never have been accepted by a population from the richer country? The CIOMS guidelines presuppose that their principle-based approach reflects 'universally applicable ethical standards'. However, they go one step further than the Belmont Report and require that 'cultural values' need to be respected. Participating countries are allowed to accept different standards at least 'in superficial aspects' (CIOMS 2002, 6, 'Introduction') concerning individual autonomy and informed consent as well as acceptable benefit–risk ratios.

Both the Belmont Report and the CIOMS guidelines describe the principle of justice as 'fairness of the distribution' of benefits and burdens of research. Research participants should only be chosen 'for reasons related to the problem being studied' and scientific studies should 'not unduly involve persons from groups unlikely to be among the beneficiaries of subsequent applications of the research' (Belmont Report 1979). Again, the CIOMS guidelines announce a universal starting point, but acknowledge the debate about different interpretations of justice by developed countries as compared to less developed countries. In 2002, at a conference of European medical ethicists, an African epidemiologist defended the view that ethical codes drawn up predominantly by experts from developed countries should not be imposed on the rest of the world. Health research in poor countries will be paralysed if universal ethical principles of fairness and justice are interpreted dogmatically (Richards 2002). One example is the Malarone (proguanil hydrochloride with atovaquone) trials that have been carried out in Kenya, Indonesia and Gabon. The aim of the research was not to test the drugs for local use, but the results were intended to help protect those from (mostly rich) countries travelling to countries with endemic malaria. The Norwegian philosopher, R. Lie, found the trials justified, although they violated the principle of justice required by international ethical guidelines. In the beginning, the trials had been refused by ethical review boards. The local communities protested against this refusal: the trials were thought to be highly beneficial to the community because the sponsors had promised to finance free malaria treatment and to build clean water wells.[7] According to classical research ethics, 'justice' means that individuals from less well-off countries should not be exposed to research risks if the benefits of this research are intended for individuals who do not bear the burdens of the research. From the viewpoint of the 'exploited' countries, 'justice' means that they should not be deprived of accepting research that makes them better off than before, even

---

7    R. Lie quoted in Richards (2002, 796).

if the research implies lower standards of justice than research accepted according to classical international criteria. As a matter of fact, the different viewpoints on justice do not so much reflect cultural values, but are influenced by the situation. If the Western ethicists were in the same situation as those in poor countries who lack basic resources such as clean water, they might adopt a different view on justice and prefer to take moderate research risks if this could enable them and their children to survive (in general small children are the first to die of infectious diseases caused by contaminated water).

The explanations of the CIOMS guidelines concerning the principle of justice reflect these different viewpoints. On the one hand, research should be responsive to the health needs of populations; on the other hand it could be globally sufficient that the research project leaves 'low-resource countries or communities better off than previously or, at least, no worse off' (CIOMS 2002, 9). CIOMS guideline 3, entitled 'ethical review of externally sponsored research', announces the 'dogma', that is, that ethical standards applied concerning a project to be carried out by an external sponsor should be 'no less stringent than they would be for research carried out in the country of the sponsor'. However, in the commentary to guideline 3, they allow the host country's commission to judge 'whether material benefits or inducements may be regarded as appropriate'. The involvement of the host country's commission probably does not reflect the acceptance for culturally[8] different viewpoints on justice, but only the pragmatic awareness of the complexity of the issue: the CIOMS guidelines acknowledge that 'the borderline between justifiable persuasion and undue influence is imprecise' (CIOMS 2002, 21).

The Declaration of Helsinki and the Convention on Human Rights and Biomedicine, hereafter Bioethics Convention, use the term 'principle' in a somewhat different way than the Belmont Report and the CIOMS guidelines. 'Basic principles for all medical research' (WMA 2008, title of section B) or 'the principles contained in this Convention' (COE 1997b, Art. 16) do not refer to abstract ethical principles, but to the concrete recommendations of the guidelines. Some of the recommendations refer to principles such as informed consent or confidentiality. These principles could be called 'secondary' or derived principles because they serve to put into practice some of the more basic ethical principles.[9] Although the Declaration of Helsinki does not contain a theoretical reflection on its underlying ethical framework, its recommendations are clearly influenced by the framework of classical medical research ethics. The principle of autonomy, and to some extent also the principle of justice, is represented by the references to 'respect for all human beings'. The principle of beneficence is contained in the imperative to protect the health and well-being of the human subject. The

---

8    As we have discussed above, the opposite views on justice are not primarily influenced by cultural difference, but are influenced in an important way by the situation from which a person judges.

9    Informed consent and confidentiality, for example, are mainly derived from the principle of autonomy.

'beneficence/non-maleficence rule' cited by the Belmont Report and the CIOMS guidelines to maximize benefits and minimize harms is present in Article 21 of the Declaration of Helsinki (2008) which indicates that the importance of the objective needs to outweigh the risks and burdens of the subject. The Declaration of Helsinki (2008) provides relatively little guidance on justice issues, apart from Article 17 which underlines that populations in which the research is carried out should benefit from the results of the research.

The European Bioethics Convention (COE 1997b) dedicates several articles to medical research, although it has a scope that is not restricted to health research ethics. The convention adopts an approach based on human rights and fundamental freedoms combined with the principle of beneficence and some new aspects of justice.[10] This approach is compatible with the classical 'Georgetown Mantra' principlism, while adding some new elements. The human rights and fundamental freedoms referred to in the preamble of the Bioethics Convention and its Additional Protocol Concerning Biomedical Research can be interpreted as following from the principle of autonomy or the principle of respect for persons. The fact that the texts are framed by referring to the legal traditions and documents about human rights rather than ethical principles reflects the status of the Bioethics Convention as a legal as well as ethical document. Using this legal framework, the Bioethics Convention reaches similar provisions as the Belmont Report and the CIOMS guidelines as regards the requirements of informed consent, confidentiality and privacy. The ethical requirement of beneficence, which means in the ethical documents a favourable risk–benefit ratio, appears in the Bioethics Convention in the form of the concept of 'proportionality', highly valued by legal scholars: 'research may only be undertaken if the risks which may be incurred by that person are not disproportionate to the potential benefits' (COE 1997b, Art. 16).

Both the Declaration of Helsinki and the Bioethics Convention provide a specific explanation as regards the balancing of individual and collective benefit: the well-being of 'the human subject' (WMA 2000)[11] or 'human beings' (Bioethics Convention) should take precedence/shall prevail over the interests of science and society.[12] This article of the Declaration of Helsinki has been cited in the CIOMS guidelines (2002). A similar provision is not present in the Belmont Report.

---

10   The Additional Protocol Concerning Biomedical Research (COE 2005) contains the same approach based on human rights and fundamental freedoms, while providing more detailed recommendations concerning different forms of biomedical research. See also the literature on human rights and biotechnology (Brownsword 2007; Francioni 2007a and 2007b; Millns 2007).

11   The World Medical Association Declaration of Helsinki (2000, para. 5). Interestingly, in the 2008 version this topic is framed more broadly: 'In medical research involving human subjects, the well-being of the individual research subject must take precedence over all other interests' (WMA 2008, para. 6).

12   The '*sole* interest of society and science' (COE 1997b, Art. 2, italics B.E.).

The Bioethics Convention puts the exercise and protection of individual rights first, but allows some relatively vague restrictions 'such as are prescribed by law and are necessary in a democratic society in the interest of public safety, for the prevention of crime, for the protection of public health or the protection of the rights and freedoms of others' (COE 1997b, Art. 26). However, according to Article 26, these restrictions do not apply to the prohibition of financial gain from the human body and its parts, the articles on organ and tissue removal from living donors and the main articles (Articles 16 and 17) on scientific research.

The Bioethics Convention introduces a new element to the objective to maximize benefit. It refers to the 'benefit of present and future generations' and to the 'need to respect the human being both as an individual and as a member of the human species' (COE 1997b, preamble). This is a first step away from individualism towards a collective good of the human species. Another interesting, somewhat anti-individualistic, new element in the Bioethics Convention, as compared to the 'older' Belmont Report, is the notion of 'responsibilities' of all members of society.

The recommendation to take into account the benefit for future generations can be seen as one form of distributive intergenerational justice or 'justice across time'. In its articles on research, the Bioethics Convention does not contain the elements of distributive justice detailed in the CIOMS guidelines and the Belmont Report. Indirectly, some considerations of justice are present in the Convention when it refers to the group of human rights that are often called social or economic, but these human rights do not directly refer to research. Furthermore, the Bioethics Convention contains another unique concept of very far-reaching, albeit vague, distributive justice in its statement that '*all humantiy* may enjoy the benefits' (COE 1997b, preamble, italics B.E.).

In contrast to the other classical guidelines on medical research ethics, the Declaration of Helsinki (WMA 2008, B. para. 11) and the Bioethics Convention (preamble) refer to the concept of 'the dignity of the human being' or 'human dignity'. The principle of respect for human dignity, proclaimed in Article 1 of the Universal Declaration of Human Rights,[13] has been said to have either too many vague meanings or 'no meaning beyond what is implied by the principle of medical ethics, respect for persons' (Macklin 2003, 1419). Adding the term 'dignity' is therefore judged useless by many ethicists (Macklin 2003, 1419). As a matter of fact, neither the Bioethics Convention nor the Declaration of Helsinki contains any concrete provisions for health research ethics that differ from the provisions of the other classical documents and that would follow from the supplement of referring to human dignity.

---

13   See the Universal Declaration of Human Rights, Article 1: 'All human beings are born free and equal in dignity and rights. They are endowed with reason and conscience and should act towards one another in a spirit of brotherhood.'

*The Ethical Foundations of Guidelines Concerning Research Using Human Genetic Databases*

The guidelines that deal more specifically with ethical questions related to research involving genetic databases contain more or less elaborated parts on their ethical foundations. Tables 3.4–3.12 show the ethical principles mentioned in the different guidelines.

The guidelines differ with respect to the extent to which an ethical framework is described. Professional guidelines such as the Statement of the European Society of Human Genetics, the Statement of the American College of Medical Genetics (1995), the statements of the American Society of Human Genetics on DNA Banking and DNA Analysis: Points to Consider (1988) and on Informed Consent for Genetic Research (1996), and the US National Center for Human Genome Research guidelines (1996, 1998) contain almost no reference to a broader ethical framework. These professional guidelines all mention 'secondary' principles, especially informed consent and confidentiality.

Table 3.3 shows that the term 'principle' is used in several different senses. The term 'principle' refers, first, to classical ethical principles such as those of the 'Georgetown Mantra' and to other general more or less new and unique principles such as solidarity, freedom of research, altruism and familial mutuality, as well as to secondary or derived principles such as informed consent. Second, 'principle' refers to the content of concrete recommendations such as the 'principles and procedures' in the Network of Applied Genetic Medicine (RMGA) document and the 'principles' of the Bioethics Convention or the UNESCO document.

In the following we limit our analysis to the ('primary') ethical principles. We examine which principles are cited, whether principles given by the guidelines differ, and whether the types of principles used and the way the principles are defined, interpreted and balanced is related to the recommendations made by the guidelines.

Guidelines which contain explanations on their ethical framework are all based either on the principles of the 'Georgetown/Belmont Report Mantra' (WHO 1998; TC; HGC; NC; RCP; NBAC; CAP) or on a human rights approach (UNESCO; COE 2006; HUGO; NARC). Most of the guidelines based on the principles of the Belmont Report refer occasionally either to international documents on human rights or mention non-specifically the 'rights of the research subjects'.

*Respect for persons/autonomy*
The importance of the individual is underlined in all guidelines. Most of the guidelines based on a human rights approach also mention the principle of 'respect for persons'. However, in the guidelines on research involving genetic databases, one finds less often than in the classical health research guidelines an explicit statement as to how the respect for persons should be balanced against the interest of society, that is, that respect for persons outweighs society's interests (COE 1997b; WMA 2000; CIOMS 2002). This balancing goes back to the Code

of Nuremberg and the Universal Declaration of Human Rights (United Nations 1948). The latter, adopted by the General Assembly of the United Nations in 1948, has obtained legal as well as moral force through the International Covenant on Civil and Political Rights, which the General Assembly adopted in 1966. Article 7 of the Covenant states: 'No one shall be subjected to torture or to cruel, inhuman or degrading treatment or punishment. In particular, no one shall be subjected without his free consent to medical or scientific experimentation.' This statement affirms the fundamental human value that is supposed to govern all research involving human subjects – the precedence of the rights and welfare of the individual research participant over the interests of science and society.

Only less than half of the guidelines that give recommendations pertinent for research involving human genetic databases contain any explicit statement reminding of the precedence of the individual. The guidelines from UNESCO (2003), the COE (2006), the CEST (2003) and the Medical Research Council (MRC 2001) statements are the only ones which contain a sentence similar to the Declaration of Helsinki. The guidelines of the Human Genetics Commission contain a similar statement: 'individual persons have the highest moral importance or value'.

An explanation for the lack in many guidelines of such an explicit balance between the interests of society and the individual could be that this balancing is taken for granted since it has been expressed by the Declaration of Helsinki, the value of which is not contested by any guideline. In addition, in several professional guidelines the lack of such a balancing could be explained by their general silence about the ethical foundations of their recommendations. However, this leaves some international and professional guidelines which give room to ethical reflections of a different kind. They are different in that they seem to indicate the opposite balance, giving more weight to 'community values' (see Table 3.10) than to an approach centred on the individual.

The reason for this shift away from the precedence of the individual could be that research involving tissue or information, without the consent of the donor, does not seem as 'cruel' or 'degrading' as other medical experimentation carried out directly with human subjects. If Article 7 of the International Covenant on Civil and Political Rights were tailored to human tissue, it might state: *No human tissue shall be subjected to what would amount to torture or cruel, inhuman or degrading treatment or punishment of its donor. In particular, no human tissue shall be subjected without the free consent of the donor to medical or scientific experimentation.* Intuitively, many might say that society should never have the right to enforce human subjects' direct participation in research, but that it does not seem justified to attribute the same weight to individual autonomy in research using tissue or information as in research directly involving human beings. The French guidelines state, for example (CCNE 2003, 37, annexe 1), that French law does not give priority to the principle of autonomy (and ownership) concerning tissue or information, although one cannot ignore that other societies do not use the same reasoning.

Interestingly, most guidelines relevant for research involving human genetic databases cite not only the principle of 'respect for persons', but refer in addition to the concept of 'human dignity'. This seems related to the same reasons that have motivated so many readers of the *British Medical Journal* to react to Ruth Macklin, who claimed that the concept of human dignity is 'useless' because it does not imply anything more than the principle of 'respect for persons' (Macklin 2003). Several authors of the rapid responses referred to the usefulness of 'human dignity' outside the context of the living person, for example, in the context of cadavers (Caplan 2003; Capron 2003; D'Oronzio 2003; Giannet 2003; Scott 2003; Woods 2003; Häyry 2004; Häyry and Takala 2005).[14] The authors of the guidelines might have mentioned 'human dignity' because they thought that concerning research involving human genetic databases, the principle of respect for persons is not sufficient and needs to be supplemented by the concept of dignity. The concept of respect for persons is used to argue for a right to influence what is done with the samples. Agreement exists that donors have the right to decide against uses that could harm them. A more controversial issue is whether donors have the right not to be wronged if they are not harmed. However, simply referring to the concept of dignity does not resolve this controversy. Another explanation could be that human samples are conceived as being different from 'things' because of the 'dignity' of the human body to which some guidelines refer (see Table 3.5).

The guidelines of the Nuffield Council on human tissue express the opinion (Nuffield Council on Bioethics 1995, 39) that argumentation based on the perspective of human rights is not helpful since human rights proponents have argued in favour of as well as against extended rights of individuals to control the use of their body parts. In the United States, it has been argued that human rights include individuals' right to make profit from their body parts. Conversely, in Europe the opinion is predominant that respect for human rights includes the non-commercialization of body parts and DNA (Nuffield Council on Bioethics 1995, 39). The Nuffield Council guidelines therefore reject the human rights approach and propose 'a more practical ethical stance' based on a consequentialist approach, namely 'the avoidance and limitation of injury' (Nuffield Council on Bioethics 1995, 39–40).

In line with a consequentialist approach, the concept of human dignity is more often used to limit the respect for persons than to increase it. Particular uses of human tissue such as cloning or obtaining financial gains are restricted because they are incompatible with 'human dignity'. The wishes of donors who request these uses would therefore not be respected.

Important for the governance of human genetic databases are not only the rights of donors about their tissue, but more specifically the rights of donors concerning information derived from their tissue and from other sources, either research health questionnaires or medical records. The concept of dignity has been extended in some guidelines (Nuffield Council on Bioethics 1995; Tri-Council

---

14   See D'Oronzio (2003); Giannet (2003); Woods (2003); Scott (2003) and Capron (2003). See also Häyry (2004).

1998; National Bioethics Advisory Commission [NBAC] 1999) from the dignity of human beings to the dignity of the human body and its parts. However, so far no author or commission has claimed the dignity of 'human' information. If this is due to a moral difference perceived to exist between tissue and information, donors' rights concerning information about them might not be limited by any concerns about dignity. The human rights or respect for persons approach could therefore be sufficient to regulate the use of information contained in human genetic databases. However, when comparing the different guidelines, it becomes clear that, although all are in favour of respect for persons, the extent to which individuals have the right to control the uses of 'their' information and the access to it is highly controversial. These differences will be discussed in more detail in the sections on consent, access and re-contacting.

Independently of whether guidelines mention the principle of respect for persons or the respect of human rights, they all list the principle of confidentiality, a secondary principle that is in general derived from the broader principle of respect for persons.[15]

*Beneficence, non-maleficence and justice*
All guidelines relevant to the establishment and use of human genetic databases contain some reference to 'benefits' and 'risks'. While in the therapeutic context the principles of beneficence and non-maleficence are mostly limited to the individual patient, this is not the case in the context of research ethics. Therefore, the mere announcement of these principles in research ethics does not indicate more than the commitment to involve consequentialist reasoning. Indeed, all guidelines relevant for research implying biobanks agree that a purely deontological approach is obsolete and that an evaluation of the risk–benefit ratio is important.

Most guidelines do not indicate either a theoretical concept or a practical way how to balance the benefits and harms that fall unto different stakeholders, such as sample donors, the participating population, other populations, patients, societies and, sometimes evoked, future generations. In addition, many guidelines do not propose a particular theory of justice. This leads to a broad spectrum of concrete recommendations all based on the principles of beneficence and non-maleficence. Several guidelines state explicitly that general 'rules' of balancing either do not exist or are not feasible, because each research project involving human genetic databases is so complex and unique that the research ethics committee needs to decide on a case by case basis.[16] However, to a certain extent the guidelines' concrete recommendations concerning a particular situation or controversial issue indicate how the ethical principles are used and balanced. We will discuss the

---

15    In addition, the principle of confidentiality is based on consequentialist arguments; see Chapter 4.

16    The role of ethics committees concerning biobanks has been recently investigated in Canada (Gibson et al. 2008) and France (Auray-Blais and Patenaude 2006; De Montgolfier et al. 2006; Moutel et al. 2004).

different ways of balancing below, after the description of the whole range of ethical principles contained in the guidelines.

Tables 3.7 and 3.8 show the range of different 'goods' to be promoted: the maximum protection to DNA donors (NHC),[17] the interests, well-being, welfare and health of the individual sample donor (COE 2006; UNESCO; WHO; MRC; HGC, and so on), the future benefit of all participants (ESHG 2002; ESHG 2003),[18] the welfare of families, the health of populations (WHO) or the immediate benefits to the sampled populations (NARC), benefits for public health and health care (MRC), and the 'collective good and well being of humanity' (CCNE).[19] Guidelines differ as to which stakeholder is associated the most often with the term 'benefit'. There are first guidelines which focus only on the benefits of the donors, such as the guidelines of the American Society of Human Genetics (ASHG), and especially the US National Center for Human Genome Research (NCH) guidelines, which aim at a 'maximum protection to DNA donors'. Second, there are guidelines which focus on individual and population benefit (WHO; TC; NBAC) and, third, guidelines which mention benefit predominantly with respect to populations (NARC; CAP), public health and humanity (RMGA; MRC; CCNE).

The majority of the guidelines relevant to the establishment and use of human genetic databases contain the term 'justice'. The interpretation of justice in classical research ethics[20] comprised two important requirements, first that, if not the individual research subject, at least the participating populations should benefit from research, and second that burdens and benefits of research should be distributed equally. These ideas are expressed in a number of the guidelines relevant to human genetic databases, although not explicitly in all. Examples are the TC guidelines (Tri-Council 1998). They mention distributive justice in the sense that benefits and burdens of research should be distributed in a fair way, which implies especially the protection of vulnerable populations against unfair discrimination and exploitation.[21] Similarly, the National Bioethics Advisory Commission (NBAC) states: 'Justice requires the fair and equitable distribution of benefits and burdens in research.' The guidelines refer to the explanations of one of the most influential textbooks in medical ethics written by T.L. Beauchamp and J.F. Childress (Beauchamp and Childress 2008) and cite 'formal criteria' of justice such as 'treating similar cases in a similar way' and mention the existence of 'various material criteria that specify relevant similarities and differences among individuals and groups'. The NBAC does not clarify which similarities and differences are relevant.

---

17    For the abbreviations, see Table 3.1.

18    More information on the ESHG expert meeting has been published (Godard et al. 2003).

19    In French: 'le bien collectif et le bien-être de l'humanité'.

20    See Table 3.6 in Belmont Report (1979), WMA (2008) and CIOMS (2002).

21    It should be noted, however, that in this general form, the principle of justice is of limited guidance to research ethics committees.

The term most often used in the guidelines concerning genetic databases to describe 'justice' is 'equity' (WHO 1998; CEST; TC; RMGA; NBAC); the next most often used term is 'fairness' (WHO; TC; RMGA; NARC; NBAC). The adjective 'unfair' appears most often in the context of 'unfair discrimination'. A rarely used term is 'equality' (UNESCO).

The CEST guidelines mention the need for equity concerning the following three issues: equity implies that nobody should suffer from discrimination or stigmatization based on genetic characteristics, benefits should be shared in an equitable way, and the knowledge derived from research using genetic databases should be shared and made public. The CEST's examples of benefit sharing show that making reference to equity does not guide towards *one* solution. The solution to compensate donors through monetary benefits proportional to the gains of the biotechnology industry is refuted in the CEST guidelines, not on the grounds of lack of equity but because it transforms the donor's generosity in a commercial operation without sense.[22] The other solutions that are mentioned, namely contributions to humanitarian projects, compensation of the population through access to health care, as well as new medications and better infrastructure, are all considered equitable in the CEST guidelines. The guidelines conclude that sharing the benefits of research in some form with society ('avec la collectivité') is a sufficient criterion for equity, if researchers, donors and the population are satisfied with the conditions and agree to them before the research starts.

Several other guidelines (HGC; COE) use the concept of 'fairness' in relation to discrimination in the same sense as the CEST guidelines. They indicate that discrimination based on genetic characteristics is 'unfair'. Similarly, the NBAC mentions in the context of genetic research that risks of discrimination concerning health insurance and employment raise significant questions about whether institutions and policies are just. '[U]njust social prejudices and arrangements' would be those that 'burden individual choice or degrade the worth of certain groups defined in invidious ways'.[23]

The guidelines of the National Bioethics Advisory Commission (NBAC 1999) spend almost two pages (49–50) on justice. For the NBAC, justice extends not only to individuals, but also to populations. The guidelines recommend procedures to ensure 'fair participation on the part of a particular group in designing research protocols that may have a negative impact on that group'. In this context, the guidelines also raise the issue of 'intergenerational justice', that is, justice concerning succeeding populations.

The UNESCO International Declaration on Human Genetic Data (UNESCO 2003, 9) mentions the principle of equality without any explanation. The principle of fairness is used in the context of access to data. Access should be 'fair', fostering 'international medical and scientific cooperation'. Similarly, the guidelines of

---

22    '[L]a transformation d'un geste de générosité en une opération commerciale dépourvue de sens' (CEST 2003, 52).

23    See NBAC (1999, 50) citing a book on justice in genetics (Murphy and Lappe 1994).

the Human Genetics Commission (HGC) consider that it is 'very important for equitable research access to be maintained at all times' (HGC 2002, 103).

The WHO guidelines (WHO 1998, 3) announce that 'the principle of distributive justice should ensure that scarce resources are utilized equitably *on the basis of need*'. Concerning genetic databases, they define equity somewhat differently than the CEST guidelines, that is, they do not require an approach in which the entire society must benefit. Instead, the benefit of the donors could be sufficient: '[E]quity requires that the donors, or the community generally, should receive some benefit' (WHO 1998, 14).

The Network of Applied Genetic Medicine (RMGA) considers all forms of payment to participants in exchange for participation 'unacceptable'. 'For the sake of equity', however, the population of Quebec should 'profit from the resulting benefits' through medical supplies and 'humanitarian causes'. Furthermore, the RMGA uses the principle of equity to defend the right to keep local copies of the tissue and the database: 'In consideration of the voluntary participation and the universal nature of the Quebec health care system, and by virtue of the principle of equity (fairness), copies of the genetic material and information of participants should be kept in Quebec' (RMGA 2000, 15).

The Tri-Council guidelines cite the principle of justice (TC 1998, i.6) when they refer to fairness and equity in the context of the ethical review process. The ethical review requires procedural justice in the form of 'fair methods'.

The guidelines of the North American Regional Committee (NARC) use the concept of fairness in order to condemn exaggerated promises of benefit that might be used as a persuasion to participation: 'But it is fundamentally unfair to tell a community that this research will "cure" their diabetes, or even to couch an explanation of the research in a way that allows the community to believe a cure will result' (NARC 1997).

The examples demonstrate that, in addition to the 'classical' use of the principle of justice in health research ethics, in the guidelines concerning human genetic databases, the principle of equity is used to defend detailed practical requirements that differ according to each guideline. The different ways of benefit sharing are a typical example. Based on the principle of equity, either a range of solutions for benefit sharing or only some solutions are recommended. Reference to the principle of equity in this form is not helpful in this context, because benefit sharing is reduced to the idea of 'sharing', without providing guidance as to whether some forms of sharing are preferable over others and why some forms should not be permitted. General reference to equity also does not clarify with whom one should share: with donors, the entire population, only those in need (humanitarian causes), or even all humanity.

The topics described above are taken from classical health research ethics, although guidelines relevant for biobanks adapt these topics to the new problems raised by genetic research in general and research involving genetic databases in particular. In addition, biobank guidelines contain new principles that have not appeared in the classical guidelines before.

*New principles: Respect for the human body*

Biobank guidelines focus on research involving tissues and information, and not on 'classical' research. In line with this new focus, some guidelines mention a new principle: 'respect for the human body' (TC; MRC; NC; NBAC; see Table 3.5). More rarely, reference is made to the 'dignity of the human body' (TC; NC; NBAC; see Table 3.6). Interestingly, the principle of respect for the human body can be in conflict with the respect for persons. The NBAC explains that from the respect for human tissue follows in general the restriction of selling tissue (see Table 3.5). The prohibition of financial gains is recommended in many other guidelines and regularly the reason why financial gains are prohibited is 'respect for the human body'. This means that the autonomy of persons is limited not only by the respect for the autonomy of others, but also by the respect a person owes to his or her own body. This new principle is somewhat problematic because different cultures define the limits and requirements of respect for the human body in different ways. Respect for the human body is part of the mainstream of North American culture. However, due to the strong support for the rules of the market system, the idea of making profit from human tissue is clearly more widely accepted in the United States than in Europe (Harrison 2002). Therefore, in an international context reference to the abstract principle is only of limited guidance.

*New principles: Freedom of research*

The principle of freedom of research is not mentioned in any of the classical guidelines on health research ethics. A reason could be that this principle seems to be contrary to the intent of the guidelines to explain the ethical framework imposed to limit the freedom of (unethical) research. In the context of genetic research and research involving human genetic databases, the principle is used in two distinct ways. First, this principle, sometimes also called 'freedom of science' or 'academic freedom', has been formulated in response to the growing privatization, especially of genetic research, that promises great profits. The collaboration of publicly funded research with private sponsors, and the restrictions imposed by patenting, have created concerns about limitations to scientific freedom with regard to the choice of research subjects, the publication of results and access to samples and data (CEST 2003, 22). Second, the principle is used to justify why, in research involving genetic databases, a compromise must be found between the promotion of scientific freedom and the respect and protection of research subjects through confidentiality and informed consent (RMGA 2000, 4). The principle of scientific freedom seems in this sense to reflect an at least slight shift away from the automatic primacy of the rights of the individual at all costs to the valorization of research. Not all restrictions imposed on research might be ethically defendable in the light of academic freedom. This case is not different from conflicts between other ethical principles. The ethically 'right' balance between the freedom of science and conflicting principles such as beneficence and respect for persons still needs to be described and defended.

*New principles: Respect for populations*

The new (2002) version of the CIOMS guidelines reflects a growing tendency in research ethics: the focus is not only on individual research subjects, but on populations. As stated by the NBAC:

> justice, along with the other two Belmont principles, should be interpreted to include communities as well as individuals. Just as beneficence may require attending to group harms, and respect for persons may necessitate attending to their communities, so justice may mandate the provision of procedures for group participation in the planning of research (NBAC 1999, 50).

The focus on populations reflects partly changing practices in research due to the growing technical possibilities and increased interest in population genetics.

*New principles: Community values*

Community values, such as 'familial mutuality' (RMGA) and 'solidarity' (UNESCO; HUGO; COE, and so on; see Table 3.10), seem to have arrived in two steps in medical research ethics. First, with respect to genetic tests in general, it has been recognized that the results of such research do not only concern an individual, but also all genetically related members of his or her family. For many years now, geneticists have struggled with the question whether and up to which point confidentiality has to be maintained towards family members. A slight shift towards a higher willingness among geneticists to inform family members against the wish of the subject that has been tested has been observed (Fletcher 1989; Wertz, Fletcher and Mulvihill 1990; Nippert et al. 1996; Wertz 1997). This could be interpreted as another example of a cultural evolution away from the predominance of individualism. However, until now, a duty to disclose has only been defended in rare circumstances, such as those specified by the President's Commission.[24] Although it seems exaggerated to speak in this case of a duty of the physician, the principle of familial mutuality announces, if not a legal duty, at least a moral ideal away from individualism and towards motivating the individual to share the information with members of his or her family. The principle of 'familial mutuality' has been the most clearly expressed in the guidelines established at a WHO meeting. The authors proclaim 'moral duties to disclose a genetic status' (WHO 1998, 5) and indicate that 'control of DNA may be familial, not only individual' (WHO 1998, 13).

The second step has been triggered by questions related to research involving biobanks and human genetic databases, or more generally related to genetic research involving populations. The value of such research depends on the willingness of the members of a group to participate, even if the benefits and risks of the studies are often uncertain. In order to obtain the benefits, it is not sufficient

---

24   The violation of confidentiality is justified if several cumulative conditions apply: the risk of harm is imminent, the harm is important and cannot be prevented other than by the breach of confidentiality (President's Commission 1983).

to show solidarity towards one's own family. One 'needs the help of all' to obtain valuable results in population database research. 'Genetic solidarity' (HGC; see Table 3.10) is required in order to act as 'motivation for allowing the use of one's biological materials and personal data in biomedical research' (COE/CDBI; see Table 3.10). In addition, the principle of solidarity is used to justify the protection of the genetically disadvantaged or vulnerable (TC; see Table 3.10) against the risks of discrimination and stigmatization (RMGA 2000, 13).

Another principle introduced by a number of guidelines in the context of research involving tissue banks and genetic databases is 'altruism'. This refers most often to the idea that the donor provides his or her tissue to be used in research as a gift, that is, without direct monetary compensation. Several guidelines mention as reason for the new principles of solidarity and altruism the fact that the human genome is part of the common heritage of humanity (see Table 3.10).

The principles of solidarity and altruism are open to different interpretations which are rarely discussed. On the one hand, such community values could serve only as an ideal intended to motivate future donors to participate in research. On the other hand, these values could also be used to justify limitations to the individualistic principle of respect for persons or even to the principle of beneficence.

Although many guidelines use the terms 'solidarity' and 'altruism', it is remarkable that all these are guidelines from Europe or Canada, or, in the case of HUGO and UNESCO, international guidelines. The term does not appear in the American guidelines included in the analysis, such as the NBAC, NARC and CAP guidelines. It might be worth remembering in this context that most European countries and Canada dispose of national or obligatory health care systems based on solidarity. The underlying idea seems to be that 'human health is a common public good the care of which should be managed by the public and in the public's interest'. In line with this cultural perception of health, the concept of a public good is extended to health research involving biobanks.[25]

*New principles: Respect of the democracy*
Only the Commission from Quebec (CEST 2003, 36) proposed to add the value 'respect of the democracy'. The Commission motivates the necessity to add this value by its observation that, first, this is a fundamental value prevalent in the society of Quebec and, second, that this is the only value that permits reflection of the   future changes of the population's opinion towards ethical problems concerning human genetic databases.

*Duties reconsidered: Modern individualism versus Kant*
According to the classical guidelines about health research ethics, the welfare and interests of the individual always outweigh those of society. The guidelines of the

---

25   See the principles cited by Pullman and Latus (2003c, 556) as typically Canadian (from inside a public health care system), and the discussion of the public good argument (Chadwick and Wilso 2004).

Royal College of Pathologists (RCP) present a somewhat different opinion. These guidelines contain a unique paragraph about the conflict perceived to exist between the Kantian categorical imperative and the principles of modern society. According to the guidelines (RCP 2001, Introduction, 9): 'if everyone refused to allow their tissues to be used for teaching, quality assurance and research, the health services they need and have benefited from, and which produced the samples, could not exist'. The Royal College of Pathologists (RCP 2001) is of the opinion that this is not in accordance with the Kantian categorical imperative because:

> [the] act cannot be universalized, which indicates that to act this way is immoral [...] Recent events demonstrate that in the UK, society has chosen not to follow these arguments. Nevertheless, their existence serves to emphasize the point that the wishes of a single individual cannot invariably be assumed to be paramount: such wishes cannot take precedence over the rights of large groups of individuals without reason. A balance needs to be found which invites and respects reasonable individual objections but which allows work for the common good to continue (RCP 2001, Introduction, 10).

The RCP guidelines do not give more details of which reasons should be considered 'reasonable' and acceptable and how the mentioned balance can be found, that is, which criteria should be used to evaluate the balance. In the following, we examine guidelines that provide explanations about ways in which conflicting principles should be balanced, or how a solution can be found when principles conflict and when controversial opinions exist about the right balancing.

*Ways of balancing: Principles in conflict*
Only some guidelines give more or less detailed theoretical explanations on the way in which conflicting principles should be balanced. Not only is it interesting to compare the theoretical rules of balancing provided by different guidelines; in addition, it is worthwhile examining which concrete recommendations are given in the guidelines, for example, concerning informed consent, on the grounds of different ways of balancing individual rights against the benefit to society.

The guidelines of the Canadian Commission (CEST 2003, 37) contain a paragraph which summarizes theoretical reflections on balancing. According to the Commission, the balancing rules are supposed to facilitate decisions that are beneficial for the individuals and for the future of the human species, the future of the society of Quebec and its maintenance among the most advanced contemporary societies.[26] Further objectives are to avoid any social and individual harm ('éviter toute dérive nuisible sur les plans social et individuel'). It has to be noted that the Commission named the benefit to individuals first, but concerning harms, social harms are listed

---

26 '[D]es décisions qui soient à la fois bénéfiques pour les personnes et le devenir du genre humain, et pour l'avenir de la société québécoise et son maintien au nombre des sociétés contemporaines les plus avancées' (CEST 2003, 37).

before individual harms. The Commission admits that the process of finding the right balance is not always easy ('pas toujours aisé'). The guidelines indicate that the ethically ideal solution has to be somewhat sacrificed in order to satisfy the general interest in future benefits of genetic research for medical treatments.[27] The ethical ideal may be abandoned and some inconveniences to individuals are permitted if no social or individual harm results. However, research will not be entirely free. Some restrictions on research must be in place to avoid harm.[28]

Interestingly, although the theoretical balancing seems to give room for some decrease of respect for the individual in the name of potential health benefits for all, the concrete recommendations of the guidelines do not reflect this decrease. On the contrary, in comparison to other guidelines, the recommendations are relatively strict. The classical standard of informed consent is maintained. Recommendation 7 states that, for any future use of the sample that has not been explained in the original consent form, new consent should be obligatory. The classical standard is maintained, if not increased, for example, through the requirement for consent not only from the legal representative, but also from the incapacitated themselves and through the requirement to provide to future subjects the possibility of receiving genetic counselling *before* entering research involving human genetic databases. A third important restriction (recommendation 9) imposed by the Canadian Commission is that only irreversibly anonymized information is allowed to be released to regions outside of Quebec, and that participants must be informed about this possibility.

A characteristic of the guidelines of the Network of Applied Genetic Medicine (RMGA) is that they add explicitly in their introduction the most complete list of 'community values' to the classical principles of research ethics. These guidelines contain only scarce theoretical reflections on balancing. They describe their objectives as 'seeking to promote freedom of genomic research while respecting and protecting the different parties involved'. They use the principle of solidarity explicitly, not to justify a decrease in respect for the individual, but to prohibit genetic discrimination and to promote the protection of individuals from adverse effects that might result from participation in research (RMGA 2000, 3–4). In their recommendations concerning consent, they require high standards of informed consent and demand that subjects be provided with the possibility of making informed choices about the uses of the samples (RMGA 2000, 6). Subjects also have the possibility of obtaining access to results if they keep their addresses updated (RMGA 2000, 9).

---

27   'Tout en poursuivant un idéal éthique, la Commission ne saurait faire abstraction de l'intérêt que peut présenter la recherche en génétique humaine dans le traitement de la maladie et dont les avantages pour les personnes pourraient se révéler supérieurs aux inconvénients envisagés' (CEST 2003, 37).

28   'La mise en place de balises normatives et éthiques capables d'encadrer adéquatement l'action des principaux acteurs et d'éviter toute dérive nuisible sur les plans social et individuel [...] apparaît cependant fondamentale' (CEST 2003, 37).

The College of American Pathologists (CAP) proposed a different balancing than the Canadian Commission (CEST). The guidelines do not contain any theoretical reflection on balancing, but the paragraph about consent contains information on the reasons for this concrete form of balancing. First, in contrast to the CEST, the CAP recommends 'simple (general or unspecified) consent'. The CAP is aware of the conflict between the 'current informed consent doctrine which requires detailed information about benefits and risks' and the interest of society and researchers in maximizing benefits resulting from research: 'Society has a strong interest in research involving the use of human tissue, and such research may be hampered by well-intended but intrusive regulations.' Interestingly, the guidelines do not argue that, for the benefit of all members of society, the balancing should involve some decrease in individual rights. At least according to the argumentation in the guidelines, the reason for decreasing the standards of informed consent are not a different balancing of the principles of respect for persons versus beneficence, but a different evaluation of what counts as 'sufficient for protection of patients' rights' (Grizzle et al. 1999, 299). The argumentation of the guidelines goes as follows: research, teaching and quality control testing that use only excess human tissue, that is, tissue 'not required for maintaining the integrity of the patient's medical record', should be permitted with general consent because:

- this research does not involve patient therapy (use of the excess tissue does not imply any physical risk) and therefore general consent 'should be regarded as sufficient for protection of patients' rights';
- it is 'an unreasonable burden for the patient and the researcher' to give 'a description of each and every research protocol that might be performed in the (sometimes distant) future on a patient's tissue'.

The CAP states explicitly that general consent includes consent to genetic testing. According to the CAP, genetic information 'should be subject to the same standards of privacy, confidentiality, and security as nongenetic medical information' (Grizzle et al. 1999, 297).

The difference between the CEST and the CAP does not seem to consist of a different balancing of the principles of respect for persons and the overall benefits to individuals and society, but in a different appreciation of the empirical risk of harm to subjects. For the CEST, classical informed consent to all uses of the samples is necessary to prevent social and individual harm. For the CAP, general consent gives 'sufficient protection' if the classical standards of privacy, confidentiality and security are maintained. Although some disagreement might concern the question to what extent patients' rights need 'sufficient protection', the main disagreement seems to be about the empirical question 'how great are the risks?'

The objectives of the guidelines of the Human Genetics Commission (HGC) are to protect 'interests in genetic privacy and confidentiality [...] in a way which does not harm comparably important interests of others' (HGC 2002, 9). The

Commission believes that it is 'quite possible to achieve a balance between public interest and individual concerns' (HGC 2002, 9). The HGC guidelines contain theoretical reflections on the balancing of principles. Although the guidelines stress the 'benefits of altruistic conduct', they state that 'generally' the principle of 'genetic solidarity and altruism' will 'take second place to the principle of respect for persons'. However, in 'exceptional circumstances' the balancing might be in the opposite way. The exceptions are justified 'where the social interest is thought to exceed the individual interest'. It will 'sometimes […] be appropriate to use personal genetic information for the public good' (HGC 2002, 9). However, in these cases 'it is necessary to ensure that other interests of the individual remain protected, such as ensuring that their information is not used inappropriately' (HGC 2002, 94).

The interpretation of the guidelines' balancing will depend on the criteria used to judge when the social interest exceeds appropriately the individuals' interest. By allowing exceptions in this general way, the balancing contradicts the statement of the Declaration of Helsinki and the Convention on Human Rights and Biomedicine that the interests of society and science should never take precedence over those of the individual.

The concrete recommendations of the Human Genetics Commission (HGC) are in line with the theoretical balancing. Since there is a 'strong social interest' (HGC 2002, 94) in research involving genetic databases and since the requirement to recontact sample donors for further consent (re-consent), as well as the right of donors to withdraw samples at any time, would 'hamper' or 'compromise' research (HGC 2002, 94 and 96), all personal interests of a donor cannot be respected. The person might be interested in controlling all future uses of his or her samples and information. However, the Commission believes that it is reasonable not to permit such detailed control if the use of the information is 'unlikely to cause harm'. The guidelines therefore judge general consent 'for use in medical research' (HGC 2002, 93 and 95) to be sufficient if data and samples are anonymized either in an irreversible or in a reversible way (see Chapter 4). The guidelines acknowledge another limitation of individual rights: the right to withdrawal from research involving genetic databases may be limited. If future research procedures have no physical impact on a living subject but only on the donor's tissue, the right to terminate participation is interpreted to be 'less clear' (HGC 2002, 95). The Commission considers the possibility acceptable that donors lose any claim on their samples after donation, as long as they are informed about these conditions at the moment of donation (HGC 2002, 96). Moreover, the guidelines state that the practical difficulties in providing individuals access to their individual results outweigh the individuals' interests in finding out their genetic characteristics.

Another document from the United Kingdom (The Nuffield Trust 2000)[29] goes even further in its balancing. The authors of this document express the opinion

---

29   See The Nuffield Trust (2000, chapter IV, 17; The international dimension and human rights).

that a number of international bodies have overreacted to existing 'anxieties'. The 'absolute commitment to the principles of human dignity, individual autonomy and informed consent and confidentiality in the application of human genetics' in international guidelines such as the Bioethics Convention and the Universal Declaration of the Human Genome and Human Rights (UNESCO) seems exaggerated to these authors. They believe that 'the principle of inalienable individual rights that lies at the heart of most [...] protocols [...] about data protection may not be in the best interests of the health of the population'. According to these authors, individuals should not be considered to have an absolute right to give or to withhold information about their genetic status, and equally they should not have an absolute right to prevent their stored genetic data being transmitted to a third party for the purpose of research, since this research might assist in securing health benefits for a large number of other people. The benefit to the well-being of families suffering from genetic diseases or to 'some wider social grouping' should, according to this document, outweigh the interests of the individual.

The French National Ethics Committee (CCNE 2003) believes that obtaining a benefit from the advances in genetics and the biotechnologies as regards genetic databases presupposes the collaboration of the population. The idea of a common genetic heritage ('patrimoine') leads to the necessity of solidarity between individuals, succeeding generations and humanity. These ideas need to be developed in addition to the rights of the individual (CCNE 2003, 29–30). The CCNE explains in the Rapport No. 77 which is attached to the Avis No. 77 that the principle of solidarity justifies a derogation of the rules and laws intended to protect individual rights (CCNE 2003, 25). However, the Committee stresses that it has in mind 'true solidarity', which means that all acts need to be voluntary.

Based on this type of balancing, the statement justifies a simplification of the classical informed consent doctrine for the use of tissue in databanks.[30] The simplification would be a form of general consent of the donor to future uses of his or her tissue/information without re-contacting and new consent.

The US American National Bioethics Advisory Commission (NBAC) takes a different view than that expressed in the documents from the UK. The NBAC recognizes that the protection of donors and others from 'wrongs and harms' will probably require increased expenditure for research. However, according to the Commission, this investment is needed to ensure a just distribution of the burdens of research and to reduce the wrongs and harms. The Commission believes that this investment is finally useful to society and researchers because public trust will be increased and individuals will be encouraged to contribute their tissue to important research (NBAC 1999, 50).

The concrete recommendations of the NBAC allow donors who wish so a maximum of control. The Commission was divided on the question whether donors who do not wish any control should be permitted to sign a general or

---

30 'Il semble donc concevable de simplifier l'exigence du consentement' (CCNE 2003, 25).

'blanket' consent. Concerning the tissue donors' right to have access to results of the research, the NBAC has a rather restricted view, favouring beneficence rather than the respect for individuals' rights. Results should not be communicated to donors, except in exceptional situations if three conditions apply: the findings are scientifically valid and confirmed, the findings have significant consequences for the donor's health, and a course of action, for example, prevention or treatment, to interfere with these consequences is available.

The NBAC guidelines attribute a relatively important place to individual rights, at least concerning consent, as compared to most statements from Europe and the CAP. This different balancing seems to be motivated by the fact that the NBAC takes seriously the 'risks of discrimination in health insurance and employment' (NBAC 1999, 50) which are particularly significant in a country such as the United States without a right to health insurance.

To sum up, we have made three main observations:

- First, theoretical discussion on balancing is scarce and often the need to decide on a case by case basis is expressed.
- Second, the theoretical explanations concerning balancing in a particular guideline do not permit prediction of its concrete recommendations. The variation of these recommendations, in spite of similar balancing of the abstract principles, seems to be due to a different evaluation of empirical questions, mainly related to the risks involved and the burdens or disadvantages that new informed consent will impose on research.
- Third, cultural differences about how many resources a particular society is willing to spend on the protection of individual rights also seem to play a role.

The Canadian documents (CEST; RMGA) show that in theory the possibility of restricting individual rights for the benefits of health, science and society is acknowledged and that an important weight is given to community values. The concrete recommendations concerning informed consent and access to the results demonstrate, however, that in practice, priority is given to individual rights concerning informed consent and access to the results. The principle of solidarity is used not to diminish individual rights, but to argue for the altruistic contribution of all to pay not only for a national health system, but also to accept the costs for the protection of the rights of research participants.

The statements from the United Kingdom and from France demonstrate the greatest willingness to implement solidarity. Compared to the use of the term 'solidarity' in the Canadian guidelines, the principle of solidarity has a somewhat different meaning here: it is interpreted as the duty to increase the common good, a duty which implies sacrificing individual rights to a certain extent. The guidelines from the United Kingdom might also mirror public opinion in the country. The UK spends a relatively small percentage of its national growth product on the National Heath Service, compared to other countries' expenditure for health care.

The 'typical British', that is, 'pragmatic', opinion documented in some public consultations is that the costs for health should be limited and that one should not spend too many resources only to uphold the ethical ideal of giving subjects the greatest possible control over their donated tissues.

While Canadian guidelines value individual rights and Europeans (French and British) express willingness to sacrifice individual rights for the health of society (because the latter is believed to benefit from research involving genetic databases), the NBAC takes an intermediate position. It has to be noted that the NBAC does not at all use the idea of solidarity in its approach to balancing. Similarly to Canadians from Quebec, the American National Bioethics Advisory Commission accepts that individual rights and justice have a price which should be paid for the 'good' to live in an ethical society. However, in contrast to the Canadian position, the idea of offering the donor not only the option of new consent to future projects, but also the option of blanket consent, has been supported by some members of the US Commission. On the other hand, the position of the NBAC concerning the feedback of research results is rather restrictive as regards autonomy rights of donors. This restrictive position is based, first, on the paternalistic view that scientifically unclear results could harm the donor and that this harm needs to be avoided; and, second, on the practical reasoning that communicating results is not cost-effective if the results will not change the medical care of the donor. How can the NBAC's opposite tendencies be explained: on the one hand a strong tendency to respect individual rights concerning consent, and on the other hand a restrictive tendency towards access to results? The context of the American health care system seems to be the easiest explanation. Since risks of refusal by insurance companies due to genetic testing are relevant, it is consistent to ask for high standards of consent and at the same time to limit access to results.

*Ways of balancing: Procedures to guarantee the right balancing*
Almost all guidelines state that the concrete balancing is difficult to find and should be done on a case by case basis. Since a universal way of balancing cannot be announced from the beginning, the guidelines spend many pages on explanations about procedures to reach the right balancing. These involve in general: (1) traditional research ethics committees (NBAC guidelines); (2) special independent oversight bodies (CEST guidelines); or (3) governmental control through central bodies or trustees (CCNE avis). Another process to come to a decision is mentioned several times, named 'the principle of democracy' or public consultation (United Kingdom, CCNE).[31]

The ethics committees or oversight bodies are encouraged to decide on the basis of the recommendations set out in the guidelines. The historical example

---

31    The principle of democracy has been associated especially with genetics (Brito 2001; Launis 2007; Launis and Räikkä 2007) and includes biobank governance (McCarty et al. 2008; Secko, Burgess and O'Doherty 2008; O'Doherty and Burgess 2009; Secko et al. 2009).

of the Estonian Ethics Committee shows what this might mean in practice. The mandate of this Committee was described as follows: 'The aim of the [Estonian] Ethics Committee is to assist in ensuring the protection of the health, human dignity, identity, security of person, privacy and other fundamental rights and freedoms of gene donors and the resolution of general ethical problems related to human gene research' (Rannamäe 2003, 23). If guidelines, similarly, only list principles and are not more explicit on the reasons for and the ways of balancing, it is not clear how committees with different expertise should come to well-informed and well-argued decisions.

The difficulties of providing ethical guidance concerning the use of human genetic databases might be related to the fact that a principle-based approach is too vague and unsuited for the issues raised. We therefore now examine briefly the critics of principlism as dominating ethical approaches concerning research involving human genetic databases.

## The Limits of Ethical Principles in Research Involving Human Genetic Databases

The principle-based approach has always produced criticism, in bioethics in general and in health research ethics in particular. General criticisms have been that the approach using the 'Georgetown Mantra' principles is too simple. It has been argued that the rational balancing of principles does not take into account situational variations and the fact that principles are culturally shaped. One response to this criticism could be to complement rational balancing: it could be helpful to find out empirically how much value real individuals or groups give to each principle in real cases (Robertson 2003).

In spite of its shortcomings the principle-based approach has obtained wide consensus so far and, consequently, has dominated health research ethics until now. Therefore, reasons not to use this approach for research involving human genetic databases must be particularly strong.

Critics of a principle-based ethics for genetic research have doubted that classical principles are sufficiently robust to address the risks of genetic discrimination. According to the critics, the principles should be supplemented by a code of ethics more specifically focused on questions unique to research involving genetic testing. This code would need to address discrimination based on predictive knowledge and implications of genetics for families and groups (Australian Law Reform Commission 2003, 6.29). Critics have also pointed out that the classical ethical approach based on principles tends to perpetuate too easily the interests of researchers and the commercial interests of medical–industrial collaborations, because the principle of beneficence is in general based on the assumption that scientific progress is automatically for the good of humanity.[32]

---

32    See Submissions G141, G052, G021, G056 and G143 (6.35–6.37) to the Australian Law Reform Commission (Australian Law Reform Commission 2003).

If one agrees that a principle-based ethical approach has successfully governed classical research ethics, it seems adequate for research involving human genetic databases as well, until the contrary has been proven. Ethical questions raised by human genetic databases are not fundamentally different from questions of research using human subjects in general. When trying to determine ethical ways to establish, maintain and use human genetic databases, one has to take into account the autonomy rights of participants, balance harms and risks and make sure that benefits and burdens of research involving the databases are distributed fairly.

Some have argued that the (secondary)[33] principle of informed consent is not 'adapted' to research involving human tissue, because the concept was originally based on tangible physical harm, whereas 'harm to data or samples' represents a different category (Buchanan 1999). This standpoint does not disqualify fundamentally the principle-based approach. It might be sufficient to adapt the evaluation of the seriousness of harm in the balancing process. Questioning the appropriateness of classical informed consent (Beauchamp and Faden 1995, 1238) in research involving data and samples does not mean questioning the principle-based approach altogether.

Limits of the principle-based approach concern classical research ethics as well as research ethics dealing with human genetic databases. In both cases, ethics committees have to decide whether a particular research project is acceptable and need concrete guidance on how to balance conflicting principles. In the context of decisions involving the new biotechnologies, McDonald (2000, 10) has proposed that the aim of the balancing should be to make reasonable choices based on 'good moral reasons'. To be defined as good and moral, reasons need to be 'impartial, promote human well-being, non-arbitrary and overriding considerations of self-interest' (McDonald 2000). In order to make reasonable choices, moral arguments should be used that 'all affected parties can reasonably endorse' and that 'should be justifiable interpersonally'. McDonald's (2000) approach is interesting and worth a try for members of a research ethics committee. However, these members will need to take into account the fact that in a pluralistic society, no impartial definition of human well-being exists. Indeed, the wide acceptance of the principle of respect for autonomy or respect for persons is not a mere coincidence. The acceptance of the principle testifies that pluralistic societies attribute a lot of weight to individual self-interest and to individual evaluations of well-being. The crucial task remains to find a way, acceptable to all, of deciding where the limits to individual autonomy are. These are necessary to make sure that the very foundations of a democratic pluralistic society are not endangered (Macedo 1995 and 2001).

The limits of a principle-based ethics for research involving human genetic databases become apparent at the point where evaluations of well-being or benefit need to be decided at the population level. This is illustrated by the benefits that have been mutually agreed to by pharmaceutical companies and the Icelandic population

---

33   Informed consent is a secondary principle derived in particular from the mid-level principle of respect for autonomy.

(Chadwick 1999, 444). Hoffmann-La Roche had offered access to free medication. Should only such financial advantages and health gain for the population count as adequate benefit, or should more intangible benefits such as prestige to the country be taken into account, too? The decision on how to define benefit cannot be left to the individual but has to be made in some way for the whole community.

The reason why many guidelines provide new principles, especially principles based on community values, might be that adding those principles is seen as one way to counterbalance the limits of the traditional principle-based approach and to adapt principlism to the new problems. In the following section, we will examine whether the new principles are different from the old and whether they are helpful and/or necessary to guide the establishment of an ethical framework for research involving human genetic databases.

*Traditional Principles and Frameworks Versus the 'New' Principle of Solidarity*

Why is it difficult to reach a consensus concerning the ethical framework of research involving genetic databases? As we have seen, the area of genetic testing has introduced crucial new elements to the ethical discussion. Due to the sharing of genes between families and genetically related communities, all decisions will automatically affect more than one individual. As a consequence it is not possible to limit the decision to one individual and refer solely to his or her right to take an autonomous decision. This questions the traditional individualistic foundations of Western bioethics, in particular the most widely accepted framework: the ethics of *prima facie* principles such as respect for autonomy, beneficence, non-maleficence and justice. In this ethical framework it has so far been more or less possible to resolve conflicts by respecting the autonomous choices of individuals. If patients and physicians disagree on moral questions, the wish of a competent patient has to be respected, as long as it does not interfere significantly with the autonomy of others or cause a significant danger to the interests of others. Conflicts between the principles of autonomy and beneficence or non-maleficence become not so much fundamentally ethical, but practical problems of how to be sure whether patients are competent and whether their wishes are truly autonomous. Controversial discussion in biomedical ethics is presently related to two problems. The first is 'biological entities' for which the ethical status and their right to be respected are not clear, such as, for example, embryos. The second is related to the principle of justice. This principle is controversial, because a more complex way to balance the interests and preferences of several autonomous patients or citizens is needed in comparison to the 'simple' individualistic approach of 'patient autonomy goes first'. A similar ethical problem exists concerning genetic databases. In order to achieve the expected benefits to all from this kind of research, some form of collaboration is needed. Relying on traditional individualism is not just one cost neutral choice among others. Choosing a maximum of autonomy for the individual can only be achieved through a decrease of the benefits expected to arise for the health and well-being of many others. In addition, the fact that family members, members of the same population and eventually all human beings share some amount of their own genetic information makes it impossible to completely separate one individual and his/her interests from another. Recognizing that the traditional principles do not provide answers to the ethical questions of genetic databases, adherents to the principle-based approach have tried to add 'new' principles. As described above, the most common propositions are a 'principle of solidarity' or a 'principle of altruism'. Adding this kind of principle is ethically problematic because many of the new principles are in conflict with the principles of traditional research ethics that are enshrined in the Declaration of Helsinki. The most central point of this declaration is that the interests of society and science must never prevail over the interests of the research subject.

Building an ethical framework for genetic databases is part of the global endeavour of health research ethics. It could be that the ethical questions related to genetic databases cannot be resolved within the traditional framework of health research ethics because the issues raised are new and require a novel approach. However, if this is the case, it needs to be defined which aspects of human genetic databases render ethical questions different from the questions addressed by traditional health research ethics. As said before, arguments need to be particularly strong to show that the traditional values of health research ethics are not valid for the ethical problems related to human genetic databases, but have to be replaced by new ones. A more easily acceptable alternative would be to assume as a starting point that the ethical framework of traditional health research ethics is valid for solving ethical problems related to human genetic databases. Only if this traditional framework proves not to be able to address the relevant questions, should it be supplemented by new elements which help to deal with new questions that are specific to genetic databases.

The questions that need to be answered are therefore: are the general guidelines concerning medical research ethics (1) adequate and (2) sufficient for genetic research in general and research using human genetic databases in particular? The most complete classical international guidelines on health research ethics, the guidelines of the Council for International Organizations of Medical Sciences (CIOMS 2002), seem to consider that new problems are raised by genetic research and that the present CIOMS guidelines are not able to deal adequately with these new problems. The guidelines state explicitly that they do not address genetic research, except in the commentary to one guideline. Instead, the Council treated the ethics of genetic research in a commissioned paper and commentary.[34]

The need for a specific paper demonstrates that, in the eyes of the members of the Council, significant differences exist between 'classical' research and genetic

---

34 'Certain areas of research are not represented by specific guidelines. One such is human genetics. It is, however, considered in Guideline 18 Commentary under *Issues of confidentiality in genetics research*. The ethics of genetic research was the subject of a commissioned paper and commentary' (CIOMS 2002, commentary to guideline 18; introduction, 7).

research, differences which might justify substitution or supplementation of the classical guidelines.

The guidelines of the French National Ethics Committee not only distinguish between research involving living subjects and research involving tissue, but acknowledge two categories within biobank research. They state that a distinction needs to be made between the general situation of research implying the use of human body parts and the specific aspects of genetic research (CCNE 2003, 38). The more categories that are created, the more complex becomes the task to supplement or adapt the classical framework.

## The Differences Between 'Classical' Human Subject Research and Research Using Human Genetic Databases

Research involving genetic databases is part of genetic research and might, only for this reason, require a different framework as compared to classical human subject research. In addition, research using genetic databases might possess specific characteristics which distinguish it even from other types of genetic research. Several national and professional bodies have judged it necessary to write special guidelines concerning research involving human tissue (NBAC 1999; MRC 2001; Nuffield Council 1995). This type of research has apparently been considered to create particular ethical problems that have not been sufficiently addressed by documents regulating classical health research ethics. The special aspects of research involving human genetic databases are related to the particularities (1) of genetic research and (2) of research using human tissue. We will examine more closely these differences and describe whether they are qualitative or rather quantitative.

### New risks of harm

One difference between research using human genetic databases and 'classical' medical research is that the risks related to this research differ in quality, quantity and certainty from most risks of 'classical' research. In research involving human genetic databases, the risk of direct physical harm is very low, that is, related to taking the tissue sample, most often blood or tissue left over from biopsies. The risks are related to the information contained in the samples about the donor. The information exists in different forms. The sample itself contains information about genes, but this information needs first to be made available through genetic testing. Genetic information entered into a database can range from the entire sequence of the donor's genome to specific information on a gene locus obtained from a particular gene test. Technical advances have made it possible to do a multitude of tests at the same time, for example, by using DNA chips. Genetic databanks contain different amounts of additional data, for example, demographic or health-related information about the donor. Harm may result from a lack of privacy concerning the information. The magnitude of the risk depends on the specific circumstances. It is related to the size of the databank, the size of the sampled population and to the frequency of certain characteristics in this population. In the Swiss Pediatric Oncology Group Tumor Bank, it might be possible to identify the donor of a sample if the donor suffers from a rare tumour with only a few cases per canton. The risks also depend on the mechanisms to secure confidentiality and on local or international anti-discrimination laws. Risks might be psychological related to stigmatization. Donors' self-esteem could decrease if they learn that they carry genes which predispose to disease. Risks can also be physical and severe if in a country without a right to at least basic health care, individuals are refused health insurance because of their genetic risks. If these individuals develop health problems, they might die or suffer other serious physical damages because of the lack of access to health care. Risks to donors who have contributed samples for biobank research have a particular characteristic: the great uncertainty about the type and magnitude of the risks.

In addition, a characteristic of research involving genetic databases is risks to groups – in contrast to risks to individuals. These risks are not completely new. They exist if research populations are identifiable (Andrews 2005, 24). Epidemiological or sociological research involving identifiable groups has always implied the risk that information might be published which could stigmatize a group or lead to discrimination of its members. Such information could be a high prevalence of HIV or other stigmatizing diseases in this group. CIOMS has published International Guidelines for Ethical Review of Epidemiological Studies in 1991 which have recently been revised. In its general research guidelines from 2002, CIOMS has also discussed the need to plan such studies in a way that maintains group confidentiality. CIOMS suggested that this could mean 'in certain circumstances not to publish' the results (CIOMS 2002, 24).

Genetic databases, in contrast to other types of genetic research, create special risks if it is planned to add later new information to the database, for example, about the diseases individuals develop or do not develop in the future. This might increase the threat to confidentiality because it requires at some moment breaking the code or matching new coded health data with the data already in the database.

*Controversial wrongs*

Research on human genetic databases raises not only questions about the risk of harm but also about the risk of being wronged. Education, strict confidentiality and anti-discrimination laws might reduce harms to zero. If this were possible, individuals could still claim the right to know and to influence what is done to their tissue. Pro-life activists might not want their tissue to be used for research that might in any way favour abortions. They could be wronged if their tissue is used without their consent. Others might not want their tissue to be involved in research about cloning or 'enhancement' medication such as Fluoxetine (Prosac) or Sildenafil (Viagra). The history of the molecule Sildenafil shows that indicating the purpose of research might not protect against such wrongs since Viagra was originally discovered in studies about cardiovascular disease. The autonomy rights of individuals to control what is done with their 'detached' body parts are not immediately evident to everybody and therefore stir controversy. This controversy concerns not only research using human genetic databases but all types of research involving 'detached' human tissue or information as opposed to living human beings.

*Benefits depend on participation*

A particular problem of research involving certain types of human genetic databases, especially population-based studies, is that the benefits can only be obtained if a significant number of individuals participate. Low participation creates the risk that results become less valuable due to some form of selection bias. In the past, many epidemiological studies have been carried out with anonymous samples without consent, in order to avoid such a selection bias. Researchers who plan projects involving population biobanks face the dilemma that it might be impossible to design research protocols which use the highest standards of informed consent, while, at the same time, obtaining the greatest benefit. This may force researchers or community leaders to decide between two alternatives: either the benefit is sacrificed in order to maintain individual rights or less weight is given to individual rights in order to obtain a maximum benefit. It should be noted that this problem is not completely new. Similar dilemmas have been faced by other population studies not involving genetic databases. However, its importance became more visible and accentuated in biobank research.

*Informed consent might be impossible or particularly costly*

Some research projects using human genetic databases might not require the participation of a substantial proportion of the population. However, since future advances in the medical sciences are not foreseeable in detail, projects promising great benefit might be developed which have not been included in the original consent form signed by the donors when they provided tissue and data to the genetic database. Classical health research ethics has reflected on trade-offs between informed consent and possible benefits of research. The burden of obtaining informed consent has been taken into account and traded off against expected benefits and possible risks of the research (CIOMS 2002, guideline 4). Research directly involving human beings rarely generates this kind of problem because the subjects are physically present and either competent and able to consent or they are incompetent. In the latter case, specific considerations of research on incompetent subjects apply. Most of the research studies that require such trade-offs concern research on medical records, non-genetic health databases or left-over tissue not originally collected for research. In the case of health databases, the World Medical Association (WMA 2000) states that '[a]pproval from a specifically appointed ethical review committee must be obtained for research using patient data, including for new research not envisaged at the time the data were collected'. The committee should decide whether patients' new informed consent is necessary or whether it is 'acceptable' to use the information for the new purpose without further consent. The World Medical Association guidelines on health databases do not make explicit which uses are 'acceptable' under which conditions. They mention only that ethics committees decide 'in accordance with applicable national law' and 'conform to the requirements of this statement' (Art. 21). Among these requirements is the statement's guiding principle that it should be ensured that 'secondary uses of information do not inhibit patients from confiding information for their own health care needs' (Art. 6). The guidelines also declare that databases 'are valuable sources of information' for 'secondary uses' in medical research, including retrospective epidemiological studies (Art. 5). This might authorize all kinds of secondary uses as long as public trust is not undermined. Such a large interpretation of authorization is in contrast with the guidelines' requirement for patient consent which should include 'the purposes for which their information may be used' (Art. 16). Article 16 does not specify how precisely the purposes should be defined. If 'medical research' is given as the purpose, this would amount to blanket or general consent for research and might not be called 'informed consent'. Interestingly, the World Medical Association's guidelines do not use the term 'informed consent', only the term 'consent', although they specify what kind of information patients should receive. They should be informed about the fact that data will be stored and about future purposes for which it will be used.

It is not clear to what extent the World Medical Association's guidelines apply to genetic databases. The guidelines' definition of 'database' as 'a system to collect, describe, save, recover and/or use personal health information from more than one individual' includes genetic databases. In addition, genetic databases are nowhere in the text explicitly excluded. It might be claimed that genetic databases should not be handled according to the 'classical' guidelines on health databases on the grounds that they require a stricter use of a more specific 'informed' consent, due to the distinct and greater risks associated with genetic information than with non-genetic information. It might also be argued that they require, in addition, consent of the family or the community to the extent to which this information involves individuals and has possible adverse consequences not only for them, but for relatives and the genetically related community as well.

*The potential of profit and the question of benefit sharing*

Research on new treatments or diagnostic techniques implies burdens for research subjects, but can often also generate benefits. Classical research ethics has discussed the ethical problems associated with benefits and burdens. The mainstream opinion has been that individuals should not receive any financial benefit from participation in research except reimbursement for any costs and time spent. The reason for this has been the fear of undue inducement. In-kind benefits to the participating group or community have been declared acceptable in certain circumstances. This is the case if sponsors might make great profit based on the research and especially if external sponsors from rich countries finance research in poorer countries (CIOMS 2002, general ethical principles, justice). Genetic research has pushed the debate one step further, for two main reasons. First, it is widely recognized that the patenting of particular gene sequences and of gene tests has enabled some companies to make enormous profits (Dickenson 2004). As the Human Genome

Organization states: 'expenditures by private industry for genetic research now exceed the contributions of government'. Second, the feeling that genetic resources belong to all humans has increased the sensitivity to distributive injustice and led to a call for benefit sharing. It has been considered just to share benefits either with research participants who are often patients suffering from genetic disease or with populations, especially if these populations are disadvantaged in respect to access to health care. It is not immediately evident why benefit sharing would be justified only for genetic research. We all share the same or at least very similar morphologic structures and hormone or drug receptors; why should benefit sharing not be justified for anatomical, endocrinological or all pharmacological research? A special status has been attributed to genes, or more mystically to the 'genome', as compared to other parts or molecules of the body, not only by the public, but also by scientific bodies such as the Human Genome Organization (HUGO). In its Statement on the principled conduct of genetics research and in the Statement on benefit-sharing, the first (out of four) principle is the 'recognition that the human genome is part of the common heritage of humanity'. HUGO argues in favour of benefit sharing using the 'concept of human heritage' which 'also resonates under international law (e.g. the sea, the air, space …)' (HUGO 1995 and 2000).

At least in the eyes of those who defend a special status of genes, research involving human genetic databases, as well as other types of genetic research, creates the new ethical problem as to whether and how benefits should be shared, or at least accentuates the growing claim for 'more' distributive justice in research.

*Re-contacting, families and populations*
Genetic research, but also genetic testing outside a research setting, raises the new question as to whether researchers or clinicians have a duty to re-contact sample donors when new genetic information becomes available or, formulated differently, whether patients have a right to know this information. Since the genetic information might also be important for relatives and even spouses, the right to know (or not to know) might extend to them, either in general or only in specific circumstances, such as the death of sample donors or their durable incompetence. The 'classical' framework of the World Medical Association's Declaration on ethical considerations regarding health databases, as well as classical data protection laws, provide that 'patients have the right to know what information physicians hold about them, including information held on health databases' (WMA 2002, Art. 9). Although the World Medical Association's Declaration contains argumentation referring to the therapeutic privilege (Art. 11),[35] exceptions to the right to be informed are only justified in 'rare, limited circumstances' (Art. 11). The issue of re-contacting has been raised so far mostly outside, or at least independent from, research settings in the case of a duty to warn

---

35   The therapeutic principle means that it is permitted to restrict or withhold information for therapeutic reasons, that is, if there is a significant risk that patients will be harmed by the information.

(HIV contamination), or a duty to 'recall' in the case of defective drugs or devices (Knoppers 2001, 277).

Classical health research guidelines did not directly address the question before 2005. The Bioethics Convention, which contains only three short articles on the regulation of medical research, does not contain any notice about re-contacting. The Declaration of Helsinki (Art. 10) states that it is 'the duty of the physician in medical research to protect the life, health [...] of the human subject'. From this could be deduced a duty to re-contact if the new results have important consequences for the life and/or health of the sample donor. The guidelines of the Council for International Organizations of Medical Sciences (2002) address the question of re-contacting in order to obtain additional consent, but they do not discuss re-contacting in order to inform participants about results.

Finally, in the Additional Protocol Concerning Biomedical Research (COE 2005) which entered into force only recently, in 2007, the Council of Europe takes a position in favour of re-contacting. Article 27 of the Additional Protocol stipulates a right to be offered not only information relevant for the future health of individual research participants, but also information relevant for their quality of life:

> Article 27 – Duty of care. If research gives rise to information of relevance to the current or future health or quality of life of research participants, this information must be offered to them. That shall be done within a framework of health care or counselling. In communication of such information, due care must be taken in order to protect confidentiality and to respect any wish of a participant not to receive such information (COE 2005).

### *Reconsideration or Supplementation?*

In light of the specific and more or less new ethical problems related to research involving human genetic databases, are we 'forced to reconsider, reinterpret, or enrich our understanding of cherished values and principles' (Chadwick 1999, 444)? As Chadwick and Berg (2001, 318) state, the existing ethical principles like informed consent 'might not be ideally equipped to deal with the issues that arise in large-scale population genetic research', but a new ethical framework could 'provide a relevant and valuable perspective' (Chadwick and Berg 2001). The new framework based on solidarity (participation in research for the benefit of others; see Caplan 1984) and equity (sharing the benefits of research) is described as a valuable 'alternative'. This implies some form of reconsideration and replacement of the old framework. Chadwick and Berg seem to limit the application of the new perspective to the new type of large genetic databases because, in their opinion, they differ from small genetic registers. The latter 'have generally benefited individuals, families and societies' (Chadwick and Berg 2001, 318). Authors of other documents in favour of the 'new principle of solidarity', such as the HUGO Statement on benefit-sharing, also seem to believe in the necessity not only to supplement, but to reconsider the existing framework. They refer to two new and only one old principle (common inheritance, solidarity and justice) (HUGO 2000; Ortúzar 2003). In the following sections, we will first examine the meanings of the new principles and then discuss whether any reconsideration or supplementation of the classical health care ethics is appropriate.

*Value and Limits of the 'New' Approach: Solidarity, What Does It Mean?*

The principle of solidarity is not mentioned in any of the classical texts on medical research ethics. Only the Convention on Human Rights and Biomedicine mentions, besides the rights of individuals, some form of duty, that is, the 'responsibility' of the members of society.

The principle of solidarity as it is used by most guidelines is a form of duty. In line with the tradition of the Declaration of Helsinki, many guidelines acknowledge the duty of *researchers* to promote the well-being and health of their patients. By contrast, the principle of solidarity implies a duty of the members of society to participate in research and to donate samples, or the duty to 'facilitate research progress and to provide knowledge that could be crucial to the health of others' (Chadwick and Berg 2001, 320). 'To provide knowledge' could, for example, mean that individuals have a duty to tell family members about genetic information that is important for those family members, too.

The principle of solidarity has a second meaning in some guidelines (RMGA 2000, 13). It describes the duty of members of society to counteract the natural 'genetic lottery'. All members of society should share the burden of health insurance or to a certain extent of life insurance, to ensure medical treatment of those disadvantaged by their genes: solidarity requires the prohibition of discrimination based on genetic characteristics.

Solidarity has a third meaning which refers to a theory of distributive justice and is also described as 'equity'. Solidarity in this sense implies the duty of participants and researchers to share the benefits of the research. The principle of solidarity does not specify whether the benefits should be shared either with the local community, or generally with the rest of mankind, or especially with the least well-off, that is, according to need. The last form has been proposed by HUGO. In its guidelines on benefit sharing, HUGO recommends that 1–3 per cent of the benefits resulting from genetic research should be attributed to humanitarian programmes. In this form, the third meaning of solidarity would be close to the second. The intention would be again to counteract the natural lottery, but furthermore also the social lottery, since humanitarian programmes are directed towards those who are worse off in the social and natural lottery.

*Value and Limits of the 'New' Approach: Is Solidarity a Solution for the Ethical Questions Raised by Human Genetic Databases?*

The principle of solidarity is often defended by arguments that are not convincing. It has been claimed that the foundation of the principle of solidarity is inheritance ('solidarity and altruism in relation to inheritance', HGC 2002, 37). Similarly, HUGO describes the genome as the common heritage of humanity and deduces the principle of solidarity from this shared ontological entity (HUGO 2000). The Human Genetics Commission (HGC) proposes in addition a somewhat different foundation. According to this Commission, the principle of solidarity and altruism is based on 'shared interests in medical progress and the conquest of disease'.[36]

The first problem with these arguments is the naturalistic fallacy. There is no reason why ontology, the existence of shared characteristics or shared interests, constrains a society to deduce an 'ought' from an 'is'.

The second problem with the described arguments is their restriction to genetics. Concerning the argument of common heritage, it is not convincing why solidarity should govern only genetic research. Human beings share a common morphology, common pattern of diseases, common hormones and all sorts of common other molecules, apart from nucleic acids forming genes. The same is true for a common interest in medical progress. Shared interest and shared ontology would both suggest that the principle of solidarity is valuable for research ethics in general. However, classical research ethics does not contain the idea of solidarity, because it has focused on the primacy of the individual. Research participants should not be put under pressure for the good of society.

We think that the principle of solidarity is not useful to resolve the ethical problems associated with research using genetic databases. The first reason is the unclear and partly opposite definition of solidarity.[37] In the first meaning, solidarity is used as a justification to limit individual rights and to decrease the standards of consent in the name of the common good (for example, CCNE 2003, 19ff). In the second meaning it is used in the opposite way, in order to promote greater protection of donors through classical informed consent (for example, RMGA).[38] These opposite meanings of the principle explain why guidelines provide completely different recommendations although they value the same principle (see above).

The second reason is that referring to solidarity as an *ethical principle* is not helpful, even if we restrict the principle to one meaning. Solidarity has been praised and named as one of the ideals and foundations of society, although interestingly it is the last of three.[39] The question is not so much whether solidarity is a valuable principle, but which are the concrete types of solidarity that are not only ethically sound, but that should also be legally enforced. To take an example from the Swiss context, the obligation to help a person who is injured or in danger,

---

36   See HGC (2002, 37).

37   See also Häyry (2003): 'solidarity can be interpreted in many ways'.

38   See RMGA (2000, V. 4.): 'The principle of solidarity requires that those responsible for the universal health care system ensure that the affected individuals and families are protected against all forms of discrimination resulting from their participation in the research. The researcher should defend the participants in any case of potential discrimination.'

39   See, for example, the French tradition of 'liberté, égalité, fraternité', which contains the element of solidarity (fraternité) among the three main principles.

if the circumstances permit this without unreasonable danger to the helper, is part of Swiss criminal law. Article 128 announces that a person who does not provide help in such circumstances will be punished. The requirement for solidarity in this situation can be compared to the criteria of the President's Commission that determine when it is justified to breach confidentiality: the existence of an important danger to a concrete identified person and the ability of another person to prevent the harm. Only in these concrete circumstances is it justified to restrict the rights of the individual through the obligation to act in a certain way. Creating a *legal* duty to solidarity concerning the donation of tissue would not fulfil the described criteria because neither the benefits of the research nor the risks to the donor are determined. Such a *legal* duty would be contrary not only to the existing body of human rights law but also to the tradition of classical research ethics: participation in research, even if this 'participation' concerns 'only' a donor's human tissue, cannot be undertaken without consent.

If enforcing a *legal* duty to solidarity is not justified in these circumstances, would the proclamation of an *ethical* duty be justified and 'useful'? A socially recognized ethical duty to solidarity might create social pressure, but an ethical duty would not be sufficient to limit negative individual rights such as the right to refuse participation in research and the right to withdrawal (opt out). It must be left to individuals to make the decision whether they will increase the benefits of further research or whether they prefer to avoid risks to themselves. The only ethically acceptable way of action is to provide unbiased information and to let people decide for themselves. Individuals might be allowed to agree to a presumed consent model (Elger and Mauron 2003) in which they have the possibility of being informed about further research projects and to opt out, without being forced to take an active part in the decision if they do not want to. However, it cannot be imposed on individuals to have only once the opportunity to decide about all future uses of their tissues, that is, at the moment of donation, without any right to future withdrawal.

'Solidarity' is not a helpful principle in finding a solution when the term is used in its first meaning, but it could be helpful in its second and third meaning. It may be used to justify the prohibition of genetic discrimination.[40] Furthermore, it could be a guiding principle for benefit sharing because it provides some 'thicker flesh' around the 'thin bones' of the word 'justice'. It might not help in choosing the details of who should benefit to what extent. However, it indicates clearly that benefits should not only be provided to participants, but to some larger group or community.

---

40 This seems to be the prevailing meaning of the concept in Europe, referring to the welfare state and a health care system in which solidarity helps to counteract the natural (and social) lottery; see Houtepen and Meulen (2000a and 2000b), Pasini and Reichlin (2000), Ashcroft, Campbell and Jones (2000), Bergmark (2000). See also Häyry and Häyry (1990).

## Interest-based Ethical Reflections

The principle-based approach is used in the majority of guidelines. It has been argued that a principle-based ethics does not permit a convincing response to the controversial issues related to research involving biobanks. To fill the gap, several recent publications about the ethical issues of human genetic databases have adopted a different approach based on interests (Buchanan 1999; Hansson 2001; Merz et al. 2002; Elger and Mauron 2003).[41] It seems important, therefore, to examine the answers of an interest-based approach to the controversial ethical questions, in order to find out whether this approach has any advantages over the use of principles.

A significant number of the guidelines that have been included in the analysis of principles (see Tables 3.2–3.12) also use the term 'interest'. We will, first, describe the interest-based ethical frameworks contained in the guidelines and, second, discuss critically whether an approach based on reflections about interests (see Table 3.13) is helpful in building a globally acceptable ethical framework.

*Interests, Principles, Rights and Values*

The term 'interest' is used by the great majority of guidelines (see Table 13.3), although clearly more frequently by some (MRC; HGC; TC; NBAC) than by others. Many guidelines mention principles as well as interests. For instance, the guidelines of the NBAC, which are dedicated to the principles of classical medical research ethics, also contain reflections on interests. Certainly, this confirms that principles and interests, as well as values and rights, are related. Statements about principles and rights are the conclusions of a moral deliberation about the interests that should be protected. The principle of the respect for persons/respect of autonomy indicates that the interests of the autonomous individual should be respected. The Universal Declaration of Human Rights (United Nations 1948, Art. 1-30) lists individual rights that deserve special legal protections against the interference of states or societies and therefore indirectly gives a list of interests which merit protection.

Buchanan (1999, B-5) distinguishes between welfare interests and ulterior interests. Welfare interests are the basic interests that need to be fulfilled for a human being's 'flourishing', such as access to food, physical security, liberty of action and access to information. Welfare interests can be objectively determined for all human beings, at least within certain limits. Individuals are only able to pursue ulterior interests if their welfare interests are satisfied to a minimum. Ulterior interests relate to the different ways by which individuals seek to live their personal lives and to pursue personal goals. Ulterior interests mirror therefore what a person values.

---

41 See also Tugendhat (1984, 127): 'Es ist Ergebnis der Aufklärung, "daß alle höheren Wahrheiten ihre intersubjektive Überzeugungskraft verlieren." Einzig verbleibende Begründungsmöglichkeiten von Moral "sind die eigenen Interessen der Individuen, das, was jeder mit Rücksicht auf sein Wohl und das Wohl derer, denen er affektiv verbunden ist, will".'

An approach based on interests could have several advantages over a principle-based approach when it comes to evaluating the ethical problems related to the use of genetic databases. First, an interest-based approach provides a direct way to integrate the reality of a pluralistic society into the ethical deliberation. A pluralistic society needs to balance the interests of different individuals if they are in conflict. At this point, the principle of autonomy is of limited help, because the autonomy of one person stands against the autonomy of another. In the classical principle-based approach of Beauchamp and Childress (2008), the principle of justice has been used to balance the autonomy rights of different individuals. The analysis of interests and the attribution of different weights to different interests is a transparent way of establishing a 'thick' theory of justice that could be accepted by various members of a pluralistic society.

Second, an interest-based approach is useful in order to describe more clearly what is meant by the idea of an 'interest of society'. Societies are composed of individuals. An interest shared by all individuals in the society becomes a 'common interest'. However, on the level of the individual, the same individual might have several conflicting interests. In the case of genetic databases, the same donor is interested in guaranteeing a maximum of privacy rights and protection against possible harms *and* in obtaining a maximum of future health benefits resulting from the research. Analysing interests will enable each individual to define his or her own priorities of interests. It might turn out that, although all individuals share a strong interest 'in medical progress and the conquest of illness', they all give a higher priority to the protection of privacy and the avoidance of risks. In this case, it will be misleading to speak of the value of research as an important interest of society, since everybody agrees that it is less important than other interests.

*Different Meanings of the Term 'Interest' Inside the Same Guidelines*

In the guidelines (see Table 13.3), the term 'interest' is most frequently used to refer to the interests of the research subjects and to the fact that these interests should be protected. Consensus seems to exist that it is acceptable to use tissue for research if the research does not affect the donor's interests (RCP 2001). The problem is that the term 'interest' is used in many different meanings even within the same guidelines. The term 'interest' may refer within one single guideline to (1) entirely subjective or at least ulterior interests, (2) a reasonable person's interests, as well as (3) legitimate interests that are or should be legally protected. Interestingly, compared to the term 'wish', the 'interests' of a donor or subject seem to be perceived as less arbitrary and imply at least some notion of moral or psychological legitimacy (Hoerster 2003).[42]

---

42   See Hoerster (2003, 37ss) who distinguishes 'wishes' from 'enlightened interests'. In this context, see also the HUGO Statement on DNA sampling (1998): 'These shared biological risks *create special interests* and moral obligations with respect to access, storage and destruction that may occasionally *outweigh individual wishes*' (italics B.E.).

The term 'best interest' refers in general to the interests of incapacitated or not autonomous persons. The best interest is therefore determined according to a reasonable person standard and takes into account, if possible, previous interests of a known individual. When guidelines mention the rights and interests of research subjects, interests – mentioned separately from rights – seem to refer most often to ulterior or subjective interests, since all welfare interests are in general so important as to deserve protection by rights. Since most guidelines refer to interests without further explanation, it is not clear whether they wish to protect all interests of an individual or whether some interests of research subjects are not worth protecting. The Medical Research Council (MRC) states that 'the assumption by the donor is that nothing will be done that would be detrimental to his or her interests, or bring harm to him or her' (MRC 2001, 8). This indicates that interests are more than the avoidance of harm. At other places, however, the MRC seems to restrict interests to the idea of physical harm: on page 10 it states, for example, that 'provided there is no possible way to link the results of tests to identifiable individuals their interests cannot be compromised'. In this quotation the MRC does not seem to value the interest of individuals not to be wronged. Individuals could feel wronged either because they would have liked to know the uses of their tissue or because their tissue or the information derived from it is used in studies that the donor would not want to be done. In the case of religiously motivated interests, the wrongs might even turn out to be harms if the use of a donor's tissue for abortion research or research to develop contraceptives is considered a sin that might have harmful consequences for the donor before and after his or her death (for example, exclusion from the religious community or no resurrection). Even independently from religious ideas, being wronged could imply harm. A very broad definition of harm is used by Feinberg who holds that all harms might be viewed as setbacks to interests (1984, 51–5). In line with this definition, 'being harmed' does not mean that an individual suffers from adverse physical or psychological consequences. 'Being harmed' might not even imply that the person is still alive, because some interests survive the death of the donor (Gesang 2003).[43]

The Tri-Council policy statement (Tri-Council 1998) and the Human Genetics Commission (HGC 2002, 94) acknowledge interests that are not related to physical harm. They state that the interests of individuals, families or communities 'may be adversely affected through research uses of their anonymous tissue'. 'Some individuals may not want their tissue used for any research purposes regardless of anonymity' (Tri-Council 1998, 10.4). The Nuffield Council (1995, 5) seems to have a somewhat critical view of some interests which are 'claimed' by individuals. The Council refers to interests in removed tissue or 'products derived from it'. According to the Nuffield Council guidelines, such a claim has not received legal attention in the United Kingdom, because it is generally admitted that 'a person from whom tissue is removed has not the slightest interest in making any claim

---

43  See Gesang (2003, 35); NBAC (1999, 49). See also the discussion by Hoerster (2003, 31–3).

to it once it is removed' (Nuffield Council 1995, 68). On the other hand, some interests in the dead body or its parts are legally protected, such as the right to a decent burial (Nuffield Council 1995, 68). It is interesting to notice that the 'legal attention' in the UK has shifted about a decade later, when the UK implemented the Human Tissue Act (Ironside 2006) which provides a greater protection to interests in removed tissue than was the case in 1995.

In spite of its restricted use of the term 'interest', the Medical Research Council (MRC 2001) does not limit the use of the term 'interest' to best interests or interests shared by all human beings. On page 18, it is stated that participants have individual interests which they need to define themselves after having received adequate information. For this reason, the guidelines caution researchers not to assume that 'they, rather than the individuals concerned, are best placed to determine what information is of interest to donors on a case-by-case basis' ( MRC 2001, 18). Researchers might see a need to inform donors only of genetic risks for which prevention or the possibility of changing the outcome exists. Research participants might want to know predictive genetic information, even if this knowledge will not have any health consequences for them. Researchers would define interests in this case as welfare interests related to health risks, whereas donors might value ulterior interests or reproductive interests. The classification of reproductive interests is difficult. They are in general valued as 'rights' because they represent fundamental objective interests of all human beings. Most individuals would only feel 'happy' if their reproductive interests are fulfilled. On the other hand, the satisfaction of reproductive interests is not to the same degree a prerequisite in order to pursue ulterior interests as is the case for the satisfaction of welfare interests. Reproductive interests could therefore best be classified as lying somewhat between welfare interests and ulterior interests.

The guidelines written by the Human Genetics Commission (HGC 2002) are another example which illustrates that the term 'interest' is used in different meanings. The HGC recognizes the donor's 'interest in being properly informed and consulted, and in remaining in control of personal biological material and information' ( HGC 2002, 10). The HGC considers this interest important and describes it as a '*strong* interest in what happens to the sample' ( HGC 2002, 90, italics B.E.). In this passage, the HGC seems to refer to a personal interest. In contradiction to this use of the term 'interest', the HGC pronounces on page 96 its 'view on the absence of interest which the donor has in the DNA that is contained in developed cell lines'. Here, the term 'interest' seems to refer to a legitimate or legal interest, as compared to a personal interest. This interpretation is confirmed by the following sentence, in which the HGC states that donors should be informed of the fact 'that their interest in the donated material is to cease once the donation is made'.

The Tri-Council policy statement (1998, i.5) provides the following description of the interests of subjects that should be protected: 'the multiple and interdependent interests of a person – from bodily to psychological to cultural integrity'. While 'bodily and psychological integrity' seems to refer to some objective standard of scientific medicine or psychology, 'cultural integrity' implies some non-universal standards which are shared by a group of individuals. Indeed, the interest in tissue which is removed from the body is shaped by different cultural perceptions (Tri-Council 1998, 10.1).

The College of American Pathologists (CAP) (Grizzle et al. 1999) always employs the term 'interest' in the sense of objective or legitimate interests. The first indication of this meaning is that the term 'best interests' of patients and the public is used independently from the fact of whether patients are competent or not. The guidelines take the position that the interests of patients in the use of their bodies for therapeutic interventions are completely different from the interests of donors in the use of their tissue for research (Grizzle et al. 1999, 298–9). In the latter case, donors have, according to the CAP, no interest in being informed about their individual results which are part of a single project, because one study does not establish irrefutable scientific facts, whereas society's interest in accumulated research findings is 'great' or 'strong' (Grizzle et al. 1999, 299).

A number of guidelines do not only refer to the interests of participating individuals, but also to the interests of participating groups, such as communities, populations, 'all research subjects', or to a national interest in the case of large-scale genetic databases, such as the UK Biobank (HGC 2002, 19). The interests of these groups are often determined by benefits that would be available primarily to the participating community.

The term 'interest' is frequently used in relation to society, also referred to as an 'important public interest' (UNESCO 2003). The following interests of 'society' are mentioned: the 'interest of public safety' (COE 1997b), the interest 'in the advancement of knowledge' (RMGA 2000), the 'common interest in maintaining the highest ethical and scientific standards' (Tri-Council 1998, 1.11), a 'shared interest in medical progress and the conquest of illness' (HGC 2002, 37) or 'in treating disease and developing new therapies' (NBAC 1999, iii), and the 'vital interest of society that human tissue can be used in NHS hospital laboratories' (RCP 2001). Such public interests are in general taken for granted. Only the NBAC provides a critical discussion of the interests of society and demonstrates that more nuances about society's interests are necessary, because the various interests might not be shared equally by all of its members: 'If the distribution of benefits is grossly inequitable, it is misleading to speak of a common interest in medical progress.' Those who 'lack access to important health care benefits because they cannot afford them' will not agree to provide samples and to tolerate increased risks to their interests 'for the sake of society's interests in medical progress' because they will never have the possibility of benefiting from this medical progress (NBAC 1999, 50).

In some places, the 'interests of society' stand for national interests; in others they refer more broadly to 'the interests of all concerned' (CIOMS), or of 'humanity'. According to the guidelines of the North American Regional Committee (NARC 1997), 'humanity' has an interest in knowledge (similar to 'society' in the RMGA guidelines). Another interest of humanity which is only mentioned explicitly in the guidelines of the North American Regional Committee (NARC 1997) is the interest in 'confidence in science'.

Interestingly, interests are not only attributed to persons and groups, but also to an abstract entity: science. Several interests are shared by society and science. Interest in confidence in science (NARC 1997) is an example of an interest shared by humanity and science, as well as interest in the progress of medical knowledge.

In addition to the aforementioned interests of research participants, the communities of research participants, society and science, interests of 'others' are discussed in the guidelines, or also called 'third party interests'. Most often 'others' are the family,[44] researchers and companies. According to the Human Genetics Commission (HGC 2002, 103), companies have 'legitimate interests'. Part of these legitimate interests is to have 'exclusive access to particular information in order to allow a reasonable period for commercial opportunities' (HGC 2002, 103).

*How Do Guidelines Balance Interests?*

The HUGO Statement on DNA sampling (1998) describes how the interests of donors and present and future relatives should be balanced: 'These shared biological risks create special interests and moral obligations with respect to access, storage and destruction that may occasionally outweigh individual wishes' (HUGO 1998). Criteria which indicate when individual wishes do not have priority are not specified. Instead, the possible areas in which interests might conflict are described. Such areas are the 'very fact of participation in research or not', 'the decision to refuse to warn at-risk relatives', the decision to 'withdraw', or the 'failure to provide for access after death' (HUGO 1998).

The National Bioethics Advisory Commission (NBAC 1999) proposes to 'identify and, whenever possible, assign weights to various interests of both individuals and groups'. Moreover, 'rather than simply trying to present those interests in the abstract', the NBAC considers them 'in relation to the principles, regulations, and guidelines that already identify many of the relevant harms and assigns them some weights relative to each other'. However, as we have shown before, the problem with research involving genetic databases is in particular that the weight of the different 'harms' and 'wrongs' related to tissue and genetic information still needs to be defined in an uncontroversial way.

One hypothesis is that we only need to find the appropriate empirical solution to avoid any conflict of interests. The solution would consist of finding appropriate means by which privacy will be efficiently protected without hampering research. According to this hypothesis, no real conflict of interests exists. This seems to be the opinion of the Human Genetics Commission: '[I]nterests in genetic privacy and confidentiality can be protected in ways that do not harm comparably important interests of others' (HGC 2002, 13). Similarly, the National Bioethics Advisory Commission states that 'fundamentally the interests of subjects and those of researchers are not in conflict' (NBAC 1999, ii).

---

44    '[F]amily's interests' (MRC 2001, 3.5, 11 and 25) or 'vital interest of a relative' (ESHG 2002, 23).

A closer look at the solutions proposed by the Human Genetics Commission (HGC 2002) and the National Bioethics Advisory Commission (NBAC 1999) shows that the authors of the guidelines are not convinced that the ideal empirical means can be found. Instead, the implicit or explicit assumption is that everybody will agree that the protection of privacy and confidentiality does not need to be or even cannot be absolute. The aim is not complete protection. Instead, incomplete protection is considered acceptable because interests of 'the patient, relatives or wider public might be more important' (HGC 2002, 15). The Tri-Council guidelines give the following example of balancing: 'The public interest thus may justify allowing researchers access to personal information' in the case of 'compelling and specifically identified public interests' such as the 'protection of health, life and safety' (Tri-Council 1998, 3.1). Similarly, the Human Genetics Commission believes that 'there may be circumstances in which we would seek to balance the demands of autonomy (for example with respect to the right to keep personal genetic information confidential) with the interests of others whose welfare may be affected by access to such information' (HGC 2002, 40). The underlying idea seems to be that welfare interests of others are more important than ulterior interests of the donors. According to the HGC (2002, 40), the 'pursuit of individual fulfillment at the expense of the claims of others' may 'find few defenders in a society based on ideas of mutual co-operation and inter-dependence'. The HGC holds that the use of anonymized samples and genetic data in research will not cause harm to the donors, but will only interfere with some of their interests in privacy and in control over their tissue. This restriction of individual autonomy would be justified since the 'process of balancing interests is a common one in a range of privacy issues, where public interest may justify a limiting of the individual's right to privacy (for example, in issues of freedom of the press or criminal justice' (HGC 2002, 40).

In addition to this general form of balancing, a frequently mentioned approach is the balancing of interests on a case by case basis by the ethical review committee. The Nuffield Council believes that the 'notion of public decency' could be useful in the balancing process because it could help to define the limits of research that is said to be in the public interest. Limits would need to be established for those forms of banking and research involving human tissue that offend public decency (Nuffield Council 1995, 65). However, overall the concept of 'public decency' remains vague and would need to be defined on a case by case basis.

## Rules for Balancing Interests and Principles: Proposition of an Ethical Framework for Research Involving Genetic Databases

*The Ethical Framework Concerning the Use of Human Genetic Databases: Conclusions from the Guidelines*

Based on the discussion in the previous sections, we defend the following conclusions:

1. The framework of classical research ethics is sufficient to guide ethical questions related to human genetic databases. The foundations of this framework need not and should not be replaced by a new framework.

2. The classical principles of research ethics are broad milestones that do not give detailed guidance but that eliminate at least some choices and direct towards a limited number of alternatives. The first two milestones are the absolute respect of autonomy in the case of refusal to participate in research and some paternalistic restriction of the freedom to participate in research considered too dangerous. The third milestone is the active collaboration of involved communities. This milestone reflects the acceptance of some cultural differences in the weighing of benefits and harms.

3. Principles are not sufficient to resolve controversial issues in detail. Referring at this point to ethics committees and leaving them the task of resolving the controversial issues means only transferring the problem. It is well known that distinct ethics committees come to different conclusions for the same research protocol (Dziak et al. 2005) and the aim of guidelines is precisely to harmonize practice. Therefore, guidelines should provide to members of ethical review committees at least some rules or indications how to balance conflicting principles. For ethical problems that involve classical conflicts between two parties, typically the patient and his or her physician(s), rules for balancing conflicting principles are at present well established. However, in the case of a more complex structure involving a multitude of parties which have different interests, it is helpful to complement the principle-based approach by an analysis and a balancing of the interests involved. In addition to rules for balancing principles, guidelines should provide rules or indications how to balance interests. Balancing interests is not a new approach. Most classical guidelines on medical research ethics have discussed some form of balancing of interests. The rule most frequently adopted was that the interests of research participants always outweighed the interests of society or science.

4. The basic rule for the balancing of the classical three principles of health research ethics is the following: priority should be given to respect for autonomy, as long as the welfare interests of others are not in danger.[45]

---

45    See also Mill's harm principle (Mill 1956): '[...] the sole end for which mankind are warranted, individually or collectively, in interfering with the liberty of action of any of their number, is self-protection. That the only purpose for which power can be rightfully exercised over any member of a civilized community, against his will, is to prevent harm from others.' One can find a sort of 'harm principle' already in Kant (1982 [1797]). For Kant, the liberty and autonomy of every human being are limited by the liberty of all others. As he puts it in his famous definition: 'Freiheit (Unabhängigkeit von eines anderen nötigen der Willkür), sofern sie mit jedes anderen Freiheit nach einem allgemeinen Gesetz zusammen bestehen kann, ist dieses einzige, ursprüngliche, jedem Menschen, kraft seiner Menschheit, zustehende Recht (Kant 1982 [1797], 345). Protecting welfare interests translates into

This means that precedence is given to the negative rights of those who do not want to participate over the positive rights of those who are interested in the benefits of the research. Research projects can only be carried out with the free and uncoerced participation of individuals. The burden lies on the researchers to propose projects that are ethically acceptable to the participants. The progress of research might even be greater and faster if the interests of participants are fully respected. Even if it were true that the progress of medical research is somewhat slower due to ethical restrictions, this represents neither a measurable nor a preventable danger to the welfare interests of identifiable individuals or groups.

5. The claim that research involving genetic testing that is part of genetic databases needs to be governed by a new framework based on community values such as solidarity, altruism and familial mutuality lacks sufficient justification. Medical research has always had implications for others than the individuals involved. The sharing of common genes does not impose a duty of solidarity when solidarity is meant to imply a restriction of personal rights. Solidarity in a different meaning might be a useful concept for research in general, not only genetic research. This concept of solidarity can help to obtain a consensus about a form of distributive justice that implies the prevention of genetic discrimination, as well as some form of redistribution of benefits to the worst off in the natural and social lottery.

6. New principles, such as solidarity, are not needed to guide the balancing of principles and interests when it comes to biobank research. What has to be done is a further examination of how the balancing of interests can complement the 'classical' balancing of principles. In the following section we provide concrete rules for how interests should be balanced in order to resolve the controversies about ethical uses of human genetic databases.

*Rules for Balancing Interests in Biobank Research*

• All interests of research participants or donors should be considered, that is, objective welfare interests, common ulterior interests and other more subjective ulterior interests.

• Reproductive interests need to be taken into account, too, because they are a particularly important type of common ulterior interest.

• Religious interests referring to non-physical harms or wrongs should be respected as much as possible, since not respecting them would deprive entire groups or communities of participation in research involving biobanks.

• Different weight should be given to these interests according to criteria already in use in medical ethics, such as, for example, the criteria used to justify breaches of confidentiality.

---

negative and positive rights, but both can be summarized under the harm principle: a person is harmed by a violent act (right to non-interference) and by a lack of food (positive right).

- The various interests of the different stakeholders are not of equal weight. First, welfare interests outweigh ulterior interests. Therefore, it is permitted to give less priority to some interests because they are clearly secondary, such as the interest of a researcher to obtain interesting results and to publish them (ulterior interest), the interest of a pharmaceutical company to make profit (ulterior interest), or the interests of insurance companies and of employers to know about genetic risks in circumstances that do not affect the welfare interests of anybody involved.

This leaves two situations in particular where one needs to balance important interests: welfare[46] and reproductive interests:

1. The conflict between, on one side, the confidentiality and privacy interests of a donor and, on the other side, the possible *health (welfare) and reproductive interests of family members* if the donor is found to carry disease-causing mutations.
2. The conflict between the confidentiality, privacy and non-interference interests of a donor on one side and, on the other side, the interests of present and future patients suffering from genetically influenced diseases that could be prevented or cured due to the advances in research.

*Rules for balancing in the first situation*
The classical criteria used to justify a breach of confidentiality in different situations have been established by the President's Commission (President's Commission 1983) and supported by a growing number of health care professionals and ethicists (Andrews et al. 1994; Privacy Commissioner of Australia 1996; Reilly 1997; ASHG 1998). Disclosure against the wishes of the donor is justified if the probability is high that identifiable individuals would otherwise suffer from serious, avoidable harm (President's Commission 1983, 44). It is important to define what constitutes 'serious harm'. In the context of the balancing of interests we define serious harm as harm related to welfare interests or to reproductive interests. Including the latter would mean that possible serious harm to offspring which would have influenced the reproductive choices of family members might be considered a sufficient reason to justify a breach of confidentiality.

---

46 Several classical research ethics guidelines (Declaration of Helsinki: WMA 2008; Convention on human rights and biomedicine: COE 1997b) do not state that the *interests* of individuals outweigh the interests of society, but that the *well-being* or *welfare* of individuals outweigh the interests of society. This is in accordance with the idea that immediately identifiable welfare interests have more weight than ulterior interests and that ulterior interests of subjects might not always outweigh the interests of society. Interestingly, the documents more particularly concerning research involving human tissue or genetic databases (UNESCO 2003; COE 2006; MRC 2001) mention both the interests of individuals and their welfare, stating that the 'interests and welfare of the individual' outweigh the interests of society.

*Rules for balancing in the second situation*

The improvement of health could be considered a welfare interest of those suffering present y or in the future from genetically influenced disease. The following problem exists when one tries to balance these interests against the interests of the donor at the moment of donation: when the donors provide their tissue, it is not clear whether the particular research project will in the future, and at what point in time, influence the health of present or future patients. No identified person is in immediate and preventable danger. Consequently, no strong reason exists to override the privacy and protection interests of donors or to restrict the interests of donors who wish to remain in control of their samples and information.

Harris (1999, 77–91, especially 83–4) comes to a different conclusion concerning the conflict between the interests of research participants and present and future patients who will benefit from the research. He contests the principle set out in the Declaration of Helsinki that the interests of research participants always outweigh the interests of society, society here being interpreted as present and future patients. He provides the following example to justify mandatory participation for public good: a captain is called to rescue passengers from another ship in danger. This rescue attempt will impose a small amount of risk to the passengers of the captain's own ship. It is justified for the captain to rescue the passengers from the foreign ship without the consent of his own passengers because the benefit for the passengers in danger outweighs the small increase in risk for his own passengers. In our opinion, this example is not relevant because it contains two important differences compared to research involving human genetic databases. First, the passengers in danger are identified persons in immediate danger and the probability that they can be saved is high. Second, in order to rescue the passengers in danger, the captain is forced to use his ship together with all participants. The option to offer passengers the opportunity to leave the ship does not exist in the middle of the sea. This means that, automatically, all passengers on the ship will be exposed to the small increase in risk. Conversely, genetic research using human genetic databases can produce valuable results without the participation of all subjects. This shows that there is a danger in limiting the personal rights of research participants based on inappropriate justifications, for example, when the need for the participation of all is exaggerated or when stakeholders disagree about the empirical question of how best to use genetic databases.

A different question in this respect is the amount of control over future information that one grants to participants. Although a research participant might have an interest in knowing the results, it might be too costly or not feasible to provide these results, especially if standards of care would require genetic counselling together with the transmission of the information. The difference between this issue and an obligation to participate in research is that interest in not participating concerns a desire for non-interference, whereas interest in knowing the results is a request for an 'active behaviour'. The researcher, or a panel of experts in genetics, might argue based on the available evidence that disclosure of unproven research findings could do more harm than good to the patient. In this case, the autonomy rights of the researcher might outweigh the autonomy rights of patients. As with other harmful medical procedures, good medical practice guidelines might set limits to the ulterior interests of research participants if compliance with the interests requires the active participation of the researcher (see the section about re-contacting).

The balancing of principles and interests in research involving human genetic databases is complex. In order to harmonize balancing, it is necessary to examine arguments, principles and interests in more detail concerning the most controversial issues. In the following chapter we will first provide an overview about the debate and proposed different solutions to the ethical problems. We will analyse the involved principles and interests and apply some of the formulated rules of balancing in order to guide the discussion towards one or at least a restricted number of acceptable solutions.

The discussion of selected issues of consensus and controversy not only permits us to show the most popular positions, but is also of particular interest in looking at unique and original ideas defended in single guidelines, because some ideas are easily overlooked or forgotten in spite of their potential to solve the existing ethical problems.

Finally, the following chapter will also show how the positions held by different policy makers and scholars evolved over time towards some degree of harmonization. Chapter 5 discusses the potential for further harmonization.

## Table 3.1    Guidelines examined (the following abbreviations are used)

| Abbreviation | Guideline |
|---|---|
| **1. Classical international guidelines for medical research ethics (on human beings)** | |
| Helsinki | Declaration of Helsinki (WMA 2000; WMA 2008) |
| Belmont | Belmont Report (1979) |
| CIOMS | Council for International Organizations of Medical Sciences (2002; 2009) |
| CHRB or Bioethics Convention | Convention on human rights and biomedicine. Council of Europe (COE 1997), and the Additional Protocol Concerning Biomedical Research (COE 2005) |
| **2. Specific guidelines concerning biobanks/genetic databanks** | |
| **International recommendations:** | |
| UNESCO | International Declaration on Human Genetic Data (UNESCO 2003) |
| WHO 1998 | World Health Organization. Proposed International Guidelines on Ethical Issues in Medical Genetics and Genetic Services (WHO 1998) |
| WHO 2000 | WHO's guideline for obtaining informed consent for the procurement and use of human tissues in preparing a research project proposal 3rd edn (WHO 2000) |
| WHO 2001 | World Health Organization Regional Office for Europe: Genetic Databases: Assessing the benefits and the impact on human and patient rights. Report for Consultation (WHO 2001) |
| HUGO 1995 | Statements of the Human Genome Organization<br>• Human Genome Organization. Ethical, Legal, and Social Issues Committee Report to HUGO Council. Statement on the principled conduct of genetics research (HUGO 1995) |
| HUGO 1998 | • Human Genome Organization. Statement on DNA sampling: control and access (HUGO 1998) |
| HUGO 2000 | • 2000: Human Genome Organization. Ethics Committee. Statement on benefit-sharing (HUGO 2000) |
| **European recommendations:** | |
| COE | Council of Europe Rec(2006)4 of the Committee of Ministers to member states on research on biological materials of human origin (COE 2006) |
| CDBI Explanatory Report | Council of Europe Steering Committee on Bioethics. Proposal for an instrument on the use of archived human materials. Explanatory Report (CDBI 2002b) |
| ESHG | European Society of Human Genetics (ESHG et al. 1 November 2002; ESHG 2003) |
| **National recommendations:** | |
| **Canada** | |
| CEST | Commission de l'Éthique de la Science et de la Technologie. Quebec 2003 |
| TC | Tri-Council policy statement. Ethical conduct for research involving humans. Canada 1998 |
| RMGA | Network of Applied Genetic Medicine. Statement of principles: human genome research. Version 2000 |
| **United Kingdom** | |
| MRC | Medical Research Council. UK 2001 |
| HGC | Human Genetics Commission. UK 2002 |
| NC | Nuffield Council. UK 1995 |
| RCP | Royal College of Pathologists. UK 2001 |
| **USA** | |
| NBAC | National Bioethics Advisory Commission. USA 1999 |
| NARC | North American Regional Committee. USA 1997 |
| CAP | College of American Pathologists. USA 1999 |
| NCH | US National Center for Human Genome Research. USA 1996, update 1998 |
| ACMG | American College of Medical Genetics 1995 |
| ASHG | American Society of Human Genetics<br>• 1988 DNA Banking and DNA Analysis: Points to Consider<br>• 1996 Statement on Informed Consent for Genetic Research |
| **France** | |
| CCNE | Comité Consultatif National d'Ethique, Avis et rapport No. 77. France 2003 |

**Table 3.2    Explanations in relevant 'classical' international documents about the ethical framework of medical research ethics**

| Guideline | Ethical principles | Principles mentioned |
|---|---|---|
| Belmont Report, United States 1979 | Yes | Basic ethical principles:<br>• respect for persons (two elements: 'individuals should be treated as autonomous agents' and 'persons with diminished autonomy are entitled to protection'). 'Respecting persons, in most hard cases [e.g. should prisoners have the right to volunteer for research], is often a matter of balancing competing claims urged by the principle of respect itself.'<br>• beneficence ('two general rules': 'do not harm' and 'maximize possible benefit and minimize possible harms')<br>• justice: 'fairness of distribution' of the benefits and burdens of research. Research should not be done using systematically individuals from certain classes only because of their 'easy availability, their compromised position, or their manipulability'. They should be chosen 'for reasons directly related to the problem being studied'. Research 'should not unduly involve persons from groups unlikely to be among the beneficiaries of subsequent applications of the research'.<br>Applications:<br>• 'informed consent', 'assessment of risks and benefits', 'selection of subjects' |
| Declaration of Helsinki 2008 | The declaration does not refer directly to principle-based ethics, but announces 'basic principles for all medical research' | A 3. 'It is the duty of the physician to promote and safeguard the health of patients.'<br>A 6. 'In medical research involving human subjects, the well-being of the individual research subject must take precedence over all other interests.'<br>A 9. 'ethical standards that promote respect for all human subjects and protect their health and rights'<br>'B. Basic principles for all medical research'<br>11. 'It is the duty of physicians who participate in medical research to protect the life, health, dignity, integrity, right to self-determination, privacy, and confidentiality of personal information of research subjects.'<br>12. 'Medical research involving human subjects must conform to generally accepted scientific principles ….'<br>14–18. 'research protocol', 'appropriate scientific training', 'careful assessment of predictable risks and burdens'<br>21. 'Medical research involving human subjects should only be conducted if the importance of the objective outweighs the inherent risks and burdens to the subject.'<br>22. 'Participation by competent individuals as subjects in medical research must be voluntary.'<br>23. 'Every precaution must be taken to<br>• protect the privacy of research subjects and<br>• the confidentiality of their personal information and<br>• to minimize the impact of the study on their physical, mental and social integrity.'<br>24. on (classical) informed consent<br>25. (new in the 2008 version compared to the previous version): 'For medical research using identifiable human material or data, physicians must normally seek consent for the collection, analysis, storage and/or reuse. There may be situations where consent would be impossible or impractical to obtain for such research or would pose a threat to the validity of the research. In such situations the research may be done only after consideration and approval of a research ethics committee.' |

**Table 3.2** Continued

| Guideline | Ethical principles | Principles mentioned |
|---|---|---|
| Council for International Organizations of Medical Sciences (CIOMS). International ethical guidelines for bio-medical research involving human subjects 2002 | Yes. Chapter on 'General ethical principles' | Introduction: 'research involving human subjects must not violate any universally applicable ethical standards, but acknowledge that, in superficial aspects, the application of ethical principles, e.g. in relation to individual autonomy and informed consent, needs to take account of cultural values, while respecting absolutely the ethical standards.' 'General ethical principles. All research involving human subjects should be conducted in accordance with three basic ethical principles, namely': <br>• 'respect for persons' (referring to the two considerations of the Belmont Report: respect the choices of individuals having the capacity of self-determination and protect persons with diminished autonomy) <br>• 'beneficence': the 'ethical obligation to maximize benefits and minimize harms' and <br>• 'justice': the 'equitable distribution of both the burdens and the benefits of participation in research. Differences in distribution of burdens and benefits are justifiable only if they are based on morally relevant distinctions between persons; one such distinction is vulnerability.' <br>'these principles [have] in the abstract [...] equal moral force [...] In varying circumstances they may be [...] given different moral weight.' |
| Convention for the protection of human rights and dignity of the human being with regard to the application of biology and medicine: convention on human rights and biomedicine, Council of Europe 1997 | No direct reference to the classical form of an ethics of principles. Instead, the document contains an approach based on human rights and freedoms | The term 'principle' appears three times in the document referring to 'the principles contained in this Convention.' <br>Art. 23: 'Infringement of the rights or principles. The Parties shall provide appropriate judicial protection to prevent or to put a stop to an unlawful infringement of the rights and principles set forth in this Convention at short notice.' <br>Art. 31: 'Protocols may be concluded in pursuance of Art. 32, with a view to developing, in specific fields, the principles contained in this Convention.' <br>Principles referred to in the preamble: <br>• referred to twice: 'maintenance and further realisation of human rights and fundamental freedoms', 'safeguard [...] the fundamental rights and freedoms of the individual' <br>• referred to twice: 'importance of ensuring the dignity of the human being', 'safeguard human dignity' <br>• 'need to respect the human being both as an individual and as a member of the human species' <br>• 'benefit of present and future generations' <br>• 'so that all humanity may enjoy the benefits of biology and medicine' <br>• 'promoting a public debate' <br>• 'rights and responsibilities' of 'all members of society' <br>General provisions: <br>• Art. 1: 'protect the dignity and identity of all human beings and guarantee [...] respect for their integrity and other rights and fundamental freedoms.' <br>• Art. 2: 'The interests and welfare of the human beings shall prevail over the sole interest of society or science.' <br>• Art. 3: 'equitable access to health care of appropriate quality' ... 'taking into account health needs and available resources ... ' <br>• Arts 5–9: on consent <br>• Art. 10: 'respect for private life in relation to information about health', affirmation of the right to know and the right not to know <br>• Art. 16: 'Protection of persons undergoing research [...] research [...] may only be undertaken [...] if [...] the risks which may be incurred by that person are not disproportionate to the potential benefits of the research.' |

**Table 3.3 Explanations on the ethical framework in guidelines relevant for research involving human genetic databases**

| Guideline | Ethical principles | Principles mentioned |
|---|---|---|
| UNESCO 'Draft report on collection, treatment, storage and use of genetic data' Paris, 2001 *and* UNESCO International declaration on human genetic data. Final version adopted 16 October 2003 | Yes, p. 2s<br><br>Yes | The UNESCO 'Draft report on collection, treatment, storage and use of genetic data' Paris, 3 September 2001, contained a section 'VII. Principles', followed by 'VIII. Application of the principles'. The section 'Principles' explained in more detail six principles (respect for human dignity, autonomy, privacy, property, equality, justice) and four 'processes and fair procedures', also called 'process values', to deal with conflicts between principles. The 'process values' listed were: transparency of process, public involvement in decision-making, public education, quality control (of laboratories undertaking genetic testing). In the final version, a slightly different list of principles is only cited, without explanation, in the introduction part.<br>*Noting* that the interests and welfare of the individual should have priority over the rights and interests of society and research'<br>*Reaffirming*<br>- the principles established in the Universal Declaration on the Human Genome and Human Rights and the principles of<br>- equality, - justice, - solidarity, - responsibility [*], - respect for human dignity, - human rights and fundamental freedoms<br>- freedom of thought and expression, - freedom of research, - privacy [*], - security of the person [*]'<br>All, except the principles marked [*], are repeated in Art. 1 of the declaration.<br>Additional principles are introduced in Art. 20: 'Monitoring and management [...] based on the principles of<br>- independence, - multidisciplinarity, - pluralism and, - transparency as well as, - the principles set out in this Declaration.'<br>*Proclaims* the principles that follow [...]' (all recommendations of the declaration). |
| The Advisory Committee on Health Research (ACHR): Genomics and World Health 2002 | No reference to ethical principles but to 'ethical issues in genetic research' p. 147 | '[E]ven these familiar ethical issues require some specific consideration in the context of genomics and cannot be simply addressed by standard approaches in medical ethics for two reasons':<br>1. 'genetic information' is 'different' ... 'in degree and [..] in kind'.<br>2. 'the importance of the social context'; 'appropriate uses [...] depend critically on social, political, economic and cultural context' (p. 148)<br>- Ethical issues: 'Informed consent', - 'Confidentiality', - 'Gender issues', - 'Eugenics' |
| WHO. Proposed int. guidelines on ethical issues in medical genetics 1998 | Yes, p. 2 | • 'Respect for the autonomy of persons: respecting the self-determination of individuals and protecting those with diminished autonomy;'<br>• 'Beneficence: giving highest priority to the welfare of persons and maximizing benefits to their health [...] Beneficence also bears upon a goal of medicine to improve the health of populations with the voluntary cooperation of the populations involved.', - 'Non-maleficence', - 'Justice' |
| WHO Regional Office for Europe. Genetic databases. Assessing the benefits and the impact on | Yes, complemented by 'values' p. 7 | 'Fundamental guiding values:<br>• The pursuit of human well-being<br>• The quality of human dignity, including fundamental human rights and the principle of non-discrimination<br>• The principle of respect for persons, including the imperatives of beneficence and non-maleficence<br>• The principle of respect for individual autonomy<br>Various means exist by which these values are embodied in social and legal norms. Two important examples are those of respect for individual privacy, and the recognition of the individual interest in controlling certain intimate adjuncts to one's |

**Table 3.3**  Continued

| Guideline | Ethical principles | Principles mentioned |
|---|---|---|
| human and patient rights 2001 | | personality, such as the use and dissemination of personal information. These values, and the means to protect them, equally underpin this report. They inform the debate that is contained herein, and they govern the formulation of the recommendations that are offered' (p. 7). <br> Balancing of principles or values: <br> p. 3 'We have, then, a fundamental tension between the possibility of considerable public good on the one hand, and the potential for significant individual and familial harm on the other. The basic interests that lie in the balance are those between human dignity and human rights as against public health, scientific progress and commercial interests in a free market.' <br> p. 8: 'a common measure seen in these international instruments, as a counter-balance to individual rights, is the public interest in the advancement of scientific knowledge and the promotion of public health. It is frequently on this ground that (genetic) databases are justified by the state and commercial bodies. More broadly, it is an appeal that it is often made to override individual rights or to reduce the protection afforded to them. Accordingly, the role of the public interest requires close scrutiny in tandem with any examination of individual rights. No individual rights are absolute. Inevitably, therefore, a balance of legitimate interests is required.' <br> p. 8 'The value of databases derives from the collective nature of their data. Often, the prospect of direct individual benefit is minimal. Thus, the justification for a database is more likely to be grounded in communal value, and less on individual gain. And, while this is not to say that individual protection should be ignored, it leads to the question whether the individual can remain of paramount importance in this context. Although protections can and should be instituted for individuals who surrender personal data, the achievement of optimal advances in the name of the collective good may require a reconsideration of the respective claims so as to achieve an appropriate balance between individual and collective interests, including those of ethnic minorities, from a multi-cultural perspective.' <br> p. 13 'The principle of respect for autonomy and the doctrine of informed consent prescribe that consent should be obtained from sample sources before any research is undertaken. However, this is not an approach of universal application, and exceptions can be justified in rare circumstances.' |
| HUGO principled conduct 1995 | Yes <br> p. 1 | Recommendations are based 'on the following four principles: 1. Recognition that the human genome is part of the common heritage of humanity; 2. Adherence to the international norms of human rights; 3. Respect for the values, traditions, culture, and integrity of participants; and 4. Acceptance and upholding of human dignity and freedom.' |
| Council of Europe (COE). Recommendation Rec(2006)4 of the Committee of Ministers to | No direct reference to an ethics of principles. The document refers to human rights. Some principles are mentioned in | Preamble: <br> Primacy of the human being: 'the interests and welfare of the human being whose biological materials are used in research shall prevail over the sole interest of society or science.' <br> Justice: 'donations of biological materials made in a spirit of solidarity should not be monopolised by small groups of researchers'. <br> Article 1 - Object: 'protect' - the 'dignity' [of all human beings]; - the 'identity of all human beings', - 'without discrimination', - the 'right to private life', - 'other rights and fundamental freedoms' <br> Chapter II: |

**Table 3.3**  Continued

| Guideline | Ethical principles | Principles mentioned |
|---|---|---|
| member states on research on biological materials of human origin | a specific context: Preamble, Article 1 and Chapter II: General provisions | • Private life: 'risks for the persons concerned and, where appropriate, for their family, related to research activities, in particular the risks to private life, should be minimized […] Furthermore, those risks should not be disproportionate to the potential benefit of the research activities.'<br>• Non-discrimination: 'Appropriate measures should be taken, in the full range of research activities, to avoid discrimination against, or stigmatization of, a person, family or group.'<br>• Prohibition of financial gain: Biological materials should not, as such, give rise to financial gain.'<br>• Justification of identifiability: 1. Biological materials and associated data should be anonymised as far as appropriate to the research activities concerned. 2. Any use of biological materials and associated data in an identified, coded, or linked anonymised form should be justified by the researcher.'<br>• Independent review: 'Research should only be undertaken if the research project has been subject to an independent examination of its scientific merit, including assessment of the importance of the aim of the research, and verification of its ethical acceptability. National law may additionally require approval by a competent body.'<br>• 'Confidentiality and right to information: The principles of chapter VIII (confidentiality and right to information) of the Additional Protocol concerning biomedical research should be applied to any research project using biological materials and associated personal data.' |
| COE Steering Committee on Bioethics (CDBI) 2002. Draft Explanatory report | Same as above | 'This instrument builds on the principles embodied in the Convention on Human Rights and Biomedicine […] with a view to protecting human rights and dignity in relation to research on biological materials' (p. 2).<br>'The purpose […] is to set out and safeguard fundamental rights of individuals whose biological materials are used in biomedical research, while recognising the importance of freedom of research' (p. 3). 'Their [the donors'] integrity and private life must be guaranteed, while at the same time the continued benefits of research should be ensured'. |
| European Society of Human Genetics. Data storage and DNA banking 2002 | Yes, referred to without explanation, no special section on ethical foundations | • 'Ethical principles have been introduced […] quality assurance', no storage 'without a good reason', 'voluntary nature of gene donation', 'confidentiality of the identity of gene donors' (pp. 3–4, citing other laws and guidelines)<br>• The 'principle of quality assurance' (p. 6), – The 'principle of consent' (pp. 8, 9, 21)<br>• The 'principle that population consent, as well as individual consent, should be sought for genetic research' (p. 11, citing the Canadian Tri-Council)<br>• The 'principle of inalienable individual rights' (p. 14)<br>• The 'principle of autonomy' (p. 14)<br>• 'Ethical principles concerning the protection of individuals participating in research projects state that consent must be informed and confidentiality and private life must be protected' (p. 20).<br>'Consent, confidentiality and coding are the key principles for DNA banking' (p. 24). |

**Table 3.3**  Continued

| Guideline | Ethical principles | Principles mentioned |
|---|---|---|
| Commission de l'Éthique de la Science et de la Technologie. Avis. Les enjeux éthiques des banques d'information génétique. Québec 2003 | Based rather on values and interests, citation of the principles mentioned in other declarations (p. 36) | • The 'avis' cites all principles from the UNESCO declaration on human genetic data (see above), and other Canadian recommendations (RMGA, Tri-Council) stating that 'A tous ces principes et valeurs […] elle [la commission] attache une grande importance'.<br>• 'la Commission a ajouté le respect de la démocratie',[1] - 'principe de l'équité' (p. 53) values and interests are mentioned before principles (p. 66: 'sur quelles valeurs, sur quels principes, voire sur quelles préférences s'appuie cette opinion.' Subchapter titles: p.19: 'Une multitude d'intérêts à concilier', p. 35: 'la délicate question des valeurs' The principles are cited as 'enjeux':<br>- 'L'enjeu de la transparence' (p. 37), - 'L'enjeu de la légitimité des banques' (p. 39), - 'L'enjeu de l'autonomie' (p. 42) -<br>- 'L'enjeu de la confidentialité' (p. 50), - 'L'enjeu de l'équité' (p. 51), - 'L'enjeu de la propriété de l'information génétique' (p. 53), - 'L'enjeu de la solidarité: l'impact sur le système de santé' (p. 56) |
| Tri-Council policy statement. Ethical conduct for research involving humans. Canada 1998 | Yes. Part 'C. Guiding ethical principles' | • 'A moral imperative: respect for human dignity' (i.4) the 'cardinal principle of modern research ethics' (i.5) 'aspires to protecting the multiple and interdependent interests of the person - from bodily to psychosocial to cultural integrity. This principle forms the basis of the ethical obligations in research that are listed below.'<br>• 'Respect for free and informed consent', - 'Respect for vulnerable persons'<br>• 'Respect for privacy and confidentiality': […] In many cultures, privacy and confidentiality are considered fundamental to human dignity.'<br>• 'Respect for justice and inclusiveness: Justice connotes fairness and equity. Procedural justice requires that the ethics review process have [sic] fair methods […] distributive justice means that no segment of the population should be unfairly burdened with the harms of research.' Avoid the risk of burdening vulnerable individuals … 'distributive justice also imposes duties neither to neglect nor to discriminate against individuals and groups who may benefit from advances in research' (i.6).<br>'Balancing harms and benefits: […] require a favorable harms-benefit balance - that is, that the foreseeable harms should not outweigh anticipated benefits.'<br>• 'Minimizing harm' (non-maleficence), no 'unnecessary risks', 'scientifically and societally important aims'<br>• 'Maximizing benefit' (beneficence): 'produce benefits for subjects themselves […] In most research, the primary benefits produced are for society and for the advancement of knowledge.'<br>• 'A subject-centred perspective': 'collaboration' with subjects, subjects should 'not be treated simply as objects', information tailored to the individual, take into account that research participants might be influenced more by 'trust' and the 'hope for other goals' than by 'assessment of the pros and cons of participation in the research'. 'This places extra demands on the researcher for accuracy, candour, objectivity and sensitivity in informing potential subjects about proposed research' (i.7).<br>• 'Academic freedom and responsibilities': 'To secure the maximum benefits from research, society needs to ensure that researchers have certain freedoms': 'freedom of inquiry', 'freedom to challenge conventional thought', 'freedom from institutional censorship'. 'With freedom comes responsibility' and 'duties of honest and thoughtful inquiry, rigorous analysis', and 'accountability to society' (i.8). |

**Table 3.3** Continued

| Guideline | Ethical principles | Principles mentioned |
|---|---|---|
| | | The following explanations are given on how to deal with conflicting principles: 'Researchers and REBs must carefully weigh all the principles and circumstances involved to reach a reasoned and defensible conclusion' (i.5). 'If the application of principles yields conflicts, then such conflicts properly demand probing ethical reflection and difficult value choices [...] In their best uses, principles serve as short-hand reminders of more complex and context-specific moral reflection' (i.9). 'Putting principles into practice' (i.9) – effective application of principles means that they 'must operate neither in the abstract, nor in isolation from one another', not in 'formulaic ways', but, – 'applied in the context', – principles 'admit flexibility and exceptions'; – 'the onus for demonstrating a reasonable exception to a principle should fall on those claiming the exception', – decisions should be made by 'multidisciplinary ethics committees', based on 'a dynamic relation between ethical principles and procedures'. 'Principles are short-hand reminders of more complex and context-specific moral reflection.' |
| North American Regional Committee (NARC). Human Genome Diversity Project. Proposed model ethical protocol 1997 | Yes, I. p. 3 | 'Three principles have guided our consideration of the ethical issues raised by this Project: – informed consent, – respect for the participating population's culture, and – adherence to international standards of human rights.' 'These principles combine to help us ensure that the Project not only does no harm to the participating communities, but, where possible, brings it benefits [...] Different field situations will necessarily produce different answers in applying ethical principles and rules [...] The precise form of the interaction should and must vary with the circumstances, but any researchers who want to participate in this Project in North America must accept the principles and rules discussed below.' • Reasons to respect the principles (p. 26): – will 'enhance [...] confidence in science', – non respect for the rights of those who participate and non protection of their rights may lead to 'a disaster – not for humanity, but for science'. |
| Network of Applied Genetic Medicine (RMGA) Statement of principles: human genome research. Version 2000 | Yes, p. 3ss | Classical ethical principles: – 'respect for human dignity' (! not for autonomy), – 'beneficence', – 'non-maleficence', – 'justice' 'In addition to these principles which reflect the fundamental rights of all those participating in research involving humans, the RMGA seeks to promote certain community values inherent to genetic information, notably – 'Professional reciprocity', – 'Familial mutuality', – 'State solidarity', – 'Equity (fairness) with regard to the benefits of research', and – 'The universality of the human genome' Comprehensive principles proposed: The aim of these principles is 'to promote freedom of genomic research while respecting and protecting the different parties involved' (p. 4) • 'I. Informed participation. Principle: Respect for the self-determination of the participants is primordial.' • 'II. Participation without prejudice. Principle: The participant has the right to choose to participate and to be informed or not of the results. The participant is free to withdraw from the research project at any time. These decisions should not limit or restrict the quality of care and services he is entitled to.' |

**Table 3.3**   Continued

| Guideline | Ethical principles | Principles mentioned |
|---|---|---|
| | | • 'III. Confidentiality. Principle: Respect for privacy is fundamental. Given the personal and familial nature of genetic information, the researcher should put in place prospective measures designed to safeguard the greatest degree of confidentiality.'<br>• 'IV. Professionalism. Principle: Participants in research have the right to expect professional behaviour, competence and quality on the part of the researchers and the members of the researcher team. Professionalism is based on the *principle of reciprocity* that allows the free exchange and shared confidence between participant and researcher' (italics: B.E.).<br>• 'V. Contribution to the scientific development of Quebec. Principle: The universal nature of the Quebec health care system allows researchers to collect genetic material and information. By virtue of the principle of solidarity, the population may rightfully expect that this research will serve to improve knowledge in the fields of biology and health in Quebec.'<br>• 'VI. Commercialization. Principle: The researchers, institutions and sponsors can aspire to the acquisition of intellectual property rights over the inventions derived from genetic material. All forms of payment to participants in exchange for participation are unacceptable. For the sake of equity (fairness), however, in return for its participation, the population of Quebec should profit from the resulting benefits of the scientific breakthroughs they contributed to.'<br>• 'VII. Contribution to international scientific development. Principle: Genomic knowledge should serve humanity as a whole and is essential to the understanding of the determinants of health.' |
| MRC. Human tissue and biolo-gical samples for use in re-search. 2001 | Yes, section 1.2 | 'general ethical principles' for research involving 'human participants, material' and 'personal information' (1.2):<br>- 'benefits' must outweigh any associated risks, the 'interests of research participants should always take precedence over those of science and society', 'in most circumstances [...] full and informed consent', - 'confidentiality', - 'respect for the human body', - 'respect for the known wishes of the donor of the material', 'Researcher must always ensure that their use of human material will not compromise the interests of the donor' |
| Human Genetics Commission (HGC). Inside information. Balancing interests in the use of personal genetic data UK 2002 | Yes, chapter 2 | 'certain basic principles that underpin our conclusions'; 'The source of the principles':<br>• 'values from different sources': 'human rights', 'goals and methods of medicine and biology [...] moral values of particular religious and philosophical traditions which have long been accepted in British society', 'defended [...] by moral conviction and by the common law'<br>• 'European Convention on Human Rights and Fundamental Freedoms'<br>• 'domestic legislation such as the Human Rights Act 1998'<br>• Declaration of Helsinki and other guidelines (HUGO, Nuffield Council, General Medical Council, NBAC, UNESCO, Council of Europe). These guidelines 'provide a clear core of values which, although not universally agreed, represent a high degree of contemporary consensus.'<br>• 'Overarching principles' ... 'reached after an extensive effort to ascertain moral views in this country'<br>• The principles are for the most part 'concerned with safeguarding the individual'.<br>• 'We feel that it is important [...] to see the individual as a member of society with a shared interest in medical progress and the conquest of illness.' |

**Table 3.3** Continued

| Guideline | Ethical principles | Principles mentioned |
|---|---|---|
| Nuffield Council on Bioethics. Human tissue. Ethical and legal issues. 1995 | Yes, 'elaborate relevant basic ethical principles' | 1. 'Genetic solidarity and altruism': 'We share the same basic human genome [...] sharing of our genetic condition not only gives rise to opportunities to help others but it also highlights our common interests in the fruits of medically-based research.' 2. 'Respect for persons': 'affirms the equal value, dignity and moral rights of each individual. Each individual is entitled to lead a life in which genetic characteristics will not be the basis of unjust discrimination or unfair or inhuman treatment.' 3. 'Privacy': 'in the absence of justification based on overwhelming moral considerations, a person should generally not be obliged to disclose information about his or her genetic characteristics.' 4. 'Consent': 'private genetic information about a person should generally not be obtained, held or communicated without the person's free and informed consent.' 5. 'Confidentiality': 'private personal genetic information [...] should not be communicated to others without consent except for the weightiest of reasons.' 6. 'Non-discrimination': 'No person shall be unfairly discriminated against on the basis of his or her genetic characteristics.' A 'central task' of the report has been 'to identify the ethical principles that should govern the uses of human tissue' (p. 39) and 'the treatment of the human body with respect and dignity' (p. ii). 'elaborate relevant basic ethical principles, which are sufficiently general to apply not only to existing uses but also to future developments' (p. 39), – a 'practical ethical stance' based on principles. 'Ethical principles: - respect for human lives and the human body' (p. 39), - 'avoidance and limitation of injury' is 'a central element of the undefined, yet widely endorsed, demand for respect of the human body and for respect of human dignity' (p. 40), – 'the only circumstances in which inflicting injury is acceptable is when it is done to avoid greater injury' (p. 40), – 'consent [...] is not the primary consideration. In particular, consent cannot justify injury.' |
| The Royal College of Pathologists. Transitional guidelines to facilitate changes in procedures for handling 'surplus' and archival material from human biological samples. 2001 | No, but 'value of individual autonomy' | • '[S]ome practices in pathology departments were out of date [...] Urgent changes have been made [...], continuing the trend we have seen throughout medicine to put greater emphasis on the value of individual autonomy' (Introduction 2). • 'requirement for consent from the tissue donor' (Introduction 3); 'as far as possible maximize the rights of patients to control how their tissue samples are used but [...] permit the NHS [...] and its biomedical research projects to continue to function' (Introduction 11). • '[T]he Kantian "categorical imperative"' (Introduction 9): 'if everyone refused to allow their tissues to be used for teaching, quality assurance and research, the health services they need and have benefited from, and which produced the samples, could not exist. The act cannot be universalised, which indicates that to act this way is immoral.' 'Recent events demonstrate that in the UK, society has chosen not to follow these arguments. Nevertheless, their existence serves to emphasise the point that the wishes of a single individual cannot invariably be assumed to be paramount: such wishes cannot take precedence over the rights of large groups of individuals without reason. A balance needs to be found which invites and respects reasonable individual objections but which allows work for the common good to continue' (Introduction 10). |

**Table 3.3** Continued

| Guideline | Ethical principles | Principles mentioned |
|---|---|---|
| | | • 'Generic consent [...] *must* be accepted' (15) |
| | | • 'Seeking consent, recording objections' (33) |
| | | • 'The need for oversight' (21, 45) |
| National Bioethics Advisory Commission (NBAC). Research involving human biological materials: ethical issues and policy guidance. USA 1999 | Yes. Chapter 4 'Ethical perspectives on the research use of human biological materials' | The guidelines refer to the three principles of the Belmont Report (p. 41):<br>• 'beneficence'<br>• 'respect for persons'<br>• 'justice'<br>'excessively individualistic interpretations of the ethical principles and rules governing research involving human subjects' could 'fail to address the needs of relevant groups and communities' (p. 42).<br>'it is not always necessary to pit the interests of future beneficiaries of current research against the interests of those who have provided the human biological materials' (p.42).<br>Ad beneficence:<br>• 'Promoting benefits' (greater access to samples for purposes of conducting clinically beneficial research) and (p. 42)<br>• 'minimizing harms and wrongs' ('potential harms from breaches of privacy and confidentiality', 'group-related harms'): 'protection' for subjects<br>Ad respect for persons (p. 47):<br>• 'informed consent' (e.g. about future uses): 'control' of subjects over the use of the samples<br>• expression about 'preferences': 'objectionable, unacceptable, or questionable research' (p. 49; e.g. from a religious or cultural standpoint)<br>• 'commodification of the body and its parts: issues of justice and respect for persons' (p. 50)<br>In case of conflicting principles: a 'defensible balance' is needed. The balancing will depend 'on the identifiability of the sample sources and on the probability and magnitude of various wrongs and harms that may occur' (p. 51).<br>'Rather than assuming that a necessary conflict exists between promoting important research and protecting biological sample sources against various wrongs and harms, NBAC holds that policymakers should seek [...] to develop policies that avoid tradeoffs, while [...] setting procedures to deal with situations that sometimes necessitate such tradeoffs, especially those involving less weighty interests.'<br>The guidelines proposed by the NBAC are intended to 'both promote important research and provide sufficient safeguards for the rights and welfare of sources of biological materials and their families, groups and communities' (p. 52). |
| ACMG Statement on storage and use 1995 | The term 'principle' does not appear | 'These guidelines do not contain a part on ethical foundations or principles. In the introduction, the importance of 'defining the scope of informed consent' is mentioned: 'The objective of informed consent is to preserve the individual's right to decide whether to have a genetic test. This right includes the right of refusal should the individual decide the potential harm (stigmatization or undesired choices) outweighs the potential benefits.' |

**Table 3.3** Continued

| Guideline | Ethical principles | Principles mentioned |
|---|---|---|
| ASHG DNA Banking and DNA Analysis 1988 | The term 'principle' does not appear | • 'Users should rely on their own professional judgment.'<br>• 'help ensure that patients and families affected by genetic disease obtain and understand the information they need and desire'<br>• 'health professionals involved in counseling, banking, or analysis must recognize their individual responsibilities.' |
| ASHG. Statement on Informed Consent for Genetic Research 1996 | The term 'principle' does not appear | • The ASHG 'is committed to protecting the rights and welfare of those who participate in genetic research as subjects'<br>• Consideration is required 'of new ways to achieve the goals of expanding knowledge, and, at the same time, respecting the interests of those who volunteer themselves to be subjects'<br>• The ASHG 'affirms traditional research practices in human genetics and recommends new ones'<br>• 'informed consent' and 'confidentiality' |
| College of American Pathologists. Recommended policies for uses of human tissue in research, education, and quality control. 1999 | Yes, p. 298 | 'The 3 ethical principles of the Belmont Report […] - respect for persons, - beneficence, - justice are aspects of the ethical foundation of practice for pathologists and guide decisions involving how tissues will be used.'<br>The following other details of an ethical framework are mentioned:<br>• The law recognizes 'the autonomy of patients' decisions over their bodies as well as related medical information' (p. 298).<br>• The aim is to discuss 'balancing the needs of customary medical practice and research using human tissues with the legitimate concerns about protecting the rights and privacy of human subjects' (p. 296).<br>• 'the doctrine of informed consent' (p. 298)<br>• 'confidentiality and privacy rights' (p.297) |
| NCH-DOE. Guidance on Human Subject Issues in Large-Scale DNA Sequencing. 1996 | No direct reference to principles | 'The guidance provided in this statement is intended to afford maximum protection to DNA donors and is based on the belief that protection can best be achieved by a combination of approaches.'<br>The document addresses, among others, the following issues (subtitles):<br>• 'Benefits and risks of genomic DNA sequencing'<br>• 'Privacy & confidentiality'<br>• 'Informed consent'<br>• 'IRB [institutional review board] approval' |
| Comité Consultatif National d'Ethique. Avis 77. Problèmes | Yes, but rare. The document is centred on the *rights* of the tissue donors. | Principles:<br>'Quelques principes d'organization' (p. 34)<br>• 'il faut respecter les principes que sont l'indisponibilité du corps humain et le caractère non commercial' (p. 34).<br>• 'L'intérêt scientifique […] ne doit pas occulter l'extrême sensibilité d'un tel matériel au regard de principes éthiques importants, respect de la vie privée, autonomie et dignité des personnes' (p. 17). |

**Table 3.3    Continued**

| Guideline | Ethical principles | Principles mentioned |
|---|---|---|
| éthiques posés par les collections de matériel biologique et les données d'information associées: 'biobanques', 'biothèques' 2003 | | • 'Les règles régissant la réunion et l'utilisation de telles collections doivent en effet respecter deux principes, parfois contradictoires. L'un est celui de leur usage optimal pour l'intérêt collectif, notamment à des fins scientifiques, médicales et de santé publique ; l'autre est d'éviter pour autant de parvenir à une assimilation de telles collections à un bien public qui serait en quelque sorte socialisé, nationalisé, ou, à l'inverse, totalement marchandisé. En d'autres termes, les donneurs doivent être informés, pour l'essentiel, du type d'études qui sera mené grâce à leurs dons, et du cadre dans lequel ces études pourront s'effectuer' (p. 19).<br>• 'Le principe de solidarité vient en ce sens justifier cette dérogation aux règles destinées à protéger l'individu, mais il s'agit d'une vraie solidarité qui regroupe des comportements volontaires' (p. 19).<br>• 'les obligations' sont 'identiques que l'opérateur soit public, privé ou agisse en partenariat' (p. 29).<br>• la collection de tissu et de données constitue 'un bien collectif [….] qui doit être gérée en commun dans un intérêt de solidarité' (p. 29).<br>• 'les pouvoirs publics' devront dessiner 'une autorité indépendante' pour la supervision des banques et 'la mission de mettre au point concrètement les réponses nécessaires à leurs problèmes de fonctionnement' (p. 30).<br>• 'Les droits des personnes dont proviennent les éléments biologiques' (p. 4).<br>• Le 'consentement des personnes' (p. 23).<br>• Le 'droit de retour' (p. 24).<br>• 'l'exigence de la confidentialité' (p. 26).<br>• 'Consultation préalable des populations' (p. 27).<br>• 'Consentement, droits des personnes et usage commun'.<br>'Les droits dont pourrait se prévaloir la collectivité nationale sur les éléments et informations collectés' (p. 28). |

*Note:* 1 See Commission de l'Éthique de la Science et de la Technologie (2003, 36): 'À tous ces principes et valeurs auxquels elle attache une grande importance, la Commission a ajouté le respect de la démocratie qu'elle considère comme une valeur fondamentale au sein de la société québécoise, la seule en mesure de refléter l'évolution des valeurs dans la population, et qu'elle inscrit à la base de sa réflexion sur les enjeux éthiques des banques d'information génétique.'

**Table 3.4   Respect for persons**

| Respect for persons | Principle of autonomy | Individuals should be treated as autonomous | Protection for the incapacitated | Respect privacy/ confidentiality |
|---|---|---|---|---|
| Belmont | Belmont ('autonomy') | Belmont | Belmont | Terms not in the report |
| Helsinki ('respect for all human subjects') | Does not contain the word 'autonomy' | Helsinki | Helsinki | Helsinki |
| CIOMS 2002 | CIOMS 2002 ('respect for autonomy') | CIOMS 2002 | CIOMS 2002 | CIOMS 2002 |
| CHRB | Does not contain the word 'autonomy' | Does not contain the word 'autonomous' | CHRB ('protection of persons not able to consent to research') | CHRB |
| Term not used in the UNESCO Declaration 2003 | Term not used | Term not used | UNESCO ('adult not able to consent') | UNESCO |
| WHO 1998 (p. 3) | WHO 1998 ('principle of respect for autonomy') | WHO 1998 | WHO 1998 (p. 2) | WHO 1998 |
| WHOROE (p. 7) | WHOROE (p. 7) | WHOROE | WHOROE (p. 12 referring to the CIOMS and Helsinki guidelines) | WHOROE (pp. 16ff) |
| Not HUGO 1995 (only: 'respect for the integrity of participants') | Term not used | Term not used | – | HUGO 1995 |
| Not COE 2006 (only: 'respect for private life') | Term not used | COE 2006 | COE 2006 ('persons not able to consent') | COE 2006 |
| ESHG (citing the HGC) | ESHG | Not explicitly addressed | Not explicitly addressed | ESHG |
| CEST (p. 36: 'respect de la personne') | CEST | CEST | CEST ('inaptes', 'autonomie partielle') | CEST |
| TC (2.8) | TC (2.12) | TC (2.12) | TC ('respect for vulnerable persons') | TC ('in many cultures…') |
| Term not used in the RMGA text | Term not used in the RMGA text | Not explicitly addressed | Not explicitly addressed | RMGA |
| NARC does not mention explicitly 'respect for persons' but 'for the population' | NARC ('autonomy of the population'/'community') | Not explicitly addressed | Not explicitly addressed | NARC |
| Term not used by the MRC | Term not used by the MRC | Term not used by the MRC | Term not used by the MRC | MRC 2001 |
| HGC | HGC | HGC | HGC | HGC |
| Term not used | NC | NC | NC | NC |

**Table 3.4**  Continued

| Respect for persons | Principle of autonomy | Individuals should be treated as autonomous | Protection for the incapacitated | Respect privacy/confidentiality |
|---|---|---|---|---|
| Term not used in the RCP guidelines | RCP ('value of individual autonomy') | RCP | RCP | RCP |
| NBAC | NBAC | NBAC | NBAC | NBAC |
| – | – | – | – | ACMG |
| – | – | – | – | ASHG 1996 |
| CAP | CAP ('respect for personal autonomy', 'autonomy of patient's decision over their body') | Not explicitly addressed (indirectly in 'respect for personal autonomy') | Not explicitly addressed | CAP |
| – | CCNE (p. 28: autonomy of persons is described as the principle for the common use of informed consent)[1] | – | – | CCNE |

*Note:* 1 However, p. 37: 'le droit français ne part pas d'un principe d'autonomie de la personne ou de propriété individuelle de ces éléments ou données d'information').

## Table 3.5 Human rights

| Classical Research Ethics | | | |
|---|---|---|---|
| **Human rights** | **Fundamental freedoms** | **Respect for the human body** | **Respect for the known wishes and interests of the donor*** |
| Belmont ('the subject's rights') | Belmont ('freedom to act on his judgments') | – | – |
| Helsinki ('protect [...] rights') | – | – | – |
| CIOMS 2002 (human rights are mentioned in the introduction) | CIOMS 2002 ('freedom of choice', 'freedom to consent') | – | CIOMS 2002 ('request the permission of subjects') |
| CHRB | CHRB | Term not used but financial gains prohibited (CHRB) | – |
| **Guidelines Relevant for Research Involving Biobanks** | | | |
| **Respect human dignity** | **Respect for integrity** | **Protect the identity of all human beings** | **Dignity of the human body** |
| UNESCO | UNESCO | – | UNESCO (9c) |
| Term not directly used in the WHO text | WHO 1998 ('freedom of choice') | – | – |
| WHOROE p. 7 | – | WHOROE (p. 8: 'The intimate and unique relationship that individuals have with body samples or information derived from them deserves full recognition and proper respect.') | WHOROE (p. 8: 'Individuals are entitled to control over the use of their samples and information, in a manner akin to a property right. This right may, however, be subject to waiver or certain limits, such as when anonymization occurs (and so the relationship is lost), or when certain uses may cause harm to others.') |
| HUGO 1995 | HUGO 1995 ('human [...] freedom') | – | HUGO ('respect for the choices') |
| COE 2006 ('other rights', CDBI Explanatory Report: 'human rights', 'fundamental rights of individuals') | COE 2006 | Term not used but financial gains prohibited (COE) | CDBI Expl. Rep. (p. 3: [of concern is] 'the autonomy one has over one's own body and over the biological material once it has been removed from the body') |
| ESHG ('principle of inalienable individual rights') | ESHG: citing other guidelines | ESHG: citing laws | ESHG (p. 25) |
| CEST (refers to the Universal Declaration of Human Rights) | CEST (p. 51: 'libertés fondamentales') | Term not used but financial gains prohibited (CEST) | CEST (p. 47) |
| TC (only referring to the legal context) | TC (referring to the law) | TC (10.1) | TC partially (10.3)** |

**Table 3.5    Continued**

| Respect human dignity | Respect for integrity | Protect the identity of all human beings | Dignity of the human body |
|---|---|---|---|
| RMGA cites the Declaration of Human Rights | RMGA ('freedom of participation') | – | RMGA |
| NARC | – | – | NARC |
| The MRC text does not contain the term 'rights' | – | MRC 2001 (in addition: no financial gains) | MRC 2001 |
| HGC | HGC | – | HGC |
| NC (cites human rights as non-conclusive approach) | – | NC | NC |
| RCP ('rights of large groups', 'of patients') | – | – | RCP |
| NBAC ('rights of subjects') | – | NBAC ('As such, human tissues would warrant some measure of respect, which is the basis often expressed for restricting sales of human tissues') | NBAC |
| ACMG (the 'individual's right to decide') | – | – | ACMG (the 'right to decide' and 'to refusal') |
| ASHG 1996 ('protect rights') | – | – | – |
| CAP | CAP ('freedom from uninvited and unwarranted intrusions'; 'freedom to live as one desires') | – | CAP |
| CCNE (p. 4: 'droits des personnes') | CCNE (p. 29: les 'libertés de la personne') | CCNE indirectly (p. 2: 'l'indisponibilité et non-commercialisation du corps humain et de ses éléments') | CCNE |

\* In contrast WHO 1998 p. 13: 'Control of DNA may be familial, not only individual.'
\*\* Tri-Council policy statement (10.3): 'pay special attention to concerns that some individuals may have about certain types or applications of research.'

**Table 3.6    Human dignity**

| Respect human dignity* | Respect for integrity | Protect the identity of all human beings | Dignity of the human body* |
|---|---|---|---|
| CIOMS 2002 (twice in commentaries to guidelines 2 and 4) | CIOMS 2002 (only when citing the Code of Nuremberg) | CIOMS 2002 ('protect' subjects' 'identity') | – |
| Helsinki ('duty to protect […] dignity […] of research subjects') | Helsinki ('protect […] integrity') | – | – |
| CHRB | CHRB | CHRB | – |
| UNESCO | – | – | – |

**Table 3.6　　Continued**

| Respect human dignity* | Respect for integrity | Protect the identity of all human beings | Dignity of the human body* |
|---|---|---|---|
| WHO 1998 (p. 1: 'human life and dignity') | WHO 1998 ('preservation of family integrity') | – | – |
| WHOROE (p. 7) | – | – | – |
| HUGO 1995 | HUGO 1995 ('integrity of populations, families and individuals', 'integrity of participants') | – | – |
| COE 2006 | COE 2006 | COE 2006 ('protect the identity of all human beings') | – |
| ESHG | ESHG (p. 22) | – | – |
| CEST | CEST (p. 32: 'l'intégrité des sujets de recherche') | CEST ('Préserver l'idéntité de la personne participante') | – |
| TC ('the cardinal principle') | TC | TC | TC (only: 'human tissue itself deserves some degree of respect, for reasons of the dignity of the person') |
| RMGA | – | RMGA ('protect the identity of the participants') | – |
| The term dignity is not used in the NARC guidelines | – | NARC (identity of the community) | – |
| HGC | – | HGC | – |
| NC 1995 | NC ('unconsented interference with bodily integrity is unlawful') | – | NC 1995 |
| NBAC (p. 43: 'concerns about the dignity with which human beings are treated'; p. 47: 'Concerns about privacy often are closely related to concerns about dignity, because in most, if not all, cultures, some modes of exposing the body in some contexts are considered undignified and demeaning, and some intimate information is considered embarrassing and even shameful'). | NBAC ('integrity of the body') | – | NBAC ('Concerns about privacy often are closely related to concerns about dignity, because in most, if not all, cultures, some modes of exposing the body in some contexts are considered undignified.') |

* The Belmont Report, the MCR report, the RCP, the ACMG, the CAP statement and the NCH guidelines do not contain the term 'dignity'. The WHO guidelines (1998) ask for 'respect for human diversity' (p. 4). The HGC report (2002) mentions the idea of 'safeguarding the individual'.

**Table 3.7    Beneficence/non-maleficence (1)[1]**

| Beneficence | Do not harm/non-maleficence | Maximize benefits and minimize harms | Promote health/welfare/protection | Well-being/interests/welfare of individuals outweighs interests of science and society[2] |
|---|---|---|---|---|
| Belmont | Belmont | Belmont | – | – |
| ** 'communities' should 'benefit' | – | – | Helsinki ('duty to protect health') | Helsinki ('well-being') |
| CIOMS 2002 | | CIOMS 2002 | – | CIOMS 2002 (with reference to Helsinki) |
| ** Term 'beneficence' not used | – | – | – | CHRB ('interests and welfare') |
| ** Term 'beneficence' not used | – | – | UNESCO (welfare of the individual) | UNESCO |
| WHO 1998 | WHO 1998 | – | WHO 1998 (p. 2: 'welfare of individuals and families', 'improve the health of populations') | This balancing does not appear in the WHO guidelines |
| WHOROE (p. 7) | WHOROE (p.7) | WHOROE | WHOROE (p. 7: 'pursuit of human well-being') | This balancing does not appear |
| ** Term 'beneficence' not used | COE 2006 ('avoid discrimination [...]') | – | – | COE 2006 ('interest and welfare') |
| ** ESHG term 'beneficence' not used | – | – | ESHG (p. 13: 'future benefits of all participants') | ESHG description of the Icelandic Act# |
| CEST p. 36 | CEST p. 36 | – | CEST (p. 49: 'bénéfices [...] risques individuels', p. 52: 'bénéfices collectifs'/'de la population') | CEST: cites the sentence of the Declaration of Helsinki |
| TC | TC | TC | TC ('intended to produce benefits for subjects themselves, for other individuals or society as a whole, or for the advancement of knowledge') | The TC cites the Declaration of Helsinki without specific reference to this point |
| RMGA | RMGA | – | RMGA ('Humanity has the right to benefit from scientific progress', 'allowing the Quebec population to profit from the benefits') | A similar balancing is not found |
| RCP | RCP | – | RCP ('for the benefit of other patients and society as a whole', 'produce some benefit for humanity') | A similar balancing is not found |
| ** Term 'beneficence' not used | – | – | MRC ('benefits for public health and health care') | MRC 2001 ('interests') |

**Table 3.7    Continued**

| Beneficence | Do not harm/non-maleficence | Maximize benefits and minimize harms | Promote health/welfare/protection | Well-being/interests/welfare of individuals outweighs interests of science and society[2] |
|---|---|---|---|---|
| ** Term 'beneficence' not used | NC 1995 ('avoidance and limitation of injury') | – | – | A similar balancing is not found |
| ** Term 'beneficence' not used | HGC ('avert substantial harm to others') | – | HGC (p. 39: 'Concern for the welfare of others') | HGC ('individual persons have the highest moral importance or value') |
| NBAC | NBAC | NBAC | NBAC ('societal and individual benefits') | A similar balancing is not found |
| ** Term 'beneficence' not used | – | – | ASHG 1996 ('protect welfare', 'interests') | A similar balancing is not found |
| NARC ('researchers must carefully consider the immediate benefits they plan to provide to the sampled population, including particularly medical benefits') | NARC ('These principles combine to help us ensure that the Project not only does no harm to the participating communities, but, where possible, brings it benefits.')[3] | – | – | A similar balancing is not found |
| CAP | – | – | CAP ('health benefit that will accrue to the population') | A similar balancing is not found |
| ** Term 'beneficence' not used | – | – | NCH ('maximum protection to DNA donors') | A similar balancing is not found |
| ** Term 'bienfaisance' not used | – | – | CCNE (p. 27: 'bien-être de la population concernée et de l'humanité', p. 35: 'bien collectif') | The CCNE contains an opposite statement.[4] |

** The Declaration of Helsinki, the UNESCO declaration (2003), the CHRB, the COE guidelines, the ESHG, MRC, NC, HGC, ASHG, NHC and CCNE do not contain the term 'beneficence', but only 'benefit' (e.g. CHRB: 'benefit of present and future generations').

*Notes*: 1 Tables 3.7 and 3.8 are not exhaustive: only the most important aspects of beneficence and non maleficence are mentioned.
2 Not contained in HUGO, NARC, but contained in the Icelandic Act (see # in the same column of the table) on Biobanks 2000 (which is described by the ESHG).
3 The principles referred to by the NARC guidelines are 'informed consent, respect for the participating population's culture, and adherence to international standards of human rights'.
4 CCNE p. 30: 'Il n'est pas impossible que ces réflexions conduisent la société française à accepter l'idée que le contenu des banques est une forme de *patrimoine scientifique à mettre en commun* si l'on veut progresser; cette conception, *mieux qu'un retour sur les droits de l'individu*, devrait permettre de trouver les bonnes solutions […]' (italics B.E.).

**Table 3.8    Beneficence/non-maleficence (2)**[1]

| Classical Health Research Guidelines | |
|---|---|
| **Benefit should outweigh harms** | **Benefit of future generations** |
| Belmont (implicitly) | – |
| CIOMS | – |
| Helsinki ('objective outweighs the inherent risks') | – |
| CHRB | CHRB (benefit) |
| **Guidelines Relevant For Biobanks** | |
| Concept not explicitly mentioned in the UNESCO declaration on human genetic data | – |
| COE 2006 (no risks 'disproportionate to the potential benefit') | – |
| CEST (only implicitly) | CEST (p. 46, intérêts) |
| ESHG (p. 8: 'ensure an acceptable balance between risks and benefits') | – |
| NARC ('if the potential benefits are sufficiently great') | – |
| NBAC | NBAC (p. 50, benefit) |
| TC ('favorable harm-benefit balance') | TC (benefit) |
| ACMG ('The following factors, among others, should be considered in deciding whether it is appropriate to use previously collected samples without contacting the individual: are or will the samples be made anonymous?; the degree to which the burden of contacting individuals may make it impracticable to conduct research; existence and content of prior consent; and risks and benefits.') | – |
| MRC 2001 ('Research should only go ahead if the potential benefits outweigh any potential risks to the donors of the samples.') | – |
| Concept not explicitly mentioned in the HGC report | HGC (help) |
| CAP ('potential risks should be balanced by the health benefit that will accrue to the population by the research') | – |
| Concept not explicitly mentioned in the CCNE avis | Rapport CCNE: 'solidarity' with future generations (benefit not particularly mentioned) |

*Note*: 1 Another form of benefit in the form of 'security' of the person is mentioned in the UNESCO declaration on human genetic data and in the CCNE avis.

**Table 3.9    Justice**

| Classical Health Research Ethics Guidelines | | | | |
|---|---|---|---|---|
| **Justice** | **Participating population should benefit** | **Equal distribution of benefits and burdens** | **All humanity may enjoy the benefits** | **Equality/fairness/equity** |
| Belmont | Belmont | Belmont | – | Belmont ('justice in the sense of "fairness" or "what is deserved"') |
| The word justice does not appear in the Declaration of Helsinki | Helsinki | Helsinki (implicit) | – | – |
| CIOMS 2002 | CIOMS 2002 | CIOMS 2002 | – | CIOMS 2002 ('fair share' of burden/benefit, 'equity requires'...) |
| | | – | CHRB | – |
| **Guidelines Relevant for Research Involving Biobanks** | | | | |
| UNESCO | UNESCO | – | – | UNESCO ('equality', 'fair access' to data) |
| WHO 1998 (p. 3: 'distributive justice on the basis of need') | – | WHO 1998 (p. 2) | – | WHO 1998 (fairness, equity) |
| Term not used in the WHOROE guidelines | WHOROE (p. 13: 'Research must be shown to hold the reasonable prospect of benefiting the class of persons to which the particular subject belongs, either in the immediate or the foreseeable future.') | – | – | WHOROE (p. 19: 'equitable return as a form of benefit sharing') |
| COE 2006: term not used | – | – | – | COE 2006 ('avoid discrimination') |
| | – | – | – | ESHG (citing 'unfair' discrimination) |
| CEST (p. 36) | – | – | CEST (p. 53: 'partage des retombées de la recherche avec la collectivité') | CEST (p. 53: 'équité') |
| TC (i.6) | – | TC (5.1: 'no segment of the population unfair burdened', 'fair distribution of benefits and burdens') | – | TC (i.6: 'fairness and equity') |

**Table 3.9    Continued**

| Justice | Participating population should benefit | Equal distribution of benefits and burdens | All humanity may enjoy the benefits | Equality/fairness/equity |
|---|---|---|---|---|
| RMGA | RMGA ('Participants have the right to expect to benefit from research') | Not explicitly addressed – | RMGA ('humanity has the right to benefit') | RMGA ('equity', 'fairness' with regard to the benefits) |
| NARC (Justice means that researchers should 'help the communities that help them') to participating communities')[1] | NARC ('researchers should and will want to provide some tangible benefits | | | NARC ('fairness') |
| HGC ('unjust discrimination') | HGC ('In return for altruistic public involvement in such research, there should be some benefit for the participants, or, in the widest sense, the community from which they are drawn.') | – | – | HGC ('unfair discrimination', no 'unfair treatment', 'use of genetic information in a fair [...] way') |
| – | – | – | – | NC ('provide fair and adequate compensation') |
| RCP | – | – | RCP ('produce some benefit for humanity') | – |
| NBAC | – | NBAC ('Justice requires the fair and equitable distribution of benefits and burdens in research.') | – | NBAC ('fair', 'equitable') |
| CAP | – | – | – | – |
| – | – | CCNE (p. 27: 'repartir risques et avantages') | CCNE (the aim is the 'bien-être de l'humanité') | – |

*Notes:* The MRC report does not contain the terms 'justice', 'fairness', 'equity' or 'equality'.

1 NARC: 'The provision of benefits to the participating community in connection with collection of samples is an important part of any ethical research design, but it raises complex issues. For example, at the extreme, providing benefits in return for participation can vitiate the community's informed consent, by "bribing" it into agreement. The line between an appropriate return for the community's participation and inappropriate bribery cannot be drawn in the abstract and will necessarily vary with each population and each researcher.'

**Table 3.10    Principles related to 'community values'**

| Responsibilities/responsibility | Solidarity | Other 'community values' or duties to the community | Human genome is part of the common heritage of humanity | Altruism |
|---|---|---|---|---|
| Belmont (of researchers) | – | – | – | – |
| Helsinki[1] (of researcher) | – | – | – | – |
| CIOMS (of researchers) | – | – | – | – |
| CHRB (of members of society) | – | – | – | – |
| WHO 1998 ('moral duty to disclose a genetic status') | – | WHO 1998 ('Control of DNA may be familial, not only individual') | – | – |
| UNESCO (of members of society) | UNESCO | – | (Indirectly by referring to the UNESCO declaration on the human genome) | – |
| WHOROE (p. 8) | – | WHOROE (p. 9: 'Thus duties might be owed to (i) the community, (ii) certain institutions acting in the public interest, or (iii) one's own family. The strength of the imperative grows as we move closer to the family unit.') | WHOROE (p. 3: 'Thus, those who share a common genetic heritage also share a common interest in how their genetic information is used.') | – |
| – | HUGO 2000 (Statement on benefit sharing) | – | HUGO 1995 | – |
| – | CDBI (expl. rep.: 'the motivation for allowing the use of one's biological materials and personal data in biomedical research may be out of solidarity.') | – | – | – |
| ESHG (custodian of the biobank) | ESHG (only citing the HGC) | – | ESHG (only citing HUGO) | ESHG (only citing the HGC) |
| CEST (p. 63: 'des commissions d'éthique, du gouvernement') | CEST | CEST (p. 52: 'réciprocité') | – | CEST (p. 52: don est 'altruiste', 'générosité') |
| WHOROE (p. 9) | – | – | – | – |

**Table 3.10  Continued**

| Responsibilities/responsibility | Solidarity | Other 'community values' or duties to the community | Human genome is part of the common heritage of humanity | Altruism |
|---|---|---|---|---|
| TC (researchers) | TC (1.5: 'solidarity' towards 'vulnerable persons') | — | — | TC (10.1: 'use of tissue for research depends on an individual's altruism')[2] |
| — | RMGA ('Principle of solidarity', 'State solidarity') | RMGA ('professionnal reciprocity, familial mutuality') | (RMGA 'universality of the human genome') | — |
| NARC (researchers) | — | — | — | — |
| MRC (of the custodian of the samples) | — | — | — | — |
| — | HGC ('genetic solidarity') | HGC ('duties can include doing things to help') | — | HGC, (p. 9: 'benefits of altruistic conduct') |
| — | — | — | — | NC ('sustain the altruism of donors') |
| RCP ('patients have a responsibility to facilitate the smooth running and development of the system') | — | — | — | — |
| NBAC (researchers, repositories, Institutional Review Boards) | — | — | — | — |
| ASHG 1988 (health professionals) | — | — | — | — |
| CAP (physician, professionals) | — | — | — | — |
| CCNE (p. 31: researchers, 'curateur') | CCNE (pp. 35, 30: 'solidarité entre individus et entre générations successives qu'il faut respecter') | CCNE (p. 30: 'le contenu des banques est une forme de patrimoine scientifique à mettre en commun.') | CCNE (p. 30: 'patrimoine commun, sinon de l'humanité, au moins entre des groupes de population.') | — |

*Notes:* 1 The Declaration of Helsinki does not contain the terms 'solidarity' and 'altruism'.

2 TC (10.1: 'use of tissue for research depends on an individual's altruism in donating the tissue with the expectation that social good will be advanced and human knowledge increased').

**Table 3.11  Other principles (1)[1]**

| Take account of cultural values | Universally applicable standards | Respect the human being as member of the human species | Freedom of research | Principles of monitoring and management |
|---|---|---|---|---|
| – | – | – | – | Helsinki ('independent' 'review committee') |
| CIOMS 2002 | CIOMS 2002 | – | – | CHRB ('independent examination' of the acceptability of the research project) |
| – | CHRB ('Universal Declaration of Human Rights') | CHRB | – | |
| UNESCO ('pluralism') | UNESCO ('Universal Declaration of Human Rights') | – | UNESCO | UNESCO ('transparency', 'independence' etc.) |
| WHO 1998 ('respect the diversities of culture') | – | – | – | – |
| HUGO ('respect for values, traditions, culture') | HUGO (refers to the international norms of human rights) | – | – | HUGO 1995 ('honesty' and 'impartiality') |
| – | – | – | CDBI 2002 (Explanatory Report) | COE 2006 ('transparency') |
| WHOROE (p. 7: 'the achievement of optimal advances in the name of the collective good may require a reconsideration of the respective … interests, including those of ethnic minorities, from a multicultural perspective.') | WHOROE (p. 7: 'the universalisability of human rights') | – | – | WHOROE (p. 14: 'privacy measures must be transparent and subject to ethical approval by a suitable body.') |
| ESHG ('culturally appropriate') | ESHG (only citing documents which refer to the Universal Declaration of Human Rights) | – | ESHG (p. 24: 'freedom of science') | ESHG (p. 25: 'transparency') |
| CEST (valeurs de la société au Quebec) | CEST (refers to the Universal Declaration of Human Rights) | – | CEST ('liberté académique', 'liberté de la recherche') | CEST ('transparence') |
| TC (2.6) | – | – | TC (1.8) | – |

**Table 3.11    Continued**

| Take account of cultural values | Universally applicable standards | Respect the human being as member of the human species | Freedom of research | Principles of monitoring and management |
|---|---|---|---|---|
| – | – | – | RMGA ('freedom of genomic research') | – |
| NARC ('respect for the participating population's culture') | – | – | – | NARC ('honesty, appropriateness') |
| MRC ('cultural differences') | – | – | – | – |
| – | HGC (respect for persons 'is accepted by most religions and cultures') | – | – | – |
| NC ('persons from different cultures may have very different views of what would constitute degrading forms of medical treatment') | – | – | – | – |
| | RCP (Kant: 'golden rule') | – | – | – |
| NBAC ('cultural differences can be significant') | – | – | – | – |
| | – | – | – | CCNE (p. 27: 'transparence') |

*Notes*: 1 The Belmont Report does not contain these terms.

## Table 3.12     Other principles (2)

| Respect of democracy | Kant's categorical imperative | We all have a moral imperative to share our genetic information |
|---|---|---|
| CEST | – | – |
| – | RCP ('golden rule': you should donate samples because not donating could not be universalized) | – |
| – | – | WHOROE (p. 9: 'if some, or any, of these ends can be furthered', e.g. public interest, public health) |

## Table 3.13     Guidelines referring to 'interests'

The term 'interest(s)' is marked in bold.

| Guideline | References to interests |
|---|---|
| Belmont Report 1979 | 'subject's best **interest**'; 'On the other hand, **interests** other than those of the subject may on some occasions be sufficient by themselves to justify the risks involved in the research, so long as the subjects' rights have been protected.' |
| Declaration of Helsinki 2008 | 4: 'A physician shall act in the patient's best **interest**.'<br>6: 'In medical research involving human subjects, the well-being of the individual research subject must take precedence over all other **interests**.'<br>14/24/30: '[P]otential conflicts of **interest**' of the researcher should be declared. |
| CIOMS 2002 | Commentary on guideline 2: Any 'conflict of **interest**' of members of the ethical review committee should be avoided.<br>*Commentary on guideline 4*: 'Medical records and biological specimens taken in the course of clinical care may be used for research without the consent of the patients/subjects only if an ethical review committee has determined that the research poses minimal risk, that the rights or **interests** of the patients will not be violated, that their privacy and confidentiality or anonymity are assured, and that the research is designed to answer an important question and would be impracticable if the requirement for informed consent were to be imposed.'<br>*Commentary on guideline 8*: 'considerations related to the well-being of the human subject should take precedence over the **interests** of science and society'; 'Research […] may present risks to the **interests** of communities, societies, or racially or ethnically defined groups' … data should be published 'in a manner that is respectful of the **interests** of all concerned.' … 'The ethical review committee should ensure that the **interests** of all concerned are given due consideration.'<br>*Commentary on guideline 13*: Vulnerable populations or persons are those unable 'to protect their own **interests**'. |
| CHRB (Bioethics Convention) 1997 | Art. 2 – Primacy of the human being. 'The **interests** and welfare of the human being shall prevail over the sole **interest** of society or science.'<br>Art. 6: The authorization of the representative to an intervention may be withdrawn at any time 'in the best **interest**' of a person 'not able to consent'.<br>Art. 10: The therapeutic privilege applies in exceptional cases: '2. Everyone is entitled to know any information collected about his or her health […] 3. In exceptional cases, restrictions may be placed by law on the exercise of the rights contained in paragraph 2 in the **interests** of the patient.'<br>Art. 26: 'No restrictions shall be placed on the exercise of the rights and protective provisions contained in this Convention other than such as are prescribed by law and are necessary in a democratic society in the **interest** of public safety […].' |
| UNESCO 2003 | The '**interests** and welfare of the individual should have priority over the rights and **interests** of society and research.' |

## Table 3.13    Continued

| Guideline | References to interests |
| --- | --- |
| | Art. 8: 'The legal representative should have regard to the best **interest**' of a 'person incapable of giving consent'. |
| | Art. 11: 'Genetic counselling should be non-directive, culturally adapted and consistent with the best **interest** of the person concerned.' |
| | Art. 16: 'Human genetic data, human proteomic data and the biological samples collected for one of the purposes set out in Article 5 should not be used for a different purpose that is incompatible with the original consent, unless the prior, free, informed and express consent of the person concerned is obtained according to the provisions of Article 8(a) or unless the proposed use, decided by domestic law, corresponds to an important public **interest** reason and is consistent with the international law of human rights.' |
| WHO 1998 | The term 'interest' is not used. |
| World Health Organization Regional Office for Europe: (WHOROE) 2001 | 3: 'those who share a common genetic heritage also share a common **interest** in how their genetic information is used.' 7: 'Although protections can and should be instituted for individuals who surrender personal data, the achievement of optimal advances in the name of the collective good may require a reconsideration of the respective claims so as to achieve an appropriate balance between individual and collective **interests**, including those of ethnic minorities, from a multi-cultural perspective.' 9: ' It is also apposite to consider the legitimacy of obtaining and using genetic samples and data derived from them for the purposes of criminal investigation and prosecution. While a clear public **interest** can be furthered in this regard, it remains subject to the need for stringent safeguards of individual liberties and human rights. A consideration of such a model in detail is beyond the scope of this report, whose focus is genetic data obtained and used for research and health purposes.' 9: 'balance of **interests**': 'This is in no way to suggest that individuals should be forced to share their genetic information. Rather, it is to stress the need for a balance of **interests**. This is the most ethically justifiable approach to the management of genetic information. Moreover, it acknowledges that in certain circumstances the balance of **interests** might weigh more heavily towards public **interests** and away from more traditional ways of respecting individual rights. For example, access to archived genetic material can further a number of important research ends that might hold considerable promise of public benefit, but it might prove impossible to obtain informed consent from the sample sources. Should we depart in such cases from the requirement of informed consent? This is discussed below, but it is important to note that a strong case can be made that the balance of **interests** here should be tipped in favor of the public **interest**, subject always to protection of privacy, except where the health of a particular identifiable individual is at stake. However, in all circumstances, a suitable and rigorous process of weighing and balancing of **interests** must be undertaken to ensure adequate respect and protection for individuals. This is an imperative from which no departure is permissible.' 11: 'The fundamental **interest** that individuals have in their samples and/or genetic information must never be forgotten.' |
| COE 2006/CDBI Expl. Report 2002 | Preamble: 'the **interests** and welfare of the human being whose biological materials are used in research shall prevail over the sole **interest** of society or science.' Explanatory Report, 3: 'There is a need for a common international framework, especially in the perspective of increasing cross border flow of human biological materials and data and in the light of important third party **interests** (e.g. the pharmaceutical and biotechnology industries).' 6: 'Only in the case of an overriding **interest** of a third party, the duty of confidentiality might be overridden.' |

**Table 3.13     Continued**

| Guideline | References to interests |
|---|---|
| | 12: 'individuals have an **interest** in knowing whether their doctors have any ulterior financial **interests** that might influence their professional conduct.' |
| ESHG 2002 | 8: Pharmaceutical companies have 'major **interests** in the collection of biological samples'. |
| | 21: 'The commercial **interests** in DNA banks have risen.' |
| | 21: '[I]t appears necessary [...] to insure that DNA banking can perform its function without impinging on the rights and **interests** of individuals who have their DNA sample or DNA data in a bank.' |
| | 23: 'If storage of a patient's sample is in the vital **interest** of a relative, it might be ethically acceptable to keep the sample.' |
| | 25: It is 'essential to respect the **interests** of those who participate as research subjects in regard to deciding control over and subsequent use of sample'. |
| CEST 2003 | In the chapter entitled 'Une multitude d'**intérêts** à concilier', it is mentioned (p. 24) that conflicting interests have been analysed in the literature, but that the Commission considers that examining empirical interests in detail is speculative. The guidelines restrict its scope to the identification of the different stakeholders involved without analysing the particular interests of these stakeholders in detail. |
| RMGA 2000 | In order 'to ensure an equitable level of protection of the **interests** of participant, as much as possible, consent forms should be standardized'. |
| | '[T]he RMGA is aware that its *Statement of Principles: Human Genome Research* considers the researcher as a professional intermediary between the **interests** of the participant in research and the **interests** of society in the advancement of knowledge.' |
| Tri-Council Policy Statement 1998 | i.5: 'The cardinal principle of modern research ethics, as discussed above, is respect for human dignity. This principle aspires to protecting the multiple and interdependent **interests** of the person – from bodily to psychological to cultural integrity.' |
| | 1.5: '[R]esearch warrants [...] provision for the protection of the **interests** of prospective subjects.' |
| | 1.11: 'The process of a continuing ethics review should be understood as a collective responsibility, to be carried out with a common **interest** in maintaining the highest ethical and scientific standards.' |
| | 2.6: The research ethics committee should 'require stringent protection for the **interests** of subjects.' |
| | 2.9: '[T]he principle of respect for human dignity entails high ethical obligations to the vulnerable populations. Such obligations often translate into special procedures to promote and protect their **interests** and dignity.' ... A means of protecting the '**interests** and dignity [of incompetent subjects] is provided through the free and informed consent of authorized representatives [...] who are acting in the **interests** of the potential subjects and are not influenced by conflict of **interest**.' |
| | 3.1: 'The values underlying the respect and protection of privacy and confidentiality are not absolute, however. Compelling and specifically identified public **interests**, for example, the protection of health, life and safety, may justify infringement of privacy and confidentiality. Laws compelling mandatory reporting of child abuse, sexually transmitted diseases or intent to murder are grounded on such reasoning; so too are laws and regulations that protect whistle-blowers. Similarly, without access to personal information, it would be difficult, if not impossible, to conduct important societal research in such fields as epidemiology, history, genetics and politics, which has led to major advances in knowledge and to an improved quality of life. The public **interest** thus may justify allowing researchers access to personal information, both to advance knowledge and to achieve social goals such as designing adequate public health programmes.' |
| | 3.4: 'the researcher should be sensitive to the **interests** of those who might suffer from stigmatization. For example, when records of prisoners, employees, students |

## Table 3.13   Continued

| Guideline | References to interests |
|---|---|
| | or others are used for research purposes, the researcher should not provide authorities with results that could identify individuals, unless the prior written consent of the subjects is obtained. Researchers may, however, provide aggregated data that cannot be linked to individuals to administrative bodies for policy decision-making purposes.'<br><br>10.1: 'Some people or cultures take little **interest** in tissue removed from their bodies.'<br><br>10.3: Previously collected tissue: 'Some individuals may not want their tissue used for any research purposes regardless of anonymity. The **interests** of biological relatives or members of distinct cultural groups or other communities may be adversely affected through research uses of their anonymous tissue. Issues may also arise concerning any duties, in extraordinary circumstances, to make traceable tissue identifiable for purposes of providing significant or beneficial information to those who have provided the tissue [...]. Researchers should address such issues to the satisfaction of the REB [Research Ethics Board or Committee].' |
| Nuffield Council 1995 | 5: '[A] person from whom tissue is removed may claim an **interest** in the tissue or products derived from it.'<br><br>59: 'Thus, when removal of tissue takes place in a non-therapeutic context, for example from a volunteer in a research project, not only must the removal be for a purpose which the law permits, that is, it must be in the public **interest** [...], but it must also be consented to explicitly and on the basis of all appropriate information.'<br><br>65: 'If treatment, archiving, banking, study/research and teaching are in the public **interest**, the question then becomes how far these general terms extend and what are their proper limits? The common law at present is silent on these specific questions. Notions of public decency would guide the court if a case arose.'<br><br>68: 'It is instructive to enquire why the question of a claim over tissue once removed has not received legal attention. The answer seems simple. In the general run of things a person from whom tissue is removed has not the slightest **interest** in making any claim to it once it is removed.'<br><br>74: 'A middle course may be to [...] propose that in the case of the incompetent adult, the courts should regard it as legally justified in the public **interest** to use tissue taken from an incompetent adult even though no consent can be obtained, provided, of course, that such use was itself a justifiable use.'<br><br>78: 'Despite the no-property rule, the common and civil law still recognized a number of **interests** that continue to enjoy legal protection today. For example, although the common law did not grant an absolute right to the control of one's body after death through one's will, it and the civil law have long recognized one's right to a decent burial.' |
| Medical Research Council 2001 | 2: 'Custodianship implies some rights to decide how the samples are used and by whom, and also responsibility for safeguarding the **interests** of the donors.'<br><br>3: 'Donors should understand what the sample is to be used for and how the results of the research might impact on their **interests**.'<br><br>4: 'Research participants have a right to know individual research results that affect their **interests**, but should be able to choose whether to exercise that right.'<br><br>5: 'MRC recognizes that many existing collections of human material are immensely valuable for research, and that using these collections may be ethical, and in the **interests** of both patients and the public.'<br><br>6: 'The **interests** of research participants should always take precedence over those of science and society [...] Researchers must always ensure that their use of human material will not compromise the **interests** of the donor.'<br><br>8: 'The assumption by the donor is that nothing will be done that would be detrimental to his or her **interests**, or bring harm to him or her.'<br><br>10: '[P]rovided there is no possible way to link the results of tests to identifiable individuals their **interests** cannot be compromised [...] Patients need sufficient |

**Table 3.13    Continued**

| Guideline | References to interests |
| --- | --- |
|  | information to understand how (if at all) the research might affect their **interests**, and how their confidentiality will be protected. Where surplus material is to be used in a way that allows research results to be linked to the individual patient, individual informed consent must be obtained if there is any possibility that such results might affect the patient's **interests**.'<br>11: 'If individual written consent cannot be obtained, research using samples of material surplus to clinical requirements is only acceptable if the results cannot affect the patient's or their family's **interests**. The patient must also have been informed at the time the sample was taken that their material might be used for research, for example by clearly displayed notices, by distribution of leaflets, or on the clinical consent form itself.'<br>15: '[I]t is important that donors have sufficient understanding not only of the process involved in obtaining the sample and any associated physical risks, but also of what the sample is to be used for and how the results of the research might impact on their **interests**.'<br>18: 'Research results obtained on anonymized unlinked samples cannot have any impact on the **interests** of an individual donor, and cannot be fed back.'<br>18: 'Tests done on samples of human material in the course of research may reveal information that has implications for the donors' future health or healthcare, or otherwise impacts on their **interests**. It is important to decide before the start of a research project what will be done if this arises. Researchers should be cautious about assuming that they, rather than the individuals concerned, are best placed to judge what information is of **interest** to donors on a case-by-case basis. For instance, some researchers may take the view that information should only be fed back if there is a treatment or preventive intervention available. However, research participants might wish to know predictive information about their future health, even if there is no treatment available, for example to take it into account when making important life decisions, such as whether to have children' [...]<br>18: 'When participants are asked to make a decision on whether or not they want results to be fed back to them they must be given sufficient information to allow them to decide what their **interests** are and to make any refusal meaningful.'<br>19: 'Where samples may subsequently be used for secondary studies, a mechanism should be put in place to allow participants the opportunity to seek individual results that might impact on their **interests**. It is acceptable for the onus to be on the participant to seek the information rather than on the researcher to be pro-active in providing it.'<br>25: '[S]ome research results (e.g. from genetic studies) may have implications for the surviving family members. The potential implications for relatives of any research to be done using linked samples must be discussed, and they must be given the opportunity to learn about any research results that might impact on their **interests**.' |
| Human Genetics Commission (HGC) 2002 | 5: 'In the subtitle of this report we talk of balancing **interests**. This is an important aspect of our work [...] We have tried here to take account of a wide spectrum of views and have attempted to reach conclusions which are morally defensible and sensitive to the different **interests** involved.'<br>9: 'It is quite possible to achieve a balance between public **interest** and individual concerns. The two objectives can co-exist, and we have set out a number of principles to achieve this.'<br>10: The 'legitimate goal of medical science – improved health – should be achieved in such a way which recognizes the rights of the individual, including his or her **interest** in being properly informed and consulted, and in remaining in control of personal biological material and information.'<br>13: 'Our aim in this report is to suggest how **interests** in genetic privacy and confidentiality can be protected in a way that does not harm comparably important **interests** of others. We have set out a number of principles to achieve this, many |

**Table 3.13    Continued**

| Guideline | References to interests |
|---|---|
| | of which are laid down in international declarations and conventions which seek to establish a common ethical framework.' |
| | 15: 'The general duty to maintain the confidential nature of personal genetic information is not an absolute one. We note circumstances where it may not be appropriate, such as where consent is given or where it is in the **interest** of the patient, of relatives, or of the wider public (3.62).' |
| | 17: 'In other cases, if testing of samples from the dead is not justified by weighty reasons such as the significant **interests** of other family members or of the wider public, then such testing should be regarded as unethical (4.73).' |
| | 19: '[L]arge-scale population genetic databases, established with and supported by public funding, constitute a national asset. This means that national benefit and **interest** should be taken into account in determining the terms upon which access is to be granted to such databases.' |
| | 37: The principle of solidarity is based on the 'shared **interest** in medical progress and the conquest of illness'. |
| | 40: 'The autonomy of the individual, although important, is of course not the only value to be taken into account. Individuals live in society, and the **interests** of others must be considered in the exercise of individual autonomy. The pursuit of individual fulfilment at the expense of the claims of others for moral consideration may find few defenders in a society based on ideas of mutual co-operation and inter-dependence. In the context of personal genetic information, then, there may be circumstances in which we would seek to balance the demands of autonomy (for example with respect to the right to keep personal genetic information confidential) with the **interests** of others whose welfare may be affected by access to such information.' |
| | 42: 'There will be circumstances in which competing **interests** of the State or others outweigh the right of privacy. The earlier example of the forensic use of DNA tests applies here as a justification for the ordering of tests on a suspect.' |
| | 43: 'The pursuit of public health goals or the seeking of advances in medical research may give rise to the argument that the consent of the individual should take second place to these laudable objectives. In some cases, public health goals do outweigh the right of the individual to withhold consent, as in extreme cases where examination and isolation of a person with infectious disease may be enforced in the public **interest**. In general, our society has preferred to stress the rights of the individual to make his or her own decisions relating to the body, allowing people to pursue unhealthy lifestyles if they wish or even to embark on self-destruction if that is their firm decision. This involves a rejection of coercion, even if the coercion is motivated by paternalistic motives. The especially promising nature of any particular area of medicine or biology – such as genetics – should not be allowed to eclipse this well-established principle in bioethics.' |
| | 90: 'any system of regulation should take into account the link between the information and the original sample of genetic material. The sample is the route to the genetic information, and while the information itself may have potent implications, the individual may still have a continuing strong **interest** in what happens to the sample, as genetic information may continue to be extracted from it in the future. Controlling what is done with a sample is therefore part of the necessary control on access to genetic information.' |
| | 94: 'This argument assumes that a person has the right to control what is done with information about himself or herself; the fact that information is anonymized becomes irrelevant in this view: it is still something in which the individual feels that he or she has some personal **interest**. The degree of recognition given to this personal **interest**, though, will depend on other factors. Provided that the use of this anonymized information in research is unlikely to cause harm to the person in question and there is a strong social **interest**, we think that it is reasonable that |

**Table 3.13    Continued**

| Guideline | References to interests |
|---|---|
| | research use of such anonymized data be permitted. This process of balancing **interests** is a common one in a range of privacy issues, where public **interest** may justify a limiting of the individual's right to privacy (for example, in issues of freedom of the press or criminal justice).' |
| | 96: 'If the provision of a sample is regarded as a "gift" or donation [...] then the donor could be seen as foregoing any further claim on the sample. There are scientific reasons in favor of this approach: it could compromise research progress if samples were reclaimed after significant work had been done on them. It should also be borne in mind that the nature of samples may change radically after they have been subjected to research procedures. This may affect any moral **interest** which the donor has in them. Resolving this matter requires the balancing of the **interests** of the donor and those of the researcher. A single rule might be too blunt an instrument here, and the right to withdraw might depend on the nature of the research involved. In all cases, we consider that best practice requires that the consent should clearly specify the arrangements for withdrawal from the study and the subsequent fate of samples and data.' |
| | 96: 'The House of Lords Select Committee on Stem Cell Research has addressed this issue in relation to embryonic stem cells and recommends that no specific constraint should be placed by prospective donors on the future use of cell lines generated from their donation. This is compatible with our view on the absence of **interest** which the donor has in the DNA that is contained in developed cell lines. Again we emphasise how important it is that donors be given adequate explanation of the fact that their **interest** in the donated material is to cease once the donation is made.' |
| | 97: 'We believe that the public **interest** in the use of such material is a strong one, and that such research should be allowed in those cases where the donors cannot possibly be harmed by it. We therefore endorse the advice given by the Medical Research Council that samples from historical collections may be used subject to certain conditions. In terms of this advice, historical samples may be used where consent cannot be obtained.' |
| | 103: 'However, this is not incompatible with recognising the legitimate **interest** of companies in having exclusive access to particular information in order to allow a reasonable period for commercial opportunities. We also believe it to be very important that databases of this nature are seen and understood to be bringing at least some benefits to public-domain medical knowledge rather than being solely designed for commercial exploitation.' |
| Royal College of Pathologists (RCP) 2001 | 'It is in the vital **interests** of society that human tissues can be used in NHS hospital laboratories.'<br>'The MRC has recently expressed the opinion that implied consent (as explained above) is ethically acceptable for the research use of surplus tissue if there is no possibility of the research affecting the patient's **interests**.' |
| NARC 1997 | 'Once informed, the researchers can approach the population to determine whether it is **interested** in participating in the Project.'<br>The 'North American Regional Committee intends to establish a system of contractual protection of the population's **interest**, through the population's choice of its own control, control by a charitable third party (such as UNESCO), or a fixed-percentage royalty.'<br>'[C]ase law [...] from California, implies that individuals have very limited property **interests** in their cells' (NARC note 16).<br>The 'community **interests** and concerns [...should be] truly considered in the Project' (X).<br>The 'North American Regional Committee intends to establish a system of contractual protection of the population's **interest**' (IX.A).<br>'If the Project is conducted according to these principles, it should enhance not only humanity's knowledge of itself, but also humanity's **interest** in, knowledge |

## Table 3.13    Continued

| Guideline | References to interests |
|---|---|
| | of, and confidence in science. If conducted poorly, without respect for and protection of the rights of those who participate, it may prove a disaster – not for humanity, but for science.' |
| ACMG | The term 'interest' is not used. |
| American Society of Human Genetics | Consideration is required 'of new ways to achieve the goals of expanding knowledge, and, at the same time, respecting the **interests** of those who volunteer themselves to be subjects' (ASHG 1996). |
| US NCH 1996 | Of 'special importance' is the 'possible extension of risk to family members of the donor or to any group or community of **interest** (e.g., gender, race, ethnicity) to which a donor might belong'. |
| College of American Pathologists (CAP) 1999 | 296: 'As recipients of tissue and medical specimens, pathologists and other medical specialists regard themselves as stewards of patient tissues and consider it their duty to protect the best **interests** of both the individual patient and the public [...] The decision to provide human tissue for such purposes should be based on the specific (ie, direct patient care) and general (ie, furthering medical knowledge) **interests** of the patient and of society [...] This document proposes specific recommendations whereby both **interests** can be fostered safely, ethically, and reasonably.' 297: 'Implicit in the pathologist's stewardship is the [...] fiduciary duty, not to disclose the information to others without the person's consent, actual or implied, or otherwise in his or her **interest**.' 297: 'Privacy includes both the notion of respect for personal autonomy and an **interest** in freedom from uninvited and unwarranted intrusions. It implies freedom to live as one desires in one's own space.' 298–9: 'Although federal regulations (45 CFR 46) apply this informed consent doctrine to research with human tissues, the **interests** of the patient are fundamentally different from those in which therapeutic intervention is at issue. The **interests** of a patient in the results of research are generally not specific to the individual. Usually, in fact almost always, a single research project does not establish irrefutable scientific fact, and the results of a single investigation have no applicability to an individual patient. Disclosure of a single research project's results to a patient is at best not beneficial, and at worst could be misleading or even harmful. Nonetheless, the societal **interest** in accumulated research findings is great. In the case of research on medically or surgically removed tissues, autopsy tissues, and body fluids (tissue research), research projects do not immediately benefit the patient's health or alter treatment.' 299: 'Society has a strong **interest** in research involving the use of human tissue, and such research may be hampered by well-intended but intrusive regulations.' |
| National Bioethics Advisory Commission (NBAC) 1999 | 50: 'If the distribution of benefits is grossly inequitable, it is misleading to speak of a common **interest** in medical progress. Consequently, the case for tolerating increased risks to the **interests** of those who provide specimens for the sake of society's **interest** in medical progress becomes weaker if some people – including some who provide the biological materials – lack access to important health care benefits because they cannot afford them.' i: 'Is it appropriate to use stored biological materials in ways that originally were not contemplated either by the people from whom the materials came or by those who collected the materials? Does such use harm anyone's **interest**?' ii: 'Where identifying information exists, however, a well-developed system of protections must be implemented to ensure that risks are minimized and that the **interests** of sample sources are protected.' ii: 'Properly interpreted and modestly modified, present federal regulations can protect subjects' rights and **interests** and at the same time permit well-designed research to go forward using materials already in storage as well as those newly collected by investigators and others. Fundamentally, the **interests** of subjects and those of researchers are not in conflict.' |

**Table 3.13    Continued**

| Guideline | References to interests |
|---|---|
| | iii: '[S]ociety's **interest**' ('Given the importance of society's **interest** in treating disease and developing new therapies, a policy that severely restricts research access to unidentified and unlinked samples would severely hamper research and could waste a valuable research resource.') |
| | 7: '[A] person's rights and **interests**' ('It stands to reason that a person's rights and **interests** are better protected if that person has some form of control over his or her removed biological material, especially if it remains identifiable.') |
| | 8: 'A stable consensus must strike the right balance between the desire to increase knowledge and the necessity of appropriately protecting individual **interests**. On the one hand, there are those who think that emphasis should be placed on the distinctive nature of personal and familial medical information, the right of personal choice regarding the continual use of one's body or its parts (and, therefore, the information inherent in the materials taken from it), and the necessity of being able to exercise a measure of control over the research that can be conducted with one's DNA and tissues. On the other hand, others believe that in an era of increasing professional and legal regulations as well as an increasing emphasis on individual autonomy, renewed consideration must be given to the more extensive use of this invaluable and often irreplaceable research resource.' |
| | 34: 'A common position seems to be emerging that a person's rights and **interests** are best protected if that person has some form of control over his or her removed biological material. Nonetheless, a rich diversity of positions exists on how to control access to and use of human biological materials and the data obtained from them. A greater standardization of policies with regard to the use of DNA samples certainly would facilitate future international cooperation in biomedical research.' |
| | 37: 'a person's privacy **interest**' ('state legislative initiatives [...] attempt to protect an individual's privacy **interest** by preventing the dissemination of personal information and do so by restricting the ability of those who hold medical records, such as hospital pathology laboratories, to give out information from the records and by restricting the ability of investigators to conduct such research except in certain circumstances.') |
| | 38: 'public **interest**' ('a privacy right' is balanced against 'other recognizable public **interest**'). |
| | 39: informed consent is a required but insufficient protection of both the **interests** of the research subject and the investigator. |
| | 42: 'All harms may be viewed as setbacks to **interests** (Feinberg 1987). But it is also necessary to identify and, whenever possible, assign weights to various **interests** of both individuals and groups. Rather than simply trying to present those **interests** in the abstract, this chapter considers them in relation to the principles, regulations, and guidelines that already identify many of the relevant harms and assigns them some weights relative to each other, sometimes by establishing certain presumptions and indicating the conditions under which those presumptions can be rebutted.' |
| | 42: '**interests** of future beneficiaries of current research' ('In making ethical judgments about the research use of human biological materials, it is not always necessary to pit the **interests** of future beneficiaries of current research against the **interests** of those who have provided the human biological materials. [...] virtually all parties to the discussion acknowledge both the value of biomedical research and the need to minimize harms and wrongs to subjects. Indeed, the challenge is not to trade off the potential health benefits from research against the protection of sources and others, but rather to find ways in which to maximize the opportunities for developing new knowledge and new treatments while, at the same time, ensuring appropriate protections from harms and wrongs.') |
| | 43: 'Individuals have an **interest** in avoiding the unnecessary exposure of their bodies to the view of others and in not having intimate or embarrassing facts |

**Table 3.13    Continued**

| Guideline | References to interests |
|---|---|
| | about themselves disclosed, even if such exposure or disclosure does not threaten other of their **interests**.'<br>44: 'legitimate **interests**' ('What counts as a justifiable limitation or exception to confidentiality will depend upon a complex weighing of conflicting legitimate **interests**.')<br>45: 'balance between **interests**' ('If federal and state laws prohibiting insurance and employment discrimination on the basis of genetic and other medical information are passed and effectively implemented, the balance between **interests** that weigh in favor of more restricted access to and greater source control over biological samples, on the one hand, and those that weigh in favor of freer access and more permissive research uses of those samples, on the other hand, would shift accordingly.')<br>49: '**interests** that survive their death' ('individuals may have **interests** that survive their deaths, such as the **interest** in what happens to their children and grandchildren after they themselves die.') |
| CCNE Avis et rapport No. 77 2003 | 5: 'Des formules doivent être mises en place [...] qui permettent de…protéger les **intérêts** d'une personne disparue.'<br>16: 'Cette fonction [du curateur] doit faire une place à un mécanisme de médiation ou de conciliation en raison des difficultés qui peuvent apparaître, garantissant tout autant les **intérêts** des personnes que les **intérêts** des chercheurs.'<br>19: 'L'un est celui de leur usage optimal pour l'**intérêt** collectif, notamment à des fins scientifiques, médicales et de santé publique ; l'autre est d'éviter pour autant de parvenir à une assimilation de telles collections à un bien public qui serait en quelque sorte socialisé, nationalisé, ou, à l'inverse, totalement marchandisé.'<br>19: 'De plus, on ne sait pas par avance quand la recherche souhaitera analyzer les caractéristiques génétiques. A un moment donné, inconnu, elle peut mettre en jeu les **intérêts** de tiers, la descendance, la fratrie ou un groupe partageant une caractéristique génétique commune.'<br>21: 'Traditionnellement [dans les situations où la personne est mineure ou incapable de consentir], il y a lieu dans ce cas d'interroger une personne responsable ; il peut s'agir des parents ou d'une personne désignée avec toutes garanties pour protéger les **intérêts** de la personne, et on voit mal quelle autre solution s'appliquerait au cas des biobanques. Mais comment ignorer le fait que l'acte en cause est compliqué, car les **intérêts** à préserver ne sont pas, comme il en est de la simple intervention médicale, faciles à discerner et à prévoir? Comment ignorer qu'une collection faite à partir de prélèvements obtenus chez des enfants engage nécessairement une connaissance sur toute une vie future?'<br>24: 'Il est de l'**intérêt** général de bénéficier aussi rapidement que possible des bienfaits escomptés d'un succès des recherches entreprises. Par conséquent, dans le respect des droits des investigateurs initiaux et des personnes prélevées, des dispositions doivent être prises afin d'optimiser cette utilisation des collections d'échantillons biologiques. L'**intérêt** collectif peut parfois entrer en conflit avec celui des autres partenaires, tel le droit des personnes prélevées à l'information et à la non nationalisation ou privatisation économiques de leurs échantillons biologiques, déjà abordé plus haut ; mais aussi, le droit de la collectivité d'éviter que de très larges collections d'une dimension nationale ne soient exclusivement utilisées pour répondre aux **intérêts** commerciaux d'un partenaire industriel auquel aurait été concédée une exclusivité d'accès.'<br>25: 'Les investigateurs initiaux, appartenant au monde académique consentent souvent des efforts considérables dans la réunion d'une collection de matériel biologique à des fins d'enquête génétique: préparation du projet, établissement des critères précis d'inclusion, organization, entretien et mise à disposition des échantillons de la collection [...] Il apparaît dès lors qu'une revendication deces investigateurs de disposer d'un temps raisonnable pour pouvoir, avec tous les moyens dont ils disposent, profiter des fruits scientifiques de leurs efforts, |

**Table 3.13   Continued**

| Guideline | References to interests |
|---|---|
| | est acceptable. Cependant, ce droit légitime peut entrer en contradiction avec celui des participants à la collection d'optimiser la recherche menée grâce à leur générosité conjointe.' |
| | 25 (suite): 'Un compromis entre ces deux types d'**intérêts** légitimes passe par la précision de la durée durant laquelle les investigateurs auront un accès privilégié à la collection qu'ils ont réunie, et du délai à partir duquel il semble impératif d'ouvrir cette collection à d'autres équipes, éventuellement mieux à même de mener la recherche initialement envisagée, ou tout autre type de recherche du même type que celle à laquelle ont consenti les personnes.' |
| | 29: 'la collection […] doit être gérée en commun dans un **intérêt** de solidarité' ('Dans tous les cas, il détient une collection qui n'a pu légalement en France être achetée; elle est régie au départ par les règles d'indisponibilité du corps humain et est hors commerce. Le CCNE propose de compléter ce raisonnement en affirmant clairement que la collection contribue à constituer un bien collectif, une ressource qui doit être gérée en commun dans un **intérêt** de solidarité. Ceci ne signifie nullement que le travail pour conserver cette ressource ne doit pas être rémunéré, et que si s'exerce une œuvre d'invention et qu'elle aboutit à la création d'un test ou d'un médicament, la mise en banque interdise les conséquences financières normales de cette activité.') |

# Chapter 4

# Selected Issues of Consensus
# and of Controversy

## Consent and Withdrawal

*The Controversy*

The problem of consent to research projects involving human genetic databases[1] is among the most debated in recent biomedical research ethics.[2] Although agreement exists that some form of consent is necessary to allow research involving human genetic databases, the form that this consent should take is open to debate (Trouet 2003; Porteri and Borry 2008). The controversy is so difficult to resolve that even authors of the same article do not find a consensus. Deschênes et al. state: 'The authors of this text are divided on both the issues of consent to future unspecified research using anonymized samples and on consent to the use of coded samples for future unspecified research with or without recontact' (Deschênes et al. 2001, 223). Similarly, the report of the National Bioethics Advisory Commission on 'Research involving Human Biological Materials' has added a long note (NBAC 1999, 65) to the recommendation on this issue (recommendation 9) because some commissioners disagreed with the majority opinion on consent to future research.

The evolution of the discussion about the use of presumed consent in Iceland demonstrates that a consensus emerges about the necessity of written informed consent at least once to permit individuals to consent actively to the fact that their samples and information from their medical records will be included in a genetic database. It is also widely accepted that it is adequate, under certain conditions (COE 2006), to use already existing or historical collections of data and samples for which it is impossible to obtain informed consent because the donors cannot be

---

1   The debate about consent in biobanks has been ongoing for some time (Baumann 2001; Caulfield, Upshur and Daar 2003; Elger and Mauron 2003; Hoeyer 2003; Corrigan 2004; Hoeyer 2004; Hoeyer and Lynoe 2004; Hoeyer et al. 2004; Kaye 2004; Knoppers 2004; Williams and Schroeder 2004; Clayton 2005; Helgesson and Johnsson 2005; Hoeyer et al. 2005; Knoppers 2005; Petersen 2005; Hansson et al. 2006; Maschke 2006; Shickle 2006; Cambon-Thomsen, Rial-Sebbag and Knoppers 2007; Kristinsson and Arnason 2007; Phillips et al. 2007; Elger 2008a and 2008b; Seoane and Da Rocha 2008; Allen and McNamara 2009; Hofmann 2009; Secko et al. 2009).

2   The question of consent is important independently of whether one considers it to reflect the expression of personal rights or the object of property rights concerning DNA samples or data. See Knoppers et al. (1998, 385–7) for a discussion of the legal status of DNA samples.

traced. This could happen if they changed address or are deceased, or if material and data are irreversibly unlinked to personal information which would permit identification of donors.

Still controversial is whether, from now on, informed consent should be required in order to allow inclusion of all tissue samples taken during clinical or research activities in genetic databases, whether this tissue can be used without consent after it has been irreversibly anonymized,[3] how much information a donor should receive, how a right to withdrawal of consent should be framed and put into practice, and whether consent of the individual needs to be complemented by consent of others concerned, such as the family or community.

The following discussion will be restricted to the most controversial issue: the re-use of samples or data for further research that has not been specified at the moment of consent.[4] The justification of some consent procedures is based on particular interpretations of the right to withdrawal. Therefore, we also take into account different approaches to withdrawal, especially if guidelines contain a discussion or recommendations about this point.

If even authors of the same publications and guidelines are divided on the subject of consent to future research using genetic data banks, not surprisingly, guidelines from different places and organizations also do not reach a consensus on this point. The different positions can be summarized as two extremes and different intermediate solutions.

*The Extreme Positions*

'Blanket consent' and 'new informed consent' to each new project are the two extreme positions that are defended in guidelines. Blanket consent was among the earliest solutions proposed for the consent problem in biobank research:

> A blanket informed consent that would allow use of a sample for genetic research in general, including future as yet unspecified projects, appears to be the most efficient and economical approach, avoiding costly recontact before each new research project. The consent should specify that family members may request access to a sample to learn their own genetic status but not that of the donor (WHO 1998, 13).

---

3   See Trouet (2004), who criticizes the draft guidelines from the Council of Europe (CDBI 2002b; COE 2006) because they require consent only for identifiable (linked anonymized or coded) and identified tissue, but not for unlinked anonymized and anonymous tissue. In line with Trouet's critics, legislation in some European countries or proposals for such legislation provide the possibility for donors to influence the use of their biological materials, even in the case of unlinked anonymization (see Act on Biobanks 2000; Trouet 2004, 101).

4   The issue of 're-consent' has been identified as being of 'major concern' by Caulfield in his summary presentation at the OECD conference on human genetic databases in Tokyo, 26–27 February 2004 (Caulfield 2004a).

It has to be noted that the term 'blanket informed consent' used in this WHO document is a contradiction in itself because the donor is supposed to consent without being informed about future projects, although the guidelines add that '[a]ttempts should be made to inform families, at regular intervals, of new developments in testing and treatment. Donors should inform DNA banks of current addresses for follow-up' (WHO 1998, 13). These WHO guidelines do not discuss a right to withdrawal.

Some form of blanket consent is also defended in a more hidden form in later guidelines. In contrast to the earlier guidelines (WHO 1998), they were not written by geneticists but by patient advocates, the 'European Partnerships on Patient's Rights and Empowerment' in the WHO Regional Office for Europe (WHO May 2001). These guidelines seem to defend a strict position when they state that 'blanket consent is only permissible in circumstances where anonymity of future data can be guaranteed' (WHO 2001, 14, recommendation 9). However, a closer look at the definition of anonymity shows that the guidelines opt for the concept of '*proportional* or *reasonable anonymity*' (WHO 2001, 11, italics in the original text). This means that it is considered sufficient that data are 'linked', as long as 'access to the link is restricted appropriately'. In conclusion, these guidelines agree to the use of blanket consent, under the condition that data is protected by a secure code that is known only by a few authorized persons. However, since data remain linked, they still represent personal data because it is possible for those who are authorized to have access to the link to identify the donor. In order to limit abuse, in light of this relatively low standard of consent, the guidelines furthermore suggest the 'use of sunset clauses, whereby consent will only be valid during a finite period of time' (WHO 2001, 14). In addition, the following criteria are proposed to limit the use of blanket consent:

> Those who would seek to depart from the practice of requiring active informed consent prior to participation in the creation of a genetic database must justify this position in strong ethical terms. As a minimum the following criteria must be satisfied: (a) a clear, realisable and significant public health benefit must be identified, (b) the widest possible educational programme must be instituted among the population that will participate, including an opportunity for public debate, (c) strong privacy protection measures must be implemented, (d) individuals must at all times be given the opportunity to refuse to participate, and (e) every stage of the process must be subject to the most stringent ethical scrutiny (WHO 2001, 16).

Most other guidelines are opposed to the idea of blanket consent, although as we will discuss below, the difference between blanket consent (which is considered not acceptable) and general consent (which could be acceptable under certain conditions) is not always clear.

If blanket consent is unpopular to guideline writers and policy makers, interestingly, the other extreme of the range of opinions is even more unpopular.

The most extreme concept has been described by legal scholars (Annas, Glantz and Roche 1995a and 1995b) in the proposed federal legislation called 'Genetic Privacy Act (GPA)'. Annas et al. base their proposal on the idea that DNA samples are the property of the donor, an idea which is rejected by most other guidelines. The Act states that the donor must provide written consent in advance to proposed use(s) of the sample if tissue samples or data will be identifiable. According to the Act, the donor has, furthermore, the right to be informed at least 45 days in advance, and he/she must consent to the transfer of a DNA sample to other scientists for future research purposes.

Most guidelines do not follow the recommendations of Annas and his colleagues. Some guidelines adopt a strict position, including informed consent to each new use, but without granting the full range of donor rights that is described by Annas et al. One example in favour of strict informed consent is the guidelines of the Commission de l'Éthique de la Science et de la Technologie (CEST 2003). The CEST guidelines recommend explicitly that before any future research project can be realized that has not been determined at the moment of the original consent, the new consent of the donor is necessary. The guidelines do not accept a form of general consent for unknown future projects, because they require consent to be informed. Donors need to receive information about the aim of the study, the way in which samples are used and what kind of information is obtained from them, as well as the implications that the use of the tissue and information will have for the individuals, their families and the community (CEST 2003, 47 and recommendation No. 7, xviii). The right to withdrawal exists at any moment and it is the responsibility of the researcher to destroy all information ('retirer toutes les données concernant la personne'). The Commission is aware that withdrawals might influence the results of the research, but this is not used as an argument against the right to withdrawal. Instead, the Commission recommends that donors receive genetic counselling about the impact a withdrawal will have on the research, in order to enable them to make informed decisions (CEST 2003, 48).

Two other examples of guidelines which oppose blanket consent and favour new informed consent to each future project are the UK Advisory Committee statement (UK Advisory Committee 1998)[5] and the French Canadian guidelines of the Network of Applied Genetic Medicine (RMGA 2000). The RMGA guidelines do not state explicitly that blanket consent is inappropriate, but specify the requirement for recontacting and new informed consent for 'other research than that specified in the original consent' (RMGA 2000, 8). In the case of coded samples, 'the participant should be able to choose whether or not to be recontacted in order to authorize the analysis of his DNA for other research [...] At that time the procedures of this Statement apply.' According to these procedures, 'informed consent and choices' are required (RMGA 2000, 5).

---

5   '[B]efore any genetic test is carried out as part of medical research prior consent must have been obtained for each test' (UK Advisory Committee 1998, 7).

In spite of the strict requirement for informed consent, there is some room for interpretation of these guidelines. First, 'informed' consent could mean that general information about future uses is sufficient. This would allow for a range of different studies without new consent. In addition, attention must be paid to the exceptions related to anonymization. Policies that require strict consent often permit linked anonymized samples and information to be used without new consent (OHRP 2004).

Concerning the right to withdrawal, the RMGA guidelines specify that this right exists and that it follows from the principle of 'freedom of participation'. It has two implications:

> Firstly, the participant should be able to withdraw from the research project at all times, without prejudice. Secondly, the participant should be able to request that his sample be destroyed. The exercise of the right of withdrawal is not possible in the case of anonymized samples and the participant should be informed of this in the consent form (RMGA 2000).

The RMGA guidelines do not specify whether all information already entered in a database will be destroyed or instead irreversibly anonymized. Indeed, it would be necessary to specify whether 'withdraw from the research project at all times' means that all data from ongoing projects will be destroyed at any time. This seems to be highly impractical and inefficient for research, because already started research projects would at any time need to repeat statistical analyses without the data from the withdrawn samples, that is, an important part of the research would need to be repeated.

*Intermediate Positions*

*General consent*
An increasingly popular intermediate position is *general* – also called *broad* (ESHG 2003) or *unrestricted* (WHO 2000) – consent. For example, the Human Genetics Commission considers that general consent is sufficient in cases where 'irreversible or reversible anonymization of data and samples'[6] is guaranteed (HGC 2002, 95). Consent at the outset is judged important, but 'repeated processes of re-consent for subsequent use are impractical and, moreover, may be considered as unnecessarily invasive' (HGC 2002, 94–5). The extent to which blanket consent differs from general consent is open to debate. The HGC states that participants should be given at the outset 'a clear explanation of the potential scope of the research that may be carried out on their sample or data'. Re-consent would be required for research that is of a 'fundamentally different nature' (HGC 2002, 94), at least for identified samples. The HGC seems to be of the opinion that reversible anonymization, for example, coding of the sample and data, is a sufficient protection to allow for future

---

6   For the terminology concerning anonymization, see Table 4.1.

research without re-consent. The HGC is somewhat critical concerning withdrawal. It recognizes that international and national guidelines on the use of human subjects in research have stressed the right of a participant in medical research to withdraw from a study at any time, and for any reason. The HGC believes, however, that '[t]he same right has not been as clearly established in cases where participation is limited to the donation of bodily materials' (HGC 2002, 95). Since future research on samples does not have any physical impact on the donors, in contrast to classical research involving human subjects, the HGC judges the right to withdrawal to be less obvious or less morally required. The donor could be seen as 'foregoing any further claim on the sample', if the sample is considered a gift. In addition, a right to withdrawal could 'compromise research progress if samples were reclaimed after significant work had been done on them'. Since the balancing of the interests of the donor and those of the researcher might vary according to the type of research, the HGC considers that the right to withdraw 'might depend on the nature of the research involved'. The guidelines recommend that the consent document should 'clearly specify the arrangements for withdrawal from the study and the subsequent fate of samples and data' (HGC 2002, 96). The French guidelines (CCNE 2003, 4) take a similar position in favour of general consent to future research, if the data and samples are anonymized. The term 'anonymization', as it is used by the CCNE, seems to include both reversible and irreversible anonymization. The CCNE states that the notion of consent needs to be adapted ('il y a lieu d'adapter la notion de consentement'). First, the establishment of genetic databases leads to the need to reinforce consent requirements.[7] This means that the donor, before consenting to any storage of samples, should receive full information about storing, the aims and nature of research projects, publications, patents and commercialization planned, and consequences foreseen. However, concerning *future* uses of anonymized samples, it is conceivable to simplify ('Il semble donc concevable de simplifier l'exigence du consentement', CCNE 2003, 24–5). If the donor provides consent, according to the CCNE, the use of samples and information for other research will be possible without new consent. This consent is best characterized as general consent, because it is given without any detailed information about future projects. In this respect, the 2003 statement has become less strict than the CCNE guidelines from 1991 concerning genetic testing. In 1991, the CCNE stated that for genetic research of a different aim ('finalité') than that described in the original consent form, new consent should be required.

In 2003, the CCNE added a unique requirement for the original consent to storage. The donor should be informed that the genetic databank has put in place a 'council' ('instance conseil') that donors are allowed to contact at any time in order to know exactly what has happened to their samples and information.

The position of the UNESCO guidelines seems to imply at least some form of general consent. When looking at the Declaration's definition of consent, one might

---

7   'L'apparition des banques conduit à *un renforcement des exigences liées au consentement de la personne*' (CCNE 2003, 5, italics in the original text).

conclude that blanket consent would not fulfil the definition of 'consent' (UNESCO 2003, 3). Consent is defined as a 'freely given specific, informed and express agreement of an individual to his or her genetic data being collected, processed, used and stored'. The term 'informed [...] agreement' used in this definition could be interpreted to mean informed consent in its traditional sense, which implies that detailed information about research projects should be provided to sample donors. However, the UNESCO guidelines require consent to include only information which specifies 'the purpose' for which data is 'being derived from biological samples' and 'used and stored'. Although UNESCO recommends a strict requirement for new informed consent for 'purposes' that are 'incompatible' with the original consent, it is not clear how detailed the 'purpose' needs to be described in the beginning. The purposes mentioned in Article 5 of the Declaration are extremely broad and do not contain any detail about specific research projects. Consent to the purposes mentioned, such as 'diagnosis and health care, including screening and predictive testing', or to 'medical and other scientific research, including epidemiological, especially population-based genetic studies, as well as anthropological or archaeological studies' without further details, could at best be called general consent and might even be called blanket consent to 'medical research' or 'health purposes'. Moreover, the UNESCO Declaration leaves room for not clearly defined limitations[8] of the requirement for consent. Limitations are mentioned in Article 16 ('Change of purpose'). New consent would not be necessary if the new 'proposed use, decided by domestic law, corresponds to an important public interest reason and is consistent with the international law of human rights'. Even samples and data collected for purposes other than health care or research might be used for research without the consent of the donors if regulated by domestic law. This law 'may provide that if such data have significance for medical and scientific research purposes, e.g. epidemiological studies, or public health purposes, they may be used for those purposes' (UNESCO 2003, Art. 17) without consent after approval of an '[i]ndependent, multidisciplinary and pluralist ethics committee' (UNESCO 2003, Art. 6b). Furthermore, changing the purpose for which data and samples are used is allowed without consent if samples are irretrievably unlinked and if certain procedures are respected, for example, involvement of an ethics committee (UNESCO 2003, Art. 16b).

The UNESCO Declaration upholds a right to withdraw consent. In the case of withdrawal, the data and samples 'should no longer be used unless they are irretrievably unlinked to the person concerned'. The data and samples should be 'dealt with in accordance with the wishes of the person'. The range of acceptable or feasible wishes is not clear and seems to be open to various limitations, because the Declaration states further: 'If the person's wishes cannot be determined or are not feasible or are unsafe, the data and biological samples should either be irretrievably unlinked or destroyed' (UNESCO 2003, Art. 9).

---

8   Article 8 of the Declaration explains that limitations 'should only be prescribed for compelling reasons by domestic law consistent with the international law of human rights' (UNESCO 2003, Art. 8).

*Consent limited to a list of diseases or the same research domain*
Other intermediate strategies consist in using similar forms of a general or
'semi-blanket' consent, although the type of consent is declared as being closer
to informed consent. New research is authorized if it concerns the same overall
domain (CCNE 2003) or the same condition (Tri-Council 1998). Both statements
insist on the importance of new consent to future research (Tri-Council 1998, Art.
10.3, 10.4) and claim that the consent form they propose is close to the requirement
of new informed consent for each future research project. The French Committee
explains this strategy in a report from 1995. This report states: 'Should there be
an extension of research to a domain not foreseen at the time of sampling, consent
must again be obtained' (CCNE 1995, recommendation 3). Similarly, the Tri-
Council (1998)[9] has proposed that consent including future research about the
same condition is an adequate option.

*Multiple options (multi-layered consent)*
Bioethics commissions from North America adopt a different position. The
characteristic of this third intermediate strategy is that donors are given a great
amount of choice. This 'multi-layered consent' is proposed by the National
Bioethics Advisory Commission (NBAC 1999), the Canadian Tri-Council (1998),
the Network of Applied Genetic Medicine (RMGA 2000), and also the National
Institutes of Health (NIH), advocacy groups such as the National Action Plan
for Breast Cancer,[10] but also the WHO guide from 2000. The latter recommends
general ('unrestricted') consent, but finds it justified only if donors have two other
options: 'fully restricted' consent (to the present research project) and 'partially
restricted' consent (to research of a certain type). The consent form proposed
by the National Bioethics Advisory Commission (NBAC) offers donors the
possibility of choosing from a larger number of options than the WHO guide.
Donors can choose to give permission to have their samples and data used only
if both are unidentified or unlinked, to give permission to have their coded or
identified data and samples used only for the present study, or in addition also
for future studies that investigate the same condition as the present study for
which the sample was originally collected. Donors also have the choice of being
recontacted for other studies or not, and of permitting research for conditions other
than the one specified for the original research project. On a long list, donors can
exclude research areas for which their samples should not be used, for example,
research about genetic predisposition to psychiatric diseases. In contrast to most
North American guidelines, the National Bioethics Advisory Commission (NBAC
1999) includes – similar to the WHO guide (2000) – blanket consent among the
options that a donor is allowed to choose. One might ask whether blanket 'consent'

---

9   See the options mentioned before of consent to future 'use restricted to the condition'
(Art. 8.6, 8.7).
10   These documents are cited on page 66 of the National Bioethics Advisory
Commission guidelines (NBAC 1999).

becomes more acceptable if it is not offered as the only option, but as one among five others.[11] The guidelines contain a footnote stating that some commissioners disagreed with providing this sixth option.

Positions in the US have somewhat evolved over the years, as is witnessed by the recommendation from the NCI (C.2.2.7), which is not completely against tiered consent but also warns about its disadvantages for research:

> While a tiered system of consent will provide the human subject with greater specificity about future research, it also can lead to ambiguities in terms of how to classify certain types of inter- or multidisciplinary research. Tiered consent also may be inappropriate if the purpose of the biospecimen resource is to provide biospecimens to a very broad range of research, in which case providing human subjects with a list of potential types of research would be burdensome and uninformative. Tiered consent only should be used if a sophisticated system capable of tracking the levels of consent for each human subject is in place (NCI 2007).

The TC guidelines (Tri-Council 1998, Art. 8.6, 8.7) are in favour of multi-layered consent. They state that: '[s]uggested methods of handling secondary use of genetic material or research data include a comprehensive consent form, which allows the research subject to choose from a number of options [...], or a more limited consent form, which specifies arrangements to maintain contact with the subject regarding future uses. Either method must be clearly explained during the free and informed consent process.'

Similarly, the Network of Applied Genetic Medicine (RMGA 2000, 6) guidelines recommend that '[w]here applicable, the participant should be provided with options so that he can choose the type of test or examination (additional examinations, DNA sampling, banking of tissue or DNA and cellular transformation, etc.)'. The 'participant should also be able to choose whether or not to be recontacted in order to authorize the analysis of his DNA for other research than that specified in the original consent' (RMGA 2000, 8).

Most guidelines in favour of multi-layered consent are also in favour of a right to withdrawal. As already mentioned, the RMGA guidelines include a right to withdrawal from research projects and the right to destruction of samples. The guidelines of the Tri-Council state that the 'right to withdraw from a research study is a necessary component of the free and informed consent process'. The guidelines recommend that researchers discuss the options with the donor, that is, withdrawal either in the form of destruction of genetic material or research data, or in the form of removal of all identifiers (Tri-Council 1998, 8.6). The National Bioethics Advisory Commission (NBAC) document does discuss the right to

---

11   The National Bioethics Advisory Commission (1999) recommends that consent forms provide six options, the sixth being blanket consent for coded use of any kind of future study.

withdrawal for cases where donors have signed one of the options permitting relatively large uses of their samples.

*Waivers of consent*

The possibility of waivers is a fourth intermediate strategy. Within this strategy, new consent is a general requirement for each future study, but exceptions are permitted based on several criteria. The problematic aspect of waivers is that criteria are not always clearly defined, and even if they are defined in more detail, the application of the criteria is open to interpretation on a case by case basis. For example, if ethical review committees in Australia consider waiving the requirement to obtain consent, they will take into account several elements, among which are:

- the risks to the participant;
- the proposed measures of protection of privacy;
- the nature of previous consent: if future research is refused in the beginning (on the informed consent form of the original research), the possibility of a waiver is not given, because the sample must be destroyed;
- the justification of the waiver.[12]

Consent waivers are a possibility for circumventing strict consent requirements as is the case, for example, in the CIOMS guidelines for epidemiological studies (CIOMS 2009)[13] and in the guidelines of the American Society of Human Genetics (ASHG 1996). The latter guidelines are an example of a position strongly opposing blanket consent. However, they also contain the possibility of a waiver of consent. According to these guidelines, it 'is inappropriate to ask a subject to grant blanket consent for all future unspecified genetic research projects [...] if the samples are identifiable in those subsequent studies'. The guidelines encourage obtaining informed consent for all studies involving identified DNA samples, all prospective research involving identifiable DNA samples, as well as all retrospective studies on identifiable (coded) DNA samples, 'except if a Yes waiver is granted' (ASHG 1996, Table 1). The ASHG document does not explain any further under which conditions a waiver may be granted.

Waivers are also proposed as a strategy in the National Bioethics Advisory Commission (NBAC) guidelines. The criteria for waivers are already defined by current federal regulations in the United States. The requirement of informed consent can be waived if:

- the research involves no more than minimal risk to the subjects;
- the waiver or alteration of consent will not adversely affect the rights and welfare of the subjects;

---

12   See Australian Law Reform Commission (2003, Chapter 15). See also Deschênes et al. (2001, 224).

13   See in particular guideline 24 on the use of samples and data (CIOMS 2009).

- the research could not practicably be carried out without the waiver or alteration;
- whenever appropriate, the subjects will be provided with additional pertinent information after participation.[14]

The WHO guide (2000) and the COE (2006) guidelines permit waivers for samples obtained without consent for future research. In these cases researchers should try to obtain consent from the original donors or their proxies for future studies. 'Where this is not practicable, and the research is expected to produce important public health benefits, the researcher should request the research ethics committee to waive the informed consent requirement' (WHO 2000).

The criteria of consent waivers concerning tissue research have been enlarged more recently (OHRP 2004). For the National Bioethics Advisory Commission (NBAC), a waiver is not a sufficient reason not to obtain consent. If a waiver is granted, 'it is still appropriate to seek consent however, in order to show respect for the subject, unless it is impracticable to locate him or her in order to obtain it' (NBAC 1999, 66). As an 'additional measure of protection', the NBAC mentions that donors should have the option to withdraw (opt out) from a study that has been granted a waiver of informed consent (NBAC 1999, 70).

According to the ACMG statement on storage and use of genetic material (ACMG 1995), in order to decide whether a waiver is appropriate, one needs to link the requirement of informed consent for the use of coded samples to the questions how burdensome it would be to obtain consent and how high the risks of the research are. The greater the risk for donors, the greater should be the responsiblity that the researcher would need to accept for recontacting subjects for new consent (ACMG 1995; Wendler 2002).

*Implicit consent and the possibility of opting out*
The 'Statement on DNA sampling' of the Human Genome Organization (HUGO 1998)[15] proposes a fifth intermediate strategy. This is a form of 'opt out' or 'presumed consent'. The HUGO document states that: 'Research samples obtained with consent and stored may be used for other research if: there is general notification of such a policy, the participant has not objected, and the sample to be used by the researcher has been coded or anonymized.' According to the interpretation of Deschênes et al. (2001, 225), '[t]his procedure offers a theoretical right of refusal for the participant. It requires the creation of a mechanism by which the refusal of the participant could be registered and observed.' The HUGO statement proposes somewhat different opt-out procedures for 'routine samples, obtained during medical care and stored' and 'research samples obtained with consent and stored'.

---

14  See 45 CFR 46.116(d), cited in NBAC (1999, 66).

15  However, in appendix C of the NBAC guidelines (1999), the HUGO statement is interpreted as requiring new informed consent for every new research.

The common approach for both clinical and research samples is that they may be used for research if three conditions are fulfilled:

- there is general notification of such a policy;
- the patient/participant has not objected;
- the sample to be used has been irreversibly anonymized or coded.

The criteria for routine samples obtained during medical care and stored *before such notification* of this policy are stricter than the criteria mentioned. These samples may be used for research only if the sample has been *irreversibly anonymized* prior to use.

The policy described by this HUGO statement is similar to a form of presumed or implied blanket consent. The difference between this form of consent and other forms of general consent is that the HUGO guidelines state explicitly that written consent is only required for samples obtained originally for research, but not for samples obtained during clinical care. The guidelines justify this approach by granting to the patient the right to object before the sample is taken and also the right to refuse further use of coded samples at any time in the future through an opt-out process.

*Two-layered consent combined with general consent and waivers*
The Medical Research Council (MRC 2001) recommends another intermediate strategy. This strategy combines elements of general consent and a two-layered consent with the idea of waivers. The MRC states that it opposes blanket consent. Although it does not use the term 'general consent', it seems to accept some form of general consent because donors are permitted to consent to unforeseen research without having received detailed information at the time of consent. Whether new consent is required depends on the future research and its impact on the interests of donors and their families. These interests are not defined. According to the MRC, new consent is rarely absolutely required. It is obligatory for genetic research if future results are of clinical value and for research in areas of 'particular concern', such as behavioural genetics and genetic testing about sexual orientation or intelligence (MRC 2001, 6.4, 16). Future research without an impact on the donor's interests might be done if the donor has consented to future research in a more or less general form and if the research is approved by an ethics committee. The difference of this approach to the US American waiver strategy is that at least some general form of consent is obligatory and that the idea of 'minimal risk' is replaced by the concept of 'absence of an impact on the donors' interests'. Whether in practice both approaches differ depends on the criteria used to define these concepts.

The position of the Medical Research Council (MRC) unfolds in a multifaceted manner that is not completely without contradictions. Blanket consent, described as 'unconditional' consent to 'all biological or medical research', is explicitly opposed (MCR 2001, 15). Unless the sample is (irreversibly) anonymized, explicit and informed consent of the donor to the research project is necessary. Donors should 'understand what the sample is to be used for and how the results of the research might impact on their interests', and they should be informed whether the sample will be used for any form of genetic testing. The donor should have the possibility of providing a 'two part' consent (MRC 2001, 15), first to the original research and second to other future studies. If the sample is stored in a form that can be linked to the individual, the donor should be informed about the types of studies that may be done, the types of diseases that could be investigated, and the possible impact of the research on donors. The MRC is aware that future research is partly or totally 'unforeseen'. This contradicts the idea of providing detailed information at the beginning. In addition, the guidelines seem to allow that future research is carried out without the new specific consent of the donor, if the project is approved by an ethics committee and if the results will not have direct clinical implications for the donor.

Explicit consent is required for the use of medical information for research (MRC 2001, 13). Prior to consent, patients need to be informed about who will use the information and how, and about how confidentiality is assured. Furthermore, the MRC proposes variations of other intermediate strategies discussed above. It admits the use of samples without explicit consent of the donor (consent waiver) if the sample has been left over from clinical uses and if obtaining written consent is 'impossible', if the research 'will not affect the patient's or family's interests', and if patients have been notified of this practice (for example, by 'clearly displayed notices', MRC 2001, 11). This strategy is almost identical to some of the recommendations of the Human Genetic Organization (HUGO 1998). However, the MRC does not specify a procedure to opt out, as does the HUGO document (see above). The possibility of withdrawal is only mentioned in the example of a consent form (MRC 2001, 33) and does not apply to research carried out after having obtained a consent waiver. The consent form contains the wording: 'I agree […] that I am free to withdraw my approval for use of the sample at any time without giving a reason and without my medical treatment or legal rights being affected.'

Concerning anonymous and unlinked samples, the MRC proposes a stricter approach than most other guidelines. Anonymous samples cannot be used without consent for genetic research in the areas of particular concern mentioned above (MRC 2001, 6.4, 16). For other areas, research on samples left over from clinical practice is allowed if the samples are anonymous or unlinked. The MRC does not clearly state whether unlinked means that the process is irreversible or not.

*Family, community and population consent*
Another intermediate strategy consists of reinforcing the incomplete and (perhaps too) general individual consent by adding community consent.

The results obtained from studies involving genetic databases might not only have an impact on individuals, but also on their families. Moreover, anonymization will only prevent the identification of individuals who show different characteristics from the overall participating population. Anonymization of individuals will not grant anonymity of groups. Indeed, the results of the research will show typical characteristics of the genetic 'make-up' of the population or group that has been investigated. The results will therefore reveal relevant information about all participants and even about members of the same population who did not participate in the study. This implies a risk of discrimination and stigmatization of the entire population, a risk that cannot be prevented by anonymization, only by keeping results secret, by publishing only parts of it, or by publishing them in a form that does not permit the identification of the involved population or community. The latter is probably difficult to achieve, if the names of the authors are revealed, because it cannot be kept secret on which research projects the authors have worked. Furthermore, in the name of transparency and accountability, it is ethically and medically not desirable to encourage this type of secrecy in health research.

In light of the aforementioned risks to families and groups, a number of guidelines recommend obtaining not only the consent of the participating individuals, but also the consent of all those who share the risks, or at least consulting the groups or populations involved. In most ethical and legal frameworks, family consent is not a requirement.[16] Article 8.1 of the Tri-Council guidelines addresses the question whether in genetic research the requirement for free and informed consent needs to be extended. '[G]enetic research involves the family and/or the community [...].' Therefore, 'free and informed consent shall also involve those social structures, as far as is practical and possible [...] When the wishes of the family or a group are in conflict, enhancing communication is preferable to compelling either the group or the individual to overcome their reluctance' (Tri-Council 1998, 8.1). The idea of community consultation is not limited to genetic research or research involving genetic databases.[17] The Tri-Council guidelines discuss the requirement for community consultation when they address research involving aboriginal people (Tri-Council 1998, 6.2). They recognize the necessity to determine 'when it is legitimate for researchers to interview individuals in their own right as individuals, without regard to the interests of the group as a whole and without seeking permission from any group authority or spokesperson or, conversely, when the approval of the community as a whole should be required'.

The CIOMS guidelines state that when epidemiological, genetic or sociological studies imply risks to groups, 'often it will be advisable to have individual consent

---

16    One rare example is the Swedish Medical Research Council (Anonymous 1999; Swedish Medical Research Council 1999; Eriksson 2004).

17    It has long been recognized that it is fruitful for research to have patient communities or groups participate in the research design, especially if groups of patients are at risk of stigmatization, as in the case of HIV or hereditary breast cancer. Evans (1994, 1086) describes the valuable involvement in research decision making of patient groups suffering from breast cancer: 'exclusion of patients from research decision-making will rapidly become the exception' (Evans 1994).

supplemented by community consultation' (CIOMS 2002, commentary on guideline 8; see also CIOMS 2009, 37–9).

In the United States, community consultation has been recognized as beneficial for research projects, but no formalized procedures have been elaborated. Community consultation is required in the United States by two sets of federal regulations (NBAC 1999, 8). Firstly, research carried out in emergency circumstances should be preceded by a consultation process which involves representatives of the communities in which the research will take place and from which the subjects will be selected. In addition, prior to enrolling subjects, the nature of the research, risks and benefits needs to be disclosed to the public, as well as results once the study is completed. Moreover, investigators are under an obligation to disclose to the involved community the research plans, as well as the risks and expected benefits, prior to initiation of the research. Secondly, a policy of the Indian Health Service requires researchers to obtain approval from the tribal government before carrying out research projects in American Indian communities.

In Canada, the Network of Applied Genetic Medicine (RMGA) Statement of Principles on the Ethical Conduct of Human Genetic Research Involving Populations recommends 'prior and ongoing public consultation' for genetic research with populations. Research involving a given population should be 'based upon open dialogue between the population and the research team', in order to respect 'the principles of reciprocity and accountability' (RMGA 2003, 2).

Concerning genetic databases, a form of community consultation is proposed by the Canadian guidelines (CEST 2003). Recommendation 15 states that a process of consultation of the public is necessary in order to enable the population of Quebec to pronounce a democratic decision.[18] Similarly, the French CCNE proposes a large consultation among the French population before starting to build up a national genetic database project (CCNE 2003, 6). Likewise, the Explanatory Report (CDBI 2002b) to the Council of Europe's recommendation (COE 2006) refers to community consultation: 'When appropriate, the researchers should consult with the potentially affected groups in regard to the design of the research and its foreseen publication' (CDBI 2002b, 8). The 'competent body' (ethics committee) should 'alert researchers to such potential problems in their research projects' (CDBI 2002b, 8).

The UNESCO Declaration on Human Genetic Data recommends the involvement of 'society at large':

> States should endeavour to involve society at large in the decision-making process concerning broad policies for the collection, processing, use and storage of human genetic data […], in particular in the case of population-based genetic studies. This decision-making process, which may benefit from international experience, should ensure the free expression of various viewpoints (UNESCO 2003, 5).

---

18  '[Q]ue la population québécoise puisse se prononcer démocratiquement sur la mise en place de banques populationnelles d'information génétique' (CEST 2003, xix).

The HUGO statement on the principled conduct of genetics research (HUGO 1995) does not only recommend consultation of the community, but introduces the notion of family or community *consent*:

> [I]nformed decisions to *consent* to participate can be individual, familial, or at the level of communities and populations. An understanding of the nature of the research, the risks and benefits, and any alternatives is crucial. Such consent should be free from coercion by scientific, medical, or other authorities. Under certain conditions and with proper authority, anonymous testing for epidemiological purposes and surveillance could be an exception to consent requirements (HUGO 1995).

Similarly, the guidelines of the North American Regional Committee (NARC 1997) specify the necessity not only of consultation, but of group *consent*, that should supplement individual consent:

> In addition to individual informed consent, the North American Regional Committee believes that a further consent process is required. The Project intends to study populations, not individuals. As a result, we believe that the populations, as well as the individuals, must give their free consent to participate (NARC 1997, A.2).

Conversely, the guidelines of the German Nationaler Ethikrat oppose the idea of group consultation or consent, although the German Council admits that risks to groups of patients exist. The opposition to group consultation or consent seems to be based partly on the argument that the particular problems related to aboriginal populations do not exist in Germany. Apparently the Council agrees that certain kinds of (indigent or aboriginal) groups might need to be consulted.[19]

*Discussion: Ways Out of the Consent Dilemma?*

The debate about consent concerning genetic databases unfolds in two directions. Firstly, it is claimed that classical informed consent at the outset of a project is not enough and should be supplemented by family or community consent; and secondly, it is claimed that the standard of informed consent should be decreased to allow for a more general consent to future projects.

---

19　See Nationaler Ethikrat (2004, 9): '24. Genetische Analyzen an Spenderproben können zu Aussagen über die genetischen Besonderheiten und Risiken von Patienten führen, die an einer bestimmten Krankheit leiden, oder von ethnischen Gruppen, in denen solche Krankheiten gehäuft auftreten. Die Betroffenheit dieser Gruppen kann nicht dazu führen, dass zusätzlich zur Einwilligung der Spender eine Gruppeneinwilligung erforderlich ist. Die besonderen Probleme im Zusammenhang mit der Forschung an indigenen Populationen (sog. Ureinwohnern) stellen sich für Deutschland nicht.'

*Increased requirements of consent: supplementing individual informed consent*
It is important to note that the idea of community consent is not restricted to genetic research. Thus, the claim of the Consortium on Pharmacogenetics that group participation in the informed consent process is not justified in pharmacogenetics, because this would be an example of genetic exceptionalism (Consortium on Pharmacogenetics et al. 2002, 14), cannot be supported. Indeed, the involvement of communities through some form of consultation has been discussed, independently from research involving genetic databases, especially for all research that implies risks to a community, or for research for which individual consent is difficult to obtain, for example, research in emergency circumstances, but also for all types of research involving aboriginal communities (Tri-Council 1998, chapter 6) or the HIV community (Weijer and Miller 2004, 14).

A growing number of research ethics guidelines seem to support a new requirement, especially in the context of population studies involving genetic testing: the idea of community 'consent' instead of consultation. This evolution demonstrates the perception that consultation is not enough and that the classical framework based on individual consent needs to evolve.

Among the reasons in favour of a formal requirement of community consent to research protocols is the idea that populations are an identity that can be 'attacked'. Populations are understood to have the right to 'autonomy' (NARC 1997, IV.A.2) which should be respected. The underlying assumption is that a community is more than the sum of individual interests, because the community has 'separable interests' (Weijer and Miller 2004). This leaves the question of which type of interest, those of the community or those of the individuals, should be overriding. Some have argued that when the Navajo nation decided not to participate in a particular research project and to forbid participation of their members, the Navajo nation leaders violated the rights of those Navajos who would have preferred to participate. Similarly, the Consortium on Pharmacogenetics opposes group consent that 'trumps the individual's right to participate' (Consortium on Pharmacogenetics et al. 2002, 15). However, it has to be noted that the foundation of the argumentation supporting the Navajo nation's standpoint is that the risks of the research will automatically be shared by the whole population. This fact is demonstrated by the recent discussion in the United States concerning Ashkenazi Jews. According to recent cancer genetics, the prevalence of genetic mutations predisposing to breast, ovarian and colon cancers is high among Ashkenazi Jews. Jewish leaders have called for protections against discrimination, because 'anyone with a Jewish-sounding name could face discrimination in insurance and employment as companies struggle to keep down health-care costs' (Lehrman 1997).[20] In the case of shared risks, it seems appropriate to adopt a rather risk-averse position among all the controversial opinions that exist among members of the population as regards the adequate risk–benefit ratio, even if this could limit the chances of obtaining benefits. The reason for choosing the rather

---

20   This position has been supported by other publications (Struewing et al. 1995; Laken et al. 1997; Weijer, Goldsand and Emanuel 1999).

risk-averse position is that negative rights, such as the right not to participate, have always been given precedence over positive rights, unless an immediate or at least clearly foreseeable danger could be prevented by taking active steps, and if these steps would only impose a reasonable burden (somewhat increased risk) on others.[21] Different ways to justify the decision of the Navajo nation exist: first, it has been argued that members of certain communities do not view themselves as atomistic entities. Second, communities curtail the autonomy of its members in other fields. Communities obligate members to pay taxes or decide which school their children must attend. The basis for the limitation of individual autonomy is that the authority of the community is legitimate. The extent of the curtailment is culturally shaped. In a democratic European state that has signed the Universal Declaration of Human Rights, the curtailment of individual autonomy is limited by the respect for human rights and individual freedoms, the interpretation of which might be open to some variation. As we have already seen, in research ethics it is not conceivable to curtail the individual right to refuse participation in research. Similarly, if participation in a study promises direct health benefits to an individual, the position of the Navajo nation is also difficult to defend. However, in population studies without any benefit to the individual, the risks to the community could outweigh the autonomy rights of individual members to participate in the research study.

Another reason mentioned in favour of the supplementation of individual informed consent by group consent is the perception that individual informed consent does not sufficiently protect vulnerable groups. According to Fortun (2003, 3), if all donors provide informed consent for each new research project, this means that each individual decides in an isolated way. He regrets that '[n]o one has even *imagined*' reflecting on 'a mechanism for ongoing, collective education; a mechanism for deliberation; a mechanism for decision making'. According to Fortun, the ethical idea of informed consent and protection of privacy, 'in part through its grounding in the liberal ideal of autonomy', leads to and maintains atomization. A similar debate about the limits of individual informed consent has taken place between Sigurdsson and Kari Stefansson, founder of deCode Genetics. The latter claimed that decisions concerning the ethical framework of genetic databases should not be made by ethicists but left to the individual citizen who makes 'intelligent choices'. Against Stefansson, Sigurdsson defends the opinion that individual informed consent is not a sufficient protection against risks and exploitation. The 'atomized societal vision' that follows from the individual informed consent doctrine 'takes advantage of vulnerable populations, such as the elderly in Iceland. They go to their physicians, many of whom are collaborating with deCode at the local level, and sign informed consent forms. What would an intelligent choice be in their case?'[22]

---

21   This is in accordance with the argumentation of Article 128 of the Swiss criminal law ('omission de prêter secours').

22   See Sigurdsson (2003, 9). See also Merz et al.: 'informed consent cannot reasonably be relied upon to fix ethical problems in research. Informed consent is but the last and quite

The concept of community consent, as opposed to community consultation, is problematic in several respects. It is not always easy to determine the relevant population. In order to use community consent, the community 'must have a legitimate political or cultural authority that is empowered to speak authoritatively for, and make binding decisions on behalf of the community', that is, 'more than mere representation' is required (Weijer and Emanuel 2000, 1142–4). In a democratic society, procedures have been defined how to ensure the participation of the public in the decision-making process. These procedures are used to make many other important decisions that might eventually result in limitations for or risks to the members of the community. They are used, for example, to define what counts as acceptable risk when thresholds are established concerning the security of roads or the use of nuclear energy, or the detention of potentially dangerous psychiatric patients or criminals. There seems to be no reason why other procedures should be used when defining acceptable risks related to the health care system and the research that is part of this system. The important point is that community consent can never be a substitute for individual consent. However, community refusal should be allowed to override individual consent. This 'paternalistic' approach is not fundamentally different from the classical paternalism in health research ethics which permits ethics committees to override individual consent in the case of research judged too dangerous. Research ethics committees are often supposed to represent the ethical 'conscience' of society, and in general at least one of their members should be a non-medical representative of the community.

Using community consultation before initiating a research project is advisable, not only because it respects the rights of communities, but also because the research will benefit from the fact that the community is involved (Weldon 2004). The question that needs to be asked is: which are the criteria that mandate formal community consent instead of consultation? One argument against formal community consent that has been defended by researchers is that procedures are cumbersome and time-consuming and might unduly hamper research or make it more costly. Until now, even epidemiological studies that have involved the entire population of a Swiss canton have been approved by ethics committees and not by the cantonal parliament. On the other hand, the biobanks created in Iceland, Estonia and the planned UK Biobank have been debated in parliament, and Iceland and Estonia have voted laws specific to the particular biobank projects, while the UK has established a broader law, the Human Tissue Act. Policies should acknowledge the heterogeneity of communities and the heterogeneity of research or genetic database projects.

No compelling reason exists why research involving genetic databases should be treated differently from other types of research. The mechanism that should be used to decide whether a research project or a biobank project requires community consent or consultation should be the same and should be based on the following questions:

---

imperfect check on researcher [sic] – and in this case, State – authority and power' (Merz, McGee and Sankar 2004b, 1213).

- Is a community identifiable? Studies that include race, ethnicity or country as variables in order to analyse the explanatory power of these variables with respect to the study questions do not examine separate communities, but could still generate stigmatizing results. If these studies include a representative sample from identifiable communities and have an impact for this group, community consultation and consent should be considered.
- Does the research affect the interests of the community, that is, do risks to the community exist? The community's appreciation of the meaning and importance of risks might differ from that of researchers.
- Does the community have a political authority or other legitimate structures to make decisions on behalf of the community members (procedures for decisions concerning research or structures that are already in place for areas other than research)?

The degree to which consent or consultation is formalized will depend on these three factors. For high-risk research in communities with strongly legitimate political authorities, it is recommended to use both community consent and community consultation simultaneously. For research associated with medium or low risk, one or both might be sufficient. If the research concerns a community without legitimate representatives, consultation should involve a statistically representative sample of the members in order to evaluate the lower borders of acceptable risks.

*Decreased requirements of consent: How can lower standards than classical informed consent be defended and which consent form is the most adequate?*
A common characteristic of the debate about consent to research involving genetic databases is the discussion and defence of particular consent forms such as blanket consent, general consent or presumed consent. These consent forms accept lower consent standards than informed consent. One has to have convincing arguments in order to justify lower standards because informed consent is considered one of the cornerstones of classical research health ethics.

*Consent in classical health research ethics: The interests at stake*
In all types of research, a conflict exists between, on one side, researchers' and societies' interests in simplifying procedures in order to obtain maximal benefit and to minimize costs ('efficiency–benefit interest') and, on the other side, participants' and societies' interest in maximizing the self-determination of participants and protecting them against possible harms ('autonomy–harm-reduction interest'). The requirement of explicit informed consent has never been absolute in classical research ethics, although the CIOMS guidelines consider waivers of informed consent exceptional: 'Waiver of informed consent is to be regarded as uncommon and exceptional, and must in all cases be approved by an ethical review committee.'[23] The balancing between the efficiency–benefit interest and

---

23 See CIOMS (2002, guideline 4).

the autonomy–harm-reduction interest in classical research has mainly considered the harm-reduction* component and the efficiency–benefit component. The criteria to allow for a waiver were 'minimal risk' and 'individual informed consent would make the conduct of the research impracticable (for example, where the research involves only excerpting data from subjects' records)'.[24] The prerequisite for a waiver is the approval of an ethical review committee. In this form of balancing, no reference is made to autonomy or self-determination rights of patients who might be wronged although they are not harmed, or who might feel harmed in a form that the majority of society would not consider to be harmful. An example would be a retrospective study of records about sexual behaviour or any study in the area of abortion. Having their samples and data participate in such a study could be considered a sin by religious individuals who would, according to their religious views, be harmed because of this sin.

Article 321bis of the Swiss criminal law[25] contains a balancing between the 'legitimate interests of individuals' and the 'interests of research' (Art. 321bis alinea 2

---

24   See CIOMS (2002, guideline 4): 'Waiver of informed consent is to be regarded as uncommon and exceptional, and must in all cases be approved by an ethical review committee.' See also CIOMS (2002, commentary on guideline 4): '*Waiver of the consent requirement.* Investigators should never initiate research involving human subjects without obtaining each subject's informed consent, unless they have received explicit approval to do so from an ethical review committee. However, when the research design involves no more than minimal risk and a requirement of individual informed consent would make the conduct of the research impracticable (for example, where the research involves only excerpting data from subjects' records), the ethical review committee may waive some or all of the elements of informed consent. *Renewing consent.* When material changes occur in the conditions or the procedures of a study, and also periodically in long-term studies, the investigator should once again seek informed consent from the subjects. For example, new information may have come to light, either from the study or from other sources, about the risks or benefits of products being tested or about alternatives to them. Subjects should be given such information promptly. In many clinical trials, results are not disclosed to subjects and investigators until the study is concluded. This is ethically acceptable if an ethical review committee has approved their non-disclosure. *Cultural considerations.* In some cultures an investigator may enter a community to conduct research or approach prospective subjects for their individual consent only after obtaining permission from a community leader, a council of elders, or another designated authority. Such customs must be respected. In no case, however, may the permission of a community leader or other authority substitute for individual informed consent.'

25   Art. 321bis* (Etat le 1 Avril 2009): 'Secret professionnel en matière de recherche médicale. 1 Celui qui, sans droit, aura révélé un secret professionnel dont il a eu connaissance dans le cadre de son activité pour la recherche dans les domaines de la médecine ou de la santé publique sera puni en vertu de l'art. 321. 2 Un secret professionnel peut être levé à des fins de recherche dans les domaines de la médecine ou de la santé publique si une commission d'experts en donne l'autorisation et si l'intéressé, après avoir été informé de ses droits, n'a pas expressément refusé son consentement. 3 La commission octroie l'autorisation dans les cas où: a. La recherche ne peut être effectuée avec des données

to 5). The legitimate interests of individuals include autonomy and self-determination interests, such as, for example, the interests to maintain confidentiality and to give explicit consent. According to this article, a commission of experts is allowed to grant researchers access to patient data without the explicit consent of the patient, but only a form of presumed consent. If patients have been informed about their rights and have not explicitly expressed their refusal, the use of their data will be authorized by the commission if particular criteria are fulfilled. These criteria refer in the first place to the efficiency–benefit interest: the research cannot be carried out using anonymous data, it is impossible or particularly difficult to obtain consent, and the interests of the research outweigh the interest to maintain confidentiality. Autonomy and harm-reduction interests are indirectly considered when referring to the 'legitimate interests' of the individual concerned and the interest to maintain confidentiality. Article 321bis refers to data, but one might ask whether it could in the future be extended to include access to tissue, if tissue is understood to contain information protected by confidentiality laws. It is difficult to predict whether the commission would consider a possible project such as a 'Swiss health database', similar to the Icelandic health database, a case in which it is particularly difficult to obtain the consent of the individuals concerned (Art. 321 3b) and in which the interests of research outweigh those of maintaining complete confidentiality (Art. 321 3c). In projects that plan – similar to the Icelandic Health Sector Database, the UK Biobank and the Swiss Pediatric Oncology Group Tumor Bank – to add future health data to the database, the research cannot be carried out with irreversibly anonymized data, but only with reversibly anonymized or coded data (Art. 321 3a). The international reaction to the Icelandic Health Sector Database has shown that the use of coded data without explicit patient consent is considered to be not in line with European data protection laws and international ethics: the World Medical Association declaration on ethical considerations regarding health databases (WMA 2002) and other guidelines (MRC 2001) agree that explicit consent is necessary before including information from health records in genetic databases.

*Consent for research involving genetic databases: Areas of consensus*
Consensus exists that donors need to consent to blood taking or to the surgical act, that is, the violation of their bodily integrity, when providing tissue for clinical or

anonymes; b. Il est impossible ou particulièrement difficile d'obtenir le consentement de l'intéressé; c. Les intérêts de la recherche priment l'intérêt au maintien du secret. 4 La commission grève l'autorisation de charges afin de garantir la protection des données. Elle publie l'autorisation. 5 La commission peut octroyer des autorisations générales ou prévoir d'autres simplifications si les intérêts légitimes des intéressés ne sont pas compromis et si les données personnelles sont rendues anonymes dès le début des recherches. 6 La commission agit sans instructions. 7 Le Conseil fédéral nomme le président et les membres de la commission. Il en règle l'organisation et la procédure.'

'* Introduit par le ch. 4 de l'annexe à la LF du 19 juin 1992 sur la protection des données, en vigueur depuis le 1er juillet 1993 (RS 235.1).'

research purposes. International consensus also exists that explicit consent from patients is obligatory before transferring information contained in health records to databanks in which individuals are identifiable through a code, such as the Icelandic Health Sector Database.

The type of consent judged adequate depends on the primary purpose of the tissue collection. Consensus exists that the donor has to give informed consent to the original research project, if the primary use of the tissue is research. For example, future mothers should give explicit written consent to the use of the placenta for research. If tissue is taken during clinical practice, in most countries consent is limited to the clinical purpose, although it is known that tissue will be stored in repositories, most often institutes of pathology. Although the primary reason for storage is clinical (the possibility of confirming or refining diagnosis, comparison with later samples, and so on), it is widely known that these repositories are treasures for future research on samples for which the clinical course of the disease is known. Some guidelines recommend that such secondary uses for research should be communicated by general notification and patients should have the possibility of opting out (HUGO 1998). Other guidelines recommend a two-part consent, separating consent to clinical and possible future research uses (MRC 2001).

The type of consent required depends on the degree of anonymization of the samples and data. Most guidelines make a difference between consent for identifiable samples/data and those that are unlinked anonymized. A wide, but not entire, consensus exists that the latter can be used without the consent of the donor, since the use of irreversibly anonymized tissue does, principally, not entail any risk for the donor. Informed consent for the use of unlinked anonymized samples and information, and complete control of the uses, is under discussion, but in general not recommended.[26]

Conversely, the use of identifiable samples or information requires at least some form of consent. This could be classical informed consent according to international standards. Classical research ethics documents, such as the Declaration of Helsinki and the CIOMS guidelines, assimilate research using identifiable samples with human subject research. However, a change towards less

---

26   It is not recommended in most guidelines. However, in the literature the position is defended. Deschênes et al. (2001) announce that future research using unlinked anonymized samples is an area of dissent among the authors of that article. Sade explains that research subjects might have valuable reasons not to want an (irreversibly) anonymized sample to be used in a research project believed to be important: 'For example, personal information systems have been used by governments in the past to identify and locate a target race or ethnic group, both in Germany to identify Jews and others in the 1930s and in the United States to identify and detain Japanese Americans [...] Today, one could imagine an Arab American declining to allow personal biological samples or genetic information, stripped of personal identifiers but perhaps still containing racial or ethnic information, to be used for research designed to develop identifiers of Arab Americans in a genetic database' (Sade 2002, 1440).

strict consent standards has been observed in the 2008 revision of the Declaration of Helsinki (WMA 2008). In Article 25, consent waivers are permitted for research involving samples and data 'in situations where consent would be impossible or impractical to obtain for such research or would pose a threat to the validity of the research. In such situations the research may be done only after consideration and approval of a research ethics committee' (WMA 2008, Art. 25). European data protection laws require that (with some exceptions) any identifiable information, that is, personal data, can only be collected and used with the 'unambiguous' consent of the individual whose information is processed.[27]

*Consent for research involving genetic databases: Areas of disagreement*
The consent problem is complex. Controversy arises because of the definition problems of what constitutes anonymous or anonymized samples, because the type of consent that is considered adequate depends on the degree of anonymization. Three main issues need to be clarified in this respect.

First, a principal problem of DNA is that it is never completely anonymous, but permits the identification of the individual or family ties. In theory, no sample containing DNA could be treated as entirely anonymous unless it is ancient and no comparative DNA is available from living relatives.

Second, any information stored without or together with samples differs in the degree of identification even if names and addresses are stripped. The degree of identification depends on the size of the community sampled and the frequency of different types of information. The smaller the community and the less frequent some types of information are – for example, a patient suffers from a rare disease or has an unusual or unique profession – the greater is the risk of identification.

Third, a number of guidelines differentiate between irreversibly and reversibly anonymized samples and information (UNESCO 2003; COE 2006). They state that the existence of a reversible code makes information and samples identifiable and puts donors at greater risk than if anonymization were irreversible. Others (OHRP 2004; MRC 2001; HGC 2002) hold that coded samples should be treated as if they were anonymous, if those using the coded information and samples do

---

27　See European Parliament and the Council (1995), Directive 95/46/EC. 'Article 7: Member States shall provide that personal data may be processed only if: (a) the data subject has unambiguously given his consent, or (b) processing is necessary for the performance of a contract to which the data subject is party or in order to take steps at the request of the data subject prior to entering into a contract, or (c) processing is necessary for compliance with a legal obligation to which the controller is subject, or (d) processing is necessary in order to protect the vital interests of the data subject, or (e) processing is necessary for the performance of a task carried out in the public interest or in the exercise of official authority vested in the controller or in a third party to whom the data are disclosed, or (f) processing is necessary for the purposes of the legitimate interests pursued by the controller or by the third party or parties to whom the data are disclosed, except where such interests are overridden by the interests or fundamental rights and freedoms of the data subject which require protection under Article 1(1).'

not have the possibility of accessing the code. A number of guidelines use the term 'anonymized' without always making clear whether anonymization is considered irreversible or not (MRC 2001; HGC 2002). Thus, it is not clear how the guidelines' recommendations about the adequate type of consent should be interpreted (see the section below: 'Confidentiality, Access to Data and Assessment of Risks'). We will discuss the problems related to the definitions of anonymization in more detail in the section on confidentiality.

In this section, we focus on the most important area in which no consensus exists: the question of donors' consent to future research done using their samples and information.

*Ethically acceptable balancing of interests concerning consent to future research projects involving DNA banks*
Blanket consent and new informed consent for each future project are extreme forms of balancing the involved interests. The WHO guidelines (1998) explicitly mention the efficiency–benefit interest as a main argument for adopting blanket consent. In his article commissioned by the US National Bioethics Advisory Commission, Korn describes the magnitude of the efficiency–benefit interest in respect to future research projects (Korn 1999). In the 1970s and early 1980s, the National Cancer Institute sponsored clinical trials in the field of lung cancer. These trials provided evidence that the then available diagnostic procedures could detect some presymptomatic earlier stage cancers, but were not sufficiently sensitive to lower overall lung cancer mortality. Meanwhile, cancer biology has progressed and increased knowledge is available about specific changes in gene structure and patterns of gene expression during the progression of different populations of normal cells to neoplasia (Korn 1999, E7). Not only have genetic changes been identified, but in addition, by using monoclonal antibodies, it is possible to demonstrate altered patterns of gene expression in neoplastic cell populations (Korn 1999, E8). Human lung cancer has been shown to express such a presumptive 'cancer neoantigen'. This antigen is found in sputum cytological samples at least two years prior to clinical diagnosis.

> To try to initiate prospective studies de novo for each new promising candidate marker for each of the varieties of human neoplasia would not only be extraordinarily costly in dollars and human effort, but would also require study periods of many years, or even decades, before definitive endpoints could be reached. In contrast, being able to apply such new technologies to archival materials, where clinical course, therapeutic response, and outcome are already known, represents an incredible collapse of the time and money, to say nothing of the human suffering, required to evaluate the technologies […] (Korn 1999, E8).[28]

---

28   Others have confirmed the usefulness of studies involving archived tissue and have discussed the ethical problems related to the lack of adequate consent (Struewing et al. 1995; Garvin et al. 1996 and 1997; Vlastos et al. 2009).

It is important to note that those who defend blanket consent admit that they value highly efficiency–benefit interests. Interestingly, they also state that they do not believe that efficiency–benefit interests outweigh the self-determination and harm-reduction interests of donors. Instead, they think that blanket consent grants simultaneously the 'most efficient and economical approach, avoiding costly recontact before each new research project' (WHO 1998, 13) *and* respect for donors' rights because it still counts as consent: the donor has the right to refuse overall participation at the outset. Controversy unfolds about the question whether blanket consent should be considered *valid* consent. At least the description 'informed' consent in the classical sense in which it is used in research ethics is not justified because when blanket consent is given, the information about the nature, risks and benefits of future projects is not available. The donor is not in a position to evaluate their personal harm–benefit ratio and make an autonomous decision about participation in the research. For this reason, Buchanan proposes that blanket consent and informed consent should not be confounded: '[B]lanket consent [...] should not be expected to perform the functions of informed consent. In most cases [...] key features of informed consent, including disclosure and comprehension of relevant risks and benefits, will not be present' (Buchanan 1999, B29).

Others consider that an 'open-ended consent' such as blanket consent is a 'breach of the participants' personal autonomy' (Deschênes et al. 2001, 223f). The door is open for a 'disrespect of the personal values of the participants', and for future harm of a different nature, including the fact that 'the sample is used in a way that is contrary to the values of the participant' (Deschênes et al. 2001, 223f). Certainly one has to conclude that, although blanket consent does not completely 'disrespect' autonomy–harm interests, it sacrifices a great deal of these interests in favour of efficiency–benefit interests.

In contrast, new consent for each new research project represents a balancing in the opposite sense. The self-determination of donors is granted at the expense of efficiency–benefit interests. Indeed, recontacting donors for new consent is costly and response rates will never be 100 per cent, even under ideal conditions. A loss of donor material and information will inevitably be the result.

In the classical framework of research ethics, new informed consent is judged to be the best way to reduce harms. The underlying assumption is that competent persons are best situated to protect their own well-being (Brock 1987). This assumption may be based on two different arguments. First, individual harms vary from one person to another. A pianist will be particularly concerned about risks to his/her ability to play the piano. The risk of genetic discrimination varies significantly between individuals. The magnitude of the risk can only be exactly judged by individuals, because they are the only ones who have access to the most complete information. The second argument is that, apart from knowing the individual situation best, the donor is the only person to evaluate the benefits and harms, because this evaluation is subjective. In the clinical context, when physicians provide information about the risks and benefits of surgical procedures or other treatments to patients, most of them use the reasonable person standard. It could be justified to use a higher standard in research, that is, the subjective person standard instead of the reasonable person standard. The justification would be that research subjects are not supposed to benefit from the research. They should be able to judge, according to their own subjective standard, whether they want to participate in the research project or not.

In conclusion, obtaining new consent for each future research project maximizes the autonomy–harm-reduction interests of donors, while it sacrifices efficiency–benefit interests. An example is the NHANES III research project. Beginning in the 1980s, scientists from the Center for Disease Control and Prevention (CDC) had, by about 10 years later, collected almost 20,000 blood samples stored in liquid nitrogen and immortalized cell lines from approximately 8,500 people. When the study was originally planned, a complicated consent statement had been proposed. This was later abandoned in favour of a simple, less technical statement. The final statement provided only very limited information to participants, including the fact that a small sample of their blood was to be kept in long-term storage. The purpose of the storage was described vaguely as 'for future testing'. Since such blanket consent was later judged to be insufficient for research involving genetic testing, obtaining more specific consent seemed to be the only acceptable solution. However, this new consent has not been finally realized because the costs were estimated to amount to two million dollars and the risk of decreasing the value of the immense collection of nationally representative DNA samples was judged too high.[29]

When looking for a solution, one should try to find out, in the first place, whether it is possible to avoid the conflict between efficiency–benefit interests and autonomy–harm-reduction interests. If the conflict cannot be avoided, it might be possible to reduce it, for example, by choosing a solution in which autonomy and harm-reduction interests are maximized, while losses for efficiency and benefit remain minimal.

The conflict would be reduced if the following conditions could be met in order to maximize *autonomy* interests:

- Donors are granted the possibility of staying informed about future research if they so desire.
- Donors are free to decide whether they want to be informed or not about details of future research.
- Donors maintain the option to withdraw or to opt out of further research (Gertz 2008).
- Donors are able to control whether they are informed about any individual results.

The conflict would also be reduced if the following conditions could be met in order to maximize *harm-reduction interests*:

---

29   See Weir (1998 and 1999, F4); Weir, Olick and Murray (2004); Eiseman and Haga (1999); and Eiseman (2003 and 1999, D22–D23).

- It is ensured that donors' participation in a genetic databank does not entail any risk.
- Donors are granted the possibility of withdrawing from any future research project that is associated with risks.

The conflict would also be reduced if the following condition could be met in order to maximize *efficiency–benefit* interests:

- · The measures listed above to maximize the autonomy and harm-reduction interests will only minimally increase the costs of research and will only minimally interfere with the interpretation of the results.

Attempts should always be made to reduce the conflict between the interests in an ethically defensible way that maximizes both efficiency–benefit interests and autonomy–harm-reduction interests, and models have been described previously which fulfil the conditions explained above (Elger and Mauron 2003).

*Maximizing efficiency–benefit interests: In search of technical solutions*
Technical solutions could help to reduce the conflict between autonomy–harm-reduction interests and efficiency–benefit interests. Research in information technology (IT) should be encouraged in order to find measures to secure autonomy and harm-reduction interests with only minimal increase in the costs of research and only minimal interference with the interpretation of the results. This could be reached through secure one-way coding procedures which maximize anonymity and IT systems which guarantee that the links are maintained for opt-out of participants. Further research should evaluate the costs of different forms and mechanisms for opt-out procedures and for generating accessible and ongoing information about donors who want to know details about future research projects once the projects have been developed. Providing the possibility for donors to opt out of specific projects would limit less the general value of the biobank, and might be technically feasible without the often claimed elevated costs (Eriksson and Helgesson 2005) when computer systems are used. Making the IT systems of different national and international biobanks compatible could facilitate technical solutions. The aim should be to standardize information and opt-out procedures, not only in Switzerland, but in Europe, or even worldwide.

## Confidentiality, Access to Data and Assessment of Risks

*The Importance of Confidentiality*

Without exception, guidelines mention that the 'secondary' principles of confidentiality and/or privacy should be respected (see Chapter 3). Confidentiality is in general judged to be important for three reasons. First, from the principle of respect for persons follows the right of the individual that information about him or her is kept confidential and only divulged to others with his or her consent.[30] Second, it is in the interest of public health that confidentiality is granted to ensure that patients do not lose trust, but consult their physicians in order to be treated for their disease.[31] This argument is consequentialist. If patients feared negative consequences due to a lack of confidentiality, they might not consult and diseases might be untreated and spread to the community. A third argument is also consequentialist and is not only important for the clinical context, but also especially important for research. If patients feared that information might be released to third parties without their consent, either they might not tell their physicians the truth, or physicians might feel pressured to keep double records. According to Korn (2000, 968), surveys in the United States indicate that as many as 15 to 20 per cent of adult patients have paid for medical treatment themselves in order to prevent their medical information being transmitted to their insurance, or have withheld 'sensitive' information from their caregivers (Korn 2000). In a letter to *The Lancet*,[32] Q.B. Deming expresses his opinion that the physician who creates the medical record is the only person to efficiently protect the patient from damage; 'nothing should be written in the record the physician and the patient are not prepared to see in the *New York Times*. The physician must have a well trained memory. It may also mean the physician must sometimes keep double records' (Deming 2002, 84). Such practices will seriously threaten the results of biobank research, if phenotype information noted in the records is incomplete or not accurate. Therefore, it is clearly in the interest of research to accept some higher costs for confidentiality, in order to maximize the benefit resulting from the research. Inaccurate research results based on incomplete information will not be of much use to the health of future patients.

*Risks to Confidentiality and Privacy: A Problem of Definition*

Comparing different guidelines and publications on the issue of confidentiality is complicated by the fact that guidelines use different and not always clear definitions of different degrees of anonymization of data and samples. The main

---

30   See the Council of Europe Steering Committee on Bioethics Explanatory Report (CDBI 2002b): 'Worries about the access to and the protection of data and public scandals concerning the use of human biological materials without the knowledge of the subjects of the research, have increased the need for international regulation. The primary goal of this instrument is to protect the rights and fundamental freedoms of those whose biological materials could be included in a research project.'

31   See also the Council of Europe Steering Committee on Bioethics Explanatory Report (CDBI 2002b): 'Strengthening confidence, which is the basis of the patient–physician relationship, is another aim of this instrument. The instrument supports the idea that it is good practice to inform and request consent from patients and research subjects when human biological materials are used for research purposes.'

32   See Deming (2002, 84).

problem is the use of the term 'anonymized'. It could mean reversibly anonymized, that is, a special form of coded,[33] or irreversibly anonymized. This terminology refers principally to *direct* identification through a link with personal data (name, address, and so on). Another problem is how to deal with the probability that *indirect* identification might be possible in spite of anonymization (Lowrance and Collins 2007). The risk of *indirect* identification concerns coded data/samples, as well as data that have been stripped of identifiers with the intent of irreversible anonymization. Some guidelines use the term 'coded', 'reversibly anonymized' or de-identified only to indicate that *direct* identifiers such as name, birth date and address are reversibly detached and can be reattached through a code. Coded data/samples in the latter sense might still be 'easily identifiable' if they are from a small community and contain information about specific characteristics which third parties could know or identify. Other guidelines use the same terms in a stricter way: coded or de-identified in these guidelines means that demographic data have been detached to the point that *indirect* identification is not possible, that is, that it is not possible to identify a person 'easily' (HGC 2002) without knowing the code. This might, in small communities, mean that all rare characteristics or rare combinations which might permit identification of a person must be stripped. In larger communities, in general fewer characteristics need to be taken off, depending on the frequency of a certain characteristic in the community. An example of the difficulties in determining the risk of re-identification in de-identified data is the new US federal medical privacy rule (Kulynych and Korn 2002a, 2002b and 2002c). According to the rule's legal standard, the data must be stripped of a large quantity of information, including most ZIP codes, birth and discharge dates and other unique identifiers. The remainder may not be useful for research (Annas 2002). An alternative way to define de-identification, according to the new US federal medical privacy rule, is to prove that 'a person with appropriate knowledge

---

33     The difference between linked (reversibly) anonymized (in the French translation 'réversiblement anonymisé') and coded is, according to the Council of Europe (COE 2006; CDBI 2002a and 2002b), that in the first case the researcher using the samples or data does not have access to the code, whereas 'coded' means that the researcher using the material/ information knows the code (see Table 4.1). Others use the term 'coded' to describe what the Council of Europe guidelines call 'linked anonymised' (OHRP 2004). This means that the terms 'anonymized' and 'coded' are used with significantly different meanings by different authors. Others, for example, the HUGO and RMGA guidelines and Deschênes et al. (2001), consider coded and reversibly anonymized as one category which is separate from 'true' (irreversible) anonymized. The most important problem is that the Council of Europe puts both types of anonymization in the same category, because both are considered 'identifiable' (personal information), whereas in the US, reversibly anonymized samples and information (OHRP writes 'coded' but explains that researchers do not have access to the code) are considered to be *non-identifiable* and therefore research with reversibly anonymized samples is not human subject research and does not require consent or ethics committee approval (Elger and Caplan 2006). See also the discussion of this problem in Chapter 5.

of and experience with generally accepted statistical and scientific principles and methods' determines that the risk of identification is 'very small' and provides documentation of 'the methods and results of the analysis' (Kulynych and Korn 2002a).

Depending on the degree of de-identification and the method used to 'prove anonymization', it is not clear whether such anonymized data/samples should be considered personal data/samples, independently from the question of reversibility. They would not be personal data/samples for somebody who does not have access to the code, if sufficient demographic information is detached. However, they are personal data/samples if the unique combination of attached data permits identification of the individual, even though classical identifiers, such as name, birth date and address, are stripped. An example would be a person suffering from a tumour type that has occurred in only two persons from the same region (for example, a state or county) during the past five years. If the persons are of different sex, knowing only the sex and region would be sufficient to identify the individuals.

It is also not clear whether coded or reversibly anonymized data should be considered personal[34] data/samples or whether they should be treated as if they were completely anonymous.[35] They might be equivalent to anonymous data for those who do not have access to the code, but personal data for those with legitimate and illegitimate access to the code.

From a pragmatic point of view, this creates at least two major issues. First, ethics committees would need to request a statistical expert opinion for each study in order to determine whether anonymization is sufficient or if information and samples still fall into the category of 'personal data'. This leaves a problem of 'standard' because the facility to identify depends on the effort and technical possibilities that change over time.[36] Second, it is intellectually and legally

---

34    See the definition of personal data (CDBI 2002a): Art. 2 Definitions: 'iii) Personal data shall mean data that are identified or identifiable. [...] v) Identifiable shall mean linked anonymized or coded. vi) Linked anonymized shall mean human biological materials or personal data that are anonymous to the people who receive or use them but contain information that would allow others to link them back to identifiable individuals. vii) Coded shall mean human biological materials or personal data that have a coded identification that would allow the user to link them back to an identifiable individual. viii) Unlinked anonymized shall mean human biological materials or data that, alone or in combination, contain no information that could reasonably be used by anyone to identify the individuals to whom they relate.'

35    The decision of the Icelandic Supreme Court (Abbott 2004; Anonymous 2004; Law Review 2004; Jost 2007, 197) seems to indicate that coded data are considered personal data by the Court. This contradicts the evaluation of the guidelines of the Nationaler Ethikrat, which treat coded data for which the user does not know the code as if they were anonymous (see Nationaler Ethikrat 2004, 3).

36    The most recent European standard has been set by the Data Protection Working Party in 2007: '"Anonymous data" in the sense of the Directive can be defined as any

unsatisfactory to have data and samples that have two different denominations: 'personal data' for those who have access to the code and 'not personal data' for the researchers who do not have access to the code.

In light of the technical uncertainty, other guidelines try to use definitions that are independent from the unresolved empirical questions about which code system is efficient and how much data must be stripped to assure true anonymization. These guidelines use the terms 'non-identifiable' and 'untraceable' to indicate the result, without describing in each case how this can be technically guaranteed.

An additional question is whether definitions should differentiate between samples and information. A particular problem of DNA samples is that, theoretically, they always contain sufficient information to identify a person. Samples are said to be anonymous if they are taken from a person without any information attached. However, if samples consist at least partially of DNA, comparison of the information contained in the DNA with other samples or with information from other banks still permits identification. An important difference between samples and information is that the information contained in a DNA sample is itself 'a code', that is, the genetic code first needs to be analysed in order to establish the nucleic acid base sequence. Second, the significance of polymorphisms or of a particular gene or sequence needs to be determined before this information can be interpreted. Although the significance of information contained in a medical record may also change with time, if new risk or prognostic factors are proven, the significance of information contained in a DNA sample will certainly change to a much greater extent in the future with the increase in knowledge about the predictive value of genetic information.

A different problem, already discussed in the earlier section about consent, is that even if data are completely and irreversibly anonymized, they might still threaten the privacy and confidentiality, not of individuals, but of groups – as far as information or samples permit identification of ethnic, racial or other group characteristics. These groups need not be equivalent to populations or communities. If DNA permits identification of approximate height and hair colour, and studies show that individuals with red hair carry certain disease genes, this might stigmatize and harm all red-haired individuals.

### Proposition of a definition

The definitions with a distinction between 'unlinked anonymized' and 'linked anonymized' proposed by the Council of Europe (2006), and the similar terminology used by the Human Genetics Commission (HGC 2002) and UNESCO (2003), might be misleading because intuitively the term 'anonymized' is associated with irreversible anonymization and not with the existence of a (more or less accessible) code. On the

---

information relating to a natural person where the person cannot be identified, whether by the data controller or by any other person, *taking account of all the means likely reasonably to be used either by the controller or by any other person* to identify that individual' (Data Protection Working Party 2007, 21).

other hand, the adjectives 'irreversible' or 'reversible' help to classify anonymization and they are more self-explanatory than some of the new terms created to explain reversible anonymization.[37] Indeed, the term 'anonymized' is only misleading if it is used without clarification. The risk could be that the term 'anonymized' is used to make patients assume that irreversible anonymization has taken place, whereas a link to the identity is kept because 'anonymized' may also mean 'linked anonymized'.

In the following text we use the terms 'anonymized' and 'coded' in the way suggested by the guidelines of the Council of Europe (COE 2006) and add 'irreversibly/unlinked' or 'reversibly/linked' to the term 'anonymized' in order to clarify the meaning of anonymization.[38] The terms are used with the understanding that anonymization of most combinations of data, and especially that of samples containing DNA, can never be 100 per cent complete but that, in line with the Data Protection Working Party (2007, 21), anonymization indicates that identification is not possible 'taking account of all the means likely reasonably to be used'.

The following other terms cover more than one category (see Table 4.1): confidential (includes all medical information); personal data (includes identified, coded as well as reversibly anonymized data, at least for those who have access to the code); de-identified (could mean irreversibly anonymized, reversibly anonymized or coded). The term 'encrypted' could mean either reversibly anonymized or coded, but another dimension is added which means that even the reversibly anonymized data are not readable for those who do not have the encryption key.

The terminology brings to mind the Tower of Babel story (Knoppers and Saginur 2005; Elger and Caplan 2006) because the same term is used with different meanings, and different terms are used in order to indicate the same degree of anonymization. While the German Ethics Council has created the term 'pseudonomyzed' (Nationaler Ethikrat 2004) which means that a 'pseudonym', that is, a code, is attached, the British Department of Health has coined the term 'pseudoanonymized' (UK Department of Health 2001). It is likely that the MRC (2000 and 2001) and the Council of Europe (CDBI 2002a and 2002b; COE 2006) prefer to use 'reversibly anonymized' because 'pseudoanonymized' has the connotation of deception: the data were only 'pseudo' (that is, not really sufficiently) anonymized (Pownall 2007).

---

37    The German National Ethics Council uses the term 'completely anonymized' ('vollständig anonymisiert') to describe irreversibly anonymized samples of data, and 'pseudonomisiert' for 'reversibly anonymised' data, explaining that, if at all possible, the researcher in contact with information or samples should not have access to the code (see Nationaler Ethikrat 2004, 3).

38    It could be argued, however, that making a difference between reversible anonymization and coding is not only somewhat artificial, but implies that the same data will be characterized at the same time as coded and linked anonymized, depending on which person is considered. In general, only the principal researcher (or the responsible person at the biobank) has access to the code. For him or her, data/samples will be called 'coded', and for all other researchers, data/samples would need to be called 'linked anonymized'. This makes the labelling of data and samples not only complicated but also confusing.

**Table 4.1    Terminology used in various guidelines concerning different types of storage of data/samples**

| Degree of anonymization | Equivalents or similar terms |
|---|---|
| **I. ANONYMOUS** (**Anonymous** in the strict form) | Samples without any information attached and for which no possibility of comparison (finger-printing) exists. This is in the strictest form only the case for a certain type of historical samples. |
| **II. IRREVERSIBLY ANONYMIZED (not personal data)** Data are 'quasi anonymous'; they cannot be linked to an identifiable individual. Completely anonymized data are in general not considered as personal data although, through DNA fingerprinting, it would still be possible to compare one sample with another from a known individual and to confirm the identity of the donor who provided the sample. | • Anonymized (ASHG; 1988, RMGA 2000)<br>• Irreversibly anonymized (HGC 2002)<br>• Permanently de-linked (House of Lords 2001)<br>• Irretrievably unlinked to an identifiable person (UNESCO 2003)<br>• Completely anonymized (Nationaler Ethikrat 2004)<br>• Unlinked anonymized (COE 2006 English version)<br>• Irréversiblement anonymisé (COE 2006 French version)<br>• Unlinked (NBAC 1999): information is in general not identifiable: depending on the amount of attached demographic information a risk of identification persists<br>• Unidentified (NBAC 1999; WHO 2000): the amount of attached demographic information has been tested and indirect identification is not possible<br>• Not traceable (Tri-Council policy statement) |
| **III. REVERSIBLY ANONYMIZED** (personal identifiers such as name, birth date and address detached and replaced by a code, but researchers and users do not have access to the code[§]) | • Pseudoanonymized (UK Department of Health 2001)<br>• Pseudonomisiert (Nationaler Ethikrat 2004)<br>• Linked anonymized (COE 2006 English version; MRC 2000)<br>• Réversiblement anonymisé (COE 2006 French version; CEST 2003)<br>• Reversibly anonymized (HGC 2002) |
| **IV. CODED** (personal identifiers such as name, birth date and address detached and replaced by a code known by the users/researchers) | • Coded (only the following guidelines use the term coded in this restricted sense: CEST 2003; COE 2006; MRC 2000) |
| Terms that do not distinguish between III (reversibly anonymized) and IV (coded), so the listed terms can mean both | • Coded (NBAC and all other guidelines not mentioned under IV)<br>• Traceable (Tri-Council policy statement)<br>• Identifiable (NBAC)<br>• Linked (NBAC)<br>• *Data unlinked to an identifiable person* (UNESCO 2003, 4: 'Data that are not linked to an identifiable person, through the replacement of, or separation from, all identifying information about that person by use of a code')<br>• Encoded<br>• *Data linked to an identifiable person* (UNESCO 2003, 4: 'Data that contain information, such as name, birth date and address, by which the person from whom the data were derived can be identified') |
| **V. IDENTIFIED** (the identifying information such as name, address, etc. is attached directly to the sample or data)* | • Identified (NBAC)<br>• Nominative<br>• Directly identified (Clayton et al. 1995)<br>• Fully identifiable |

*Notes*: § For those who distinguish between reversibly anonymized (HGC) and coded samples/data (COE) (CEST 2003; COE 2006), it is under discussion whether HGC or COE samples and data are to be treated as irreversibly anonymized data, because they cannot be identified by those who use them (personal identifiers such as name, birth date and address are detached and replaced by a code which is NOT known by the users/researchers).

* For example, an identifying tag is on the specimen (as is usual in institutes of pathology) or the identifying information is in the same data table.

*Should reversibly anonymized data be considered non identifiable?*

If reversibly anonymized data are considered non identifiable, that is, non-personal data, this has important consequences for the protection of sample donors because researchers could use these samples and data without consent and without the need for ethics committee approval, as is presently the case in the US (OHRP 2004). Those who propose creating two categories for linked (or coded) data and samples – that is, 'reversibly anonymized' or 'linked anonymized' to describe whether the code is known by the users of the data and samples, or not – justify this terminology because they want to indicate that reversible anonymization implies a higher degree of security than 'simple' coding. Those who consider reversibly anonymized data and samples to be non-identifiable claim that this degree of security is similar to that of irreversibly anonymized data. However, we agree with the Council of Europe's position which makes a distinction between 'coded' and 'reversibly anonymized', but maintains that reversibly anonymized samples and data are identifiable (personal data). Indeed, the degree of security is not the same for reversibly and irreversibly anonymized samples and data. If a link is kept (for example, by the custodian of a biobank), this is done because one anticipates occasions when this link will be useful. If not, no reason exists to keep the link. The existence of a link always implies an increased risk of identification at the moment when the process of linking is carried out (for example, when new phenotypic information is added or when individual results are fed back).

The discussion whether a distinction between 'coded' and 'reversibly anonymized' is useful signifies that the preoccupation is with knowing who has access to the code. This might distract attention from the fact that the degree of protection depends on many other factors: on the security of the code (functioning firewalls, sufficient digits), on the frequency of the occasions in which decoding is carried out, on the authority or body that is responsible for coding, and on the risk of indirect identification.

*Privacy, Confidentiality and Genetic Databases: An Overview of the Different Positions*

Concerning the regulation of genetic databases, the issue of confidentiality needs to be examined in two respects. First, although all guidelines stress the importance of confidentiality and privacy, controversy exists about how and to what degree they should be protected. The principal question is: to what extent should databases be made secure enough to guarantee participants' privacy? One aspect of security could be anonymization. It is therefore interesting to know whether and how anonymization is discussed in different guidelines and which kinds and degrees of anonymization or coding are considered adequate in different circumstances.

The second controversy exists about how access to the data by third parties should be regulated. Data held in a biobank are potentially of interest to a number of third parties. The most important of these are: relatives, the police (and the entire justice system), insurers, employers, schools, and other researchers. The aspect of access to results by relatives will be discussed in another section (see the section on the feedback of results). In this section, we discuss recommendations concerning access by all other third parties mentioned.

In the following we will describe the debate about the degree of confidentiality and the way in which it should be ensured. The most important positions concerning the different issues will be mentioned.[39] After the summary of the different positions, we analyse where the points of consensus and controversy lie and where issues mainly seem not to have been sufficiently clarified. Then we provide our own answer to the controversies.

*The degree of adequate confidentiality: How is it determined and by whom?*
The guidelines of the Medical Research Council (MRC) state that donors need to be informed about the use of their data and the way in which confidentiality is ensured:

> People who donate samples for research must be told what information about their medical history or other personal details will be used in the research, who it might be shared with, and what safeguards are in place to preserve confidentiality. They should give explicit consent to these arrangements. [...] Researchers should normally have each person's explicit consent to obtain, store and use information about them (MRC 2001, 5.2, 13).

In addition, according to the MRC guidelines, independently from the degree of anonymization, ethics committee approval is mandatory: 'All medical research using identifiable personal information or anonymized data from the NHS that is not already in the public domain must be approved by a Research Ethics Committee' (MRC 2001, 5, 13–14). Concerning the role of ethics committees, similar positions are held by most other guidelines (for example, NBAC 1999; COE 2006; CIOMS 2002; CEST 2003). These guidelines also agree that donors have the right to know about the arrangements made concerning confidentiality, before consenting. However, guidelines are in general not explicit about the amount of details that should be explained to donors.

The guidelines of the WHO Regional Office for Europe (WHO 2001) recommend that 'any anonymization process be overseen by an independent body that would have the following obligations: (1) To scrutinise and ensure the legitimacy of requests to the database; (2) To act, where possible, as an intermediary between the creators and the users of the database, in respect of decoding apparatus [sic] used to anonymise and/or link data held on the database; (3) To maintain standards and keep anonymisation processes under review' (WHO 2001, 13).

---

39   Many guidelines are silent on several of the questions. Guidelines are only mentioned if they deal with the particular question.

*Is coding enough? Coding (or reversible anonymization) versus irreversible anonymization*

According to the CIOMS guidelines, 'secure coding' may constitute sufficient protection, if combined with 'restricted access to the database'.[40]

The Council of Europe's guidelines indicate that the way in which confidentiality should be protected cannot be decided in general, but depends on the type of research: 'Biological materials and associated data should be anonymised as far as appropriate to the research activities concerned' (COE 2006, Article 8).

Both UNESCO and the COE seem to consider that irreversible anonymization is the best protection. They specify that not using irreversibly anonymized samples and data needs to be justified:

> Human genetic data, human proteomic data and biological samples collected for medical and scientific research purposes can remain linked to an identifiable person, only if necessary to carry out the research and provided that the privacy of the individual and the confidentiality of the data or biological samples concerned are protected in accordance with domestic law [...] Human genetic data and human proteomic data should not be kept in a form which allows the data subject to be identified for any longer than is necessary for achieving the purposes for which they were collected or subsequently processed (UNESCO 2003, Art. 14, 'Privacy and Confidentiality').

> Any use of biological materials and associated data in an identified, coded, or linked anonymised form should be justified by the researcher (COE 2006, Art. 8).

The problem with these recommendations is that it needs to be defined what constitutes justified necessity. Coding and reversible anonymization might put a significant additional workload and financial burden on researchers. Moreover, the purposes for which data and samples are collected are often not defined exhaustively at the onset of a biobank. Consequently, for many genetic databases it might be difficult to define clearly whether it is justified to unlink data and samples or not. It is also not clear whether unlinking should be irreversible in the long run or whether it would be acceptable to keep data and samples in a coded form for a long duration. Coding allows the data subject to be identified by those who know the code. It implies higher risks to privacy than irreversible anonymization, but on the other hand it is advantageous for most biobank research because it permits the addition of data and keeps the range of future research opportunities large.

---

40   See CIOMS 2002 commentary on guideline 18. This commentary examines specifically the issues of confidentiality and genetic testing: 'When biological samples are not fully anonymized [...], the investigator in seeking informed consent should assure prospective subjects that their identity will be protected by secure coding of their samples (encryption) and by restricted access to the database, and explain to them this process.'

UNESCO states further that in addition to the protection provided by anonymization (for example, unlinking), the 'necessary precautions should be taken to ensure the security of the data and biological samples'. However, these precautions are not defined:

> Human genetic data, human proteomic data and biological samples collected for the purposes of scientific research should not normally be linked to an identifiable person. Even when such data or biological samples are unlinked to an identifiable person, the necessary precautions should be taken to ensure the security of the data or biological samples (UNESCO 2003, Article 14).

The HUGO guidelines (1995) recommend that 'recognition of privacy and protection against unauthorized access be ensured by the confidentiality of genetic information'. However, HUGO gives only vague guidance about how confidentiality should be achieved. This guidance is limited to the recommendation to implement coding, procedures for access, and policies for transfer and conservation: 'Coding of such information, procedures for controlled access, and policies for the transfer and conservation of samples and information should be developed and put into place before sampling' (HUGO 1995).

Further guidelines (HUGO 1998) underline that '[d]ata protection is of the utmost importance' and 'can be facilitated and ensured by avoiding the use or transmission of identifiable samples wherever possible'. These guidelines also recommend coding: 'The coding of samples is a technique that protects confidentiality provided that stringent mechanisms are put in place.' The value of (irreversible) anonymization for confidentiality is recognized, but balanced against the limitation which might result from anonymization for future uses: 'Another avenue is the anonymization of samples which would make tracing back impossible. While necessary demographic and clinical data may accompany the anonymized sample, careful consideration should be given before proceeding to strip samples of identifiers since other unknown, future uses may thereby be precluded as well as may the validation of results.' In addition, the guidelines require that '[s]ecurity mechanisms must be put into place to ensure the respect of the choices made and of the desired level of confidentiality'. They do not specify what kind of security mechanisms are meant and how they can be realized.

The guidelines of the North American Regional Committee (NARC 1997, chapter VII 'Privacy and Confidentiality') are another example where the scientific value of rich data is balanced against the risks for confidentiality. The NARC states that 'the HGD Project's standard ethnographic protocols call for the collection of some cultural and ethnographic information from individual donors, including names and other information that could be used to identify a donor'. The NARC does not require that no personally identifying information should be collected, although this would be the most efficient way to make breaches of confidentiality impossible. 'Such a draconian rule' is rejected because it 'would make impossible a number of scientifically useful analyses that could depend on cultural characteristics of individual donors and, in some cases, even on the ability to re-contact a particular donor'. The guidelines propose that '[t]he basic rule must be protection of the confidentiality of all individual donors, but we believe that it should be done through control over personally identifying information, not its total exclusion'.

According to the Canadian Science and Technology Commission (CEST 2003, 50–51), the degree of security should be adapted to the degree of risk, and the degree of risk should not be higher than the scientific quality of the research project demands. The CEST guidelines indicate, therefore, similarly to the UNESCO guidelines, that the lowest possible degree of identification compatible with the aim of the research should be adopted.

The Tri-Council guidelines state: 'Family information in databanks shall be coded so as to remove the possibility of identification of subjects within the bank itself' (Tri-Council 1998, Article 8.2, 'Privacy, Confidentiality, Loss of Benefits and Other Harms').

According to the guidelines of the Medical Research Council (MRC), the degree of anonymization should be as high as possible and achieved as early as possible: 'All personal information must be coded or anonymized as far as possible and as early as possible in the data processing.' The MRC recognizes that protection through anonymization is never absolute. The guidelines add, therefore, a call for ethical behaviour of researchers and other users: 'Users of anonymized samples of human material must undertake not to attempt to identify individual research participants' (MRC 2001, 5.4, 14).

The Human Genetics Commission (HGC 2002, 17) admits that '[t]he very nature of DNA limits the process of complete anonymization, because it makes it possible to link a sample by use of "DNA fingerprinting"'. The HGC nonetheless considers that 'for practical purposes the concept of anonymization is valid'. The Commission states that the ethical implications of dealing with genetic material and information depend on the degree of anonymization and the security of the data: 'It is important that satisfactory techniques of encryption be used where the anonymization is to be reversible. We recommend that the Government gives a firm commitment to funding research and development initiatives on this important aspect of data security' (HGC 2002, 17 and Art. 5.14).

The guidelines of the WHO Regional Office for Europe distinguish between 'absolute' anonymity and 'proportional or reasonable' anonymity. They express the opinion that coding can be a way of reasonable and acceptable anonymization, as long as anonymization procedures are adequately reviewed by an independent body (WHO 2001, 13). They introduce a sliding scale for the need for privacy protection through various means: 'The greater the impact that use or misuse of the information might have, the greater the sensitivity it carries, and so the greater the need for its protection' (WHO 2001, 16).

The report of the National Bioethics Advisory Commission (NBAC 1999) issues the following recommendations: the protection of confidentiality should be assessed by the research ethics committee (in the US called 'IRB', that is, institutional review board). This should require the investigator to set forth 'a full description of the mechanisms that will be used to maximize the protection against inadvertent release of confidential information' (NBAC 1999, recommendation 5, iv). Recommendation 10 of the same report states that coding might be sufficient to grant confidentiality:

> IRBs should operate on the presumption that research on coded samples is of minimal risk to the human subject if a) the study adequately protects the confidentiality of personally identifiable information obtained in the course of research, [and] b) the study does not involve the inappropriate release of information to third parties (NBAC 1999, recommendation 10, v).

The problem with this definition is that it will only be possible to assess retrospectively whether confidentiality has been adequately protected, because 'inappropriate release of information to third parties' is in general not actively planned at the beginning of the study, but happens accidentally.

The NBAC recommends in addition that researchers should obtain the consent of donors before publishing research results with identifiable information in scientific journals and elsewhere, because such publications imply a risk to the privacy and confidentiality of individuals who provide samples for research (NBAC 1999, 44).

The guidelines of the College of American Pathologists reflect in some detail on standards of confidentiality:

> There is no controversy among health care workers and researchers regarding the privacy rights of patients and the obligation to safeguard confidentiality [...] The operational challenge is, thus, one of security. Security is the notion of unlikelihood of undesired disclosure or leakage of confidential information, intentional or not. Since patient information of any kind is presumed to be confidential unless disclosure is permitted expressly by the patient (or the patient's legal representative) or is required by law, organizations and individuals must operate under rules of conduct and use physical systems that reasonably protect this information from inappropriate or unregulated disclosure. Specimens (referred to also as tissues, including cells and bodily fluids) removed from patients and sent to the pathology laboratory for examination essentially become part of the patient's medical record, either through processing into durable materials (eg, slides, blocks, and reports) or through maintenance in some form for storage (eg, preserved in formalin, frozen, or as tissue culture) (Grizzle et al. 1999, 297).

The guidelines state further that the 'challenges' that pathologists face in granting confidentiality today are 'both social and technological in nature. The number of individuals and institutions with legitimate access to medical records is large, and information technology has placed more and more components of medical records in electronic form, adding new dimensions to the need for security of information.'

The guidelines do not propose any particular form of anonymization, but rather written procedures that regulate access to samples and data:

> We therefore recommend that pathology departments must have a written policy concerning confidentiality and privacy rights. The policy should include specific procedures for access to the medical record; confirmation of IRB approval of research involving tissues when appropriate; a description of safeguards to prevent unauthorized access; procedures for the release of information; methods of assuring that everyone with access or who may gain legitimate access embraces the need for privacy, confidentiality, and security of patient information; procedures specific for records kept in electronic form; and procedures that specifically apply to the release of information for research (Grizzle et al. 1999, 297).

The CCNE guidelines identify security and anonymization as key aspects in gaining public confidence in genetic databases. Legal guarantees against discrimination are, according to the CCNE, based on the technical means available to grant anonymity. Only sufficient technical investment and training of personnel will ensure the respect of the legal requirement for confidentiality.[41] The idea of the CCNE seems to be that anonymization is reversible and controlled by an authority of mediation ('instance of mediatization') which oversees access to the code. This authority informs research participants at their request about what happened to their samples and data, and controls that donors are only recontacted in justified cases.[42]

The most extreme position concerning confidentiality is held by the US National Center for Human Genome Research (NCH) guidelines (NCHGR-DOE 1998). The guidelines acknowledge that:

> one of the most effective ways of protecting volunteers from the unexpected, unwelcome or unauthorized use of information about them is to ensure that there are no opportunities for linking an individual donor with information about him/her that is revealed by the research [...] no phenotypic or demographic information about donors should be linked to the DNA to be sequenced.

---

41    '[I]l est certain que le respect de garanties de sécurité et d'anonymat est la cheville ouvrière de la confiance du public et d'un bon fonctionnement des banques. Il appelle d'ailleurs des exigences particulières, sur lesquelles le CCNE insiste en matière d'investissement technique et de formation des personnes appelées à traiter des échantillons et données ; c'est sur elles que reposent la réalité des garanties légales qui interdisent par exemple que toute personne fasse l'objet de discrimination à raison de ses caractéristiques génétiques' (CCNE 2003, 6).

42    '[O]n peut soutenir qu'une formule de substitution, confiée à l'instance de médiation dont la création a été suggérée, permettrait de ne rechercher la personne que dans les cas justifiés; toute personne pourrait cependant s'adresser à tout moment à cette instance pour savoir ce qu'il est advenu du matériau et des échantillons la concernant' (CCNE 2003, 6).

The guidelines require that '[n]ot only should others be unable to link a DNA sequence to a particular individual, but no individual who donates DNA should be able to confirm directly that a particular DNA sequence was obtained from their DNA sample' (NCH 1996, Privacy and Confidentiality). The NCH guidelines even propose an additional safeguard that consists in establishing gene libraries that contain 'mosaics' or 'patchworks' of sequenced regions derived from a number of different individuals, rather than of a single individual. On the other hand, the guidelines recognize that in the future technology that will allow unambiguous identification of individuals from their DNA sequences will mature and become a potential means to easily identify individuals. 'Thus,' continue the guidelines, 'for the foreseeable future, establishing effective confidentiality, rather than relying on anonymity, will be a very useful approach to protecting donors.'

*Who is responsible for granting confidentiality?*
Responsibility is assigned to a range of different people and bodies. The UNESCO Declaration on Human Genetic Data states that the 'privacy of an individual participating in a study using human genetic data, human proteomic data or biological samples should be protected and the data should be treated as confidential' (UNESCO 2003, Art. 14 'Privacy and Confidentiality'). A particular aspect of the Declaration is the announcement of a responsibility of the state concerning confidentiality: 'States should endeavour to protect the privacy of individuals and the confidentiality of human genetic data linked to an identifiable person, a family or, where appropriate, a group, in accordance with domestic law consistent with the international law of human rights' (UNESCO 2003, Art. 14).

The guidelines of the CEST (2003, 50–51) require that the administrator of a genetic databank and the researchers using the data and samples guarantee the security of the personal data.

The WHO Regional Office for Europe announces that 'the onus of ensuring adequate protection of privacy falls on the shoulders of those who gather and use genetic information and samples, especially if this is with a view to storage in a database' (WHO 2001, 16).

The guidelines of the UK Medical Research Council state that all medical information should be treated confidentially: 'Doctors and researchers should treat any information about an individual, however derived, as confidential. This is what the public expects' (MRC 2001, 13–14). The responsibility for granting confidentiality is with the researchers and all other individuals in contact with the data:

> Each individual entrusted with patient information is personally responsible for their decisions about disclosing it. Personal information should only be handled by health professionals or staff with an equivalent duty of confidentiality. Principal investigators have personal responsibility to ensure that procedures and security arrangements are sufficient to prevent breaches of confidentiality (MRC 2001, 13).

According to the guidelines of the College of American Pathologists, the responsibility for ensuring confidentiality is assigned to the pathologist:

> Implicit in the pathologist's stewardship is the duty to maintain the confidentiality of the information contained in the patient's medical record. Confidentiality means that information will not be disseminated freely. This implies that the information will be held in confidence and constitutes a trust, if not a fiduciary duty, not to disclose the information to others without the person's consent, actual or implied, or otherwise in his or her interest (Grizzle et al. 1999, 297).

*Group confidentiality*

The requirement of group confidentiality is stated in the UNESCO Declaration on Human Genetic Data (2003) and the guidelines of the North American Regional Committee (1997). Article 14 ('Privacy and Confidentiality') of the UNESCO Declaration on Human Genetic Data requires that the state should not only protect the confidentiality of individuals, but also that of groups. This means that coding and anonymization are not sufficient means, because they do not guarantee the protection of groups. The NARC guidelines identify a conflict in the wish of populations to remain unidentifiable: 'At the extreme, of course, this runs counter to the goals of the HGD Project. It cannot study the history and diseases of individual populations without knowing what populations provided the DNA samples' (NARC 1997, VII. Privacy and Confidentiality, C). The guidelines recommend that researchers should reveal geographic coordinates about the sample site:

> with only limited precision, to the degree rather than the minute or second of longitude or latitude. The individual samples will contain other information about the individuals, but, except in the case of very small populations, that information should not allow researchers to identify the precise settlement from which the samples were taken […]. The issue of disclosure of community location should be discussed with the group before beginning sampling. After a full discussion of the possible consequences, the group should choose between complete disclosure and confidentiality, along with a variety of intermediate positions.

Among the guidelines that express concern about group confidentiality are those of the MRC. They state that 'families or groups should not be identifiable from published data' (MRC 2001, 5.4, 14). The National Bioethics Advisory Commission is also concerned about group confidentiality. The report recommends that '[i]nvestigators' plans for disseminating results of research on human biological materials should include, when appropriate, provisions to minimize the potential harms to individuals or associated groups' (NBAC 1999, recommendation 19, vii).

A different approach is taken by the College of American Pathologists (CAP). Although the CAP guidelines acknowledge the importance of risks for groups, they do not recommend group confidentiality. Instead, they stress that laws should prevent the misuse of information:

> Research can develop information on all Caucasians or all females or all septuagenarians that may damage or otherwise put at risk individual members of the class. The risk here is primarily social (stigmatization, insurance discrimination, and so on) and should be addressed through social mechanisms (eg, law, regulation, or code) (Grizzle et al. 1999, 299).

*Limits of confidentiality*

Several guidelines mention that confidentiality has limits. According to the CIOMS, the 'investigator must establish secure safeguards of the confidentiality of subjects' research data. Subjects should be told the limits, legal or other, to the investigators' ability to safeguard confidentiality and the possible consequences of breaches of confidentiality' (CIOMS 2002, guideline 18). The CIOMS guidelines do not explain any further what exactly legal and other limits are and whether criteria exist to determine justified limits.

According to the guidelines of the North American Regional Committee, confidentiality is not absolute. Unfortunately, the recipients of the information are not described in more detail. It is not clear whether only other researchers are meant or also other third parties:

> The discussion above of both individual and population confidentiality noted circumstances where disclosure may be appropriate [...]. Neither the central repository nor the particular researchers should normally be empowered to make a decision to release additional identifying information. Instead, the information should be released only if both the researchers and the HGD Project, acting perhaps through a regional HGD ethics committee, agree that it should be released. In addition, if the community or individuals can be contacted, their views should also be sought. The decision should be made only after full discussion of the circumstances of the request, the circumstances of sampling in that population, and guarantees from the recipients of the information that they will appropriately protect the confidentiality of the sampled individual or populations (NARC 1997, D. Control of Confidentiality).

The Human Genetics Commission considers that the principles of privacy and confidentiality should generally be respected. However, the Commission admits that 'for the weightiest of reasons' or 'based on overwhelming moral considerations', information might be 'communicated without consent' or a person could be 'obliged to disclose information about his or her genetic disease' (HGC 2002, 14). Among the reasons to override confidentiality 'in exceptional cases' are mentioned 'public safety' and 'substantial harm to others' (HGC 2002, 3.72 and 15).

The report of the National Bioethics Advisory Commission acknowledges that US federal research regulations provide confidentiality protections, but that 'nothing in the regulations will provide complete protection against the inadvertent disclosure of such information' (NBAC 1999, 44). Similar to the HGC, the NBAC states that from an ethical standpoint, rules of confidentiality are rarely considered absolute: 'What counts as a justifiable limitation or exception to confidentiality will depend upon a complex weighing of conflicting legitimate interests' (NBAC 1999, 44).

The final version of the guidelines of the Council of Europe does not contain a discussion of the limits to confidentiality, but the more elaborate precursor version, the CDBI proposal (2002) refers, at least indirectly, to the limits of confidentiality contained in European data protection laws. The CDBI proposal treats the issue of confidentiality in several articles (Articles 6, 9, 18, 19, 20). Article 18 states that '[a]ny information of a personal nature obtained during the research shall be considered as confidential and treated according to the rules relating to the protection of private life and subject to law on the protection of individuals with regard to processing of personal data'. In addition to reference to the law, the justification of limits is explained as a form of balancing: the protection of privacy is not absolute, but is weighed against potential benefits: as stated in Article 6 ('Private life'), '[r]esearch shall not involve risks to the private life of individuals or a group of individuals disproportionate to its potential benefit'. The guidelines do not provide further explanation on details of where the thresholds of proportionality lie.

*Access of third parties in general*
The HUGO guidelines (1998) state that authorization by law and consent are the conditions necessary to authorize access by third parties: 'Unless authorized by law, there should be no *disclosure* to institutional third parties of participation in research, nor of research results identifying individuals or families. Like other medical information, there should be no disclosure of genetic information without appropriate consent' (HUGO 1998, emphasis in the original). Since laws vary in different countries and since the content of the laws is not specified, this exception could be interpreted in various ways. Although the HUGO guidelines add that '[i]nternational *standardization* of the ethical requirements for the control and access of DNA samples and information is essential' (HUGO 1998, emphasis in the original), the guidelines do not provide specific guidance on the content of such standardization concerning access by third parties other than family members.

According to the guidelines of the WHO Regional Office for Europe:

> it should be the role of an independent body to oversee and regulate access to genetic databases. This same body should hold the key to any anonymization methods that have been used. The body should receive applications for access, and these should be considered in light of the nature and purposes of the database. Moreover, the body must be satisfied that the party seeking access is able to make responsible use of the data and to continue to respect their status. The use of finite resources such as genetic samples must equally be regulated by ethically appropriate means (WHO 2001, 18, recommendation 17).

The Tri-Council policy statement does not differentiate between access by different third parties. They regulate access through donors' consent. Article 8.2 of these guidelines ('Privacy, Confidentiality, Loss of Benefits and Other Harms') requires free and informed consent before the transmission of any information to third parties (the 'researcher and the REB shall ensure that the results of genetic testing and genetic counselling records are protected from access by third parties, unless free and informed consent is given by the subject').

Similarly, the guidelines of the RMGA underline the importance of consent. The guidelines state:

> Access to genetic information is subject to the consent of the participant. The principal researcher is responsible for controlling access to genetic material and information. Controlling access is similar to the control exercised over delegated medical acts. Authorized persons having access to the genetic material and information, should, therefore, be overseen by the principal researcher. Controlling access extends to, among other things, the identification of phenotype, access to the participant's personal and familial data and results and finally, to coded information (RMGA 2000, III 2).

The report of the ASHG also regulates limits of confidentiality exclusively through donors' consent:

> [R]esults of DNA tests, like those of other medical tests, are subject to the traditional principles of medical confidentiality and should be released to third parties only with the express consent of the individual [...]. The DNA laboratory must obtain express consent before transmitting patient DNA to a third party. Unless immortalized cell lines have been established, patient DNA is exhaustible and the patient's needs should take priority (ASHG 1988, 4/5).

The guidelines of the MRC stress in particular the rights of those who have collected the samples. The MRC requires that '[u]se of samples by third parties must be on terms that do not disadvantage those involved in making and maintaining the collection or unnecessarily hamper or restrict future uses' (MRC 2001, 9.2, 21). The MRC does not specifically discuss access by insurance companies or employers. Instead, the guidelines mention the problem of discrimination by these third parties in the context of the feedback of results to donors. The underlying assumption seems to be that the problems consist not so much in the direct access by these third parties, which can be prohibited, but in the knowledge of donors themselves. This is so because it is difficult not to grant insurance companies the right to know what donors already know.

The report of the Human Genetics Commission does not focus on technical solutions to restrict access to third parties, but on the prohibition of discriminatory effects of such access:

No person shall be unfairly discriminated against on the basis of his or her genetic characteristics [...] We recommend that consideration be given to the creation of a criminal offence of the non-consensual or deceitful obtaining and/or analysis of personal genetic information for non-medical purposes [...] We believe that it would be sensible to conduct our review of direct access to genetic tests in the light of our recommendation relating to a new criminal offence (HGC 2002, 14–15).

In the section that is specifically dedicated to databases, the HGC notes that the:

confidentiality of the information stored in the databases is a major concern for participants. We recommend that the operators of all genetic research databases should be required to take rigorous steps to ensure that unauthorized access or disclosures are prevented [...] We recommend that genetic research databases established for health research should not be used for any purpose other than such research and that this be put beyond any doubt, by legislation if necessary (HGC 2002, 19 and 5.49–5.50).

Since public safety is mentioned as an exception which could justify access to data, it is not clear how the recommended legislation needs to be understood. Access to data by the police or the justice system might be justified by public safety. As long as the HGC guidelines do not explain in more detail under which conditions the exceptions are valid, their recommendation concerning legislation is of limited help.[43]

*Access of the police (justice system)*
Access by judicial authorities is rarely explicitly discussed in the various guidelines. Article 10 of the Convention on Human Rights and Biomedicine, entitled 'Private life and right to information', affirms that '[e]veryone has the right to respect for private life in relation to information about his or her health' (COE 1997b). However, as the explanatory report to the Convention states (COE 1996):

certain restrictions to the respect of privacy are possible for one of the reasons and under the conditions provided for in under [sic] Article 26.1. For example, a judicial authority may order that a test be carried out in order to identify the author of a crime (exception based on the prevention of a crime) or to determine the filiation link (exception based on the protection of the rights of others) (COE 1996, para. 64).

Similarly, the WHO guidelines admit that 'there should be no access for institutions without the donor's consent' except 'for forensic purposes or instances when the information is directly relevant to public safety' (WHO 1998, 13).

---

43    One might wonder whether the case of Stephen Kelly could be considered justified (Dyer 2001). See Staley (2001, 21) and the description of the case of Stephen Kelly above (Chapter 2: 'Ethical and Legal Objections to the UK Biobank Database').

*Access of insurers, employers, schools and other state agencies*

The strictest position is adopted by the WHO guidelines (WHO 1998, 13). They state that '[i]nsurance companies, employers, schools, government agencies and other institutional third parties that may be able to coerce consent should not be allowed access, even with the individual's consent'. The interesting difference between most other guidelines and the position of the WHO guidelines is that in the latter even the consent of the individual is not sufficient to transmit the information. In addition, the WHO guidelines state (1998, 4) that 'prevention of unfair discrimination or favoritism in employment, insurance or schooling based on genetic information (non-maleficence) is part of the ethical principles that apply for the field of genetic testing'.

The UNESCO Declaration on Human Genetic Data (2003, Art. 14) states that '[h]uman genetic data, human proteomic data and biological samples linked to an identifiable person should not be disclosed or made accessible to third parties, in particular, employers, insurance companies, educational institutions and the family'. Several exceptions are mentioned which allow disclosure: first, 'an important public interest reason in cases restrictively provided for by domestic law consistent with the international law of human rights', and second, 'the prior, free, informed and express consent of the person concerned has been obtained provided that such consent is in accordance with domestic law and the international law of human rights'. The last sentence could be interpreted in the sense that in some cases, similar to the recommendations of the WHO guidelines, even the consent of the donor is not sufficient to transmit information. Furthermore, the UNESCO guidelines require that:

> Every effort should be made to ensure that human genetic data and human proteomic data are not used for purposes that discriminate in a way that is intended to infringe, or has the effect of infringing human rights, fundamental freedoms or human dignity of an individual or for purposes that lead to the stigmatization of an individual, a family, a group or communities [...] In this regard, appropriate attention should be paid to the findings of population-based genetic studies and behavioural genetic studies and their interpretations.

It is not mentioned explicitly that countries should have anti-discrimination laws.

The Human Genetics Commission recommends that 'the Government consider in detail the possible need for separate UK legislation to prevent genetic discrimination and that this evaluation form part of a long-term policy review on the use of personal genetic information in insurance and employment' (HGC 2002, 20 and 6.41).

The report of the National Bioethics Advisory Commission explains that the degree of restrictions on access to genetic information differs according to the type of society. In 'societies in which powerful institutions pose significant threats of discrimination on the basis of genetic or other medical information, greater restrictions on access to such information will be needed than in societies in which such threats are absent'. Therefore:

[i]f federal and state laws prohibiting insurance and employment discrimination on the basis of genetic and other medical information are passed and effectively implemented, the balance between interests that weigh in favor of more restricted access [...] and those that weigh in favor of freer access and more permissive research [...] would shift accordingly [... and] any policies developed now may require revision in the future (NBAC 1999, 45).

*Access of researchers*
The guidelines of the Council of Europe allow for the transfer of biological material and data ('Transborder flows'): 'Biological materials and associated personal data should only be transferred to another state if that state ensures an adequate level of protection' (COE 2006, Art. 16). It remains open to definition how the level of protection will be measured and what kind of proof has to be provided by researchers for justifying the transfer of data or samples. The Council of Europe encourages access of researchers to population biobanks: 'Member states should take appropriate measures to facilitate access by researchers to biological materials and associated data stored in population biobanks' (COE 2006, Art. 20). The conditions of access are the same for all researchers, although some non-defined 'appropriate' conditions may be added: 'Such access should be subject to the conditions laid down in this recommendation; it may also be subject to other appropriate conditions' (COE 2006, Art. 20).

Article 18 ('Circulation and international cooperation') of the UNESCO Declaration on Human Genetic Data requires states to grant *fair* access to data in the international context: 'States should regulate, in accordance with their domestic law and international agreements, the cross-border flow of human genetic data, human proteomic data and biological samples so as to foster international medical and scientific cooperation and ensure fair access to this data' (UNESCO 2003, Art. 18). UNESCO's further explications seem to imply that fair access includes that both industrialized and developing countries cooperate:

States should make every effort, with due and appropriate regard for the principles set out in this Declaration, to continue fostering the international dissemination of scientific knowledge concerning human genetic data and human proteomic data and, in that regard, to foster scientific and cultural cooperation, particularly between industrialized and developing countries (UNESCO 2003, Art. 18).

The standards of data security in cross-border flow of data and samples are not specified, except by the vague term 'adequate protection': 'Such a system should seek to ensure that the receiving party provides adequate protection in accordance with the principles set out in this Declaration' (UNESCO 2003, Art. 18).

The WHO guidelines (1998) are more specific on this aspect. They state that 'qualified researchers should have access if identifying characteristics are removed' (WHO 1998, 13). Removing identifying characteristics could mean a form of coding or an irreversible anonymization of the data and samples.

The HUGO guidelines (1995) state that 'collaboration between individuals, populations, and researchers and between programs in the free flow, access, and exchange of information is essential not only to scientific progress but also for the present or future benefit of all participants. Co-operation and co-ordination between industrialized and developing countries should be facilitated [...] Loss of access to discoveries for research purposes, especially through patenting and commercialization' is a concern and should be prevented.

The guidelines of the CEST (2003) specify that any cross-border flow of data to other researchers, that is, any transfer of data outside of Quebec where they have been gathered, is only authorized if, first, data are irreversibly anonymized, and, second, the other countries or the institutions in these countries ensure the same degree of protection of confidentiality required in Quebec (CEST 2003, xviii, recommendation 9). The guidelines require further that the donors be informed about the fact that their data will be used by researchers outside Quebec (CEST 2003, 51 and xviii).

The guidelines of the North American Regional Committee balance group confidentiality against the importance that other researchers have access to the study results:

> We do not believe that researchers should normally encourage populations to seek complete confidentiality. As with individual confidentiality, however, there may be circumstances under which later researchers have good reasons for needing to know the identity of the sampled populations. Normally, even when communities choose to protect their identity, a reasonable degree of protection would be to allow disclosure of that identity to other researchers upon demonstration, to the HGD Project and, where possible, to the community, of such a good reason. That disclosure would, of course, have to be coupled with guarantees that the new set of researchers will keep the information appropriately confidential. Of course, if the community finally chooses absolute confidentiality, the researchers must either abide by that wish or abandon the effort to study samples from this community (NARC 1997, VII. Privacy and Confidentiality, C).

The RMGA states that '[i]f the participant's genetic material and/or information is to be sent to other researchers, the participant should be notified at the time of consent to participation' (RMGA 2000, II 2). In addition, the 'researchers, institutions and sponsors should promote the sharing of scientific breakthroughs within the international and Quebec scientific communities by making the research results available in a timely manner' (RMGA 2000, VI 2).

According to the guidelines of the MRC in the UK, the sharing of data is essential for scientific progress: 'Custodians of established collections are encouraged to ensure that they are used optimally, and to allow access to other researchers wherever practicable, provided this is consistent with the consent that was obtained and confidentiality is not breached' (MRC 2001, 10.1, 23). Access should be possible to researchers without discrimination, except for a starting period which permits the initiators of the collection to finish the original research projects:

> The value of a collection for research will usually be significantly increased if all the data relating to the samples are stored together and made available in an anonymized form to all users. Custodians of collections of human material are encouraged to make it a condition of access to the samples that copies of all data generated by other users are provided to the custodian for inclusion in a common database. A suitable period of exclusive access may be allowed, to give sufficient time to analyze the data and prepare publications. The requirements of confidentiality and data protection must of course be met. This sharing of data is an essential requirement where sample collections are being managed as a resource for multiple users.[44]

Three conditions must be fulfilled before access is granted to other researchers: 'appropriate consent'; the fact that the interests of the donor are not threatened; and documentation:

> The MRC wishes to promote sharing of useful collections with bona-fide academic researchers undertaking high-quality research, provided that appropriate consent has been obtained and that such use is not against the interests of the donor [...] Proper records of sample distribution must be kept and users must agree to return or destroy material surplus to their requirements and not use it for additional studies or pass it on to others (MRC 2001, 9.2 and 9.3, 21).[45]

The MRC guidelines authorize the transfer of data to other researchers either in anonymized form or with the consent of the donor:

> Data that have not been anonymized should not be transferred without informed consent. The responsibility lies with the custodian to ensure that all data related to samples of human material are unidentifiable before release to other researchers or inclusion in a common database. It is good practice to store, process and analyze personal data in a form that does not allow individuals to be identified. Personal information should only be accessible to staff who have a formal duty of confidence to the research participants. Researchers handling personal

---

44   See MRC (2001, 5.5, 14). See also, in the same guidelines, 9.2, 21: '[I]t will usually be appropriate for the investigators making the collection to have priority access and the right to control use of the collection for the duration of the initial study.'

45   Valid consent from the donor is also required for access to the samples by other researchers or a biobank (MRC 2001, 8): 'When central banking facilities are available, there may be a requirement for the investigator to split the sample and provide a portion to the bank as a condition of research funding. Valid consent from the donor will of course be required to share a sample with other researchers in this way.'

information should have a duty of confidence to research participants included in their contract of employment (MRC 2001, 5.3, 14).

The transfer of identifiable data to countries inside the European Economic Area (EEA) is possible. However, 'identifiable data should not be transferred to a country outside the EEA unless it has an equivalent data protection regime' (MRC 2001, 5.3, 14). Concerning the transfer of samples, the position of the MRC is not clear, because besides the agreement of the institutions involved,[46] it requires that 'contributors to the collection must be consulted where possible'. The term 'consultation' seems to indicate that the process does not imply consent. The condition 'where possible' needs to be specified. Contacting contributors is often possible if the necessary funding is provided, but is impossible without the necessary resources.

The guidelines of the American Society of Human Genetics allow for the access of other researchers with the consent of the donor:

> Subjects involved in studies in which the samples are identified or identifiable should indicate if unused portions of the samples may be shared with other researchers. If the subject is willing to have the sample shared with other researchers, it is the responsibility of the principal investigator to distribute the sample, so as to ensure that the agreement embodied in the informed consent is upheld. Finally, subjects should decide if subsequent researchers may receive their samples as anonymous or identifiable specimens (ASHG 1996).

The guidelines of the College of American Pathologists assign a responsibility to the pathology laboratory that stores material to ensure that researchers have access to such stored material. This access is regulated by the approval of the research ethics committee (institutional review board):

> The laboratory that provides the primary diagnostic analysis of specimens is responsible for the maintenance and integrity of this part of the medical record. Included in maintenance responsibility is a parallel responsibility to provide appropriate material for research studies that have received institutional (i.e., institutional review board [IRB]) approval (Grizzle et al. 1999, 297).

The guidelines of the CCNE (2003, 25) propose two possible ways to regulate access to samples and data by researchers. The relationship between researchers and biobanks will be made explicit by a contract. Either this contract provides a particular initial right to use the samples to the researchers who have collected them in the first place, or, on the other hand, the CCNE discusses whether such

---

46 'When a researcher wishes to move samples to a new location, the agreement of the current and the future host institution must be sought, and contributors to the collection must be consulted where possible' (MRC 2001, 10.1, 23).

contracts are justified. The privilege concerning access could indeed be interpreted as discrimination against other researchers. The CCNE believes that a compromise could be to grant privileged access during a limited time. Free access for all, according to the CCNE, does not imply that access is without any fee. The only accepted criteria to regulate access would be the quality of the research. The donors have the right to be informed about the immediate and delayed projects for which their samples and data will be used. New groups of researchers should have access to collections if the researchers who have gathered the material are not able to attain the collection's objectives.

*Access with respect to commercial purposes and intellectual property rights*
Most guidelines admit the possibility that data and samples are used for research implying commercial purposes, and patenting is permitted. Open to controversy is the question whether donors have to be informed about commercial uses.

The guidelines of the North American Regional Committee note that the Human Genome Diversity Project has no position on questions of patentability, but that the Project holds clear positions about the commercial use of its samples and of the information derived from them. Access by researchers for commercial purposes is possible:

> Three different approaches seem most plausible. Under the first approach, no one could make use of the Project's samples or data in a patent application or a commercial product without the express written permission of the sampled populations involved, and subject to whatever conditions they impose for that permission. Under the second, anyone making commercial use of the Project's samples or data would pay a set percentage royalty to a designated body, to be used for the benefit of the sampled populations. Under the third, anyone making commercial use of the Project's samples or data would have to negotiate a reasonable financial payment with a trustee for the sampled populations, with the proceeds to be used for the populations' benefit (NARC 1997 IX, Questions of Ownership and Control A, Patenting and Commercial Use).

The authors of the guidelines issued by the WHO Regional Office for Europe believe that '[p]artnership between public and private enterprises would currently seem to be the optimal means to realise public benefit from research in genetics'. According to the guidelines, access to databases by commercial companies is not regulated differently than access by public institutions. Intellectual property rights are admitted since they 'can ensure both private and public interests' (WHO 2001, 19).

The Tri-Council guidelines permit access to genetic data for commercial use with informed individual consent and, maybe, group consent and under the condition that, 'at the outset of a research project', the researcher has discussed with the research ethics committee and the donor 'the possibility and/or probability that the genetic material and the information derived from its use may have potential commercial uses'. It is not further specified under which circumstances 'the researcher may have to seek further permission from the group. The fact of commercial sponsorship of genetic research should be revealed to the subject at the beginning of the project. Similarly, possible commercialization occurring after involvement in research should also be revealed at the outset if possible' (Tri-Council 1998, Art. 8.7, 'Commercial Use of Genetic Data').

The RMGA admits access to data and material for commercial purposes:

> The researchers, institutions and sponsors can aspire to the acquisition of intellectual property rights over the inventions derived from genetic material and information, even though they are not the owners of the material [...] When a patent has been awarded, the researchers, institutions and sponsors should promote the transfer of technologies through licensing or other available means (RMGA 2000, VI 3, Intellectual Property).

The guidelines of the MRC, as well as the WHO guide (2000) require that donors be informed regarding 'if their samples might be used in commercial research' (MRC 2001, 3). In addition, 'if a cell line is to be made and used for commercial purposes the donor must be consulted and consent obtained' (MRC 2001, 4.4, 12). Access by the commercial sector to samples collected in the course of MRC-funded research is not only possible but 'should be facilitated, where it is consistent with our mission' (MRC 2001, 4.4, 12). Some limitations of access for commercial purposes exist. For example, 'it is not appropriate for any one company to be given exclusive rights of access to a collection of samples made with the benefit of public funds, nor is it acceptable for any individual to profit financially from providing samples of human material to a third party' (MRC 2001, 4.1, 12). On the other hand, access of commercial companies to data is allowed to be exclusive as permitted by European patent law:

> It is important to distinguish between the samples themselves and the data or intellectual property derived from research using them. Exclusive access to data arising directly from a company's experiments for sufficient time to secure patent protection or other commercial advantage is acceptable, as is ownership by a company of any intellectual property rights arising from their own research using samples of human material (MRC 2001, 4.3, 12).

Commercial companies are not allowed to buy samples, but this applies only if samples have been collected with MRC funding. 'Researchers may not sell for a profit (in cash or in kind) samples that they collected with MRC funding' (MRC 2001, 9).

In contrast, '[i]ntellectual property rights (IPR) arising from research using human samples may be sold or licensed in the same way as other IPR' (MRC 2001, 3) or 'in the usual way' (MRC 2001, 2.5, 9). Patenting requires the written agreement of custodians of collections, but apparently not of donors: 'Custodians of collections of human biological material should ensure that a written agreement covering access to data and ownership of intellectual property rights is secured before allowing access to samples by either commercial companies or academic researchers' (MRC 2001, 4.5, 12).

The Human Genetics Commission proposes interesting limitations to access by commercial companies. These limitations are the three conditions of (1) health-related research, (2) public benefit and (3) consent of the donors:

> Access to samples and personal genetic information may need to be made available to commercial organizations engaged in health-related research of public benefit [...] best practice requires that the question of commercial involvement in research or access to genetic databases should be fully explained at the time of obtaining participants' consent. This should include a brief explanation of any intellectual property issues (HGC 2002, 18).

These limitations are motivated by 'public disquiet' on the issue of commercial uses. The Commission justifies access by commercial organizations by the fact that 'the development of medicines and treatments is largely a commercial undertaking and would be severely limited if commercial access were denied' (HGC 2002, 5.25 and page 18).

The French guidelines (CCNE 2003, 26–7) also admit the possibility of commercial uses of samples and biobanks. If the researchers who have collected the material are not able to attain the objectives of the collection, new groups of researchers should have access to those collections. This concept is valid independently of whether the first are academic researchers and the second belong to a commercial organization or vice versa.

*Discussion of the Guidelines: Consensus and Controversy*

*Technical safety, protection of confidentiality and protection from discrimination*
The concern about confidentiality and privacy with respect to genetic databases is motivated mostly by the objective to avoid harm to the donors that could result when third parties have access to the data. Adverse consequences in the case of such access could be a family conflict, loss of insurance or employment, and other forms of discrimination and stigmatization. There is some controversy as to which is empirically the best way to protect donors. Three principal ways of protection exist. The first is protection by technical means. These range from the most complete form of anonymization to the development of sophisticated coding systems. The second and the third way rely on legal (or ethical) provisions. Donors are protected by laws which punish breaches of confidentiality and by anti-discrimination laws. Confidentiality laws have varying contents. Traditionally, the violation of medical confidentiality is punished in most countries. A particular form of more strict research confidentiality has been proposed in the guidelines of the German Ethics Council (Nationaler Ethikrat 2004) and is known in the United States in the form of Certificates of Confidentiality. With this certificate, researchers

cannot be forced to disclose information that may identify a donor, even by a court subpoena, in any federal, state or local civil, criminal, administrative, legislative or other proceedings (Personalized Medicine Research Project 2009).

Among the three ways to protect the confidentiality and privacy of donors, *technical safety* is discussed by all guidelines, but only the CCNE guidelines state explicitly that the technical means available to grant anonymity are the most important legal guarantees against discrimination.

A broad consensus exists among different guidelines that irreversible anonymization is not a solution that should be generally adopted, even if this would increase confidentiality and the security of the data. The only exception is the US National Center for Human Genome Research (NCH 1996) which not only recommends anonymization, but even suggests the use of mosaics and patchworks of DNA sequences. However, these guidelines foresee that even these methods are not completely secure and propose for the future reliance on confidentiality rather than on anonymization.

Most guidelines propose coding or reversible anonymization. No clear consensus exists as to when it is acceptable not to use any coding. Most guidelines either generally recommend coding (HUGO 1998) or favour the lowest possible degree of identification compatible with the aim of the research (MRC 2001); or they require that data be 'not normally linked to an identifiable person' and that the absence of coding must be justified by the fact that not coding is necessary to carry out the research (UNESCO 2003; COE 2006). Less frequently, recommendations concerning coding are also made with respect to the 'time' factor: (reversible) anonymization should be carried out as early as possible in the data processing (MRC 2001) or data should not be identified any longer than necessary (UNESCO 2003).

*Legal protection of confidentiality* is explicitly mentioned in the UNESCO guidelines which require 'States' to 'endeavour to protect the privacy of individuals and the confidentiality of human genetic data linked to an identifiable person, a family or, where appropriate, a group' (UNESCO 2003, Art. 14). Most professional and national guidelines included in our analysis do not recommend a degree of confidentiality that is stricter than traditional confidentiality laws in their respective countries. The latter provide the possibility for states to access data for reasons such as public safety and protection is therefore never absolute. The NBAC guidelines (1999) do not explicitly discuss the legal means by which confidentiality should be ensured and whether existing legislation should be adapted. According to the NBAC, the ethics committee has to judge the particular way in which a research project or a biobank protects confidentiality on a case by case basis. The Certificate of Confidentiality is a legal possibility that exists in the US in order to protect confidentiality. The German recommendations concerning research biobanks (Nationaler Ethikrat 2004) seem to be the only guidelines which favour stricter confidentiality laws for research involving biobanks than for clinical practice, in the form of a special research confidentiality ('Forschungsgeheimnis').

*Anti-discrimination laws*, that is, the prohibition of discriminatory effects of insufficient confidentiality and access of third parties to data, are only explicitly recommended in a few guidelines (for example, HGC 2002). The report of the National Bioethics Advisory Commission refers to the possibility that 'federal and state laws prohibiting insurance and employment discrimination on the basis of genetic information [...] are passed and effectively implemented'. Such laws are not explicitly recommended, but indirectly, since such laws would make it possible to 'weigh in favor of freer access and more permissive research'. The WHO guidelines (1998, 2001), and similarly the UNESCO guidelines (2003), mention prevention of discrimination as an 'ethical principle' or 'effort' to be made, without recommending any legal framework.

*Group confidentiality*

Group confidentiality is clearly a point of controversy. Some guidelines believe that it is very important to assure group confidentiality, for example, in publications (NARC 1997; MRC 2001), whereas others express the opinion that this is either not feasible or would put too many limits on the researchers (Grizzle et al. 1999). The underlying reasoning is that risks to groups should be prevented by anti-discrimination laws rather than by restrictions on researchers. Still other guidelines acknowledge the problem, but do not take any clear position, such as the NBAC guidelines which vaguely require 'provisions to minimize the potential harms to [...] groups' (NBAC 1999, vii).

*Who is responsible for granting confidentiality?*

Guidelines mention the state (UNESCO 2003), the administrator of the biobank (CEST 2003), the pathologist who, according to the understanding of the guidelines of the College of American Pathologists (Grizzle et al. 1999), functions as the administrator of the pathology repositories, and finally researchers and all other individuals in contact with the data (MRC 2001). It is not clear whether the answers of the guidelines reflect a true controversy because one could imagine that all the entities mentioned, that is, the state, the administrator of the biobank, and researchers and other individuals in contact with the bank, are in some respect responsible for granting confidentiality. In part, the answer to this question is linked to the three ways to protect donors from harm that was mentioned above. Most guidelines seem to recommend all three ways of protection and give more or less weight to particular aspects. The state is responsible for the legal framework that protects confidentiality and punishes discrimination. Administrators of biobanks and researchers might, in addition to the legal obligations, be bound by an ethical duty to protect confidentiality. This duty is sometimes understood to comprise not only that the transmission of information to third parties should be prevented by technical means and restriction of access, but also the duty for researchers 'not to attempt to identify individual participants' (MRC 2001).

*The degree of adequate confidentiality: How is it determined and by whom?*

The consensus seems to be that researchers propose a project for which they explicitly specify the degree of confidentiality. Then, an ethics committee decides whether the degree of confidentiality proposed is adequate, and at the end donors agree to participate under the proposed conditions of confidentiality or not. Rarely, guidelines recommend a form of ongoing control regarding confidentiality, such as, for example, the guidelines of the North American Regional Committee (NARC 1997). These suggest that any transmission of data after collection should be discussed not only with researchers and ethics committees but also with the participating groups of donors.

Although in this area consensus seems to prevail, one point is not clear. Guidelines pay different attention to the question of to what extent donors need to be informed about the details of confidentiality. The guidelines of the MRC require donors to be informed in detail about the people who will have access to the data. As shown by the discussion regarding the UK Biobank, different opinions exist about whether donors have the right to be informed about possible access by the police and the state. Since many guidelines do not discuss these questions explicitly, it remains unclear what their concrete position is and controversies might be greater than they presently appear.

*Limits of confidentiality*

Access to data and samples depends on the extent to which confidentiality is perceived as absolute or as overriding other principles or interests. All guidelines agree that confidentiality is never absolute, but that overriding confidentiality should be exceptional. However, reflections on the balancing of confidentiality with other interests are rather scarce. Among the reasons proposed to justify overriding confidentiality are: public safety and substantial harm to others (HGC 2002); potential benefit if risks to confidentiality are proportional (CDBI 2002a and 2002b); consent of the sampled groups and the involved researchers (NARC 1997). These scarce theoretical reflections of guidelines on the limits of confidentiality do not permit us to conclude whether guidelines truly disagree or not. It is necessary to look in more detail at the recommendations concerning access of different third parties in order to determine whether and where guidelines take opposite positions.

*Access of third parties*

Consensus among guidelines seems to exist regarding the general principle: information should only be transmitted to third parties with the consent of the donor. The consent of groups with respect to confidentiality is only mentioned explicitly by the guidelines of the North American Regional Committee (NARC 1997). If one looks at the details of consent, several points are open to controversy or remain unclear.

First, is consent always sufficient? The WHO guidelines (1998) and the UNESCO guidelines (2003) defend the idea that in certain situations the consent of the donor is not sufficient. The WHO guidelines explicitly consider consent as not sufficient if information is requested by institutions such as insurance companies, employers, state agencies and schools that have the possibility of coercing individuals.

The second question again concerns the limits of confidentiality: do situations exist in which information should be or can be transmitted against the wishes of the donor? The answers in the guidelines are controversial: many guidelines accept the traditional form of confidentiality which permits access by the police, justice system or the state, if public safety is concerned (HGC 2002; UNESCO 2003). Some guidelines would allow exceptions to confidentiality even more generally, for the prevention of crime or other forensic purposes, such as the determination of paternity. Still other guidelines do not permit any access without the consent of the donor, except if significant harm could be prevented (HGC 2002). How should 'prevention of significant harm' be interpreted?[47] Did the fact that the crime of a prisoner, Stephen Kelly, had been proven, after violating confidentiality in two research studies, prevent harm? The answer to this question can only be speculative. Since the crime had already been carried out, that is, he had infected a woman with HIV, the harm is not reversible. The punishment itself cannot be considered to reduce harm unless one argues that five additional years of imprisonment will hinder him in infecting further individuals with HIV during this time. However, he is not considered dangerous in this respect, and the probability is low that this would happen in particular in the next five years compared to all the years of liberty during which he will be able to infect others, once released from prison. In addition, if he wanted, he could also infect other inmates during the time of imprisonment. The argument that punishing him will have a preventive effect on others to commit similar crimes is also weak. The only consequence might be that future criminals will not consent to participation in research in order to avoid the risk of being convicted on the grounds of evidence obtained from their tissue or data. In conclusion, the understanding of what constitutes harm would need to be made more explicit.

The strictest position is proposed by the German guidelines. The general recommendation is that the state should not have access to information contained in biobanks. However, the guidelines recognize that the prevention of serious crimes could constitute an important interest that might need to be balanced against the strictest form of special research confidentiality ('Forschungsgeheimnis'). The German Ethics Council still needs to provide a final conclusion regarding to what extent the 'Forschungsgeheimnis' should be absolute (Nationaler Ethikrat 2004, 51 and 8, point 20).

Access by researchers and for commercial purposes is generally admitted by all guidelines. Several issues of controversy exist. The first question is whether the researchers who have collected material and information should always have privileged access to the genetic databank, or only during a limited period, or even never.

---

47   The forensic uses of medical biobanks are manifold (Kaye 2001a). 'When crime scene samples do not match anyone in a search of forensic databases, the application of indirect methods could identify individuals in the database who are close relatives of the potential suspects. This raises compelling policy questions about the balance between collective security and individual privacy' (Bieber, Brenner and Lazer 2006).

Although the exclusive licence of one commercial entity has been publicly condemned in Iceland and similar exclusive licences are criticized in the guidelines of the MRC, other guidelines do not share this criticism and might condone such exclusive access. However, many guidelines give preference to an exclusive control of access to material by non-commercial institutions, such as academic researchers, not-for-profit funding organizations or public biobank administrations (CCNE 2003). A frequent example is the idea of allowing privileged use of the biobank by researchers from the country in which the material has been collected (CEST 2003; CCNE 2003). Only guidelines from international organizations (HUGO 1995 and 1998; UNESCO 2003) defend the position of universal access which should not discriminate against countries with a lower degree of development. The only requirement for access accepted by all guidelines is that the standards of confidentiality in the recipient country need to be equivalent to the standards recommended in the guidelines.

The second question is how confidentiality should be assured when data are shared. The answers in the guidelines vary from prohibition of samples leaving the country to the possibility of transfer of irreversibly anonymized data or even identified data. Most frequently, the recommended procedure is to transfer reversibly anonymized data and samples, that is, data and samples are coded but the receiving researchers are not permitted to know the code.

Third, it is open to debate what kind of consent from donors is needed to allow transfer to researchers from the same or other countries. Although the consent of the donor is generally a prerequisite, guidelines vary in the extent to which they require explicit consent to the transfer (ASHG 1996), general consent (MRC 2001) or accept waivers approved by an ethics committee (NBAC 1999). The CCNE (2003) defends the idea that consent is linked to the purpose and not to the identity or localization of the researchers. Therefore access should be granted to those researchers who are most likely to use the data and samples the most efficiently for the purpose to which the donor has consented.

A fourth question is whether it should be mandatory to inform donors about possible commercial uses of their samples and/or data. Some guidelines require such information (Tri-Council 1998; MRC 2001; HGC 2002); others do not, or at least avoid providing a definite answer (NARC 1997; CCNE 2003).

Finally, should access by other researchers be limited according to the restrictions provided by patent law? Guidelines vary between explicit acceptation of the present patent laws (MRC 2001; WHO 2001) and explicit criticism (HUGO 1995; NARC 1997; Nuffield Council on Bioethics 2002).

*Formulating Adequate Recommendations about Confidentiality: What Ethics Can Contribute to the Discussion*

*Information of the donor*
From the point of view of an ethics based on the classical principles of research ethics, respect for the donor's autonomy requires that he or she is adequately

informed about the risks to confidentiality before participating in a biobank.[48] This information should include details concerning possible access to the data or samples by commercial entities and by the police, the justice system or the state. No important reason exists not to provide this information. Two reasons against providing this information are presently discussed. The first is that informed consent will become too difficult or costly if too much information has to be given. The second is that the information about commercial uses or police access will defer potential participants. This argument is used in two variants. Either the case is made that potential participants will be unnecessarily hindered from taking part in the study because the information creates disproportionate fears; or it is argued that potential participants should not know the details because too many would refuse to participate (for good reasons). In both cases, research would be severely hampered and the benefits expected to result from the research would be lost. Both variants of the argument are based on unproven empirical assumptions about the reactions of donors. The argument that adding the information about commercial use has adverse consequences, because too much information is costly, is not convincing. Indeed, the information about access by third parties does not need to contain a large amount of details. The relevant facts can be summarized in one or two sentences in an understandable way. As far as the second argument is concerned, it has not been empirically proven that information decreases willingness to participate, because of either unreasonable or justified fears of the donor. Indeed, here we face again the conflict between different interests: on the one side the autonomy and harm-reduction interests, and on the other side the efficiency–benefit interests. Since the opinion of those who argue against complete information is based on expected negative consequences of the information, that is, a decrease in participation, the first way to try to settle the controversy would be to examine the probability that this consequence would take place. This is an empirical question: will donors refuse to participate if they know about access by the police and the state, and about commercial uses? Data from Sweden indicate that use of medical biobanks by the police does not decrease trust (Bexelius, Hoeyer and Lynoe 2007). Rates of refusal to participate in biobanks vary: refusals were infrequent in Sweden (Kettis-Lindblad et al. 2006 and 2007; Johnsson et al. 2008), while the response rate in the UK was only 10 per cent (Watts 2007). Some information from consultations with the public in the United Kingdom indicates, however, that members of the public are able to understand the conflicting interests of confidentiality and public safety and accept the trade-off proposed in favour of public safety.[49] In addition, it is likely

---

48    Concerning the question how to deal with the empirical problem, Lavori et al. give the answer: do not overstate: 'It is important not to overstate the ability of the Bank to guarantee the research subject's privacy' (Lavori et al. 2002, 226). A special, and not yet sufficiently examined, problem arises if databases are aggregated/combined (Karp et al. 2008).

49    See Chapter 2: 'you have to accept that there is a risk, [but as] this is for the greater good then surely that's a good enough reason to say all right I'll go with this … [as] this is gonna help us over the longer period of time' (Opinion Leader Research 2003, 11).

that those who oppose commercial involvement will not participate anyway if they believe that they have not been correctly informed on this point. It is important to realize that the alternatives are not between high participation of an uninformed public and low participation of an informed public. The efficiency of a biobank is better served if the bank or research project includes a smaller number of donors who have made informed choices than if it includes a high number of uninformed donors who later discover important details and opt out, independently of whether the fears of the donor are realistic or unreasonable. To sum up, the analysis of the empirical consequences shows that the arguments used are rather fragile.

The second way to settle the controversy is to define which is the adequate balancing of the conflicting interests. Although we might not be able to assign absolute and definite values to the different types of interests, it has rarely been contested that autonomy and harm-reduction rights are important. As shown in Chapter 3, harm-reduction rights, and to a significant extent autonomy rights, serve to protect basic welfare interests which should outweigh purely ultimate interests. This means that the unclear benefits of future research are not sufficient to significantly limit autonomy and harm-reduction rights. In order to override such important interests, the arguments that are based on unproven negative consequences are not sufficient. The evidence would need to be more convincing: in order to justify overriding of important autonomy and harm-prevention interests, it would be necessary to prove with a higher level of certainty that the expected negative consequences will take place. In conclusion, our ethical analysis does not show support for a position against complete information of donors.

*Keeping a link versus irreversible anonymization*
Genetic research with directly identified, that is, nominative, samples is rarely justified. It is not recommended by the great majority of guidelines because of the high risk of information abuse (Deschênes et al. 2001, 223; Tri-Council 1998, 8.2). The question remains whether samples should be irreversibly (unlinked) anonymized or whether it is justified or even advisable to keep a link by using a code that permits identification of the donor.

Directly identified samples or information differ from coded samples concerning the degree to which efficiency–benefit interests and autonomy–harm-reduction interests are respected. If samples are not coded at all, this implies a higher amount of possible harm, which can rarely be justified. In order to simplify the analysis, we assume here that unlinked anonymized samples are not indirectly identifiable: it has been verified that sufficient variables have been stripped to make it impossible to identify sources. If the risk of identification is very low, these samples can be considered as 'sufficiently' or 'reasonably' anonymized.

In many cases using linked (coded) samples has the greatest number of advantages and the lowest number of disadvantages (Elger and Mauron 2003, 279, Table 2). Concerning the efficiency–benefit interest, irreversibly anonymized samples have the advantage that there are no costs for informed consent. A disadvantage is the impossibility of going back to sample sources and adding clinical course data. Concerning the autonomy interest, it is a disadvantage that there is no possibility of sample sources influencing whether certain types of research are carried out with their tissue. Finally, concerning the harm-reduction interest, it is advantageous that the risks of discrimination or stigmatization are very low. On the other hand, it is a disadvantage that it is impossible to inform sample sources if preventable or treatable diseases are detected. If samples and data remain identifiable (coded or reversibly anonymized samples and data), the advantages are the possibility of going back to sample sources and adding clinical course data, the possibility of sample sources influencing whether certain types of research are carried out with their tissue, and the possibility of informing sample sources if preventable or treatable diseases are detected. The disadvantages are the costs for informed consent and a higher risk of discrimination and stigmatization.

It is clear that the type of research influences advantages and disadvantages. Furthermore, protection against insurance and employer discrimination and against stigmatization varies in different societies and according to the type of research. The balance is more in favour of coding as compared to irreversible anonymization in countries with universal basic health insurance and with a strong anti-discrimination legislation as regards employment and basic life insurance than in a country without universal health coverage, for example, the United States. In addition, the balance depends on the probability that the research will generate information useful to prevent harm. This is again an empirical question that will only be answered more precisely in the future. Some philosophical positions are centred mainly on the idea of future harm prevention and use this expected benefit to defend the proposition that donors need always remain identifiable (Buchanan 1999). In contrast, the National Bioethics Advisory Commission (NBAC) does not consider such harm-prevention as being of overriding importance, because the possibility of preventing harm through the communication of research results is judged to occur infrequently:

> these guidelines should reflect the presumption that the disclosure of research results to subjects represents an *exceptional* [italics: B.E.] circumstance. Such disclosure should occur only when all of the following apply: (a) the findings are scientifically valid and confirmed, (b) the findings have significant implications for the participant's health concerns, and (c) a course of action to ameliorate or treat these concerns is readily available (NBAC 1999, 72).

Based on this evaluation, the NBAC guidelines permit unlinking if this 'will not unnecessarily reduce the value of the research'. This shows how opposite estimates for outcomes for which we do not have any empirical evidence certainly at present motivate opposite ethical and legal frameworks. The NBAC might be right that the probability that the research will generate findings that would require disclosure to sample donors or their relatives in the interest of harm prevention is low at the moment. But these probabilities could change between the moment of banking and the future, when researchers will use data and samples for new studies.[50] Moreover, adding future phenotypic information is an important prerequisite for many research projects. If anonymization has been irreversible, the genetic databank will be worthless for at least some, but perhaps many, further research projects.

On the other hand, keeping linked samples and data might not be the most advantageous degree of identification for a number of research projects in which clinical course data are not needed. However, if these projects use irreversibly anonymized data or samples, the results of this research cannot be integrated in the original genetic databank. This contradicts the idea that the benefit expected from genetic databanks will rely in particular on the linking together of a great number of different phenotypic and genotypic information. Efficiency–benefit interests should not be judged on the basis of a single project, but based on the overall benefit that genetic databases or biobanks will produce when they are used for a great number of different projects. The irreversible anonymization of samples and data, even if this entails no loss of beneficence for the original research project, may well provide diminished value for the entire genetic database project and many future research studies.

Another argument exists in favour of coding, that is, for maintaining identifiability: as explained above, granting irreversible anonymity for DNA and related information is virtually impossible.[51] Irreversible anonymization would therefore not necessarily be a significantly more secure solution to prevent harm, as compared to sophisticated coding techniques.

---

50   Recent advances have increased the understanding of several genes and the specific gene-line mutations responsible for carcinogenesis. This provides more and more possibilities for specific prevention ('Orphan diseases demand orphan prevention measures!'; see Muller et al. 2003, 235). This prevention is not restricted to 'classical' surgical or chemo prevention (Muller and Scott 1995), but includes new forms of prevention based on enlarged knowledge of the mechanisms of carcinogenesis (impediment of somatic mutations, induction of selection barriers which arrest the outgrowth of cancerous cell clones, and so on; see Muller, Heinimann and Dobbie 2000). In parallel, the possibilities of early non-invasive prenatal detection of genetic disease increase (Holzgreve and Hahn 2002, 86; Holzgreve and Hahn 2001), as well as the possibilities of early treatment (Surbek and Holzgreve 2002).

51   See the Tri-Council policy statement (Tri-Council 1998, 10.2.): 'genetic testing has greatly narrowed the concept of anonymous tissue'. See also the NCHGR-DOE guidelines (NCH 1996, Art. 2.): 'Large-scale DNA sequence determination represents an exception [to the possibility of protection by anonymization alone] because each person's DNA sequence is unique and ultimately, there is enough information in any individual's DNA sequence to absolutely identify her/him.' Similarly, the Human Genetics Commission (HGC 2002, 91) states: 'For example, if a person had access to a database which contained details of the DNA of a group of identifiable individuals, and if this same person had a quite separate anonymized sample of DNA, provided that the donor of the anonymized sample was on the other database, it would be possible to match the two and reach a conclusion as to identity.'

Last, but not least, when anonymization is irreversible, it will not be possible for donors to exercise their right of withdrawal. Even in the absence of any risk of harm, a person might object to certain types of research for moral or religious reasons. Typical examples are genetic research projects, the results of which might in any way encourage abortion or cloning (Campbell 1999, C12–C15). For these individuals, irreversible anonymization is contrary to their autonomy interests.

In conclusion, if one takes into account the consequences of the different degrees of identification on the conflicting interests, it can be defended that samples should be coded or reversibly anonymized rather than irreversibly anonymized. In exceptional circumstances, if otherwise the research project could not be realized, other forms of identification might be used with the consent of the donors.

*Protection of confidentiality versus prevention of discrimination*
Fears and Poste (1999, 267f) express the opinion that 'it seems preferable to act on the misuse of information rather than to promulgate further laws to protect privacy, which if poorly drafted, as in the case of considerable state law in the United States, may constrain research'.[52] Guidelines stress in general both the importance of confidentiality and the principle of non-discrimination.[53] Theoretically, even if risks of discrimination exist, these might be acceptable as long as the researchers guarantee donors complete compensation for possible harms through a particular insurance contract.[54] The analysis of consent forms shows that in many countries such insurance is not always granted (Personalized Medicine Research Project 2009). The consent form of the Marchfield Clinic (Personalized Medicine Research Project Consent 2009, 4) informs donors that risks exist for which the Research Foundation of the clinic does not provide compensation. 'While Wisconsin laws prohibit discrimination based on genetic testing, they do not apply to all types of genetic information and are difficult to enforce' (Personalized Medicine Research Project Consent 2009). The practical problem in such a case is how to prove harm which is due to stigmatization and discrimination. An example is the case of Terri Seargent. In April 1999, she went to her doctor with slight breathing difficulties. A genetic test confirmed that she had alpha-1 deficiency, which had caused the death of her brother. The test probably saved her life because the condition is treatable if detected early. But when her employer found out, she was fired (Martindale 2001; Staley 2001). Terri Seargent thinks that her employer dismissed her because of the supposed high costs of health care due to her genetic disease, but employers often declare other reasons, or other reasons might exist in addition to the genetic disease, which make it difficult to prove genetic discrimination. More importantly, some risks might not be compensated for at all, such as several years of additional

---

52   See also other authors (for example, Reilly and Page 1998).

53   See, for example, WHO (2001, 7). See also Article 6 ('Non-discrimination') of the Council of Europe (COE 2006) guidelines.

54   In Switzerland, federal law requires such insurance policies for all types of medical research.

imprisonment for Stephen Kelly (Dyer 2001; Staley 2001, 21). This was the consequence of the lawful breach of confidentiality, because law enforcement officers have access to confidential research data, according to the British Data Protection Act of 1998.

The analysis and evaluation of consequences will certainly show differences between countries, depending on the laws and the availability of social insurance which will reduce the risk of harm. No compelling reason exists against the adoption and implementation of efficient anti-discrimination legislation. The difficulty of protecting efficiently against discrimination in practice underlines the importance of additional protection of confidentiality through other measures such as confidentiality laws and efficient coding. Another argument against the proposition of Fears and Poste (1999, 267) to rely mainly on anti-discrimination laws is that, although laws can limit open forms of discrimination, they do not influence stigmatization which can cause significant harm to a subject and might be even more difficult to prove than discrimination.

*Group confidentiality*
Respect for the autonomy of persons, the principles of beneficence and non-maleficence and the principle of justice, all underscore the justification of group confidentiality. The autonomy and harm-reduction interests of groups and their members are in conflict with the efficiency–benefit interests of biobank research. It is not a solution, as proposed by some guidelines (Nationaler Ethikrat 2004), to refer to the fact that in a certain number of Western countries the population is rather homogenous and is therefore not confronted with the same ethical issues as the United States or Australia concerning Indian or Aboriginal tribes. This view neglects the fact that the problem of group confidentiality is not limited to ethnic groups, but also concerns groups of individuals suffering from the same disease or having been exposed to the same environmental factors. Using efficiency–benefit interests as an argument against group confidentiality is only marginally justified. Indeed, if coding of the group identity and all usual forms of protection of confidentiality are employed with scrutiny, the most important problem specific to group confidentiality remains the publication of the research results. A way to limit or at least to control harm would be to require approval of an ethics committee before publication. This requirement can be waived routinely at the onset of the study for all research projects that do not deal with sensitive group characteristics.

*The degree of adequate confidentiality: How is it determined and by whom?*
The acceptable degree of what constitutes adequate confidentiality will vary from country to country. However, in light of the benefits of international collaboration in research projects, the objective should be to require standards of confidentiality that are sufficient in the areas of the world where the risk of harm is the greatest. The price of such international standards will be an increased cost for the research, that is, a setback to the efficiency–benefit interest. As an alternative solution it may

be justified to limit collaboration to countries with social insurance and functioning anti-discrimination legislation. Such limitations of collaboration might be a way to motivate some countries to adopt social conditions comparable to those in many European countries. However, setting very high standards of (costly) confidentiality will also have a discriminatory effect on developing countries, because they may not have the means to provide for efficient confidentiality. A way out of this dilemma consists in requiring funding agencies from rich countries to provide the additional costs for securing confidentiality in order to permit collaborations with poor countries.

Before the controversy about adequate confidentiality is settled, the only solution is to act according to what most guidelines recommend: the degree of confidentiality needs to be evaluated and described at the onset of each project. Then an ethics committee decides whether the proposed degree of confidentiality is adequate, and finally donors have the choice of agreeing to participation under the explained conditions of confidentiality or not.

An ongoing form of group control regarding confidentiality, as proposed by the guidelines of the North American Regional Committee (NARC 1997), is problematic due to the same problems that one encounters with group consent or consultation. Ongoing control could be beneficial if the group has any legitimate authorities or structures which permit determination of the preferences of the group in a valid way. In light of these difficulties, the same criteria should apply as for group consent versus consultation: it will depend on the characteristics of the group. Ongoing control regarding confidentiality is less important than group consent at the onset of the research, because in the latter case the group has the possibility of determining before the project starts which conditions are acceptable for confidentiality. If the project and the surrounding conditions do not change, the need for ongoing control is low. It can be left to the ethics committee, as explained above (under 'Group confidentiality'), to decide whether the planned publications pose a threat to confidentiality and whether, therefore, the group needs to be involved again.

*Who is responsible for granting confidentiality?*
Ethical responsibility for granting confidentiality lies with all persons in contact with samples or data. All those who deal with samples and data should try to avoid harm and respect the autonomy of donors. This leaves the empirical problem how the ethical conduct of all possible researchers and auxiliary personnel involved should be controlled. Details of this control need to be tailored to the existing structure and organization of the biobank. A question of justice is involved if the implementation of this control requires substantial amounts of resources which would need to be taken from other fields or distributed between competing projects, for example, the costs of verifying whether a coding system is secure. However, this problem is in principle not specific to research. Regulating responsibility in medical and research confidentiality is not a new problem and the control of these responsibilities does not require different structures than those that exist already.

*Limits to confidentiality: What constitutes legitimate access?*
The protection of confidentiality has technical limits: it is impossible to exclude completely accidental violations of confidentiality and illegitimate access. In addition, access to the data and samples of a biobank is legitimate and even ethically required in some circumstances. We do not discuss here access by drug regulatory authorities and audits that control research. This type of access is part of classical research ethics and is justified by the necessity of quality control. We will not discuss here the classical foundations on which limits to medical confidentiality are based in most ethical and legal frameworks. Instead, we will restrict our analysis to the question whether access to samples and data in biobanks should be regulated more strictly than it is according to the traditional standards of medical confidentiality. Classical limits to ethical and legal principles are listed in the Convention on Human Rights and Biomedicine. According to this Convention, legitimate limits on ethical principles and protective provisions are those that are 'prescribed by law and are necessary in a democratic society in the interest of public safety, for the prevention of crime, for the protection of public health or for the protection of the rights and freedoms of others' (COE 1997, Art. 26). However, '[t]he restrictions contemplated in the preceding paragraph may not be placed on Articles 11, 13, 14, 16, 17, 19, 20 and 21'. These articles stipulate non-discrimination on the grounds of genetic heritage (Art. 11), the prohibition of genetic modification in germ cells (Art. 13), the prohibition of sex selection (Art. 14), the protection of persons undergoing research (Arts 16 and 17), the protection of living donors in organ and tissue removal for transplantation purposes (Arts 19 and 20) and the prohibition of financial gain from the human body and its parts (Art. 21). The protection of persons undergoing research and non-discrimination on the grounds of genetic heritage are apparently thought to be of such importance that, in this case, usual legitimate limits are not justified.

We argue that in the case of genetic databanks a stricter form of confidentiality is justified for deontological and consequentialist reasons: first, non-discrimination for genetic reasons has been recognized as a principle overriding other legitimate interests which exist in a democracy (COE 1997, Arts 11 and 26). As shown above, even in the presence of anti-discrimination laws, protection of the genetically worst-off is not guaranteed. As a consequence, confidentiality must be secured and access must be limited more strictly in all clinical and research activities that generate information about hereditary characteristics. Second, a characteristic of research involving biobanks as compared to other research is that, in general, donors provide their samples for a vast array of purposes and for a long period. At the same time, since biobank research does not involve donors themselves in person, they are not able to control physically what happens to their DNA. This extended power of biobanks must be compensated by a higher threshold for reasons that constitute legitimate limits to confidentiality. Third, from a consequentialistic view, no major reason exists to grant the state, the police, the justice system, insurance companies or employers access to data or samples. The investigation of crimes can in general be ensured by other means than access to research material. Paternity tests can serve as an example: if the presupposed father does not agree to provide a blood sample, he is treated as if he were the father. For very few crimes will access to biobanks be the only means to assure proof finding and in even fewer cases will crime prevention rely on access to biobanks. Allowing general access by the state, the police or the justice system is of little benefit compared to the consequences that such access might have on the public image of biobanks. Granting access to employers, insurance companies or schools is even less beneficial. Only extremely few situations exist in which the harm that could be prevented using data or samples from biobanks will be so important as to justify access. Such examples, for example, related to public health in the case of life-threatening diseases or to the true prevention of severe crimes (significantly different from the case of Stephen Kelly, see Dyer 2001; Staley 2001, 21), should be defined clearly with regard to the degree of harm that is considered an acceptable threshold to permit overriding confidentiality. In order to have a realistic idea what their participation in a biobank implies, donors should be informed about this threshold: typical cases should be described in which confidentiality will be overridden.

Except for these rare situations defined in advance, the consent of the donor should always be required before third parties may obtain access to samples and data for other than medical or research purposes. From an ethical point of view, this consent should be informed, given freely and without coercion. The WHO guidelines (1998) warn that this might not be the case if access to the data or samples is requested by institutions that have the power to coerce individuals, such as the state, schools, insurance companies and employers. However, this risk of coercion cannot justify an absolute ban on the transmission of information. Donors have the right, although not without limits, to know about data obtained from their samples and to communicate the results to another person. A way to solve the dilemma is to examine whether the third party has any important reason to know the data. As discussed with regard to access by the state, the crucial question is where the threshold should be set. Important arguments exist to choose a high threshold. This means that only the avoidance of immediate and significant harm should justify access. For schools and employers, such situations do not exist. If an employer decides to screen individuals for genetic diseases that may create risks to others, it is justified to let candidates start work only after they have consented to a test. An example would be a possible test for hereditary heart disease causing sudden death in a school bus driver. Access to genetic databanks is not necessary.

Insurance companies claim that if they do not know the results of genetic tests that are known by an individual, they will not be able to calculate adequately the actuarial risk for this person. They claim that companies may go bankrupt or that the insurance premiums will be so high that low-risk individuals will not be able or interested to buy insurance. In the first place, this does not seem to constitute any significant immediate harm, especially since measures exist to cover the period of empirical evaluation during which it is examined whether the consequences predicted by the insurance companies will be of the alleged importance. Such a measure could be to involve reassurance companies that might be backed up by public money. Whether higher insurance premiums to all are acceptable depends on the extent to which an insurance type is perceived to be a basic social good. In many countries, the burden of health insurance is shared equally between healthy and ill individuals. If not being able to buy life insurance disadvantages individuals in an important way, life insurance, at least up to a moderate amount of coverage, should become part of an obligatory social insurance system.

We conclude that the third parties mentioned do not have sufficiently important reasons to access the data kept in biobanks. However, prohibiting the direct access of third parties to biobank data or results does not completely protect donors against genetic discrimination. If donors have been informed about data or results, institutions might address a request to individuals to transmit these data. Even if there is no obligation to inform insurance companies, discrimination will result from the fact that those with low risk will agree to transmit their data. This means that insurance companies might charge higher premiums to all individuals who do not agree to transmit results. Two ways exist to protect donors against this risk of discrimination, but both have drawbacks. The first is to decide that donors will not be informed at all about their results. This is problematic because it is contrary to the principle of autonomy or respect for persons, reflected in European data protection laws and the Oviedo Convention (COE 1997): these stipulate that individuals should have the possibility of knowing the information stored about them. In addition, not informing donors at all would hinder them in receiving information that might be useful for them to prevent diseases or to plan their life. The second way to protect donors is to punish the use of genetic information by insurance companies. However, as with other anti-discrimination laws, this kind of protection is not absolute, since it would not always be possible to prove that the refusal of insurance is motivated by reasons related to genetic characteristics.

*Acceptable solutions for access of researchers and access for commercial purposes*
This title encompasses a number of important and timely questions.[55] First of all, should the researchers who have collected material and information have privileged access to the genetic databank during a limited period or in general? Guidelines from international organizations (HUGO; UNESCO) claim that access to biobanks should be universal and should not discriminate against countries with a different degree of development. Different arguments may be used in favour of universal access. The first refers to the fact that humans share most of their genes. According to this argument, from the sharing of genes it follows that DNA stored in biobanks is a common resource and should be accessible by researchers from all over the world. However, this argument is based on the naturalistic fallacy, and can therefore be easily criticized. The second argument refers to the principle of justice and is problematic too, because the principle of justice can be used to

---

55   See a selection of publications on these issues (Anonymous 2007; Lenk, Hoppe and Andorno 2007; Clement, Chene and Degos 2009; Pennisi 2009) and of practical aspects (Shevde and Riker 2009, 6.2).

support many different positions. Equality could be interpreted as equal access for all, or equality for equals.[56] The former idea of justice supports universal access, whereas the idea of equality for equals could be used to defend privileged access for the researchers who have collected the material or for researchers coming from or working in the same country as the donors who have contributed their DNA. A third argument is based on the idea of scientific freedom. As shown in Chapter 3, several guidelines list 'freedom of research' or 'scientific freedom' among their basic values. Freedom of research is not only a principle founded on a deontological or human rights approach. It is also based on the consequentialist argument that 'free access to scientific knowledge and data is essential to scientific progress' (Bourne 2003, 786). According to the International Council for Science (ICSU), 'there would be few, if any circumstances in which the principle should be overridden' (Lubchenco, Rosswall and Warren 2003, 785). The fourth argument refers to the benefit of the research. The assumption is that hindering access to genetic databanks will hamper the progress of science. The opposite view is held by those who defend privileged access to the samples for the institutions and researchers who have collected the material, as well as access limits based on patent laws and the concept of intellectual property. Those who support limited access are convinced that research will advance faster if incentives exist such as profit from privileged access and through patenting. This consequentialist argument is of limited value, because it is difficult to prove whether one or the other hypothesis is true (Nuffield Council on Bioethics 2002).

In conclusion, it is not possible to resolve the controversy by referring to robust data about consequences. The references to justice or to the common genetic heritage of mankind are of limited value as well. They could even support the opposite views. So we are left with the principle of scientific freedom: if interpreted in a quasi absolute way, it speaks in favour of universal access to databases. Such an ethical requirement could come into conflict with the legal concept that data can be owned by a biobank and samples, although they cannot be sold (COE 1997, Art. 7), can be stolen, that is, access to samples requires at least the consent of the institution where they are stored. From a legal point of view, the principle of scientific freedom is rather a right to non-interference[57] and does not include a positive right to universal access to databases. In contrast to such a legal approach, an ethical approach based on a virtue ethics could go further and require researchers to grant, if possible, universal access. Empirical studies

---

56　See Aristotle book V 3 (Aristotle 350 BCE) or in the German version, page 202ss (2. Das objektiv Gerechte).

57　See also Trouet (2004, 101) who argues that freedom of scientific research 'should be interpreted correctly'. This means that scientific freedom does not imply a positive right. Trouet does not refer to the example of universal access, but to the use of scientific freedom as an argument to justify a positive right for researchers to the use of tissue. 'Freedom of research does not imply a (legal or moral) obligation for patients of research subjects to have their tissue used for research' (Trouet 2004, 101).

designed to clarify the uncertain consequences of various access policies would certainly be helpful in this debate. In the absence of such evaluation, a modest degree of privileged access by those who have collected the DNA contained in a biobank, or financed its collection, seems a reasonable compromise.

A second question is how confidentiality should be assured when data are shared. Should it be required that samples or data leave the country only if they are irreversibly anonymized, is reversible anonymization or coding sufficient, or should even the transfer of identified data be possible? In previous paragraphs of the section on confidentiality we have concluded that, even in the presence of anti-discrimination and confidentiality laws, the protection of the anonymity of samples and data through information technology (IT) is important. We have also shown that the use of irreversibly anonymized data has important disadvantages. From this it follows that data should best be transferred in a reversibly anonymized form where access to the code is restricted to the custodians of the biobanks or an independent third party. Empirical research should take place in order to define the security of different coding systems. Only if the use of coded samples or data implies significant risks to confidentiality might the use of irreversibly anonymized data or anonymous samples be preferable.

A third question exists as to which kind of consent from donors is needed to allow the transfer of samples or data to researchers from the same or from other countries. Projects of transfer are part of further research or storage projects. Consent to these projects should be handled in the same way as consent to future research projects in general. To foster universal access by researchers, the possibility of the transfer of data or samples should be explained to donors when consent is obtained to the storage of their DNA and their personal information.

A fourth question is whether it should be mandatory that donors are informed about possible commercial uses of their samples and data. Two reasons speak in favour of informing donors. First, for a sizeable percentage of possible donors, the element of 'commercial use' is relevant and influences their decision whether to participate or not. Informed consent to research signifies that information which is relevant to the decision of a reasonable person is provided. Second, not informing about commercial uses might diminish participation even more than informing, because donors who do not want to support commercial research would be forced to renounce participation in all research involving tissue banking.[58] The

---

58   It is sometimes argued that separating commercial and non-commercial uses is virtually impossible, because (1) even public institutions will claim intellectual property rights and use royalties in their interest, and (2) many public institutions depend partly on private funding. It is also argued that scientists 'have a duty to explore ways in which their results can be applied'. Therefore, researchers are encouraged to work with commercial companies as described by Evans (1996, 1828) where she reports an interview with George Radda. However, these practices can be changed. Exploring ways to apply scientific results can be done outside the context of commercial companies. Intellectual property rights can be used strictly to fund new research with or without claiming royalties from patents.

opposite consequences are predicted by opponents of complete information about commercial uses. They claim that informing donors on commercial uses will diminish participation (Parliamentary Office of Science and Technology 2002). Empirical studies about participation might help to settle this controversy.[59] Although one could imagine offering donors the possibility of specifically opting out of certain types of commercial research, this requires complicated tracking methods of donors' wishes and might not be realistic in light of the frequent entanglement of public and private interests in biobank research.

Finally, the question remains as to whether access by other researchers should be limited according to the restrictions foreseen by patent law. This question is similar to the previously discussed question whether researchers who have collected material and information should have privileged access to the genetic databank during a limited period of time. While the empirical consequences of more or less restrictive patenting are not clear, the ideal of scientific freedom points towards avoidance of patenting or less restrictive patents. This position has been voiced by several guidelines. The adequate answer is probably not for or against patenting, but in favour of some adaptation of patent laws in the direction of limiting privileges and favouring public interests. Some clarification of the consequences should be attempted: studies should try to define a methodology by which the consequences of more or less universal access, compared to more or less restrictions through patenting, could be evaluated for different research projects. Although it seems difficult to construct a scenario in which the same kind of project could be compared under different conditions, some conclusions might be drawn from the observations of different projects under different conditions.

---

Examples of patient associations show that alternatives exist which would probably be accepted by most of those who declare themselves being 'against commercial uses'.

59    The study by Danzer et al. (2003) indicates that it is very important for donors to be informed exhaustively about future uses and to ensure that donors can trust that their tissue is not used for purposes to which the donor has not consented. Although the study has not tested attitudes towards commercialization, the results concerning anxiety in the population that tissue will be used for purposes to which they did not agree might be generalized. The authors have distributed standardized, anonymous questionnaires to women six months after unrelated cord blood donation (for allogeneic stem cell transplantation). Most of the women who filled in the questionnaire (participation 59.5 per cent) stated that they would donate cord blood again, but 63 per cent reported experiencing anxiety and having objections about improper use or abuse of donated blood for genetic testing and manipulation or cloning. With regard to the risk of 'experimentation' and genetic testing of the donated samples, a significant correlation (p = 0.01) existed between these negative attitudes and the decision not to donate umbilical cord blood again. If the aim is to avoid 'irrational fears' (Muller 1991) in the public, the first step is to inform correctly about all purposes. This is the only way to prevent 'irrational legal restrictions imposed by an ill informed public' (Muller 1991, 1751).

*Confidentiality and Access: Many Questions and Many Answers*

Protection of confidentiality remains the backbone of biobank research. Finding the right balance between protection of donors and the advancement of science through global sharing of genetic databases among researchers is crucial. Many questions persist and different forms of balancing can count as justified answers. The most important ethical imperative is perhaps not to find a single best answer, but to ensure that the process of how this balance is defined is transparent, to search for new technological solutions (Reischl et al. 2006) and to require that the consequences of different protections, such as coding and anonymization, be measured with scrutiny in order to guide further decisions. Confidentiality is a major concern when it comes to the feedback of study results to sample donors. This complex issue justifies a separate discussion in the following section.

## Feedback to Study Participants

Guidelines provide different answers to the question whether participants should be informed about the results of research projects involving genetic databases and under which conditions the feedback of results should take place (for example, availability of genetic counselling).

*The Right to Know of Research Participants*

*Classical research ethics guidelines*
Among the classical guidelines for biomedical research, the Convention on Human Rights and Biomedicine (COE 1997) and its Additional Protocol Concerning Biomedical Research (COE 2005) address the issue explicitly. Based on the 'right to information', the Convention takes a position implying a *right to know and not to know*: 'Everyone is entitled to know any information collected about his or her health. However, the wishes of individuals not to be so informed shall be observed' (COE 1997, Art. 10, para. 2). 'In exceptional cases, restrictions may be placed by law on the exercise of the rights contained in paragraph 2 in the interests of the patient.' The Additional Protocol Concerning Biomedical Research explains the right to know in more detail. To begin with research participants should have access to aggregated results. The 'conclusions of the research shall be made available to participants in reasonable time, on request' (COE 2005, Art. 28). Furthermore, the Additional Protocol stipulates the duty to offer individual health-relevant information to research participants:

> If research gives rise to information of relevance to the current or future health or quality of life of research participants, this information must be offered to them. That shall be done within a framework of health care or counselling. In communication of such information, due care must be taken in order to protect

confidentiality and to respect any wish of a participant not to receive such information (COE 2005, Art. 27 'Duty of care').

During the past five years a certain shift has been observed. With few exceptions (Forsberg, Hansson and Eriksson 2009), more weight has been given to the right to be informed about research results (Knoppers et al. 2006).[60] While the most recent version of the Declaration of Helsinki contains only a right to be informed about general research results ('the outcome of the study', WMA 2008, para. 33), the guidelines for epidemiological research (CIOMS 2009) strongly support the right to know. These guidelines state (CIOMS 2009, guideline 5) 'that subjects have the right of access to their data on demand, even if these data lack immediate clinical utility (unless the ethical review committee has approved temporary or permanent non-disclosure of data, in which case the subject should be informed of, and given, the reasons for such non-disclosure)'. This text is remarkable for two reasons. First, the guidelines acknowledge the right to know, not only for clinically relevant data, but also for data that 'lack immediate clinical utility'. Second, the information about individual results is considered the default approach. Researchers who do not plan to inform research participants have to obtain ethics committee approval for their practice and must inform research subjects about the 'reasons for such non-disclosure'.

In spite of the recent reinforcement of the *right to know*, it is almost never granted without any restrictions. Information might be withheld if this is in the interest of the patient. Not to inform patients is justified, for example, if the information is likely to cause serious harm to them. In legal terms, this exception is called the 'therapeutic privilege'. Indeed, the Convention on Human Rights and Biomedicine (Oviedo) states that the exceptions must be authorized 'by law'. Although international legal documents such as the Oviedo Convention and international guidelines stress the right to know, studies show that it only occurs infrequently that researchers offer to return individual results to research participants.[61]

*The right to know in guidelines relevant for research involving biobanks*
The WHO Regional Office for Europe mentions the right of research participants to obtain access to their data and underlines that access should be in line with the

---

60    In parallel, an 'evolution in liability' has been observed in the clinical context (Burke and Rosenbaum 2005).

61    Several studies show that although the feedback of research results to participants is increasingly considered an ethical obligation (Knoppers et al. 2006; Ravitsky and Wilfond 2006), it is rarely done, due to financial costs and the difficulty of retaining contact with study participants (Fernandez et al. 2003a and 2003b; Fernandez, Kodish and Weijer 2003c; Fernandez et al. 2005; Rigby and Fernandez 2005; MacNeil and Fernandez 2006; Fernandez et al. 2007; Kozanczyn, Collins and Fernandez 2007; MacNeil and Fernandez 2007; Fernandez 2008).

Convention on Human Rights and Biomedicine and with European data protection laws:

> Where personally identifiable information is held in a database, then subject access rights to this information should be granted. These rights should be akin to those embodied in international data protection instruments, such as the EC Directive on the Protection of Individuals with Regard to the Processing of Personal Data and on the Free Movement of Such Data (WHO 2001, 18).

Another declaration that clearly affirms the right to know individual results is the UNESCO Declaration on Human Genetic Data (2003). This right is not absolute and may be limited by domestic law 'in the interest of public health, public order or national security'. Another exception, 'unless such data are unretrievably unlinked', is not based on ethical but on practical grounds. It is self-evident and one wonders why it needed to be mentioned.[62]

The Tri-Council statement mentions a general obligation of the 'genetics researcher' to report results 'if the individual so desires' (Tri-Council 1998, 8.1). The guidelines do not specify whether individual results or overall research findings need to be reported and in which form. They recommend broadly that '[the] genetics researcher shall report results to that individual'.

The Council of Europe (2006) refers to the provisions in the Additional Protocol Concerning Biomedical Research (COE 2005), in particular Article 27 (see above) and Article 26, which both underline the right to information:

> 1. Research participants shall be entitled to know any information collected on their health in conformity with the provisions of Article 10 of the Convention. 2. Other personal information collected for a research project will be accessible to them in conformity with the law on the protection of individuals with regard to processing of personal data (COE 2005, Art. 26).

The Explanatory Report (CDBI 2002b) notes that the right to be informed does not necessarily imply personal information: research results could be communicated 'by way of general information such as a newsletter' and 'should not necessarily consist of a personal communication with each participant, which would often be impracticable'. In addition, the Explanatory Report mentions as a possible exception research for which 'contacting the research subjects to inform them of the availability of research results would [...] be impracticable'.

The Medical Research Council affirms not only that participants have a right to know results, but states, in line with Article 27 of the Additional Protocol, that

---

62   See UNESCO (2003, Art. 13): 'Access: No one should be denied access to his or her own genetic data or proteomic data unless such data are irretrievably unlinked to that person as the identifiable source or unless domestic law limits such access in the interest of public health, public order or national security.'

the researcher has a 'duty of care' to communicate results in certain circumstances: 'Research participants have a right to know individual research results that affect their interests, but should be able to choose whether to exercise that right. If research results have immediate clinical relevance, there is a clear duty of care to ensure the participant is informed' (MRC 2001, 18).

*Communication of results to the community*
The guidelines of the North American Regional Committee (NARC 1997), which are mostly concerned with population research, recommend informing participants about results. However, instead of referring to a right to know, the NARC bases its recommendations on the consequentialist argument that such a practice might avoid resentment and make the public more knowledgeable about science.

Researchers should make, and keep, a commitment to the community which includes the reporting of research results at specified times and in specified manners (NARC 1997, part X.C.). The recommendation mentions only the communication of results to the community. The rights of the individual to receive personal results are not defined.

*Restrictions to the right to know: Feedback of general results only*
Some guidelines recommend that participants should not be informed about individual results, but only about the general results of the research. Others state that it should depend on the study type whether results should be communicated or not. The second is often, but not always, associated with the first.

The most pronounced example of guidelines which recommend only the *feedback of general results* are the guidelines of the Human Genetics Commission (HGC 2002). '[We] would encourage general feed-back on the overall progress of the research [...] through the use of newsletters' (HGC 2002, 106). The HGC bases its opinion on the evaluation that results of most research would not be 'relevant to the individual participant's health'. Feedback is not considered practical because it is difficult to make individual contact and to offer genetic counselling to all who wish to receive their results. Since the HGC admits that, for some research, results might be 'relevant to the individual participant's health', the second idea that feedback should depend on the study is also expressed. A similar position is held by the HUGO Statement on benefit-sharing. It recommends that participants 'should [...] receive information about the general outcome(s) of research in understandable language. The ethical advisability of provision of information to individuals about their results should be determined separately for each specific project' (HUGO 2000).

The College of American Pathologists (CAP) takes the most extreme standpoint. According to the CAP, a single project does not generate irrefutable scientific facts. Therefore, information about results obtained in only one project is not recommended. Feedback should be restricted to information about scientific progress in general in order to satisfy the interest of society to be informed about robust evidence-based research findings (Grizzle et al. 1999, 299).

Unlike the guidelines of the College of American Pathologists, the guidelines of the British pathologists stress that feedback should not be restricted to general forms. The Royal College of Pathologists (RCP 2001, 67) recommends that communication of results to individuals should not be excluded. The RCP argues that not transmitting beneficial information (for example, informing about idiosyncratic drug reaction which could be life-saving) is as bad as providing information that causes harm. The position of the RCP is compatible with the recommendations of the Human Genetics Commission, depending on the criteria used to define under which conditions feedback is beneficial. The MRC goes one step further (MRC 2001, 19–20). It holds that general information about the results is 'good practice' but 'may not be appropriate in all circumstances'. Feedback of results that 'might impact on the donors' interests' should be offered. First, general information should be provided via newsletters or websites. Second, these documents should indicate to donors the possibility that they might contact the researcher to know individual results. The onus to obtain the information would lie on the participant. The MRC seems to distinguish between results that 'impact on the donors' interests' and results that 'have immediate clinical relevance' (MRC 2001, 18). Researchers have a duty to communicate the latter (see above). For results that 'impact on the donors' interest', general information in newsletters is considered sufficient. However, this practice would mean that donors are allowed to act in a way that might not be in their interest: that is, they might not read the newsletters and therefore not learn about results which impact on their interests.

*Restrictions to the right to know: Strict criteria to define which results should be fed back to the individual*
Common opinion is that the informing of participants about the results of research should depend both on the project and on the type of results generated by the research (Renegar et al. 2006). Several guidelines define criteria in order to limit the situations in which feedback of results should take place. A closer look shows that in most guidelines the precise definition of the criteria is open to interpretation.

The ASHG statement on the principled conduct of genetic research (1996) grants the right not to know, but believes that the right to know depends on the study. The most important condition for feedback is the validity and certainty of research findings ('results may not allow definite answers [...]. Under such circumstances, results cannot be communicated expeditiously'). We have already mentioned above the criteria provided by the RCP and the MRC: 'beneficial' information should be fed back (RCP 2001) as well as information that might impact on the interests of donors (MRC 2001). More precisely, for the MRC the following conditions indicate whether feedback is appropriate: immediate clinical relevance and the predictive value of the results. The MRC cautions, however, that these criteria are not clear-cut because it is not easy to define when a research hypothesis becomes a fact (MRC 2001, 8.4, 19).

The National Bioethics Advisory Commission (NBAC 1999) proposes more elaborate and strict criteria. Disclosure should only take place if the following conditions are fulfilled simultaneously: the findings are valid and confirmed, significant implications for the subject's health concerns exist, and a course of action to ameliorate or treat these concerns is readily available.

The Network of Applied Genetic Medicine (RMGA) guidelines require the return of general results to all participants. Individual results should only be returned if they fulfil criteria that are almost identical to those of the NBAC: 'When results are scientifically valid, have significant implications for the health of the participant and prevention or treatment is available, these results should be communicated to the participant by his treating physician, unless the participant has chosen not to receive any results' (RMGA 2000, IV 2 and 3).

*Information about the provided feedback before the donor consents to participate*
Independently from the degree to which guidelines support feedback, consensus exists that the possibility and type of feedback should be explained to subjects before they give their consent to participation in the research.

The UNESCO guidelines recommend that 'the information provided at the time of consent should indicate that the person concerned has the right to decide whether or not to be informed of the results' (UNESCO 2003, Art. 10). HUGO states that '[c]hoices to be informed or not with regard to results or incidental findings should also be respected. Such choices bind other researchers and laboratories. In this way, personal, cultural, and community values can be respected' (HUGO 1995). The NARC guidelines state that '"results" usually take much longer and are much less informative than the research participants expect. The researchers must make sure that the community has a realistic understanding of what results can be expected and in how many years.' The ASHG (1996) recommends informing participants about the available means of communicating results, possible outcomes, limitations, what information might reasonably be expected, and about the possibility of unexpected findings. The CEST guidelines include the possibility of informing participants, in general via their physician, about some results.[63] According to the CEST, the consent form should mention whether the possibility of being informed about results exists or not, and whether the donor wishes to know the results or not.

The HGC (2002, 105) requires that it 'should be made clear whether or not there is to be any feed-back and what form this will take'. Since participants need sufficient information in order to make an informed decision about whether they would like to be informed of the results or not, researchers must decide before the study starts whether any feedback will take place and in what form. The HGC does not discuss the difficulty, characteristic of biobanks, that future studies are not yet defined and how to deal with the right to know and not to know for unknown research.

---

63 'Lorsque les données n'ont pas été anonymisées de façon irréversible, il est possible de retracer la personne participante, généralement par l'entremise de son médecin, afin de l'informer de certains résultats de la recherche qui la concernent' (CEST 2003, 48).

*The Right Not to Know of the Participant*

Most guidelines affirm a *right not to know* research results.[64] The right not to know is part of Article 10 of the Convention on Human Rights and Biomedicine (COE 1997) which is part of the human rights framework defended by the Council of Europe. Interestingly, in its Explanatory Report, the CDBI (2002b, 14) seems to suggest that persons who prefer not to know results ought not to participate in research:

> The individual's exercise of the right not to know this or that fact concerning his or her health is not regarded as an impediment to the validity of his or her consent. However, if relevant information is expected in the process, and the information might help prevent or cure a disease and the person does not want to find out, then this could be regarded as an impediment to performance of the research. In such cases, it would be better not to involve such persons in research projects.

This is in line with the duty to inform about health-relevant results that is found in Article 27 of the Additional Protocol Concerning Biomedical Research (COE 2005). It shows a shift in the preoccupation of the COE towards the transmission of beneficial information as a default solution.

Similar restrictions of a right not to know are found in the guidelines of the MRC with regard to 'incidental clinical findings':

> Where a result that can be linked to an individual has immediate clinical relevance (for example, if it reveals a serious condition for which treatment is required), the clinician involved has a clear duty of care to inform the research participant, either directly or via the clinician responsible for his or her care. The clinician responsible for care should always be notified, and *participants should be informed that this will occur* (MRC 2001, 18/19: 8.3).

The MRC seems to imagine a consent form even more restrictive than the one used by the Swiss Pediatric Oncology Group Tumor Bank (SPOG, see Chapter 2): according to the MRC, donors would need to be informed that incidental findings that have important impacts on their health will imperatively be communicated to their physician, whereas participants in the SPOG biobank are informed that feedback of these results will occur *if they do not object*. Indeed, although the underlying assumption is that the wish not to know is unusual or even unreasonable, the SPOG consent forms provide the possibility of exercising the right not to know.

---

64   See, for example, WHO (2001, 17), UNESCO (2003). HUGO (1995) states: 'Choices to be informed or not with regard to results or incidental findings should also be respected. Such choices bind other researchers and laboratories. In this way, personal, cultural, and community values can be respected.'

A particular problem concerning biobanks results from the fact that in order to exercise the right not to know in an informed manner, the type of future results or incidental findings, as well as the consequences of knowing these results, would have to be clear. However, this is only partially the case at the onset of a project or of storing. The guidelines of the WHO (2001) contain a detailed reflection on criteria which help to decide when incidental findings should be fed back to individuals, even if it is not known whether they would like to receive this information:

> Adequate account must be taken of the privacy interest that individuals have in not knowing information about themselves. Before any unsolicited approach is made, the following factors must be considered: (1) the availability of a cure or therapy; (2) the severity of the condition and likelihood of onset; (3) the nature of the genetic disease; (4) the genetic nature of the disease, i.e. – that it might have significant implications for blood relatives; (5) the nature of any genetic testing that will be required; (6) the question of how the individual might be affected if subjected to unwarranted information, and whether the individual has expressed any views on receiving information of this kind (WHO 2001, 17, recommendation 16).

*To Know or Not to Know: The Mechanism for Participants to Change Their Minds*

Rarely do guidelines recommend that procedures should be in place for participants to change their mind, for example, via contact phone numbers (MRC 2001, 19: 8.4). Guidelines which reflect on practical issues such as the updating of addresses state that it is the duty of participants and not of researchers or the biobank to update addresses (MRC 2001; RMGA 2000; ASHG 1988).

*The Right to Know or Not to Know of Relatives*

Guidelines disagree about the right of relatives to know research results. Theoretically, three different ways to inform relatives exist. The most direct way (1) would be to tell them the donor's results and explain to them how these findings change their own genetic risks. Another way would be to tell the relatives that some genetic diseases had been found in the study carried out with the donor's material. However, to give the relatives the possibility of making an informed decision on whether they wanted to be tested themselves, they would need to know details on the given diseases. In order to maintain the confidentiality of donors, all relatives of all donors would need to receive the same general information (2a). If the relatives of donors carrying a mutation were informed specifically about the genetic disease (2b), they would automatically know that the donor from their family must be affected. A third possibility (3) would be to require the donor's consent. If the donor refused, or was not able to give consent (because he or she was durably incompetent or dead), one would permit access to the donor's material only if, for clinical purposes, the use of this material was necessary to benefit a family member. Apart from the one possibility (2a) which is not related to specific research results, almost all the positions [(1), (2b) and (3)] require, in practice, a breach of confidentiality with regard to the donor.

### The extreme positions

*General access*   The most extreme position in favour of general access is expressed in the WHO guidelines (1998). They affirm the right of families to be informed: 'Consent should specify that family members may request access to a sample to learn their own genetic status but not that of the donor' (WHO 1998, 13). As discussed above, the problem is that the restriction in only granting family members the right to know about their own status, but not the results of the donor, does in practice not always protect the confidentiality of donors. Certain results in family members definitely reveal the carrier status of donors for particular genes or mutations. This problem is not discussed in the WHO guidelines.

*Access only for an important public interest reason*   The UNESCO guidelines (2003) take the most extreme opposite position, that is, against a right to know of relatives. Article 14b states that human genetic data 'should not be disclosed or made accessible to [...] the family, except for an important public interest reason'. Apparently, benefits to the health of a single relative do not justify disclosure of information to a relative against the donor's wishes. In addition, in Article 10 relatives are also granted only a limited right *not* to know. The guidelines recognize the right not to know 'where appropriate' of 'identified relatives who may be affected by the results'. Readers of Article 10 might ask themselves what are identified and unidentified relatives. Furthermore, the text is open to interpretation, because the conditions under which it will be appropriate to inform or not to inform relatives are not specified.

### The intermediate positions

*Broadly defined conditions for access: If results might impact on the relatives' interests*   The MRC is supportive of the rights of families. 'The potential implications for relatives of any research to be done using linked samples must be discussed, and they must be given the opportunity to learn about any research results that might impact on their interests' (MRC 2001, 25). These guidelines indicate relatively wide conditions under which informing relatives is appropriate because results that 'might impact on their interests' are not restricted to health or other welfare interests or to reproductive interests.

*Occasional access: If 'the benefit of disclosure substantially outweighs the patient's claim to confidentiality'*   The Human Genetics Commission takes the view that 'disclosure of sensitive personal genetic information for the benefit of family members in certain circumstances may occasionally be justified'. The criteria given by the Human Genetics Commission are that 'the benefit of disclosure substantially outweighs the patient's claim to confidentiality' (HGC 2002, 64).

*Restricted conditions for access: In the case of serious disorders for which prevention or treatment is available*   The HUGO Statement on DNA sampling restricts the access of relatives to serious disorders for which prevention or treatment is available. The guidelines stipulate that:

> Where there is a high risk of having or transmitting a serious disorder and prevention or treatment is available, immediate relatives should have access to stored DNA for the purpose of learning their own status. These exceptional circumstances should be made generally known at both the institutional level and in the research relationship (HUGO 1998).

Several other guidelines restrict the right to know of relatives. The ASHG and RMGA guidelines represent an intermediate position which is between the extremes of the WHO and UNESCO guidelines. Both the ASHG (1996) and the RMGA (2000, 10–11) recommend that relatives should not have a right to know. They require the written consent of the donor to transmit research results to relatives. The exceptions explicitly mentioned by these guidelines are those specified by the President's Commission (1983, 44). Disclosure against the wishes of the donor is justified when the probability is high that identifiable individuals would otherwise suffer from serious, avoidable harm (see also Chapter 3).[65]

Guidelines that mention spouses do not grant them the same right to know as they do concerning blood relatives. The RMGA guidelines (2000, 11) specify that spouses do not have a right to information. Similarly, the WHO guidelines specify a difference between the right of relatives and the interest of spouses. According to the WHO guidelines, spouses should only be informed by the donor. However, donors should be reminded that they have 'a moral obligation' (WHO 1998, 13) to inform their spouses if they desire to have children.

*Adequate Conditions of the Feedback: The Need for Genetic Counselling*

Again, the UNESCO guidelines have issued a recommendation (2003, Art. 11) that leaves open a wide range of interpretations because the conditions of appropriateness are not specified: 'genetic counselling should be made available in an appropriate manner'. Even more vaguely, the Council of Europe Steering Committee on Bioethics Explanatory Report recommends that the framework of communicating results to participants foresees 'appropriate medical advice' (CDBI 2002b). For the RMGA, genetic counselling is only one among several conditions for feedback that might be outweighed or complemented by the others: 'In communicating results to the participant, the choices of each participant, the

---

65   See also WHO (2001, 13).

extent of available clinical services, the availability of counselling, and the familial implications should be taken into account' (RMGA 2000, IV 3).

The MRC (2001, 18) recommends even more vaguely that the 'ability to provide feedback linked to counselling and clinical care must also be considered'. According to these guidelines, incidental findings should be communicated to the treating physician because 'a research result should not be relied on as the sole basis for diagnosis, since quality control standards in research laboratories generally differ from those used for clinical testing'. Similar to the US, where results need to be confirmed by a laboratory approved by the Clinical Laboratory Improvement Amendments (CLIA) (HHS 2009) before they can be given to patients, the Canadian guidelines affirm that feedback needs to be part of standardized clinical care and physicians or researchers should seek 'a repeat or confirmatory test by a clinical diagnostic laboratory where possible' (RMGA 2000). The ASHG (1996) guidelines add another explicit condition. They require any disclosure of results to be done with the involvement of a specialist in genetic counselling: 'all genetic research studies involving identified or identifiable samples in which disclosure of results is planned [should] have medical geneticists or genetic counselors involved'.

The Canadian Ethics and Technology Commission (CEST) guidelines take a unique position and recommend genetic counselling before donors consent to a study in order to help them determine whether they want to know the possible results of the research or not (recommendation 8).

*Informing the Ethical Review Committee About the Provisions Concerning Feedback*

A substantial number of guidelines specify that the ethical review committee should be informed about whether and under what conditions research participants will be informed about the results. Research ethics committees (RECs) should know the 'ways in which the research results will be published, and how the subjects will be informed of the results of the research' (Tri-Council 1998, 10: 2.7). The Council of Europe guidelines refer in Article 24 to the Additional Protocol Concerning Biomedical Research. This stipulates that RECs should be informed about 'arrangements foreseen for information which may be generated and be relevant to the present or future health of those persons who would participate in research and their family members' (COE 2005, Appendix, xv). The Explanatory Report of the CDBI (2002b), which addresses research involving biological samples, specifies that the 'research protocol submitted for review should foresee research findings that could require communication to the research subjects and a framework for such communication'.

The MRC takes a similar position. The guidelines recommend the involvement of the ethical review committee in the decision about feedback: 'Researchers must decide at the beginning of a project what information about the results of laboratory tests done on samples should be available to the participants, and agree these plans with the Research Ethics Committee' (MRC 2001, 4). Moreover, the MRC adds advice relevant for the review committee: 'If research results have immediate clinical relevance, there is a clear duty of care to ensure the participant is informed' (MRC 2001, 4).

To sum up, the obligation to inform the ethical review committee about the provisions concerning the feedback of results is not specific to research involving genetic databases, but is part of classical research ethics guidelines.[66]

## Discussion

### Arguments in favour of and against a right to know

Guidelines disagree about whether participants in research involving genetic databases have a right to know the results of the research and, if yes, what kind of results and in what form. It is therefore important to discuss the arguments in favour and against a right to know.

Veatch (1981) has argued that individuals have the right to know the information that others have obtained about them in a research project and that this implies the right of the subject to know interim results. In patient care the right to know is well established. Paternalistic withholding of information in the clinical context is neither beneficial – based on the available empirical evidence (Elger 2002) – nor ethically defendable (Elger 1998a). In contrast, classical research ethics incorporates paternalism explicitly. Subjects are not allowed to participate in a project judged too dangerous. The principle of beneficence dominates the principle of autonomy. Since paternalism is admitted concerning the request for participation in research, it might seem logical to admit it as well concerning the request of a subject to be informed about the results of the research. However, as the following considerations will show, paternalism concerning the withholding of research results is not justified. One difference between both situations is that the reason why participation is considered too dangerous for the subject is in general the risk of physical harm by a toxic medication or a risky new procedure. In contrast, the harmful 'substance' in the case of the feedback of study results is 'information'. The problem here, which affects genetic databases, is the controversy as to whether providing health-relevant information to donors causes harm. Paternalistic concerns are widespread among genetic service providers. In an empirical study about recontacting in a clinical setting, 46 per cent of participating members of the American Society of Genetics thought that recontacting should be the standard of care. Among those who did not support feedback, 82 per cent

---

66   See COE (2005) and CIOMS (2002), Appendix 1: 'Items to be included in a protocol (or associated documents) for biomedical research involving human subjects [...] Plans to inform subjects about the results of the study.' See also CIOMS (2002) commentary on guideline 4: 'In many clinical trials, results are not disclosed to subjects and investigators until the study is concluded. This is ethically acceptable if an ethical review committee has approved their non-disclosure.'

named anxiety and stress as the reasons against informing, and nearly the same percentage (81 per cent) named concerns about health insurance (Fitzpatrick et al. 1999). Studies carried out during recent years show that the concerns of genetic service providers are probably exaggerated. Providing information about a genetic predisposition to a person who wants to be informed is beneficial for the direct physical and psychological welfare of the subjects.[67] It is true that future risks that might have consequences on the physical well-being of donors due to the loss of health (or other) insurance are largely unpredictable, but the perception of whether such remote risks might be sufficient reasons to justify a paternalistic approach varies among different evaluators. In light of the lack of evidence of serious harm, the position against a right to know the results of studies involving human genetic databases cannot be defended predominantly on paternalistic grounds, at least in societies which put an emphasis on autonomy rights in other fields.

The right to know is well established in the field of medical ethics and is increasingly also discussed in the research context (Manolio 2006). However, this right includes the right to receive relevant and meaningful information which is important to help the patient make autonomous decisions. Although in many countries patients have the right to see their medical records, this does not necessarily include the right to know about and understand all irrelevant and unconfirmed details. On similar grounds, it can be claimed that donors do not have the right to know irrelevant and uncertain research findings from projects involving human genetic databases. The Convention on Human Rights and Biomedicine contains a 'right to information'. A whole range of different types of information exist which others might have gathered about an individual and to which the right to know could apply. In the Convention, the right to information is narrowed down: 'Everyone is entitled to know any information collected about his or her health' (COE 1997, Art. 10 para. 2).

The right to know[68] depends on the definition of what is considered to be 'any information collected about his or her health'. Interpreted in a broad way, this could include irrelevant and uncertain information. From the standpoint of a more narrow definition, it could be argued that irrelevant and uncertain facts do not provide valid information about health and should therefore not be included in the right to know. In order to define more clearly what is meant by the right of an individual to know 'any information about his or her health', it is helpful to look at the interests that this right intends to protect. Buchanan (1999, B-5) lists 'access to information' among the welfare rights. This means that this information is

---

67   This has been confirmed in several studies, of which some examples are: Wiggins et al. (1992); Broadstock et al. (2000a); Broadstock, Michie and Marteau (2000b); Bonadona et al. (2002); Bozcuk et al. (2002); Green et al. (2009).

68   We will, in the first place, leave aside the possibility of exceptions which is mentioned in paragraph 3: 'In exceptional cases, restrictions may be placed by law on the exercise of the rights contained in paragraph 2 in the interests of the patient' (COE 1997, Art. 10).

supposed to be a basic need: the individual has to know this information to pursue any ulterior interests. In this case the information is of a kind that increases the individual's ability to make informed decisions. Knowing irrelevant and uncertain facts will not influence the decisions of an individual. It can not be in the interest of an individual, therefore, to know this type of meaningless 'information'. No good reason exists to protect a right to know information if this knowledge is not supposed to have any consequence on the individual's well-being or decisions.

The problem now is to define which type of information is irrelevant and sufficiently uncertain not to have any consequences on the individual's well-being or decisions. An example is the information that an individual has a particular sequence of nucleic acids on one gene locus, for example, ATAT, if it is completely unknown whether this sequence has any significance. The information might be useful later if one knows more about its significance, but for the time being the knowledge of being an ATAT carrier at this locus does not change anything for the individual. This is a clear case of information that would not need to be protected by a right to know. More problematic is any probabilistic information. People clearly differ in their appreciation of whether a 1 per cent risk of suffering from a certain disease would be worth cumbersome changes in their life. Cultural differences shape this question. A research team (Eisinger et al. 1999) has examined the differences between the American and French recommendations for women at risk of breast and ovarian cancer due to BRCA1 or BRCA2 mutations. Both guidelines mention prophylactic surgery as an option for the women, although, for the time being, the evidence about the benefit of surgery is incomplete. The American document leaves the decision whether to have surgery or not to the woman. The French guidelines permit surgery only for women older than 30 (mastectomy) or 35 years (oophorectomy), and only if the risk of breast cancer is more than 60 per cent and the risk of ovarian cancer is more than 20 per cent. The reason is that under French law, a physician cannot invade a patient's bodily integrity, even with the patient's consent, unless there is a clear therapeutic justification. What constitutes a clear therapeutic justification seems to vary between the two countries. In addition, cultural differences explain why, in cases with uncertain outcomes, patient autonomy has a higher priority in the US than in France.

Information is not only important for clinical choices, for example, to have surgery or not. Certain kinds of probabilistic information are important for other choices in life, such as which type of profession one envisages, reproductive decisions, and so on; there is no cultural or philosophical consensus as to when an event is 'likely enough' to influence the choices of a reasonable person. Thus, it might be justified to conclude that the right to know comprises the right to know *all* probabilistic information, even information of limited certainty, that will influence the decision of some, but not all, individuals. This interpretation of the right to know would respect personal, cultural and community values as proposed by HUGO (1995). In the United States, the personal preferences of a sample of Americans have recently been evaluated (Wendler and Emanuel 2002; Chen et al. 2005). Wendler and Emanuel found that 89 per cent of participants wanted to be informed and wanted their physicians to be informed about 'results of uncertain clinical significance'. The exact question was: do you want to be informed 'if the researcher learned something about you, but wasn't sure if it might affect your health'. Participants were either Medicare beneficiaries or healthy individuals who had a first degree relative suffering from Alzheimer's disease. The authors of the study note that the recommendations of the National Bioethics Advisory Commission[69] are not in line with the wishes of the participants and that researchers 'should consider appropriate mechanisms to allow sources who want such information to obtain it'. The question used in the study by Wendler and Emanuel (2002) indicates that the information seems to be clear. It is, however, uncertain whether this information will affect health. In order to capture the full meaning of the right to know, one would want to frame an enlarged question which, in line with Article 27 of the Additional Protocol (COE 2005), also refers to information which is supposed to affect not only health, but also quality of life and other life decisions. The reason for this enlargement is that it seems justified to define the right to know research results in the following way: the right to know includes the type of information that reasonable persons would want to know in order to make autonomous decisions. Indeed, the right to know protects the reasonable interest of a person to make informed and autonomous decisions. In this way the extent of the right to know is defined in relation to an interest which is worth protection. This definition is in line with paragraph 3 of Article 10 of the Convention on Human Rights and Biomedicine (COE 1997) which addresses exceptions, because these exceptions are also defined on the basis of the interests of the patient: 'In exceptional cases, restrictions may be placed by law on the exercise of the rights contained in paragraph 2 in the interests of the patient.'

It is noteworthy that in Article 10 the exceptions are justified paternalistically, that is, if they are in the interest of the patient, not in the interest of society. However, Article 26 of the same Convention specifies the restrictions on the exercise of any of the rights. In this Article, the Convention allows for restrictions 'on the exercise of the rights and protective provisions contained in this Convention' that are 'prescribed by law and are necessary in a democratic society in the interest of public safety, for the prevention of crime, for the protection of public health or for the protection of the rights and freedoms of others'. The question is whether arguments used to restrict the right to know fulfil the conditions of Article 26: apart from paternalistic arguments about the invalidity of the information and the risk of harm related to it, the most often used argument against the feedback of results is the associated costs. As noted by the HGC, feedback is not considered practical because of the difficulties of making individual contact and because of the problem of granting genetic counselling for all who wish to receive their results. In principle, neither public safety nor public health are in danger if research is more

---

69   See NBAC (1999), discussed above, which recommends that feedback should be regulated by strict criteria (valid and confirmed information, significant implications for the donor's health, and whether amelioration or treatment is possible).

costly due to the necessity to feed back the results. The question to be asked is whether the rights and freedoms of others suffer if feedback was made obligatory. Should it be permitted to balance the right to information of the donor against the 'right of others' to reduce the costs of research or against the 'freedom' of researchers? It seems justified to allow for some restriction of the definition of what is to be considered information that is in the interest of an individual and that he or she should have the right to know. One might argue that risks below a certain probability will not change the decisions of a reasonable person. However, some individuals who desire children might be interested to know even remote risks. International or local bodies should describe the type of results that reasonable persons should have the right to know. Individuals who would like to receive more information than the reasonable person could react to this description. According to the reasons why they ask for more information, they could either be allowed to receive feedback according to broader criteria or they might choose not to participate in the research project.

The discussion in the previous paragraph permits us to critically evaluate the restrictions of the right to know that have been proposed in various guidelines. The argument of the Human Genetics Commission (HGC 2002, 106) that 'many would find this [individual feedback] intrusive' is not convincing if donors are allowed to decide at the beginning of each study whether they want to be informed about the results, according to the criteria based on the preferences of a reasonable person. Biobanks could publish details on their website about the expected results of different studies and donors could receive a personal 'account' in which they update their wishes to be informed or not. With modern technology, it does not seem to add enormous costs to establish individualized procedures. Such practice would be in line with the recommendation of the MRC to give donors the opportunity to change their minds. The opinion of the HGC relies on a number of assumptions which concern empirical questions and could therefore be tested. It can only be judged whether it is true that feedback is not 'practical because of the difficulties of making individual contact', and because of the 'problem [of] grant[ing] genetic counselling for all who wish to receive their results', if different forms of feedback are tried in practice. Efforts to develop efficient and practical forms of feedback should not be suppressed at the outset.

In light of the preceding arguments, it cannot be recommended that the general rule should be not to provide any individual feedback. As we have mentioned, empirical evidence exists that information about genetic tests is beneficial, and that evidence continues to increase. If transparent criteria are developed to define standards of certainty and relevance, it is not adequate to call all resulting information 'at best not beneficial' or 'at worst misleading or harmful' (Grizzle et al. 1999, 299). The arguments put forward by the CAP, the HGC or the NBAC in favour of a rule not to provide feedback are too general. It might be true for many research projects that 'interests in results are generally not specific to the individual' or that 'no irrefutable scientific facts' are produced (Grizzle et al. 1999, 299). Even if this was confirmed for the majority of projects, it would still be necessary to establish transparent criteria concerning feedback for the minority of studies that might produce relevant findings. It does not seem justified to limit these criteria to results 'valid for the clinical care of the individual' (Grizzle et al. 1999, 298) or 'relevant to the individual participant's health' (HGC 2002), since results without impact on clinical care might still be important for reproductive decisions and professional or personal life plans.

*Arguments in favour of and against a right* not *to know*
Most guidelines agree that participants in research involving genetic databases have a right *not* to know the results of the research.[70] However, some European guidelines and international recommendations restrict this right (for example, MRC 2001; COE 2005, see above). In our study among medical and law students, we found that law students in particular think that individuals at risk of genetic disease have a duty to know the results in order to behave in a responsible way (Elger and Harding 2003; Rhodes 2006). In Europe and elsewhere, a growing tendency seems to exist to restrict the right not to know.[71] Another recent example from Switzerland demonstrates this tendency: the Swiss law about genetic testing involving human beings affirms the right not to know, but includes restrictions: 'Each individual has the right to refuse to be informed about results concerning his or her genome, with the exception of Art. 18, paragraph 2' (Swiss federal law 8.10.2004, Art. 6, translation by B.E.). Article 18 of the same law contains the restriction that the 'physician has the obligation to inform an individual immediately about a test result, if an immediate physical danger exists for this individual, an embryo or a foetus that could be prevented'. On 15 September 2003, the Swiss Commission on Science, Education and Culture (Kommission für Wissenschaft, Bildung und Kultur) had even announced in a press report that it recommended the deletion of Article 6 from the law project. The Swiss Commission seemed to have been concerned that Article 6 might be interpreted as justifying not

---

70    The right not to know (Appel and Friedman 2004) and not to be recontacted concerning new information about genetic testing available in clinical practice has also been debated elsewhere (Hunter et al. 2001; Knoppers 2001).

71    These restrictions are defended by referring to Kant and the way he conceived the principle of autonomy. According to one modern interpretation of Kant's philosophy, the principle of autonomy implies the duty to live responsibly and to be autonomous, which includes the duty to be informed (Harris and Keywood 2001; Rhodes 2006). However, as Häyry and Takala show, in contemporary bioethics, the principle of autonomy is rather founded on John Stuart Mill's idea of self-determination: individuals have the right to make their own decisions using the amount of information they prefer, as long as these decisions do not result in harm to others (Häyry and Takala 2001, 411). It should be added that one needs to be careful about what may be considered as 'harm'. Giving birth to a child suffering from a genetic disease does not mean harming this child because, for the child, the alternative to a life with the disease would have been no life at all, either through the avoidance of conception, non-implantation (if the embryo was discovered to be affected during in vitro fertilization) or abortion (Elger 1998b; Häyry and Takala 2001, 410).

informing individuals about test results. In its guidelines about genetic testing of human beings (SAMS 1993), the Swiss Academy of Medical Sciences had affirmed that a person has the right not to know the results of gene tests. In a letter written in January 2004, the Academy reminded the Commission of the existing national and international guidelines confirming the right not to know and asked the Commission to reconsider its decision (Stauffacher and Leuthold 13 January 2004). Finally, Article 6 has been maintained, albeit with the restriction explained in Article 18, and is now part of the implemented Swiss federal law on the genetic testing of human beings.

The following arguments are in favour of Article 6 and the right *not* to know. The first argument refers to the coherence of the traditional framework of patient rights. Changes to this framework need to be in line with ethical practice in other areas of medicine, and the burden of proof is on those who want to make changes. Those who propose changes need to provide sound arguments. In other fields of medicine, patients have the right to withdraw consent to any medical test or procedure at any time. Creating a different standard for genetic testing would constitute a threat to the present framework of patients' rights. There is no reason why, in respect to genetic testing, traditional patients' rights should be limited. Patients have the right to ask not to be informed about their diagnosis and prognosis even if this will result in harm to themselves. Independently from the possibility of carrying out gene tests, other forms of 'predictive medicine' are part of routine medical care, based on known environmental risk factors such as diet and physical training. For the time being, nobody is forced to receive detailed explanations from his or her physician about all the risk factors to avoid as regards cardiovascular disease or cancer, although these risk factors and the effectiveness of preventive measures are well established (Hobbs and Bradbury 2003). No reason exists why information about genetic risk factors should be obligatory and information about other risk factors should not. Another argument is based on the principle of beneficence: concerning untreatable severe diseases such as Huntington's chorea, the right not to know is important to protect individuals who are at risk of the disease from harm.[72] Studies have so far only shown that those who wish to know benefit from the knowledge and the evidence is not clear for those who do not want to know. The majority of persons at risk of Huntington's disease have expressed the desire not to know and could be harmed by the information. Moreover, society could be negatively affected by a restriction of the right not to know. Such a restriction could have adverse consequences on the willingness of the public to participate in genetic research. Many patients might fear unwanted confrontation with test results and refuse the donation of samples for research. This reaction could seriously hamper medical research.

---

72    See also the argumentation mentioned in the previous note: public policy concerning the right not to know should be guided by Mill's ideas on liberty and the prevention of harm (Takala and Häyry 2000; Häyry and Takala 2001).

We conclude that a broad international consensus exists to maintain the right not to know. The arguments of those who favour restrictions of the right not to know are based on the principle of beneficence. For the time being the evidence indicates that the abolition of the right not to know will create more harm than benefit. Those who propose important restrictions to individuals' and patients' rights need to provide strong evidence for the benefit of their approach before making any changes.

Concerning research involving biobanks, from an ethical and pragmatic point of view we defend the solution of informing donors that, unless they object, results will be fed back to them, if an ethics committee decides that the information is sufficiently valid and relevant for important health and life decisions. The ethics committee should publish any decisions made in this respect. Researchers should inform the ethics committee about any results that might fulfil these criteria. The committee's decisions will be based on the choices of average reasonable persons.[73] The biobank may choose not to include the samples and data of donors who object to this feedback procedure.

*Arguments in favour of and against a right to know (and not to know) of relatives*
Guidelines agree that relatives and spouses have an interest in knowing or not knowing results.[74] Different views exist concerning the weight of this interest when it has to be balanced against the interest of the donor and the interest of society. Donors might be interested in keeping any information concerning themselves confidential against their relatives' wishes to know. Donors might also want to tell the results to a relative who does not want to know. The latter problem has so far not been discussed in any guideline. It does not involve the researcher and is left to the private relationship between family members. The most far-reaching proposition in this respect has been made by the Swedish Medical Research Council (Eriksson 2004). The Council states that if research implies important interests of relatives or groups, informed consent should be obtained from 'anyone who could be directly affected by the results'. In this case, relatives would be able to express their wish not to know any results. If such guidelines concerning

---

73   It should also be noted that studies have shown that biobank participants are interested in receiving individual results. 'Only 10% of participants explicitly stated they had no expectation for personal benefit, and when asked whether they expected to be contacted with study results, respondents were split between having no expectation (39%), being hopeful for results (37%) and expecting to be contacted with results (12%)' (Ormond et al. 2009, 188).

74   See the discussion about informing relatives (ASHG 1998; Deftos 1998a and 1998b; Skene 1998; Sulmasy 2000; Dugan et al. 2003; Parker and Lucassen 2003; Lucassen and Parker 2004; Parker and Lucassen 2004; Arar et al. 2005; Clarke 2005; Clarke et al. 2005; Hallowell et al. 2005; Hamilton, Bowers and Williams 2005; Harris, Winship and Spriggs 2005; Sulmasy 2005; Godard et al. 2006; Lucassen, Parker and Wheeler 2006; Schneider et al. 2006; Forrest et al. 2007; Kohut et al. 2007; Wolff et al. 2007; Forrest et al. 2008; Lacroix et al. 2008); and also an evaluation of the needs of spouses (Metcalfe et al. 2002).

research involving human genetic databases were enforced by law, it might become possible to punish donors for informing a relative against his or her will. One might disagree about the requirement and its feasibility and claim that it is often impossible to obtain informed consent from all relatives concerned who are 'identified' (UNESCO 2003). However, if one wants to grant a right not to know for relatives, it is necessary to ask them whether they want to be informed about the results *before the results are generated*. In this case, the right of relatives not to know is in conflict with the interest of society to limit the costs of research projects.[75] Practical problems of respecting the right not to know of relatives are evident. Should donors provide a list of relatives of whom they are aware and know the addresses? Should the researcher have the right or obligation to contact them (De Wert 2005; Aktan-Collan et al. 2007)? Should only close relatives be included or where should limits be set? The most comprehensive alternative in the age of genetic databases would be to increase public awareness of the issue and to advise citizens to inform their treating physicians about their preferences in the case of foreseen or incidental findings, so that, if results are given to their physicians, the latter know whether they should pass them on to the patients or not. An ethically justified and feasible alternative could be to adopt a publicly known strategy, for example, in favour of information, similar to the proposition in Article 18 paragraph 2 of the Swiss law about genetic testing, and then to allow disagreeing individuals to manifest their wish not to be informed in some form of 'advanced directive'. These alternatives might turn out to be less costly to the researcher and society. It does not seem impossible to find ways to respect the right of relatives that impose only minimal burdens on researchers.

Whereas the right *not* to know of relatives has only been affirmed explicitly by the UNESCO guidelines, two other documents (WHO 1998; MRC 2001) stipulate the right to know of relatives. These guidelines do not discuss explicitly how this right should be balanced against the donor's right to confidentiality. The justification for a right to know of relatives would, as in the case of the right to know of donors, be based on the importance of the information. One would need to evaluate how important the information is for the welfare interests or reproductive interests of individual relatives and for their capacity to make autonomous and well-informed decisions. Therefore, the same criteria as defined above for the donor's right to know apply for the definition of information (relevance, degree of certainty) that relatives would want to know, that is, their wish to know is justified by an interest which is worth protection. Some have argued that being part of a family creates moral obligations towards relatives (Hardwig 1990). As shown in Chapter 3, many guidelines conclude that the sharing of genes implies a duty of solidarity (HGC 2002, 64) or familial mutuality. As we have already discussed (Chapter 3), the argument that an ethics of familial mutuality follows from the sharing of genes is not well

---

75   This is similar to the CEST's idea (2003) of genetic counselling when donors provide consent to their samples being included in a biobank which also implies significant additional costs.

grounded, because it is based on the naturalistic fallacy. Others (Hardwig 1990; Eriksson 2004) base the principle of familial mutuality not primarily on genetic relatedness, but on relational closeness. However, again a naturalistic fallacy is involved. Eriksson writes that in 'real world situations, an obligation to inform relatives is dependant on the quality of the relationship'. He cites studies which demonstrate that individuals are more likely to discuss issues with close relatives (D'Agincourt-Canning 2001; Claes et al. 2003; Peterson et al. 2003). However, the fact that human beings are more willing to disclose their results to close than to distant relatives, and, independently from the degree of relatedness, in many cases probably more easily to relatives with whom they have a good relationship than to those with whom they are in conflict, is not a reason to conclude that it is ethically adequate to disclose information only to some relatives. It is more adequate to balance the interests that a donor has in confidentiality of the results against the interests of relatives to know this information using ethical criteria which are less subjective and which are generally applicable in society, for example, in other fields of medicine. Among such criteria would be the rule of rescue (Jonsen 1986). Article 128 of the Swiss Criminal Code indicates that a person who has not provided assistance to an injured person or a person in danger, when this could be reasonably expected from the first person in light of the circumstances, will be punished by imprisonment or a fine. In this Article no difference is made between the obligation to provide assistance ('de prêter secours') to a relative or to an unknown person. The Article only exempts a person from the obligation to help if this help puts the helper himself/herself at disproportional risk. No compelling reason exists to balance the right of relatives to know results from genetic databases against the right to confidentiality of the donor differently than in another situation where confidentiality has to be balanced against other interests. Sometimes the threshold allowing for breaches in confidentiality in genetics is put higher than for other cases. The reason given for this is that in genetics the donor is not actively involved, whereas, for example, in sexually transmitted diseases, persons who infect others have taken some active step which engages their responsibility and diminishes their right to confidentiality. However, this argument does not seem convincing for cases in which the persons suffering from a disease have engaged in 'normal' activity without knowing that they are infected and could infect others. For example, it would be justified to breach the confidentiality of an individual against his/her wishes in order to inform those living in the same house that this individual suffered from SARS (Severe Acute Respiratory Syndrome) without having been diagnosed, and did nothing more than touch the elevator buttons and in this way transmitted the virus (imagine a small house in which it would be possible to identify the individual who has been coughing and sneezing, and that the person suffering from SARS might not wish that others be informed because of a fear of stigmatization). The only relevant difference between genetics and other fields of medicine is the fact that genetic diseases can be 'transmitted' to the offspring. This means that the relatives' interests that need to be protected are not limited to their own health but include reproductive interests. We therefore conclude that the criteria of the

President's Commission should be completed by two others: reproductive interests should be included among the reasons to breach confidentiality, and the risk to the donor resulting from a breach of confidentiality should be taken into account. This risk (discrimination and stigmatization inside or outside the family) will in general not be sufficient to outweigh important dangers to the health of others. The right to confidentiality and the risk to the individual resulting from the disclosure will, however, be sufficiently important to limit breaches of confidentiality to cases in which information is relevant and confirmed.

As a conclusion, we maintain that the right of relatives to receive feedback about research results is similar to the right of donors to receive feedback about information, if the donor agrees that relatives can be contacted. The burden of contacting relatives could be shared between the donor who provides the addresses, the researcher who sends an invitation and the relatives who would be required to take an active part in the process. They should be asked to confirm that they request information. The right to know of relatives should be judged according to higher standards if the donor desires to keep the information confidential. In this case, an immediate risk to the health or the reproductive rights of an identified person would need to be demonstrated, as well as the possibility of reducing these risks through the breach of confidentiality without imposing disproportional risks on the donor.

However, it has to be noted that this view is not entirely shared by all persons concerned. A sample of American Jewish women has been asked whether a physician should inform at-risk family members against a patient's wishes. In the case of an easily preventable genetic disease, only 18 per cent of the participants thought the physician should inform relatives against the wishes of the patient, in the case of a predisposition to breast cancer for which prophylactic surgery is the only measure of prevention, the figure was 22 per cent, and it was 16 per cent in the case of a non-preventable genetic disease (Lehmann et al. 2000; Plantinga et al. 2003). Of a sample of medical geneticists who faced the dilemma of patients refusing to notify their at-risk relatives (Falk et al. 2003), only 25 per cent considered disclosure to the relatives against the patient's wishes, and only 3 per cent actually warned relatives. The reasons cited not to warn were emotional issues, the value of confidentiality and eventual case resolution by other means. These empirical results do not question the theoretical ethical conclusions, but remind us that in most cases no risk of immediate urgency exists for relatives and trying to convince patients or donors should be tried intensively. The discussed criteria for breaching confidentiality would only be fulfilled after such attempts have taken place for a substantial period of time.

*Informing populations, ethics committees and other issues related to the feedback of results*
The importance of informing the ethical review committee about the arrangements made for or against feedback, and the right of participants to be informed about these arrangements, seems to be widely acknowledged and has not been contested in any guideline.

Other issues have only been raised by one or a few guidelines, such as the requirement to inform not only individuals, but also populations or their representatives about results (NARC 1997), the requirement of a mechanism that provides the possibility for donors to change their minds about the feedback of results (MRC 2001), and the requirement to provide to participants the opportunity of genetic counselling *before* they donate their tissue to research (CEST 2003) or *at the moment* of feedback (UNESCO 2003; ASHG 1988; MRC 2001 which uses the term 'medical advice' instead of genetic counselling).

Informing populations about general results of a study is compatible with the idea of most guidelines to provide at least general feedback and seems therefore not to create any controversy, although the details of this requirement would still need to be specified.

The two other aforementioned issues will predictably stir controversy, since they could add costs to research. However, as has been discussed above, the right of donors to change their minds concerning feedback of study results protects important interests and its realization does not seem to add significant costs to research, provided most donors do not change their minds frequently.[76] By contrast, the requirement for genetic counselling, before and/or after the research, will add significant costs. Not surprisingly, guidelines from professional organizations which represent the interests of researchers recommend avoiding cumbersome requirements such as genetic counselling. Some internal contradiction in the arguments used should be noted. On the one hand, these guidelines argue in favour of restricting participants' rights (for example, to informed consent and to far-reaching control of samples and information) for the benefit of society from research. This research is supposed to discover interactions between genes and environmental factors. The results of these findings will be used to improve the health of the members of society. Genetic counselling is likely to be an important factor in order to achieve the benefits of the same research. If the welfare of society is truly the objective used to guide reflections on an ethical framework for genetic databases, genetic counselling should not be considered only as a cumbersome impediment on research, but as a benefit for society that should be favoured in the same way as research itself.

## Benefit Sharing

*Payments Versus Benefit Sharing with Human Subjects of Medical Research*

In international debates, benefit sharing has been a recurrent and controversial issue for many years.[77] In spite of the long-lasting debate, the concept of benefit

---

76    Studies from other fields show that patient choices tend to be stable (Everhart and Pearlman 1990; Emanuel et al. 1994; Carmel and Mutran 1999; Wolfe et al. 1999).

77    The debate was fuelled in 2000 by the publication of the HUGO recommendation (Anonymous 2000b; Anonymous 2000a; Alvarez-Castillo and Feinholz 2006) as well as by

sharing has not yet been clearly defined (Schroeder 2007, 205). Traditionally, research subjects have participated in medical studies for idealistic reasons without receiving any monetary benefit. The underlying idea has been that 'any research on human beings should be developed in a context of absolute freedom – not expecting any reward in order to avoid coercion – and in search for advances in human knowledge and for the benefit of mankind' (Ortúzar 2003, 477). The guidelines of the Swiss Academy of Medical Sciences on research on human beings state, in accordance with this idea, that, in principle, participation in research does not include payment. In certain cases, costs can be reimbursed, such as for the lost salary during participation (SAMS 1997). In other guidelines, the idea of some form of financial benefit ('honoraries') for research subjects is more explicitly admitted. An example is the ICH Guideline for Good Clinical Practice (ICH 2002) which does not exclude payment to the subject. 'The anticipated prorated payment, if any, to the subject for participating in the trial' must be among the written information provided to subjects (ICH 2002, Art. 4.8.10 k). The International Ethical Guidelines for Biomedical Research Involving Human Subjects of the Council for International Organizations of Medical Sciences (CIOMS 2002) discuss this point in more detail. They try to describe criteria to distinguish between unjustified 'material inducement' to participation and justified payments or benefits. According to the CIOMS guidelines, the following types of payment or 'benefit' are 'acceptable' (CIOMS 2002, guideline 7 and commentary on guideline 7):

- reimbursement for lost earnings, travel costs or other expenses incurred in taking part in a study;
- those 'who receive no direct benefit from the research may also receive a small sum of money for inconvenience due to their participation in the research';
- subjects may receive medical services unrelated to the research or have procedures and tests performed free of charge.

The following types of payment or 'benefit' are 'unacceptable', according to the CIOMS guidelines:

- payments in money or in kind to research subjects, if the payments are 'so large as to persuade them to take undue risks or volunteer against their better judgment';
- payments or rewards that 'undermine a person's capacity to exercise free choice' (CIOMS 2002, commentary on guideline 7).

The CIOMS guidelines admit that it is not easy to differentiate between suitable recompense and undue influence to participate in research. It is therefore proposed

---

the innovations inspired by the Human Genome Project (Sheremeta 2003; Sheremeta and Knoppers 2003).

that the ethical review committee should judge what constitutes the justified type of recompense in a particular study. This is in accordance with the Declaration of Helsinki. It states that the protocol which should be submitted to the ethical review committee should include 'information regarding [...] incentives for subjects' (WMA 2008, Art. 14). The question of undue inducement (Grant and Sugarman 2004) arises in particular for research which does not include the prospect of direct benefit to the subject resulting from the research, but which at the same time presents more than minimal risk to the participant (Barnbaum 2002; Kopelman 2004). In this type of research, vulnerable subjects, such as the poor or indigent, might be induced to accept risks which they would otherwise not if they were not in need of the payment or of the non-monetary benefit provided.

Concerning the risk of undue inducement, it does not necessarily matter whether payments or direct or indirect benefits in various forms are used. The payments for 'the inconvenience' might be an undue inducement for an unemployed person, and both payments and benefits could persuade subjects or donors 'to take undue risks or volunteer against their better judgment' (CIOMS 2002, commentary on guideline 7). In addition, the classical guidelines seem to admit a relation between benefits and payments because payments are suggested to replace direct benefits, in the case of the participation of volunteers who will 'receive no direct benefit'.[78]

Hence, the important task is to define the border between undue inducement and appropriate benefit sharing or payment. The Declaration of Helsinki states that '[m]edical research involving a disadvantaged or vulnerable population or community is only justified if [...] there is a reasonable likelihood that this population or community stands to benefit from the results of the research' (WMA 2008, Art. 17). Expecting some form of benefit from the research is a justified attitude of communities and individuals who are approached for participation. Denying any benefit to research subjects and relying only on altruism is not in the interest of society because it could cause decreased participation in research. The improvement of health through medical research ultimately depends on the willingness of individuals to participate. Research about causes, prevention and treatment of some rare genetic diseases will not be possible if the few families suffering from the condition all over the world do not agree to participate. The answer to the empirical question what actually motivates research subjects is not clear. Is it really altruism, or rather direct benefit or some other form of non-monetary or even monetary benefit? Evidence exists that altruism is involved

---

78  See CIOMS (2002) guideline 7: 'Subjects may be reimbursed for lost earnings, travel costs and other expenses incurred in taking part in a study; they may also receive free medical services. Subjects, particularly those who receive no direct benefit from research, may also be paid or otherwise compensated for inconvenience and time spent. The payments should not be so large, however, or the medical services so extensive as to induce prospective subjects to consent to participate in the research against their better judgement ("undue inducement"). All payments, reimbursements and medical services provided to research subjects must have been approved by an ethical review committee.'

(Schron, Wassertheil-Smoller and Pressel 1997; Koblin et al. 1998; Sugarman et al. 1998; Welton et al. 1999; Koblin et al. 2000; Karlawish et al. 2001; Halpern, Karlawish and Berlin 2002, 360). However, a study showed that in a clinical population, altruistic desire to help research was lower than in a registry population. In the clinical population, motivation related to personal benefit from the research was predominant over altruistic motivation (Geller et al. 1999). Similarly, David F. Horrobin, a well-known researcher who died of cancer, defended the view that many patients, especially those receiving a diagnosis of a lethal disease, want foremost research from which they will benefit themselves instead of research that will benefit other patients in the future (Horrobin 2003). The importance of direct benefit to the research subject as a motivating factor cannot be denied. An example is Interferon for hepatitis C which, a few years ago, was likely to be beneficial, but was first only offered through clinical studies. The motivation of patients in such cases is influenced by the fact that they receive the benefit of an experimental treatment when other treatments have failed, or are not available or not reimbursed. Another form of motivation is the expectation of patients or groups that they will later receive indirect benefits through the development of treatments or diagnostic tests. In non-lethal chronic diseases, research subjects might themselves benefit from the development of new treatments. In other diseases, it might happen that only future patients who suffer from the same conditions are likely to benefit from the research.

Recent changes have 're-initiated' and further nourished the discussion and shifted attention towards benefit sharing. First, in the Western secular individualistic culture, a growing tendency exists to value altruism less than self-interest. For research this means that altruistic participation is not taken for granted anymore and that the idea of sharing the benefit with research subjects is not rejected outright.

Second, due to the inequality of health care distribution, some people are significantly more in need of adequate health care than others and the gaps continue to widen. The differences are noteworthy between patients in developed countries and patients in third world countries (Schuklenk and Kleinsmidt 2006) and, in countries without a right to universal health care such as the United States, between insured and uninsured patients. Individuals from families suffering from severe genetic diseases are especially in need of expensive treatment, but might not be able to afford it because they have been refused health insurance on the basis of their known increased health risk.

Third, the growing commercialization of the biotechnology and genetic industries, and the enormous present and potential profits observed, create a feeling of injustice and a call for distributive justice. The gap between the unfortunate and suffering patients who agree to participate in research and the profit of commercial companies from these patients has widened to a point that it cannot be overlooked. This gap is felt to be disproportionate and largely unacceptable.

The Human Genome Organization Ethics Committee acknowledges the changing attitudes towards benefit sharing: 'In the interest of justice, the last decade has witnessed an emerging international consensus that groups participating in research should, at a minimum, receive some benefit' (HUGO 2000).

*Benefit Sharing Concerning Research Involving Genetic Databases: Consent and Dissent*

The question of benefit sharing has aroused particular interest concerning genetic research on populations (Simm 2007). A specific argument cited in the field of genetics is that all humans share 99.9 per cent of their genetic structure. The human genome is said to be a common good and benefits resulting from genetic research should be made available to participants in research, and even to all mankind (Ortúzar 2003, 475; Taylor 2007). In various guidelines, the issue of benefit sharing is not always addressed explicitly.[79] Consent exists that it is acceptable to pay reimbursement for costs and inconvenience caused by participating in research, and to pay compensation for harm caused by participation. It is also widely accepted that human tissue should be treated differently than other materials that have a market value. Allowing individuals the private sale of their tissue would put vulnerable populations such as the poor and indigent at risk of exploitation.

Dissent exists, first, as to whether, apart from reimbursement and direct benefits resulting from participation in the study, any form of benefit sharing is acceptable; second, about the form of benefit sharing; third, about the quantity of acceptable benefit sharing; and, fourth, about the individuals or populations entitled to receive benefit from a particular study. In the following section, the different propositions are described.

*The extreme positions*
*Against benefit sharing* According to this position, benefit sharing is not acceptable, with the exception of direct benefits and of reimbursement for costs and inconvenience caused by participating in research. A position of this type is recommended by the Medical Research Council in the UK:

> One of the major concerns in allowing commercial access to human material originally collected for research projects funded by the public or charity sectors is the potential to damage the gift relationship between scientists and research participants. Research participants may be particularly sensitive to the idea of a company or an individual making a profit out of research material that they have freely donated. It is important that research participants are made aware of the potential benefits of allowing commercial access, and that the role of any one individual's sample in the generation of future profits is likely to be minimal as well as impossible to quantify. Given the possible sensitivities, it is essential that

---

79   Among the guidelines that do not discuss the issue are: Grizzle et al. (1999); Belmont Report (1979); NBAC (1999); Nuffield Council (1995); ASHG (1988 and 1996); ACMG (1995); and RCP (2001).

research participants know that their sample or products derived from it may be used by the commercial sector, and that they will not be entitled to a share of any profits that might ensue (MRC 2001, 4.2).

Arguments against benefit sharing in research involving genetic databases or biobanks are that, first, it would provide incentives which put vulnerable individuals and groups at risk through participation against their interests.

Second, donors should not obtain financial gains from 'selling' their tissue, because human material is not a commodity that can be sold by the patient who provided it. In line with this argument, a divided California Supreme Court rejected the claim of the patient John Moore that his property rights had been violated (Harrison 2002). Moore's physician and others had used the patient's surgically excised spleen cells and had created cell lines and other products from it, without the patient's permission and without sharing the commercial profits.[80]

Third, benefit sharing implies additional work for researchers and companies, and for research ethics committees if they are asked to judge the fairness of the benefit sharing. This additional work adds additional costs to research and hinders the advancement of human knowledge in the long run.

Fourth, it is claimed, that the participation of sample donors in the profit which is later obtained from commercial uses of the research results poses too many practical problems of recompense because of the time gap between participation and the potential benefit linked to the profit (Berg 2001, 241).

*In favour of benefit sharing* The most extreme position in favour of benefit sharing with participants would be to consider human tissue as a private property and to allow individuals to make profit from the tissue and the information derived from it. As has been said before, this position is rarely defended in the literature in the most extreme way and has not been recommended in any of the existing guidelines on biobanking.

Another extreme position would be to distribute benefits equally to 'all mankind', since all humans share the same genes. One could imagine every human being receiving a small percentage of the commercial profits of the biotechnology industry using DNA, for example, one dollar to everybody. This position has the disadvantage of being highly impractical, besides defending an extreme viewpoint of justice. Indeed, positions in the literature in favour of some form of redistribution of benefits to individuals other than those having participated in the research have so far been almost exclusively based on need. They intend to use benefit sharing specifically in order to relieve, at least partially, the present unequal distribution of access to health care.

Finally, the guidelines of the WHO Regional Office for Europe contain a noteworthy standpoint which strongly favours benefit sharing. They appreciate the idea that persons own their samples and consider this to be an important

---

80   Moore v. Board of Regents of California. See also Harrison 2002, 77–83.

concept, from which it follows that at least some form of benefit should be shared. However, this benefit does not need to be individual, but may be attributed to the community. On the other hand, it should be noted that the guidelines clearly admit the possibility that individual benefit occurs:

> Serious consideration should be given to recognising property rights for individuals in their own body samples and genetic information derived from those samples. In all circumstances, the provision of research materials, including DNA samples, should be on the undertaking that some kind of benefit will ultimately be returned, either to the individual from whom the materials were taken, or to the general class of persons to which that individual belongs (WHO 2001, recommendation 19).

*Intermediate positions*
*Benefit sharing to help families in need because the genetic disease has caused financial and social problems*    Another argument on behalf of benefit sharing is based on the principle of equity (Merz et al. 2002, 970) or distributive justice. These principles are used to defend a duty to help those in need, especially if those not in need profit from research done with the tissue of individuals who are less well off than those who conduct the research or profit from it.

Berg (2001), among others, argues in favour of some form of direct or indirect benefit sharing with those participants in genetic research who are disadvantaged in financial or social respects because of genetic diseases running in the family. If pharmaceutical companies make a profit from research in which such families have participated, part of the profit should be used to compensate for the natural (genetic) and social injustice. In this view, benefit sharing is not based on a principle of return for contribution, but on a principle of justice that requires palliating existing inequalities. Other subjects without financial and social difficulties would be expected to participate in research out of 'solidarity with one's own genetic group' (Berg 2001, 242).

*Benefit sharing as a return to the nation (or community)*    This position is defended by several guidelines. The Human Genetics Commission states:

> In return for altruistic public involvement in such research, there should be some benefit for the participants, or, in the widest sense, the community from which they are drawn. All we would affirm at this stage is that large-scale population genetic databases, established with and supported by public funding, constitute a national asset. This means that national benefit and interest should be taken into account [...] We would be concerned, for example, if no benefit for the National Health Service could be demonstrated in the proposed setting up of BioBank UK. [... We consider] it to be very important that databases of this nature are seen and understood to be bringing at least some benefits to public-

domain medical knowledge rather than being solely designed for commercial exploitation (HGC 2002, 103: 4.55, see also 17–18).

The Network of Applied Genetic Medicine (RMGA 2000, VI) states that:

> All forms of payment to participants in exchange for participation are unacceptable. For the sake of equity (fairness), however, in return for its participation, the population of Quebec should profit from the resulting benefits of the scientific breakthroughs they contributed to […] The researcher should inform the participant at the time of consent, that he is not entitled to any financial benefit from his contribution to research, including any commercialized product which may eventually derive from research. This does not preclude the eventual sharing of benefits with the community (e.g. medical supplies, humanitarian causes, etc.).

The guidelines of the Commission de l'Éthique de la Science et de la Technologie (CEST) defend a similar position. The 'collectivité' to which they refer is, in the context of the guidelines, often the population of Quebec which should be involved in all decisions through the democratic process:

> Quelles que soient les solutions [du 'benefit sharing'] envisagées, la Commission est d'avis que les plus intéressantes sur le plan éthique devraient être axées sur un partage des retombées de la recherche avec la collectivité. Il lui apparaît également important que toute forme de partage soit discutée entre les responsables de la recherche (ou les promoteurs d'un projet d'envergure) et les sujets de recherche ou la population, avant le début de la recherche, afin d'éviter les incompréhensions et les insatisfactions des sujets de recherche ou de la population en général une fois les résultats connus. Enfin, l'équité commande aussi le partage des connaissances.[81]

Similar forms of benefit sharing as a return to the community are also defended in the literature (Soejarto et al. 2005; Schroeder and Lasen-Diaz 2006; Schulz-Baldes, Vayena and Biller-Andorno 2007).

---

81   English translation: 'Whatever are the planned solutions [of benefit sharing], the Commission believes that those most interesting from an ethical point of view should be based on a sharing of research benefits with the community. It also seems important that any form of benefit sharing is discussed among those responsible for the research (or those promoting substantial projects) and the research subject or population, before the beginning of the research, in order to avoid incomprehension and dissatisfaction amongst the research subjects or the population in general once the results become known. Finally, equity also requires the sharing of knowledge.'

*Benefit sharing as a contribution of 1–3 per cent of research profits to humanitarian projects (HUGO 2000)*[82]    In addition to the proposition of in-kind benefits to communities discussed in the previous paragraph, the HUGO ethics committee adds a new aspect: 'the possible use of a percentage of any royalties for humanitarian purposes' (HUGO 2000, 1). This proposition goes further than all previous positions in that it not only recommends benefit sharing as a form of compensatory justice based on the factual contribution of individuals or communities to the research. HUGO's proposition to give, in addition, 1–3 per cent of profits to humanitarian projects represents a form of distributive justice based on needs. Compared to the position centred on the needs of donors or research subjects suffering from genetic disease, HUGO's position addresses needs in a more global perspective. Given 'the inequality between the rich and poor nations' (HUGO 2000, 2) and the 'vast difference in power between those carrying out the research and the participants', as well as the 'possibility of substantial profit [...] considerations of justice support the desirability of distributing some profits to respond to health care needs'. As a conclusion, the committee recommends that 'profit-making entities dedicate a percentage (e.g. 1%–3%) of their annual net profit to healthcare infrastructure and/or to humanitarian efforts'.[83] It is not clear whether the humanitarian efforts are mainly intended to benefit the communities in which research has been done, or whether the 1–3 per cent of the profit could also be distributed to other communities chosen according to criteria such as need.

*Towards a universal definition of benefit sharing according to need: The role of a World Fund for Genetics*    Ortúzar (2003, 475) criticizes the relativistic definition of benefit provided by positions that define it according to the subjective or culturally different desires of individual communities. She considers this relativistic view to be in contradiction to universal justice. Although HUGO has put forward the idea of some form of more or less general contribution to humanitarian efforts, the guidelines focus mostly on benefit as a reward that a population will receive in exchange for its contribution to the research. Ortúzar criticizes this approach for two reasons. First, it is difficult to define the interests of a genetic community because this type of community is not equivalent to a political community. Relying on community consent for benefit sharing implies the risk that individual interests are not respected. International corporations have initiated research in countries mainly 'in exchange for "rewards" for participating doctors and institutions' (Ortúzar 2003, 477). The second argument against community-defined benefit sharing is, according to Ortúzar, the universality of the human genome, because it implies that all humans should benefit from research using DNA. Based on John Rawls' theory of justice as fairness, Ortúzar argues

---

    82    This position is also among the different forms of benefit sharing that could be acceptable, according to the guidelines of the CEST (2003, 52–3): '1% de ses profits nets à une fondation caritative au bénéfice de l'ensemble de la population.'
    83    See HUGO (2000, 3). A similar position is defended by Berg (2001, 243).

that 'if each institution sets up different principles for solving local issues, the result may be global unfairness' (Ortúzar 2003, 480). The only just solution would be an impartial redistribution of goods to those less advantaged in the natural and social lotteries. In practice, Ortúzar proposes the creation of an international treaty charged to assure equity of access in genetics and universal benefit sharing. A 'World Fund for Genetics' should be created, similar to the WHO fund related to AIDS. All private companies obtaining commercial benefits from genetic research on human populations would be obliged to pay a percentage of their profits to the fund. An international ethics commission should be created in order to regulate the distribution of the benefits to the 'worst-off' in developing countries in respect to health and genetics. The advantage of this approach is that in this form the benefits are not directly related to the population participating in research and do not risk acting as an inducement.

*Benefit sharing: Multiple forms are acceptable*
In the previous sections, we have tried to distinguish different positions on benefit sharing and have cited guidelines which defend one or the other position. It has to be noted, however, that many guidelines do not defend a single approach, but provide a list of possible acceptable forms of benefit sharing. Examples are the HUGO guidelines on benefit sharing (2000), the guidelines of the North American Regional Committee (NARC 1997) and the CEST guidelines (2003). It is not clear whether these guidelines consider all approaches equally justified, or whether it will depend on the research project whether one or the other approach is acceptable.

   Another example of a document which provides a list of acceptable forms of benefit sharing is the UNESCO Declaration on Human Genetic Data (2003). The UNESCO guidelines propose a distribution of benefits not only to 'society as a whole', but also to the 'international community':

> In accordance with domestic law or policy and international agreements, benefits resulting from the use of human genetic data, human proteomic data or biological samples collected for medical and scientific research should be shared with the society as a whole and the international community. In giving effect to this principle, benefits may take any of the following forms: (i) special assistance to the persons and groups that have taken part in the research; (ii) access to medical care; (iii) provision of new diagnostics, facilities for new treatments or drugs stemming from the research; (iv) support for health services; (v) capacity-building facilities for research purposes; (vi) development and strengthening of the capacity of developing countries to collect and process human genetic data, taking into consideration their specific problems; (vii) any other form consistent with the principles set out in this Declaration. (b) Limitations in this respect could be provided by domestic law and international agreements (UNESCO 2003, Art. 19).

The position of the UNESCO guidelines is difficult to classify because it is open to interpretation. It could be compatible with most positions that have been discussed above. Although it mentions in particular in-kind benefits, it might even include the most extreme position described above (royalties or other direct payment to participants)[84] because any type of monetary benefit could also be, under some conditions, 'consistent with the principles set out in this Declaration' (UNESCO 2003, Art. 19).

*Bridging the Dissent: Towards a Generally Acceptable Position Concerning Benefit Sharing*

The question remains as to whether the cited positions are mutually exclusive or whether a universally acceptable form of benefit sharing could be found. Clearly, adopting the extreme position that any form of benefit sharing except compensation for time and inconvenience is prohibited is not compatible with all other positions. It is timely, therefore, to examine whether important and overwhelming reasons exist to adopt this extreme position. Hence, we will here discuss in more detail the possible arguments against benefit sharing.

The most frequent concern is that benefit sharing could represent an inducement which puts at risk vulnerable individuals and groups who might be driven to participate in research against their interests. This argument is important, but for the following reasons it might not be sufficient to prohibit benefit sharing on ethical grounds:

- It is generally accepted that research participants, in particular if they are vulnerable, should receive some form of at least indirect benefit from the research (WMA 2008, Arts 17 and 27). Since some form of benefit or at least compensation for time spent or inconvenience due to participation is already allowed, it is more important to determine which type of benefit provided will constitute an inducement and which type will not. This is an empirical question and should be evaluated in more detail in the future.
- The risk of inducement, and of possible negative consequences to research subjects caused by this inducement, must be balanced against positive consequences of benefit sharing. Among possible positive consequences are the just redistribution of benefits, the limit-setting to disproportionate commercial gains, the advance of research if the percentage of profit obtained is fed back to further research, and the influence on access and pricing of the developed treatments (Merz et al. 2002, 970).
- Forms of benefit sharing exist which imply a low risk of inducement. An example which implies a particularly low risk is the contribution of a percentage of the researcher's or company's profit to a universal fund that will finance humanitarian efforts. Some other forms of benefit sharing might imply some risk of inducement. Examples are forms of benefit sharing that

---

84　See above the position that benefit sharing implies royalties or post-profit payment directly to participants for providing samples or for participation.

are directed to improvement of health care needs and health infrastructure in the country where the research takes place, and even more risky, in-kind benefit directed to individual donors in particular. As shown by trials involving malaria treatment – the Malarone (proguanil hydrochloride with atovaquone) trials carried out in Kenya, Indonesia and Gabon (Richards 2002) – it is not clear whether the communities involved were realistically in a position to refuse the free malaria treatment and the clean water wells to be built in return for the research participation of the community.

Another widely held concern is that benefit sharing related to the use of DNA or other human material will increase the commercialization of the human body. The commercialization of the human body can either be opposed on deontological grounds referring to human dignity, or on consequentialist grounds referring to the risk of exploitation of vulnerable populations who might be induced to sell their bodies and health. Again, this concern is important, but it only serves to exclude particular forms of benefit sharing such as direct payment to the individual for contributing his/her own tissue.

Clearly, benefit sharing might imply additional work for researchers and companies, and for ethics commissions, and this could increase the costs of research. Again, however, this argument helps to exclude particular forms of benefit sharing, such as those associated with high administrative costs, and those posing practical problems, such as certain forms of participation of individual study participants in the profit made later by the commercial use of research results. These practical problems are in particular caused by the time gap and the difficulties of identifying or tracing sample donors.

To sum up, the arguments against benefit sharing do not seem to provide sufficient grounds to prohibit it. However, they are helpful in narrowing down the list of acceptable specific forms of benefit sharing.

The next question is whether – if agreement can be reached that some form of benefit sharing is acceptable – some types of benefit sharing exist that could be universally acceptable to defenders of all the intermediate positions described. It cannot be denied that the various intermediate positions reflect different cultural traditions, as well as specific values from different types of contexts, which are not shared internationally. The proposition to implement benefit sharing from genetic research by contributing financial or in-kind benefits which permit the improvement of the local health care system presupposes (1) the existence of a public health care system from which all members of the community will benefit, and (2) the shared belief that health is a public good. This typically European or Canadian position (Pullman and Latus 2003c) is not generally shared among American scholars, who frequently defend legislation to protect the interests of individuals in controlling the benefits resulting from their own DNA. Similarly, strong American libertarians will not support a form of distributive justice that compensates for unjust distribution of goods and needs due to the natural and social lottery (Nozick 1974). These incompatibilities of opinion exclude for the time being the adoption of robust details about what constitutes appropriate benefit sharing. However, the following minimal framework might be internationally acceptable:

- Benefit sharing from research involving human DNA should not be based on property rights leading to the commodification of the human body.
- Benefit sharing which is not based on property rights and which does not lead to undue inducement is justified.
- DNA has the unique property of being shared by individuals from the same family and from the same genetic community. From this empirical fact it follows that risks related to the donation of DNA will be shared by families and genetic communities. Since risks are shared, it seems adequate not to limit benefits to participants, but to ask in addition for some sharing of benefits among the entire population concerned.
- Taking into account the three preceding points, an adequate form of benefit sharing must be decided together with the community or group in which the research is carried out. According to the local culture, different forms of benefit sharing can be judged acceptable.
- An ethics committee specialized in benefit sharing should determine whether the specific form of benefit sharing proposed by a researcher or a company is within the universally acceptable framework. Pullman and Latus have come to the conclusion that ordinary research ethics committees 'will neither have the time nor expertise to consider whether or not genetic studies include an adequate benefit sharing' (Pullman and Latus 2003c, 559). They have proposed to create, as part of a 'provincial approval model', a Standing Committee on Human Genetic Research in Newfoundland and Labrador. Since different countries do not have the same possibilities of setting up such a particular committee, an alternative not discussed by Pullmann and Latus would be to offer to local ethics committees the possibility of sending protocols for advice to an international committee specialized in benefit sharing in various cultural contexts (for example, a WHO committee, see below).

*Benefit Sharing: Conclusions and Recommendations for a Particular Cultural Context – The European Perspective*

For countries with universal access to health care (as is the case in many countries in Europe), there is no compelling argument for benefit sharing with individual participants because the participants, even if they suffer from a genetic disease, are not in particular need since they will in principle receive adequate health care.[85] If this is the case, the duty to help individuals in need does not apply. In this context it

---

85    See also Schroeder and Lasen-Diaz (2006) and Pullman and Latus (2003a and 2003b).

might be more risky to harm vulnerable groups or to induce biased research results if benefit sharing creates incentives for economically disadvantaged persons to participate in research more often than persons from the rest of society.

In these countries it is, however, justified for health institutions and health care systems to ask for some global form of benefit sharing if the biotechnology or pharmaceutical industries use public resources such as hospital or community-based biobanks or databases. The benefits should be redistributed in a form to increase the public good, that is, by sponsoring further research or improving the health care system. An example of this kind of benefit sharing is the UK Biobank. The biobank announced that samples and information will be available to commercial entities if their projects are judged to be beneficial to health care and if the companies pay a fee. This payment is then reinvested by the biobank into further research projects.

In these countries it is also justified for research ethics committees to require that companies using human genetic resources provide a general contribution of 1–3 per cent of their profit to humanitarian projects, in accordance with the provisions of the HUGO guidelines. However, it is difficult to name a particular reason why only profit from genetic research should be the object of such a form of benefit sharing. Other types of commercial research implying the participation of human subjects or the use of any human material should also be included.

The difficulty will be to decide in which humanitarian projects the money should be invested. Should the humanitarian projects be limited to the country where the research takes place or should some other principle of equity be used, according to which the 'benefit-sharing money' coming from all types of research is distributed in a more general way among populations in the world according to criteria such as health need or need for genetic services, and so on. It can be argued that, based on the differences between countries, a need exists in less well-off countries and that there is a duty to share all benefits arising from 'gifts' or altruism with those in need. It would presuppose that those who participate in research agree to this kind of distributive justice and to the humanitarian projects. The projects could be planned and funds could be distributed through a WHO committee according to health needs defined according to some internationally agreed standard.

Commercial and non-commercial research involving human genetic databases must fulfil two criteria: first, as for all medical research, it must be expected to produce benefits and the benefits need to outweigh the risks to the participants. Second, direct monetary benefit sharing or offering royalties to research subjects are not recommended, because the risk that they will have the same effect as an inducement is too high. Some general form of benefit sharing to the community is acceptable if there is no danger that (1) this benefit sharing creates an incentive to consent in spite of risks, or that (2) it will cause a biased evaluation of risks because the latter are balanced against the possible non-medical (for example, monetary) benefits. Some have argued that many Icelanders accepted presumed consent and the monopoly of deCode mainly because they hoped that they would get a personal economic benefit from the biobank project due to both a general rise in Iceland's economy and the free access to drugs promised by deCode. A statement on benefit sharing should figure in any protocol for commercial and non-commercial research, except for research in which, with certainty, no profit can be made. For research projects that might give rise to substantial profit, at least part of the benefit sharing should occur after the profit has been made, and the amount of benefit sharing should be proportional to the quantity of the profit.

For an individual research project, whether the conditions of benefit sharing are acceptable and do not risk creating inducement can best be decided by an ethical review board specialized in such questions. At least some of its members should have detailed knowledge about the cultural context of the country where the research will take place and the type of participants to be recruited for the research. Additional community consent about benefit sharing is important if a clearly identifiable community or group will be involved in the research.[86]

---

86   See above (in Chapter 4) the section on community consent and community consultation.

# Chapter 5
# Ethical Issues of Human Genetic Databases and the Future

**Lessons Learned: The Productive Dialogue**

Guidelines from the past 20 years in Europe and North America, as well as from international bodies, are reactions to the more or less troubled birth and life stories of different biobanks. The guidelines mirror the search for local as well as global values and principles. They also try to find practical solutions that permit the ethical and legal foundations of Western societies to be honoured, and an ethical justified balance between the legitimate interests of different stakeholders on a global level, including poor countries and indigent populations.

From the beginning, in the 1980s, different frameworks existed: on the one hand, those that give almost unlimited priority to patients' and research participants' autonomy rights, and on the other hand, those that attribute a varying amount of weight to solidarity with family members and society. The public discussion about biobanks started when this controversy already existed, but the media interest about the Icelandic, the Estonian and the UK biobanks brought it to the forefront of the international debate. In light of what precedes, it is not surprising that there is not what could be called a 'history of guidelines', in the sense that old guidelines disappeared and were replaced by new guidelines. Most of the texts are still posted on the internet and in use, although some of them were written 10 to 20 years ago. A pessimist might say that this shows to what little extent there seems to be 'progress' in the form of a fundamental change in the arguments and in the overall ethical framework. But instead, this finding should be judged positively. It is very reassuring and speaks in favour of the authoritative power of the classical framework of research ethics which was created in an era, immediately after the Second World War, when respect for human rights encountered wide international agreement which is much less obvious nowadays (Nys et al. 2007; Goffin et al. 2008).

It is very reassuring to see that what was written in the 1980, 1990s and at the beginning of the twenty-first century is not outdated at the end of the first decade of the new millennium. Indeed, this book was also written in order to show the richness of the existing guidelines and to honour the work of those involved in the drafting of the guidelines. Many of the ideas and reflections are precious and should not be drowned in an overall negative judgment. Instead of seeing the multitude of guidelines and conflicting ideas as problematic, one should rather look at the details and admire the impressive degree of agreement on many basic questions. Indeed it might come as a surprise that, although guidelines are from different times and contexts (NARC 1997; ASHG 1988; UNESCO 2003; different European countries, and so on), the similarities throughout different texts are noteworthy, whereas controversies can only sometimes be clearly attributed to countries or a particular context.

The guidelines accompany the birth and childhood of existing biobanks and show that the dialogue was fruitful in the long run. Human rights organizations, international courts and international bodies, as well as human rights-related concerns of the population, have influenced the debate and put limits on some of the earlier governance structures of population biobanks. Smaller biobanks, such as the Swiss Pediatric Oncology Group Tumor Bank, have not aroused public attention, perhaps because they were less visible, but certainly also because they took into account and did not repeat the mistakes of earlier biobank initiatives. Indeed the individualistic human rights approach has prevailed. Although the discussion about solidarity and altruism (Knoppers and Brand 2008; Knoppers 2009) has been ongoing for 20 years, community values have not overruled the human rights framework of research ethics. This needs to be firmly recognized as deeply reassuring because it increases trust in the present regulatory structures which were able to maintain the protection of research subjects as their priority and have so far not been overrun by the pressure of commercialization, commercial progress and the worldwide competitiveness of biotechnology research. In the era of modern bioethics and post Tuskegee (Bates and Harris 2004; Curtis 2004; Katz et al. 2008), the idea that the good of society could sometimes outweigh the rights of research subjects continues to be rejected in Europe and North America, so far.

Biobanks are a sort of trial and error: new ethical questions emerged and different biobanks created ethical governance frameworks that were tested in real-life scenarios. Countries and their populations responded by legislations and guidelines, and the different solutions continue to be tested in practice. In this somewhat Darwinian way, biobank frameworks were created and selected because only some finally 'passed' in the long run. Overall, the storm that brewed over gene banks (Frank 1999) has calmed down. Ten years after the mediatized outcry about the Iceland and Estonian databases, we pass a rather quiet afternoon at UK Biobank (Anonymous 2009) where a few inconveniences are the major issue, as well as some doubts about the cost–benefit ratio of this possibly too ambitious biobank. Clearly, good humour is back when biobanks envision Walt Disney pictures ('10001 Dalmations: Croatia launches its national biobank'). One imagines cute puppies playing peacefully (Rudan et al. 2009) rather than stormy and thorny debates about human rights. Nevertheless, crucial ethical questions remain on the agenda for the future:

> The idea of setting biobanking guidelines is analogous to the standardization of Europe's rail system [...] Every country pays for its own train line, but they have agreed to put their rails at the same distance so it's easy to go from the Netherlands to Greece without changing trains (Ballantyne 2008, quoting Gert Jan van Ommen, Head of Human Genetics at Leiden University Medical Center in the Netherlands).

**Ethical Issues of Human Genetic Databases: A Challenge to Classical Health Research Ethics?**

It is evident that research involving samples and data has characteristics that differ from research involving directly human subjects. These differences have motivated the ethical debate about the question whether the framework of classical health research ethics needs to be changed or supplemented in order to be applicable for biobank research. The applicability of the classical framework indeed has limits when it comes to biobanks. Even the Declaration of Helsinki introduced a new paragraph in the 2008 version (WMA 2008, Art. 25) that points towards the search for a compromise. In summary, we have noticed in the preceding chapters that problems related to the feasibility of future biobank research have produced two major propositions to change or adapt the classical framework. One is the proposition to enlarge the definition of what is considered 'identifiable' biological material and data (OHRP 2004), and the other is the proposition to broaden the concept of consent (Caulfield et al. 2003; Arnason 2004; Elger and Caplan 2006; Artizzu 2007). The Helsinki Declaration has taken up the consent issue and added a cautious article which permits waivers of consent for some research with identifiable samples or data. This Declaration has not defined whether reversibly anonymized samples should be considered identifiable (COE 2006) or not (OHRP 2004). One might conclude that there has finally been an adaptation of expectations. New informed consent is no longer considered the gold standard for biobanks: even Helsinki changed. It should be noted that broadening the definition of 'identifiable' and broadening consent do not need to be conflicting approaches. Both methods help to adapt classical research ethics to the realities of biobank research and both could be used together: within this twofold adapted framework, research subjects would be asked to provide general consent to future research implying reversibly anonymized samples. The problematic point with broadening the definition of 'identifiable' is not that it permits future studies to be undertaken without new consent; the difference compared to general consent is that research ethics committee approval is waived if research with reversibly anonymized samples is declared to be research on non-identifiable samples and, hence, is no longer human subject research. In the future, this will be the most important issue to be tackled. The era of biobanks is first and foremost the era of diversity: the binary choice between human subject research and non-human subject research should not mean that the aim is to escape regulations by stating that research involving data and samples is not human subject research. Instead, the standards for ethics committee approval should be adjusted. Some creative approaches are presently being tested, for example, in the UK. A novel ethics approval mechanism exists for tissue banks in this country (Clark 2007; Elger, Hofner and Mangin 2009a). It includes the possibility of biobanks requesting a form of general approval. The biobank is allowed to operate the bank, to obtain samples according to an approved protocol, and to provide tissue to researchers without new approval if these activities stay within the scope of the biobank's approved range of projects. Researchers who receive samples from the bank do not need to apply for ethics approval individually, but their activities are covered by the bank's general authorization. Biobank research is indeed a challenge to classical research ethics. However, solutions exist to maintain the classical framework while allowing for minor adjustments.

From the stormy history of biobanks, recent managers of genetic databases have learned that the classical framework cannot and should not be changed fundamentally. Solidarity cannot be imposed. However, biobank managers do not give up. They adapt to public perceptions and the persistence of the classical values of research ethics (Haimes and Whong-Barr 2004). The message is some indirect form of moral pressure. Biobanks are described as a means to achieve 'better healthcare' (Riegman et al. 2008). Therefore the plea for altruism is justified – be nice and participate: '354,271 people are already helping' (UK Biobank 2009c). References to altruism are prevalent on biobank websites and in the titles of biobank-related conferences: 'Biobanks – a part of me for research' (Förderverein Humangenomforschung und Biotechnologie e.V. 2004; BioValley Science Day 2005).

**The Future: Old and New Challenges**

Some old challenges seem under control. If Iceland went overboard with presumed consent, general consent is emerging as an accepted solution (Wendler 2006; Hansson 2009). Furthermore, countries continue to build their own biobanks with much less 'outcry', probably also because many population biobanks are now mainly publicly funded. Some general challenges persist (Gottweis and Zatloukal 2007; Gottweis 2008): for many presently debated issues, it must be clarified to what extent the controversial recommendations of international bodies and ethicists are due to disagreement on fundamental ethical questions, as compared to a different evaluation of the empirical facts and the lack of a practical solution to the problems. The sharing of data among researchers (Kaye et al. 2009) recently experienced a significant drawback when, in 2008, the NIH had to adapt its policies and restrict access based on the findings of new studies about the risk of identification of individual participants (Couzin 2008; Homer et al. 2008; NIH 2009). While ELSI (ethical, legal and social issues) research has been gaining support among major funding agencies in the biotechnology landscape, empirical research on the consequences of different ethical frameworks is still underfunded and is not a recognized part of the ELSI domain, probably also because it is fundamentally interdisciplinary and requires input from empirical sciences as well as philosophical, ethical and legal scholars. Consent and withdrawal of consent, confidentiality, feedback of results and benefit sharing remain issues where empirical research of this type is important to identify the most beneficial approaches for the future.

The new challenges are found predominantly in three fields: first, ethical issues are taken up more and more in national legislations as well as in international law.

In particular issues pertaining to ownership, commercialization and patents are presently being tackled in different countries and on the international level. The challenge is to avoid conflicting legal frameworks in different countries which will sensibly hamper international collaboration (Kaye 2006; Kaye 2007; Zika et al. 2008). The forthcoming, but yet unpublished, OECD guidelines are an example of the international search for a global approach.

Second, new biomedical developments change the ethical debate, and biobank frameworks have to adapt to scientific progress. Complex multiple-gene tests are being introduced (Gewin 2007; Pickles, Maughan and Wadsworth 2007, 85). The WHO and others have recognized the problems of postgenomic medical research (Reymond et al. 2002 and 2003). Not only genetic, but also epigenetic, factors are now being recognized as influencing the development of disease (Pickles, Maughan and Wadsworth 2007, 86–7) and epigenetic research has become an integral part of modern biobanks (IARC 2009; IMPPC Biobank 2009; STYJOBS/EDECTA 2009). The ethical analysis of epigenetics has only recently started and has not yet been extended explicitly to biobank research (Rothstein, Cai and Marchant 2009a and 2009b). Even less attention from ethicists is observed concerning the influence of metagenomics and metagenetics (Aharoni 2009; Handelsman 2009)[1] on the conception and objectives of future biobanks and the need for future adjustments of the ethical and legal frameworks.

Finally, the ethical dimension of technical aspects and of the necessary funding (Ballantyne 2008; Barnes et al. 2008) needs to receive greater attention. Storing samples of the highest possible quality is an ethical imperative related to the principle of beneficence and respect for sample donors. If donors provide biological material and data and accept some risks to confidentiality, then researchers and funding agencies have the obligation to ensure that the greatest possible benefit is obtained from these collections. Standardized sampling and storing techniques need to be defined which permit the quality and comparability of samples and data to be ensured on an international level (NCI 2007). In addition, ethical standards must extend to the definition of confidentiality concerning new electronic forms of shared data. Indeed, besides information and samples, digital radiological images are important elements in certain types of biobanks (Aneurist 2009) and the efficient reversible anonymization of electronic CT-scans and x-rays is only starting to be examined (Elger et al. 2009b). Again, the analysis of these questions requires close interdisciplinary collaboration between information technology experts, clinicians, biologists, ethicists and legal scholars.

As regards technical aspects, as well as the influence of epigenetics and metagenetics, the borders between human and non-human biobanks are becoming

---

1   Mutant analysis needs to be extended to the community context. 'Let's call this "metagenetics", to highlight the concept of an analysis that transcends individuals ("meta" in Greek means "transcendent"). Metagenetics provides a parallel with metagenomics – genetics and genomics deal with single organisms and metagenetics and metagenomics both apply to analysis of a multigenome unit, or community' (Handelsman 2009, 138).

blurred and international initiatives are trying to ensure global harmonized technical as well as ethical standards which transgress the traditional borders between human-subject (human biobanks) and non-human-subject (non-human biobanks) research (Day and Stacey 2008; ISBER 2009).

The present analysis of existing guidelines illustrates the richness of local and international approaches and the struggle to find shared solutions in spite of conflicting and overlapping ethical and legal guidance. This problem will not be solved by pessimism and inertia. Recent initiatives to propose consensus papers (Caulfield et al. 2008), projects in search of global guidelines involving WHO researchers (Elger et al. 2008), and harmonization efforts from national and international associations (NCI 2007; ISBER 2009) are praiseworthy and need to receive more support. The creation of international ethics guidelines and standard operating procedures for biobank research must stay on the agenda of a global civil society and research community which feels responsible for protecting research subjects while maintaining respect for human rights and global justice.

# References

Abascal Alonso, M., de Abajo Iglesias, F.J., Campos Castello, J., Feito Grande, L., Herrera Carranza, J., Judez Gutierrez, J. et al. 2007. [Recommendations on the ethical aspects of specimen collections and human biobanks for biomedical research purposes], *Rev Esp Salud Publica*, 81(2), 95–111.

Abbing, H.D. 2004. International Declaration on Human Genetic Data, *Eur J Health Law*, 11(1), 93–107.

Abbott, A. 1999. 'Strengthened' Icelandic bioethics committee comes under fire, *Nature*, 400(6745), 602.

Abbott, A. 2000. Iceland's doctors rebuffed in health data row, *Nature*, 406(6798), 819.

Abbott, A. 2003. DNA study deepens rift over Iceland's genetic heritage, *Nature*, 421(6924), 678.

Abbott, A. 2004. Icelandic database shelved as court judges privacy in peril, *Nature*, 429(6988), 118.

ACMG. 1995. Statement on storage and use of genetic materials. American College of Medical Genetics Storage of Genetics Materials Committee, *Am J Hum Genet*, 57(6), 1499–1500.

Act on Biobanks. 2000. No. 110/2000: <http://www.bibliojuridica.org/libros/5/2292/57.pdf> (accessed 20 July 2009).

Act on a Health Sector Database. 1998. No. 139/1998. Passed by Parliament at 123rd session, 1998–99: <http://brunnur.stjr.is/interpro/htr/htr.nsf/pages/gagngr-log-ensk> (accessed 5 September 2004).

Adalsteinsson, R. 2004. Human genetic databases and liberty, *Jurid Rev*, 2004(1), 65–74.

Advisory Committee on Health Research [ACHR]. 2002. *Genomics and World Health. Summary*. Geneva: WHO.

Aharoni, A. 2009. Mining for new enzymes, *Microbial Biotechnology*, 2(2), 128–9.

Aktan-Collan, K., Haukkala, A., Pylvanainen, K., Jarvinen, H.J., Aaltonen, L.A., Peltomaki, P., Rantanen, E., Kaariainen, H. and Mecklin, J.P. 2007. Direct contact in inviting high-risk members of hereditary colon cancer families to genetic counselling and DNA testing, *J Med Genet*, 44(11), 732–8.

Allen, J. and McNamara, B. 2009. Reconsidering the value of consent in biobank research, *Bioethics* (e-publication ahead of print).

Allore, R. 2007. Research in human genetics: technology, information, therapeutic promise, and challenge, in *Ethics and the New Genetics: An Integrated Approach (Lonergan Studies Series)*, D. Monsour (ed.). Toronto: University of Toronto Press, 19–27.

Alvarez-Castillo, F. and Feinholz, D. 2006. Women in developing countries and benefit sharing, *Dev World Bioeth*, 6(3), 113–21.

Anderlik, M. 2003. Commercial biobanks and genetic research: ethical and legal issues, *Am J Pharmacogenomics*, 3(3), 203–15.

Andersen, B. 1998. Icelandic health records, *Science*, 282(5396), 1993.

Andersen, B. and Arnason, E. 1999. Iceland's database is ethically questionable, *BMJ*, 318(7197), 1565.

Anderson, R. 1998. The deCODE proposal for an Icelandic health database: <http://www.cl.cam.ac.uk/~rja14/iceland/iceland.html>. PDF at: <http://www.cl.cam.ac.uk/~rja14/Papers/iceland.pdf> (accessed 30 July 2009).

Anderson, R. 1999. Iceland's medical database is insecure, *BMJ*, 319(7201), 59.

Anderson, R. 2001. Undermining data privacy in health information, *BMJ*, 322(7284), 442–3.

Andorno, R. 2006. Biobancos poblacionales: un analisis juridico a partir de las experiencias islandesa y estonia [Population biobanks: a juridical analysis based on Icelandic and Estonian experience], *Law Hum Genome Rev*, 25, 55–76.

Andrews, L.B. 2005. Harnessing the benefits of biobanks, *J Law Med Ethics*, 33(1), 22–30.

Andrews, L.B., Fullarton, J.E., Holtzman, N.A. and Motulsky, A.G. 1994. *Institute of Medicine Committee on Assessing Genetic Risks. Assessing Genetic Risks. Implications for Health and Social Policy*. Washington, DC: National Academy Press.

Aneurist. 2009. Integrated biomedical informatics for the management of cerebral aneurysms: <http://cilab2.upf.edu/aneurist1/> (accessed 10 August 2009).

Annas, G.J. 2000. Rules for research on human genetic variation: lessons from Iceland, *N Engl J Med*, 342(24), 1830–33.

Annas, G.J. 2002. Medical privacy and medical research: judging the new federal regulations, *N Engl J Med*, 346(3), 216–20.

Annas, G.J., Glantz, L.H. and Roche, P.A. 1995a. Drafting the Genetic Privacy Act: science, policy, and practical considerations, *J Law Med Ethics*, 23(4), 360–66.

Annas, G.J., Glantz, L.H. and Roche, P.A. 1995b. The Genetic Privacy Act and Commentary, unpublished model law, February, 1995, cited in R.F. Weir, The ongoing debate about stored tissue samples, research, and informed consent. Commissioned paper, in *Research Involving Human Biological Materials: Ethical Issues and Policy Guidance, Report and Recommendations, vol. 2*, National Bioethics Advisory Commission (NBAC) (ed.). Rockville: NBAC, F1–F21, August 1999.

Annas, G.J. and Grodin, M.A. 1992. *The Nazi Doctors and the Nuremberg Code: Human Rights in Human Experimentation*. New York: Oxford University Press.

Anonymous. 1999. Swedish standards set for use of genetic 'biobanks', *Prof Ethics Rep*, 12(3), 3.

Anonymous. 2000a. Genetic benefit sharing, *Science*, 290(5489), 49.

Anonymous. 2000b. HUGO urges genetic benefit-sharing, *Community Genet*, 3(2), 88–92.

Anonymous. 2002. Commission organises data protection conference to look at key privacy issues. Brussels, 26 September 2002: <http://europa.eu/rapid/pressReleasesAction.do?reference=IP/02/1373&format=HTML&aged=0&language=EN&guiLanguage=en> (accessed 30 July 2009).

Anonymous. 2003. Bankable assets?, *Nat Genet*, 33(3), 325–6.

Anonymous. 2004. Prozesse. Sieg der Privatsphäre. *Der Spiegel* 18/2004 (26 April 2004), 63: <http://wissen.spiegel.de/wissen/dokument/dokument.html?id=306 12509&top=SPIEGEL> (accessed 10 August 2009).

Anonymous. 2006. The Domesday project: how much personal information should we reveal for the common good?, *New Sci*, 189(2535), 5.

Anonymous. 2007. Researcher access to patient samples reaches supreme court, *Ann Neurol*, 62, A12–14.

Anonymous. 2009. An afternoon at UK Biobank, *Lancet*, 373(9670), 1146.

Anonymous. 2010. Announcing the new deCode. 21 January 2010: <http://www.decode.com/news/news.php?story=112> (accessed 1 February 2010).

Appel, J. and Friedman, J.H. 2004. Genetic markers and the majority's right not to know, *Mov Disord*, 19(1), 113–14.

Arar, N.H., Hazuda, H., Steinbach, R., Arar, M.Y. and Abboud, H.E. 2005. Ethical issues associated with conducting genetic family studies of complex disease, *Ann Epidemiol*, 15(9), 712–19.

Aristotle. 350 B.C.E. Nicomachean Ethics: <http://classics.mit.edu/Aristotle/nicomachaen.html>; Nikomachische Ethik (Êthika nikomacheia): <http://www.e-text.org/text/Aristoteles%20-%20Nikomachische%20Ethik.pdf> (accessed 10 August 2009).

Arnason, E. 2002. Personal identifiability in the Icelandic Health Sector Database, *Journal of Information, Law & Technology* 2002: <http://www2.warwick.ac.uk/fac/soc/law/elj/jilt/2002_2/arnason/> (accessed 30 July 2009).

Arnason, E. 2003. Genetic heterogeneity of Icelanders, *Ann Hum Genet*, 67(Pt 1), 5–16.

Arnason, G., Nordal, S. and Arnason, V. (eds). 2004. *Blood and Data: Ethical, Legal and Social Aspects of Human Genetic Databases*. Reykjavik: University of Iceland Press.

Arnason, V. 2004. Coding and consent: moral challenges of the database project in Iceland, *Bioethics*, 18(1), 27–49.

Arnason, V. and Hjörleifsson, S. 2007. Population databanks and democracy in light of the Icelandic experience, in *Genetic Democracy: Philosophical Perspectives (International Library of Ethics, Law, and the New Medicine)*, V. Launis and J. Räikkä (eds). Heidelberg/New York: Springer, 93–104.

Artizzu, F. 2007. The informed consent aftermath of the genetic revolution: an Italian example of implementation, *Med Health Care Philos*, 11(2), 181–90.

Ashcroft, R.E., Campbell, A.V. and Jones, S. 2000. Solidarity, society and the welfare state in the United Kingdom, *Health Care Anal*, 8(4), 377–94.

Ashcroft, R.E. and Hedgecoe, A.M. 2006. Genetic databases and pharmacogenetics: introduction, *Stud Hist Philos Biol Biomed Sci*, 37(3), 499–502.

ASHG. 1988. DNA banking and DNA analysis: points to consider. Ad Hoc Committee on DNA Technology, American Society of Human Genetics, *Am J Hum Genet*, 42(5), 781–3.

ASHG. 1996. ASHG report. Statement on informed consent for genetic research. The American Society of Human Genetics, *Am J Hum Genet*, 59(2), 471–4.

ASHG. 1998. ASHG statement. Professional disclosure of familial genetic information. The American Society of Human Genetics Social Issues Subcommittee on Familial Disclosure, *Am J Hum Genet*, 62(2), 474–83.

Auray-Blais, C. and Patenaude, J. 2006. A biobank management model applicable to biomedical research, *BMC Med Ethics*, 7, E4.

Austin, M.A., Harding, S. and McElroy, C. 2003a. Genebanks: a comparison of eight proposed international genetic databases, *Community Genet*, 6(1), 37–45.

Austin, M.A., Harding, S.E. and McElroy, C.E. 2003b. Monitoring ethical, legal, and social issues in developing population genetic databases, *Genet Med*, 5(6), 451–7.

Australian Law Reform Commission. 2003. ALRC 96 Essentially yours: the protection of human genetic information in Australia: <http://www.austlii.edu. au/au/other/alrc/publications/reports/96/> (accessed 4 August 2009).

Ballantyne, C. 2008. Report urges Europe to combine wealth of biobank data, *Nat Med*, 14(7), 701.

Barbour, V. 2003. UK Biobank: a project in search of a protocol?, *Lancet*, 361(9370), 1734–8.

Barnbaum, D. 2002. Making more sense of 'minimal risk', *IRB*, 24(3), 10–13.

Barnes, R.O., Parisien, M., Murphy, L.C. and Watson, P.H. 2008. Influence of evolution in tumor biobanking on the interpretation of translational research, *Cancer Epidemiol Biomarkers Prev*, 17(12), 3344–50.

Bates, B.R. and Harris, T.M. 2004. The Tuskegee Study of Untreated Syphilis and public perceptions of biomedical research: a focus group study, *J Natl Med Assoc*, 96(8), 1051–64.

Bauer, K., Taub, S. and Parsi, K. 2004. Ethical issues in tissue banking for research: a brief review of existing organizational policies, *Theor Med Bioeth*, 25(2), 113–42.

Baumann, T.K. 2001. Proxy consent and a national DNA databank: an unethical and discriminatory combination, *Iowa Law Rev*, 86(2), 667–701.

BBC News. 25 March 2003a. MPs lambast top research body: <http://news.bbc. co.uk/2/hi/health/2882325.stm> (accessed 15 July 2009).

BBC News. 25 March 2003b. MRC response: <http://news.bbc.co.uk/2/hi/ health/2882325.stm> (accessed 15 July 2009).

Beauchamp, T.L. 1978. Paternalism, in *Encyclopedia of Ethics*, W. Reich (ed.). New York: Macmillan.

Beauchamp, T.L. and Childress, J.F. 2008. *Principles of Biomedical Ethics*. Oxford: Oxford University Press.

Beauchamp, T.L. and Faden, R.R. 1995. Meaning and elements of informed consent, in *Encyclopedia of Bioethics. Revised Edition*, W.T. Reich (ed.). New York: Simon & Schuster/Macmillan, 1238–41.

Belmont Report. 1979. The National Commission for the Protection of Human Subjects of Biomedical and Behavioral Research. The Belmont Report Ethical Principles and Guidelines for the Protection of Human Subjects of Research. 18 April 1979: <http://www.hhs.gov/ohrp/humansubjects/guidance/belmont. htm> (accessed 1 August 2009).

Benatar, S.R. 2007. Towards progress in resolving dilemmas in international research ethics, in *Readings in Comparative Health Law and Bioethics, Second Edition*, T.S. Jost (ed.). Durham, NC: Carolina Academic Press, 401–5.

Berg, K. 2001. The ethics of benefit sharing, *Clin Genet*, 59(4), 240–43.

Berger, A. 1999. Private company wins rights to Icelandic gene database, *BMJ*, 318(7175), 11.

Bergmark, A. 2000. Solidarity in Swedish welfare: standing the test of time?, *Health Care Anal*, 8(4), 395–411.

Bexelius, C., Hoeyer, K. and Lynoe, N. 2007. Will forensic use of medical biobanks decrease public trust in healthcare services? Some empirical observations, *Scand J Public Health*, 35(4), 442–4.

Bieber, F.R., Brenner, C.H. and Lazer, D. 2006. Human genetics: finding criminals through DNA of their relatives, *Science*, 312(5778), 1315–16.

BioValley Science Day. 2005. Biobanken: '... ein Stück von mir' für die Forschung? 18 October 2005 in Basel: <http://www.biovalley.ch/files/documents/ Programme_Life_Sciences_%20Week_2005_Schweiz.pdf> (accessed 3 August 2009).

Bjornsson, A., Gudmundsson, G., Gudfinnsson, E., Hrafnsdottir, M., Benedikz, J., Skuladottir, S. et al. 2003. Localization of a gene for migraine without aura to chromosome 4q21, *Am J Hum Genet*, 73(5), 986–93.

Blondal, T., Waage, B.G., Smarason, S.V., Jonsson, F., Fjalldal, S.B., Stefansson, K. et al. 2003. A novel MALDI-TOF based methodology for genotyping single nucleotide polymorphisms, *Nucleic Acids Res*, 31(24), e155.

Bonadona, V., Saltel, P., Desseigne, F., Mignotte, H., Saurin, J.C., Wang, Q. et al. 2002. Cancer patients who experienced diagnostic genetic testing for cancer susceptibility: reactions and behavior after the disclosure of a positive test result, *Cancer Epidemiol Biomarkers Prev*, 11(1), 97–104.

Bosch, X. 2004. Spain to establish national genetic database, *Lancet*, 363(9414), 1044.

Bourne, P.E. 2003. Free access to publicly funded databases is vital, *Nature*, 421(6925), 786.

Boyes, R. 2003. 'Gene bank' set to solve riddle of ill health. *London Times*, 28 August 2003: <http://www.geenivaramu.ee/index.php?id=246> (accessed 14 August 2009).

Bozcuk, H., Erdogan, V., Eken, C., Ciplak, E., Samur, M., Ozdogan, M. and Savas, B. 2002. Does awareness of diagnosis make any difference to quality of life? Determinants of emotional functioning in a group of cancer patients in Turkey, *Support Care Cancer*, 10(1), 51–7.

Brand, A.M. and Probst-Hensch, N.M. 2007. Biobanking for epidemiological research and public health, *Pathobiology*, 74(4), 227–38.

Breithaupt, H. 2001. The future of medicine. Centralised health and genetic databases promise to increase quality of health care while lowering costs. But to get there, many legal and social obstacles will have to be overcome to prevent abuse, *EMBO Rep*, 2(6), 465–7.

Brito, A. 2001. Community participation and representation in genetic studies: testing the application of fundamental ethical principles, *St Thomas Law Rev*, 13(4), 935–43.

Broadstock, M., Michie, S., Gray, J., Mackay, J. and Marteau, T.M. 2000a. The psychological consequences of offering mutation searching in the family for those at risk of hereditary breast and ovarian cancer – a pilot study, *Psychooncology*, 9(6), 537–48.

Broadstock, M., Michie, S. and Marteau, T. 2000b. Psychological consequences of predictive genetic testing: a systematic review, *Eur J Hum Genet*, 8(10), 731–8.

Brock, D.W. 1987. Informed consent, in *Health Care Ethics: An Introduction*, D. Van De Veer and T. Regan (eds). Philadelphia, PA: Temple University Press, 98–126.

Brownsword, R. 2003. An interest in human dignity as the basis for genomic torts, *Washburn Law J*, 42(3), 413–81.

Brownsword, R. 2007. Ethical pluralism and the regulation of modern biotechnology, in *Biotechnologies and International Human Rights (Studies in International Law)*, F. Francioni (ed.). Portland, OR: Hart Publishing, 45–70.

Bruce, A. and Tait, J. 2004. Values and genetic databases, in *Blood and Data: Ethical, Legal and Social Aspects of Human Genetic Databases*, G. Arnason, S. Nordal and V. Arnason (eds). Reykjavik: University of Iceland Press, 211–16.

Buchanan, A. 1999. An ethical framework for biological samples policy. Commissioned paper, in *Research Involving Human Biological Materials: Ethical Issues and Policy Guidance, Report and Recommendations, vol. 2*, National Bioethics Advisory Commission (NBAC) (ed.). Rockville, MD: NBAC, B1–B31.

Burgermeister, J. 2004. Estonia genome project lives on. *The Scientist*, 28 April 2004: <http://www.geenivaramu.ee/index.php?id=118> (accessed 1 August 2009).

Burke, T. and Rosenbaum, S. 2005. Molloy v Meier and the expanding standard of medical care: implications for public health policy and practice, *Public Health Rep*, 120(2), 209–10.

Burton, P.R., Hansell, A.L., Fortier, I., Manolio, T.A., Khoury, M.J., Little, J. and Elliott, P. 2009. Size matters: just how big is BIG?: Quantifying realistic sample size requirements for human genome epidemiology, *Int J Epidemiol*, 38(1), 263–73.

Busby, H. 2004. Blood donation for genetic research: what can we learn from donors' narratives?, in *Genetic Databases: Socio-Ethical Issues in the Collection and Use of DNA*, R. Tutton and O. Corrigan (eds). London/New York: Routledge, 39–56.

Busby, H. 2006. Biobanks, bioethics and concepts of donated blood in the UK, *Sociol Health Illn*, 28(6), 850–65.

Cambon-Thomsen, A. 2003. Assessing the impact of biobanks, *Nat Genet*, 34(1), 25–6.

Cambon-Thomsen, A. 2004. The social and ethical issues of post-genomic human biobanks, *Nat Rev Genet*, 5(11), 866–73.

Cambon-Thomsen, A., Rial-Sebbag, E. and Knoppers, B.M. 2007. Trends in ethical and legal frameworks for the use of human biobanks, *Eur Respir J*, 30(2), 373–82.

Campbell, C.S. 1999. Research on human tissue: religious perspectives. Commissioned paper, in *Research Involving Human Biological Materials: Ethical Issues and Policy Guidance, Report and Recommendations, vol. 2*, National Bioethics Advisory Commission (NBAC) (ed.). Rockville, MD: NBAC, C1–C22.

Caplan, A.L. 1984. Is there a duty to serve as a subject in biomedical research?, *IRB*, 6(5), 1–5.

Caplan, A.L. 2003. Dignity is a social construct: <http://bmj.bmjjournals.com/cgi/eletters/327/7429/1419#44060> (accessed 5 August 2009).

Capron, A.M. 2003. Indignities, respect for persons, and the vagueness of human dignity: <http://bmj.bmjjournals.com/cgi/eletters/327/7429/1419#440 60> (accessed 5 August 2009).

Capron, A.M., Mauron, A., Elger, B.S., Boggio, A., Ganguli-Mitra, A. and Biller-Andorno, N. 2009. Ethical norms and the international governance of genetic databases and biobanks: findings from an international study, *Kennedy Inst Ethics J*, 19(2), 101–24.

Carmel, S. and Mutran, E.J. 1999. Stability of elderly persons' expressed preferences regarding the use of life-sustaining treatments, *Soc Sci Med*, 49(3), 303–11.

Caulfield, T. 2004a. Human genetic research databases. Presentation at the OECD conference on human genetic databases in Tokyo, 26–27 February.

Caulfield, T. 2004b. Tissue banking, patient rights, and confidentiality: tensions in law and policy, *Med Law*, 23(1), 39–49.

Caulfield, T. and Brownsword, R. 2006. Human dignity: a guide to policy making in the biotechnology era?, *Nat Rev Genet*, 7(1), 72–6.

Caulfield, T., McGuire, A.L., Cho, M., Buchanan, J.A., Burgess, M.M., Danilczyk, U. et al. 2008. Research ethics recommendations for whole-genome research: consensus statement, *PLoS Biol*, 6(3), e73.

Caulfield, T., Upshur, R.E. and Daar, A. 2003. DNA databanks and consent: a suggested policy option involving an authorization model, *BMC Med Ethics*, 4, E1.

Cavusoglu, A.C., Saydam, S., Alakavuklar, M., Canda, T., Sevinc, A., Kilic, Y. et al. 2008. A pilot study for human tumor/DNA banking: returned more questions than answers, *Med Oncol*, 25, 471–3.

CCNE. 2003. Comité Consultatif National d'Ethique pour les sciences de la vie et de la santé. Avis No 77. Problèmes éthiques posés par les collections de matériel biologique et les données d'information associées: 'biobanques', 'biothèques'. 2003: <http://www.ccne-ethique.fr/docs/fr/avis077.pdf> (accessed 1 August 2009).

CDBI. 2002a. Council of Europe Steering Committee on Bioethics. Proposal for an instrument on the use of archived human biological materials in biomedical research 2002: <http://www.eortc.be/vtb/TuBaFrost/Ethics/CDBI-INF(2002)5E.pdf> (accessed 10 August 2009).

CDBI. 2002b. Council of Europe Steering Committee on Bioethics. Proposal for an instrument on the use of archived human biological materials in biomedical research: draft explanatory report to the proposal for an instrument on the use of archived human biological materials in biomedical research 2002: <https://wcd.coe.int/ViewDoc.jsp?id=747439&Site=COE> (accessed 2 August 2009).

CEST. February 2003. *The Ethical Issues of Genetic Databases: Towards Democratic and Responsible Regulation – Position Statement*. Quebec: Commission de l'Éthique de la Science et de la Technologie.

CEST. 2003. Commission de l'Éthique de la Science et de la Technologie. Avis. Les enjeux éthiques des banques d'information génétique: pour un encadrement démocratique et responsable. Quebec 2003: <http://catalogue.cdeacf.ca/Record.htm?idlist=1&record=19186491124919046739> (accessed 10 August 2009).

Chadwick, R. 1999. The Icelandic database: do modern times need modern sagas?, *BMJ*, 319(7207), 441–4.

Chadwick, R. and Berg, K. 2001. Solidarity and equity: new ethical frameworks for genetic databases, *Nat Rev Genet*, 2(4), 318–21.

Chadwick, R. and Wilso, S. 2004. Genomic databases as global public goods?, *Res Publica*, 10(2), 123–34.

Chen, D.T., Rosenstein, D.L., Muthappan, P., Hilsenbeck, S.G., Miller, F.G., Emanuel, E.J. and Wendler, D. 2005. Research with stored biological samples: what do research participants want?, *Arch Intern Med*, 165(6), 652–5.

Chung, T.H., Yoo, J.H., Ryu, J.C. and Kim, Y.S. 2009. Recent progress in toxicogenomics research in South Korea, *BMC Proc*, 3 Suppl 2, S6.

CIOMS. 2002. Council for International Organizations of Medical Sciences. International Ethical Guidelines for Biomedical Research Involving Human Subjects: <http://www.cioms.ch/frame_guidelines_nov_2002.htm> (accessed August 2007).

CIOMS. 2009. *Council for International Organizations of Medical Sciences. International Ethical Guidelines for Epidemiological Studies.* Geneva: CIOMS.

Claes, E., Evers-Kiebooms, G., Boogaerts, A., Decruyenaere, M., Denayer, L. and Legius, E. 2003. Communication with close and distant relatives in the context of genetic testing for hereditary breast and ovarian cancer in cancer patients, *Am J Med Genet A*, 116A(1), 11–19.

Clark, B.J. 2007. Tissue banking in a regulated environment: does this help the patient? Part 1: legislation, regulation and ethics in the UK, *Pathobiology*, 74(4), 218–22.

Clarke, A. 2005. Confidentiality and serious harm in genetics, *Eur J Hum Genet*, 13(4), 399; author reply – 400.

Clarke, A., Richards, M., Kerzin-Storrar, L., Halliday, J., Young, M.A., Simpson, S.A., Featherstone, K., Forrest, K., Lucassen, A., Morrison, P.J., Quarrell, O.W. and Stewart, H. 2005. Genetic professionals' reports of nondisclosure of genetic risk information within families, *Eur J Hum Genet*, 13(5), 556–62.

Clayton, D. and McKeigue, P.M. 2001. Epidemiological methods for studying genes and environmental factors in complex diseases, *Lancet*, 358(9290), 1356–60.

Clayton, E.W. 2005. Informed consent and biobanks, *J Law Med Ethics*, 33(1), 15–21.

Clayton, E.W., Steinberg, K.K., Khoury, M.J., Thomson, E., Andrews, L., Kahn, M.J., Kopelman, L.M. and Weiss, J.O. 1995. Informed consent for genetic research on stored tissue samples, *JAMA*, 274(22), 1786–92.

Clement, B., Chene, G. and Degos, F. 2009. A national collection of liver tumours: lessons learnt from 6 years of biobanking in France, *Cancer Lett*, 286(1), 140–44.

COE. 1996. Council of Europe. Convention for the protection of human rights and dignity of the human being with regard to the application of biology and medicine: Convention on Human Rights and Biomedicine. Explanatory report (ETS No.: 164): <http://conventions.coe.int/treaty/EN/Reports/Html/164.htm> (accessed 5 August 2009).

COE. 1997a. Council of Europe, Committee of Ministers (1997), Recommendation No. R(97)5 of the Committee of Ministers to Member States on the Protection of Medical Data: <http://www1.umn.edu/humanrts/instree/coerecr97-5.html> (accessed 30 July 2009).

COE. 1997b. Council of Europe. Convention for the protection of human rights and dignity of the human being with regard to the application of biology and medicine: Convention on Human Rights and Biomedicine. CETS No.: 164.

COE. 2005. Additional Protocol to the Convention on Human Rights and Biomedicine Concerning Biomedical Research Strasbourg, 25.I.2005: <http://conventions.coe.int/Treaty/en/Treaties/Html/195.htm> (accessed 2 August 2009).

COE. 2006. Council of Europe. Rec(2006)4 of the Committee of Ministers to member states on research on biological materials of human origin: <https://wcd.coe.int/ViewDoc.jsp?id=977859> (accessed 30 July 2009).

Coghlan, A. 2006. One million people, one medical gamble, *New Sci*, 189(2535), 8–9.

Consortium on Pharmacogenetics, Buchanan, A., McPherson, E., Brody, B.A., Califano, A., Kahn, J., McCullough, N. and Robertson, J.A. 2002. *Pharmacogenetics: Ethical and Regulatory Issues in Research and Clinical Practice*. Minneapolis, MN: Consortium on Pharmacogenetics.

Corrigan, O. 2004. Informed consent: the contradictory ethical safeguards in pharmacogenetics, in *Genetic Databases: Socio-Ethical Issues in the Collection and Use of DNA*, R. Tutton and O. Corrigan (eds). London/New York: Routledge, 78–96.

Corrigan, O. 2006. Biobanks: can they overcome controversy and deliver on their promise to unravel the origins of common diseases?, *Med Educ*, 40(6), 500–502.

Couzin, J. 2008. Genetic privacy: whole-genome data not anonymous, challenging assumptions, *Science*, 321(5894), 1278.

Currie, R. 1998. MRC funds large-scale human genetic database, *Nat Med*, 4(12), 1346.

Curtis, H. 2004. Getting ethics into practice: Tuskegee was bad enough, *BMJ*, 329(7464), 513; author reply.

D'Agincourt-Canning, L. 2001. Experiences of genetic risk: disclosure and the gendering of responsibility, *Bioethics*, 15(3), 231–47.

D'Oronzio, J.C. 2003. 'Human dignity' – prognosis positive: <http://bmj.bmjjournals.com/cgi/eletters/327/7429/1419#44060> (accessed 5 August 2009).

Danzer, E., Holzgreve, W., Troeger, C., Kostka, U., Steimann, S., Bitzer, J., Gratwohl, A., Tichelli, A., Seelmann, K. and Surbek, D.V. 2003. Attitudes of Swiss mothers toward unrelated umbilical cord blood banking 6 months after donation, *Transfusion*, 43(5), 604–8.

Data Protection Act. 1998. UK: <http://www.opsi.gov.uk/acts/acts1998/ukpga_19980029_en_1> (accessed 15 July 2009).

Data Protection Commission. 1998. Data Protection Commission's opinion on the draft Bill on a health-sector database. Letter from Data Protection Commission to Minister of Health, Ingibjörg Pálmadóttir, 4 September 1998: <http://www.mannvernd.is/english/news/Data_Protection_Commission_040998.html> (accessed January 2004).

Data Protection Working Party. 2007. Opinion 4/2007 on the concept of personal data. Article 29, WP 136: <http://ec.europa.eu/justice_home/fsj/privacy/docs/wpdocs/2007/wp136_en.pdf>.

Davis, R.L. and Khoury, M.J. 2007. The emergence of biobanks: practical design considerations for large population-based studies of gene-environment interactions, *Community Genet*, 10(3), 181–5.

Day, J.G. and Stacey, G.N. 2008. Biobanking, *Mol Biotechnol*, 40(2), 202–13.

De Montgolfier, S., Moutel, G., Duchange, N., Callies, I., Sharara, L., Beaumont, C. et al. 2006. Evaluation of biobank constitution and use: multicentre analysis in France and propositions for formalising the activities of research ethics committees, *Eur J Med Genet*, 49(2), 159–67.

De Wert, G. 2005. Cascade screening: whose information is it anyway?, *Eur J Hum Genet*, 13(4), 397–8.

Deftos, L.J. 1998a. The evolving duty to disclose the presence of genetic disease to relatives, *Acad Med*, 73(9), 962–8.

Deftos, L.J. 1998b. Genomic torts: the law of the future – the duty of physicians to disclose the presence of a genetic disease to the relatives of their patients with the disease, *Spec Law Dig Health Care Law*, (234), 9–41.

Deming, Q.B. 2002. Protecting patients' privacy, *Lancet*, 359(9300), 84.

*Der Standard*. 2003. Isländer sind 'Mäuse in einem Labor'. *Der Standard*, Print Ausgabe 12.4.2003: <http://derstandard.at/?id=1269423> (accessed 20 July 2009).

Deschênes, M. 2004. Ethics guidelines for population genetics research, *Nat Rev Genet*, 5(6), 408.

Deschênes, M., Cardinal, G., Knoppers, B.M. and Glass, K.C. 2001. Human genetic research, DNA banking and consent: a question of 'form'?, *Clin Genet*, 59(4), 221–39.

Deschênes, M. and Sallee, C. 2005. Accountability in population biobanking: comparative approaches, *J Law Med Ethics*, 33(1), 40–53.

Dickenson, D. 2004. Consent, commodification and benefit-sharing in genetic research, *Dev World Bioeth*, 4(2), 109–24.

Dugan, R.B., Wiesner, G.L., Juengst, E.T., O'Riordan, M., Matthews, A.L. and Robin, N.H. 2003. Duty to warn at-risk relatives for genetic disease: genetic counselors' clinical experience, *Am J Med Genet C Semin Med Genet*, 119(1), 27–34.

Duncan, N. 1999. World Medical Association opposes Icelandic gene database, *BMJ*, 318(7191), 1096.

Durham, N.P. and Hall, A.S. 1999. Genes and the heart: a quest for new therapeutic strategies. Cambridge Healthtech Institute's First Cardiovascular Genomics Conference. Orlando, FL, USA, 11–12 January 1999, *Mol Med Today*, 5(5), 195–7.

Dyer, C. 2000. Surgeon amputated healthy legs, *BMJ*, 320(7231), 332.

Dyer, C. 2001. Scientists fear breach of confidentiality will threaten research. *The Guardian*. 17 March 2001.

Dziak, K., Anderson, R., Sevick, M.A., Weisman, C.S., Levine, D.W. and Scholle, S.H. 2005. Variations among Institutional Review Board reviews in a multisite health services research study, *Health Serv Res*, 40(1), 279–90.

Edwards, J.H. 1999. Unifactorial models are not appropriate for multifactorial disease, *BMJ*, 318(7194), 1353–4.

Eesti geenivaramu. 2002. Who can receive information from the Gene Bank and what information can one receive? 30 November 2002: <http://www.geenivaramu.ee/index.php?id=118> (accessed 1 August 2009).

Eesti geenivaramu. 2003. Estonian Genome Project starts the main project. 27 February 2003: <http://www.geenivaramu.ee/index.php?id=118> (accessed 1 August 2009).

Eesti geenivaramu. 2004a. Estonian Gene Bank has received the data of 10000 gene donors. 2 January 2004: <http://www.geenivaramu.ee/index.php?id=118> (accessed 1 August 2009).

Eesti geenivaramu. 2004b. The Estonian Government decided to allocate funds for the Estonian Genome Project. 23 January 2004: <http://www.geenivaramu.ee/index.php?id=118> (accessed 1 August 2009).

Eesti geenivaramu. 2004c. General information. Ethics Committee of the Estonian Genome Project Foundation: <http://www.geenivaramu.ee/index.php?lang=eng&sub=72> (accessed 20 July 2004; original website not available anymore).

Eesti geenivaramu. 2004d. General information. Information about the Gene Donor Consent Form: <http://www.geenivaramu.ee/index.php?lang=eng&sub=75> (accessed August 2004; the original website is not available anymore).

Eesti geenivaramu. 2004e. General information. Introduction of the Estonian Gene Bank's questionnaire of the state of health and genealogy: <http://www.geenivaramu.ee/index.php?lang=eng&sub=76> (accessed 20 July 2004; this website is not accessible any more).

Eesti geenivaramu. 2004f. General information. What should I know about the Genome Project?: <http://www.geenivaramu.ee/index.php?lang=eng&sub=59> (accessed 20 July 2004; this website is not available anymore).

Eesti geenivaramu. 2009a. EGP questionnaire: <http://www.geenivaramu.ee/documents/egpq.xls> (accessed 1 August 2009).

Eesti geenivaramu. 2009b. Frequently asked questions: <http://www.geenivaramu.ee/index.php?id=110> (accessed 1 August 2009).

Eesti geenivaramu. 2009c. The Gene Donor Consent Form: <http://www.geenivaramu.ee/index.php?id=104> (accessed 1 August 2009).

Eesti geenivaramu. 2009d. Main provisions of the Human Genes Research Act: <http://www.geenivaramu.ee/index.php?id=105> (accessed 1 August 2009).

Eesti geenivaramu. 2009e. Supervisory Board of the Estonian Genome Project Foundation. Elected Chairman and Member of Scientific Advisory Board: <http://www.geenivaramu.ee/?id=209> (accessed 1 August 2009).

Eesti geenivaramu. 2009f. What is the genome project?: <http://www.geenivaramu.ee/index.php?id=102> (accessed 1 August 2009).

Eiseman, E. 1999. Stored tissue samples: an inventory of sources in the United States. Commissioned paper, in *Research Involving Human Biological Materials: Ethical Issues and Policy Guidance, Report and Recommendations, vol. 2*, National Bioethics Advisory Commission (NBAC) (ed.). Rockville, MD: NBAC, D1–D52.

Eiseman, E. 2003. *Case Studies of Existing Human Tissue Repositories: 'Best Practices' for a Biospecimen Resource for the Genomic and Proteomic Era*. Santa Monica, CA: RAND.

Eiseman, E. and Haga, S.B. 1999. *Handbook of Human Tissue Sources: A National Resource of Human Tissue Samples*. Santa Monica, CA: RAND.

Eisinger, F., Geller, G., Burke, W. and Holtzman, N.A. 1999. Cultural basis for differences between US and French clinical recommendations for women at increased risk of breast and ovarian cancer, *Lancet*, 353(9156), 919–20.

Elger, B. 1998a. *Le concept de paternalisme: aspects éthiques et philosophiques.* Geneva: Thèse de doctorat à la Faculté de Médecine.

Elger, B. 1998b. *Médecine prédictive et décisions procréatives et prénatales.* Geneva: Médecine et Hygiène, Livres Georg.

Elger, B.S. 2002. Ethics in clinical routine care: example of prognosis information, *Med Klin (Munich)*, 97(9), 533–40.

Elger, B. 2006. Kritische Analyse der Reglementierung von Biobanken im Vorentwurf des Bundesgesetzes über die Forschung am Menschen, *Bioethica Forum*, 49, 42–5.

Elger, B. 2008a. Consent and use of samples, in *Ethical Issues in Governing Biobanks: Global Perspectives*, B. Elger, N. Biller-Andorno, A. Mauron and A.M. Capron (eds). Aldershot: Ashgate, 57–88.

Elger, B. 2008b. Consent to research involving human biological samples obtained during medical care, in *Ethical Issues in Governing Biobanks: Global Perspectives*, B. Elger, N. Biller-Andorno, A. Mauron and A.M. Capron (eds). Aldershot: Ashgate, 89–120.

Elger, B., Biller-Andorno, N., Mauron, A. and Capron, A.M. (eds). 2008. *Ethical Issues in Governing Biobanks: Global Perspectives*. Aldershot: Ashgate.

Elger, B.S. and Caplan, A.L. 2006. Consent and anonymization in research involving biobanks: differing terms and norms present serious barriers to an international framework, *EMBO Rep*, 7(7), 661–6.

Elger, B. and Harding, T. 2003. Huntington's disease: do future physicians and lawyers think eugenically?, *Clin Genet*, 64(4), 327–38.

Elger, B.S., Hofner, M.C. and Mangin, P. 2009a. Research involving biological material from forensic autopsies: legal and ethical issues, *Pathobiology*, 76, 1–10.

Elger, B., Iavindrasana, J., Iacono, L.L., Müller, H., Roduit, N., Summer, P. and Wright, J. 2009b. Health data depersonalisation for prospective research in the life sciences, *Computer Methods and Programs in Biomedicine*, submitted.

Elger, B. and Mauron, A. 2003. A presumed-consent model for regulating informed consent of genetic research involving DNA banking, in *Populations and Genetics: Legal and Socio-Ethical Perspectives*, B.M. Knoppers (ed.). Leiden/Boston, MA: Martinus Nijhoff Publishers, 269–95.

Elliott, P. and Peakman, T.C. 2008. The UK Biobank sample handling and storage protocol for the collection, processing and archiving of human blood and urine, *Int J Epidemiol*, 37(2), 234–44.

Emanuel, L.L., Emanuel, E.J., Stoeckle, J.D., Hummel, L.R. and Barry, M.J. 1994. Advance directives: stability of patients' treatment choices, *Arch Intern Med*, 154(2), 209–17.

English, V., Heath, L., Romano-Critchley, G. and Sommerville, A. 2000. Ethics briefings: confidentiality; organ donation; insurance; the Icelandic database, *J Med Ethics*, 26(3), 215–16.

Ennis, D.P., Pidgeon, G.P., Millar, N., Ravi, N. and Reynolds, J.V. 2009. Building a bioresource for esophageal research: lessons from the early experience of an academic medical center, *Dis Esophagus*, 23(1), 1–7.

Enserink, M. 1998a. Opponents criticize Iceland's database, *Science*, 282(5390), 859.

Enserink, M. 1998b. Physicians wary of scheme to pool Icelanders' genetic data, *Science*, 281(5379), 890–91.

EPIC. 2002. Privacy International and Electronic Privacy Information Center. New report on privacy and human rights 2002: <http://www.privacyinternational. org/survey/phr2002/>; pdf at: <http://www.privacyinternational.org/survey/ phr2002/phr2002-part2.pdf> (accessed 30 July 2009).

Eriksson, S. 2004. Should results from genetic research be returned to research subjects and their biological relatives?, *TRAMES – A Journal of the Humanities and Social Sciences*, 8(1–2), 46–62.

Eriksson, S. and Helgesson, G. 2005. Potential harms, anonymization, and the right to withdraw consent to biobank research, *Eur J Hum Genet*, 13(9), 1071–6.

ESHG. 2003. Data storage and DNA banking for biomedical research: technical, social and ethical issues. Recommendations of the European Society of Human Genetics, *European Journal of Human Genetics*, 11, Suppl. 2, S8–S10.

ESHG, Godard, B., Schmidtke, J., Cassiman, J.J. and Ayme, S. 1 November 2002. Data storage and DNA banking for biomedical research: informed consent, confidentiality, quality issues, ownership, return of benefits. A professional perspective. European Society of Human Genetics, Public and Professional Policy Committee. Eurogappp project 1999–2000: <http://www.eshg.org/ ESHGDNAbankingbckgrnd.pdf> (accessed 7 August 2009).

Etzioni, A. 2006. A communitarian approach: a viewpoint on the study of the legal, ethical and policy considerations raised by DNA tests and databases, *J Law Med Ethics*, 34(2), 214–21.

European Parliament and the Council. 1995. Directive 95/46/EC of the European Parliament and of the Council of 24 October 1995 on the protection of individuals with regard to the processing of personal data and on the free movement of such data: <http://www.dataprotection.ie/viewdoc.asp?DocID=89> (accessed 30 July 2009).

Evans, I. 1994. The challenge of breast cancer, *Lancet*, 343(8905), 1085–6.

Evans, I. 1996. Leading council, *Lancet*, 347(9018), 1828.

Everhart, M.A. and Pearlman, R.A. 1990. Stability of patient preferences regarding life-sustaining treatments, *Chest*, 97(1), 159–64.

Falk, M.J., Dugan, R.B., O'Riordan, M.A., Matthews, A.L. and Robin, N.H. 2003. Medical geneticists' duty to warn at-risk relatives for genetic disease, *Am J Med Genet A*, 120A(3), 374–80.

Fan, C.T., Lin, J.C. and Lee, C.H. 2008. Taiwan Biobank: a project aiming to aid Taiwan's transition into a biomedical island, *Pharmacogenomics*, 9(2), 235–46.

Fears, R. and Poste, G. 1999. Policy forum: health care delivery. Building populations genetics resources using the U.K. NHS, *Science*, 284(5412), 267–8.

Feinberg, J. 1984. *Harm to Others: The Moral Limits of the Criminal Law*. Oxford: Oxford University Press.

Fernandez, C. 2008. Public expectations for return of results: time to stop being paternalistic?, *Am J Bioeth*, 8(11), 46–8.

Fernandez, C.V., Kodish, E., Shurin, S. and Weijer, C. 2003a. Offering to return results to research participants: attitudes and needs of principal investigators in the Children's Oncology Group, *J Pediatr Hematol Oncol*, 25(9), 704–8.

Fernandez, C.V., Kodish, E., Taweel, S., Shurin, S. and Weijer, C. 2003b. Disclosure of the right of research participants to receive research results: an analysis of consent forms in the Children's Oncology Group, *Cancer*, 97(11), 2904–9.

Fernandez, C.V., Kodish, E. and Weijer, C. 2003c. Importance of informed consent in offering to return research results to research participants, *Med Pediatr Oncol*, 41(6), 592–3.

Fernandez, C.V., Santor, D., Weijer, C., Strahlendorf, C., Moghrabi, A., Pentz, R., Gao, J. and Kodish, E. 2007. The return of research results to participants: pilot questionnaire of adolescents and parents of children with cancer, *Pediatr Blood Cancer*, 48(4), 441–6.

Fernandez, C.V., Taweel, S., Kodish, E.D. and Weijer, C. 2005. Disclosure of research results to research participants: a pilot study of the needs and attitudes of adolescents and parents, *Paediatr Child Health*, 10(6), 332–4.

Fitzpatrick, J.L., Hahn, C., Costa, T. and Huggins, M.J. 1999. The duty to recontact: attitudes of genetics service providers, *Am J Hum Genet*, 64(3), 852–60.

Fletcher, J.C. 1989. Ethics and human genetics: a cross cultural perspective, in *Ethics and Human Genetics: A Cross Cultural Perspective*, D.C. Wertz and J.C. Fletcher (eds). Heidelberg: Springer-Verlag, 1–79.

Förderverein Humangenomforschung und Biotechnologie e.V. 2004. Biobanken: '... ein Stück von mir' für die Forschung? Podiumsdiskussion am 06.05.2004 in Wiesbaden: <http://idw-online.de/pages/de/news79462> (accessed 3 August 2009).

Forrest, L.E., Curnow, L., Delatycki, M.B., Skene, L. and Aitken, M. 2008. Health first, genetics second: exploring families' experiences of communicating genetic information, *Eur J Hum Genet*, 16(11), 1329–35.

Forrest, L.E., Delatycki, M.B., Skene, L. and Aitken, M. 2007. Communicating genetic information in families: a review of guidelines and position papers, *Eur J Hum Genet*, 15(6), 612–18.

Forsberg, J.S., Hansson, M.G. and Eriksson, S. 2009. Changing perspectives in biobank research: from individual rights to concerns about public health regarding the return of results, *Eur J Hum Genet*, 17, 1544–9.

Fortun, M. 2003. Towards genomic solidarity: lessons from Iceland and Estonia. Open Democracy 10 July 2003: <http://www.opendemocracy.net/theme_9-genes/article_1344.jsp> (accessed 28 July 2009).

Fortun, M.A. 2008. *Promising Genomics: Iceland and deCODE Genetics in a World of Speculation.* Berkeley, CA/Los Angeles, CA/London: University of California Press.

Foster, M.W. and Sharp, R.R. 2005. Will investments in large-scale prospective cohorts and biobanks limit our ability to discover weaker, less common genetic and environmental contributors to complex diseases?, *Environ Health Perspect*, 113(2), 119–22.

Francioni, F. 2007a. *Biotechnologies and International Human Rights (Studies in International Law).* Portland, OR: Hart Publishing.

Francioni, F. 2007b. Genetic resources, biotechnology and human rights: the international legal framework, in *Biotechnologies and International Human Rights (Studies in International Law)*, F. Francioni (ed.). Portland, OR: Hart Publishing, 3–32.

Frank, L. 1999. Storm brews over gene bank of Estonian population, *Science*, 286(5443), 1262–3.

Frank, L. 2001. Biotechnology in the Baltic, *Nat Biotechnol*, 19(6), 513–15.

Garfinkel, S. 2001. *Database Nation: The Death of Privacy in the 21st Century.* Sebastopol, CA: O'Reilly.

Garvin, A.M., Eppenberger, U., Muller, H., Eppenberger-Castori, S. and Scott, R.J. 1997. BRCA1 mutations found in archived early onset breast tumours, *Eur J Cancer*, 33(4), 683–6.

Garvin, A.M., Mueller, H., Eppenberger-Castori, S., Eppenberger, U.R. and Scott, R.J. 1996. Informed consent and BRCA1 mutation detection in archived breast tumor specimens, *Lancet*, 347(9009), 1189.

Geller, G., Doksum, T., Bernhardt, B.A. and Metz, S.A. 1999. Participation in breast cancer susceptibility testing protocols: influence of recruitment source, altruism, and family involvement on women's decisions, *Cancer Epidemiol Biomarkers Prev*, 8(4 Pt 2), 377–83.

GenomeWeb staff reporter. 29 April 2009. Decode Genetics gets stay from Nasdaq delisting. GenomeWeb Daily News: <http://www.genomeweb.com/dxpgx/decode-genetics-gets-stay-nasdaq-delisting> (accessed 30 July 2009).

German National Ethics Council. 2004. Biobanks for research. Opinion: <http://www.ethikrat.org/_english/publications/Opinion_Biobanks-for-research.pdf> (accessed 30 July 2009).

Gertz, R. 2008. Withdrawing from participating in a biobank: a comparative study, *Eur J Health Law*, 15(4), 381–9.

Gesang, B. 2003. *Eine Verteidigung des Utilitarismus.* Stuttgart: Reclam.

Gewin, V. 2007. Crunch time for multiple-gene tests, *Nature*, 445(7126), 354–5.

Giannet, S.M. 2003. Dignity is a moral imperative: <http://bmj.bmjjournals.com/cgi/eletters/327/7429/1419#44060> (accessed 5 August 2009).

Gibbons, S.M. 2009. Regulating biobanks: a twelve-point typological tool, *Med Law Rev*, 17, 313–46.

Gibson, E., Brazil, K., Coughlin, M.D., Emerson, C., Fournier, F., Schwartz, L., Szala-Meneok, K.V., Weisbaum, K.M. and Willison, D.J. 2008. Who's minding the shop? The role of Canadian research ethics boards in the creation and uses of registries and biobanks, *BMC Med Ethics*, 9, 17.

Giles, J. 2006. Huge biobank project launches despite critics, *Nature*, 440(7082), 263.

Godard, B., Hurlimann, T., Letendre, M. and Egalite, N. 2006. Guidelines for disclosing genetic information to family members: from development to use, *Fam Cancer*, 5(1), 103–16.

Godard, B., Schmidtke, J., Cassiman, J.J. and Ayme, S. 2003. Data storage and DNA banking for biomedical research: informed consent, confidentiality, quality issues, ownership, return of benefits. A professional perspective, *Eur J Hum Genet*, 11 Suppl. 2, S88–122.

Godfrey, K. 2003. Genetic databank launches ethics framework, *BMJ*, 327(7417), 700.

Goffin, T., Borry, P., Dierickx, K. and Nys, H. 2008. Why eight EU Member States signed, but not yet ratified the Convention for Human Rights and Biomedicine, *Health Policy*, 86(2–3), 222–33.

Gottweis, H. 2008. *Biobanks: Governance in Comparative Perspective*. New York: Routledge.

Gottweis, H. and Zatloukal, K. 2007. Biobank governance: trends and perspectives, *Pathobiology*, 74(4), 206–11.

Grant, R.W. and Sugarman, J. 2004. Ethics in human subjects research: do incentives matter?, *J Med Philos*, 29(6), 717–38.

Greely, H.T. 1999. Breaking the stalemate: a prospective regulatory framework for unforseen research uses of human tissue samples and health information, *Wake Forest Law Rev*, 34(3), 737–66.

Greely, H.T. 2000. Iceland's plan for genomics research: facts and implications, *Jurimetrics*, 40, 153–91.

Greely, H.T. 2007. The uneasy ethical and legal underpinnings of large-scale genomic biobanks, *Annu Rev Genomics Hum Genet*, 8, 343–64.

Green, R.C., Roberts, J.S., Cupples, L.A., Relkin, N.R., Whitehouse, P.J., Brown, T., Eckert, S.L., Butson, M., Sadovnick, A.D., Quaid, K.A., Chen, C., Cook-Deegan, R. and Farrer, L.A. 2009. Disclosure of APOE genotype for risk of Alzheimer's disease, *N Engl J Med*, 361(3), 245–54.

Greenhalgh, T. 2005. The Human Genome Project, *J R Soc Med*, 98(12), 545.

Gretarsdottir, S., Thorleifsson, G., Reynisdottir, S.T., Manolescu, A., Jonsdottir, S., Jonsdottir, T. et al. 2003. The gene encoding phosphodiesterase 4D confers risk of ischemic stroke, *Nat Genet*, 35(2), 131–8.

Grizzle, W., Grody, W.W., Noll, W.W., Sobel, M.E., Stass, S.A., Trainer, T., Travers, H., Weedn, V. and Woodruff, K. 1999. Recommended policies for uses of human tissue in research, education, and quality control. Ad Hoc Committee on Stored Tissue, College of American Pathologists, *Arch Pathol Lab Med*, 123(4), 296–300.

Gross, M. 2006. Iceland plans reigned in, *Curr Biol*, 16(24), R1005–6.

Grotzer, M. 2002. Zentrale Tumorbank für maligne Kindertumoren der Schweizerischen Pädiatrischen Onkologie Gruppe (SPOG) an der Universitäts-Kinderklinik Zürich. Revidierte Fassung 9 July 2002.

Grotzer, M.A., Shalaby, T., Poledna, T. and for the Swiss Pediatric Oncology Group (SPOG). 2003. Establishment of the Swiss Pediatric Oncology Group (SPOG) Tumor Bank, *SIAK-SPOG*, 180–84.

Gulcher, J.R., Kristjansson, K., Gudbjartsson, H. and Stefansson, K. 2000. Protection of privacy by third-party encryption in genetic research in Iceland, *Eur J Hum Genet*, 8(10), 739–42.

Gulcher, J. and Stefansson, K. 1998. Population genomics: laying the groundwork for genetic disease modeling and targeting, *Clin Chem Lab Med*, 36(8), 523–7.

Gulcher, J. and Stefansson, K. 1999a. An Icelandic saga on a centralized healthcare database and democratic decision making, *Nat Biotechnol*, 17(7), 620.

Gulcher, J.R. and Stefansson, K. 1999b. Ethics of population genomics research, *Nature*, 400(6742), 307–8.

Gulcher, J.R. and Stefansson, K. 2000. The Icelandic Healthcare Database and informed consent, *N Engl J Med*, 342(24), 1827–30.

Gunning, J., Holm, S. and Kenway, I. (eds). 2009. *Ethics, Law and Society Volume IV*. Farnham: Ashgate.

Gurwitz, D., Lunshof, J.E. and Altman, R.B. 2006. A call for the creation of personalized medicine databases, *Nat Rev Drug Discov*, 5(1), 23–6.

Habeck, M. 2003. Northern Europe says Skol to biotechnology. *Scientist* 28 July 2003: <http://www.the-scientist.com/article/display/13996/> (accessed 1 August 2009).

Hacking, I. 2001–2002. Body parts, large and small. Brownbag research seminars 2001–2002 abstracts. York University Atkinson Faculty of Liberal and Professional Studies: <http://www.yorku.ca/sts/brownbag/abs_0102.html> (accessed 20 July 2009).

Haimes, E. and Whong-Barr, M. 2004. Levels and styles of participation in genetic databases: a case study of the North Cumbria Community Genetics Project, in *Genetic Databases: Socio-Ethical Issues in the Collection and Use of DNA*, R. Tutton and O. Corrigan (eds). London/New York: Routledge, 57–77.

Hall, S. 2006. £61m medical experiment begins, *The Guardian*, Tuesday 22 August: <http://www.guardian.co.uk/science/2006/aug/22/medicineandhealth.lifeandhealth> (accessed 10 August 2009).

Halldenius, L. 2007. Genetic discrimination, in *The Ethics and Governance of Human Genetic Databases: European Perspectives*, M. Häyry, R. Chadwick, V. Arnason and G. Arnason (eds). Cambridge: Cambridge University Press, 170–80.

Hallgrimsson, B., Donnabhain, B.O., Walters, G.B., Cooper, D.M., Gudbjartsson, D. and Stefansson, K. 2004. Composition of the founding population of Iceland: biological distance and morphological variation in early historic Atlantic Europe, *Am J Phys Anthropol*, 124(3), 257–74.

Hallowell, N., Ardern-Jones, A., Eeles, R., Foster, C., Lucassen, A., Moynihan, C. and Watson, M. 2005. Communication about genetic testing in families of male BRCA1/2 carriers and non-carriers: patterns, priorities and problems, *Clin Genet*, 67(6), 492–502.

Halpern, S.D., Karlawish, J.H. and Berlin, J.A. 2002. The continuing unethical conduct of underpowered clinical trials, *JAMA*, 288(3), 358–62.

Hamilton, R.J., Bowers, B.J. and Williams, J.K. 2005. Disclosing genetic test results to family members, *J Nurs Scholarsh*, 37(1), 18–24.

Handelsman, J. 2009. Metagenetics: spending our inheritance on the future, *Microbial Biotechnology*, 2(2), 138–9.

Hansson, M.G. 2001. In the interests of efficiency and integrity. The use of human biobanks: ethical, social, economical and legal aspects: <http://www.crb.uu.se/downloads/biobanks-report/MHansson.pdf> (accessed 1 August 2009).

Hansson, M.G. 2006. Combining efficiency and concerns about integrity when using human biobanks, *Stud Hist Philos Biol Biomed Sci*, 37(3), 520–32.

Hansson, M.G. 2009. Ethics and biobanks, *Br J Cancer*, 100(1), 8–12.

Hansson, M.G., Dillner, J., Bartram, C.R., Carlson, J.A. and Helgesson, G. 2006. Should donors be allowed to give broad consent to future biobank research?, *Lancet Oncol*, 7(3), 266–9.

Hansson, S.O. 2004. The ethics of biobanks, *Camb Q Healthc Ethics*, 13(4), 319–26.

Haraldsdottir, R. 1999a. Iceland's central database of health records, *Science*, 283(5401), 487.

Haraldsdottir, R. 1999b. Icelandic gene database will uphold patients' rights, *BMJ*, 318(7186), 806.

Hardwig, J. 1990. What about the family?, *Hastings Cent Rep*, 20(2), 5–10.

Harmon, S.H. 2009. Semantic, pedantic or paradigm shift? Recruitment, retention and property in modern population biobanking, *Eur J Health Law*, 16(1), 27–43.

Harris, J. 1999. Ethical genetic research on human subjects, *Jurimetrics J*, 40, 77–91.

Harris, J. and Keywood, K. 2001. Ignorance, information and autonomy, *Theor Med Bioeth*, 22(5), 415–36.

Harris, M., Winship, I. and Spriggs, M. 2005. Controversies and ethical issues in cancer-genetics clinics, *Lancet Oncol*, 6(5), 301–10.

Harrison, C.H. 2002. Neither Moore nor the market: alternative models for compensating contributors of human tissue, *Am J Law Med*, 28(1), 77–105.

Hauksson, P. 1999. Icelanders opt out of genetic database, *Nature*, 400(6746), 707–8.

Häyry, M. 2003. European values in bioethics: why, what, and how to be used?, *Theor Med Bioeth*, 24, 199–214.

Häyry, M. 2004. Another look at dignity, *Camb Q Healthc Ethics*, 13(1), 7–14.

Häyry, M., Chadwick, R., Arnason, V. and Arnason, G. (eds). 2007. *The Ethics and Governance of Human Genetic Databases: European Perspectives*. Cambridge: Cambridge University Press.

Häyry, M. and Häyry, H. 1990. Health care as a right, fairness and medical resources, *Bioethics*, 4(1), 1–21.

Häyry, M. and Takala, T. 2001. Genetic information, rights, and autonomy, *Theor Med Bioeth*, 22(5), 403–14.

Häyry, M. and Takala, T. 2005. Human dignity, bioethics, and human rights, *Dev World Bioeth*, 5(3), 225–33.

Häyry, M. and Takala, T. 2007. American principles, European values and the mezzanine rules of ethical genetic databanking, in *The Ethics and Governance of Human Genetic Databases: European Perspectives*, M. Häyry, R. Chadwick, V. Arnason and G. Arnason (eds). Cambridge: Cambridge University Press, 14–36.

Helgason, A., Hrafnkelsson, B., Gulcher, J.R., Ward, R. and Stefansson, K. 2003a. A populationwide coalescent analysis of Icelandic matrilineal and patrilineal genealogies: evidence for a faster evolutionary rate of mtDNA lineages than Y chromosomes, *Am J Hum Genet*, 72(6), 1370–88.

Helgason, A., Nicholson, G., Stefansson, K. and Donnelly, P. 2003b. A reassessment of genetic diversity in Icelanders: strong evidence from multiple loci for relative homogeneity caused by genetic drift, *Ann Hum Genet*, 67(Pt 4), 281–97.

Helgesson, G. and Johnsson, L. 2005. The right to withdraw consent to research on biobank samples, *Med Health Care Philos*, 8(3), 315–21.

HGC. 2000. Human Genetics Commission. Whose hands on your genes? A discussion document on the storage protection and use of personal genetic information. 2000: <http://www.hgc.gov.uk/UploadDocs/DocPub/Document/business_consultations2maintext.pdf> (accessed 15 July 2009).

HGC. 2002. Human Genetics Commission. Inside information: balancing interests in the use of personal genetic data: <http://www.hgc.gov.uk/Client/library_category.asp?CategoryId=10> and <http://www.hgc.gov.uk/UploadDocs/DocPub/Document/insideinformation_summary.pdf> (accessed 2 August 2009).

HHS. 2009. Department of Health & Human Services. Clinical Laboratory Improvement Amendments (CLIA): <http://www.cms.hhs.gov/clia/> (accessed 10 August 2009).

Hirshhorn, R. and Langford, J. 2001. Intellectual property rights in biotechnology: the economic argument. Prepared for the Canadian Biotechnology Advisory Committee Project Steering Committee on Intellectual Property and the Patenting of Higher Life Forms. Canada: Canadian Biotechnology Advisory Committee, 2001: <http://strategis.ic.gc.ca/eic/site/cbac-cccb.nsf/vwapj/EcoArgument_Hirshhorn_Langford_f.pdf/$FILE/EcoArgument_Hirshhorn_Langford_f.pdf> (accessed 20 July 2009).

Hobbs, S.D. and Bradbury, A.W. 2003. Smoking cessation strategies in patients with peripheral arterial disease: an evidence-based approach, *Eur J Vasc Endovasc Surg*, 26(4), 341–7.

Hodgson, J. 1998. A genetic heritage betrayed or empowered?, *Nat Biotechnol*, 16(11), 1017–21.

Hoerster, N. 2003. *Ethik und Interesse*. Stuttgart: Reclam.

Hoeyer, K. 2003. 'Science is really needed – that's all I know': informed consent and the non-verbal practices of collecting blood for genetic research in northern Sweden, *New Genet Soc*, 22(3), 229–44.

Hoeyer, K. 2004. Ambiguous gifts: public anxiety, informed consent and biobanks, in *Genetic Databases: Socio-Ethical Issues in the Collection and Use of DNA*, R. Tutton and O. Corrigan (eds). London/New York: Routledge, 97–116.

Hoeyer, K. and Lynoe, N. 2004. Is informed consent a solution to contractual problems? A comment on the article '"Iceland Inc."'?: On the ethics of commercial population genomics' by Jon F. Merz, Glenn E. McGee, and Pamela Sankar, *Soc Sci Med*, 58(6), 1211; author reply – 3.

Hoeyer, K., Olofsson, B.O., Mjorndal, T. and Lynoe, N. 2004. Informed consent and biobanks: a population-based study of attitudes towards tissue donation for genetic research, *Scand J Public Health*, 32(3), 224–9.

Hoeyer, K., Olofsson, B.O., Mjorndal, T. and Lynoe, N. 2005. The ethics of research using biobanks: reason to question the importance attributed to informed consent, *Arch Intern Med*, 165(1), 97–100.

Hofmann, B. 2009. Broadening consent – and diluting ethics?, *J Med Ethics*, 35(2), 125–9.

Holzgreve, W. and Hahn, S. 2001. Fetal cells in maternal circulation: what is the relationship to obstetric ultrasound? *Ultrasound Obstet Gynecol*, January, 17(1), 1–3.

Holzgreve, W. and Hahn, S. 2002. Nichtinvasive Pranataldiagnose – schon eine Tatsache? *Gynakol Geburtshilfliche Rundsch*, 42(2), 84–6.

Homer, N., Szelinger, S., Redman, M., Duggan, D., Tembe, W., Muehling, J., Pearson, J.V., Stephan, D.A., Nelson, S.F. and Craig, D.W. 2008. Resolving individuals contributing trace amounts of DNA to highly complex mixtures using high-density SNP genotyping microarrays, *PLoS Genet*, 4, e1000167.

Horrobin, D.F. 2003. Are large clinical trials in rapidly lethal diseases usually unethical?, *Lancet*, 361(9358), 695–7.

House of Lords. 2001. Committee on Science and Technology Fourth Report, Chapter 7: Ethics, privacy and consent: <http://www.parliament.the-stationery-office.co.uk/pa/ld200001/ldselect/ldsctech/57/5709.htm> (accessed 30 January 2010).

Houtepen, R. and ter Meulen, R. 2000a. New types of solidarity in the European welfare state, *Health Care Anal*, 8(4), 329–40.

Houtepen, R. and ter Meulen, R.T. 2000b. The expectation(s) of solidarity: matters of justice, responsibility and identity in the reconstruction of the health care system, *Health Care Anal*, 8(4), 355–76.

HUGO. 1995. Statement on the principled conduct of genetics research, *Eubios Journal of Asian and International Bioethics*, 6, 59–60.

HUGO. 1998. Human Genome Organisation. Statement on DNA sampling: control and access. Genome Digest March 1999; 6:8: <http://www.hugo-international.org/img/dna_1998.pdf> (accessed 20 July 2009).

HUGO. 2000. Human Genetics Organization Ethics Committee. Statement on benefit-sharing: <http://www.hugo-international.org/Statement_on_Benefit_Sharing.htm> (accessed 20 September 2007).

Human Genes Research Act. 2000. Passed 13 December 2000 (RT I 2000, 104, 685), enforced 8 January 2001, changed with the next law 14 February 2007 (RT I 2007, 22, 111) 1 April 2007: <http://www.geenivaramu.ee/index.php?id=98> (accessed 20 July 2009).

Hunter, A.G., Sharpe, N., Mullen, M. and Meschino, W.S. 2001. Ethical, legal, and practical concerns about recontacting patients to inform them of new information: the case in medical genetics, *Am J Med Genet*, 103(4), 265–76.

IARC. 2009. International Agency for Research on Cancer. Epigenetics group: <http://www.iarc.fr/en/research-groups/EGE/current-topics.php> (accessed 15 August 2009).

ICH. 2002. International Conference on Harmonisation of Technical Requirements for Registration of Pharmaceuticals for Human Use. Guideline for good clinical practice: <http://www.emea.europa.eu/pdfs/human/ich/013595en.pdf> (accessed 10 August 2009).

IMPPC Biobank. 2009. Institut de Medicina Predictiva i Personalitzada del Càncer. Director of the IMPPC BioBank (DNA and biological samples): <http://www.rticcc.org/i/DirectorIMPPCBioBankEN.pdf> (accessed 15 August 2009).

Interim Advisory Group on Ethics and Governance. 2003. UK biobank ethics and governance framework. Background document: <http://www.wellcome.ac.uk/About-us/Publications/Reports/Biomedical-ethics/wtd003284.htm> (accessed 20 July 2009).

Ironside, J. 2006. Effective implementation of the Human Tissue Act, *Lancet*, 368(9548), 1648–9.

ISBER. 2009. International Society for Biological and Environmental Repositories: <http://www.isber.org/> (accessed 10 August 2009).

Jackson, C., Best, N. and Elliott, P. 2008. UK Biobank Pilot Study: stability of haematological and clinical chemistry analytes, *Int J Epidemiol*, 37 Suppl. 1, i16–22.

Johnsson, L., Hansson, M.G., Eriksson, S. and Helgesson, G. 2008. Patients' refusal to consent to storage and use of samples in Swedish biobanks: cross sectional study, *BMJ*, 337, a345.

Joly, Y. and Knoppers, B.M. 2006. Pharmacogenomic data sample collection and storage: ethical issues and policy approaches, *Pharmacogenomics*, 7(2), 219–26.

Jonasdottir, A., Thorlacius, T., Fossdal, R., Benediktsson, K., Benedikz, J., Jonsson, H. et al. 2003. A whole genome association study in Icelandic multiple sclerosis patients with 4804 markers, *J Neuroimmunol*, 143(1–2), 88–92.

Jonsen, A.R. 1986. Bentham in a box: technology assessment and health care allocation, *Law, Medicine and Health Care*, 14, 172–4.

Jost, T.S. 2007. *Readings in Comparative Health Law and Bioethics, Second Edition*. Durham, NC: Carolina Academic Press.

Kahn, J.P. 22 February 1999. Attention shoppers: special today – Iceland's DNA. CNN. Ethics matters: <http://www.cnn.com/HEALTH/bioethics/9902/iceland. dna/template.html> (accessed 20 July 2009).

Kaiser, J. 2002a. Biobanks. Population databases boom, from Iceland to the U.S, *Science*, 298(5596), 1158–61.

Kaiser, J. 2002b. Biobanks. Private biobanks spark ethical concerns, *Science*, 298(5596), 1160.

Kant, I. 1982 [1797]. *Die Metaphysik der Sitten (Königsberg 1797)*. Frankfurt (Main).

Karlawish, J.H., Casarett, D., Klocinski, J. and Sankar, P. 2001. How do AD patients and their caregivers decide whether to enroll in a clinical trial?, *Neurology*, 56(6), 789–92.

Karlsen, J.R. and Strand, R. 2009. The ethical topography of research biobanking, in *Ethics, Law and Society Volume IV*, J. Gunning, S. Holm and I. Kenway (eds). Farnham: Ashgate.

Karp, D.R., Carlin, S., Cook-Deegan, R., Ford, D.E., Geller, G., Glass, D.N. et al. 2008. Ethical and practical issues associated with aggregating databases, *PLoS Med*, 5(9), e190.

Kattel, R. and Suurna, M. 2008. The rise and fall of the Estonian Genome Project, *Studies in Ethics, Law, and Technology*, 2(2), Article 4.

Katz, R.V., Kegeles, S.S., Kressin, N.R., Green, B.L., James, S.A., Wang, M.Q., Russell, S.L. and Claudio, C. 2008. Awareness of the Tuskegee Syphilis Study and the US presidential apology and their influence on minority participation in biomedical research, *Am J Public Health*, 98(6), 1137–42.

Kaye, D.H. 2001a. Bioethical objections to DNA databases for law enforcement: questions and answers, *Seton Hall Law Rev*, 31(4), 936–48.

Kaye, J. 2001b. Genetic research on the UK population: do new principles need to be developed?, *Trends Mol Med*, 7(11), 528–30.

Kaye, J. 2004. Abandoning informed consent: the case of genetic research in population collections, in *Genetic Databases: Socio-Ethical Issues in the Collection and Use of DNA*, R. Tutton and O. Corrigan (eds). London/New York: Routledge, 117–38.

Kaye, J. 2006. Do we need a uniform regulatory system for biobanks across Europe?, *Eur J Hum Genet*, 14(2), 245–8.

Kaye, J. 2007. The legal jigsaw governing population genetic databases: concluding remarks on the ELSAGEN legal findings, in *The Ethics and Governance of Human Genetic Databases: European Perspectives*, M. Häyry, R. Chadwick, V. Arnason and G. Arnason (eds). Cambridge: Cambridge University Press, 141–5.

Kaye, J., Heeney, C., Hawkins, N., de Vries, J. and Boddington, P. 2009. Data sharing in genomics: re-shaping scientific practice, *Nat Rev Genet*, 10(5), 331–5.

Kettis-Lindblad, A., Ring, L., Viberth, E. and Hansson, M.G. 2006. Genetic research and donation of tissue samples to biobanks: what do potential sample donors in the Swedish general public think?, *Eur J Public Health*, 16(4), 433–40.

Kettis-Lindblad, A., Ring, L., Viberth, E. and Hansson, M.G. 2007. Perceptions of potential donors in the Swedish public towards information and consent procedures in relation to use of human tissue samples in biobanks: a population-based study, *Scand J Public Health*, 35(2), 148–56.

Kleinman, I. 1994. Written advance directives refusing blood transfusion: ethical and legal considerations, *Am J Med*, 96(6), 563–7.

Knoppers, B.M. 1996. Conclusion: human genetic material – commodity or gift?, in *Legal Rights and Human Genetic Material*, B.M. Knoppers, T. Caulfield and T.D. Kinsella (eds). Toronto: Edmond Montgomery Publications, 171–7.

Knoppers, B.M. 2000. Population genetics and benefit sharing, *Community Genet*, 3(4), 212–14.

Knoppers, B.M. 2001. Duty to recontact: a legal harbinger?, *Am J Med Genet*, 103(4), 277.

Knoppers, B.M. 2004. Biobanks: simplifying consent, *Nat Rev Genet*, 5(7), 485.

Knoppers, B.M. 2005. Consent revisited: points to consider, *Health Law Rev*, 13(2–3), 33–8.

Knoppers, B.M. 2009. Genomics and policymaking: from static models to complex systems?, *Hum Genet*, 125(4), 375–9.

Knoppers, B.M. and Brand, A.M. 2008. From community genetics to public health genomics: what's in a name?, *Public Health Genomics*, 12, 1–3.

Knoppers, B.M., Hirtle, M., Lormeau, S., Laberge, C.M., Laflamme, M. 1998. Control of DNA samples and information, *Genomics*, 50, 385–401.

Knoppers, B.M., Joly, Y., Simard, J. and Durocher, F. 2006. The emergence of an ethical duty to disclose genetic research results: international perspectives, *Eur J Hum Genet*, 14(11), 1170–78.

Knoppers, B.M. and Saginur, M. 2005. The Babel of genetic data terminology, *Nat Biotechnol*, 23(8), 925–7.

Knudsen, L.E. 2005. Global gene mining and the pharmaceutical industry, *Toxicol Appl Pharmacol*, 207(2 Suppl.), 679–83.

Koblin, B.A., Heagerty, P., Sheon, A., Buchbinder, S., Celum, C., Douglas, J.M. et al. 1998. Readiness of high-risk populations in the HIV network for prevention trials to participate in HIV vaccine efficacy trials in the United States, *AIDS*, 12(7), 785–93.

Koblin, B.A., Holte, S., Lenderking, B. and Heagerty, P. 2000. Readiness for HIV vaccine trials: changes in willingness and knowledge among high-risk populations in the HIV network for prevention trials. The HIVNET Vaccine Preparedness Study Protocol Team, *J Acquir Immune Defic Syndr*, 24(5), 451–7.

Kohut, K., Manno, M., Gallinger, S. and Esplen, M.J. 2007. Should healthcare providers have a duty to warn family members of individuals with an HNPCC-causing mutation? A survey of patients from the Ontario Familial Colon Cancer Registry, *J Med Genet*, 44(6), 404–7.

Koik, A. 2003. The Estonian Genome Project: a hot media item. Open Democracy 7 July 2003: <http://www.geenivaramu.ee/?id=243> (accessed 1 August 2009).

Kopelman, L.M. 2004. Minimal risk as an international ethical standard in research, *J Med Philos*, 29(3), 351–78.

Korn, D. 1999. Contribution of the Human Tissue Archive to the advancement of medical knowledge and the public health. Commissioned paper, in *Research Involving Human Biological Materials: Ethical Issues and Policy Guidance, Report and Recommendations, vol. 2*, National Bioethics Advisory Commission (NBAC) (ed.). Rockville, MD: NBAC, E1–E30.

Korn, D. 2000. Medical information privacy and the conduct of biomedical research, *Acad Med*, 75(10), 963–8.

Korts, K. 2007. Estonia, in *The Ethics and Governance of Human Genetic Databases: European Perspectives*, M. Häyry, R. Chadwick, V. Arnason and G. Arnason (eds). Cambridge: Cambridge University Press, 47–52.

Kozanczyn, C., Collins, K. and Fernandez, C.V. 2007. Offering results to research subjects: U.S. Institutional Review Board policy, *Account Res*, 14(4), 255–67.

Kristinsson, G. and Arnason, V. 2007. Informed consent and human genetic database research, in *The Ethics and Governance of Human Genetic Databases: European Perspectives*, M. Häyry, R. Chadwick, V. Arnason and G. Arnason (eds). Cambridge: Cambridge University Press, 199–216.

Kulynych, J. and Korn, D. 2002a. The effect of the new federal medical-privacy rule on research, *N Engl J Med*, 346(3), 201–4.

Kulynych, J. and Korn, D. 2002b. The new federal medical-privacy rule, *N Engl J Med*, 347(15), 1133–4.

Kulynych, J. and Korn, D. 2002c. Use and disclosure of health information in genetic research: weighing the impact of the new federal medical privacy rule, *Am J Law Med*, 28(2–3), 309–24.

Lacroix, M., Nycum, G., Godard, B. and Knoppers, B.M. 2008. Should physicians warn patients' relatives of genetic risks?, *CMAJ*, 178(5), 593–5.

Lahteenmaki, R. 2000. Estonian parliament considers genome law, *Nat Biotechnol*, 18(11), 1135.

Laken, S.J., Petersen, G.M., Gruber, S.B., Oddoux, C., Ostrer, H., Giardiello, F.M. et al. 1997. Familial colorectal cancer in Ashkenazim due to a hypermutable tract in APC, *Nat Genet*, 17(1), 79–83.

Launis, V. 2007. The scope and importance of genetic democracy, in *Genetic Democracy: Philosophical Perspectives (International Library of Ethics, Law, and the New Medicine)*, V. Launis and J. Räikkä (eds). Heidelberg/New York: Springer, 1–8.

Launis, V. and Räikkä, J. (eds). 2007. *Genetic Democracy: Philosophical Perspectives (International Library of Ethics, Law, and the New Medicine)*. Heidelberg/New York: Springer.

Laurie, G. 2002. *Genetic Privacy: A Challenge to Medico-Legal Norms*. Cambridge/New York: Cambridge University Press.

Lavori, P.W., Krause-Steinrauf, H., Brophy, M., Buxbaum, J., Cockroft, J., Cox, D.R. et al. 2002. Principles, organization, and operation of a DNA bank for clinical trials: a Department of Veterans Affairs cooperative study, *Control Clin Trials*, 23(3), 222–39.

Law Review. 2004. Icelandic. Decision of the Supreme Court on the protection of privacy with regard to the processing of health sector databases. Attorney at Law vs The State of Iceland, *Law Hum Genome Rev*, (21), 127–38.

Lehmann, L.S., Weeks, J.C., Klar, N., Biener, L. and Garber, J.E. 2000. Disclosure of familial genetic information: perceptions of the duty to inform, *Am J Med*, 109(9), 705–11.

Lehrman, S. 1997. Jewish leaders seek genetic guidelines, *Nature*, 389(6649), 322.

Lemonick, M.D. 2006. The Iceland experiment: how a tiny island nation captured the lead in the genetic revolution, *Time*, 167(8), 50–51.

Lenk, C., Hoppe, N. and Andorno, R. (eds). 2007. *Ethics and Law of Intellectual Property (Applied Legal Philosophy)*. Aldershot: Ashgate.

Lewis, G. 2004. Tissue collection and the pharmaceutical industry: investigating corporate biobanks, in *Genetic Databases: Socio-Ethical Issues in the Collection and Use of DNA*, R. Tutton and O. Corrigan (eds). London/New York: Routledge, 181–202.

Lewis, R. 1999. Iceland's public supports database, but scientists object. *The Scientist*, 13 (19 July 1999): <http://www.the-scientist.com/article/display/18638/> (accessed 30 July 2009).

Liao, S.M. 2009. Is there a duty to share genetic information?, *J Med Ethics*, 35(5), 306–9.

Liberty. 2001. The National Council for Civil Liberties. Whose hands on your genes? Liberty's response to the Human Genetics Commission's discussion document on the storage, protection and use of personal genetic information. 2001: <http://www.liberty-human-rights.org.uk/pdfs/policy01/mar-genetic.pdf> (accessed 15 July 2009).

Lindgren, A. 2003. The law concerning biobanks is a strain on health care work, *Lakartidningen*, 100, 1730–31.

Lipworth, W. 2005. Navigating tissue banking regulation: conceptual frameworks for researchers, administrators, regulators and policy-makers, *J Law Med*, 13(2), 245–55.

Litman, M. 1997. The legal status of genetic material, in *Human DNA: Law and Policy*, B.M. Knoppers (ed.). Cambridge, MA: Kluwer Law International, 17–32.

Little, J., Khoury, M.J., Bradley, L., Clyne, M., Gwinn, M., Lin, B. et al. 2003. The human genome project is complete: how do we develop a handle for the pump?, *Am J Epidemiol*, 157(8), 667–73.

Lowrance, W.W. and Collins, F.S. 2007. Ethics: identifiability in genomic research, *Science*, 317(5838), 600–602.

Lubchenco, J., Rosswall, T. and Warren, P. 2003. Scientific freedom: new strategies are needed, *Nature*, 421(6925), 785.

Lucassen, A. and Kaye, J. 2006. Genetic testing without consent: the implications of the new Human Tissue Act 2004, *J Med Ethics*, 32(12), 690–92.

Lucassen, A. and Parker, M. 2004. Confidentiality and serious harm in genetics: preserving the confidentiality of one patient and preventing harm to relatives, *Eur J Hum Genet*, 12(2), 93–7.

Lucassen, A., Parker, M. and Wheeler, R. 2006. Implications of data protection legislation for family history, *BMJ*, 332(7536), 299–301.

Lunshof, J.E., Pirmohamed, M. and Gurwitz, D. 2006. Personalized medicine: decades away?, *Pharmacogenomics*, 7(2), 237–41.

Macedo, S. 1995. Liberal civic education and religious fundamentalism: the case of God vs. John Rawls?, *Ethics*, 105 (April), 468–96.

Macedo, S. 2001. Liberal constitutionalism and diversity: <http://www.ccsindia.org/ccsindia/macedo.doc> (accessed 4 August 2009).

Macklin, R. 2003. Dignity is a useless concept, *BMJ*, 327(7429), 1419–20.

Macklin, R. 2004. Reflections on the human dignity symposium: is dignity a useless concept?, *J Palliat Care*, 20(3), 212–16.

MacLeod, D. 2003. Medical council accused of bad management. *The Guardian*, 25 March 2003: <http://www.guardian.co.uk/education/2003/mar/25/highereducation.uk3> (accessed 20 July 2009).

MacNeil, S.D. and Fernandez, C.V. 2006. Informing research participants of research results: analysis of Canadian university based research ethics board policies, *J Med Ethics*, 32(1), 49–54.

MacNeil, S.D. and Fernandez, C.V. 2007. Attitudes of research ethics board chairs towards disclosure of research results to participants: results of a national survey, *J Med Ethics*, 33(9), 549–53.

MacWilliams, B. 2003. Banking on DNA: Estonia's genetic database promises medical advances – maybe, *Chron High Educ*, 49(33), A16, A8.

Manolio, T.A. 2006. Taking our obligations to research participants seriously: disclosing individual results of genetic research, *Am J Bioeth*, 6(6), 32–4; author reply – W10-2.

Martin Uranga, A., Martin Arribas, M.C., Jaeger, C. and Posadas, M. 2005. Outstanding ethical-legal issues on biobanks: an overview on the regulations of the Member States of the Eurobiobank project, *Law Hum Genome Rev*, (22), 103–14.

Martindale, D. 2001. Pink slip in your genes, *Scientific American*: <http://www.scientificamerican.com/article.cfm?id=pink-slip-in-your-genes> (accessed 5 August 2009).

Maschke, K.J. 2005. Navigating an ethical patchwork: human gene banks, *Nat Biotechnol*, 23(5), 539–45.

Maschke, K.J. 2006. Alternative consent approaches for biobank research, *Lancet Oncol*, 7(3), 193–4.

Maschke, K.J. and Murray, T.H. 2004. Ethical issues in tissue banking for research: the prospects and pitfalls of setting international standards, *Theor Med Bioeth*, 25(2), 143–55.

McCarty, C.A., Chapman-Stone, D., Derfus, T., Giampietro, P.F. and Fost, N. 2008. Community consultation and communication for a population-based DNA biobank: the Marshfield clinic personalized medicine research project, *Am J Med Genet A*, 146A(23), 3026–33.

McDonald, M. 2000. *Biotechnology, Ethics and Government. A Synthesis*. Prepared for the Canadian Biotechnology Advisory Committee Project Steering Committee on Incorporating Social and Ethical Considerations into Biotechnology. Ottawa: CBAC.

McGrath, D. 2002. Ethical concerns at the DNA bank. Wired News 6 May 2002: <http://www.wired.com/news/medtech/0,1286,52176,00.html> (accessed 20 July 2009).

McInnis, M.G. 1999. The assent of a nation: genethics and Iceland, *Clin Genet*, 55(4), 234–9.

Meade, T. 2003. The future of Biobank, *Lancet*, 362(9382), 492.

Meek, J. 2002. Decode was meant to save lives ... now it's destroying them. *The Guardian*, 31 October 2002: <http://www.guardian.co.uk/science/2002/oct/31/genetics.businessofresearch> (accessed 30 July 2009).

Merz, J.F., Magnus, D., Cho, M.K. and Caplan, A.L. 2002. Protecting subjects' interests in genetics research, *Am J Hum Genet*, 70(4), 965–71.

Merz, J.F., McGee, G.E. and Sankar, P. 2004a. 'Iceland Inc.'?: On the ethics of commercial population genomics, *Soc Sci Med*, 58(6), 1201–9.

Merz, J.F., McGee, G.E. and Sankar, P. 2004b. Response from Jon F. Merz, Glenn E. McGee, and Pamela Sankar to Hoeyer and Lynoe's commentary on their article '"Iceland Inc."? On the ethics of commercial population genomics', *Soc Sci Med*, 58(6), 1213.

Metcalfe, K.A., Liede, A., Trinkaus, M., Hanna, D. and Narod, S.A. 2002. Evaluation of the needs of spouses of female carriers of mutations in BRCA1 and BRCA2, *Clin Genet*, 62(6), 464–9.

Mikail, C.N. 2008. *Public Health Genomics: The Essentials (J-B Public Health/ Health Services Text)*. San Francisco, CA: Jossey-Bass (Wiley).

Mill, J.S. 1956. *On Liberty*. Indianapolis, IN/New York: Bobbs-Merrill.

Millns, S. 2007. Consolidating bio-rights in Europe, in *Biotechnologies and International Human Rights (Studies in International Law)*, F. Francioni (ed.). Portland, OR: Hart Publishing, 71–84.

Mitchell, R. and Waldby, C. 2009. National biobanks: clinical labor, risk production, and the creation of biovalue. Science Technology Human Values: <http://online.sagepub.com/cgi/citmgr?gca=spsth;0162243909340267v1> (accessed 17 August 2009).

Monsour, D. (ed.). 2007. *Ethics and the New Genetics: An Integrated Approach (Lonergan Studies Series)*. Toronto: University of Toronto Press.

Moutel, G., De Montgolfier, S., Duchange, N., Sharara, L., Beaumont, C. and Herve, C. 2004. Study of the involvement of research ethics committees in the constitution and use of biobanks in France, *Pharmacogenetics*, 14(3), 195–8.

MRC. 2000. Medical Research Council. Ethics series. Personal information in medical research: <http://www.mrc.ac.uk/Utilities/Documentrecord/index. htm?d=MRC002452> (accessed 10 August 2009).

MRC. 2001. Medical Research Council. Ethics series. Human tissue and biological samples for use in research. Operational and ethical guidelines 2001: <http:// www.mrc.ac.uk/Utilities/Documentrecord/index.htm?d=MRC002420> (accessed 1 August 2009).

MRC. 2009. Medical Research Council (UK). UK Biobank: <http://www.mrc. ac.uk/Ourresearch/Ethicsresearchguidance/Biobank/index.htm> (accessed 28 July 2009).

Muller, H. 1991. Grundlagen der Gentechnologie und Moglichkeiten der DNA-Diagnostik [Principles of gene technology and potentials of DNA diagnosis], *Schweiz Med Wochenschr*, 121(48), 1751–60.

Muller, H.H., Heinimann, K. and Dobbie, Z. 2000. Genetics of hereditary colon cancer: a basis for prevention?, *Eur J Cancer*, 36, 1215–23.

Muller, H., Plasilova, M., Russell, A.M. and Heinimann, K. 2003. Genetic predisposition as a basis for chemoprevention, surgical and other interventions in colorectal cancer, *Recent Results Cancer Res*, 163, 235–47; discussion 264–6.

Muller, H. and Scott, R.J. 1995. Familiares Kolorektal und Mammakarzinom – genetische Beratung und prasymptomatische Diagnostik [Familial colorectal and breast carcinoma – genetic counseling and presymptomatic diagnosis], *Ther Umsch*, 52, 826–34.

Muramoto, O. 2001. Bioethical aspects of the recent changes in the policy of refusal of blood by Jehovah's witnesses, *BMJ*, 322(7277), 37–9.

Murphy, T.F. and Lappe, M.A. (eds). 1994. *Justice and the Human Genome Project*. Berkeley, CA: University of California Press.

NARC. 1997. North American Regional Committee. Human Genome Diversity Project model ethical protocol for collecting DNA samples 1997: <http://www. stanford.edu/group/morrinst/hgdp/protocol.html> (accessed August 2004).

National Bioethics Advisory Commission [NBAC]. 1999. *Research Involving Human Biological Materials: Ethical Issues and Policy Guidance, Report and Recommendations, vol. 1*. Rockville, MD: National Bioethics Advisory Commission.

Nationaler Ethikrat. 2004. Biobanken für die Forschung. Stellungnahme. Berlin, 17 März 2004: <http://www.ethikrat.org/themen/pdf/Stellungnahme_Biobanken. pdf> (accessed 3 August 2009).

Nationaler Ethikrat. Pressemitteilung 03/2004, Berlin 17 March 2004. Nationaler Ethikrat veröffentlicht Stellungnahme zu Biobanken für die Forschung: <http:// www.interconnections.de/id_3112.html> (accessed 1 August 2009).

NCH. 1996. U.S. National Center for Human Genome Research and U.S. Department of Energy (NCHGR-DOE). 1996. Guidance on human subject issues in large-scale DNA sequencing: <http://www.genome.gov/10000921> (accessed 10 August 2009).

NCH. 1998. U.S. National Center for Human Genome Research and U.S. Department of Energy (NCHGR-DOE). Update of NHGRI policy for the use of human subjects in large-scale sequencing: <http://www.genome. gov/10000921> (accessed 10 August 2009).

NCI. 2007. Best practices for biospecimen resources: <http://www.allirelandnci. org/pdf/NCI_Best_Practices_060507.pdf> (accessed 3 August 2009).

Nicol, D., Otlowski, M. and Chalmers, D. 2001. Consent, commercialisation and benefit-sharing, *J Law Med*, 9(1), 80–94.

NIH. 2009. Policy for sharing of data obtained in NIH supported or conducted genome-wide association studies (GWAS): <http://grants.nih.gov/grants/ guide/notice-files/NOT-OD-07-088.html> (accessed 25 June 2009).

Nippert, I., Horst, J., Wolff, G. and Wertz, D. 1996. Ethical issues in genetic service provision: attitudes of human geneticists in Germany, *Am J Hum Genet*, 59(4), A338.

Nozick, R. 1974. *Anarchy, State, and Utopia*. New York: Basic Books.

Nuffield Council on Bioethics. 1995. Human tissue. Ethical and legal issues: <http://www.nuffieldbioethics.org> (accessed 2 August 2009).

Nuffield Council on Bioethics. 2002. The ethics of patenting DNA. A discussion paper: <http://www.nuffieldbioethics.org> (accessed 2 August 2009).

Nuffield Trust. 2000. Genetics Scenario Project. Genetics and health. Policy issues for genetic science and their implications for health and health services. Dr Ron Zimmern MA, FRCP, FFPHM and Christopher Cook BA. May 2000: <http://www.archive.official-documents.co.uk/document/nuffield/policyf/ genetics.htm> (accessed 3 August 2009).

Nutley, N.J. 2002. Roche and deCODE unveil new alliance in drug discovery and development. Current news releases, 29 January 2002: <http://www. datamonitor.com/store/news/roche_and_decode_unveil_new_alliance_in_ drug_discovery_and_development?productid=2DEA0EE0-08B6-4FE7- 97A3-EE821B8848DD> (accessed 30 July 2009).

Nwabueze, R.N. 2007. *Biotechnology and the Challenge of Property (Medical Law and Ethics)*. Aldershot: Ashgate.

Nys, H. and Fobelets, G. 2008. The regulation of biobanks in Spain, *Law Hum Genome Rev*, 29, 169–88.

Nys, H., Stultiens, L., Borry, P., Goffin, T. and Dierickx, K. 2007. Patient rights in EU Member States after the ratification of the Convention on Human Rights and Biomedicine, *Health Policy*, 83(2–3), 223–35.

O'Brien, S.J. 2009. Stewardship of human biospecimens, DNA, genotype, and clinical data in the GWAS era, *Annu Rev Genomics Hum Genet*, 10, 193–209.

O'Doherty, K.C. and Burgess, M.M. 2009. Engaging the public on biobanks: outcomes of the BC biobank deliberation, *Public Health Genomics*, 12(4), 203–15.

O'Neill, M. 2007. Estonia: small country, big ambitions, *Drug Discov Today*, 12(17–18), 683–7.

OHRP. 2004. *Guidance on Research Involving Coded Private Information or Biological Specimens*. Rockville, MD: Office for Human Research Protections.

Ollier, W., Sprosen, T. and Peakman, T. 2005. UK Biobank: from concept to reality, *Pharmacogenomics*, 6(6), 639–46.

Opinion Leader Research. 2003. Summary of the UK Biobank consultation on the ethics and governance framework (public-stakeholder-olr-report). August 2003: <http://www.ukbiobank.ac.uk/docs/public-stakeholder-olr-report.doc> (accessed 28 July 2009).

Ormond, K.E. 2006. Disclosing genetic research results: examples from practice, *Am J Bioeth*, 6(6), 30–32; author reply – W10-2.

Ormond, K.E., Cirino, A.L., Helenowski, I.B., Chisholm, R.L. and Wolf, W.A. 2009. Assessing the understanding of biobank participants, *Am J Med Genet A*, 149A(2), 188–98.

Ortúzar, M.G. 2003. Towards a universal definition of 'benefit-sharing', in *Populations and Genetics: Legal and Socio-Ethical Perspectives*, B.M. Knoppers (ed.). Leiden/Boston, MA: Martinus Nijhoff Publishers, 473–85.

Palmer, L.J. 2007. UK Biobank: bank on it, *Lancet*, 369(9578), 1980–82.

Pálsson, B. and Thorgeirsson, S. 1999. Genetic databases: decoding developments in Iceland, *Nat Biotechnol*, 17(5), 407.

Pálsson, G. 2007. *Anthropology and the New Genetics (New Departures in Anthropology)*. Cambridge/New York: Cambridge University Press.

Pálsson, G. and Rabinow, P. 2001. The Icelandic genome debate, *Trends Biotechnol*, 19(5), 166–71.

Parfitt, T. 2004. Estonian efficiency, *Lancet*, 364(9444), 1475–8.

Parker, M. and Lucassen, A. 2003. Concern for families and individuals in clinical genetics, *J Med Ethics*, 29(2), 70–73.

Parker, M. and Lucassen, A.M. 2004. Genetic information: a joint account?, *BMJ*, 329(7458), 165–7.

Parliamentary Office of Science and Technology. 2002. 'The UK Biobank'; Postnote Vol. 180 (UK): <http://www.parliament.uk/post/pn180.pdf> (accessed 20 May 2005).

Pasini, N. and Reichlin, M. 2000. Solidarity and the role of the state in Italian health care, *Health Care Anal*, 8(4), 341–54.

Pennisi, E. 2009. Data sharing: group calls for rapid release of more genomics data, *Science*, 324(5930), 1000–1001.

People Science & Policy Ltd. 2002. BioBank UK: A Question of Trust: a consultation exploring and addressing questions of public trust. Report prepared for the Medical Research Council and the Wellcome Trust. March 2002: <http://www.ukbiobank.ac.uk/docs/consultation.pdf> (accessed 20 July 2009).

People Science & Policy Ltd. 2003. UK Biobank Consultation on the Ethical and Governance Framework Report prepared for the Wellcome Trust and the

Medical Research Council 2003: <http://www.ukbiobank.ac.uk/docs/people-science-policy.pdf> (accessed 15 July 2009).

Personalized Medicine Research Project. 2009. Will my information be kept confidential?: <http://www.marshfieldclinic.org/chg/pages/default.aspx?page=chg_pmrp_faqs> (accessed 3 August 2009).

Personalized Medicine Research Project Consent. 2009. Research consent/authorization form: <http://www.marshfieldclinic.org/chg/pages/Proxy.aspx?Content=MCRF-Centers-CHG-Core-Units-PMRP-consent-form_6-6-07.1.pdf> (accessed 3 August 2009).

Petersen, A. 2005. Securing our genetic health: engendering trust in UK Biobank, *Sociol Health Illn*, 27(2), 271–92.

Peterson, S.K., Watts, B.G., Koehly, L.M., Vernon, S.W., Baile, W.F., Kohlmann, W.K. and Gritz, E.R. 2003. How families communicate about HNPCC genetic testing: findings from a qualitative study, *Am J Med Genet C Semin Med Genet*, 119C(1), 78–86.

Phillips, M.S., Joly, Y., Silverstein, T. and Avard, D. 2007. Le consentement à la recherche en pharmacogénomique, *Gen Edit*, 5, 1–10.

Pickles, A., Maughan, B. and Wadsworth, M. 2007. *Epidemiological Methods in Life Course Research (Life Course Approach to Adult Health)*. New York: Oxford University Press.

Plantinga, L., Natowicz, M.R., Kass, N.E., Hull, S.C., Gostin, L.O. and Faden, R.R. 2003. Disclosure, confidentiality, and families: experiences and attitudes of those with genetic versus nongenetic medical conditions, *Am J Med Genet C Semin Med Genet*, 119C(1), 51–9.

Porter, G. 2009. Biobanks in Japan: ethics, guidelines and practice, in *Human Genetic Biobanks in Asia: Politics of Trust and Scientific Advancement*, M. Sleeboom-Faulkner (ed.). New York: Routledge.

Porteri, C. and Borry, P. 2008. A proposal for a model of informed consent for the collection, storage and use of biological materials for research purposes, *Patient Educ Couns*, 71(1), 136–42.

Potts, J. 2002. At least give the native glass beads: an examination of the bargain made between Iceland and deCODE Genetics with implications for global bioprospecting, *Virginia Journal of Law and Technology*, 8, 1–40.

Pownall, M. 2007. Blair under attack for confidentiality stance. *DOCTOR* magazine, Sunday 11 March 2007: <http://forum.no2id.net/viewtopic.php?p=62545&sid=477446cd05002cc7d53139d5cd47ac1a> (accessed 5 August 2009).

President's Commission. 1983. *President's Commission for the Study of Ethical Problems in Medicine and Biomedical and Behavioral Research. Screening and Counseling for Genetic Conditions*. Washington, DC: U.S. Government Printing Office.

Press Release. 2009. UK Biobank recruits its 250,000th participant. 30 January 2009: <http://www.ukbiobank.ac.uk/docs/quartermillion.doc>.

Privacy Commissioner of Australia. 1996. The privacy implications of genetic testing. Information paper no. 5. Commonwealth of Australia 1996: <http://

www.privacy.gov.au/publications/oldrefive.pdf> or <http://www.privacy.gov.au/publications/HRC_PRIVACY_PUBLICATION.pdf_file.p6_4_72.44.pdf> (accessed 4 August 2009).

Public Population Project in Genomics P3G. 2003. Executive summary. 5. Appendix – project overviews. Estonian Genome Project.

Pullman, D. and Latus, A. 2003a. Benefit sharing in smaller markets: the case of Newfoundland and Labrador, *Community Genet*, 6(3), 178–81.

Pullman, D. and Latus, A. 2003b. Clinical trials, genetic add-ons, and the question of benefit-sharing, *Lancet*, 362(9379), 242–4.

Pullman, D. and Latus, A. 2003c. Reconciling social justice and economic opportunism: regulating the Newfoundland genome, in *Populations and Genetics: Legal and Socio-Ethical Perspectives*, B.M. Knoppers (ed.). Leiden/Boston, MA: Martinus Nijhoff Publishers, 543–66.

Rabino, I. 2003. Genetic testing and its implications: human genetics researchers grapple with ethical issues, *Sci Technol Human Values*, 28(2), 365–402.

Radda, G., Dexter, T.M. and Meade, T. 2002. Reply from Biobank UK, *Lancet*, 359 (29 June), 2282.

Radford, T. 2003. Gene study will provide 30 years of human data. *The Guardian*, 24 September 2003: <http://www.guardian.co.uk/uk/2003/sep/24/research.genetics> (accessed 15 May 2009).

Räikkä, J. 2007. Autonomy and genetic privacy, in *Genetic Democracy: Philosophical Perspectives (International Library of Ethics, Law, and the New Medicine)*, V. Launis and J. Räikkä (eds). Heidelberg/New York: Springer, 43–52.

Rannamäe, A. 2003. Estonian Genome Project: large scale health status description and DNA collection, in *Populations and Genetics: Legal and Socio-Ethical Perspectives*, B.M. Knoppers (ed.). Leiden/Boston, MA: Martinus Nijhoff Publishers, 17–36.

Ravitsky, V. and Wilfond, B.S. 2006. Disclosing individual genetic results to research participants, *Am J Bioeth*, 6(6), 8–17.

RCP. 2001. *Transitional Guidelines to Facilitate Changes in Procedures for Handling 'Surplus' and Archival Material from Human Biological Samples*. UK: The Royal College of Pathologists.

Reilly, P.R. 1997. Genetic information in families: rethinking confidentiality, *Microbial Comp Genom*, 2, 1–11.

Reilly, P.R. and Page, D.C. 1998. We're off to see the genome, *Nat Genet*, 20(1), 15–17.

Reischl, J., Schroder, M., Luttenberger, N., Petrov, D., Schumann, B., Ternes, R. and Sturzebecher, S. 2006. Pharmacogenetic research and data protection: challenges and solutions, *Pharmacogenomics J*, 6(4), 225–33.

Renegar, G., Webster, C.J., Stuerzebecher, S., Harty, L., Ide, S.E., Balkite, B. et al. 2006. Returning genetic research results to individuals: points-to-consider, *Bioethics*, 20(1), 24–36.

Revill, J. 2003. Pioneer DNA bank to examine lifestyles. *The Guardian*, 27 July: <http://www.guardian.co.uk/uk/2003/jul/27/humanrights.genetics> (accessed 28 July 2009).

Reymond, M.A., Steinert, R., Eder, F. and Lippert, H. 2003. Ethical and regulatory issues arising from proteomic research and technology, *Proteomics*, 3(8), 1387–96.

Reymond, M.A., Steinert, R., Escourrou, J. and Fourtanier, G. 2002. Ethical, legal and economic issues raised by the use of human tissue in postgenomic research, *Dig Dis*, 20(3–4), 257–65.

Reynisdottir, I., Gudbjartsson, D.F., Johannsson, J.H., Manolescu, I., Kristjansson, K., Stefansson, K. et al. 2004. A genetic contribution to inflammatory bowel disease in Iceland: a genealogic approach, *Clin Gastroenterol Hepatol*, 2(9), 806–12.

Reynisdottir, I., Thorleifsson, G., Benediktsson, R., Sigurdsson, G., Emilsson, V., Einarsdottir, A.S. et al. 2003. Localization of a susceptibility gene for type 2 diabetes to chromosome 5q34-q35.2, *Am J Hum Genet*, 73(2), 323–35.

Rhodes, R. 2006. Genetic testing: is there a right not to know?, *MCN Am J Matern Child Nurs*, 31(3), 145.

Richards, T. 2002. Developed countries should not impose ethics on other countries, *BMJ*, 325, 796.

Riegman, P.H., Morente, M.M., Betsou, F., de Blasio, P. and Geary, P. 2008. Biobanking for better healthcare, *Mol Oncol*, 2(3), 213–22.

Rigby, H. and Fernandez, C.V. 2005. Providing research results to study participants: support versus practice of researchers presenting at the American Society of Hematology annual meeting, *Blood*, 106(4), 1199–202.

RMGA. 2000. Network of Applied Genetic Medicine. Statement of principles: human genome research: <https://www.rmga.ca/files/attachments/0000/0055/%C3%A9nonc%C3%A9_de_principes_recherche_en_g%C3%A9nomique_humaine_en.pdf> (accessed 8 August 2009).

RMGA. 2003. Network of applied genetic medicine. Statement of principles on the ethical conduct of human genetic research involving populations (Énoncé de principes sur la conduite éthique de la recherche en génétique humaine concernant des populations) (Quebec): <http://www.rmga.ca/fr/programs_and_forms> (accessed 30 January 2010).

Robertson, I. 2003. Submission G209 to the Australia Law Reform Commission, 29 November 2002: <http://www.austlii.edu.au/au/other/alrc/publications/reports/96/> (accessed 4 August 2009).

Robertson, J.A. 1999. Privacy issues in second stage genomics, *Jurimetrics*, 40, 59–76.

Rose, H. 2001. The commodification of bioinformatics: the Icelandic Health Sector Database. London: The Wellcome Trust, 2001: <http://www.wellcome.ac.uk/stellent/groups/corporatesite/@msh_grants/documents/web_document/wtd003281.pdf> (accessed 30 July 2009).

Rose, H. 2006. From hype to mothballs in four years: troubles in the development of large-scale DNA biobanks in Europe, *Community Genet*, 9(3), 184–9.

Rothstein, M.A. 2005. Expanding the ethical analysis of biobanks, *J Law Med Ethics*, 33(1), 89–101.

Rothstein, M.A., Cai, Y. and Marchant, G.E. 2009a. Ethical implications of epigenetics research, *Nat Rev Genet*, 10(4), 224.

Rothstein, M.A., Cai, Y. and Marchant, G.E. 2009b. The ghost in our genes: legal and ethical implications of epigenetics, *Health Matrix Clevel*, 19(1), 1–62.

Rudan, I., Marusic, A., Jankovic, S., Rotim, K., Boban, M., Lauc, G. et al. 2009. '10001 Dalmatians': Croatia launches its national biobank, *Croat Med J*, 50(1), 4–6.

Sade, R.M. 2002. Research on stored biological samples is still research, *Arch Intern Med*, 162(13), 1439–40.

SAMS. 1993. *Directive on Genetic Testing of Human Beings [Genetische Untersuchungen am Menschen]*. Basel: SAMS.

SAMS. 1997. *Forschungsuntersuchungen am Menschen*. Basel: SAMS.

SAMS. 2006. *Directive on Biobanks, Obtainment, Preservation and Utilisation of Human Biological Material*. Basel: SAMS.

Schimmek, T. 2003. Patriotisches Kataster. *Die Zeit*, 28 May 2003: <http://www.geenivaramu.ee/index.php?id=240> (accessed 1 August 2009).

Schneider, K.A., Chittenden, A.B., Branda, K.J., Keenan, M.A., Joffe, S., Patenaude, A.F., Reynolds, H., Dent, K., Eubanks, S., Goldman, J., Leroy, B., Warren, N.S., Taylor, K., Vockley, C.W. and Garber, J.E. 2006. Ethical issues in cancer genetics: I 1) whose information is it?, *J Genet Couns*, 15(6), 491–503.

Schroeder, D. 2007. Benefit sharing: it's time for a definition, *J Med Ethics*, 33(4), 205–9.

Schroeder, D. and Lasen-Diaz, C. 2006. Sharing the benefits of genetic resources: from biodiversity to human genetics, *Dev World Bioeth*, 6(3), 135–43.

Schron, E.B., Wassertheil-Smoller, S. and Pressel, S. 1997. Clinical trial participant satisfaction: survey of SHEP enrollees. SHEP Cooperative Research Group. Systolic Hypertension in the Elderly Program, *J Am Geriatr Soc*, 45(8), 934–8.

Schuklenk, U. and Kleinsmidt, A. 2006. North-south benefit sharing arrangements in bioprospecting and genetic research: a critical ethical and legal analysis, *Dev World Bioeth*, 6(3), 122–34.

Schulz-Baldes, A., Vayena, E. and Biller-Andorno, N. 2007. Sharing benefits in international health research: research-capacity building as an example of an indirect collective benefit, *EMBO Rep*, 8(1), 8–13.

Schwartz, J. 1999. For sale in Iceland: a nation's genetic code. *Washington Post*, 12 January 1999: <http://www.encyclopedia.com/doc/1P2-572603.html> (accessed 30 July 2009).

Scott, T. 2003. On dignity: <http://bmj.bmjjournals.com/cgi/eletters/327/7429/1419#44060> (accessed 5 August 2009).

Secko, D.M., Burgess, M. and O'Doherty, K. 2008. Perspectives on engaging the public in the ethics of emerging biotechnologies: from salmon to biobanks to neuroethics, *Account Res*, 15(4), 283–302.

Secko, D.M., Preto, N., Niemeyer, S. and Burgess, M.M. 2009. Informed consent in biobank research: a deliberative approach to the debate, *Soc Sci Med*, 68(4), 781–9.

Senior, K. 2006. UK Biobank launched to mixed reception, *Lancet Neurol*, 5(5), 390.

Sensen, C.W. 2005. *Handbook of Genome Research, Two Volume Set: Genomics, Proteomics, Metabolomics, Bioinformatics, Ethical and Legal Issues*. Weinheim: Wiley-VCH.

Seoane, J.A. and Da Rocha, A.C. 2008. Consentimiento, biobancos y ley de investigacion biomedica [Consent, biobanks and biomedical research law], *Law Hum Genome Rev*, (29), 131–48.

Sheremeta, L. 2003. Population genetic studies: is there an emerging legal obligation to share benefits?, *Health Law Rev*, 12(1), 36–8.

Sheremeta, L. and Knoppers, B.M. 2003. Beyond the rhetoric: population genetics and benefit-sharing, *Health Law J*, 11, 89–117.

Shevde, L.A. and Riker, A.I. 2009. Current concepts in biobanking: development and implementation of a tissue repository, *Frontiers in Bioscience*, S1 (June 1), 188–93.

Shickle, D. 2006. The consent problem within DNA biobanks, *Stud Hist Philos Biol Biomed Sci*, 37(3), 503–19.

Shickle, D., Hapgood, R., Carlisle, J., Shackley, P., Morgan, A. and McCabe, C. 2003. Public attitudes to participating in UK Biobank: a DNA bank, lifestyle and morbidity database on 500,000 members of the UK public aged 45–69, in *Populations and Genetics: Legal and Socio-Ethical Perspectives*, B.M. Knoppers (ed.). Leiden/Boston, MA: Martinus Nijhoff Publishers, 323–42.

Sigurdsson, S. 1999. Icelanders opt out of genetic database, *Nature*, 400(6746), 708.

Sigurdsson, S. 2003. Decoding broken promises. Open Democracy, 6 March 2003: <http://www.opendemocracy.net/theme_9-genes/article_1024.jsp> (accessed 20 July 2009).

Simm, K. 2007. Benefit-sharing and biobanks, in *The Ethics and Governance of Human Genetic Databases: European Perspectives*, M. Häyry, R. Chadwick, V. Arnason and G. Arnason (eds). Cambridge: Cambridge University Press, 159–69.

Simoncelli, T. and Wallace, H. 2006. Expanding databases, declining liberties, *Genewatch*, 19(1), 3–8, 18.

Skene, L. 1998. Patients' rights or family responsibilities? Two approaches to genetic testing, *Med Law Rev*, 6(1), 1–41.

Skrikerud, A.M. and Grov, J. 2009. Puzzle-solving for fun and profit: the abusive potential of nongenetic health data in epidemiological biobanks, in *Ethics, Law and Society Volume IV*, J. Gunning, S. Holm and I. Kenway (eds). Farnham: Ashgate.

Sleeboom-Faulkner, M. (ed.). 2009. *Human Genetic Biobanks in Asia: Politics of Trust and Scientific Advancement*. New York: Routledge.

Soejarto, D.D., Fong, H.H., Tan, G.T., Zhang, H.J., Ma, C.Y., Franzblau, S.G. et al. 2005. Ethnobotany/ethnopharmacology and mass bioprospecting: issues on intellectual property and benefit-sharing, *J Ethnopharmacol*, 100(1–2), 15–22.

Solbakk, J.H., Holm, S. and Hofmann, B. (eds). 2009. *The Ethics of Research Biobanking*. Heidelberg/New York: Springer.

Songini, M. 2000. Hospital confirms copying of patient files by hacker. *Computerworld*, 14 December 2000: <http://archives.cnn.com/2000/TECH/computing/12/15/hospital.hacker.idg/> (accessed 15 July 2009).

Spinney, L. 2003. UK launches tumor bank to match maligned Biobank, *Nat Med*, 9(5), 491.

Staff and Agencies. 2003. Long aim for gene study. *The Guardian*, 7 April 2003: <http://www.guardian.co.uk/science/2003/apr/07/genetics.science> (accessed 28 July 2009).

Staley, K. 2001. Giving your genes to Biobank UK. Questions to ask. A report for GeneWatch UK. December 2001: <http://www.genewatch.org/uploads/f03c6d66a9b354535738483c1c3d49e4/Biobank_Report_1.pdf> (accessed 28 July 2009).

Stauffacher, W. and Leuthold, M. 13 January 2004. *Vorentwurf zum Bundesgesetz über genetische Untersuchungen am Menschen – 'Recht auf Nicht-Wissen'. Brief an den Kommissionspräsidenten der Kommission für Wissenschaft, Bildung und Kultur*. Basel: SAMW.

Stefansson, H., Einarsdottir, A., Geirsson, R.T., Jonsdottir, K., Sverrisdottir, G., Gudnadottir, V.G. et al. 2001. Endometriosis is not associated with or linked to the GALT gene, *Fertil Steril*, 76(5), 1019–22.

Stefansson, H., Ophoff, R.A., Steinberg, S., Andreassen, O.A., Cichon, S., Rujescu, D. et al. 2009. Common variants conferring risk of schizophrenia, *Nature*, 460(7256), 744–7.

Stefansson, H., Rujescu, D., Cichon, S., Pietilainen, O.P., Ingason, A., Steinberg, S. et al. 2008. Large recurrent microdeletions associated with schizophrenia, *Nature*, 455(7210), 232–6.

Stefansson, H., Sarginson, J., Kong, A., Yates, P., Steinthorsdottir, V., Gudfinnsson, E. et al. 2003a. Association of neuregulin 1 with schizophrenia confirmed in a Scottish population, *Am J Hum Genet*, 72(1), 83–7.

Stefansson, H., Thorgeirsson, T.E., Gulcher, J.R. and Stefansson, K. 2003b. Neuregulin 1 in schizophrenia: out of Iceland, *Mol Psychiatry*, 8(7), 639–40.

Stefansson, K. 2001. Health care and privacy. An interview with Kari Stefansson, founder and CEO of deCODE Genetics in Reykjavik, Iceland, *EMBO Rep*, 2(11), 964–7.

Stege, A. and Hummel, M. 2008. Erfahrungen bei einrichtung und betrieb einer biobank [Experience with establishment and operation of a biobank], *Pathologe*, 29, Suppl. 2, 214–17.

Struewing, J.P., Abeliovich, D., Peretz, T., Avishai, N., Kaback, M.M., Collins, F.S. and Brody, L.C. 1995. The carrier frequency of the BRCA1 185delAG mutation is approximately 1 percent in Ashkenazi Jewish individuals, *Nat Genet*, 11(2), 198–200.

STYJOBS/EDECTA. 2009. Observational study of early metabolic and vascular changes in obesity. Medical University of Graz: <http://clinicaltrials.gov/ct2/show/NCT00482924> (accessed 15 August 2009).

Styrkarsdottir, U., Cazier, J.B., Kong, A., Rolfsson, O., Larsen, H., Bjarnadottir, E., Johannsdottir, V.D., Sigurdardottir, M.S., Bagger, Y., Christiansen, C., Reynisdottir, I., Grant, S.F., Jonasson, K., Frigge, M.L., Gulcher, J.R., Sigurdsson, G. and Stefansson, K. 2003. Linkage of osteoporosis to chromosome 20p12 and association to BMP2, *PLoS Biol*, 1(3), E69.

Sugarman, J., Kass, N.E., Goodman, S.N., Perentesis, P., Fernandes, P. and Faden, R.R. 1998. What patients say about medical research, *IRB*, 20(4), 1–7.

Sullivan, P. 1999. Move to market gene pool angers Iceland's MDs, *CMAJ*, 161(3), 305.

Sulmasy, D.P. 2000. On warning families about genetic risk: the ghost of Tarasoff, *Am J Med*, 109(9), 738–9.

Sulmasy, D.P. 2005. Duty to warn about hereditary disease risks, *JAMA*, 293(6), 676.

Surbek, D.V. and Holzgreve, W. 2002. Vorgeburtliche Stammzelltransplantation zwischen Forschung und Klinik, *Ther Umsch*, 59(11), 619–23.

Sutrop, M. 2003. Trust, informed consent and population databases. A case study of the Estonian Genome Project. Presentation at the XVIIth European Conference on philosophy of medicine and health care. 21–23 August 2003, Vilnius, Lithuania.

Swedish Medical Research Council. 1999. Research ethics guidelines for using biobanks, especially projects involving genome research: <http://www.privireal.org/content/rec/sweden.php> (accessed 11 August 2009).

Swiss federal law, 8.10.2004. Law about genetic analysis of human beings (Loi fédérale sur l'analyse génétique humaine): <http://www.admin.ch/ch/f/rs/810_12/index.html> (accessed 12 July 2009).

Takala, T. 2001. Genetic ignorance and reasonable paternalism, *Theor Med Bioeth*, 22(5), 485–91.

Takala, T. and Häyry, M. 2000. Genetic ignorance, moral obligations and social duties, *J Med Philos*, 25(1), 107–13; discussion – 14–20.

Tasmuth, T. 2003. The Estonian Gene Bank Project – an overt business plan. Open Democracy 29 May 2003: <http://www.opendemocracy.net/theme_9-genes/article_1250.jsp> (accessed 20 July 2009).

Taylor, P.L. 2007. Research sharing, ethics and public benefit, *Nat Biotechnol*, 25(4), 398–401.

Ten Have, H. 2007. Towards global bioethics: the UNESCO universal declaration on bioethics and human rights, in *Genetic Democracy: Philosophical Perspectives (International Library of Ethics, Law, and the New Medicine)*, V. Launis and J. Räikkä (eds). Heidelberg/New York: Springer, 31–42.

Thorgeirsson, T.E., Geller, F., Sulem, P., Rafnar, T., Wiste, A., Magnusson, K.P. et al. 2008. A variant associated with nicotine dependence, lung cancer and peripheral arterial disease, *Nature*, 452(7187), 638–42.

Thorgeirsson, T.E., Oskarsson, H., Desnica, N., Kostic, J.P., Stefansson, J.G., Kolbeinsson, H. et al. 2003. Anxiety with panic disorder linked to chromosome 9q in Iceland, *Am J Hum Genet*, 72(5), 1221–30.

Traulsen, J.M., Bjornsdottir, I. and Almarsdottir, A.B. 2008. 'I'm happy if I can help': public views on future medicines and gene-based therapy in Iceland, *Community Genet*, 11(1), 2–10.

Tri-Council. 1998. Tri-Council Policy Statement. Medical Research Council of Canada, Natural Sciences and Engineering Research Council of Canada and Social Sciences and Humanities Research Council of Canada. Tri-Council policy statement: Ethical conduct for research involving humans. Ottawa: Public Works and Government Services Canada, 1998, with 2000, 2002 and 2005 amendments, art. 10.1 a). National Council on Ethics in Human Research (NCEHR). Available at: <http://pre.ethics.gc.ca/eng/policy-politique/tcps-eptc/> (accessed 2 August 2009).

Trouet, C. 2003. Informed consent for the research use of human biological materials, *Med Law*, 22(3), 411–19.

Trouet, C. 2004. New European guidelines for the use of stored human biological materials in biomedical research, *J Med Ethics*, 30, 99–103.

Trouet, C. and Sprumont, D. 2002. Biobanks: investigating in regulation, in *Baltic Yearbook of International Law, Volume 2, 2002*, I. Ziemele (ed.). The Hague/London/New York: Kluwer Law International, 3–19.

Tugendhat, E. 1984. *Probleme der Ethik*. Stuttgart: Reclam.

Tutton, R. 2004. Person, property and gift: exploring languages of tissue donation to biomedical research, in *Genetic Databases: Socio-Ethical Issues in the Collection and Use of DNA*, R. Tutton and O. Corrigan (eds). London/New York: Routledge, 19–38.

Tutton, R. and Corrigan, O. 2004. Introduction: public participation in genetic databases, in *Genetic Databases: Socio-Ethical Issues in the Collection and Use of DNA*, R. Tutton and O. Corrigan (eds). London/New York: Routledge, 1–18.

Tutton, R., Kaye, J. and Hoeyer, K. 2004. Governing UK Biobank: the importance of ensuring public trust, *Trends Biotechnol*, 22(6), 284–5.

Tzortzis, A. 2003a. Estonia sees its future in genes. DW-World.de, 10 December 2003: <http://www.geenivaramu.ee/?id=249> (accessed 1 August 2009).

Tzortzis, A. 2003b. Good science, good PR. *Boston Globe*, 19 August 2003: <http://www.geenivaramu.ee/?id=245> (accessed 1 August 2009).

Uehling, M.D. 2003. Decoding Estonia. *Bio-IT World*, 10 February 2003: <http://www.geenivaramu.ee/index.php?id=118> and <http://connection.ebscohost.com/content/article/1034109954.html;jsessionid=F0AE57E7A9B8CA2D70C611ECAB761F1A.ehctc1> (accessed 1 August 2009).

UK Advisory Committee. 1998. Statement. Advisory Committee on Genetic Testing, Advice to Research Ethics Committees, sec. 3.1., United Kingdom, October 1998. UK Department of Health: <http://www.publications.doh.gov. uk/pub/docs/doh/acgtar1.pdf> (accessed 3 August 2009).

UK Biobank. 2007. UK Biobank Ethics and Governance Framework. Version 3.0 (October 2007): <http://www.ukbiobank.ac.uk/docs/EGF20082.pdf> (accessed 28 July 2009).

UK Biobank. 2009a. Confidentiality: <http://www.ukbiobank.ac.uk/faqs/ confidentiality.php> (accessed 28 July 2009).

UK Biobank. 2009b. Consent and withdrawal: <http://www.ukbiobank.ac.uk/ faqs/consent.php> (accessed 28 July 2009).

UK Biobank. 2009c. Homepage: <http://www.ukbiobank.ac.uk/> (accessed 21 August 2009).

UK Biobank. 2009d. What happens at an assessment centre? <http://www. ukbiobank.ac.uk/assessment/whathappens.php> (accessed 28 July 2009).

UK Biobank Coordinating Centre. 2006. UK Biobank: Protocol for a large-scale prospective epidemiological resource: <http://www.ukbiobank.ac.uk/docs/ UKBProtocol_000.pdf> (accessed 28 July 2009).

UK Department of Health. 2001. Building the information core. Protecting and using confidential patient information. A strategy for the NHS: <http://www. erpho.org.uk/Download/Public/13423/1/Strategy_v7.doc> (accessed 10 August 2009).

Ummel, M., Schmidt, A., Pelet, O., Dumoulin, J.-F. and Lässer, E. 2002. *La réutilisation des tissus humains*. Université de Neuchâtel: Institut de droit de la santé.

UNESCO. 16 October 2003. *International Bioethics Committee. International Declaration on Human Genetic Data*. Paris: UNESCO.

United Nations. 1948. Universal Declaration of Human Rights: <http://www. un.org/en/documents/udhr/> (accessed 5 August 2009).

Veatch, R.M. 1981. *A Theory of Medical Ethics*. New York: Basic Books.

Veatch, R.M. and Spicer, C.M. 1994. Against paternalism in the patient–physician relationship, in *Principles of Health Care Ethics*, R. Gillon (ed.). London: John Wiley & Sons, 409–19.

Vlastos, F., Lacomme, S., Wild, P., Poulain, S., Siat, J., Grosdidier, G., du Manoir, S., Monga, B., Hillas, G., Varsovie, R., Claudot, F., Marie, B., Vignaud, J.M. and Szymanski, N. 2009. Do evolving practices improve survival in operated lung cancer patients? A biobank may answer, *J Thorac Oncol*, 4(4), 505–11.

Wadman, M. 2008. Icelandic biotech feels the pinch, *Nature*, 455(7215), 842.

Wallace, H. 2002. The need for independent scientific peer review of Biobank UK, *Lancet*, 359(9325), 2282; author reply.

Watson, J. and Cyranoski, D. 2005. Beset by practical hurdles, UK Biobank moves at sluggish pace, *Nat Med*, 11(7), 696.

Watts, G. 2006. Will UK Biobank pay off?, *BMJ*, 332(7549), 1052.

Watts, G. 2007. UK Biobank gets 10% response rate as it starts recruiting volunteers, *BMJ*, 334(7595), 659.

Wei, G. 2002. *An Introduction to Genetic Engineering, Life Sciences and the Law.* Singapore: Singapore University Press.

Weijer, C. 2000. Benefit-sharing and other protections for communities in genetic research, *Clin Genet*, 58(5), 367–8.

Weijer, C. and Emanuel, E.J. 2000. Ethics: protecting communities in biomedical research, *Science*, 289(5482), 1142–4.

Weijer, C. and Miller, P.B. 2004. Protecting communities in pharmacogenetic and pharmacogenomic research, *Pharmacogenomics J*, 4(1), 9–16.

Weijer, C., Goldsand, G. and Emanuel, E.J. 1999. Protecting communities in research: current guidelines and limits of extrapolation, *Nat Genet*, 23(3), 275–80.

Weir, R.F. 1998. *Stored Tissue Samples: Ethical, Legal, and Public Policy Implications*. Iowa City, IA: University of Iowa Press.

Weir, R.F. 1999. The ongoing debate about stored tissue samples, research, and informed consent. Commissioned paper, in *Research Involving Human Biological Materials: Ethical Issues and Policy Guidance, Report and Recommendations, vol. 2*, National Bioethics Advisory Commission (NBAC) (ed.). Rockville, MD: NBAC, F1–F21.

Weir, R.F., Olick, R.S. and Murray, J.C. 2004. *The Stored Tissue Issue: Biomedical Research, Ethics, and Law in the Era of Genomic Medicine*. New York: Oxford University Press.

Weldon, S. 2004. 'Public consent' or 'scientific citizenship'? What counts as public participation in population based DNA collections?, in *Genetic Databases: Socio-Ethical Issues in the Collection and Use of DNA*, R. Tutton and O. Corrigan (eds). London/New York: Routledge, 161–80.

Wellcome Trust, Medical Research Council and Department of Health. 2002. The UK Biobank. Ethics Consultation Workshop, 25 April 2002: <http://www. ukbiobank.ac.uk/docs/ethics_work.pdf> (accessed 20 July 2009).

Welton, A.J., Vickers, M.R., Cooper, J.A., Meade, T.W. and Marteau, T.M. 1999. Is recruitment more difficult with a placebo arm in randomised controlled trials? A quasirandomised, interview based study, *BMJ*, 318(7191), 1114–17.

Wendler, D. 2002. What research with stored samples teaches us about research with human subjects, *Bioethics*, 16(1), 33–54.

Wendler, D. 2006. One-time general consent for research on biological samples, *BMJ*, 332(7540), 544–7.

Wendler, D. and Emanuel, E. 2002. The debate over research on stored biological samples: what do sources think?, *Arch Intern Med*, 162(13), 1457–62.

Wertz, D.C. 1997. International perspectives on privacy and access to genetic information, *Microbial & Comparative Genomics*, 2, 33–40.

Wertz, D.C., Fletcher, J.C. and Mulvihill, J.J. 1990. Medical geneticists confront ethical dilemmas: cross-cultural comparisons among 18 nations, *Am J Hum Genet*, 46(6), 1200–1213.

WHO. 1998. World Health Organisation. Proposed International Guidelines on Ethical Issues in Medical Genetics and Genetic Services (Report of a meeting on ethical issues in medical genetics, Geneva, 15–16 December 1997), WHO Human Genetics programme. Geneva, 1998: <http://whqlibdoc.who.int/hq/1998/WHO_HGN_GL_ETH_98.1.pdf> or <http://www.ncbi.nlm.nih.gov/entrez/query.fcgi?db=PubMed&cmd=Retrieve&list_uids=10335346&dopt=Abstract> (accessed 9 August 2009).

WHO. 2000. WHO's guideline for obtaining informed consent for the procurement and use of human tissues in preparing a research project proposal, third edition: <http://www.who.int/reproductivehealth/topics/ethics/human_tissue_use.pdf> or (entire document): <http://www.who.int/reproductivehealth/topics/ethics/human_tissue_use_guide_serg/en/index.html> (accessed 14 July 2009).

WHO. May 2001. World Health Organization Regional Office for Europe (European Partnerships on Patient's Rights and Empowerment): Genetic databases: assessing the benefits and the impact on human and patient rights. Report for Consultation: <http://www.law.ed.ac.uk/ahrc/files/69_lauriewhoreportgeneticdatabases03.pdf> (accessed 30 July 2009).

WHO. 2005. World Health Organization. Handbook for Good Clinical Research Practice (GCP). Guidance for implementation: <http://apps.who.int/medicinedocs/index/assoc/s14084e/s14084e.pdf> (accessed 30 July 2009).

Wichmann, H.E. and Gieger, C. 2007. [Biobanks], *Bundesgesundheitsblatt Gesundheitsforschung Gesundheitsschutz*, 50(2), 192–9.

Wiggins, S., Whyte, P., Huggins, M., Adam, S., Theilmann, J., Bloch, M., Sheps, S.B., Schechter, M.T. and Hayden, M.R. 1992. The psychological consequences of predictive testing for Huntington's disease. Canadian Collaborative Study of Predictive Testing, *N Engl J Med*, 327(20), 1401–5.

Williams, G. and Schroeder, D. 2004. Human genetic banking: altruism, benefit and consent, *New Genet Soc*, 23, 89–103.

Wilson, D.H. 1994. Patients' wishes must be accepted, *BMJ*, 308, 1424.

Winickoff, D.E. 2001. Biosamples, genomics, and human rights: context and content of Iceland's Biobanks Act, *J Biolaw Bus*, 4(2), 11–17.

WMA. 2000. World Medical Association. Declaration of Helsinki, adopted by the 52nd World Medical Association General Assembly, Edinburgh, Scotland.

WMA. 2002. The World Medical Association Declaration on Ethical Considerations Regarding Health Databases. 2002: <http://www.wma.net/e/policy/d1.htm> (accessed 30 July 2009).

WMA. 2008. World Medical Association. Declaration of Helsinki, 59th WMA General Assembly, Seoul, October 2008: <http://www.wma.net/e/policy/b3.htm> (accessed 3 August 2009).

Wolfe, J., Fairclough, D.L., Clarridge, B.R., Daniels, E.R. and Emanuel, E.J. 1999. Stability of attitudes regarding physician-assisted suicide and euthanasia among oncology patients, physicians, and the general public, *J Clin Oncol*, 17(4), 1274.

Wolff, K., Brun, W., Kvale, G. and Nordin, K. 2007. Confidentiality versus duty to inform: an empirical study on attitudes towards the handling of genetic information, *Am J Med Genet A*, 143(2), 142–8.

Woods, S. 2003. Dignity not entirely useless: <http://bmj.bmjjournals.com/cgi/eletters/327/7429/1419#44060> (accessed 5 August 2009).

Wright, A.F., Carothers, A.D. and Campbell, H. 2002. Gene-environment interactions: the BioBank UK study, *Pharmacogenomics J*, 2(2), 75–82.

Zika, E., Schulte in den Baumen, T., Kaye, J., Brand, A. and Ibarreta, D. 2008. Sample, data use and protection in biobanking in Europe: legal issues, *Pharmacogenomics*, 9(6), 773–81.

Zoëga, T. and Andersen, B. 2000. The Icelandic Health Sector Database: deCODE and the 'new' ethics for genetic research, in *Who Owns Our Genes?*, L. Nielsen and C. Holm (eds). Copenhagen: Nordic Council of Ministers, 33–64.

# Index

ulterior inter
102
UNESCO *s*
S*c*
United *K*

# The Consumer Handbook on Hearing Loss and Hearing Aids

## A Bridge to Healing

## 2nd Edition

### CHAPTERS RECOMMENDED BY YOUR HEARING HEALTHCARE PROVIDER

# Dedication

To you with courage to seek change. . .

# The Consumer Handbook on Hearing Loss and Hearing Aids

## A Bridge to Healing

## 2nd Edition

**Edited by
Richard Carmen, Au.D.
Doctor of Audiology**

Auricle Ink Publishers • Sedona Arizona

Library of Congress Cataloging-in-Publication Data

The consumer handbook on hearing loss and hearing aids : a bridge to healing / edited by Richard Carmen.— 2nd ed.
    p. cm.
Includes bibliographical references and index.
  ISBN 0-9661826-2-6 (hbk.) — ISBN 0-9661826-1-8 (pbk.)
  1.  Deafness—Handbooks, manuals, etc. 2.  Hearing
disorders—Handbooks, manuals, etc. 3.  Hearing aids—Handbooks, manuals, etc. 4.  Hearing impaired—Rehabilitation—Handbooks, manuals, etc.  I. Carmen, Richard.

  RF290.C665 2004
  617.8'9—dc22

                                                    2003020383

©2004 by Auricle Ink Publishers

Second Printing

ISBN 0-9661826-1-8 (Soft Cover)
ISBN 0-9661826-2-6 (Hard Cover)

Cover Concept and Development by Jane Pirini

This book is available at special discount when ordered in bulk quantities. Contact the publisher for more information.

**Auricle Ink Publishers**
**P.O. Box 20607, Sedona AZ 86341**
**Tel (928) 284-0860**

**www.hearingproblems.com**
**E-mail: AIP@hearingproblems.com**

# TABLE OF CONTENTS

# Introduction
*Douglas L. Beck, Au.D.*

Dr. Beck received his Doctor of Audiology Degree from the University of Florida, and currently resides in San Antonio, Texas. He has been practicing audiology for 20 years. Dr. Beck is President and Editor-In-Chief of the world's largest professional website for hearing healthcare professionals, www.audiologyonline.com and the most "linked to" hearing healthcare website for consumers and their families, www.healthyhearing.com.

I was deeply honored by Dr. Carmen's invitation to prepare an Introduction to the Second Edition of this wonderful book. I have given patients and their families many copies of the First Edition, so I am quite familiar with it.

Throughout this Second Edition, I was impressed with the content, style and ease with which complicated information is transferred to those with hearing loss and their loved ones. It is a pragmatic approach to improving your quality of life and getting results if you have hearing loss. Day-to-day issues are competently addressed in simple, non-technical language.

The roster of contributors to this book includes some of the most distinguished practitioners in our profession. If you are new to hearing loss issues, hearing aids, or are an experienced hearing aid wearer, you'll find many valuable tips and tremendous guidance through the wealth of knowledge and experience offered by these contributors.

I believe this book will be the single most important educational tool you will discover in your search for better hearing! Those with a desire to seek positive changes and improve their quality of life (and the lives of their loved ones) can do so with the tools found in this book. Between the covers you'll find the inside story from the experts. They'll tell you how to maximize adjustment to hearing loss and how to most benefit from hearing aids. You'll learn who to consult, how to interpret your audiogram, and how to confront deep feelings about hearing loss. You'll read about technology breakthroughs and cutting edge science that will enrich your life. And you'll learn of some challenges that must be endured. Ultimately, you'll be able to assess your level of readiness for help, and most importantly, learn what action you can take to dramatically improve the quality of your life.

If you're a senior, you have certain requirements that come with age which deserve the attention of patient healthcare professionals. You'll learn how to identify these needs so you can remain watchful over them.

While this book can be read cover to cover, it's intended as a *handbook* from which you can pick and choose chapters and sections you find most beneficial. However you use this book, I think you'll find it to be of exceptional benefit.

Congratulations to Dr. Carmen for this wonderful gift to you, and congratulations to you for seeking a better quality of life through knowledge and perseverance.

—*Dr. Douglas L. Beck*

# CHAPTER ONE

# The Emotions of Losing Hearing and A Bridge To Healing

## *Richard Carmen, Au.D.*

---

Dr. Carmen received his Doctor of Audiology Degree from the Arizona School of Health Sciences, a division of the Kirksville College of Osteopathic Medicine. He has been practicing audiology and issuing hearing aids since 1972, during which time he pioneered research into the effects of metabolic diseases on hearing. He has written extensively in the field as a regular contributor to various hearing journals, and authored two previous consumer books. His material has appeared in such popular consumer-based periodicals as *The Saturday Evening Post, Ladies' Home Journal* and *Self Magazine*. He currently resides in Sedona Arizona where he manages his clinical practice.

---

As Quasimodo, the Hunchback of Notre Dame, lay dying in the arms of the beautiful gypsy girl La Esmeralda, a tear rolls down his cheek. On his dying breath, he realizes his greatest torment—the pain of feeling. He whispers to Esmeralda, "Why could I not have been made of stone?"

There is nothing wrong with feeling emotions. After all, they are what characterize us as human. Emotional experiences may be wonderful, painful, and sometimes perplexing. Yet, more than our physical body, feelings are the substance of our identity. Each of us reacts differently toward the varied experiences of our lives. For centuries, fields of study have been devoted to exploring this fascinating phenomenon, but the search seems to have yielded as much controversy as knowledge.

From more than three decades of clinical practice, I've observed some compelling emotions and feelings in my patients. These observations extend into my own family members with loss of hearing, so the feelings we'll be talking about touch home.

I taught an audiology course once in which I had my students wear earplugs for a full day—morning to bedtime. They were asked to log their feelings and emotions and report to the class the following week. We were all overwhelmed by two things: the similarity of their experiences and the depth of their emotions.

Students reported that they felt inadequate and incompetent. There was also a sense of limitation in areas they'd taken for granted. Simple tasks like using the telephone couldn't be performed without special focus, difficulty or strain. Common sounds like ice stirred in a glass, running water or turning a page in a book—sounds that orient us in our environment—suddenly vanished.

Driving the car was a new experience. With the absence of wind and traffic, there was a feeling of disorientation. Students quickly realized how important their vision became to compensate for what they could not hear. Yet, such compensation wasn't enough.

By the end of the day most of the students confessed they were worn out and disturbed by what they had gone through.

"What a horrible experience!" one student remarked.

An apt description I thought.

One student reported she had collapsed into bed crying. Others were unnerved or depressed. Their collective reactions were directly linked to feelings of inadequacy—a deficiency in their daily performance relative to how they were accustomed to functioning. Once the earplugs were removed, all ill feelings dissipated. Their sense of normalcy and calm had returned. If your significant other has no idea what it feels like to have a hearing loss, this might be an enlightening experience.

While this experiment was useful to normal hearing students, it revealed what you no doubt already know. Hearing is an essential human sense. Its absence would be greatly missed by anyone. And as hearing declines, similar to other sensory deficits, we humans have an extraordinary ability to compensate for the loss. Such compensation is a built-in defense mechanism that we give little thought to. It just happens. If you have a heart attack, the body works quickly to establish other arteries and connections. If you lose your sense of smell, your eyes become more probing. If vision goes, hearing usually sharpens. And when hearing deteriorates, an array of latent abilities kick in. When they do, the act of compensation can fool you. You may do well for a while with partial hearing loss, and not even recognize its presence. For example, you might cast it off as poor attention. It's for this reason that loss of hearing gives the impression of being so insidious.

"It just kind of crept up on me!" most hard of hearing people confess. Of course it didn't really just creep up. It's more that early suspicions went ignored.

Something you've probably said many times in your life, and will see repeated, rephrased and re-analyzed in this book is the complaint, "I hear but I don't understand the words clearly!" This is particularly true when trying to communicate in a group, around a few people, or in an environment with background noise such as in a restaurant or automobile. Early on, when you had problems hearing, you may have passed it off as being no more troublesome for you than for anyone else in the same situation. But as issues around poor hearing grew more apparent and the process of communication began breaking down, you must have realized the problem was not going away.

People who develop hearing loss from an explosion, accident, or other physical trauma are probably more inclined to deal with it because it is sudden and readily apparent. But if you're in generally good health and are the type of person who doesn't like to think of yourself as less capable than anyone else, you may have started blaming other people for frequent miscommunication. Typically, you may think others are not speaking clearly or loudly enough, or they "mumble" their words. It's only when sufficient numbers of people close to you suggest that it's you and not them, you usually get your first inkling of something within your personal communication system has gone awry. Some people never come to this realization and go on believing that others are the source of their communication failure. They continue to blame and are discouraged that other people do not enunciate well. This is not healthy for anyone, and why it's so important to address the core issue.

Our ego is attached to our health. We like to think of ourselves as being in shape, with a good heart, teeth, bones, vision, and good hearing. To resist the reality of having hearing loss perpetuates miscommunication and the emotions that go with it. If we try to ignore it, or stop thinking about it, the problem persists. For some people, the crossroads for acknowledging hearing difficulty and doing something about is where they get stuck, and end up doing nothing. In fact, the odds are high that prior to reading this book you've known of your hearing loss for longer than seven years. In the meantime, what problems you thought you had may now be compounded.

## Problem-Solving Ground Rules

Before we discuss feelings you may hold surrounding your hearing loss, let's first define the terms used and establish the ground rules upon which problems can be solved. A "hearing loss" is the physical condition in your ear. "Hearing difficulties" pertain to specific situations (like trying to hear someone speaking to you). A "hearing problem" is your internalization, how you process the issues surrounding these situations (like getting upset at your spouse if you miss a word).

These terms are often mistakenly interchanged. If you're in the living room watching television with your family and you realize that you're missing too much dialogue, you might ask others in the room if you can turn the volume louder, in which case you think you've solved the hearing difficulty. The reality is that inevitably your family will object to having the television too loud. This may make you angry, resentful, embarrassed, guilty, selfish, annoyed or other ill feelings—and it's a sure sign of a hearing problem. You're internalizing feelings about a hearing difficulty. As stated earlier, the first step in solving difficulties about your experience is to first acknowledge the difficulty, then recognize how you feel about your hearing loss. A willingness to consider it a fact of life will create a solid bridge to healing. This is the foundation upon which all hearing problems will find resolution.

There are two common philosophies people seem to adopt once hearing loss becomes a part of their lives: you can try to cover up the fact that you have it, or tell others when the occasion is appropriate that you don't hear well. There are many variations between both themes but if you look at yourself honestly, you'll recognize that you are more polarized one way.

The emotions a person feels when hearing loss is confirmed takes the full gamut of human experiences. Some are relieved that at last they know that this is the cause of their problem. Others are horrified—it seems an unbelievable possibility that the problem could be wholly theirs. So many of us react in so many different ways, and each of us seems to have our own specific internal (feelings) and external (people around us) influences, that predicting how we might experience hearing loss becomes quite complex.

Furthermore, your reactions to hearing loss do not necessarily equate to the degree of impairment; that is, you can have a mild loss of hearing which impacts your life more profoundly than someone with greater loss. Your reactions will be most influenced by how you feel about yourself and the world around you, the personality type you're born with, and how other people close to you feel about your problem (or who you've alienated in the process). The most important ground rule to bear in mind when looking at your issues as we progress through this chapter is: *be honest with yourself!*

# Self Inquiry

Any problem can have at least two solutions that bring about healing: (1) change the situation, or (2) change how you feel, interact or react. The problem with *changing the situation*, if you're an unaided person with hearing loss, is that you could find yourself continually changing your environment and still not hearing. You may also try to change the environment to avoid an unpleasant experience but it doesn't necessarily help you hear better.

The problem with *changing how you feel* is that it's an imposing challenge. It's very difficult to transform anger into love, frustration into understanding, or embarrassment into delight. Surely, it would seem that it doesn't happen quickly if at all. But I can tell you that it does happen. When people move past whatever has been holding them back from hearing aids, and they finally wear them, not only has a change occurred but how they feel about it becomes apparent to most people in their lives.

*The definition of "change" is "giving up something for something else."* The difficulty for anyone in making changes is that it requires giving up something to which we've grown accustomed. It is less certain, and sometimes frighteningly unfamiliar. I've always thought that there should be a course teaching students during their first year of college how to gracefully make changes in their lives. How better adjusted to life's experiences we'd all be.

Most of us find we're not skilled in making changes. It's usually something we find uncomfortable. Even good changes are known to cause stress. A move to a better house, getting a higher paying job, or even winning the lottery cause high stress. We tend to want to stick to "the familiar." Yet, going from dysfunction to adjustment necessitates change. To avoid stress, most of us unknowingly tend to stick to bad situations.

Perception has everything to do with the degree of adjustment, acceptance and solutions you embrace with regard to your hearing loss. Many people with hearing loss report they have altered their view of the world around them in an unhealthy way. People who were once soft spoken and gentle sometimes become outspoken and annoyed; others who were once alive with spirit and energy may grow pensive and withdrawn. Those close to them notice these changes and are saddened by it. If you aren't aware of such changes, if in fact they exist, it could be because they usually develop slowly over a period of years.

If you have the courage to really look at the impact hearing loss has had in your life, the following exercise may prove to be revealing. When completed, read the same list to someone who knows you well (your spouse, a grown child or a close friend) and ask this person to respond *how he or she believes you operate in the world.*

## Exercise #1

If the statements feel mostly accurate write True; if they feel mostly inaccurate write False:

1) _____ I don't hear well because other people mumble, don't enunciate clearly enough, or talk too low or softly for me to hear.

2) _____ Since I've had this hearing loss, I can't do all the things I'd like to do.

3) _____ People don't dare make jokes about my hearing trouble in my presence.

4) _____ I don't mingle with as many people (old and/or new acquaintances) as I used to because I don't hear well.

5) _____ I just can't be seen wearing a hearing aid.

6) _____ If I'm left alone in a conversation, I don't understand or trust what I hear.

7) _____ I know people think I'm not as sharp as I used to be because I don't hear as well as I once did.

8) _____ If I don't want to hear what someone says the first time, I'll remain quiet; it's a waste of my time trying to hear.

9) _____ I just can't seem to assert myself the way I used to (or as others do) since I lost my ability to hear well.

10)_____ It's difficult for me to accept that I actually have a hearing loss.

11)_____ I recognize that I'm the source of the problem because of my hearing loss; when I miss what somebody says to me, it's not their fault.

12)_____ Even though I have a hearing loss, I still do all the things I used to do.

13) _____ I have humorous things happen to me as a result of my not hearing well.

14) _____ In spite of my hearing loss, I'm careful not to give up any relationships I have in my life, or lose out on any potential relationships, by staying home too much.

15) _____ I would not think of hiding the fact that I was wearing a hearing aid.

16) _____ I feel completely at ease communicating with anyone in most environments even though I have hearing loss.

17) _____ Despite my hearing loss, other people do not think less of me than before my loss developed.

18) _____ I don't mind asking people to repeat what was said if I haven't heard it.

19) _____ As my hearing loss has developed, I have made a systematic effort to compensate for it by being more outgoing.

20) _____ It's easy for me to think of myself as having a hearing loss.

Note: Before you read the following interpretation which will give away the design of this exercise, be sure you and your partner complete it fully.

## Interpretation

Statements 1 through 10 are the reverse of 11 through 20, respectively. For example, statement 3 is opposite to statement 13. There are two built-in veracity checks: one is that however you responded to a particular statement, if you're honest with yourself, you should have responded opposite to its corresponding statement. The other check is the way in which your partner responded.

Did you respond consistently to both sides of the statements, True on one, False on the other? Did your partner agree with you? If not, you may want to look carefully at the content of those statements. Are you procrastinating? Do you spend a lot of time with negative thinking about the loss? Are you blaming others?

Or is your outlook healthy? Do you tend to think more positively in handling your hearing loss? Do you try and find the lighter side? Are you just as engaged in life as before you developed loss of hearing?

Once you've examined the way you and your partner responded to the same statements, you may well find that you are the one person who has prevented finding your own solutions. This exercise was not an attempt to change who you are, but rather to *change and improve how you react in the world.*

# Denying Hearing Loss

If your hearing healthcare provider informs you that you have an irreversible sensorineural hearing loss, despite the fact that more than 28 million other Americans have it, this is not welcomed news. However, it is quite another story if you don't believe it or choose to do nothing about it.

Most standard dictionaries define *denial* as *the refusal to believe* or *the act of disowning.* It is rejection of the notion that your hearing is an issue. This being so, you not only disown the condition, you decline help because logic dictates that you cannot seek help for something that does not exist:

- "Nobody hears everything!"
- "Don't talk to me from another room and I hear great!"
- "It doesn't bother me!"
- "I just ask people to speak up!"
- "Only my wife (or husband) complains about it!"
- "I ignore it!"

Often, early denial provides a useful function by allowing people time to recover from the initial shock of knowing they have a hearing loss. But some trap themselves here for years. To deny the notion of hearing loss is to claim that you hear well. Denial is the ultimate deception to oneself.

Mechanisms of denial can become an integral part of the way people operate in the world. The more sophisticated and highly developed their compensatory responses, the easier it may be to deny the problem. For example, they may have others help them hear, like asking others to repeat, rephrase, speak up and so forth. Without realizing it, they may even grow skilled at favoring an ear, tuning one person in and another out, repeating what they think they hear to confirm its accuracy, reducing background noises, making educated guesses, watching facial movements and expressions as well as gestures and body language. These are all excellent and necessary ways to hear and understand better, but the irony is people can get stuck believing all of this will solve their problem, and it doesn't.

If you're wondering if you're experiencing denial as you read this book, likely not. If you were in true denial, you probably wouldn't have picked up this book (although you could read it and say, "That's

10

not me he's talking about!"). If you're well aware of the loss, but deny its presence when others inquire, this isn't denial. It's concealment. So, congratulations! At least you're willing to look at the problem. This is where we must begin.

It's been said that uncorrected hearing loss is more noticeable than hearing aids because the act of concealing a hearing loss is doomed to fail. It can make a person appear foolish, inattentive, disinterested, confused, senile or mentally challenged. A person operating at this level needs to understand the serious emotional hardships imposed on oneself, the spouse, family and friends. Denying or minimizing the impact the loss has in one's life (or in the life of others) does not solve the problem. Having others "hear" for you is not the answer either. In fact, these things compound the problem in close relationships. "Why should I carry the burden?" an honest but resentful spouse asks!

You might feel annoyed that you have a hearing loss but your spouse is annoyed that you do nothing about it. You may isolate yourself from family gatherings because you can't hear, or feel foolish, or get embarrassed, but your family feels abandoned and dismissed that they aren't important enough to you. Your unwillingness to seek help can create the feeling in loved ones and friends that you are selfish or irresponsible.

## Procrastination

Something that may have tended to fool you is that sometimes you hear beautifully, other times poorly. Loved ones may also observe this to be true. This gives the false impression that you have a *listening issue*, not a hearing problem. This is the elusive nature of the condition for many people. You may believe room acoustics are the problem, or that it's other people—they talk like they have marbles in their mouth or "mumble." You may hear people differently because some voices project better than others. Men are usually easier to hear than women or children. And the environment plays a significant role. The bottom line is that the configuration of loss you have may allow you to hear some voices well, others poorly.

Putting off the hearing evaluation (or hearing aids) can be based on what seems like valid logic:
- "I'm too young!"
- "It's not bad enough yet!"
- "No one I know likes their hearing aids!"

- "We just can't afford it now!"
- "After we paint the house!"
- "Tom has a hearing loss and doesn't wear hearing aids and he gets along just fine!" (but of course Tom really doesn't).

Such people recognize the presence of the loss but try to find every excuse not to do anything about it. This is procrastination. In the presence of other health concerns, this may seem like just one more issue you may or may not eventually get to. However, in the absence of any other health problems, hearing loss may not seem important enough to address:

- After I do my teeth!"
- I don't want to spend my children's inheritance!"
- If only Medicare paid for it!"
- It's that trip to Hawaii (a new car, a child's wedding) or hearing aids!"

Any of this sound familiar? If so, it's worth reading further to explore this more thoroughly. Just buckle your seatbelt.

## Emotions Behind Hearing Loss

How you deal with hearing loss is probably how you deal with life. We all develop patterns by three to five years of age by which time they become entrenched in our personality. While you may wish to act and react differently, to a certain extent, it means deprogramming yourself. Despite such imposing challenges against change, to attempt change precludes the *desire* or *intent* to change. As you are about to discover, failure to change by not seeking help for your hearing loss is now linked to a myriad of emotional problems, some permanent, but most preventable.

As you explore your internal emotional processes, if you feel you don't deal with them in the way you would like, you would be well advised (individually or as a couple) to consider consulting a psychotherapist. I am not suggesting long-term therapy, but a few sessions where an unbiased, arbitrary, properly trained therapist can act as your personal sounding board. This can prove to be a very rewarding, productive and nurturing experience.

## The Effects of Sensory Deprivation

Sensory deprivation research was popular in the 1950s and told us much about the human experience in the absence of stimulation. John Lilly, MD[1] authored a few pop culture books on this subject matter, as well as scientific papers that were informative and fascinating. He was the creator of the "Lilly Tank," where one floated on Epson salts sealed inside a tank, had no body awareness, no light and no sound.

As auditory, visual and sensual input diminishes with less stimulation to corresponding neural centers in the brain, the brain is not happy. Lilly's students subjected to these experiments generally could not tolerate the absence of sensory stimulation longer than a few hours or a few days. Besides altered realities, other complaints included feelings of disorientation and inability to concentrate. You should know that people who suffer from hearing loss (which is auditory deprivation) also report *the same symptoms*.

Solitary confinement in prisons is sensory deprivation to the extreme. Over time, it has been shown to cause permanent problems, most profoundly, *intolerance to social interaction*. Obviously, this effect is counterproductive to a society that desires paroled inmates to be re-acclimated into society. By no coincidence, symptoms found among many people with untreated hearing loss (auditory deprivation) also include *intolerance to social interaction*.

Much of reality (what little we understand of it) is based on our very delicate sensory systems. Impairment to any one of our five senses *does result in an altered state of reality*. If you miss portions of communication and perhaps do not realize it, you are experiencing one thing while something else entirely may have been intended. When you experience auditory deprivation, your natural instinct is to avoid social situations because just like students in Lilly's experiments, not many people like living in an altered state of reality.

Furthermore, there is now reliable scientific evidence to document the fact that untreated hearing loss can lead to a variety of unhealthy emotional conditions. The Hearing Instrument Association in conjunction with the National Council on Aging ran a study with over 2,000 hard of hearing adults and over 1700 family members.[2] (Dr. Kochkin will discuss this further in Chapter 4.)

This study concluded that people who suffer from hearing loss were more likely to experience increased anger, frustration, paranoia, insecurity, instability, nervousness, tension, anxiety, irritability, discontentment, depression, being temperamental, fearful, more likely to be self-critical, suffer from a sense of inferiority, social phobias, be perceived as confused, disoriented or unable to concentrate. Experiencing only one of these would seem enough to inspire one to seek help, but unfortunately, many people with hearing loss tend to experience a variety of these unhealthy emotional states.

In addition, research has shown that failure to stimulate hearing (the auditory portion of the brain) by not wearing hearing aids may result in a more rapid decline in speech recognition.[3-4] These reports were based on a substantial number of subjects who possessed at least a moderate degree of hearing loss in both ears but received only one hearing aid. As a result of auditory deprivation in the unaided ear, a reduction in speech recognition occurred. In some cases, this was reversible by adding a second hearing aid.

If hearing loss is not addressed as a major health issue, the risks of negative emotional impact are far too great. These are consequences that can be avoided, but often are not because people do not realize the influence of untreated hearing loss. What follows will give you a sense of this impact.

## Isolation, Avoidance, Anxiety & Social Phobias

As we age and begin to lose longtime friends and loved ones, we find ourselves more isolated. Impaired hearing only adds to this isolation, and compounds matters. The experience of separation from others is not limited to the over-fifty crowd. Many patients in their twenties and thirties give up their favorite activities because of their inability to hear adequately. I've seen high school students refuse to wear hearing aids because they feared peer ridicule. They sadly preferred to be left alone and miss out on social interaction than risk being seen wearing hearing aids.

Social phobias can and do commonly develop from untreated hearing loss.[5] A social phobia is a form of anxiety; a persistent fear of social or performance situations in which embarrassment may occur. For example, if you avoided a particular social obligation with your significant other because you feared the embarrassing consequences of your hearing loss, and these types of things were persistent and excessive for more than six months, you would have a diagnosable social phobia.

If you have noticed that you've been avoiding social situations as described, you have reason to be concerned. Fundamentally, you're cutting yourself off from the very nurturing people who make you feel loved in the world. Clearly not a healthy choice. Apart from hearing loss, these anxiety disorders are serious medical conditions affecting more than 19 million American adults and can grow progressively worse if untreated. Through the 1990s, anxiety disorders in the U.S. grew by more than 50 percent and now pose a major public health concern. Interestingly, according to the National Institute on Deafness and Other Communication Disorders (NIDCD), hearing loss is the third most prevalent chronic condition in older Americans. So, if you're an older American experiencing hearing loss, you have much greater risk for isolation and avoidance of common pleasures in life.

## Depression

More than 22 percent of Americans ages 18 and older suffer from a diagnosable mental disorder in a given year,[6] and major depressive disorder is the leading cause of disability in the U.S. and established market economies worldwide.[7] The average age of onset is in the twenties with twice as many women as men affected by depressive disorders. A fact you should know is that those who suffer from hearing loss have a greater likelihood of also suffering from depression.[8]

These are staggering statistics. Despite these facts, depression is *not* a natural part of aging. It can be prevented, and is treatable in about 80 percent of older adults. A major source of depression, especially in older adults, can be untreated hearing loss. The simple action of wearing hearing aids can resolve depression associated with untreated hearing loss. In older adults, this should be pursued aggressively, since depression is also commonly associated with anxiety and other simultaneously occurring ailments. As we age, our normal coping abilities diminish. It is so important to restore as much normal functioning as we can, at any age, but especially in these later years.

So often we think that what we feel inside remains hidden there. It's easy to forget that those we love can usually see past this thin veil of illusion. And rest assured, if depression is there, they'll eventually see it, and no doubt be suffering right along with you.

## Anger

Anger is a kind of stepchild to depression. In clinical terms, anger is often described as *depression turned inward.* When left untreated, people with depression can be difficult to be around, but something you may be surprised to hear is that you have a right to be angry! It's your body. Hearing is a needed and vital sense. Its loss influences almost every aspect of socialization. Every time you ask people to repeat themselves, it's a quiet reminder of a problem that does not go away.

The problem with anger is that it typically finds its vent outwardly. Eventually, you can become resentful and angry at others over your own need to have things repeated. Worse yet, you may become angry when a family member suggests you should get help. You already know that, you just don't want to hear it from anyone. For some, it's just too painful.

The dynamics of this emotion can be fairly simple. You become angry that you're not hearing. The family is upset that this "stubborn person" isn't doing more about the hearing loss. Some hard of hearing people, oblivious to the impact their hearing loss has on others, may ask to have things repeated in a blaming manner. This leads others to feel that the communication problem extends *to them,* and therefore gets them angry!

If you recognize that anger is an issue for you, you may find that you're as angry with the world as you are with yourself. Perhaps you desperately want to make a change but don't know how or where to turn. Indecision can keep you angry and upset. If you continue ignoring the problem, the issues surrounding it are further perpetuated. If you find solace in reverting to denial of the problem, it's a reprieve—but short-lived—you've already awakened to the truth of your situation.

For most people, unexpressed inner turmoil finally shifts from its simmering, hidden view, to boiling over. People around you are less likely to understand from where this hostility arises if you yourself are not in touch with it. You risk friends and family support diminishing as rapidly as your quality of life.

Once you become attuned that your upset originates from how you feel about yourself (that is, the anger that you carry because of what hearing loss has done to your life), and are willing to do something about it, you may discover a renewed sense of calm.

## Selfishness and Resentment

Living with someone who refuses to get help, regardless of the condition, is a challenge. But coming to terms with hearing loss can be a very slow journey for many. If you expect others to compensate for your loss of hearing instead of assuming this responsibility yourself, you could be setting up a fertile environment for strained family relationships. Your negligence may rightfully be seen as a selfish act. Of course you're entitled to expect others not to speak to you from another room, or in the presence of such cacophony as a loud television, a vacuum cleaner or music. But in the absence of wearing hearing aids, the family shouldn't be expected to manipulate the household for your convenience, especially when it's at the expense of others you care about.

If you're out socially and you're unaided, you already know how fed up your friends and loved ones are over seeing you miss out on conversation. If you're in a movie theater (if in fact you're not avoiding theaters altogether) and your spouse or friend must continuously repeat the on-screen dialogue, you might be hearing a lot of, "Shhh!" from those seated near you. In the meantime, you, your partner and maybe others around you have just missed another line of dialogue.

## Frustration and Defeat

In any family where a member has hearing loss, you'll find frustration. For someone who doesn't have hearing loss, it's almost impossible to conceptualize the depth of this problem. After all, there's no physical sign—no bandages on the head, no fractured bones, no walker. Because you give the general appearance of looking so normal, others may expect you to *hear normally*. Your spouse may continue to talk to you from other rooms, or with a back turned or with a pencil in the mouth.

Worse, you tell your physician that you believe you have a hearing loss and are surprised what you're told. Research has shown that, first, your physician will not test you nor will he or she likely refer you. To add insult to injury, you are probably told: "Don't worry about it. Everyone eventually has some. I have a little myself but I just ignore it!" If your physician has told you ignore it, it is well meant but incorrect and misguided information that will merely add to your mounting frustrations. You should know you are not alone. Eighty-six percent of doctors in the U.S. still *do not* screen for hearing loss![9]

Early in your experience of hearing loss you may have actually laughed at many of the misheard words. I was with my wife at the hardware store when I thought I heard her say, "Do you need some *coffee?*"

I was insulted because I took it to mean she thought I was not paying attention, but she had said, "Do you need some *caulking!*"

Another time when I asked my wife about what I should wear to a particular party, she said, "Leave your clothes!" Hardly, I thought! I only heard it correctly when she repeated it. "*Leisure* clothes!" Good thing she repeated it!

Worse yet is when you think you hear everything quite clearly but none of it makes sense, perhaps mixed with other thoughts you heard perfectly. Repeating doesn't help because with a hearing loss at specific frequencies, the same words are generated at the same frequencies you do not hear well.

My 7-year-old daughter was in the backseat of the car and hollered up front, "Daddy, did you see my new *minty mouth wash?*"

Now that made perfect sense to me, but when I told her she had to keep it in her bathroom cabinet, not laying around the counter, she was dumbfounded. "Why would I do that?" she asked.

"Because that's where minty mouth wash belongs!"

"Dad! I didn't say my minty mouth wash. I said *Mickey Mouse Watch!*"

Over time, the humor of mistakes seems to dwindle. What remains are still day-to-day frustrations. Eventually, it can lead to a culmination of mixed emotions as we've discussed, especially annoyance and anger fueled by frustrations.

A frequently heard comment by the person with hearing loss, as well as the family, is, "I can't stand it anymore!" In fact, the longer untreated hearing loss persists, the greater the frustrations <u>for everyone</u>.

In addition to frustration, it's easy to feel defeated and not know what else to do. You struggle to hear despite how attentive you are. You're playing an odds game—sooner or later you're going to miss some conversation. Defeat could be your fate if there was no help available. Not taking advantage of professional help is not defeat, *it's self-defeat.* It is resignation, concession, submission and surrender. It does nothing to lessen the problem. (If you already wear hearing aids and feel defeated, explore all other options available to you, *many included in this book.*)

## Embarrassment

Of the array of emotions you can go through with loss of hearing, something common to everyone is embarrassment. Second-guessing what you think you hear, offering inappropriate responses, missing the punch line to a joke, or getting wrong directions are small examples of what you and loved ones experience. If you're not comfortable with your communication skills, your subtle cues of awkwardness will put others ill at ease.

People often do not pursue help for themselves because the thought of wearing hearing aids is embarrassing. Ironically, failure to do so usually proves to be more embarrassing. With the advent of the CIC (completely-in-the-canal) hearing aids in the early 1990s, this trend has shifted. The cosmetic appeal of these exceptionally inconspicuous hearing aids have attracted wearers who would never have considered amplification on any other basis.

Hopefully, with continuing technology, embarrassment about hearing aid use will become a thing of the past. In the hearing healthcare world of today, hearing aids and other appropriate amplification accessories offer anyone with loss of hearing the most efficient avenue to independent hearing. These devices allow you to break free of your dependence on others, and can make all the difference in strengthening your relationship with those around you rather than fueling unrewarding emotions.

## Rejection

Bill was a likeable but boisterous man. He told funny jokes but he told them with such volume that strangers thirty feet away laughed. He was a source of constant entertainment as well as embarrassment to his wife and friends. Sitting in a restaurant, he'd talk about people's personal problems. It wasn't that his friends didn't want their problems discussed, they just didn't want the entire restaurant to hear about it. It was as if Bill had no sense of what was appropriate. No one suspected, until I met Bill, his wife and others for lunch one day, that he had a marked loss of hearing. Bill knew it, but he wasn't about to let anyone else in on his secret. His refusal for help cost him the relationships of people who once truly loved and appreciated him. However, his friends simply could no longer tolerate the humiliations that went with the friendship.

Many hard of hearing people are rejected by others who do not recognize their condition. When others remain uninformed about why you may behave or interact the way you do, they're forced to draw wrong conclusions that carry undesirable consequences. You don't have to be vulnerable to social rejection. You have to experience this only a few times to know how painful it is.

## Spouses & Significant Others

If you're an average person with hearing loss, you know that your own impatience at times has caused you to be harsher on loved ones than you'd like, or insensitive, unkind or unfair. Once you've realized what you've done, you may feel guilty. You may wish you could have handled the situation differently but you just couldn't control yourself. You may feel like it's a vicious cycle—you expect loved ones to be your ears, and those around you get fed up doing the hearing for you. No one wins.

When I consult with a person experiencing hearing loss, I turn to the spouse or companion and ask for his or her feelings. The common response is, "I'm so tired of repeating myself!" What you might not know is that everyone feels the same. As stated earlier, others can feel resentful that they must do your work.

Only 20 percent of people who suffer from hearing loss seek treatment through hearing aids. This speaks volumes about what spouses endure. It does not only mean louder television, repeating yourself throughout the day, and filling in parts of important conversations, it dangerously raises the level of anxiety in a healthy spouse married to someone with untreated hearing loss. Your spouse will develop her or his own anxiety around your issues, which can start with annoyance and lead to anger, intolerance, a sense of hopelessness, and can even lead to depression. In some cases it ends in divorce. Struggling to communicate under these circumstances can be exhausting.

Many people with untreated hearing loss feel they are not ready for hearing aids. Inspiring you to seek this needed help may be the most challenging task your spouse and family face. Change can only begin with your readiness, but the rewards can dramatically improve lives and transform relationships.

## Expectations Versus Actual Performance

If you're a person living in a non-amplified world, you no doubt have expectations about hearing that may not align with your performance. I've known people with hearing loss refuse to get hearing aids, then go into situations expecting to hear. At the end of the evening, I'd point out how much conversation was missed.

People who haven't yet come to terms with their loss of hearing, or who have not fully admitted this to themselves, mistakenly believe that *they hear all they need to hear.* The truth is, *you only hear what your hearing capacity permits.* The illusion to oneself is two-fold: you not only fail to get important information but you don't even know it. The illusion to others is that they believe communication has occurred when in fact it hasn't. Thus, we have multiple altered realties!

## Exercise #2

Here's a little exercise that can help you better understand hearing loss. Divide the top of a blank sheet of paper into three sections: on the left, title it "Situations;" in the middle "Expectations;" and on the right, "Actual Performance."

List three to five situations or environments where you expect to hear regardless of whether or not you actually can. Your task is to rate the items under the "Expectations" and "Actual Performance" columns by selecting one of the following ratings:

# NEVER - RARELY - SOMETIMES - OFTEN - ALWAYS

After you've completed this, take another piece of paper and list the same situations. Then have your spouse or someone close to you complete how they think your expectations versus actual performance pan out. This makes for good and healthy discussion, and for excellent comparisons. The more truthful you are with yourself, the more you'll gain from these insights.

## Interpretation

If you've rated everything in the exercise the same for all situations, either you're an amazingly well adjusted person with hearing loss, or you're kidding yourself. It's unlikely that all hearing situations on your list will be evaluated equally even if you are well adjusted.

So, take a closer look at your list. Bear in mind that people with normal hearing will rate the situations of expectations and performance differently because of their varying listening environments. The difference indicates the magnitude of the problem; the greater the difference, the greater the problem. For many people with loss of hearing, it's typical to have expectations higher than performance levels. As a result, reactions to environmental situations that prove difficult can lead to the emotions we've discussed.

## Acceptance and Moving On

Do you want better communication? Do you want to do more to help yourself? Is the quality of *your* life important enough to *you* to make positive changes? Do you care enough about loved ones to make these changes?

Acceptance of hearing loss allows you to move on. It's that easy. You already recognize the trials and tribulations of insufficient hearing. You know that despite all efforts to compensate for not hearing, nothing gets you through. This realization is essential before you can move on with clear vision. Coming to terms with the emotions surrounding your hearing builds that bridge to healing; and acceptance of your hearing loss allows you safe passage.

## References

1. Lilly J. *The Center of the Cyclone: An Autobiography of Inner Space.* New York: Bantam Books, 1972.
2. Kochkin S and Rogin CM. Quantifying the obvious: the impact of hearing instruments on quality of life. The Hearing Review 7(1), 2000.
3. Silman S, et al. Late on-set auditory deprivation: effects of monaural versus binaural hearing aids. J. Acoust. Soc. Am. 76:1357-62, 1984.
4. Silman S, et al. Adult-onset auditory deprivation. J. Am. Acad. Audiol. 3:390-96, 1992.
5. Carmen R and Uram S. Hearing loss and anxiety in adults. The Hearing Journal 55(4), 2002.
6. Reiger DA, Narrow WE, Rae DS, et al. The de facto mental and addictive disorders service system. Epidemiologic Catchment Area prospective 1-year prevalence rates of disorders and services. Archives of General Psychiatry 50(2):85-94.,1993.
7. Klerman GL, Weissman MM. Increasing rates of depression. JAMA 261(15):2229-35, 1989.
8. Bridges JA, Bentler RA. Relating hearing aid use to well-being among older adults. The Hearing Journal 51(7):39-44, 1998.
9. Kochkin S. MarkeTrak VI: The VA and Direct Mail Sales Spark Growth in Hearing Aid Market. The Hearing Review 8(12), 2001.

CHAPTER TWO

# How to Obtain Professional Help

*Robert E. Sandlin, Ph.D.*

---

Dr. Sandlin received his Ph.D. in Clinical Audiology from Wayne State University in 1961. He serves as an Adjunct Professor of Audiology at San Diego State University. He has served as a research and clinical audiologist in several clinics and hospitals. He served as Director of the California Tinnitus Assessment in San Diego that is devoted to developing effective strategies for the non-medical management of those with subjective tinnitus. Dr. Sandlin has published over 90 articles and edited four major texts on hearing aid sciences and amplification, and contributed a number of chapters to other texts His greatest achievement has been six tremendous children and seven grandchildren who provide a constant source of satisfaction for him and his wife, Joann.

---

In the first edition of this book, I suggested procedures and reasons for finding the most qualified individual to help you along the way. You may ask, "Are there more things that I can do to help me find the best person who understands my hearing problems?"

Yes!

There are things you may want to consider in your search for professional guidance. This is especially true, in view of the improvements in hearing aid design and function. What I mean is that advances in hearing aid technology may be very helpful to those with hearing loss.

Why is this so important to you? Hearing aids with computer capability are now available that permit the hearing professional to help you in ways that were impossible before. The fancy name for this advanced hearing aid is *Digital Signal Processing.*

The task of finding the most qualified individual to manage whatever hearing problems you have is not as difficult as it might first seem. Your biggest challenge will be narrowing your search down from a lot of choices to a few options. In doing so, you'll reduce your frustrations and sharpen your focus on what's required. There is always a certain amount of frustration in seeking help for some human ailment. Questions may arise for which there are no immediate answers. For example, have you ever asked yourself any of the following questions?

- Do I need a hearing aid at all?
- Do I need two?
- How do I know if the recommended hearing aids are the best for me?
- How do I know whether the person I'm going to see is competent?
- How do I determine if the person I'm seeing really cares about me or is merely profit-motivated?
- What if I don't like the hearing aids, what action can I take?
- How can I determine whether medicine or surgery can improve my hearing?

These questions are not uncommon. The important thing is that all of them can be answered in an intelligent manner. A lot depends on whom you select to be your personal hearing healthcare manager. Your physician can tell if medicine or surgery would help. The audiologist can verify the presence or absence of a significant hearing loss and select and dispense the appropriate hearing aid. The hearing instrument specialist is also qualified to select, fit and dispense hearing aids.

Be optimistic about your potential success with hearing aids. Think of all the benefits you could experience. Look at it this way. You've already won more than half the battle just by making a positive decision to do something.

The purpose of this chapter is to suggest ways in which you can connect to the proper hearing care professionals, and understand what they can offer. This will require <u>positive action</u> on your part, defined as taking a step(s) to successfully eliminate or reduce your hearing problem.

This chapter will provide guidance to you and your family on several key issues. In the process, it should reduce your fears, apprehensions and frustrations sometimes associated with any search for better ways to manage a health problem. By the end of this chapter, you should be knowledgeable about how to move through the maze of hearing healthcare professionals. You should know who's who in this profession. You should be able to establish who is the best person to meet your particular needs. You will know how to determine the qualifications of the provider who might best serve you.

If you have doubts or problems regarding the hearing healthcare person you elected to see, get a second opinion. You know your hearing is extremely important to you. You have every right to find the best help possible. Not all hearing health professionals have the same amount of knowledge and experience. Let's review some history underlying the emergence of hearing aid dispensing as an occupation in the United States.

## History of Hearing Aid Dispensing

The selection and fitting of hearing aids has been practiced for well over seventy years. During that period of time, there have been steady improvements in the design and performance of hearing aid devices. However, less than twenty-five years ago, hearing aid dispensers were not required to have any special technical training to carry out the necessary tasks for selection and fitting of hearing aids. Nor was it required for the individual to have a dedicated place of business. Only sufficient capital to buy hearing aids from a manufacturer and go into business were needed. Further, early on, there was no sophisticated diagnostic or hearing aid measuring equipment required to validate the degree of improvement provided by hearing aids or to qualify their acoustic performance.

As the manufacturing of hearing instruments became more technologically advanced, so did the ability to measure their electroacoustic characteristics. As time passed, manufacturers initiated training programs in the proper selection and fitting of their hearing aid products. For the most part, early educational programs provided by the industry were very instrumental in improving selection and fitting skills. The manufacturer was interested, primarily, in its own product and most educational efforts were dictated by that philosophy.

Nevertheless, from the early introduction of hearing aids and the early selection and fitting practices, those who had less than positive experiences regarding hearing aid use developed some negative attitudes. While some of these attitudes may have had a basis in fact, it's important for you to know that significant and positive changes have come about within the hearing aid dispensing field. For example, by the late 1970s, most individuals who dispensed hearing instruments were licensed by the state in which they practiced. In order to receive a hearing aid dispensing license, a test of basic competency had to be passed.

Today, these tests have become more sophisticated. Area of study includes a basic understanding of the anatomy, physiology, neurology pathology of the hearing system. They also include factors contributing to hearing impairment; psychology of the hearing-impaired person; and electroacoustic measurement of hearing aid devices.

In addition, other areas of study include administering and understanding hearing tests; understanding audiometric test results for the purpose of fitting hearing aids; learning effective counseling strategies; and becoming familiar with state laws governing the professional activities of hearing instrument providers. These tests are not exhaustive ones nor necessarily overly difficult, but did cover basic educational requirements. Licensure to fit hearing aids created a higher level of competence.

There are two individual and distinct disciplines now dispensing hearing aids: the Clinical Audiologist and the Hearing Instrument Specialist (HIS). Let's look at both of these practitioners.

## Hearing Instrument Specialists

There are thousands of qualified hearing instrument specialists throughout the United States. State requirements and licensing assures that they are knowledgeable and capable of performing necessary measurements for the selection and fitting of hearing aids. Many are members of the International Hearing Society (IHS). In order to qualify and maintain membership in this group, continuing education is mandatory. The hearing instrument specialist also can pursue additional training to achieve Board Certification (BC) status. In order for members to be board certified, a written examination must be taken and passed. This examination is more demanding of specific knowledge than is the examination of individual states.

It can be stated positively that the hearing instrument specialist is much more qualified to select and fit these devices than they were at any time in the past. This qualification has been largely based on state licensure and mandatory continuing education requirements. Much of the credit is due to the continuing efforts of the International Hearing Society and its board certification program. Additionally, state certification has advanced the professional status of the hearing aid specialist and has inspired greater consumer confidence.

# History of Audiology

Although the medical profession has long been interested in the measurement of hearing loss for the purpose of diagnosis and treatment, there was no great effort until World War II to establish a separate branch of medicine dealing solely with the objective assessment of the human auditory system. At that time, hundreds, if not thousands of returning servicemen had incurred permanent hearing impairment due to the injuries of war.

Physicians recognized the value of assessing hearing because of its implications regarding medical management. It soon became evident that most hearing loss caused by battle conditions could not be treated medically or surgically. This was so because most of the injuries to the ear were caused by shell blasts and other loud, explosive noises. As an aside, do you know that once nerve cells in the ear die, they cannot be replaced? I mention this because the majority of people with hearing impairment have received damage to the ear, which causes some of the nerve cells to die.

Because of the number of servicemen and women with hearing loss, there needed to be some organized, clinical program. A program was needed which could evaluate the type and degree of hearing loss as well as develop effective rehabilitation programs. Just the sheer numbers of servicemen needing immediate attention gave need to program development. Advanced techniques of measuring hearing loss were introduced. More sophisticated equipment was developed for the measurement of hearing. Much attention was given to rehabilitation programs which would permit, as much as possible, the hard of hearing serviceman to live effectively in a hearing world. You can imagine the important role that hearing aids played in the successful rehabilitation of these servicemen and women.

Coupled with the urgency to meet the needs of the hard of hearing soldier was the need to provide expanded training for personnel working in rehabilitation programs for hearing-impaired veterans. As training programs were established and proved to be very worthwhile, a name—a professional label—had to be associated with those who performed these services. A branch of special education merged with medicine and this new academic discipline emerged as the profession of Audiology.

Since those early beginnings, the practice of audiology has expanded tremendously. The amount of audiological research is reflected in the number of scientific journals devoted solely to its study. The growth of this field is evident by the significant increase in academic programs in hearing science.

It's noteworthy that audiologists have been responsible for almost all of the formal research efforts involving hearing aid use and function. Yet, they were prevented from dispensing hearing aids for profit by their national association, the American Speech-Language-Hearing Association (ASHA).

But all businesses, whether medical or not, are profit driven, and rightfully so or they could no longer afford to keep their doors open. In the early 1970s, many audiologists recognized this. Whether it was naive of the ASHA or an outdated ideology, the time had come for hearing aids to be part of clinical audiology practice. Several clinical audiologists in the United States opposed the majority viewpoint and began to dispense hearing aids. They believed they had the right to include dispensing in their responsibilities to consumers. Those audiologists who dispensed hearing aids had their clinical certification revoked by ASHA.

However, by 1978, as more and more audiologists had adopted the dispensing philosophy, ASHA revised their Code of Ethics and accepted hearing aids as being an integral part of the services offered by audiologists. Since that time, audiology has had an enormous and positive influence on the hearing aid industry. Hearing aid evaluation and subsequent dispensing of hearing aids are now considered to be well within the scope of practice for audiologists.

## Clinical Audiologists

Audiologists are familiar with the functions of the human auditory system and trained to understand normal and abnormal functions of that system. They are trained to perform routine and, at times, highly technical diagnostic tests to determine what is causing abnormal auditory function. Their depth of understanding of the physiology, neurology, anatomy and pathology of the auditory system is greater than that of the hearing instrument specialist. This is true because of the required education.

Further, audiologists provide rehabilitation to those with hearing loss ranging in degrees from mild to profound. Over the past 15 to 20 years, the field of audiology has expanded to include the assessment of hearing loss for the purpose of selecting and fitting hearing aid devices.

The advanced training and educational requirements are

dictated by ASHA. To obtain a Master's Degree in Audiology, typically six years of study at an approved university or college are required. In addition, the student must serve a clinical fellowship year and must pass a rigorous examination. Audiologists must earn at least a Master's Degree to assume clinical or academic responsibilities.

Also, several universities offer a Doctor of Philosophy (Ph.D.) degree as the terminal degree requiring two to four years of additional study. However, in the mid-1990s, there was a concerted effort by a group of audiologists to establish one common professional degree by which all "clinical" audiologists would be recognized—the Doctor of Audiology (Au.D.). The consensus is that by around 2012, the primary degree to be granted by most audiology programs will in fact be the Au.D. The Ph.D. will then be a direction for those audiologists wishing to pursue teaching and research.

Academic preparation stresses the diagnostic procedures required to differentiate various pathologies of the auditory system. This may include anything from wax in the ear canal to a tumor resting on the eighth cranial nerve. For most academic programs, audiology also includes rehabilitation programs for the deaf and hard of hearing.

More recently, academic programs relating to the electroacoustic performance, selection, assessment and fitting of hearing aids have been added to the curriculum. Inclusion of hearing aid dispensing as an integral part of audiology practice began in the early 1980s and has continued to grow in acceptance.

## Similarities Among Providers

In those states requiring licensure, both the audiologist and hearing instrument specialist must pass the same mandatory examination and complete the required number of continuing education hours each year to maintain licensure. Members of both groups must abide by the same standards of ethical practice and are subject to the same state laws governing the dispensing of hearing aids. (Did you know that in states where licensing is mandatory, the physician must also be licensed to dispense hearing aids?)

One significant similarity is that each group has access to the same hearing instrument manufacturers and to all literature and clinical information pertaining to hearing aids and their electroacoustic performance. There are no restrictions placed on which manufacturer can provide hearing aid devices to those who dispense.

There are, however, a few manufacturers of hearing instruments who will sell their product only to approved franchises. The basic philosophy underlying a given franchise operation is that it's more efficient for the manufacturer to deal with persons dispensing only their product.

Obviously, there are pros and cons to this argument, but very active franchises do exist in today's marketplace. All practitioners have access to pertinent scientific and trade journals and may very well modify that which they do in the selection and fitting process based on information contained in specific articles. Most hearing instrument dispensers and dispensing audiologists have more than a single brand of hearing aids available to their clients.

From a humanistic point of view, I think you will find that each discipline is sensitive to your needs. Each individual will do his or her best to satisfy your needs and maintain your confidence in their abilities.

## A Difference Among Providers

The major difference as already alluded to, is that of formal education. The hearing instrument specialist does not have a formal educational background in measuring the performance of the human auditory system for purposes of diagnosis or in the rehabilitation of those with hearing impairment. He or she is more typically required to have a high school education in order to sit for the examination to qualify as a dispenser. This description of the academic requirements of a hearing instrument specialist is not intended as an indictment of the qualifications necessary to become a provider, nor is it intended as a yardstick against which to measure proficiency in the selection and fitting of hearing aid devices. Rather, it's a straightforward statement of criteria imposed by most states in granting licensure to those qualifying by examination to dispense hearing aids. There are thousands of qualified hearing instrument specialists throughout the United States. By far, the majority is knowledgeable and capable of performing necessary measurements to select the most appropriate hearing instruments.

The education required to become a clinical audiologist is extensive. It entails undergraduate and graduate school training in assessing neurophysiologic function and dysfunction of the hearing system through the administration of defined clinical tests. Audiology is, and has been for decades, a recognized academic discipline.

Inherent in the training of audiologists is courses relating to hearing aid amplification. A number of training institutions provide clinical practicum for their graduate students in hearing instrument dispensing and specific courses relating to selection and fitting of amplification devices.

It's gratifying to report to you that many more major universities are offering academic courses dealing with the selection, measurement and dispensing of hearing aids. Hearing instrument dispensing is now well within the scope of audiologic practice.

## Your Significant Other

When starting your search for qualified service providers, it may be wise to consider taking another person with you. It can be your spouse or another family member or friend. This person can be a second pair of eyes and ears to assist in the evaluation process. He or she may be able to provide a somewhat more objective observation of the hearing care provider's skills and services. This person can serve as a sounding board to respond to such questions as, "What do you think I should do?" or "Should I get one or two hearing aids?"

## Finding The Preferred Professional

In the selection of a qualified provider, you want someone who demonstrates proficiency and competence. You must realize that you'll be using hearing aid amplification for many years to come, and therefore, will want to establish a long-term relationship with whomever you choose. This is something to which you should give considerable thought.

Listed below are some of the recommended criteria you can use to select the best person in whom you can place confidence and trust. These are the essential components that you should look for when seeking a hearing care professional:

### Expectations of Your Hearing Care Provider

Hearing aid researchers agree that the interaction of the hearing aid fitter and the client is a critical element in successful hearing aid use. There are specific elements to this important relationship that are common to providers who achieve a high degree of satisfaction among their clients. Successful providers believe in the efficacy (benefit) of hearing aids and they keep up with rapid changes in hearing aid technology.

Expect your hearing health provider to have an attractive and clean office with convenient business hours. Expect him or her to act professionally, to be knowledgeable and demonstrate the benefits I will present in the next section. Expect your provider to be able to explain hearing aid options to you in simple terms. Demonstrations are often helpful which allow you to listen to a particular type of circuitry, to compare different settings in noise, or to experience the difference between monaural (one hearing aid) and binaural amplification. A good professional dispensing hearing aids never assumes that clients cannot understand complex concepts. You should be given as much information as you require in the form of discussion, videotapes, books, brochures, consumer guides, and technical articles. Currently, there's a popular phrase, "too much information." There's also a time to stop giving information. Not all patients want or need a bus load of materials. Information needs to be tailored to your needs.

Research has identified that stigma is still a very common reason why people hold back from purchasing hearing aids. It's very important that you're allowed to express your feelings about how hearing aids will look and what you think about them. Simply talking about your feelings associated with your hearing loss can be of tremendous benefit. Some people don't care what size or style of hearing aid is chosen. Others are extremely conscious about the cosmetic aspect. (Sociologist Dr. Cuzzort in Chapter 8 offers valuable insights on stigma.)

Experienced providers know how to motivate skeptical, timid hearing aid candidates. They know that proactive clients have a higher likelihood of becoming satisfied hearing aid wearers. All providers want their clients to be willing to go the distance, even if they make a few mistakes in the beginning. Sometimes the process can be difficult. A caring professional will always see you through, if you will.

Optimizing the match between your lifestyle and communication needs is an important determination by your provider, something which can have direct impact on you. We're all more likely to trust someone who we feel understands us. Therefore, effective hearing care providers are good listeners. It's important that your provider takes the time to learn what problems you have in meetings, groups, theater, with co-workers, family, and in your place of worship.

It's also important for you to express what you hope to improve in your hearing world as a result of amplification.

Once you have been fit with hearing aids, it is absolutely mandatory that the person who fit you with the hearing aids explain in detail how to care for the hearing aid, how to clean and maintain them, how to use the switches or remote (if there is one), and how to change batteries. You should receive an instructional booklet for later referral after the initial counseling or instructional session.

Especially with programmable hearing aids, it's not uncommon to come back several times in order to get "just the right fit" (physical, acoustical, audiological) for you. This is a normal part of the hearing aid fitting process. Multiple adjustments to hearing aids are normal and are not indicative of a "lemon." However, it's important that these adjustments occur during the normal trial period, and that you are satisfied the product meets your needs.

## Years of Service

If somebody has been providing hearing services for many years, it generally is an indicator that many people with hearing loss have been seen by that person. Although it may not necessarily indicate superior knowledge and care, it does suggest that this person has been in business awhile and is not likely to disappear tomorrow. As with any skill-related work, the longer you do it, the more proficient you become.

In the selection process, you may want to determine the years of service a particular practitioner has in providing amplification devices to those with hearing loss. However, I must tell you that years of service does not always mean that the person is the most qualified to work with, or the one who understands the latest in technological advances in hearing aid performance. Don't hesitate to ask anyone from whom you are seeking advice and direction to review his or her professional and academic background.

## Level of Knowledge

It's in your best interest to determine the level of skill one has in the selection and fitting of hearing aids. Just having a state license to dispense hearing instruments does not guarantee that the individual is current with technological advances in hearing aid performance. In the past decade or so, there have been significant changes in this industry. You should not feel uncomfortable, and the provider should not feel challenged, if you inquire about his or her level of knowledge as it pertains to current hearing aid selection and use.

As a matter of fact, many hearing instrument providers may display a variety of certificates indicating they've taken specific courses of study to become more competent. You should take advantage of this by carefully noting the dates on these certificates. A certificate hanging on the wall may not tell you how much the person learned, but it does indicate that he or she continues to study. If you observe that there is nothing to indicate continuing education, simply ask what his or her continuing education has been.

## Empathy and Compassion

Your hearing aid needs are best met by an empathetic person who understands what you are experiencing. There is really no substitute for empathy. If the hearing health professional is truly empathetic to your needs, he or she will do what is necessary to achieve the greatest benefit to you.

Although similar in meaning, compassion is a deep sympathetic concern or feeling for a given condition or for an individual, while empathy is more of an intellectual acceptance and understanding of an individual's need or given condition. In essence, you want services rendered by someone who really understands how you feel.

## Temperament and Likeability

For our purposes, temperament can be defined as the natural and predictable behavior of an individual. As it relates to one's needs when searching for answers to hearing loss problem, it is the overt actions of the individual. By this I mean that the hearing health professional should display patience, understanding and concern, without eliciting fear or unrealistic statements regarding hearing aid use.

Certainly, knowledge of hearing aid dispensing is fundamental to doing business and meeting hearing aid needs. But a very important and essential ingredient is also the temperament and likeability of the one with whom you are doing business. Likeability is a sense of joy or contentment in the presence of an individual who expresses a sincere interest in your needs and feelings. It is not something that can always be expressed in concrete terms. It's something you feel and experience in a very positive way.

The sense of feeling positive about the hearing healthcare professional cannot be regulated by a state agency. Like a physician with good bedside manners, you want professionals who conduct themselves in a way that allows you to feel protected. You want this person to be sensitive to your needs. You want to feel comfortable revealing your very private feelings regarding hearing aid use. You don't want to feel like you're intruding, but rather, that the hearing health professional appreciates the opportunity to serve you. It's in your best interest to gather a good sense about the person with whom you are expected to work closely.

## Dependability

Although seldom discussed in hearing aid literature, dependability is a very important attribute to successful patient management. That is, as a patient, can you depend on your hearing healthcare professional to be there when you need him or her? Does their office have predictable hours? Is the dispenser there every day of the week or just on certain days? Does the dispenser provide emergency care just in case something goes wrong with the hearing aid? You may consider talking to others who have purchased hearing aids from the dispenser and question them about dependability.

The large majority of dispensers are dependable. They are interested in providing services when you need them and want you to feel free to call them when a need arises. To the dispenser, it is simply good business practice to maintain a high level of dependability.

## Talk to Successful Users

It was stated earlier in this chapter that all hearing losses are not the same. Regardless of the degree and type of hearing loss you may have, others with permanent hearing loss can tell you of their experiences with a given practitioner and whether or not they were satisfied with the services offered and the benefits received. Ask people who have utilized hearing aids for several years. They have experienced the contributions and limitations of technological advances in hearing aid design and performance. They can be a rich resource for you.

Be careful though, because the positive experience of one person does not mean you will have a positive experience with the same hearing aid or the same professional. Conversely, the negative report by a friend doesn't preclude you will also have a bad experience. The emotional and physical needs for all with hearing loss are not the same. You may differ a great deal in your emotional reactions, as well as your acceptance and use of hearing aids.

Make it a point to talk to your friends and others who use hearing aids. Not only can these folks be supportive of your pursuit and use of amplification but you may learn from their positive, real life experiences how best to adjust to and benefit from hearing aid amplification. You may also learn a great deal from their mistakes.

## Background Check

As would be true in any profession, if you're uncertain about the audiologist, hearing instrument specialist or the physician providing services to you, contact the Better Business Bureau in your community or directly contact the state committee responsible for hearing aid licensure. You may also check with the International Hearing Society (HIS), American Speech-Language-Hearing Association (ASHA) or the American Academy of Audiology. (These institutions and more are listed in Appendix II.)

Further, in many states, hearing instrument specialists and audiologists have their own Ethics Committee. By contacting this committee, you can find out if complaints have been registered against a given provider and how such complaints were resolved.

## Spur of the Moment Decisions

At times, some people proceed with a hearing aid evaluation and the subsequent purchase of hearing aids on a spur of the moment decision. Such a spontaneous reaction in some people is exactly what is required to get the task done. But much will depend on your own temperament. If you're a person who doesn't like to spend a lot of time mulling things over, and you know what you need, such an impulsive decision to take quick action may work well for you.

On the other hand, you may need more time to think about a plan of action. Some people may have to muster the courage (or even the finances) to do something about their problem. That's okay. A few extra days of deciding what course to follow or how to arrange it won't make any difference. No doubt it has taken you years to get to this point anyway. You will find the professional person who will meet all qualifications you need and demand.

# Yellow Pages

Some consumers consult the yellow pages and select the individual whose advertisement is most visually attractive or largest or the individual who seems to have the best credentials. Others may select the first business beginning with "A." The value of yellow pages is for you to ascertain "who's who" in your community. Examine your options and proceed with optimism and faith in yourself that you have discerned the best choice.

# Medical Practitioners

Many people prefer to begin their hearing healthcare journey with the family physician whom they've known for years and whose judgment they trust. This seems like an intelligent decision because you would believe that your family physician would refer you to a hearing aid provider if needed.

However, as Dr. Carmen previously pointed out, many physicians do not refer their patients to hearing healthcare practitioners for the purpose of obtaining hearing aids. Most of these well-meaning physicians *falsely* believe you cannot be helped. If this has been your experience, I would suggest you seek a second opinion (from an audiologist or hearing instrument specialist). Some physicians are not current with state-of-the-art technology regarding hearing aids, and fail to recognize the benefit they provide to hard of hearing persons.

Nevertheless, if something about your ears or hearing is in need of specific medical attention, you could be referred to a medical specialist whose primary concern is the diagnosis and treatment of impaired hearing and diseases of the ear. Such a specialist is an otologist. The otologist restricts his or her practice to problems associated with the auditory system. The otolaryngologist is also a specialist in treating diseases of the ear, but treats nose and throat disorders as well. While either can provide you with adequate treatment, otologists are even more specialized in their training.

If your physician or medical specialist refers you to someone for hearing aids, it should be safely assumed that the practitioner knows you will receive competent care. If you have any doubts about such a referral, you should ask your physician whatever questions are on your mind.

# The Medical Waiver

If you're an experienced hearing aid wearer and you're being issued new hearing aids, federal law does not mandate that a physician see you. This is because the government takes for granted that by now you're experienced enough to recognize the presence of a problem, which needs medical attention. New users may not be as knowledgeable. In light of potential problems, federal law requires that anyone dispensing hearing aids be able to recognize a number of fairly obvious conditions of the ears. (See Chapter 8 Question & Answers number 7 for further information.) If a medical condition is recognized by your provider, you can be assured that you'll be referred for treatment prior to issuance of hearing aids.

If you're a first-time hearing aid wearer, federal law allows you to visit a hearing aid provider without first being seen by a physician, so long as you sign a waiver of medical evaluation for hearing. This essentially states, "You are being advised that the Food and Drug Administration has determined that your best health interests would be served if you had a medical evaluation by a licensed physician prior to purchasing hearing aids."

The waiver serves two solid purposes. First, it alerts you, the consumer, to the fact that a potentially serious medical problem could exist, and should not be overlooked, especially if you have any ear symptoms. Second, if you were recently seen in a physician's office and you know there's nothing wrong with your ears (other than hearing loss), you shouldn't have to go back through the medical route to obtain approval for a hearing aid purchase. Many consumers feel that a medical visit under these circumstances is both unnecessary, even redundant, and simply adds to the cost. By signing the waiver, you exercise the right to make your own decision.

# A Hearing Evaluation

There are a number of hearing tests that an audiologist or hearing instrument specialist can do to determine how severe you're hearing loss is. Please keep in mind that all tests administered are necessary in order to make the most appropriate assessment of your hearing and find the best approach to meet your hearing aid needs. In essentially all cases, you should have no pain or discomfort during the administration of diagnostic tests.

Please note that all tests performed are for the purpose of selecting and fitting hearing aids. The primary purpose of a hearing aid evaluation is simply that of determining whether you're a reasonable candidate for hearing aid use. Another purpose is that of determining the type of hearing aid most appropriate to your needs.

## Otoscopic Examination

Prior to the administration of hearing tests, your hearing healthcare provider should perform a routine otoscopic examination. Its purpose is to visually examine the status of your ear. It takes only a few minutes to complete and adds a great deal of understanding to what may have caused your hearing loss. The otoscope is a hand-held instrument about the size of a standard flashlight. Some are connected to a large-screen monitor like a TV, enabling you to see as well. It casts a sharply focused light into the ear that illuminates the canal and reveals its condition.

Some otoscopes have greater magnification and provide the examiner with a more precise view of anatomical structures. Such views may suggest problems that need to be attended to. For example, a build-up of earwax may be viewed blocking sound from entering the ear. Naturally, the greater the skill and training of the professional performing the otoscopy, the greater the chances are that existing problems will be identified.

Another major contribution of an otoscopic examination is that of assessing the status of the eardrum. For example, there could be a hole (perforation) in the eardrum due to some traumatic incident or disease process. The size and location of the hole can affect one's ability to hear well enough to understand all that is being said. Further, otoscopic examination can detect the presence of fluid in the middle ear space. Middle ear fluids can greatly reduce your ability to hear sounds at a normal level. Unfortunately, middle ear fluids can become diseased through bacterial invasion and cause serious medical problems.

Please keep in mind that an otoscopic inspection by an audiologist or hearing instrument specialist is not a diagnostic procedure. Only a qualified physician can do that. But if the hearing health professional sees something suggesting a medical condition, he or she must refer you to a physician.

## Listening for Tones

Following otoscopic examination, a number of specialized hearing tests may be conducted. The purpose of hearing tests is to determine how much hearing loss you have, if any, and what is the probable cause. Usually, the basic hearing test consists of sitting in a sound-treated chamber, listening to a series of tones, and indicating to the professional when you've heard them. Some tones will be low frequency (low pitch) and others will be high (high pitch). As you know by now, if you have a hearing loss, you won't be able to hear all of the tones at normal intensity levels. Also, you will not know how well or poorly you've done until the test is completed.

The lowest tones that the human ear can detect are very close to the sensation of feeling. At the other end of the continuum, a young healthy person can hear tones even higher than the highest violin note. We don't actually need to hear at either of these two extremes, but we do need hearing intact in the middle range where speech sounds vibrate.

Most people have greater difficulty hearing high frequencies. This is readily demonstrated by listening to (without looking at) someone repeat vowel sounds which are all low frequency, such as /a/, /e/, /i/, /o/ and /u/. Now have them produce the utterance of higher frequency sounds which make up consonants like /sh/, /ch/ and /s/ for example. Sixty-five percent of audible speech intelligibility comes from consonant (high frequency) sounds. Putting all of this in context, have someone repeat the words /sheath/, /cheap/ and /sheet/. If you can't hear the very subtle differences between these words, you will readily appreciate and recognize how important every sound is in adding information to what you hear. You might now also suspect a high frequency loss.

## Listening for Speech

As you well know, there's a direct correlation between the level of your hearing loss and your ability to understand words when presented at normal speech levels. Therefore, a couple of tests will be performed to assess your ability to understand selected words. The Speech Reception Threshold (SRT) test entails repeating two-syllable words such as "hotdog," "baseball," or "downtown."

On this particular test, the more familiar you are with the words, the more accurate the results (you just won't be able to predict which order the words will come). These words are presented at progressively weaker volume levels until you're forced to guess at what you think the words are. The value of this test is to determine how soft certain words can be made before you can only repeat them correctly 50 percent of the time. This point is called threshold. It's used as a working reference for the amount of power that eventually will be needed in your hearing aids, and can allow a certain degree of predictable success you may have in their use.

Another test is the Word Discrimination Score (WDS). Fifty one-syllable words such as "wet," "chew," or "car," are presented for you to repeat. The lower your score, the greater your difficulty in hearing and understanding people who talk with you. Usually a score poorer than 88 percent would indicate that you have at least some difficulty in some situations. None of the words on this test will be repeated if you miss them. The number of words repeated correctly reflects how well you understand speech under ideal listening conditions. Word discrimination tests are basic to good clinical practice. These tests tell us what your ability is to understand speech without hearing aids. Once you are fit with hearing aids, the same word discrimination test will tell us how much improvement occurs.

## Assessment of Middle Ear Structures

In a complete diagnostic evaluation of your hearing, other tests may be carried out to determine how well your hearing system is performing. Typically, clinical audiologists conduct these tests on highly sophisticated equipment. In certain cases, it may be important for your practitioner to know if the eardrum is moving appropriately when sounds strike it. If some disease or pathology affects the way in which the eardrum (or other structures) move, then we want to be able to identify and measure it.

Special diagnostic equipment is used through which primarily two objectives are accomplished: mobility of the eardrum (assessed by increasing air pressure into the outer ear canal), and integrity of the inner ear (by means of a series of loud tones to try to trigger your acoustic reflex). Both the pressure tests and presence or absence of the acoustic reflex add information to the final diagnosis of your hearing problem.

If these basic hearing tests confirm a loss of hearing or abnormal function, then further testing, including x-rays, blood samples, or certain brain function tests may be conducted to gain even more specific information about your hearing problem and what may be done about it. The purpose of these various tests is to compare your results with those of normal hearing persons. By making this comparison, your practitioner can quickly determine if you have normal hearing or some degree of loss.

Since you might have already suspected a hearing problem anyway, these tests will confirm your suspicions. Even though some people are apprehensive in general about taking tests, let me assure you that these diagnostic procedures recommended by your audiologist or otologist can be critical in arriving at a competent diagnosis of your problem and its proper management. In most cases, sophisticated tests are not needed to determine your hearing status or the type of hearing aids best suited to meet your needs.

So, don't be overwhelmed by all these tests. They are a necessary part of your quest for better hearing.

## Medical and/or Surgical Treatment

In many cases, hearing tests along with other information your practitioner has gathered may indicate the need for medical or surgical management. For the most part, this is good news, for it means that such intervention could resolve your problem and restore your hearing to a normal or near-normal state. If such is the case, there is usually no need for hearing aids. However, let's assume you have seen the otologist and are told that nothing medically or surgically can be done to treat your hearing problem. What can you now do to improve your ability to hear and understand? In the final analysis, when a hearing loss exists that cannot be successfully treated by medicine or surgery, the use of hearing aid amplification is the recommended path to follow.

## Conclusions

I have discussed many things you may experience in your search for professional care. It can be a highly rewarding journey if you initiate the process of help. The first step in receiving help is looking for it. And little help can be offered if you fail to deal honestly with the problem. Be assured that you'll be rewarded in your willingness to use amplification by significantly improving your ability to understand much more of your acoustic world. Your frequent requests to have conversations repeated should be markedly fewer, and your blueprint to secure a bridge to healing can at last be fulfilled.

# CHAPTER THREE
# Mapping Your Own Audiogram

## *Kris English, Ph.D.*

Dr. English earned her Doctorate in Education in 1993 from San Diego State University at Claremont Graduate University. She is an assistant professor at the University of Pittsburgh, and also teaches a class on the Internet for Central Michigan University/Vanderbilt University Bill Wilkerson Center. She has authored four books, three chapters, and over 40 papers, most lately addressing the adjustment process to living with hearing loss. She is currently developing a counseling tool to help children with hearing loss talk to audiologists about hearing aid use, friendships, and self-concept. She and her husband live in constant amazement that their two children are now adults and managing life on their own just fine.

Understanding how to read your own audiogram will assist you in better understanding your personal hearing challenges. At first, this might seem complicated, but it really is quite easy and straightforward. In my discussion with you, I will present "Mini-Summaries" of each section, provided throughout to review vocabulary and concepts, and occasionally "Audiogram Alerts" are provided to highlight a particular point of concern. In time, you will be an expert in describing your audiogram. So let's work together in this exploration.

An audiogram has three main components:
1. A range of pitches, from low to high.
2. A measurement of loudness, from soft to very loud.
3. Your hearing levels for each pitch for each ear.

## Audiogram Components

### Audiogram Component #1: Pitch

The first component of the audiogram is the range of pitches presented in the hearing test. Wearing headphones (or maybe insert earphones), you heard a series of beeps that may have reminded you of notes on a piano. Some had very low pitches (like the deep bass notes on the left end of the piano keys), some were very high pitches (similar to the far right end of piano keys), and some were in between. These pitches are lined up on the horizontal part of the audiogram, as shown in Figure 3-1.

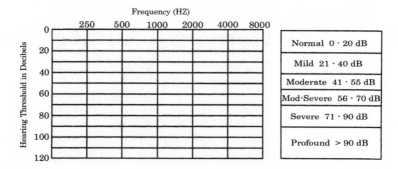

Figure 3-1: Pitch and loudness on an audiogram.

Another term used to describe these beeps is "pure tones." You may have noticed each beep was like a single note on a piano, with no chords or harmonics. The human ear can hear pure tones much lower and higher than the ones shown on the audiogram, but it would take too much time to test them all. For efficiency's sake we focus on what people are most interested in hearing—human speech. So the pure tones found in human speech are selected for testing and are the ones reported on your audiogram.

It may seem a little strange to say these pure tones have anything to do with human speech, but when analyzed electronically, each speech sound has been found to be a unique and complex combination of these pure tones. That's why your hearing care professional started with pure tone testing, as a way to describe the "building blocks" of your hearing ability.

Chances are, the term "frequency" was used during an explanation of your hearing test. For example, you may have been told you have a "high frequency hearing loss." Frequency means pitch: a way of expressing the number of cycles per second (cps) a sound wave occurs in one second. A sound that vibrates your eardrum at 500 times per second (cps) is perceived by our brain as having a low pitch, like the hum of the motor in your refrigerator. As the vibrations per second increase, the pitch of the sound will seem higher and higher, like the cheep of a bird.

A scientist named Heinrich Hertz (1857-1894) described this idea of low and high pitches having different cycles per second, and in his honor, his initials are now used to replace *cps* with *Hz*. So, for example, your hearing test may indicate that you have a hearing loss at 8000 Hz. Because this pitch (frequency) occurs in the higher end of the area for speech sounds, it can also be said to be a high frequency hearing loss.

## Mini-Summary

All of these terms mean the same thing:
- A high frequency hearing loss
- A hearing loss in the higher pitches
- A hearing loss at 4000-8000 Hz

## Audiogram Component #2: Loudness

The first question we want to answer is: how loud does each pitch have to be for you to hear it? Loudness is recorded on the vertical part of the audiogram (See: Figure 3-1). The unit of measure for loudness is the decibel (abbreviated dB). The audiogram uses increments of 5 dB mainly because the human ear is not usually able to notice differences of less than 5 dB.

This vertical measurement often causes some confusion. The softest levels of hearing are at the top, so the loudness *increases* as it goes *down* the scale. Initially, it might seem more logical to place the softest levels on the bottom and then, as loudness goes up, the scale should go up. So watch for this, and remember: when the loudness of the pitch needs to be increased, it means the hearing level is dropping downward.

## Mini-Summary

- Pitch or frequency is measured in Hertz (Hz).
- Loudness is measured in decibels (dB).
- These two measures are combined to tell us how loud (in dB) you need each frequency (Hz) to be in order to just barely hear it. This is called your hearing threshold for that frequency, and will be explained further in the next section.

## Audiogram Component #3: Your Hearing in Each Ear

Hearing tests usually start with the middle pitch, 1000 Hz. Let's say your right ear is being tested first. The tester sets the equipment to this frequency, and you raise your finger or push a button every time you hear it. The pure tone gets softer and softer, until you can barely perceive it. That level is your *threshold* for that frequency. Threshold means the softest level you could perceive it.

If your threshold for 1000 Hz is 30 dB, the tester records it with a circle at the intersection of those two values (See: Figure 3-2). Another threshold is then obtained at 2000 Hz, in this example, 40 dB. This procedure is repeated for each frequency. Then the other ear is tested in the same way.

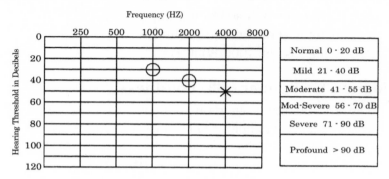

Figure 3-2: Three thresholds.

In Figure 3-2, the "X" found at 45 dB at 4000 Hz represents a threshold for the left ear. How will you remember which symbol is for which ear? The letter *R* will keep things straight: the *right* ear uses a *round* symbol (the circle). And if the hearing care professional used headphones to test your hearing, the *red* headphone went on your *right* ear. It's easy to remember because the "R" is the first letter in **r**ed, **r**ight and **r**ound—*aha!* Once you know the "round" symbols describe the right ear's hearing levels, by default you know the "X" stands for left ear hearing levels.

You may have had your hearing tested not only with headphones or inserts, but also with a bone oscillator that typically rested on your mastoid bone (behind your ear on the skull). The hearing information obtained with the oscillator would be reported with carats "<" and ">" or brackets "[" and "]." They are not included here in our first few audiograms in order to make this a bit more user-friendly; however, an example will be seen later (See: Figure 3-9).

## Mini-Summary

- Each pitch is tested to see how loud it needs to be for you to just barely hear it. This is your threshold for each pitch.
- The hearing levels for the right ear are depicted with Os, and the left ear is depicted with Xs.

46

## ⊞ Audiogram Alert!

On any given day, a person's hearing levels for pure tones can go up or down by about 5 dB. For example, on Monday a threshold at 1000 Hz could be 35; on Tuesday it could be 30, and on Wednesday it could be 40. This 5 dB-variability is normal, and can be explained by a variety of reasons. For example, if you are fatigued, your threshold could go down 5 dB because it takes a lot of concentration to keep listening to very soft tones. There's even evidence that diet plays a role in hearing. For example, the ear depends on a delicate balance of salt and potassium. If these levels are thrown off, hearing can be affected (see Chapter 8 Q&A #2).

While a 5 dB variability is not a concern, keep an eye on your first (baseline) hearing test. From one year to the next, a 5 dB shift might not seem unusual, but a 5 dB downward shift every year will have an impact on what hearing aids are selected for you.

## "Give It To Me Straight, Doc—How Bad Is My Hearing?"

Figure 3-3 shows our three audiogram components with a complete pure tone hearing test. The Os and Xs are connected with lines to help the eye track the hearing levels across the pitches. But what does it all mean? This takes us to the next step in interpreting your audiogram.

Hearing levels can be described in a progression of loss: normal, mild, moderate, moderately severe, severe, or profound. These levels of loss are added to Figure 3-3. The hearing levels depicted here are typical for many patients. Both ears start off at normal levels in the low pitches, drop to a mild loss in the middle pitches, and then end with a moderate loss in the high pitches.

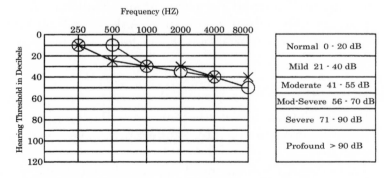

Figure 3-3: Mild to moderate hearing loss both ears.

Because there are different hearing levels (normal and also mild and moderate degrees of hearing loss) across the pitches, how would you describe this hearing loss?

Your hearing report would probably reveal close to what is written in the previous paragraph, but in conversation, you can accurately say this person has a mild to moderate hearing loss in the mid to high frequencies, both ears.

Figure 3-4 demonstrates how as the loudness increases, the hearing levels drop down the audiogram. In this example, the hearing loss we saw in Figure 3-3 has dropped about 10 to 45 dB, indicating moderate-to-severe hearing loss in both ears.

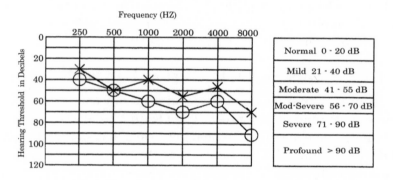

Figure 3-4: Moderate to severe hearing loss both ears.

By the way, in this chapter I am assuming that you are experiencing a hearing loss in both ears (called a bilateral loss). Occasionally, individuals have hearing loss only in one ear, with normal hearing in the other. This condition is called a unilateral (one-sided) hearing loss, and it presents unique challenges in localizing sound sources and listening in noise. Ask your hearing health professional for more information if you have a unilateral hearing loss.

## Mini-Summary

- Hearing levels can be summarized with descriptors such as normal, mild, moderate, moderately severe, severe, and profound.
- These descriptors may need to be combined to describe all the pitches (from low, middle, and high) accurately.

- How you hear pure tones is directly related to how you hear speech—the ultimate question you want to answer. Your test may have included how soft you could hear speech (speech recognition threshold, reported in decibels). These results are often included on the same form as your audiogram.

### ⊞Audiogram Alert!

Occasionally, you will hear people use percentages to describe their hearing loss, as in "I was told I have a 50 percent loss in my right ear." There are two circumstances that could explain this kind of description. First, the American Medical Association developed a percentage system years ago to describe hearing loss, and occasionally physicians still use it. However, as you look at an audiogram, you can see that decibels do not translate into percentages, and the hearing levels for each pitch are not addressed at all. So the percentage system, while intending to be helpful, does not really tell you much, and could even be misleading.

The other explanation could be confusing with some audiological testing that *is* reported in percentages. After finding out how you heard pure tones, your hearing care professional may have also wanted to know how well you hear one-syllable words. This is necessary to understand your hearing difficulties, and was touched on in the previous chapter.

## The Connection From Pure Tones to Speech Sounds

All along I have been saying that the pure tones by which you had been tested are related to how you hear and understand speech. Figure 3-5 is an audiogram with speech sounds superimposed over it. It shows how speech sounds are spread out in pitch. It has been noted that this shape vaguely resembles a banana, so it is often called the "speech banana."

Vowels are relatively low in pitch, while consonants that use voicing (for example, /l/, /m/, /n/) are in the middle range of pitches. "Voicing" means your voice helps produce the sound. To experience this, place your finger tips on your throat and hum a long "mmm." You will feel your throat vibrate. You are feeling your larynx or voice box move as air travels from your lungs to your mouth.

Many speech sounds are high in pitch (for example, /s / and /f/). These are produced without voicing, making them extremely soft as well as high-pitched. For example, put your upper teeth over your lower lip and gently blow through. This is the position for /f/. Without using your voice, try to blow harder, attempting to make the /f/ sound louder. You'll immediately notice that it cannot be done very well because the power for speech comes from your voice. The /f/ is voiceless. Now add your voice to it by humming through your lips in the same position. By doing this, you now no longer have an /f/ but a /v/ because you added vocalization, which will make this sound *much* easier to hear.

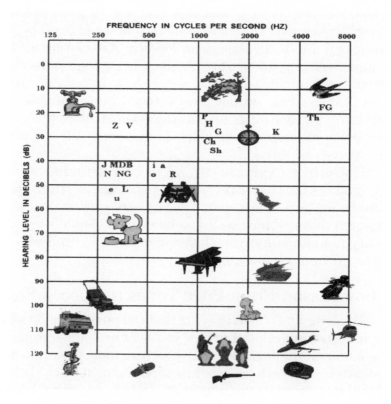

Figure 3-5: "Familiar Sounds" audiogram.

All sounds for speech vibrate at different frequencies, which is how you differentiate speech sounds. Two of the highest consonant sounds in English are /f/ and /s/. Even a mild hearing loss in the high frequencies can make either sound inaudible. If you miss hearing so much as one sound in one word in a single thought, it can be enough to miss the entire message. This is why some sounds seem garbled or muffled. It may sound like someone is mumbling. This situation explains the observation made by many people with hearing loss: "I can hear you, I just can't understand you!" Not picking up some of the speech sounds will make speech hard to understand, although general speech activity can still be heard.

As hearing levels drop, more and more speech sounds become harder to hear. This is the information your hearing care professional is looking to assess in order to appropriately fit you with hearing aids—but it all starts with those pure tones.

## ⊞ Audiogram Alert!

Your hearing care professional may have spent some time explaining your audiogram to you once the testing was completed. If you found it confusing, you may have felt too distracted or overwhelmed with the confirmation of having a hearing loss. Don't be discouraged! It's a lot of information to take in, and you should give yourself credit for getting this far in this chapter.

## More Practice

The more audiograms you see, the more sense they make. Following are four additional audiograms to consider before we take a look at your own audiogram. Figure 3-6 shows normal hearing in both ears up to 2000 Hz. Hearing levels drop to a moderate loss at 4000 Hz, and then recover to a mild loss at 8000 Hz. This type of configuration usually suggests a history of excessive noise exposure. It is such a commonly observed configuration, it has its own name: "noise notch." A person with this kind of hearing loss is strongly advised to take every measure necessary to protect against further noise exposure. Without hearing protection, this hearing loss can drop more and more, and eventually affect the middle and high frequencies.

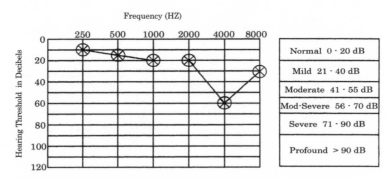

Figure 3-6: Hearing loss consistent with noise exposure.

Many hearing losses show gradual change from one frequency to the next, but some people have the kind of hearing loss shown in Figure 3-7. We see normal hearing in both ears through 1000 Hz, and then a dramatic, precipitous drop at 2000 Hz. Typically, 1500 Hz is not tested but because of the difference between 1000 and 2000, this information is important to collect. This audiogram represents a moderately severe to profound hearing loss in the mid to high frequencies, right ear worse than left.

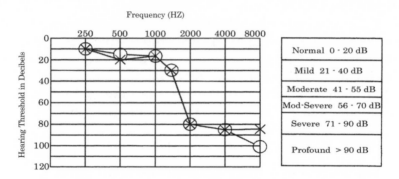

Figure 3-7: Normal hearing in low pitches with a severe precipitous drop.

In comparison, Figure 3-8 shows a severe-to-profound hearing loss in all the speech frequencies. No speech sounds produced at normal volume will be audible, although loud sounds in the environment might be barely heard.

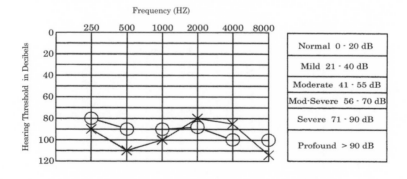

Figure 3-8: Severe to profound hearing loss both ears.

If you are a typical person with hearing loss, you have a sensorineural type of loss, meaning the sensory organ of hearing (the inner ear) is permanently losing its sensitivity. But hearing can also be temporarily affected by middle ear problems. These changes could be caused by severe head colds, allergies, damaged eardrums or other medical problems. This kind of hearing problem (called a conductive loss) will also be reflected in the audiogram, and we have one example here.

With its Os and Xs, Figure 3-9 indicates that a severe hearing loss exists in both ears in the low frequencies, recovering to a moderate hearing loss in the middle and high frequencies. However, when listening to pure tones with a bone oscillator (shown with bracket symbols), this person has better hearing levels in the low frequencies than indicated with headphones alone. Because of a middle ear problem, it is even harder than usual to hear low frequencies (note the poorer hearing levels). When a conductive loss is combined with a sensorineural loss, it is described as a *mixed loss*. Middle ear problems usually can be treated with medications or surgery. A person with an audiogram like one in Figure 3-9 will have better hearing if the conductive components are resolved (although a moderate sensorineural loss will remain in those lower frequencies).

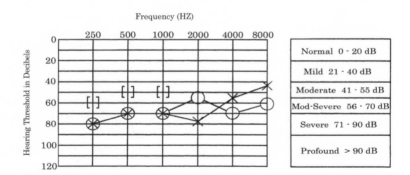

Figure 3-9: Moderate sensorineural hearing loss both ears, with additional middle ear (conductive) hearing loss in lower frequencies.

## Now It's Your Turn!

To help translate this chapter into personally meaningful information, the following questions are presented. Please locate a copy of your audiogram and follow these easy steps:

1. Carefully transcribe your audiogram's Os and Xs onto the blank audiogram in Figure 3-1.
2. Connect all the Os with a straight line
3. Connect all the Xs with a straight line.
4. Now you want to find out how well you hear within the critical range of hearing for human speech. Find your hearing threshold at 500 Hz for the right ear by looking on the graph below 500 until you see the O.
5. What is the dB level? Write it in here: _____ dB.
6. Look at the notation to the right that reveals the range from *normal* to *profound*, and write what yours is: _____.
7. Do the same for 4000 Hz as you just did for 500 Hz.
8. What is the range from *normal* to *profound* for 4000 Hz? Write what yours is: _____.
9. What are the ranges where your hearing levels start and end (for example, "*moderate* to *severe*" or perhaps even "*mild*" across all frequencies)? _____.
10. For the right ear, you should now know the range of loss you have. You can now do the same for the left ear.
11. Left ear loss at 500 Hz is: _____.
12. Left ear loss at 4000 Hz is: _____.
13. Left ear range of loss at 500 Hz is: _____.
14. Left ear range of loss at 4000 Hz is: _____.
15. What is the final range of hearing for your left ear (for example, *mild* to *severe*)? _____.
16. Now locate one of the many audiograms among Figures 3-6 through 3-20 in this chapter that most resembles your own audiogram. An easy way to match this is by noting your hearing levels for one ear at a time. Observe your loss only at these four frequencies: 500, 1000, 2000 and 4000 Hz and determine the best match for one ear.
17. You can now read the interpretation for the audiogram you matched, as described in that Figure. Ask yourself, what speech sounds are you missing? (See: Figure 3-5 to find the answer to this question.) Are you a hearing aid candidate? What challenges lay ahead for you?
18. Repeat the match for the other ear if the hearing levels differ from the first ear's best match.

We've already briefly discussed Figures 3-6 through 3-9, so let's consider the remaining audiograms. If your audiogram closely resembles Figure 3-10, you have a hearing loss of some degree in the low and perhaps middle frequencies, and normal hearing in the higher ranges. This kind of hearing loss is often caused by health conditions such as diabetes, Meniere's Disease, or labyrinthitis (an inner ear infection described in Chapter 8 Q&A #6). You could be missing as much as 30 percent of speech information, and like all hearing loss configurations, you probably find it hard to understand people in noisy situations. Hearing aids (programmable or ideally digital) can help you hear better.

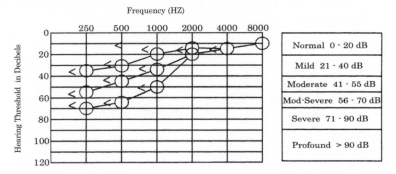

Figure 3-10: A variety of low frequency sensorineural hearing losses right ear only.

Keep in mind that the more normal your hearing across the frequency ranges, especially progressing into the higher ranges, the better you will function in your hearing world. If your audiogram closely resembles Figures 3-11, 3-12 or 3-13, you have a mild hearing loss at some of the tested frequencies. You could be missing up to 40% of speech, making it difficult to follow conversations, especially in noisy situations (restaurants, parties, etc.).

You will note that Figures 3-12 and 3-13 have hearing loss restricted to only the higher ranges. Figure 3-13 is limited to loss only in the uppermost range (furthest to the right on the audiogram). The latter indicates that someone with this loss may hear fairly well overall except when in the most challenging situations around noise or very soft female voices, and may not be the best candidate for hearing aids. Persons with audiograms similar to Figures 3-11 and 3-12 might well utilize hearing aids with only a minimum of power to pick up softer consonants that make speech clear.

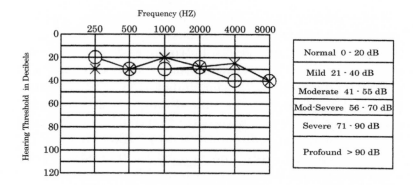

Figure 3-11: Mild hearing loss both ears all frequencies (flat mild loss).

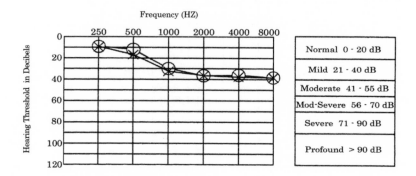

Figure 3-12: Mild mid-to-high frequency hearing loss both ears (with normal hearing in lows).

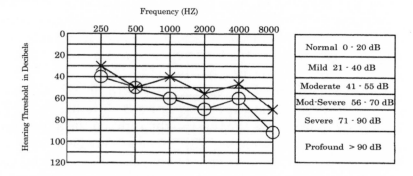

Figure 3-13: Normal hearing low and mid frequencies with a mild loss in the high frequencies.

If your audiogram closely resembles Figures 3-14, 3-15 or 3-16, you have a moderate hearing loss at some of the tested frequencies. However, depending on where your loss occurs in the frequency range, you will experience a different set of problems. Naturally, the further away you are from the conversation you are trying to hear, the more difficult it will be for anyone to understand.

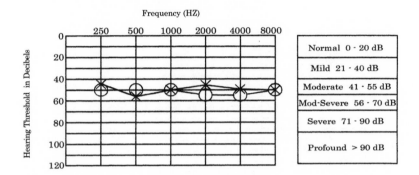

Figure 3-14: Moderate hearing loss in all frequencies (moderate flat loss) both ears.

Figure 3-14 indicates that with about equal loss across all tested frequencies, understanding almost all speech at five feet in a quiet room could prove challenging. For example, if your spouse was reading behind a newspaper, yet only five feet away, you will not have the advantage of speech cues and would likely miss most of what would be said.

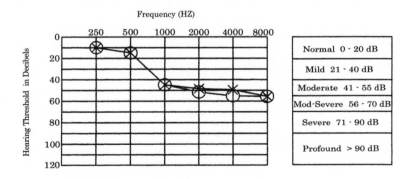

Figure 3-15: Moderate mid-to-high frequency hearing loss both ears with normal hearing in the lows.

On the other hand, if your loss is limited to only the high range (Figure 3-16), you are likely to do much better. As you have no doubt already noticed, noisy situations make hearing even more difficult. Many of these environmental intrusions you can control yourself, such as turning down the music or television. Hearing aids are especially helpful with these kinds of hearing losses since they greatly assist in bringing back the intelligibility of speech.

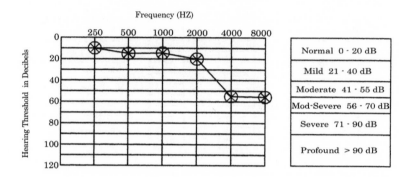

Figure 3-16: Normal hearing in low and mid frequencies, with a moderate loss in the high frequencies for both ears.

If your audiogram closely resembles Figure 3-17, you have a severe hearing loss across all frequencies. You already know that speech is not audible to you, and that hearing aids must be used in order to hear people and the sounds in your environment. The better your word discrimination ability under sound booth testing conditions *without hearing aids* the better your prognosis for benefit *with hearing aids*.

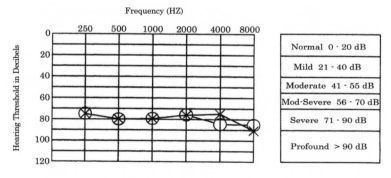

Figure 3-17: Severe hearing loss in all frequencies both ears.

If your audiogram resembles Figure 3-18, the configuration could reflect someone who spent a career around toxic levels of noise (compressors, hammers, drills, saws, etc.). You are hearing mostly vowels—lots of vocal energy with not much clarity. The intelligibility for speech (consonants) is at best very muffled. You are missing a considerable percentage of conversation and your use of hearing aids is both necessary and probably beneficial, especially if your word discrimination ability was tested and found to be good.

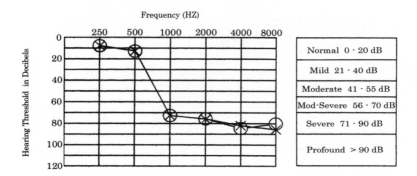

Figure 3-18: Severe mid-to-high frequency hearing loss both ears with normal low frequencies.

If your audiogram resembles Figure 3-19, your hearing levels are normal in the low and middle frequencies, but your high frequency hearing loss is severe. This audiogram includes threshold information at 3000 Hz, usually tested when the shift between 2000 and 4000 is so significant. This allows for a more accurate picture of the audiogram, and your potential hearing challenges. In this case, higher frequency consonants will be very difficult to hear (such as /f/, /k/, /s/ or /th/) and in the presence of some background noise, may even be wiped out. This type of audiogram has been seen in people who have done extensive firearms training without hearing protection for years, usually with the same or similar caliber weapon. Hearing aids can provide emphasis to the high frequencies and fill in much of what you are missing.

If your audiogram resembles Figure 3-20, you are already aware that you experience a profound loss in all frequencies. Powerful hearing aids are probably something you've been wearing for some time in order to receive as much auditory information as possible from speech and environmental sounds. If you are new to hearing aids with this kind of loss, you might consider exploring other options, such as a cochlear implant or an expanded system of assistive devices. Implants are increasingly viable options for many patients, but candidacy criteria must be discussed with your physician and hearing care professional. Assistive devices are helpful to all persons with hearing loss, and the more severe the loss, the more helpful the devices.

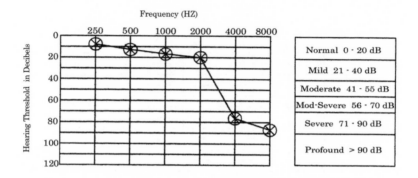

Figure 3-19: Normal hearing in mid and low frequencies with a severe hearing loss in the high frequencies both ears.

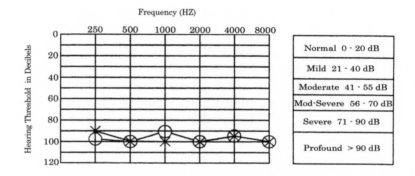

Figure 3-20: Profound hearing loss in all frequencies both ears.

## Audiograms May Not Be The Whole Story

We have spent considerable time reviewing how hearing levels are objectively measured and recorded. One final point must be mentioned: an audiogram does not always predict how you experience life. Two people can have identical audiograms but have very different reactions to the stresses and problems hearing loss causes. One person with mild to moderate hearing loss may experience a great deal of difficulty, while another person with the same hearing loss (or worse) may have fewer challenges.

Why would this be?

It seems to boil down to our individuality—the uniqueness that identifies each of us for who we are: our personality type, our perception of ourselves, our view of the world, and even our desire or motivation to communicate. A housebound reclusive person may be less likely to pursue hearing aids than an extroverted individual who continually engages with people to experience the joys of life. The truth is that some of us do not care to hear. Others are driven to solve their hearing problem.

Your hearing care professional would not assume that by knowing your audiogram, he or she also knows your listening challenges. Let your practitioner know your hearing needs and expectations so you can receive the maximum benefit with the technology now available to you. Help fill in the information that the audiogram cannot.

# CHAPTER FOUR
# Hearing Aids Positively Improve Your Quality of Life
*Sergei Kochkin, Ph.D.*

---

Dr. Kochkin is a Director of Market Development & Market Research at Knowles Electronics and past member of the Board of Directors of the Better Hearing Institute in Washington, D.C. He has published more than 50 papers on the hearing aid market and conducted customer satisfaction research on more than 25,000 hearing aid owners. He holds a Doctorate in psychology, an MBA in marketing, a Masters of Science in counseling and guidance and a BA in physical anthropology and archeology. Dr. Kochkin also maintains an interest in ancient cultures, comparative religion and meditation.

---

The number one reason why people purchase their first hearing aids is they recognize their hearing has worsened. The second reason is pressure from family members who are negatively impacted by the individual's hearing loss. As you know by now, hearing loss occurs gradually. By the time you recognize a need for hearing aids, your quality of life may have deteriorated unnecessarily. The average first-time hearing aid wearer is close to 70 years of age, despite the fact that the majority (65 percent) of people with hearing loss are below the age of 65; and nearly half of all people with hearing loss are below the age of 55.

For the vast majority of individuals who have decided to wait to purchase hearing aids *(78 percent of all people who admit to hearing loss),* I suspect that while they may be aware their hearing loss has deteriorated, they delay hearing aid purchases under the excuses: *"my hearing loss is not bad enough yet; I can get by without them; my hearing loss is mild."* A large number of people wait 15 years or more from the point when they first recognize they have a hearing loss to when they purchase their first hearing aids. This is a tragedy since they might not be aware of the impact this delayed decision has had on their life and the lives of their family, friends and associates.

The literature presents a compelling story for the social, psychological, cognitive and health effects of hearing loss. Impaired hearing results in distorted or incomplete communication leading to greater isolation and withdrawal and therefore lower sensory input.

In turn, the individual's life space and social life becomes restricted. One would logically think that a constricted life would negatively impact the psychosocial well-being of people with hearing loss.

Dr. Carmen presented a number of emotional issues in Chapter One surrounding hearing loss. Here's a quick review, with some additional ones. The literature indicates that hearing loss is associated with: embarrassment, fatigue, irritability, tension and stress, anger, avoidance of social activities, withdrawal from social situations, depression, negativism, danger to personal safety, rejection by others, reduced general health, loneliness, social isolation, less alertness to the environment, impaired memory, less adaptability to learning new tasks, paranoia, reduced coping skills, and reduced overall psychological health. For those who are still in the work force, uncorrected hearing loss must have a negative impact on overall job effectiveness, promotion and perhaps lifelong earning power. We think few would disagree that uncorrected hearing loss per se is a serious issue.

## Prior Experimental Evidence that Hearing Aids Improve Quality of Life

An effective human being is an effective communicator; optimized hearing is critical to effective communication. Modern hearing aids improve speech intelligibility and therefore communication. The benefits of hearing aids *(audiologically defined as improved speech intelligibility)* have been demonstrated in rigorous scientific research.[1] It would seem that if one could improve speech intelligibility by correcting for impaired hearing, that one should observe improvements in the social, emotional, psychological and physical functioning of the person with the hearing loss. To my knowledge there have only been a few studies to date comparing hearing aid owners and non-owners with known hearing loss. The majority of studies had small sample sizes and in general tended to confine themselves to U.S. male veterans. Let me first share these results with you before describing the exciting findings of a very large U.S. study I conducted in collaboration with the National Council on Aging in 1999 (with publication in January 2000).[2]

Harless and McConnell[3] demonstrated that 68 hearing aid wearers had significantly higher self-concepts compared to a matched group of individuals who did not wear hearing aids. Dye and Peak[4] studied 58 male veterans pre- and post-hearing aid fitting and found significant improvement on memory tests. In the most rigorous controlled study to date, Mulrow, Aguilar and Endicott[5] studied 122 male veterans and 72 patients from primary care clinics. Half were randomly chosen and fitted with hearing aids while the other half were not. After four months compared to the control group, the researchers found significant improvements in the hearing aid wearers on emotional and social effects of hearing handicap, perceived communication difficulties, cognitive functioning, and depression.

In addition, the same researchers in a follow-up study[6] published in 1992 demonstrated that the quality of life changes were sustainable over at least a year. Bridges and Bentler[7] determined in a study of 251 subjects comprised of normal hearing elderly individuals with hearing aids, and individuals with unaided hearing loss, that hearing aid wearers had less depression and higher quality of life scores compared to their unaided counterparts.

Finally, in a pre-post study *(that is the person was studied before and after a hearing aid fitting)* with 20 subjects, Crandall[8] demonstrated after three months of hearing aid use that functional health status improved significantly for hearing aid wearers.

## Research on the Positive Impact of Hearing Aids on Quality of Life

I would now like to share with you the results of the largest study in the world conducted on the impact of hearing aids on quality of life. After reading this, I hope you agree that hearing aids when successfully fit to your unique audiological needs, have the potential to literally transform your life.

Utilizing the famous National Family Opinion Panel (NFO) in 1997, I mailed a short screening survey to 80,000 panel members to find a representative sample of people with hearing loss in the United States. This short survey helped identify nearly 15,000 people with self-admitted hearing loss. The response rate to the screening survey was 65 percent. Since 1989, I have conducted research in this manner on more than 25,000 people with hearing loss and published these findings under the generic name "MarkeTrak." Working with the National Council on Aging, a sample of 3,000 individuals with hearing loss ages 50 and over were randomly drawn from the MarkeTrak hearing loss panel. Equal samples of 1,500 hearing aid owners and non-owners were drawn from the panel. What is unique about this study is that people with hearing loss as well as their significant other (usually the spouse) were studied.

Extensive questionnaires were sent to both the person with the hearing loss and the spouse or family member. The number of questions was 300 and 150 respectively. The comprehensive survey covered a myriad of topics including: self and family assessment of hearing loss, psychological well-being, social impact of hearing loss, quality of relationships, life satisfaction, general health, self and family perceptions of benefit of hearing aids *(wearers only)*, reasons for purchasing hearing aids *(wearers only)*, reasons for not purchasing hearing aids *(non-wearers only)*, and attitudes toward hearing health and hearing aids. In addition, a number of personality scales, which were deemed relevant to this study, were included in the survey.

After analyzing the returned surveys for usability (e.g. minimal missing information, hearing aid owners who wear their hearing instruments) the final sample sizes for respondents with hearing loss and family members were reduced to 2,069 and 1,710 respectively. Thus, this study involved nearly 4,000 people.

It was my goal to determine if hearing aids had an impact on hearing loss independent of the degree of hearing loss. In other words, do people with mild hearing loss derive as much benefit as individuals with more serious hearing losses? As part of the research design, in addition to quality of life items, a paper and pencil assessment of hearing loss was administered with the anticipation that the results of this assessment would be used to control for hearing loss when comparing the quality of life of hearing aid wearers and non-wearers.

The key hearing assessment tool used was the *Five Minute Hearing Test* (FMHT) by the American Academy of Otolaryngology-Head and Neck Surgery. The FMHT is a fifteen-question test measuring self-perceived hearing difficulty in a number of listening situations (e.g. telephone, multiple speakers, television, noisy situations, reverberant rooms) as well as self-assessments of some signs of hearing loss (e.g. people mumble, inappropriate responses, strain to hear, avoid social situations). Previous research has determined that the FMHT is significantly correlated with objective audiological hearing loss measures.

Based on hearing difficulty scores, all subjects in this study were grouped into five equal size groups (20 percent each—called quintiles). These ranged from quintile 1 (the 20 percent of respondents with the mildest hearing loss as measured by the FMHT) to quintile 5 (the 20 percent with the greatest hearing loss). The quintile system was utilized for all analysis as a means of controlling for differences in hearing loss between the hearing aid wearer and non-wearer samples. The use of these quintiles allowed us to achieve more valid comparisons between samples of hearing aid wearers and non-wearers.

If we were to simply compare responses of all hearing aid wearers with those of all non-wearers, without regard to degree of hearing loss, the findings would have been misleading, and even erroneous. For example, it is widely known that incidence and degree of depression have been found to increase with severity of hearing loss. Thus, even if people with severe hearing loss experience reduced depression after getting hearing aids, they might still report more depression than non-wearers overall, since hearing aid wearers tend to have more severe hearing loss. However, when hearing aid wearers are matched with non-wearers in the same quintile (non-wearers having a fairly similar degree of hearing loss), the differences between them better reflect the potential impact of the hearing aids rather than the effect of their degree of hearing loss.

While we have no audiological basis for labeling hearing loss associated with each quintile group, we did find an excellent correlation between self-perceived loss (e.g. mild to profound hearing loss) and the FMHT test. As we discuss the findings of this study with respect to the five hearing loss groups, it's appropriate to consider people in quintile hearing loss groups 1, 3 and 5 as having respectively a "mild," "moderate," and "severe /profound" hearing loss; group 2 is between mild and moderate hearing loss while group 4 should be viewed as between moderate and severe hearing loss.

## Research Findings

We will now systematically evaluate the impact that hearing aids have on quality of life. This will be done by comparing the responses of hearing aid wearers and non-wearers while controlling for hearing loss. As you evaluate the impressive findings below keep in mind the following:

- the devastating impact of hearing loss on quality of life is well-documented;
- quality of life is primarily impacted by the fact that uncorrected hearing loss results in reduced speech intelligibility;
- hearing aids when fitted correctly improve speech intelligibility and therefore can restore your ability to function more effectively in life.

## Demographics and Household Income

It should be recognized that in most respects the five hearing loss groups were well matched on key demographics: gender, marital status, employment status, and age. A striking trend was discovered when evaluating household income by level of hearing loss. Income is significantly related to both hearing loss and hearing aid usage. Figure 4-1 shows there was close to an $8,000 difference between those with mild hearing loss (quintile 1) and those with profound hearing loss (quintile 5). Note that income drops significantly only for severe to profound hearing loss groups (4 and 5—the top 40 percent of individuals with hearing loss).

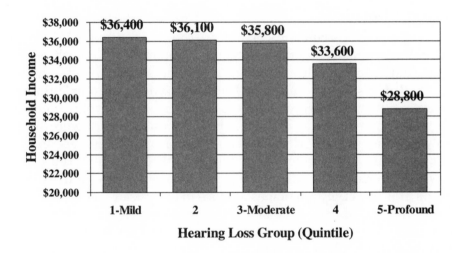

Figure 4-1: Household income is related to severity of hearing loss.

Compared to non-wearers, there was a $13,000 a year difference between the mild and profound hearing loss groups. The differential for hearing aid wearers was much less severe ($7,000). Hearing aids appeared to have a positive impact on household income, but only for individuals whose hearing loss was in the higher 60 percent (moderate-profound). People with a moderate to profound hearing loss, who did not use hearing aids, on average, experienced household incomes $5000-$6000 less than their counterparts who did use hearing aids. This is despite the fact that the higher hearing loss non-wearer groups tended to be employed slightly more often.

Hearing aid wearers also reported that they have plenty of discretionary income more often than non-wearers. For example, 22 percent of group 5 (profound hearing loss) hearing aid wearers reported they had plenty of discretionary income compared to only 8 percent of non-wearers. The discretionary income differential for samples with more severe hearing loss was a likely cause of the lower earning power. Because of higher hearing disability levels, communication is probably impacted, resulting in lower income and therefore less earning power. Finding a solution to their hearing loss is exacerbated for these groups, in that lower earning power means that the respondent was less likely to be able to afford a hearing aid to correct the hearing loss.

## Activity Level

We asked respondents to indicate the extent (times per month) to which they engaged in thirteen activities in a typical month. Six of the activities were solitary in nature while seven involved other people. Total solitary and social activity scores were calculated. Hearing aid wearers were shown to have the same level of solitary activity as non-wearers. However, hearing aid wearers were more likely to engage in activities involving other people. They were shown to have significantly higher participation in three to four of the seven activities measured. Four out of five quintile hearing aid wearer groups indicated they participated more in organized social activities while three out of five of the hearing loss groups reported they were more likely to attend senior centers if they were hearing aid wearers. The most serious hearing loss group (quintile 5) reported greater participation in four out of the seven activities if they were hearing aid wearers.

## Interpersonal relations

The survey asked 12 questions concerning the respondents' quality of interpersonal relationships with their family using a four-point scale. Twelve questions concerned negativity (e.g. arguments, tenseness, criticism) in the relationship. We found that interpersonal warmth in relationships significantly declined as hearing loss worsened. Hearing aid wearers in quintiles 1-3 (mild to moderate) were shown to have significantly greater interpersonal warmth in their relationships than their non-wearer counterparts. Also, significant reductions in negativity in family relationships appeared to be associated with hearing aid usage in quintiles 1 and 2—the hearing loss groups with the mildest hearing disability.

## Social Effects

Forty-seven items in the survey assessed the social impact of hearing loss and hearing aid usage. The majority of the items were scored on a five-point scale taking the values "strongly agree" to "strongly disagree." We also assessed average monthly contact with family and friends by phone and in person.

The stigma of hearing loss was shown to increase as hearing loss increased. All five non-wearer groups reported they would be embarrassed or self-conscious if they wore hearing aids, while all five wearer groups reported lower stigmatization with hearing aids. We are not concluding, of course, that usage of hearing aids would lead to reduced stigma; most likely hearing aid wearers have resolved their concerns about the stigma associated with hearing aid usage more so than their non-wearer counterparts.

As hearing loss increased, respondents were more likely to overcompensate for hearing loss by pretending that they heard what people said, by avoiding telling people to repeat themselves, by avoiding asking other people to help them with their hearing problem, by engaging in compensatory activities such as speechreading, or by defensively talking too much to cover up the fact that they could not hear well.

All five hearing aid wearer groups reported significantly lower overcompensation scores. The greater the hearing loss, the greater was the likelihood that respondents reported they were the target of discrimination. The greater the hearing loss, the greater the likelihood that respondents with more serious hearing losses were accused of hearing only what they wanted to hear, found themselves the subject of conversation behind their backs, were told to "forget it" when frustrated family members were not heard the first time, and so on. All hearing loss groups except quintile 1 (the mildest hearing loss) reported significant reductions in discriminatory behaviors, if they were hearing aid wearers.

We found a strong relationship between hearing loss and family member concerns of safety (e.g. cannot hear warning signs, instructions from doctor, made a serious mistake, not safe to be alone) as well as significant differences between hearing aid wearers and non-wearers. Respondents also agreed that safety concerns increased as hearing loss increased.

The data however, indicated that safety concerns were significantly higher among hearing aid wearers than non-wearers in quintiles 1-3. Perhaps the realization that mistakes were being made or that unaided hearing loss could result in possible injury motivated the current hearing aid owner to purchase hearing aids. This explanation is consistent with the findings from previous MarkeTrak research, which indicated that the number one motivation to purchase hearing aids was "the realization that their hearing loss was getting worse."

There were a number of social effects that were correlated with hearing loss but were not impacted by hearing aid usage. These were negative effects on the family (e.g., "I find it exhausting to cope with their needs"), family accommodations to the individual with hearing loss (e.g., "I have to use signs and gestures a lot of the time"), rejection of the person with hearing loss (e.g., "They tend to get left out of social activities because of their hearing loss"), and withdrawal (e.g., "They tend to withdraw from social activities where communication is difficult"). In addition, hearing aid usage was not associated with increased phone or in-person contact with family or friends.

## The Emotional Effects

Eighty items in the survey dealt with the emotional aspects of hearing loss. All five hearing aid wearer groups scored significantly lower in their self-ratings of emotional instability. In agreement with their family members, they were less likely to be tense, insecure, unstable, nervous, discontent, temperamental, and less likely to display negative emotions or traits. Four of the five hearing aid wearer groups reported significantly reduced tendencies to exhibit anger (e.g., "I sometimes get angry when I think about my hearing") and frustration (e.g., "I get discouraged because of my hearing loss"). In agreement, family members observed significantly less anger and frustration in all five hearing aid wearer groups.

The average reduction in depression associated with hearing aid usage across all five groups was 36 percent. All five hearing aid wearer groups reported significantly *lower* depressive symptoms (e.g., tired, insomniac, thinking of death) while four of the five hearing aid wearer groups (quintiles 1-4) reported a significantly lower incidence of depression within the last 12 months compared to their non-wearer counterparts.

Hearing aid wearers in quintiles 2-4 reported significantly

70

lower paranoid feelings (e.g., "I am often blamed for things that are just not my fault"). Not surprisingly, in agreement with family members, all five non-wearer groups scored higher on denial when compared to hearing aid wearers (e.g., "I don't think my hearing loss is as bad as people have told me").

Family members and respondents were asked to indicate if the person with the hearing loss exhibited anxiety, tenseness or if they worried for a continuous period of four weeks in the previous year. In addition, they were asked to indicate if they experienced anxiety symptoms (e.g., keyed up or on edge, heart pounding or racing, easily tired, trouble falling asleep). Three of the five non-wearer groups (1, 3, 5) exhibited higher anxiety symptoms. In addition, three of the five non-wearer groups (1, 2, 5) exhibited more social phobias than non-wearers of hearing aids. Clearly, the reduction in phobia and anxiety associated with hearing aid usage is more pronounced in individuals with serious to profound hearing losses (Quintile 5).

Factors *not* appreciably impacted by hearing aid usage in this study were: sense of independence (e.g., burden on family, answering for the person with hearing loss) and overall satisfaction with life. Although not as conclusive as some of the previous factors, non-wearers reported that they were more self-critical (e.g., "I dwell on my mistakes more than I should") and had lower self-esteem (e.g., "All in all, I'm inclined to feel that I am a failure"). Hearing loss was found to be highly correlated with self-criticism. There is also some evidence, though not as strong as other correlates of hearing aid use, that non-wearers were more critical of themselves (Quintiles 1, 3, 5).

## Personality Assessment

Seventy-nine items were devoted to miscellaneous personality scales in addition to the personality measures under emotional and social effects. All of the personality scales used in this study are published scales. Family members indicated that the respondents' cognitive/mental state (e.g., they appear confused, disoriented or unable to concentrate) was affected by their hearing loss, primarily if the hearing loss was "severe" to "profound" (groups 4 and 5). In this study, impressive improvements in family perceptions of the persons' mental and intellectual state were observed if the individual had a severe to profound hearing loss (groups 4 and 5 only). Non-wearers were more likely to be viewed as being confused, disoriented, non-caring, arrogant, inattentive, and virtually "living in a world of their own."

Previously we indicated that there were no significant differences in measures of "withdrawal" between aided and unaided subjects. This finding is contrary to the literature. However, family members did report that non-wearers in three of five groups (1,4, 5) were more introverted as evidenced by greater likelihood of being private, passive, shy, quiet, easily embarrassed, etc. Moderate to severe hearing loss non-wearers (quintiles 3-5) were shown to score higher on a personality variable called "external locus of control." This means they were more likely to believe that events external to them control their lives. In other words, they felt less in control of their own lives. On the other hand, hearing aid wearers felt they were more in control of their lives and less a victim of fate.

## Health Impact

The survey asked six generic questions on self-perceptions of health, prevalence of pain and the extent to which the respondent believed that hearing loss impacted their general health. In addition, from a list of 28 health problems, respondents indicated whether they experienced that health problem and the extent to which the problem interfered with their activities.

Overall assessment of health (including absence of pain) appeared to decline as a function of hearing loss with further deterioration of health associated with non-usage of hearing aids for the three most serious hearing loss groups (quintiles 3-5). Three of the five hearing aid wearer groups (quintiles 1, 3, 5) reported significantly better health compared to their non-wearer counterparts. The lowest self-rating of overall health was the non-wearer group in quintile 5 (profound hearing loss). Nonetheless, our research determined there was no consistent evidence that hearing aid usage is associated with reductions in arthritis, high blood pressure, heart problems or other serious disease states.

## Perceived Benefit of Hearing Aids

As a validation check on our comparisons of hearing aid wearers and non-wearers, both respondents and their family members were asked to rate changes they observed in 16 areas of their life that they believed were due to the respondent using hearing aids. Total findings are shown in Figure 4-2. In general, for nearly all quality of life areas assessed, the observed improvements were positively related to degree of hearing loss. Family members in nearly every comparison observed greater improvements in the respondent.

The top three areas of observed improvement for both respondents and family members were *relationships at home, feelings about self* and *life overall.* The most impressive improvements were observed in quintile 5 (profound hearing loss) in that 11 of 16 lifestyle areas were rated as improved by at least 50 percent of the respondents or family members.

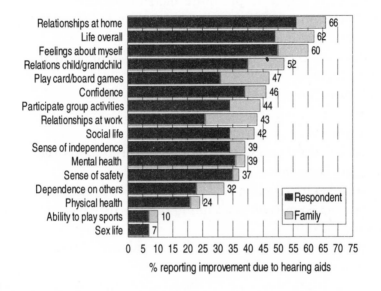

Figure 4-2: Percent of hearing aid owners and their family members reporting improvement in their quality of life in 16 areas due to hearing aids. In nearly all cases, family members report improvements due to hearing aids than hearing instrument wearers.

## Conclusions and Discussion

The results for this study are impressive. Hearing aids clearly are associated with impressive improvements in the social, emotional, psychological, and physical well-being of people with hearing loss in all hearing loss categories from mild to severe. As such, these findings clearly provide strong evidence for the *value of hearing aids* in improving the quality of life in people with hearing loss. Specifically, hearing aid usage is positively related to the following quality of life issues:

- greater earning power (especially the more severe hearing losses)
- improved interpersonal relationships (especially for mild-moderate losses) including greater intimacy and lessening of negative dysfunctional communication
- reduction in discrimination toward the person with the hearing loss
- reduction in difficulty associated with communication (primarily severe to profound hearing losses)
- reduction in hearing loss compensation behaviors
- reduction in anger and frustration
- reduction in the incidence of depression and depressive symptoms
- enhanced emotional stability
- reduction in paranoid feelings
- reduced anxiety symptoms
- reduced social phobias (primarily severely impaired subjects)
- improved sense of control in your life
- reduced self-criticism
- improved cognitive functioning (primarily severe to profound hearing loss)
- improved health status and less incidence of pain
- enhanced group social activity

In this study, both respondents and their family members were asked to independently rate the extent to which they believed their life was specifically improved due to hearing aids. All hearing loss groups from mild to profound reported significant improvements in nearly every area measured:

- relationships at home and with family
- feelings about self
- life overall
- mental health
- social life
- emotional health
- physical health

Short of stating definite causality, the evidence is quite compelling and perhaps suggestive of causality for the following reasons:

1. The sample, the largest of its kind, is nationally representative of hearing loss subjects ages 50 and over. Thus, we need not be concerned with spurious findings due to sampling methodology.
2. Many of the findings held up across all hearing loss quintiles from mild to profound.
3. The specific findings were corroborated within the study. That is, we noted significant differences between wearers and non-wearers. Also, at the end of the survey we asked respondents and their family members to specifically indicate if their life was improved as a result of wearing hearing aids in 16 quality of life areas. Both respondents and their family members indicated significant benefit due to hearing aids in most areas measured.
4. The differential efficacy between the 16 quality of life parameters noted by respondents and their family members (from a low of 4 percent to high of 74 percent improvements) indicates that a positive halo or acquiescence did not exist in this sample of respondents.
5. The survey findings are correlated well with other studies, especially the randomized control studies and pre-post hearing aid fitting studies among smaller, more narrowly defined samples.
6. The findings are consistent with the literature on factors impacting hearing loss; that is, the theoretical improvements that should occur if hearing loss is alleviated.
7. The findings are consistent with the observations of clinicians and dispensers of hearing aids.

## A Call to Action

Dr. Firman of the National Council On Aging stated in his speech to the media in the summer of 1999, "This study debunks the myth that untreated hearing loss...is a harmless condition."[9]

In focus groups conducted with physicians, the prevalent view is that hearing loss is "only" a quality of life issue. I would agree if one defined quality of life as "greater enjoyment of music." But the literature and this study clearly demonstrate that hearing loss is associated with physical, emotional, mental, and social well-being. Depression, anxiety, emotional instability, phobias, withdrawal, isolation, lessened health status, lower self-esteem, and so forth, are not "just quality of life issues." For some people, uncorrected hearing loss is a "life and death issue."

I believe that this study challenges every segment of society to comprehend the devastating impact of hearing loss on individuals and their families as well as the positive possibilities associated with hearing aid usage. We need to help physicians recognize hearing loss for the important health issue that it is. We need to help those with hearing loss who are currently in denial about their impairment, to understand the impact their hearing has on their life as well as that of their loved ones. We need to assure that hearing aids are recognized in society not just for their treatment of hearing loss, but also as a potential contributing factor to the successful resolution of other medical, emotional, social and psychological conditions.

I believe this study also demonstrates for the first time that individuals with even a mild hearing loss can experience dramatic improvements in their quality of life. This finding is significant because I believe the challenge is to demonstrate to "baby-boomers" (1946+) with emerging hearing losses that hearing aids offer something to them of value early on in their lives, and that they do not need to wait until retirement to receive the benefits of enhanced hearing.

So if you are one of those people with a mild, moderate or severe hearing loss, who is sitting on the fence, consider all the benefits of hearing aids described above. I challenge you to name another product that holds such great potential to positively change so many lives.

**Editor's Note:** The full research project this chapter is based on including detailed references, charts and figures are available at www.hearingreview.com.

# References

1. Larson V.D., et. al. (17 other authors). Efficacy of Three Commonly Used Hearing Aid Circuits, JAMA 284(14):1806-1813, 2000.
2. Kochkin S and Rogin C. Quantifying the obvious: the impact of hearing aids on quality of life. The Hearing Review 7(1): 8-34, 2000.
3. Harless E and McConnell F. Effects of hearing aid use on self-concept in older persons. Journal of Speech and Hearing Disorders 47:305-309, 1982.

4. Dye C and Peak M. Influence on amplification on the psychological functioning of older adults with neurosensory hearing loss. <u>Journal of the Academy of Rehabilitation Audiology</u> 16:210-220,1983.

5. Mulrow C, Aguilar C, Endicott J, et al. Quality of life changes and hearing impairment. <u>Annals of Internal Medicine</u> 113(3):188-194, 1990.

6. Mulrow C, Tuley M and Aguilar C. Sustained benefits of hearing aids. <u>Journal of Speech and Hearing Research</u> 35:1402-1405,1992.

7. Bridges J and Bentler R. Relating hearing aid use to well-being among older adults. <u>The Hearing Journal</u> 51(7):39-44,1998.

8. Crandell C. Hearing aids: their effects on functional health status. <u>The Hearing Journal</u> 51(2):2-6,1998.

9. Firman J. Speech to the media on May 26, 1999 based on NCOA study National Council on the Aging (NCOA). The Impact of Untreated Hearing Loss in Older Americans. Conducted by the Seniors Research Group. Supported through a grant from the Hearing Industries Association. Preliminary report, December 28, 1998. Actual press release can be seen at www.ncoa.org.

# CHAPTER FIVE
## The Leap
## From Hearing Loss to Hearing Aids
### *Barbara E. Weinstein, Ph.D.*

---

Dr. Weinstein is a Professor of Audiology at Lehman College, City University of New York (CUNY), and is a member of the doctoral faculty at the Graduate School and University Center, CUNY. She is a Fellow of the American Speech-Language-Hearing Association, and is the recipient of the 1996 Distinguished Clinical Achievement Award from the New York State Speech-Language-Hearing Association. Dr. Weinstein is the author of a text titled: *Geriatric Audiology* and has edited several books on hearing loss in the elderly. She is the co-author of the Hearing Handicap Inventory for Adults and the Elderly and has authored over 50 manuscripts on hearing loss and hearing aids in adults.

---

Responses to questionnaires that assess activity limitations and participation levels are quite important as they assist the hearing care professional in understanding the functional effects of a chronic condition such as hearing impairment. Answers to items comprising the Hearing Handicap Inventory (HHI) can help you and your hearing care provider better understand how hearing impairment interferes with a range of activities considered integral in your daily life.

As is apparent from the items shown in Tables 5-I and 5-II, responses to the questionnaires reveal perceptions of auditory and non-auditory difficulties (e.g. such as embarrassment, frustration) resulting from diminished auditory capacity. To reiterate, these self-report questionnaires provide information from your perspective about problems associated with hearing impairment. Once your hearing professional has a feel for the social and emotional consequences of your hearing loss and the impact of these changes on your independence and quality of life, it can be determined if you are a candidate for hearing aids or if you are obtaining adequate benefit from hearing aids.

## Hearing Handicap Inventories

The 10-item screening (symbolized by "-S") versions of the Hearing Handicap Inventory for Adults (HHIA-S) or for the Elderly

(HHIE-S) have gained widespread acceptance among physicians, nurses, nurse practitioners, and audiologists. The HHIE-S (Table 5-I) was standardized on adults over 65 years of age and is hence more appropriate for them. The HHIA-S, shown in Table 5-III is primarily for individuals under 65 years of age. With the exception of three items, the emotions and situations sampled are identical. The HHIE-SP/HHIA-SP (Table 5-II), where SP is short for spouse, is a companion version that enables the hearing care practitioner to elicit responses from a spouse regarding the effects of hearing loss. Evident from the items comprising the questionnaires, responses can pinpoint the social and emotional consequences of your hearing impairment as perceived by you and a significant other.

Each of the questionnaires can be completed at home using paper and pencil, by computer-assisted presentation with links to audiologists in all 50 states (www.phd.msu.edu/hearing), or by face-to-face administration with a professional asking the questions. Each form of administration has its advantages and disadvantages, but the bottom line is what is most convenient for the person with hearing impairment. Each of the scales consists of two types of questions, namely social (S) and emotional (E). The five social questions attempt to isolate the self-perceived difficulties in a given situation whereas the five emotional questions assess anxiety, frustration, and overall sense of handicap that is attributed to hearing loss.

You merely check or answer "Yes" if you experience difficulty in the situation described; "Sometimes" if you experience occasional difficulty in the given situation; or "No" if you rarely or never experience the problem. A score of "4" is awarded each Yes response, a score of "2" each Sometimes response, and a score of "0" for each No response. Points for each of the 10 items are added up and total scores can range from 0 to 40. The higher the number, the greater is the problem of hearing loss. A score of 0-10 indicates that the hearing impairment is not interfering with your daily life. The average score for new hearing aid wearers on the screening versions of the HHIE is about 18.

A score of 10 or greater signifies the necessity for referral to a hearing healthcare professional. More specifically, scores of 0-8 signify *no handicap;* scores of 10-22 signify *a mild to moderate handicap*; and scores of 24-40 suggest significant *self-perceived handicap.*

Table 5-I: Hearing Handicap Inventory for the Elderly
—Screening [HHIE-S]

**INSTRUCTIONS:** The purpose of this questionnaire is to identify the problems your hearing loss may be causing you. Answer YES, SOMETIMES, or NO for each question. To obtain a total score, add up the "yes" (4 points each), "sometimes" (2 points each), and "no" (0 points) responses. If your score is greater than 10, a hearing test is recommended.

| Yes | Sometimes | No |
|-----|-----------|-----|
| 4 | 2 | 0 |

E1 Does a hearing problem cause you to feel embarrassed when you meet new people?

E2 Does a hearing problem cause you to feel frustrated when talking to members of your family?

S1 Do you have difficulty hearing when someone speaks in a whisper?

E3 Do you feel handicapped by a hearing problem?

S2 Does a hearing problem cause you difficulty when visiting friends, relatives or neighbors?

S3 Does a hearing problem cause you to attend religious services less often than you would like?

E4 Does a hearing problem cause you to have arguments with family members?

S4 Does a hearing problem cause you difficulty when listening to TV or radio?

E5 Do you feel that any difficulty with your hearing limits or hampers your personal or social life?

S5 Does a hearing problem cause you difficulty when in a restaurant with relatives or friends?

Table 5-II: Hearing Handicap Inventory for the Elderly
—Screening [HHIE-SP]

**INSTRUCTIONS:** The purpose of this questionnaire is to identify the problems the hearing loss may be causing your spouse. Answer YES, SOMETIMES, or NO for each question. To obtain a total score, add up the "yes" (4 points each), "sometimes" (2 points each), and "no" (0 points) responses. If your score is greater than 10, a hearing test is recommended. SP=spouse.

| Yes | Sometimes | No |
|-----|-----------|-----|
| 4 | 2 | 0 |

E1 Does a hearing problem cause your SP to feel embarrassed when meeting new people?

E2 Does a hearing problem cause your SP to feel frustrated when talking to members of your family?

S1 Does your SP have difficulty hearing when someone speaks in a whisper?

E3 Does your SP feel handicapped by a hearing problem?

S2 Does a hearing problem cause your SP difficulty when visiting friends, relatives or neighbors?

S3 Does a hearing problem cause your SP to attend religious services less often than you would like?

E4 Does a hearing problem cause your SP to have arguments with family members?

S4 Does a hearing problem cause your SP difficulty when listening to TV or radio?

E5 Do you feel that any difficulty with hearing limits or hampers your SP's personal or social life?

S5 Does a hearing problem cause your SP difficulty when in a restaurant with relatives or friends?

Table 5-III: Hearing Handicap Inventory for Adult
—Screening [HHIA-S]

**INSTRUCTIONS:** The purpose of this questionnaire is to identify the problems your hearing loss may be causing you. Answer YES, SOMETIMES, or NO for each question. To obtain a total score, add up the "yes" (4 points each), "sometimes" (2 points each), and "no" (0 points) responses. If your score is greater than 10, a hearing test is recommended.

| Yes | Sometimes | No |
|-----|-----------|-----|
| 4 | 2 | 0 |

E1 Does a hearing problem cause you to feel embarrassed when you meet new people?

E2 Does a hearing problem cause you to feel frustrated when talking to members of your family?

S1 Do you have difficulty hearing/understanding co-workers, clients, customers?

E3 Do you feel handicapped by a hearing problem?

S2 Does a hearing problem cause you difficulty when visiting friends, relatives or neighbors?

S3 Does a hearing problem cause you difficulty in the movies or in the theater?

E4 Does a hearing problem cause you to have arguments with family members?

S4 Does a hearing problem cause you difficulty when listening to TV or radio?

E5 Do you feel that any difficulty with your hearing limits or hampers your personal or social life?

S5 Does a hearing problem cause you difficulty when in a restaurant with relatives or friends?

# Candidacy for Hearing Aids

We now know that your desire to purchase hearing aids is directly linked to a number of personal factors. These include:

1. your score obtained on the HHIE-S, HHIA-S, HHIE-SP;
2. your readiness for change;
3. and your motivational level

Bess[1] and his colleagues from Tennessee found that the extent of self-perceived hearing handicap on the 10-item screening version of the HHIE-S is predictive of hearing aid candidacy, in that it reliably distinguishes between people who ultimately purchase hearing aids and those who don't. Irrespective of the severity of hearing loss for pure tone signals (e.g. mild or moderate sensorineural hearing loss), persons in their study who actually purchased hearing aids were more handicapped as evidenced by higher scores on the HHIE-S, than those who did not.

Thus, the investigators concluded that when people perceive that a given hearing loss for pure tone signals is interfering with participation in and enjoyment of various activities, they are motivated to purchase hearing aids to reduce some of their communication difficulties.

Similarly, a study reported by Kochkin,[2] who sampled many hearing aid owners and non-owners across the country (presented in the previous chapter), revealed that an individual's total score on one of the hearing handicap inventories (HHI) statistically predicted ownership of hearing aids. For example, 5.7 percent of survey respondents who scored a "0" on the HHI owned a hearing aid whereas 49 percent of those with a score of "28" owned hearing aids. In general, this study revealed that the average score on the HHI of non-hearing aid owners was 13.7 out of a total score of 40, compared to 20.8 percent for hearing aid owners.

Interestingly, purchase of completely-in-the-canal (CIC) hearing aids is highly correlated to scores on the HHI as well. These studies demonstrate that self-perceived handicap, identified using a simple and easy screening tool, is linked to the decision on the part of individuals with hearing loss to purchase hearing aids. I encourage you to screen for the self-perceived effects of your loss using your hearing using one of the questionnaires included as Table 5-I or 5-II. If your total score adds up to 10 or more, you should schedule a hearing test and learn about the options available so that you don't have to miss out on hearing.

Clinically, I find that the sooner people come in for a hearing test, the more receptive they are to purchasing devices which may help overcome situation-specific difficulties such as understanding people on television or speech in large listening areas. Positive experiences with hearing assistive technologies, such as devices used with television or in theatres, often serve as an impetus to trying hearing aids.

## The Impact of Hearing Loss

I would like to further elucidate on Dr. Kochkin's previous chapter with respect to how hearing loss can impact your quality of life with respect to benefiting from self-assessment questionnaires. As you know by now, hearing loss restricts one or more dimensions in the quality of life including communication function, mental status, emotional and social function. Specifically, hearing impairment has been shown to:

- negatively impact on communicative behavior
- alter psychosocial behavior
- strain relations with friends or family members
- limit the enjoyment of daily activities
- jeopardize physical well-being
- interfere with the ability to live independently and safely
- potentially interfere with long distance contacts on the telephone
- compromise efficiency at work
- interfere with one's ability to work with co-workers, and clients
- interfere with medical diagnosis, treatment and management
- interfere with compliance with pharmacological regimens
- and interfere with therapeutic interventions across all disciplines including social work, speech-language therapy, physical or occupational therapy.

An interesting aspect of hearing impairment that afflicts adults is the large variability in response to a given hearing loss. That is to say, as stated elsewhere in this book, two individuals with the same amount of hearing loss can react very differently and can experience different behavioral consequences. Accordingly, more and more clinicians include as part of a complete hearing assessment, questions about how a given hearing loss impacts on communication, social and emotional function. The advent of digital signal processing and dual (directional) microphone technology, has revolutionized hearing aids to allow for enhanced listening comfort and optimal speech understanding in noise, and other difficult listening situations.

Data from a large scale study completed by the National Council on Aging[3] revealed objective evidence that hearing aids enable you to experience the personal stability and emotional fulfillment associated with interpersonal contacts and participation in everyday activities. Further, using change in responses to the HHI, clinicians have been able to document that hearing aids do in fact improve function in various social and emotional situations. We now know that the more hours per day one wears hearing aids, the greater the reduction in scores on the HHI—that is, the greater the improvement in social and emotional function.

## Maximizing Benefit from Questionnaires

In 1996[4] and again in 2000,[5] I did a comprehensive review of studies on hearing aid benefit and satisfaction. It showed that hearing aids, either alone or in combination with three to six weeks of counseling-oriented audiological rehabilitation, do effectively reduce or minimize the disabilities and handicaps perceived by persons with adult onset sensorineural hearing loss. Further, they are a cost effective intervention for handicapping hearing loss and declining health associated with hearing loss.

More specifically, in approximately four to five studies conducted across the country in a number of different settings including private practices, hospital clinics, and veterans administration centers, 70 to 80 percent of new hearing aid wearers experienced very dramatic reductions in the amount of their self-perceived hearing handicap. That is to say, for example, hearing impairments which were initially judged to be moderately to severely handicapping (60 percent on the HHI) improved to the point that new hearing aid wearers considered their hearing loss to be slightly or mildly handicapping (20 percent on the HHI) after only three weeks of hearing aid use.

When these new hearing aid wearers were recalled to the hearing clinics to ascertain how they were functioning with their hearing aids, in many of the studies, they derived significant benefit such that they perceived the hearing loss to be less handicapping socially and emotionally. This is depicted in Figure 5-1 that shows a graph of how percentage handicap, as judged by clients according to their responses to the HHI, changed (improved) from 60 percent before hearing aids were purchased to 20 percent after three weeks and also after one year of hearing aid use.

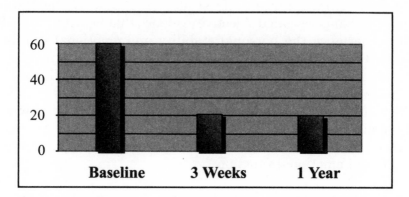

Figure 5-1: Improvement (reduction) in psychosocial handicap according to scores on the 25-item HHI following one-year of hearing aid use.

This represents a dramatic improvement and suggests that many of the problems people had when they came in for hearing aids—such as difficulty understanding friends, relatives, television and radio, or feeling upset by the hearing loss—were alleviated by hearing aid use. It is noteworthy that hearing aids did not "cure" each person's handicap.

The reality of hearing aids is that they're helpful in a variety of situations, and can alleviate feelings of isolation. However, it's unrealistic to expect "a quick fix" in all situations. Residual problems remain for which solutions are available as long as your hearing care practitioner has an open line of communication with you. Further, your expectations must be realistic so that you're not disappointed with hearing aid performance. A satisfied hearing aid wearer is one whose expectations match actual hearing aid performance.

There are times when new hearing aid wearers find they're not deriving the emotional and social benefits from hearing aids. For example, take the case of a 55-year-old teacher who recently found out that he had a mild to moderate sensorineural hearing loss. He had reported some difficulty understanding speech, especially in a noisy classroom. His score on the Hearing Handicap Inventory

(HHI) was 50 percent, suggesting that in fact he perceived his hearing loss as measured on the audiogram to be handicapping socially, emotionally and vocationally.

More particularly, he reported feeling handicapped, upset, embarrassed by and nervous from his inability to hear in a variety of situations, most notably at work (i.e. in the classroom), in movie theaters, and when socializing with friends and relatives. In light of his expenses at the time of the fitting, he decided to purchase binaural canal analog hearing aids. When he returned to his provider for the three-week follow-up appointment to determine how he was functioning with his hearing aids, he indicated that they were not helpful in the situations that mattered.

Further, he was annoyed by the sound of his voice with the hearing aids in his ears, and he noted that he heard whistling sounds a lot (feedback). His score on the long version of the HHI (i.e. 25 items) verified that the hearing aids, in fact, were not helping him, as the score remained at 50 percent, suggesting absolutely no benefit.

The hearing care professional suggested that the client try the newest technology—namely digital hearing aids with a dual microphone array and feedback controls. These units came with special earmolds that would help to make his voice sound more natural and the aids were equipped with special feedback elimination circuitry. He agreed to try them, was instructed on how to use them, was counseled regarding expected benefits, and returned one week later to pick up the hearing aids.

Three weeks later he returned for the follow-up visit. The client was quite pleased with the hearing aids, indicating that they were helpful in situations that were important to him and were alleviating some of the negative emotions attributable to his hearing loss. The aids felt more comfortable in his ear and he was not bothered by the quality of his voice or by annoying feedback. Above all, he felt less handicapped, anxious, and upset.

Responses to the HHI confirmed the client's subjective reports as his total score on the HHI improved to 10 percent suggesting a minimal hearing handicap with his new hearing aids. He continued to receive benefit after six months of hearing aid use. The pattern of findings is depicted in Figure 5-2. This case highlights the value of feedback from you, the client, and the importance of objectively quantifying performance with given hearing aids. Responses to a questionnaire, such as the HHI, can assist you in recognizing if and in what situations hearing aids are helping.

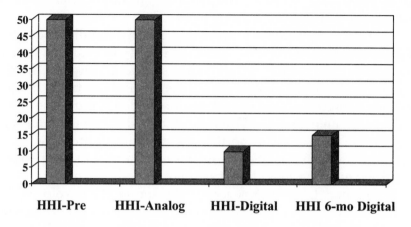

| | HHI-Pre | HHI-Analog | HHI-Digital | HHI 6-mo Digital |

Figure 5-2: Score on the 25 item HHI with analog hearing aids (3 weeks post fitting), digital directional hearing aids (at 3 weeks and 6 months post fitting).

Another interesting way in which responses to the HHI can be helpful to both the new hearing aid wearer and the provider is when hearing aids seem helpful but their value does not seem to justify the expense. A retired attorney noted that now that he was no longer confined to an office or a courtroom, he was having difficulty functioning in the variety of new situations in which he found himself. He participated in a hearing screening at a local health fair and found out he was unable to hear pure tones being presented and scored an 18 on the screening version of the Hearing Handicap Inventory.

The clinician provided a referral to a hearing healthcare professional who urged him to obtain a complete hearing test. He scheduled an appointment with a provider and underwent a series of pure tone and speech tests to determine the extent of hearing loss. Results revealed a mild to moderate high frequency sensorineural hearing loss in each ear, consistent with the type of hearing loss attributable to the aging process. The score on the 25-item Hearing Handicap Inventory suggested a moderate psychosocial handicap (score of 40 percent).

In light of the client's complaints, the configuration of hearing loss (high frequency), and its severity (mild to moderate), binaural completely-in-the-canal hearing aids were recommended. The client was instructed to return to the provider after three weeks of hearing aid use to verify the response and monitor his performance with them.

Interestingly, on the return visit the client complained that the hearing aids were amplifying too much noise, and were not helpful in situations he considered most important (namely small groups) where background noise was present. The HHI score of 38 percent verified that in fact the hearing aids were not providing him with much assistance. After slight modification to the hearing aid response, the client left expressing satisfaction.

Upon the return visit (three weeks later, six weeks from the initial fitting), the client reported that the hearing aids were helping him to function well and enjoy numerous leisure activities in which he was participating. The HHI score at this time improved some 30 points to 8 percent, suggesting a minimal psychosocial handicap attributable to the hearing loss. Once again, objective verification for the client was helpful, enabling him to justify the expenditure.

There are occasions when individuals who were previously functioning well with their hearing aids can experience a decline in performance. Take for example the case of Mr. Osborn, an 80-year-old accountant who continues to work part-time. He had worn behind-the-ear hearing aids for 10 years and up until recently was quite satisfied with them. They were helping to alleviate his difficulties understanding speech, attributable to his bilateral, moderate, sensorineural hearing loss, which he first noted on his 65th birthday. Pure tone test results at his most recent examination by his provider revealed that his hearing loss had remained the same (moderate in degree).

However, his problems understanding speech had declined dramatically, especially in noisy situations. A complete audiological work-up revealed the possibility of an auditory processing problem. Noteworthy is the pattern of findings on the HHI confirmed Mr. Osborn's subjective complaints in that he no longer was benefiting from the hearing aids. As is evident from Figure 5-3, the initial HHI score was 50 percent (prior to hearing aids), improving to 24 percent after the initial hearing aid fitting. His HHI score was between 24 percent and 30 percent over time, suggesting considerable reduction (improvement) in psychosocial handicap attributable to hearing aid use.

Four years later, at Mr. Osborn's most recent visit, the HHI score returned to 52 percent, confirming limited hearing aid benefit. His provider recommended a conventional behind-the-ear aid with

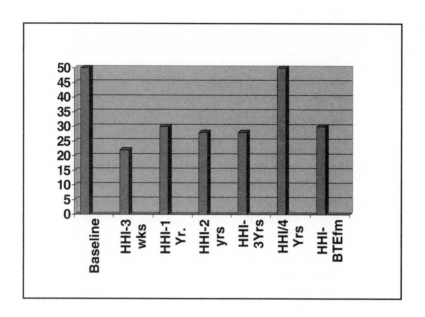

Figure 5-3: HHI scores over five-year time period with hearing aid and BTE/FM device.

an FM receiver incorporated into the hearing aid case. The advantage of an FM system is the improved signal-to-noise ratio achieved by bringing the microphone closer to the source of sound. Essentially, FM systems bridge the acoustical space between the sound source and the listener by eliminating the detrimental effects on speech understanding: distance, noise and reverberation.

The primary advantages of a BTE/FM system are that it can be used as a regular hearing aid, or as an FM receiver bringing the signal directly to the user's ear, or as both an FM system and a hearing aid. It's ideal when driving in a car, when conversing in a noisy environment, and when at a lecture or in a restaurant.

Mr. Osborn, at the urging of his wife, agreed to give the BTE/FM system a try and was immediately impressed with the clarity of the signal, especially when he was tested with noise present in the background. Mr. and Mrs. Osborn were counseled on how to use the hearing aids and upon their return visit were happy to report that speech understanding in the most difficult situations had improved dramatically. The HHI score of 28 percent verified that Mr. Osborn was deriving substantial benefit from the new device. Figure 5-3 summarizes the pattern of HHI scores over time with the hearing aids and with the BTE/FM system.

As hearing technology evolves and prices continue to rise, it is incumbent upon you to obtain information that can help you determine the value of hearing aids. Many hearing care practitioners have a variety of questionnaires at their disposal that can help you better understand how you function with hearing aids. This type of information can help to justify the high cost of present-day hearing aids. It is clear that hearing aids do provide quality of life benefits. Communication needs and expectations can be realized when hearing care professionals listen to you the consumer, either by modifying the response of a hearing aid, substituting one style hearing aid for another, or replacing a conventional hearing aid with some form of hearing assistive technology to ensure adequate benefit.

## A Final Word

To gain full benefit from hearing aids, you must be informed, have realistic expectations and patience, and you must purchase hearing aids from a professional with whom you have confidence and rapport. It is also of utmost importance to have a firm idea about what you want from hearing aids. These are your self-perceptions.

Completion of a self-report questionnaire prior to and after purchasing hearing aids can help match perceptions of what you want hearing aids to do for you, against expectations as established by your hearing healthcare professional. The closer this match, the more satisfied you will be with hearing aids. Consider the self-report questionnaire as a checklist against which to judge the extent your needs are being met.

## References

1. Bess F. Applications of the hearing handicap inventory for the elderly—screening version (HHIE-S). The Hearing Journal 48, 51-57, 1995.
2. Kochkin, S. MarkeTrak IV: 10-year trends in the hearing aid market-has anything changed? The Hearing Journal 49, 23-33, 1996.
3. National Council on the Aging. Report on the impact of untreated hearing loss in older Americans. Seniors Research Group, 1999.
4 Weinstein, B. Treatment efficacy: hearing aids in the management of hearing loss in adults. Journal Speech and Hearing Research 39,

S37-S45, 1996.

5. Weinstein, B. *Geriatric Audiology*. New York: Thieme Medical Publishers, Inc., 2000.

# CHAPTER SIX
# Hearing Aid Technology
## *Robert W. Sweetow, Ph.D.*

Dr. Sweetow is Director of Audiology and Clinical Professor in the Department of Otolaryngology at the Medical Center of the University of California, San Francisco. He received his Ph.D. from Northwestern University in 1977. He holds a Master of Arts degree from the University of Southern California and a Bachelor of Science degree from the University of Iowa. Dr. Sweetow has lectured worldwide, and has authored 20 textbook chapters and over 80 scientific articles on counseling, tinnitus and amplification for the hearing impaired.

There are many myths and misconceptions regarding hearing aids. The objective of this chapter is to prepare you with accurate up-to-date information to help in your decision to upgrade or try new hearing aids. As technology advances, and as social and workplace demands change, so do the criteria for candidacy for wearable amplification. Thirty-five years ago, many hearing healthcare professionals believed that only people with conductive hearing loss could be helped by hearing aids. Patients were often told that hearing aids could make sounds *louder* (like turning up the volume on a radio), but would not necessarily make sounds *clearer*. This thinking was reinforced by reports of unfavorable results from those hearing impaired patients who did try hearing aids and who still couldn't understand speech clearly—particularly in noisy places.

Of course, it's now recognized that early attempts to fit hearing aids on people with sensorineural loss were seriously hindered by the limited sound quality produced by these early devices; by the limited choice of electronic variations; and by poor fitting strategies used in trying to determine the best manner to amplify speech without making it too loud or too noisy.

In the early days of fitting hearing aids, professionals often tried to determine who was a candidate on the basis of the degree of hearing loss shown on the hearing test. You may recall that when your hearing was tested, the audiologist or hearing instrument specialist used beeping tones and made the sounds louder and softer until you could no longer hear them. This very softest point, the point at which you could just barely hear a sound is called your threshold. These sounds are measured in decibels (dB). Classifications used two decades ago stated that hearing better than 25 dB was normal; 26-50 dB was a mild loss; 51-70 dB was a moderate loss; 71-90 dB was a severe loss; and 91 dB and poorer was a profound loss. Strict application of these categories isn't adequate to describe the impact hearing loss has on your life. Indeed, it oversimplifies the complexities of hearing impairment. Today, we realize that *properly fitted hearing aids can provide benefit even if you have a relatively mild hearing loss.*

In addition to the previous belief among physicians and some hearing professionals that you couldn't successfully use hearing aids if you had nerve damage, it was also thought that you couldn't use hearing aids if you had normal hearing for low-pitched sounds (up to 1500 or 2000 Hz); or if you had a hearing loss in only one ear, or if your speech understanding abilities were reduced, and/or if you had difficulty tolerating loud sounds (for example, a crying baby). Advances in technology now allow for good fittings for most of these patients.

## Present-Day Candidacy For Hearing Aids

In the past several years, hearing aid technology has advanced to the point where the question of candidacy is now based more on your communicative *needs* rather than purely on the test results obtained in a soundproof room. That is, your own personal, *subjective needs*. A good litmus test is to ask yourself whether you feel stressed or fatigued after a day of straining to hear. Hearing aids may simply relieve this strain, rather than making sounds louder or allowing you to understand all speech in all listening environments. Reducing strain alone can be a very significant benefit, not only to you, but to those trying to talk to you.

Occupational and social demands vary greatly among individuals. A judge who has a mild hearing loss may desperately need amplification, while a retired person living alone with the exact same degree of hearing loss may not. You must unselfishly examine whether you're becoming a burden to others, even if you do not personally recognize difficulty hearing. *Remember that wearing hearing aids may be a symbol of courtesy to others.* Unfortunately, despite the need, you, like many people, may resist trying hearing aids. Two common factors characterizing the response in people who have been told they should wear amplification are that practically no one wants to wear hearing aids, and no one wants to spend money or waste time solving a problem unless they perceive that a problem exists and a solution is readily attainable. Opposition to wearing hearing aids usually stems from three main reasons.

First is *hearsay*. Most everyone has friends or relatives who have purchased hearing aids currently residing in their dresser drawers. These unsuccessful wearers of amplification are more than happy to spread the gospel on the limitations (some accurate, some not) of hearing aids. Often, unsuccessful experiences occurred in extremely difficult listening environments in which even people with normal hearing had trouble understanding speech.

Second, despite the fact that people of all ages have hearing impairment and use amplification, there's an undeniable *social stigma* attached to wearing hearing aids. The problem of vanity has been eased, in part, by the continuing trend toward miniaturization of hearing devices. However, not all listeners with hearing loss are candidates for very tiny completely-in-the-canal hearing aids. Thus, stigma is likely to remain a difficult hurdle to overcome.

The third main reason for opposition to hearing aid use is the perception that the relatively high cost of hearing aids is not reflected in the value and benefits they provide. When making a decision as to whether this is the right time for you to try hearing aids, you must weigh whether the financial investment can be offset by the improvement in your quality of life by reducing your hearing difficulty. Be sure to consider improvements from a social, emotional, and occupational perspective, also considering activities you would like to undertake but have given up because of communication difficulties.

It's a double-edged sword when it comes to dispensing hearing aids to a person who's not motivated to wear amplification. On one hand, a poorly motivated person is not the best candidate for amplification regardless of the degree of hearing loss. So, from this perspective, the answer to the question of whether a steadfastly reluctant patient should be forced into trying a hearing aid is probably *no*. It may be difficult to undo the damage that may be done if the borderline candidate prematurely tries, and fails with amplification. If you're absolutely opposed to trying hearing aids at this time, and if you're convinced you'll fail, it may be advisable to wait until another time when you may be more optimistic about the outcome.

On the other hand, keep in mind that it's <u>very</u> <u>possible</u> you will be pleasantly surprised. Remember that, as discussed later in this chapter, there have been more changes in hearing aids during the last few years than in the previous thirty.

# Hearing Aid Styles

In the early 1950s, you would have been limited to a choice of two styles of hearing instruments: body borne or in-eyeglass frames. These devices are rarely seen today. However, you do have options regarding hearing aid styles (see: Figure 6-1). Behind-the-ear (BTE) hearing aids sit over the outer ear and are connected to an earmold located in the concha (bowl) of the ear and ear canal. There are a variety of sizes, shapes, and models of hearing aids that fit within a soft or hard plastic shell and are worn entirely inside the ear. They include the custom in-the-ear (ITE) model (which may completely fill, or occlude, the bowl and ear canal), the thinner low profile, the partially occluding half concha, the even less occluding helix model for high frequency losses, the in-the-canal (ITC), and the tiniest of styles, the completely-in-canal (CIC) hearing aids.

Figure 6-1: Range of hearing aid styles from (left to right) completely-in-the-canal to behind-the-ear.

I strongly discourage you from selecting the style of hearing aids you're going to try strictly on the basis of cosmetic factors. While cosmetic considerations may be important, the decision as to which style hearing aids are most appropriate for you should be based on both physical as well as audiological factors.

## Physical factors

*Anatomical characteristics* may dictate the style; for example, behind-the-ear hearing aids may not be able to be used if you have deformed outer ears; the depth of your concha may determine the appropriateness of certain in-the-ear (ITE) model instruments; and in order to be able to wear the in-the-canal or the completely-in-canal types of hearing aids, your ear canal must be of sufficient diameter and must have a sharp enough bend to retain the aid, but not be so curvy that it prevents easy insertion and removal.

*Manual dexterity* is essential to handling some of the smaller style hearing aids. Not only is removal and insertion of canal hearing aids difficult for certain people, particularly as we get older, but the ability to manipulate any controls and the battery must be considered and assessed before you decide that a certain style is right for you. Also, some people need hearing aids that are large enough to accommodate a vent (hole) drilled into it, allowing air to enter the ear canal.

Without this ventilation, you may perceive a "plugged up" feeling or you may sound to yourself that you're "in a barrel" when you speak. This phenomenon is technically called the "occlusion effect." Some newer models of digital hearing aids greatly minimize the occlusion effect by allowing for more open ear fittings. In addition, if your ears produce excessive cerumen (earwax), you may be better off by not wearing canal, or even certain full ITE hearing aids.

*Medical Contraindications* such as draining ears or other medical problems may prevent the use of any hearing aid apparatus blocking your ear canals (see Chapter 8 Q&A #7 for complete medical contraindications). In this instance, you'll need open, non-occluding earmolds or possibly bone conduction-type systems. These types of hearing aids are beyond the scope of this discussion, and can be reviewed by your hearing healthcare provider if applicable to you.

## Audiological factors:

*The audiometric pattern* on your audiogram may show certain frequencies (pitches) that have normal hearing. For example, in the low frequencies, you may be best served by systems that don't occlude (block) your ear canal and thus allow low-pitched sounds to pass into your ear without being amplified.

*The degree of loss* may predict the need for a specific kind of hearing aid. For example, severe and profound hearing losses are best served by BTE-style hearing aids.

*Special features* may be indicated, such as directional or multiple microphones (which primarily amplify signals coming from in front of you) and/or the addition of a telecoil (a magnetic induction loop). Telecoils allow sound to bypass the hearing aid microphone and amplify signals received electromagnetically (from telephones). In addition to allowing a hearing aid wearer to listen to telephone signals without getting feedback (whistling), telecoils can interface with a variety of assistive listening devices (see Appendix I).

*Acoustic feedback* refers to the whistling or ringing sound often produced when you cup your hand or a telephone over your ear while wearing a hearing aid. It also occurs when the hearing aid or earmold is not properly or snugly inserted in your ear. Before discussing feedback, it would help to first describe the basic components of hearing aids.

Figure 6-2 shows the series of events that occur in conventional, non-digital hearing aids: First, sound enters into a <u>microphone</u>. Next, this sound is transformed into an electrical current as the diaphragm of the microphone moves back and forth. Then, the electrical current is fed into an <u>amplifier</u> and filtered by electrical components that establish how much relative amplification will be provided for the different frequencies. For example, most hearing aids try to amplify the high pitches more than the low pitches. The overall amount of amplification may be governed by a <u>volume control</u> . The newly formed amplified electrical signal is then fed to a <u>receiver</u>, also called a loudspeaker. The receiver turns the electrical signal back into sound waves that exit the hearing aid and enter the ear canal through the <u>earmold</u> for BTE hearing aids, or a tube in the plastic shell for custom styles.

Also, all hearing aids are run by a tiny <u>battery</u>, which generally lasts for between one to three weeks. The basic design of digital hearing aids, that will be discussed later in this chapter, differ in that they contain a signal processor rather than an amplifier and they often adjust the volume automatically without the need for volume controls.

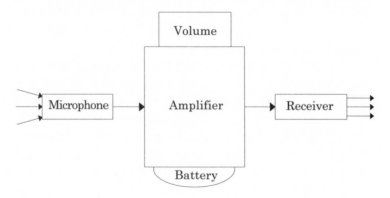

Figure 6-2: Transmission of sound through a hearing aid.

Generally speaking, the closer the microphone is to the exit point of the amplified sound from the hearing aid or earmold, the greater the likelihood of feedback. Feedback occurs when amplified sound from the earmold leaks back into the hearing aid's microphone and is re-amplified. This is a very important consideration in the selection and fitting of amplification. BTE hearing aids often have an advantage over smaller ITE or ITC styles in this regard since there's more physical distance between the microphone and the receiver.

Conventional hearing aids provide "feedback controls" which are adjustments that reduce high frequency amplification. While this does indeed accomplish the desired effect of reducing feedback, it may do so at the expense of also reducing the audibility of the vitally important high frequency consonant sounds that are essential for understanding speech. Therefore, this approach to feedback control is often not an acceptable compromise. The newest generation of advanced digital hearing aids has "active feedback management" systems. An active system detects feedback and counteracts it before it occurs by sending out counter signals to cancel the feedback.

In any case, it's important that the earmolds or hearing aid shells fit perfectly in your ears. This is why it's essential that your hearing healthcare professional takes good impressions of your ears before you obtain hearing aids. If you haven't yet had an earmold impression taken, don't worry. It doesn't hurt. Your provider will first place a cotton or foam block in your ear canal and will then inject liquid material in your ear that will harden in about five minutes. It's a similar process to getting impressions made by the dentist, except thankfully, you don't need the Novocain shot!

## Small Hearing Aids

If you're like most patients, perhaps one of the first questions you have is whether you can use one of the really small, "invisible" hearing aids (the ITC or CIC styles). Hearing aids keep getting smaller but small does not necessarily mean better. A canal-style hearing aid implies that no part of the hearing aid extends into the concha (bowl) area. There are two types: the ITC aid fills the outer half, or soft, cartilaginous portion of the ear canal while the CIC is inserted deeper in the ear canal and extends into the inner half. The CIC hearing aid is so tiny that it must be removed from the ear by pulling on a removal wire that rests at the bottom of the concha.

### *Advantages* of CIC Hearing Aids:

- They are the most *"invisible"* systems available.
- The microphone lies either within, or at the entrance of the ear canal and thus is able to benefit fully from the *natural amplification* of the outer ear bowl.
- The receiver of the hearing aid is located closer to the eardrum, where the amount of air trapped in the ear canal that needs to vibrate is less than for most other fittings. Therefore, *less hearing aid amplification is needed* to produce the same sound pressure at the eardrum. This often results in lower distortion levels and less likelihood of acoustic feedback.

### *Disadvantages* of CIC Hearing Aids:

- If the receiver stops in the outer half of the canal, it may be *subject to breakdowns* due to blockage from earwax.
- With certain basic instruments, if the receiver terminates in the outer cartilaginous portion of the canal, you may notice the "occlusion" or "barrel effect" in which your *own voice sounds hollow* as if you were in a tunnel. Digital technology can help reduce or even eliminate this effect.
- If the receiver stops in the inner, bony portion of the canal, this deeper canal placement may be *physically uncomfortable* to you because the skin is much thinner than it is at the outer part of the canal.
- Because the aid is so small, *there may not be enough space to vent the aid* in order to relieve pressure build-up, release unwanted low frequency amplification, or to house multiple microphones or telecoils.
- They are *not powerful enough to fit severe or profound losses*.
- Adequate manual *dexterity for changing the tiny batteries is essential*.

It's not unusual to find that the most important factors determining success or failure of a fitting are those unrelated to audiometric findings. In particular, you must take into consideration all of the following: your age and general physical and mental health; your motivation (as opposed to that of your family's); finances; cosmetic considerations; and your communication needs. It's heartening to note that the primary reasons for rejection of hearing aids, after people try them, are less related to finances and cosmetics, and more to do with difficulty hearing in background noise, and discomfort from loud sounds. These problems are well on the way to being lessened by modern-day hearing aids and fitting techniques.

# The Evolution of Hearing Aids

There are three basic rules that must be followed if a hearing aid fitting is to be successful: soft sounds must be made audible; normal conversational sounds must be comfortable; and loud sounds must not be uncomfortable. The reason is that if you have a sensorineural hearing loss, your hearing loss is for soft sounds but not for loud sounds. Therefore, hearing aids have changed over the past three decades in the following ways.

## 1. Linear Hearing Aids

In the past, many wearers reported that in order to hear soft sounds, they had to turn their hearing aids up quite high. This did indeed allow them to hear soft sounds but it also produced the undesirable effect of making loud sounds uncomfortable. Here's why.

Imagine that a certain level of sound enters the hearing aid, let's say 65 dB (which happens to be about the level of normal conversational speech). To make this speech comfortable, the volume of the hearing aid might be set so that it produces 25 dB of amplification. Therefore, 90 dB comes into the ear canal (65 plus 25).

Now, lets imagine that the sound coming into the hearing aid suddenly becomes much louder, as might occur in a restaurant when people at your table start to laugh at a joke. If you are wearing a linear hearing aid, the sound coming into it is now increased to 80 dB, and this type of hearing aid will still add 25 dB of amplification, so the sound in your ear canal actually becomes 105 dB. For most people, this will be entirely too loud and uncomfortable, and your reaction will be to try and turn it down using the volume control. This is why you'll see most people with linear hearing aids turning the volume control quite often when the sound intensity in the surrounding environment changes. Hearing aids which produce the same amount of amplification regardless of the loudness of the sound entering are technically categorized as *linear, one channel, conventional* hearing aids.

## 2. Non-Linear, *Single Channel*

In 1992, a new type of hearing aid was introduced using more advanced technology called <u>non-linear</u>, or <u>dynamic range compression</u>. With this system, there's more amplification given to soft sounds than there is for louder sounds. In other words, when sounds are above a certain level set in the hearing aid, it's as if an invisible finger reaches up and automatically moves the volume down for you, and vice versa, when the sound environment becomes lower than a certain level it moves the volume up for you.

This type of non-linear hearing aid basically squeezes a wide range of loudness into a narrower range, which has generated the other descriptive name of *compression hearing aids*. Going back to the earlier example, now with the non-linear type, when sounds entering the hearing aid suddenly increase to 80 dB, the amplification may be lowered from 25 dB to 10 dB. Therefore, the sound reaching your eardrum is a more comfortable 90 dB as opposed to the uncomfortable 105.

## 3. Non-Linear, *Multichannel*

While non-linear, single channel hearing aids help maintain comfortable loudness perception, another limitation remains: Your loudness growth pattern may be different from one pitch to another. That is, you might find that high-pitched sounds (like dishes clanging) seem painfully loud to you but low-pitched sounds (a refrigerator humming) do not. Therefore, the amount of compression may need to be different for various frequencies. This is where the next step up in circuitry sophistication comes in, *non-linear multiple channel*.

With multiple channels, compression characteristics of the hearing aid will be tailored to your personal needs based upon how loud you interpret certain sounds to be for various frequencies. Perhaps there will be a lot of compression for the high frequencies but very little for the low frequencies. Compression helps to make sounds appear comfortably loud for you.

The second thing multichannel compression accomplishes may be even more important. If your hearing aid system has only one channel, a loud noise made up of mostly low frequencies (as might be found in cocktail parties) would instruct the hearing aid that it needs to lower its amplification for all frequencies. This would help to keep the sound from being too loud, but it would make some of the high frequency sounds (like consonants) too soft to hear.

On the other hand, a multichannel hearing aid, in that same loud, low frequency noise situation, would decrease the amplification for low frequencies, making sound comfortable without changing the amplification for the high frequencies (thus preserving audibility of important high frequency consonant sounds). This system can actually produce additional high frequency amplification while simultaneously reducing low frequency amplification, all depending on the sound environment.

Non-linear, multiple channel hearing aids act not only as a means of loudness control, but also as a means of differentiating the amount of amplification given to different parts of the speech signal. If fitted correctly, they can dampen the strong elements of speech, such as vowels, and enhance the delicate speech elements such as the /s/, /sh/ and /f/ sounds. This will greatly improve speech clarity, especially in difficult listening environments.

## 4. Multiple Programs versus Automatic

Some people find it useful to be able to change hearing aid characteristics depending on the environment they are in. Of course, you can't keep running back to your provider each time you enter a new environment. Another option would be to have hearing aids that have several programs that you can easily select simply by touching a button located on the hearing aid or on a separate remote control. For example, one button could select a hearing aid program which is best suited to listening to one person, another program to listening in a restaurant, and yet another for music. This can also be useful if you have a fluctuating hearing loss.

Many modern hearing aids are automatic in the way they regulate volume. Often, these hearing aids regulate themselves so automatically that they don't contain a volume control. You may find this to your liking if you're the type who doesn't like to frequently adjust your hearing aids, or, you may feel that not having a volume control takes away too much control from you. This is something you should discuss carefully with your hearing healthcare provider.

## 5. Digitally-Programmable Hearing Aids

Hearing aids that are programmed, or set, by your hearing healthcare provider, via an external computer, or computer-like instrument are called *digitally programmable*. This does not mean you own a "digital" hearing aid. It merely means the computer process for programming is digitally based. The basic advantage of programmable is the flexibility for your hearing care professional to change the characteristics in the hearing aids as your needs may change. Often, preferences for sound amplification changes over time after you have used the hearing aids for a while.

For instance, if you're a new wearer, you may not want hearing aids to amplify high pitches too much because they might seem too sharp or tinny. But after you've grown accustomed to hearing sounds you may not have heard for a long time, you may want to hear some of these high-pitched sounds. With a programmable system, your hearing healthcare provider can alter the amplification in your instruments by boosting higher pitches.

## 6. Directional and Multiple Microphone Hearing Aids

Typically, you face the person who is speaking to you. Noise, however, may originate in front, behind, and/or to your sides. Many programmable and digital hearing aids contain directional or multiple microphones that "communicate" with each other so that sounds originating from the front of the hearing aid receive maximum amplification, and sounds originating from the sides or behind receive less amplification. This effectively suppresses some of the annoying background noise that may create so much difficulty for you.

Some hearing aids allow you to select whether you want most of the amplification to occur for signals in front of you or whether you want equal amplification for signals all around you. An example of when you might want amplification to occur from all around you would be when listening to music. Other multiple microphone hearing aids make these adjustments automatically for you.

## 7. Digital Hearing Aids

The most advanced hearing aids today use fully digital processing. A digital hearing aid has a computer chip performing the amplification steps instead of the traditional analog circuitry. It's actually a miniature computer in itself. This is a major breakthrough in technology because it greatly increases the amount of sound processing possible in the given amount of space.

The improvement from digital hearing aids is exciting and far-reaching because they have minimal distortion, a clearer/crisper quality, advanced feedback control, improved noise suppression, and occlusion (hollow sound) management. The first commercially available digital hearing aids took all the benefits from the advanced non-linear multichannel hearing aids and improved them even further. They have the ability to analyze the sound environment and adapt the amplification accordingly, making speech clearer. This is all done automatically without the need for volume or remote controls.

Second generation digital hearing aids that recently were introduced have more "intelligence built into the chips," allowing them to recognize the difference between the human voice versus incoming noise, and further improve speech perception. Once third and fourth generation chips are developed, they will allow for even more processing capabilities.

## Limitations of Hearing Aids

Hearing aids are meant to minimize listening fatigue and to improve ease of communication. They're not meant to allow you to "hear a pin drop," and there are going to be circumstances in which hearing aids don't give you all the benefits you'd like. The most frequent complaints voiced by hearing aid wearers are that noise is amplified too much, certain sounds become too loud to bear, and some speech remains unclear.

No hearing aids effectively eliminate all background noise. If all the sound energy that makes up noise were eliminated, important segments of speech also would be missing. And, remember that normal listeners experience background noise daily. If all background noise were eliminated, the acoustic world would be quite boring and unnatural. Even so, don't hesitate to discuss your perception of background noise with your provider so that your hearing aids can be fine-tuned to reach the best compromise. Some of the newer digital instruments have automatic modes, decreasing fatigue and only boosting amplification when speech is present.

With regard to clarity, remember that hearing aids are *aids* to hearing. They are not new ears, and they cannot correct for certain limitations in understanding that are more related to brain functioning and poor listening habits than to hearing.

You may find that your own voice sounds odd when wearing

hearing aids. The reason this occurs is that when you speak, you produce low frequency vibrations in your ear canals. When you're unaided, your ears are open, allowing these vibrations to escape from your ear canals out into the air. As touched on earlier, if your ears are blocked, these low frequency sounds are trapped in your ear canals and cannot escape. This increase in low frequency perception might make you sound as if you were talking in a barrel or experiencing an echo.

This "occlusion effect" can be minimized by: 1) keeping the ear as open as possible, perhaps by means of vents (holes) drilled into the earmold or plastic shell; 2) reducing low frequency amplification; 3) using an earmold or ITE shell that sits deeply, reaching the inner half of the canal, thus reducing vibration; 4) or in some cases, having the canal portion of the shell not set rather shallow in the ear.

As mentioned earlier, a common annoyance with all but the latest generation digital hearing aids is the presence of feedback. Feedback doesn't mean that the hearing aid is malfunctioning. There are two types of acoustic feedback: that produced internally from the hearing aid indicating the need for repair, and the more common external feedback produced by leakage of amplified sound out of the ear canal and back into the microphone of the hearing aid. Usually, external feedback can be corrected by 1) re-positioning or possibly remaking the earmold or the plastic shell; 2) plugging, or reducing the diameter of any vents; or 3) reducing the amount of high frequency amplification, which is usually an unacceptable trade-off because of the resultant loss of high frequency consonant audibility.

Another common limitation of hearing aids is that you may have more difficulty hearing when the sound source is at a distance from you. This occurs, for example, in large conference rooms or auditoriums. Loudness (intensity) decreases as physical distance increases. Unfortunately, most background noise surrounds you, so while the intensity of speech decreases with distance, the intensity of noise may not. This is one reason why hearing aids effectively transmit sound if the speaker talks right into the microphone, but at longer, more realistic distances, reception diminishes. It would be ideal if sound produced at the source transferred directly to you without losing any intensity. It's obviously impractical, however, to ask someone speaking to you to constantly move closer to your ear.

One way to achieve this effect is with direct audio input, where the person speaking holds or wears a microphone. Unfortunately, many hearing aid wearers are reluctant to ask others to use a microphone or wear a wired device. An alternative approach is to use instruments called assistive listening devices that transmit by wireless FM (like a radio), infrared, or induction loop. You may have seen these devices in auditoriums and theaters, and they can be used in combination with your hearing aids.

## Realistic Expectations with New Hearing Aids

As I mentioned earlier, hearing aids are not new ears; they are electronic devices; they are not perfect; and for the most part, they do not eliminate background noise. Since many patients with sensorineural hearing loss deny the presence of a hearing impairment, or lack sufficient motivation, they often demand to be convinced of the improvement that hearing aids might offer. Since the main goal of amplification is to facilitate the ease of communication, don't be disappointed if you experience only minimal benefit during the initial trial with amplification.

The benefit derived from amplification may be subtle. Depending on your hearing loss, the goal of the hearing aids may not be to make sounds louder. That is, especially where only high frequency amplification occurs, there are only a few English language sounds in this range (such as /s/, /sh/, /t/, /th/, /f/, and /k/). Therefore, your hearing aids are designed to pick up only these consonants and since we're talking about relatively few sounds, the benefits of amplification may not be readily apparent. It's important to note here that even though we're speaking of a few sounds, these sounds are critically important.

You also need to recognize that prediction of guaranteed long-term benefit from amplification is difficult to determine. A period of initial adjustment and a learning process is required for most new hearing aid users. It may take several weeks before you adjust to the new pattern of sound and learn new "recognition" cues that you probably have not heard for a long time. As a new wearer, you need to be oriented to the world of amplification. You may require a gradual "break-in" wearing schedule (a few hours the first day, six hours the second, nine hours the third, etc.), or you may be encouraged to wear the hearing aids immediately during all your waking hours. You may require additional counseling and training, either individually, or in groups with others with hearing loss, and family members.

You must accept that time is required for adapting to hearing aids. Your ability to understand amplified speech can continue to grow for as long as three months following the use of new hearing aids.

Most hearing healthcare professionals will give you a one-month trial period with new hearing aids. If market conditions allow, trial periods may be extended. My advice is, if a trial period is not offered, take your business elsewhere!

It's important that you read the instruction manual that comes with your hearing aids. Hopefully, your provider will have told you everything you need to know about inserting and removing your hearing aids, checking the batteries, cleaning and maintaining the instruments, and using hearing aids with the telephone. But often, too much information can overload the brain! Take the hearing aids home, read the instruction manual, and then call your provider if you have any questions. Then go out and wear them in a variety of listening environments. When you return to your hearing healthcare provider, discuss the situations with which you may have had difficulty so that possible adjustments and fine-tuning can be achieved.

Also remember that hearing aids are sophisticated electronic devices that spend most of their time in a rather unfriendly environment—your ear. Can you imagine what would happen if you placed your home stereo system in a rainforest? Well, your ear canal is somewhat like a rainforest in that it is very warm (about 98.6 degrees), it's moist (with earwax), and it doesn't always receive enough fresh air. As such, hearing aids do require occasional repair. Blockage from earwax is the most common cause for hearing aid malfunction. Ask your hearing aid provider about some of the modern "wax traps" that can help keep earwax out of your hearing aids. You can minimize the need for repair if you are conscientious about cleaning them daily according to instructions and possibly storing them every night in a container that soaks up any excess moisture (see Chapter 9 on maintenance).

## Conclusions

Now you have the facts, at least as they stand early in the 21st century. Remember, in order to have the best chance of succeeding with hearing aids, be patient with yourself and maintain realistic expectations. You and your brain have consciously and subconsciously created many behaviors to compensate for your hearing loss over the years. Some of the habits you have picked up have truly helped your ability to communicate, but some may have actually impaired your communication skills.

108

# CHAPTER SEVEN
# Why Some Consumers Reject Hearing Aids But How You Could Love Them!
## *Sergei Kochkin, Ph.D.*

Dr. Kochkin is a Director of Market Development & Market Research at Knowles Electronics and past member of the Board of Directors of the Better Hearing Institute in Washington, D.C. He has published more than 50 papers on the hearing aid market and conducted customer satisfaction research on more than 25,000 hearing aid owners. He holds a Doctorate in psychology, an MBA in marketing, a Masters of Science in counseling and guidance and a BA in physical anthropology and archeology. Dr. Kochkin also maintains an interest in ancient cultures, comparative religion and meditation.

Recent research in the United States indicates that close to 29 million people have a hearing loss, or nearly one in ten Americans. In addition, about 1.2 million school-age children have a hearing loss. The early identification and treatment of hearing loss in children is particularly critical since hearing is synonymous with normal development of speech. It is important that you understand the prevalence of hearing loss, and that it cuts across all age groups. In focus groups with people who have rejected hearing aids, some people with hearing loss have come to the erroneous conclusion that they are a rare or obscure individual, "since so few people have hearing loss." When shown that they are not alone, they tend to be more accepting of their hearing loss and therefore more willing to seek out a hearing aid solution.

From conversations with experts in other countries, it's generally recognized that close to ten percent of the populations in developed countries have problems with their hearing. I happen to believe this figure may be higher, because most studies do not include hearing loss populations in institutional settings such as nursing or retirement homes, the military, and prisons. Among the elderly, hearing loss is the third most serious health issue, following arthritis and hypertension.

The vast majority *(close to 90-95 of people with hearing loss)* can be helped by hearing aids. There have been major breakthroughs in hearing aid technology in recent years, and we can now do a better job of matching technology with a candidate's lifestyle and communication needs. Yet, some hearing aids still end up in a drawer.[1]

The good news is that many of the problems with hearing aids have been solved, and wearers can now expect improved communication with hearing aids as the rule, not the exception.

Why do some individuals have difficulty adjusting to hearing aids while others are doing so well that people around them don't even notice they're wearing them? What's different about successful hearing aid wearers? And why do only one in five individuals with hearing loss use hearing aids despite the proven value of amplification. Some interesting facts are now coming to light, which may answer these questions.

## Why Some People Reject Hearing Aids

More than 22 million people in the United States have never tried hearing aids as a solution to their hearing loss. In one research investigation, close to 3,000 individuals with self-reported hearing loss were polled regarding their reluctance to try hearing aids.[2] Here are some of the reasons why consumers have declined to pursue them.

### 1. Inadequate information

Many people are not aware they have a significant hearing loss and therefore are in need of information that would help them recognize it. Most people lose hearing gradually. In most cases, it's slowly progressive. During this time, the person with hearing loss and family members learn to adapt to it, often not even realizing that they're doing this. The number one reason why people buy their very first hearing aid is the "recognition that their hearing got worse;" usually this means they made embarrassing mistakes in society due to their untreated hearing loss. Thus, one of the first things individuals with suspected hearing loss should do is determine if they exhibit some of the signs of hearing loss.

### 2. Stigma and Cosmetics

Some people reject hearing aids because they are concerned with the stigma of hearing loss or are in a state of denial, and thus try to hide it from others. It's unfortunate, but many people, because they have less than perfect hearing, believe they are inferior, unintelligent, or simply less lovable. They believe other people will think they're getting older or that they will be viewed as less competent, less attractive, and so on. They may have shame regarding their hearing loss. This is partly due to the fact that we live in a youth-oriented, airbrushed society where physical perfection is stressed as an important human attribute.

As you previously read in this book, cosmetics no longer need to be a barrier to obtaining amplification. Since the 1990s, technological advances have permitted the hearing aid industry to develop hearing instruments like the completely-in-the-canal (CIC) devices, which are essentially not very visible (see Figure 6-1 page 96). In fact, research shows that 90 percent of consumers perceive these CICs to be completely invisible. Based on your hearing needs and the physical characteristics of your ears, you might be a candidate for these "invisible devices." If you're not, rest assured that in-the-canal (ITC) devices, although larger, are available to fit many hearing losses and are not terribly noticeable.

Understand though, that once you begin hearing through amplification and once your quality of life is enhanced, cosmetics will be of lesser concern to you. Research shows that people who have come to enjoy their hearing aids rate even the largest hearing aids as cosmetically appealing as compared to some of the smaller, in-the-ear models.[3] Some hearing instruments even come in bright colors—dispelling the myth that they are something to be ashamed of or hide!

## 3. Misdirected Medical Guidance

Many people have received misinformation about their hearing loss from well-intending physicians, and the extent to which it can be helped. For instance, many physicians have recommended to their patients that they're not candidates for hearing aids if they have hearing loss in one ear and good hearing in the other *(unilateral hearing loss)*; if they have "nerve deafness" *(an obsolete term for sensorineural hearing loss)*; or if the hearing loss still allows them to conduct a conversation in quiet. Many times the doctor's opinion will be based on the fact that the patient and doctor are able to conduct a face-to-face conversation while in the secluded and usually quiet exam room. Much of this misinformation is given unintentionally by family physicians who do not specialize in hearing problems. In fact, most physicians (except ear, nose and throat specialists) receive very little training in medical school in the areas of hearing loss and hearing aids.

## 4. Not Realizing the Importance of Hearing

Another reason for rejection of hearing aids is that people have forgotten how important hearing is to their quality of life. We live in such a visually oriented society that often hearing plays a secondary role. As you know from your own experience, or from reading this book, people who cannot hear well, often have lives filled with anxiety, insecurity, isolation and depression. People gradually withdraw from family and friends because without auditory contact they lose the feeling of being connected. In essence, they grow numb to the world around them. But in the world, communication is critical. We interact with one another through communication.

I am aware of a CEO who lost more than a million dollars in business because he misunderstood a client's needs; learning from this mistake he always wears his hearing aids when meeting with clients especially when negotiating a contract. I am aware of a grandfather who was thought to be senile instead of hearing impaired. He was able to compensate for his hearing loss with hearing aids and began to effectively interact with his family again. Most hearing healthcare professionals know of horror stories of children being misdiagnosed as slow, retarded, hyperactive, or having poor attention spans when in fact it was impaired hearing.

## 5. Misbelief that Hearing Aids Don't Work

A significant number of people with hearing loss mistakenly believe that hearing aids are not effective for what they are designed to do. Many people judge hearing aids based on what they've seen their grandparents wear—a large, clunky box about the size of a pack of cigarettes with wires coming out of it.

Recent research with consumers utilizing a variety of hearing aids *(high technology as well as older technology aids 1-5 years old)* indicates that 76 percent of hearing aid wearers report satisfaction *(defined as satisfied or very satisfied)* with the ability of the hearing aid to improve their hearing, and 66 percent report that hearing aids have significantly improved the quality of their life.[4] If this research had been conducted twenty years ago, this high satisfaction factor probably would not have even been 35 percent. A significant number of people report satisfaction with their hearing aids in quiet situations (87 percent) as well as in very difficult situations such as restaurants, places of worship or large groups.

In research with more than 25,000 consumers I have learned

that not everyone benefits equally in all listening situations, nor do all types of hearing aid circuitry perform the same in difficult listening situations. As an example, the average hearing aid achieves a 30 percent satisfaction rating in noisy situations; yet some technologies, notably programmable hearing aids with multiple microphones *(known as directional hearing aids)*, achieve satisfaction ratings as high as 67 percent.[3] Similarly, only about 41 percent of consumers are satisfied with hearing aids on the telephone, yet, some instruments, such as completely-in-the-canal (CIC) hearing aids perform better on the phone as well as outdoors because they're located just inside the entrance of the ear canal and produce less feedback while on the phone. Much of this satisfaction may also be due to diminished wind noises outdoors, a sense of more natural amplification, and the need for somewhat less power resulting in increased tolerance while in the presence of background noise.

## 6. Failure to Trust in a Hearing Aid Dispensing Professional

Another key reason some people hold off their purchase is: "I do not trust hearing health providers who fit hearing aids!" The data show that nearly 90 percent of consumers are satisfied with their hearing aid dispensing professional.[4] It is certainly worth mentioning that the training, education and experience among dispensers of hearing aids has greatly increased over the years for both audiologists and hearing instrument specialists (see Chapter 2).

## 7. Unrecognized Value of Hearing Aids

Many people who have avoided amplification tend to believe there is little value in hearing aids. By low value they mistakenly assume that "hearing aids will not work for them" and therefore they will not derive any benefit. Both consumers and physicians have little knowledge of the potential benefit of hearing aids. Since the new millennium, large-scale research has been published on the impact of hearing aids on quality of life for people who use hearing aids in the United States.[5] While I have devoted a full chapter to this research, it is important that we summarize this impact here.

In my humble opinion, I cannot think of a consumer product with such an impressive list of potential benefits: greater earning power, improved interpersonal relationships, reduced discrimination toward the person with the hearing loss, reduced difficulty in communicating, less need to compensate for hearing loss, reduced anger and frustration, reduction in depression and anxiety, enhanced emotional stability, reductions in paranoid feelings, reduced social phobias, greater belief that you are in control of your life, reduced self-criticism, increased self-esteem, improved perceptions of mental acuity, improved health status, greater level of outgoingness (e.g. extroversion) and greater likelihood of participating in groups. I challenge anyone to name a product or a service with this impressive list of benefits. When I presented these findings to a group of medical doctors, one prominent physician stated, *"I was not aware of the seriousness of hearing loss and the potential for hearing aids to alleviate the problem. Every doctor in the world must be made aware of these findings!"*

### 8. Feeling Priced Out of the Market

Some people with hearing loss simply do not have the disposable income that would enable them to afford today's modern hearing aids. Based on the known benefits of hearing aids in improving quality of life there is some effort to see if more government programs such as Medicare will cover hearing aids. If the person with a hearing loss is a child many local and state governments offer hearing aids at no or reduced cost. Check to see if you qualify for free, or a reduced price for hearing aids through your union, employer, the Veterans Administration, your insurance provider, local HMO or your local Lions Club.

## Ten Ways to Optimize your Chances of being a Satisfied Hearing Aid Wearer

There is nothing more important to the manufacturers of hearing aids and hearing healthcare professionals than your satisfaction with their product and services. Like any smart professionals , they know that satisfied clients lead to repeat business and to positive word-of-mouth advertising for their products. The hearing aid industry is interested in delighting you, in meeting your needs and exceeding your expectations. The hearing aid industry is people-oriented in that it allows significant interaction and communication between the person with the hearing loss and the hearing health professional to assure that they have done all things possible to meet your needs. It is important to emphasize that you have a roll to play in assuring your satisfaction with hearing aids.

So, I would like to offer some suggestions for optimizing the chances that you will be one of these delighted hearing aid wearers.

## 1. Meeting Your Needs

Simply stated, satisfaction is having your needs, desires or expectations met. Another way of looking at satisfaction is that you are fulfilled, based on a promise which may have come from the hearing care provider, literature, a website, advertising or a mixture of these sources. You have very specific needs and the purpose of the hearing healthcare provider is to find out what your needs are and how to meet them. Thus, during the process of rediscovering your hearing it is important to determine what your needs are, what outcomes you are looking for, and most importantly, how you'll know when you've fulfilled your needs. Many people go into their hearing healthcare practitioner with a vague concept of their need: "I can't hear," or "It seems as if people are mumbling more," or worse yet, "My wife says I don't listen to her."

I believe you will have a more fulfilling hearing aid experience if you dig deeper to comprehend the impact your hearing loss has had on your life emotionally, behaviorally, mentally and socially. There are a number of chapters in this book that can help you in this task. Write the issues down because they will become a roadmap for both you and your hearing healthcare professional. Also, many hearing healthcare professionals have assessment scales that will help you understand problems caused by your hearing loss (as described in Chapter 5). Once you know your problems, you can better identify your expected outcomes. It's your personal needs list and when it's fulfilled it will bring a smile to your face and the faces of your loved ones. This list also becomes a contract between you and your hearing care professional.

Identification of communication situations that cause you the most difficulty is a critical first step in solving your hearing loss problems. If you can describe difficult listening conditions, your hearing care provider can address the problems and develop strategies to help you manage them. If you need more information, ask for it. Some people want highly technical information about hearing aid systems and hearing loss, while others just want a brief overview of hearing aids and their function. Most providers will be happy you asked, and will give you information such as consumer literature, data sheets, brochures, videotapes and other types of instructional materials. Ask for clarification if you need it. Many complex concepts can be explained in an uncomplicated way.

## 2. Motivation

Advanced hearing aid technology can now compensate for most hearing losses, but there are still millions of hearing aid candidates who are not ready to accept this fact. Is there a missing link? I think so. People with hearing loss are in different stages of readiness. At one extreme the individual is in denial about the hearing loss. If either a family member or a professional insists on hearing aids at this point, behavior is unlikely to change and most likely such a person would be dissatisfied if pursuing hearing aids.

Individuals highly motivated to improve their hearing have an infinitely better chance of success with hearing aids. Such motivated people recognize their hearing loss and are open to change. They tend to seek out relevant information related to their hearing loss and the technology needed to alleviate the hearing problem. The most highly motivated hearing aid candidates have a willingness to discuss their feelings about their hearing problem and explore some hearing options that might be available to them. When they are fitted with hearing aids, they eagerly explore their new technology, discuss problems during follow-up visits with their hearing healthcare professional, and patiently learn to adapt to their technology.

## 3. Positive Attitude

The most important personality trait that one could possess is a positive attitude, not just toward the process of obtaining hearing aids, but toward life in general. Motivation is a key to success with amplification. This means a willingness to try hearing aids, adapt to new solutions, and keep frustration at a minimum when obstacles arise. If you view your circumstances as beyond your control, there's a higher probability that you'll be less successful in adapting to change, including hearing aid use.

Hearing aid studies have shown that people who have a positive outlook on life do better with hearing aids.[6] They have a positive self-image and believe they're in control of their life. My recommendation is take charge and be determined to improve the quality of your life with today's modern hearing aids!

## 4. Age of Your Hearing Aids

It is human nature to want to keep your hearing aids as long as possible in order to maximize value. However, it should be kept in mind that hearing aids do break down over time, ear canals change in shape, and your hearing loss is likely to change in time. In the research that I have conducted, customer satisfaction is at its highest in the first three months of use (69 percent). After five years of use, satisfaction drops significantly to 46 percent and after fifteen years of use even lower to 35 percent.[7]

So, it's important that you make sure that both the physical and audiological fit of your hearing aids is optimized for your hearing loss today rather than the way it was five, ten or fifteen years ago. I would recommend that you replace your hearing aids every four years; if your hearing aids are programmable you may be able to keep them longer since your hearing care provider can usually adjust them to the degree of hearing loss you currently have.

## 5. Choice of Technology

I have conducted extensive research across dozens of technologies. There is no doubt that customers are more satisfied with programmable technology.[3,8] Advanced programmable technology allows the dispenser to adjust the hearing aid to your specific hearing loss characteristics with more precision. If the product does not meet your needs then the hearing healthcare professional can adjust the hearing aid at their location versus sending it back to the manufacturer for adjustment.

With advancements in hearing aid technology, there has been a corresponding improvement in computer software that acoustically fits your hearing instruments to your specific needs. For example, some manufacturers store hundreds of "real world" sounds in the computer and allow you to see how your hearing aids will sound in those situations. This tremendous feature allows the hearing aid dispenser to dynamically adjust the hearing aids based on your personal reaction to sounds. If you can afford advanced technology, do not hesitate to purchase programmable hearing aids.

A second advanced feature to consider is directional hearing aids. They have either two or three microphones in them. Because of their design they are able to reduce some annoying background noise and have been proven in both the lab and in the real world to improve your ability to understand speech in many difficult listening situations. I have conducted three studies on directional hearing aids. I found a 17 percent customer satisfaction improvement in two studies and a 26 percent improvement in another.[3,4,8] The latter achieved a 90 percent customer satisfaction rating, the highest I have ever seen in a hearing aid. If you are an active person, then directional hearing aids could be suitable for you.

## 6. Controls on Your Hearing Aid

Your goal is to purchase a hearing aid that never needs adjustments. It should graciously determine the volume you need and adjust its directionality by sensing if you are in quiet or a variety of noisy situations. If you have a completely digital hearing aid, when it comes across steady state noise like in an airplane cabin or around an air conditioner, it should improve your hearing comfort in these situations by making the sounds more tolerable. In addition, it should not give you feedback (whistling, buzzing or squealing) as it amplifies sounds around you. It should restore your ability to enjoy some soft sounds (e.g. leaves rustling, bubbling of a fish tank, etc.) while sensing very loud sounds and making them comfortable for you (loud sounds should never be painful to your ears).

While the industry has in principle developed automatic hearing instruments, some people need to personally control their hearing instruments. Research has shown, especially among experienced wearers, that some people (roughly a third) still need either a volume control, multiple memory switch (quiet versus noisy situation switch) or a remote control in order to control volume or to access different hearing aid strategies for handling different listening environments. Some people need control of their hearing aid for the following reasons: the automatic feature does not meet their needs in 100 percent of listening situations; psychologically the hearing aid wearer simply must have control of their hearing aids; or they are long-term hearing aid wearers who are used to a volume control and are therefore unwilling to part with it through habit.

It is very important that you determine your needs with respect to control of the hearing aid. You don't want to fiddle with your hearing aids every ten minutes but then again you don't want to be frustrated because your hearing aids work well in most situations but not in ten percent of your favorite situations (e.g. listening to soft music). This is an area that needs to be explored with your hearing health professional.

118

## 7. Sound Quality

One of the most important aspects of an enjoyable hearing aid experience is that you like the sound quality of hearing aids. So when you test-run your hearing aids, make sure that you consider the following dimensions of sound quality:

- Do you like the sound of your voice?
- Is the sound clean and crisp (sound clarity)?
- Is the sound too tinny?
- Does your hearing aid plug up your ears and muffle sound?
- Does it make some pleasant soft sounds audible to you?
- Are loud sounds uncomfortable to you?
- Are your hearing aids natural sounding?
- Does music sound pleasant and rich in texture?
- Does the world sound like you are in a barrel?
- Does your hearing aid whistle, buzz or squeal on its own?

With today's modern digital hearing aids, most of these problems should be solved. If you notice any of these problems during the trial run and in your follow-up visits, by all means talk to your hearing healthcare professional about these issues. Such professionals are now capable of adjusting your hearing aids to your satisfaction. The extent to which all of the possible sound quality issues can be resolved is, of course, governed by the severity of your hearing loss. In other words, some types of hearing losses are simply more conducive to restoration of rich sound quality in many listening environments while others are not.

## 8. Do not Purchase Based Only on Cosmetics

Since the 1990s, the hearing aid industry has reduced the size of hearing aids to near invisibility. People can now wear them with greater comfort and we're finding very small CIC hearing aids have their distinct advantages such as on the telephone and in outdoor situations. Some people are concerned with cosmetics and prefer the least noticeable hearing aids, in the way that you might choose contact lenses instead of framed eyeglasses. The problem is that the smallest hearing aid may not be the most suitable hearing solution for you for a variety of reasons. Your specific hearing loss may require more power than is available in CICs.

Because of hearing loss stigma or embarrassment, many

consumers come into hearing healthcare offices and start off the dialog with, "I would like one of those invisible hearing aids that I saw on TV." A likely response may be something like: "We carry invisible hearing aids, but I first need to examine your ears, measure your hearing loss, assess your lifestyle and manual dexterity and then discuss how your hearing loss is impacting the quality of your life. You may or may not be a candidate for these hearing aids." If it is determined that you are not a candidate for CIC hearing aids and you still insist on buying them, the professional hearing health provider will not fit you with the product because in essence they would be giving you the wrong prescription for your hearing loss.

## 9. Have Realistic Expectations during the Trial Period

Follow the instructions you are given during the initial stages of adjustment. These are designed to help in formulating realistic expectations of what to expect from your hearing aids. You may need a specific wearing schedule for hearing aids. One experienced in-the-canal hearing aid wearer obtained CIC instruments a few years ago. He was in his early 30s and had used hearing aids since he was a teenager. When he returned for his two-week recheck, he was asked how long he could wear the instruments in the beginning. He said that he could only use them for fifteen minutes at a time. Within two weeks he was wearing them full-time and they were completely comfortable. Had he not been counseled that the deep insertion of the shell tip with CIC hearing aids may take extra time to fully adjust to, he might have become discouraged and given up on that particular style of hearing aids.

Be patient with yourself. If you have the best hearing aids for your hearing loss and your lifestyle, hang in there. Make sure you're comfortable with the advice you've been given. Ask questions. Remember, your provider is your advocate. Satisfied hearing aid wearers are not shy when it comes to telling others about their success, but unfortunately, neither are the ones who are dissatisfied. No two people are alike, and it's not a good idea to assume if someone has had a bad experience, all hearing aids are bad. You could very well be one of the overwhelming majority who has a good experience! There are many reasons why someone may not have been successful, so don't project these conditions and improbabilities onto yourself. Also, do not expect someone else's hearing aids to work for you. Would you wear their eyeglasses and decide whether you could be helped based on this experience?

Be realistic. Hearing aids will not permit you to hear the flapping of hummingbird wings over a lawnmower. Remember that it takes time to get used to hearing aids, especially if you're a new wearer. Keep in mind that background noise is almost always part of your environment, and adjustment to it is required. In time, you will tune out many of these everyday sounds. It's important not to become disappointed or frustrated while your brain begins to adjust to a whole new world of sound. If you're an experienced wearer trying new hearing aids, understand that they might not sound like your old ones. Before you reject them, allow neural hook-ups in the auditory system to adapt to these new sounds. You just might find that you like this new sound better than the old one.

## 10. Earwax Protection

One of the common causes of hearing aid failure is that moisture and earwax fill up the receiver tubing of the hearing aid causing the hearing aid speaker to no longer function correctly.

I strongly suggest that you purchase hearing aids with proven methods of keeping earwax out of the hearing aid. I have personally studied more than 90,000 hearing aid owners over a two-year period and determined that it is possible to reduce hearing aid repairs by 50 percent due to receiver failure by using a wax guard at the end of the hearing aids.[9]

# 12 Reasons to Purchase <u>Two</u> Hearing Aids Instead of One

Research with more than 5,000 consumers with hearing loss in both ears demonstrated that binaurally fit subjects (two hearing aids) are more satisfied than those monaurally fit (one hearing aid).[10]

When given the choice and allowed to hear binaurally, the overwhelming majority of consumers choose two hearing aids over one.

Consequently, binaural users tend to communicate better in their place of worship, in small group gatherings, large gatherings and even outdoors. Naturally, a person's ability to enjoy hearing aids will differ based on the specific hearing loss and the type of technology used in the hearing aids.

Nevertheless, if you have a hearing loss in both ears and there is useable hearing in your poorer ear, budget permitting, I would recommend a hearing aid for both ears. Many hearing healthcare providers can demonstrate the binaural advantage on your very first visit, under headphone testing or even with a programmable fitting.

Based on a review of the literature and my own research with thousands of consumers with hearing loss in both ears, here are many reasons why you should purchase a binaural hearing system when two are indicated.[11]

**1. Keeps both ears active, resulting in less hearing deterioration.** As Dr. Carmen identifies in Chapter One, research has shown that when only one hearing instrument is worn, the unaided ear tends to lose its ability to hear and understand. This is clinically called the auditory deprivation effect. People wearing two hearing instruments keep both ears active. In fact, wearing one hearing aid (when two are indicated) could result in greater deterioration of hearing in the unaided ear than if wearing no hearing aid at all.

**2. Better understanding of speech.** By wearing two hearing instruments rather than one, selective listening is more easily achieved. This means your brain can focus on the conversation you want to hear. Research shows that people wearing two hearing aids routinely understand speech and conversation significantly better than people wearing one.

**3. Better understanding in group and noisy situations.** Speech intelligibility is improved in difficult listening situations when wearing two hearing aids. However, advanced binaural technology (programmable analog or digital) tends to perform better in noise than older (analog) technology.

**4. Better ability to tell direction of sound.** This is called localization. Research shows that in binaural use, there's an average of a 15 percent shift in increased satisfaction in "ability to tell the direction of sounds." This is a substantial improvement! In a social gathering, for example, localization allows you to hear from which direction someone is speaking to you. In traffic, you can tell from which direction a car or siren is coming.

**5. Better sound quality.** When you listen to a stereo system, you use both speakers to get the smoothest, sharpest, most natural sound quality. The same thing can be said of hearing aids. By wearing two hearing instruments, you increase your hearing range from 180 degrees reception (with just one instrument) to 360 degrees. This greater range provides a better sense of balance and sound quality.

**6. Smoother tone quality.** Wearing two hearing instruments generally requires less volume. This results in less distortion and better reproduction of sounds.

**7. Reduced feedback and whistling.** With a lower volume control setting the chances of hearing aid feedback is reduced.

**8. Wider hearing range.** It's true. A person can hear sounds from a further distance with two ears, rather than just one. A voice that's barely heard at ten feet with one ear can be heard up to forty feet with two ears.

**9. Better sound identification.** Often, with just one hearing instrument, many noises and words sound alike. But with two hearing instruments, as with two ears, sounds are more easily distinguishable.

**10. Hearing is less tiring and listening more pleasant.** More binaural hearing aid wearers report that listening and participating in conversation is more enjoyable with two instruments. This is because you do not have to strain to hear with the better ear. Thus, binaural hearing can help make listening (and therefore life) more relaxing.

**11. Feeling of balanced hearing.** Two-eared hearing results in a feeling of balanced reception of sound, also known as the stereo effect, whereas monaural hearing creates an unusual feeling of sounds being heard in one ear.

**12. Tinnitus Masking.** About 50 percent of people with ringing in their ears report improvement when wearing hearing aids. If you have a hearing aid in only one ear, there will still be ringing in the unaided ear.

## How to Align Your Expectations
## with Hearing Aid Performance

Here are some issues you should keep in mind as you develop appropriate expectations about what your hearing aids can and cannot do for you:[12-13]

- No matter how technically advanced, in most cases hearing aids cannot restore your hearing to normal except is some very mild hearing losses.

- Not all hearing aids perform the same with every type of hearing loss.

- No hearing aid has been designed which will filter out all background noise. Some hearing instruments can reduce amplification of some types of background noise or make you more comfortable in the presence of noise.

- Where appropriate, directional microphones can often improve your ability to hear in noise.

- When directional hearing instruments are coupled with digital signal processing, you can be assured that your hearing instruments are optimized for improving your quality of life in noisy environments.

- Since you are purchasing custom hearing instruments, you should expect the fit to be comfortable; ideally you should not even know they are in your ears. There should not be any soreness, bleeding, or rashes associated with your wearing hearing aids. If there is, go back to your hearing health provider to make adjustments to the shell of the aid or earmold.

- Hearing instruments should allow you to:
  (1) hear soft sounds (e.g. child's voice, soft speech) that you could not hear without amplification—this is part of the enjoyment of hearing aids;
  (2) understand speech in quiet situations—many people will derive some additional speech intelligibility in noise with advanced technology;
  (3) prevent loud sounds from becoming uncomfortably loud for you, but very loud sounds that are uncomfortable to normal hearing people may still be uncomfortable to you.

- Hearing aids may squeal or whistle when you are inserting them into your ear (if you do not have a volume control to shut it off); but if it squeals after the initial insertion, then most likely you have an inadequate fit and should tell your hearing health provider.

- Do not expect your friend's hearing aid brand or style to work for you.
- Do not expect your family doctor to know very much about hearing loss, brands of hearing aids and whether or not you need them.
- Expect your hearing aids to provide benefit to you during the trial period. By benefit, I mean that your ability to understand speech has demonstrably improved in the listening situations important to you (with realistic expectations though). This is what you paid for, so you should expect benefit. If you do not experience an improvement, then work with your hearing health professional to see if the instrument can be adjusted to meet your specific needs. Never purchase a hearing aid that does not give you sufficient benefit.
- Expect to be satisfied with your hearing instruments; expect the quality of your life to improve due to your hearing instruments.
- Expect a 30-day trial period with a money-back guarantee if your hearing aids do not give you benefit. (There might be a small nonrefundable portion for some services rendered.)
- Give your hearing aids a chance, being sure to follow the instructions of the hearing health provider. Most people need a period of adjustment (called acclimatization) before they are deriving the maximum benefit from their hearing instruments (even up to four months).

## Common Myths about Hearing Loss and Hearing Aids

There are many common myths still prevalent about hearing loss and hearing aids. I would like to dispel these myths now that you are living in the 21st Century.

### Your hearing loss cannot be helped.

In the past, many people with hearing loss in one ear, with a high frequency hearing loss, or with nerve damage have all been told they cannot be helped, often by their family practice physician. This might have been true many years ago, but with modern advances in technology, nearly 95 percent of people with a sensorineural hearing loss *can* be helped with hearing aids.

### Hearing loss affects only "old people" and is merely a sign of aging.

Only 35 percent of people with hearing loss are older than age 64. There are close to six million people in the U.S. between the ages of 18 and 44 with hearing loss, and more than one million are school age. Hearing loss affects all age groups.

### If I had a hearing loss, my family doctor would have told me.

Not true! Only 14 percent of physicians routinely screen for hearing loss during a physical. Since most hearing-impaired people hear well in a quiet environment like your doctor's office, it can be virtually impossible for your physician to recognize the extent of your problem. Without special training in, and understanding of the nature of hearing loss, it may be difficult for your doctor to even believe that you have a hearing problem.

### The consequences of hiding hearing loss are better than wearing hearing aids.

What price are you paying for vanity? I go back to the old adage that an untreated hearing loss is far more noticeable than hearing aids. If you miss a punch line to a joke, or respond inappropriately in conversation, people may have concerns about your mental acuity, your attention span or your ability to communicate effectively. The personal consequences of vanity can be life altering. At a simplistic level, untreated hearing loss means giving up some of the pleasant sounds you used to enjoy. At a deeper level, vanity could severely reduce the quality of your life.

### Only people with serious hearing loss need hearing aids.

The need for hearing amplification is dependent on your lifestyle, your need for refined hearing, and the degree of your hearing loss. If you are a lawyer, teacher or a group psychotherapist, where very refined hearing is necessary to discern the nuances of human communication, then even a mild hearing loss can be intolerable. If you live in a rural area by yourself and seldom socialize, then perhaps you are someone who is tolerant of even moderate hearing losses.

**I'll just have some minor surgery like my friend did, and then my hearing will be okay.**

Many people know someone whose hearing improved after medical or surgical treatment, and it's true that some types of hearing loss can be successfully treated. With adults, unfortunately, this only applies to five to ten percent of cases.

**My hearing loss is normal for my age.**

Isn't this a strange way to look at things? But, do you realize that well-meaning doctors tell this to their patients everyday. It happens to be "normal" for overweight people to have high blood pressure. That doesn't mean they should not receive treatment for the problem.

**I have one ear that's down a little, but the other one's okay.**

Everything is relative. Nearly all patients who believe that they have one "good" ear actually have two "bad" ears. When one ear is slightly better than the other, we learn to favor that ear for the telephone, group conversations, and so forth. It can give the illusion that "the better ear" is normal when it isn't. Most types of hearing loss affect both ears fairly equally, and about 90 percent of patients are in need of hearing aids for both ears.

**Hearing aids will make me look "older" and "handicapped."**

Looking older is clearly more affected by almost all other factors besides hearing aids. It's not the hearing aids that make one look older, it's what one may believe they imply. If hearing aids help you function like a normal hearing person, for all intents and purposes, the stigma is removed. Hearing aid manufacturers are well aware that cosmetics are an issue to many people, and that's why today we have hearing aids that fit totally in the ear canal (essentially not noticeable unless someone is staring directly into your ear). This CIC style of hearing aid has enough power and special features to satisfy at least 50 percent of individuals with hearing impairment. But more importantly, keep in mind that "a hearing loss is more obvious than a hearing aid." Smiling and nodding your head when you don't understand what's being said makes your condition more apparent than the largest hearing aid.

**Hearing aids will make everything sound too loud.**

Hearing aids are amplifiers. At one time, the way that hearing aids were designed, it was necessary to turn up the power in order to hear soft speech (or other soft sounds). Then, normal conversation indeed would have been too loud. With today's hearing aids, however, the circuit works automatically, only providing the amount of amplification needed based on the input level. In fact, many hearing aids today don't have a volume control.

## Conclusions

Hopefully, you now recognize the value of hearing aids and the significant impact they can have on your life, as well as the life of your family and associates. I also hope you realize that hearing aids may not necessarily be an instant cure for your hearing difficulties, but with patience, you will find they can be your bridge to healing.

Enjoy the experience!

## References

1. Kochkin S. MarkeTrak V: Why my hearing aids are in the drawer: the consumer's perspective. The Hearing Journal 53(2): 34-42, 2000.
2. Kochkin S. MarkeTrak IV: correlates of hearing aid purchase intent. The Hearing Journal 51(1): 30-41, 1998.
3. Kochkin S. Customer satisfaction and subjective benefit with high-performance hearing instruments. The Hearing Review 3(12): 16-26, 1996.
4. Kochkin S. MarkeTrak VI – 10 year customer satisfaction trends in the U.S. hearing instrument market. The Hearing Review 9(10): 14-25, 46, 2002.
5. Kochkin S and Rogin C. Quantifying the obvious: the impact of hearing aids on quality of life, The Hearing Review 7(1): 8-34, 2000.
6. Singer J, Healey J. and Preece J. Hearing instruments: a psychological and behavioral perspective. High Performance Hearing Solutions 1, 1997.
7. Kochkin S. MarkeTrak VI database, Knowles Electronics: Itasca, IL. (Unpublished).
8. Kochkin S. Customer satisfaction with single and multiple microphone digital hearing aids, The Hearing Review 7(11): 24-29, 2000.

9. Kochkin S. Finally a solution to the cerumen problem. <u>The Hearing Review</u>: 9(4): 2002.

10. Kochkin S. and Kuk F. The binaural advantage: evidence from subjective benefit and customer satisfaction data. <u>The Hearing Review</u>:4(4): 29,30-32,34, 1997.

11. Kochkin S. *Binaural Hearing Aids: The Fitting of Choice for Bilateral Loss Subjects.* (An unpublished technical paper.) Itasca, IL: Knowles Electronics, 2000.

12. Allen, Rose. Reasonable Expectations for the Consumer. <u>www.healthyhearing.com</u>. August, 2002.

13. Stypulkowski P. Realistic expectations: a key to success. <u>High Performance Hearing Solutions</u> 1, 1997.

# CHAPTER EIGHT

# The Questions and Answers
# What the Experts Say
*Richard Carmen, Au.D.*

---

Dr. Carmen received his Doctor of Audiology Degree from the Arizona School of Health Sciences, a division of the Kirksville College of Osteopathic Medicine. He's been practicing audiology and issuing hearing aids since 1972, during which time he pioneered research into the effects of metabolic diseases on hearing. He has written extensively in the field as a regular contributor to various hearing journals, and of his previous book publications, two were written for the consumer. His material has appeared in such popular consumer-based periodicals as *The Saturday Evening Post, Ladies' Home Journal* and *Self Magazine*. He has maintained his present clinical practice in Sedona, Arizona since 1990.

---

While this book strives to address the most important issues pertaining to hearing loss and hearing aids, this section covers questions and answers not addressed elsewhere in this book. The questions developed were ones you yourself may have wanted to ask. As a result, the most seasoned and tenured professionals were invited to answer them. Here's what the experts had to say!

## 1. From your research, what have you discovered about the process of *listening*?

**Richard Halley, Ph.D.**, Professor of Communication at Weber State University, Ogden, Utah, is considered an expert on the topic of listening. He has been a longtime board member of the International Listening Association and has written many papers and a few books on this subject matter. Among newsworthy attention directed to Dr. Halley's work, he has been a repeated guest on ABC's "20/20."

The most obvious connection between hearing and listening is that if one does not hear the sounds, we cannot expect that person to interpret the meaning of the sounds with any accuracy. One of the things we know about listening is that people tend to hear what they want to hear (or more accurately what they expect to hear). Each individual literally creates in their mind a fairly accurate mathematical model of what they expect a message to be like. This capacity makes it possible for us to predict something about what a person is likely to say.

The advantage is that often when we're listening and we don't hear a small part of a sentence, we can guess quite accurately at what the rest of the sentence is. However, if you lose some hearing, you still have the mathematical models in your head and the predictions for what comes next in a message remain pretty strong. Yet, if you're not hearing accurately or are missing some of the sounds (some of the words even), your capacity to accurately predict is greatly reduced. If you have a hearing loss, you must learn to be conscious of the effects it has on your ability to predict. If you're careful, prediction can help you understand because your brain often knows how to fill in some of the missing parts. But if you assume this process is still as accurate as it was before your hearing loss, and you interpret messages based on what was heard with the old models, the number of interpretation errors you make will increase dramatically.

One of the things we know is that men and women process information differently. Thus, it's important that we not talk as though all of our advice will work exactly the same for both sexes. One of the major differences is that men better than women are often able to stay focused on one speaker and ignore others in the environment. This has the advantage that many men may be able to work in situations that are noisier than many women can tolerate. It has the significant disadvantage that men often do not hear someone call to them when they are concentrating on a message such as a TV program, or more specifically, like Monday night football! This is true for men with good hearing. If you are hard of hearing, listening becomes that much more difficult.

On the other hand, women far more often than men tend to check their environment for other important messages. The advantage is that women can often work on one task and be able to check another task often enough that they can also complete the second task. For example, many women can fix dinner or work on some other task while staying aware of a small child without putting the youngster at risk. Their multi-focus ability exceeds that of men. The disadvantage is that when women listen to a message that requires a great deal of concentration (perhaps because the material is new or difficult), they will still check their environment for other messages and may miss critical parts of that difficult message and thus become confused or misunderstand the message.

So, listening requires focus despite your gender, and whether you have good hearing or not. Hearing loss merely makes the listening process more challenging.

## 2. Is there a relationship between *exercise* and *better hearing*?

**Helaine Alessio, Ph.D.** Professor, Department of Physical Health, Health and Sports Studies at Miami University, is a Fellow of the American College of Sports Medicine and a Scripps Gerontology Fellow, and the recipient of several NIH grants.

**Kathleen Hutchinson, Ph.D.**, Professor and Chair, Department of Speech Pathology and Audiology at Miami University, is Chair of the Department of Speech Pathology and Audiology, and has authored several articles on personality attributes related to hearing aid use and aural rehabilitation.

**Dr. Alessio and Dr. Hutchinson** have co-authored more than twenty research papers and are currently working on a longitudinal study on cardiovascular health and hearing sensitivity.

In plain English, <u>Yes</u>! Recent advances in medicine and positive changes toward healthy lifestyles have challenged some long held assumptions about "inevitable aging changes"—including hearing loss. Impaired hearing in older years has always been considered as something to be expected. Although significant hearing loss is present in approximately 1 out of every 3 Americans aged 65 years and older, we've learned that hearing sensitivity can be maintained very well into those "older" years if:

- you were not exposed to loud noises at work or home for long periods of time;
- you wore ear protection when exposed to loud noises;
- you did not take certain ototoxic medications;
- and if you maintained a healthy cardiovascular fitness level.

The exception to these findings would be a hearing loss with a genetic component or a family history of hearing impairment. Research from our laboratory and several others in the U.S. have consistently reported a positive relation between the cardiovascular system and functional ability of the organs and tissues in the inner ear. Much of the explanation behind the protective effects of cardiovascular fitness lies in enhanced circulation of blood that is needed to supply the bones and muscles of the inner ear. When blood flow is impeded, then nutrients (like antioxidants and protective heat shock proteins) will not be available. Blood flow can be impeded by cholesterol build-up in the walls of the artery, and vasoconstriction (narrowing) that has been correlated with high blood pressure, smoking, stress, and some personality types.

The U.S. Surgeon General's report on *Physical Activity and Health* recommends that everyone engage in aerobic exercise. Figure 8-1 shows the benefits to aerobic exercise in most age groups when cardiovascular fitness is attained.

This means large muscle movements, such as walking, bicycling, and swimming, for at least 20-30 minutes at a time, five days per week. When examining exercise that is performed on a one-time only basis, aerobic exercise may divert blood flow from metabolically less active parts of the body (like organs and tissues of the inner ear) to metabolically more active parts (like skeletal muscles engaged in exercise). This may at first appear to be harmful. However, exercise on a regular basis has been shown to result in blood that is well-stocked with nutrients (like vitamins, antioxidants, and adequate levels of sugar), protective proteins (like heat shock proteins), as well as blood that is not littered with cholesterol, triglycerides, or too much sugar.

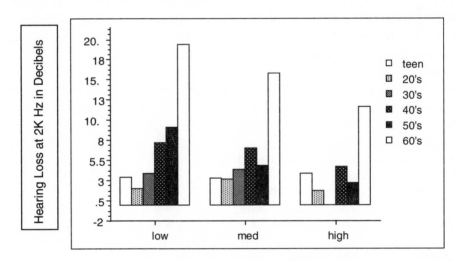

Figure 8-1: The higher the cardiovascular fitness, the better hearing in most age groups.

When performed regularly, aerobic exercise results in blood vessels that tend to be more supple, allowing for transitions in blood flow from rest to exercise, and resilient to withstanding blood pressure changes without suffering major impairments to the walls of the arteries. These changes to the vessels that carry blood impact every square inch of the body because cells live or die by blood supply and debris removal.

Our research during the past decade on over a thousand subjects ages 8-88 have resulted in the following conclusions:

1) hearing loss occurs with age, but noticeable hearing loss does not appear until after age 50;

2) having low cardiovascular fitness at any age is associated with poorer hearing sensitivity compared to those with medium or high level cardiovascular fitness; and

3) persons older than 50 who have moderate or high cardiovascular fitness levels maintain their hearing sensitivity comparable to persons who are in their 30's.

We speculate that the association of hearing loss and cardiovascular fitness are related by the common mechanism of improved blood circulation.

**3. We know that the heart carries nutrition throughout the body, including the ear. Without absorption of nutrients critical to hearing, its function would stop. For example, many people who have gone on a starvation diet as a political protest have lost some of their hearing. Since Americans have become so vitamin and mineral conscious, is there anything you can recommend that has been shown to positively impact hearing?**

Martin Dayton, D.O., is Past-President of the International and American Association of Clinical Nutritionists. Dr. Dayton is in clinical practice in Miami, Florida.

Unfortunately, no specific nutritional treatment is generally used or known to address hearing loss in all people. However, strategies do exist which may address the needs of the individual with impaired hearing, in accordance with the unique circumstances of the person. These circumstances are governed by the inherited and acquired strengths and weaknesses of the individual and the conditions under which the person exists.

A child may have an inherited predisposition to allergies and live in an environment where junk food is a staple. This child may be prone to develop a form of "stuffed ears" known as serous otitis media. Fluid accumulates in the middle ear due to allergy-mediated inflammation, swelling, and closure of the Eustachian tube. Dysfunctional pressures may develop in the ear. Infection may take hold in part due to impaired transport of immune factors to the area and impaired drainage of toxic fluids from the ear due to swelling.

On the other hand, an elderly person with an inherited predisposition to hardening of the arteries who eats the nutritionally sub-optimal standard American diet may develop progressive hearing loss. This is due to auditory nerve tissue deterioration associated with impaired circulation—accelerated with aging. Perhaps, accumulation of environmental or pharmaceutical toxic materials with time is also a role in the manifestation of hearing loss.

These two cases illustrate how diverse the contributing circumstances can be in regard to the manifestation of hearing loss. Each case must be handled differently in the use of nutrition to address the same goal of improved hearing. The child in the first example needs to avoid foods which may trigger allergies. Wheat, cow's milk, peanuts, chocolate, eggs, and soy are frequent offenders. Various methods are used to determine which foods need to be avoided, when and how often. Various methods may be used to reduce such sensitivities. Plant extracts from stinging nettles, aloe vera, citrus and seeds of grapes may reverse the allergic processes. Vitamins, such as C and pantothenic acid may also be useful. Addressing deficiencies of various substances improves overall resistance to disease.

The older person in the second example needs to improve circulation and, in part, to reverse processes which lead to deterioration. Plant extracts such as Ginkgo biloba improves efficiency and function of tissues subject to sub-optimal circulation. Niacin increases blood flow via dilation of blood vessels and may restore cholesterol to a more optimal state. Turmeric (Curcuma longa) reduces the tendency to build-up of blockages within the walls of arteries, and helps prevent deterioration of tissues.

Various substances help prevent tissue deterioration and foster repair. Optimal repair of nerve tissue needs an abundance of the components found in such tissue cofactors which make them work. Lecithin contains materials needed for cell wall repair, and chemicals needed for communication between nerve cells. Vitamin B12, alpha-lipoic acid, and thiamin are co-factors that help maintain and repair nerve tissue. Various nutritional substances help to directly remove toxins, or fortify the detoxification organs of the body so they are more effective in achieving their intended purpose. Adequate detoxification is necessary for normal function and repair. Vitamin C, garlic, and chlorella, are helpful. And many nutritional substances have multiple benefits.

Animal and plant substances may be used in various ways. For example, extracts from fetal (unborn young) sheep tissues, such as from the fetal auditory nerve, may be taken by injection to stimulate organization and regeneration of human tissues associated with hearing. Fetal tissue is programmed by nature to generate into fully functioning organ systems. After peak reproductive years, bodily tissues are programmed to disorganize and deteriorate to eventually make room for the next generations to come. The use of fetal tissue appears, in part, to counter this trend.

The most important aspect of nutritional care in regard to ear problems lies between the ears in taking care of the needs of the rest of the person who is attached to the ears.

### 4. Most of us would assume, once hair cells die, the condition is permanent with irreversible sensorineural hearing loss. Would you share with readers what you've discovered, and any implications it might hold for restoration of hearing in humans?

Edwin W Rubel, Ph.D., is Virginia Merrill Bloedel Professor of Hearing Science, and Professor in the Departments of Otolaryngology—Head and Neck Surgery, Physiology/Biophysics, Neurological Surgery and Psychology at the University of Washington. Dr. Rubel has published over 200 scientific articles and edited three books on various topics related to development and plasticity of the auditory system.

Research on hair cell regeneration was not a major topic of research in hearing science until 1986-87. At that time, my group was one of two that discovered mature birds had the remarkable natural ability to reform their inner ear hair cells. This occurred after either damage produced by loud noises or after damage produced by certain therapeutic drugs like antibiotics (see Figure 8-2). This was quite startling to us as well as to the rest of the scientific community. Confirmation through DNA technology supported what we were seeing. After damage occurred, there were indeed new hair cells generated by renewed cell division in several species of fully mature birds.

We now know that all vertebrates, *except mammals*, can regenerate new hair cells in the inner ear after native hair cells are damaged or destroyed. In some parts of the inner ear of some animals, there is ongoing production and death of hair cells (like the "turnover" of skin cells) throughout life, while in others new cells are produced only when there is damage to the native ones. We and others are working hard to understand the molecular chain of events responsible for hair cell regeneration in the species where it occurs. This may provide the clues for how to make it happen in humans and other mammals.

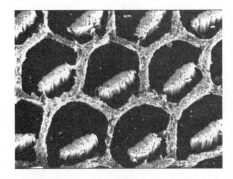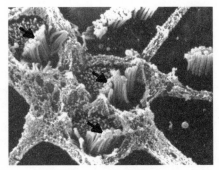

Photomicrographs provided courtesy of Edwin W. Rubel, Ph.D., Virginia Merrill Bloedel Hearing Research Center, University of Washington. Used by permission.

Figure 8-2: Left photo shows normal hair cell clusters. Right photo arrows show hair cell regeneration after being destroyed.

The work on mammals now is at a point where we can induce a small amount of cell division in the inner ear in a dish (that is, in culture), as well as in vivo (occurring within a living organism). This has been done on mice, guinea pigs and rats using a variety of growth-promoting molecules. We have also discovered one gene (and there will be others) that is responsible for turning off the production of hair cells during development and may be involved in preventing regeneration.

Therefore, we at least know that it's *possible* to induce the first stage of regeneration to a limited extent in the inner ear sensory epithelium of mature mammals. The sensory epithelia make up parts of the inner ear that cause the initial response to sound and balance. So, most of the success has been done in the balance parts of the inner ear, but we and others are working on the cochlea. In fact, a team of researchers has recently used new findings from research on development of the inner ear to induce a few new cells in the guinea pig cochlea to become hair cells, again proving that it will be possible.

The good news is that for the first time in history, there are teams of investigators worldwide exploring the possibility that hair cell regeneration can be induced in the mammal and human cochlea. In the mid-1990s, there were only two laboratories exploring this possibility. Now there are probably 20 or 30. The bad news is funding. It's a real problem. Until we actually find candidate molecules for use in humans, this research won't be taken over by pharmaceutical companies. Once they step in, they will heavily invest in developing human therapies. But, until then, the entire cost of this research must be borne by the federal government and private foundations.

I feel that within five to ten years, we could easily find out if it's possible to regenerate hair cells at robust levels, sufficient to restore hearing in mammals if the funds were available to support large multi-investigator teams working on this problem. Unfortunately, such funding does not exist at this time so small groups are struggling along to get one grant after another and do one experiment at a time. From discovery of molecules that could induce regeneration in laboratory animals, it could be as little as another 10 years until we achieve hair cell regeneration in humans. If successful, it could eliminate some of the need for hearing aids and cochlear implants as we now know them.

When I started this work, somebody said to me that I'd never be able to restore the complexity and intricacies of hair cells in humans or other mammals. My response hasn't changed: "You could be right, but without trying, it surely won't happen. If our goal is to actually restore hearing—it's the only game in town."

## 5. How can we change present prejudices and misunderstanding about hearing loss and the use of hearing aids?

Ray P. Cuzzort, Ph.D., Boulder, Colorado. Dr. Cuzzort has taught sociology at the University of Colorado in Boulder for the past 30 years. As a leading Sociologist, he's written extensively on social theory, and published books and articles on this subject matter, specifically focusing on how people deal with stigmatic conditions.

I can answer this best by asking another set of questions: hearing aids have been shunned by a number of people with serious hearing problems, while eyeglasses are often worn by people with no meaningful loss of vision. Why is a prosthetic device avoided in one instance and welcomed in the other?

The foremost concern with any prosthetic device is how effectively it deals with the physical defect it seeks to correct. This is a relative matter and not as simple as it might first appear to be. If a defect is seriously debilitating, a moderately effective prosthetic device will be relied on. However, if a defect is modest, only a superbly effective prosthetic device is likely to be preferred by a wearer. Complicating the issue is the extent to which revealing the defect is considered stigmatizing by the person involved. If the defect is not

138

seriously stigmatizing, then a prosthetic device is more likely to be utilized. For example, teenagers wear dental braces despite their mildly disfiguring appearance because ill-formed teeth are not seriously stigmatizing. Wearing a hearing aid, however, suggests that the wearer could be socially handicapped.

People commonly wear glasses when they don't need them. Sunglasses are worn in dark cafes by men and women who want to look "hip." Similarly, "bop" glasses are worn by ghetto youngsters who want to look like jazz musicians. The obvious point being made here is that glasses are not only a prosthetic device, but a stylistic one—a part of one's attire, so to speak. Like any other item of attire, glasses can enhance the image one is trying to project. They can also detract from it.

Another consideration to deal with is the folk history of a prosthetic device and how that history is perceived by the person faced with using the device. What associations does such a history bring to mind? For one thing, glasses are associated with intellectuals, office clerks, and bookish people. These are not strong positive associations, nor are they terribly negative ones either. Glasses don't threaten the image an individual is trying to sustain.

In light of the above comments, we can turn our attention to hearing aids. Its history, for many people, goes back to a time when a huge, trumpet-like device was waved by a crotchety old person in the direction of someone talking. It was commonly used by women in the advanced stages of senility. Note: this perception does not have to be accurate—it only has to exist in order to have some effect. (For both functional reasons and to rid the hearing aid of this onus, its design has moved quickly toward extremely small and relatively-easy-to-hide versions.)

Glasses have no age-specific associations, but hearing aids are seen as an indication of the infirmities that come with being older. In modern America, protests to the contrary, being old is a problem with respect to being stigmatized. It's very likely the case that when an individual is confronted with the choice of being stigmatized by a prosthetic device or being helped by it, avoidance of the stigma will be equally, or more important, as the value of the device. At the same time, it should also be recognized that stigmatization is a social creation. What is stigmatizing in one social context is not necessarily stigmatizing in another. (The classic example of this is the jagged facial scar that means one thing if it comes from an automobile accident and another if it comes from a duel of honor.) If this is so, then shifting attitudes toward aging as a stigmatizing condition will possibly bring about shifting attitudes toward the use of amplification.

Any campaigns toward changing public perception of hearing aids might consider the following possibilities. First, show more young people, even children, in situations where hearing aids are of benefit. More broadly, show people of varied ages and in different social contexts who are relying on hearing aids.

Second, provide specific and compelling measures of the effectiveness of hearing aids. This is a primary concern in any campaign to improve acceptance.

Third, direct some attention to the non-hearing aid wearer. Social interactions, even of a very informal nature, are stressful. If hearing aid wearers are convinced that people will shun them because they have hearing problems, they will be more likely either to put their hearing aids aside, or avoid people. If hearing aid wearers can be persuaded that non-hearing aid users are not inclined to perceive them as stigmatized, then the hearing aid will be more acceptable.

Fourth, in a modern social context in which a variety of physical handicaps have been granted more tolerant social perceptions, deafness should be defined as a condition that can be effectively dealt with by the use of hearing aids, by sensitivity on the part of all involved with those who are hearing-impaired, and by a willingness on the part of the hearing-impaired person to remain a participating member of the human community.

## 6. Most people have heard of the condition of Meniere's Disease, but few, including those suffering from it, have a good understanding of the problem. Can you help clarify this disorder, and how it might differ from the similar condition of labyrinthitis?

Dennis Poe, M.D., Massachusetts Eye and Ear, Boston. Dr. Poe is an otolaryngologist specializing in neurotologic surgery and is Editor of, and Contributor to *The Consumer Handbook on Dizziness and Vertigo* (Auricle Ink Publishers, 2005). He is a Past-Board member of the Prosper Meniere's Society and considered a foremost expert on Meniere's Disease.

Dizziness and balance disorders are very common and rank among the most frequent problems seen on a daily basis by health care providers of all types. The most common causes of sudden vertigo or imbalance are Vestibular Neuritis, an inflammation or irritation of the balance nerve, Labyrinthitis, inflammation or irritation of the inner ear, Migraines, causing reduced blood flow to the balance centers in the brain, and Meniere's Disease, a disruption of the inner ear due to fluid swelling. Labyrinthitis and Meniere's Disease may be associated with varying degrees of hearing loss.

Medical professionals define vertigo as any hallucination of movement when in fact no real movement has occurred. The most common form of this is the spinning sensation that results after rapidly rotating oneself and stopping quickly. If vertigo is severe enough, it can cause secondary symptoms of nausea, vomiting, and cold sweats. It's estimated that about one third of the population will experience a significant bout of sudden vertigo during their lifetime, and the vast majority of these are due to vestibular neuritis or labyrinthitis. Still, Meniere's is common enough to affect as many as one out of 50 individuals.

Vestibular neuritis is presumably caused by viral inflammation of the vestibular (balance) nerve that brings inner ear information to the brain and results in vertigo and balance disturbances without hearing loss. More severe cases may also damage hearing or the cochlear nerve. Viral inflammation of the inner ear itself is called Labyrinthitis and usually causes both vertigo and hearing loss. Severe cases of neuritis or labyrinthitis can cause sudden unexpected vertiginous attacks with a complete loss of balance that is made worse by any head movements or by watching anything move.

These symptoms can often last for hours causing nausea, vomiting, sometimes diarrhea, all of which can be a profoundly frightening experience. The episodes are usually quite harmless and completely resolve on their own in a few days without any treatment. Like many viral illnesses, it normally will not recur. More severe forms may cause a few after shock spells of lesser magnitude within a few days of the original attack. Once the acute vertigo attacks have subsided, there's a period of dysequilibrium—a sensation that the balance is off, and may last for hours, days, or many weeks, depending on the severity of the attacks. Treatment is usually limited to symptom relief with medications to quiet the balance system. A regular exercise program is recommended to speed up the recovery process after the balance injury by stimulating the natural process of *vestibular compensation.*

Even if some degree of permanent injury were to have occurred, the brain can use information from the injured balance organ or nerve and combine it with information from the normal side. The new balance signals are integrated with the vision and senses of position and feeling in the limbs to recreate an effective balance system. Exercising speeds up this compensation process.

Meniere's Disease is believed to be the long-term result of an injury to the labyrinth, such as severe labyrinthitis that has failed to heal properly and has gone on to become a recurring cause of vertigo attacks and hearing injury. Symptoms of Meniere's Disease include recurring vertigo attacks, fluctuating hearing loss, abnormal noises in the ear (tinnitus), and pressure or fullness in the ear. This can be caused by a condition known as endolymphatic hydrops (swelling of the endolymph). This is the fluid that fills the innermost compartment of the inner ear. The excessive pressure is believed to result from a breakdown in the pressure-regulating mechanisms and can be simplistically likened to water on the knee years after an injury. When the inner ear fluids swell, it causes some strain that initially may be mistaken for pressure in the middle ear, as might be experienced with infections, or airplane travel. If the swelling continues, hearing loss, especially in the lower frequencies, may fluctuate and be associated with tinnitus, the warning noises the ear creates when injured.

Ultimately, unprovoked episodes of spinning vertigo can develop, sometimes even waking someone from sleep with a violent sense of rotation, nausea, and vomiting. The attack can last for minutes or hours and usually subsides, leaving the person exhausted and very unstable with significant dysequilibrium for many more hours, days, or even weeks, going through the same vestibular compensation recovery as occurs after a labyrinthitis spell.

Meniere's is much more disabling because these spells recur unexpectedly and with variable frequency, creating a tremendous loss of confidence in oneself. If the vertigo attacks occur frequently enough, there may be insufficient time between spells for vestibular compensation to occur and the person will experience chronic dysequilibrium with intermittent vertigo attacks, never having a chance to fully recover. Healthcare professionals and patients have difficulty sorting out the difference between spontaneous vertigo attacks, and the head movement or position-induced vertigo and dysequilibrium during the compensation phase.

In its early stages, Meniere's Disease can be exceedingly difficult to diagnose but early recognition and treatment may be useful in arresting the progression of the disease from its natural course of hearing and balance degeneration. Each time a hydrops (accumulation of fluid) episode occurs, it does a small amount of cumulative permanent damage to the inner ear.

Treatment for Meniere's Disease is directed toward controlling the endolymphatic fluid swelling since in 90 percent of patients no active cause will be identified. The body uses sodium as its principal regulator of fluid balance, so a strict 2000-milligram daily sodium-restricted diet is recommended. A sodium guidebook is recommended to learn about packaging labels and natural sodium content in foods. Simply removing the saltshaker from the table is inadequate to treat this disorder and strict regular adherence to a 2000 mg diet is strongly recommended while symptoms are active. Most people who do adhere to their diet notice a substantial difference when they eat out and cannot control their sodium intake, experiencing more symptoms within one or two days afterwards.

The second most important factor in controlling Meniere's is controlling stress. The hormonal release associated with stress has a profound effect on aggravating Meniere's Disease, although, the mechanism for this is poorly understood. It's quite obvious that an increase in spells occurs during times of crises, injury, or illness. Gaining emotional control over Meniere's Disease is a critical issue in preventing oneself from falling into the trap of becoming a victim to the condition. Victims live in the constant fear that an attack may occur, and the very stress of this fear actually creates more attacks. Many people who understand this situation find that they can exert their will over spells, and sometimes avert them. Caffeine, nicotine, and other powerful stimulants have also been known to aggravate Meniere's. Decaffeinated beverages and cessation of smoking are always recommended.

Physicians will often add a diuretic (water pill) to the treatment regimen to reduce the inner ear fluid pressure. Diuretics are often used for several months, and discontinued if the condition can be controlled by diet alone. If the spells cannot be adequately managed, then vestibular suppressants are often prescribed. These medications are all central nervous system depressants in nature, trying to slow down the abnormal impulses within the balance system, or anti-nausea medications that also help stabilize balance. Such medications are for symptom assistance only and do not prevent vertigo attacks. They may be used on a daily, even round-the-clock basis for short periods of time.

Medical treatment for Meniere's is generally successful in controlling the attacks, limiting them to one or two significant attacks per year, and most people don't require surgery. About 20 percent of Meniere's patients ultimately fail medical treatment and desire surgical intervention to stop the vertiginous attacks. Most of the procedures are designed to deaden the affected balance nerve so that the abnormal imbalance signals no longer reach the brain, and the vertigo attacks cease. Newer less invasive treatments are being developed but remain investigational. When there are no further disturbances in the balance system, vestibular compensation can occur as the opposite inner ear adjusts to the new balance arrangement.

## 7. Under what circumstances should people be concerned enough about their hearing disorder to be seen medically by a family physician, otologist or otolaryngologist?

Charles Krause, MD is Past-President of the American Academy of Otolaryngology—Head and Neck Surgery. Dr. Krause has taught internationally, has more than 100 scholarly publications to his credit, and serves on five editorial boards.

Many individuals notice a problem with their ears, and wonder whether they should see a physician before being evaluated for hearing aids. Though no guidelines are correct for every circumstance, the following situations should be reason for evaluation by an ear, nose and throat specialist (otologist or otolaryngologist). These conditions are essentially what the Food and Drug Administration recommend that your hearing care professional consider prior to fitting you with hearing aids:

a) *A visible congenital or traumatic deformity of the ear.* Many of these are accompanied by hearing loss, and most can be improved both functionally and in appearance.

b) *A history of active drainage from the ear,* particularly if it's foul smelling. Except for earwax, most drainage from an ear is caused by active infection. Left untreated, the infection can cause permanent damage.

c) *A history of sudden or rapidly progressive hearing loss.* Except when caused by a plug of earwax, a sudden loss of hearing needs careful evaluation, especially if it occurs in one ear.

d) *Acute chronic dizziness,* particularly "spinning," is caused by a problem in the inner ear, and may be associated with a hearing loss.

e) *Unilateral hearing loss of sudden or recent onset within the past ninety days.* The sooner one seeks treatment, the more hopeful the outcome.

f) *A conductive hearing loss* (air-bone gap on audiometric testing) of at least 15 dB at 500, 1000 and 2000 Hz. Such a hearing loss can usually be restored with medical treatment.

g) *Visible evidence of a plug of earwax or foreign body* in the ear canal. Such an obstruction is best removed using careful extraction rather than irrigation.

h) *Pain or discomfort in an ear.* This is usually caused by infection in the external or middle ear. Medical evaluation and treatment usually result in rapid resolution of the pain.

By applying these guidelines, you'll have a more informed idea of when a medical specialty evaluation is necessary.

## 8. Cochlear implants have been around now for a number of years. As an expert on this, can you tell us what a cochlear implant is, who is a candidate, and the latest achievements in this area?

William Luxford, M.D. is a physician at the House Ear Clinic in Los Angeles, and Clinical Associate Professor of Otolaryngology at the University of Southern California School of Medicine. He has been performing implant surgeries for years and is extensively published in this area.

In general, cochlear implant candidates have a bilateral severe-profound sensorineural hearing loss, receive little or no benefit from conventional hearing aids, are in good physical and mental health, and have the motivation and patience to complete a rehabilitation program. A cochlear implant is an electronic prosthetic device that is surgically placed in the inner ear, under the skin behind the ear to provide sound perception to selected severe-to-profound hearing-impaired individuals.

In addition to the internal component of the system, the cochlear implant has external parts that are worn outside the ear, including the microphone, speech processor, headpiece antenna and cable. A cochlear implant is NOT a hearing aid (see Figure 8-3). A hearing aid amplifies acoustic signals, thereby making sounds louder and clearer to the person with hearing loss. Hearing aid-amplified acoustic signals are delivered to the ear and converted into electrical impulses by hair cells of the inner ear in exactly the same manner as sounds that are transmitted to the normal hearing ear.

A cochlear implant, on the other hand, converts acoustic sound vibrations into electrical signals, which are then coded and patterned in a manner designed to enhance speech perception. Through an externally worn antenna and internally implanted receiver, these coded electrical signals are then transmitted to an electrode in the inner ear which directly stimulates the auditory nerve fibers, thus bypassing the damaged hair cells of the cochlea. The electrical impulses are delivered to the brain where they are interpreted as meaningful sounds.

Potential candidates for cochlear implants include both children and adults with a wide age range. For the most part, children are at least 12-months old, while there are many people in their 80s who are successful users. Candidates undergo a very thorough evaluation, including medical, audiological and radiological assessment. The medical evaluation includes a complete history and

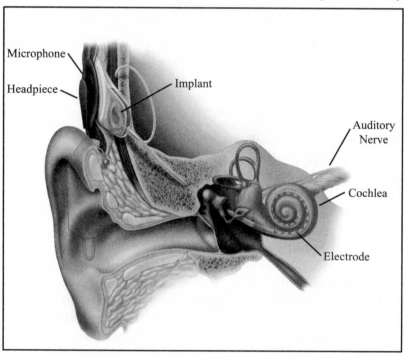

Illustration reprinted courtesy of Cochlear Ltd.

Figure 8-3: Illustration of a cochlear implant.

physical examination to detect problems that might interfere with the patient's ability to complete either the surgical or rehabilitative measures of implantation. In adults, the cause of deafness would not seem as important as its onset. Adults who become deaf later in life, and who have fully developed speech and language before losing their hearing, are able to make better use of the implant than those who are born deaf or lose their hearing very early in life. On the other hand, the prelingually deafened child, if implanted early in life, can receive a great deal of benefit from a cochlear implant.

Counseling is important so that the patient and the family will have realistic expectations regarding benefits and limitations. Support from family and friends is essential in the rehabilitative process. The definition of success is different from person to person, and family to family. Memory of sound appears to be one of the most important factors for success in adults. Early implantation, and placement in an educational program that emphasizes development of auditory skills appear to be important factors for success in children.

Initially, only those patients who were stone deaf in both ears were considered implant candidates. With significant improvements in implant technology and signal processing, the benefits gained by implanted patients, both children and adults, have markedly improved. These improvements have led to a broadening of the criteria for implant patients. Selected patients with severe hearing loss receiving some benefit from appropriately fitted hearing aids are now considered possible implant candidates. Hearing aid technology has also improved. Most likely, patients with mild and moderate hearing loss will be candidates for hearing aids. Patients with severe loss will be candidates for either a hearing aid or cochlear implant, depending upon how well they function with the appropriate device. Patients with profound hearing loss will probably receive the best benefit through the use of a cochlear implant.

**9. If you could offer one important idea to readers with loss of hearing, a mechanism that would enhance their hearing ability and improve their lifestyle (in addition to hearing aids), what might that be?"**

David G. Myers, Ph.D., is professor of psychology at Michigan's Hope College and the author of fifteen books, including *A Quiet World: Living with Hearing Loss* (Yale University Press, 2000).

Without hesitation I would offer to double the usefulness of their hearing aids by enabling them to serve as customized, in-the-ear loudspeakers for the broadcast of sound from PA systems, televisions, and telephones. With the mere push of a button—no hassle, no conspicuous headset—our hearing aids would broadcast phone conversation through *two* ears (all the better to hear you with, my dear!), our TV loudspeakers would be inside our ears, our public venues would broadcast sound not from speakers 40 feet from our eardrums, but from a fraction of an inch. Moreover, the sound would be customized for our own needs, by our own hearing aids.

In this dreamed-of future, doubly useful hearing aids would be more widely welcomed. With doubled usefulness—and doubled usage—the stigma of hearing loss and hearing aids would diminish. Hearing aids would come more and more to be seen as "glasses for the ears." Support for insurance and Medicaid/Medicare reimbursement for hearing aids would increase. The end result: improved quality of life for millions of people with hearing loss.

Is this an impossible dream? Actually, it's en route to becoming reality. In the UK, Scandinavia, and Australia nearly all hearing aids now come equipped with telecoils (or "audio coils," as Dr. Mark Ross suggests we rename them, to convey their broader usefulness beyond telephones) that can receive this broadcast sound. And most public venues—including virtually all churches, cathedrals, and public lecture halls that I have visited in my sojourns in Britain—have equipped themselves to broadcast directly to hearing aids (as does my own home television and office phone, through inexpensive induction loop systems).

Here in Holland, Michigan, most of our major churches and public facilities now offer hearing aid compatible assistive listening. It's common observation that the existing hearing aid incompatible assistive listening systems (transmitting signals to cumbersome receivers and then on to headsets) rarely get used. A number of churches that have switched to hearing aid compatible assistive listening are reporting a tenfold increase in assistive listening use (and who knows how many people are invisibly using this inconspicuous form of assistive listening?).

Thanks to publicity and word-of-mouth enthusiasm, hearing aid compatible assistive listening is now spreading elsewhere in west Michigan. One Grand Rapids, Michigan church sound engineer observes that, "Slowly the members of our congregation have been updating their hearing aids and (in four months) we've gone from one user originally to over ten now. Several members have commented on the clarity and ease of use."

For more information on hearing aid compatible assistive listening, including where it works, how much it costs, and links to vendors, visit www.hearingloop.org.

## 10. Is there a problem in the United States regarding the unintentional swallowing of hearing aid batteries, and if so, what consumer protection would you recommend?

Rose Ann G. Soloway, RN, is a board-certified clinical toxicologist with the National Capitol Poison Center. She is also Associate Director of the American Association of Poison Control Centers. The National Button Battery Ingestion Hotline Telephone Number is 202-625-3333 (collect if necessary).

It's hard to imagine swallowing a hearing aid battery, but it happens more than 1,000 times each year. And it's easier than you might think. Since Toby Litovitz, M.D. established the National Button Battery Ingestion Hotline and Registry in 1982, she and the Hotline staff have managed more than 6,000 cases of battery ingestion accidents. It occurs in children and adults.

Children swallow hearing aid batteries for the same reasons they swallow other things within reach. They're curious, they explore everything within reach, and anything can end up in the mouth. They swallow batteries pried from their own hearing aids or their family member's hearing aids, or those that may be merely left on tables or in drawers. They also have been known to locate them in the trash. But hearing aids are only one source of this problem for children. They'll swallow batteries from toys, cameras, calculators, jewelry and so forth. Protection is available by using child-resistant hearing aids and by keeping batteries in their original packaging, stored out of children's reach. To dispose of batteries, wrap them securely in something before discarding, so they can't be easily retrieved.

Adults are apt to swallow batteries by mistaking them for pills. Sometimes, they're put in the same pockets as pills. People think they're swallowing pills but are later surprised to find pills and no batteries in their pocket! A similar mistake occurs when loose batteries are stored in old pill bottles. Adults who mistakenly think they can test a battery's charge by placing it on the tongue, also wind up swallowing a tiny, slippery battery. The same thing happens to adults who put them in their mouths to keep them handy while they change batteries.

While it's unusual for swallowed batteries to cause harm, injury and death have occurred in a few cases. Most of the time, a swallowed battery passes through the esophagus and into the stomach. Gradually, it works its way through the intestinal tract and is eliminated in the stool. Rarely, the battery gets stuck in the esophagus. This situation doesn't always cause symptoms right away, but is very dangerous because it can cause a lot of bleeding. Also rarely, a battery that passes through the esophagus and stomach later gets stuck somewhere in the intestinal tract.

If someone swallows a battery, immediately call the 24-hour National Button Battery Ingestion Hotline at 202-625-3333. You may call collect. You may also call your physician or local poison center, and ask them to call the Battery Hotline. The nurses at the Hotline will ask you to have a chest x-ray immediately. If it shows that the battery has passed through the esophagus into the stomach, nothing needs to be done—or should be done—except watching and waiting for its passage. In young children, this could occur in just a day or two; in elderly people, such passage could take two or even three months. If the battery hasn't been seen within a week, another x-ray will usually be recommended to be sure it is moving. The Hotline staff will stay in touch with you until the battery has passed, then ask you to mail it in for evaluation. Of course, if you develop any symptoms, the Hotline nurses will work with your physician to decide if any treatment is necessary.

Keep in mind that it is rarely necessary for surgery to be done! Be sure to contact the Battery Hotline immediately if someone suggests surgery to remove a battery.

# CHAPTER NINE

# Problem-Solving and Extending the Life of Your Hearing Aids

*Thayne C. Smedley, Ph.D.\**
*Ronald L. Schow, Ph.D. \**

Dr. Smedley is currently Professor Emeritus of Audiology at Idaho State University in Pocatello. He received his Ph.D. in Audiology from Stanford. He is nationally published in areas of hearing aid satisfaction and self-assessment issues. In his many years of clinical audiological practice, he has also dispensed hearing aids. He was Chief of the Audiology Section of the Veterans Administration Medical Center in San Francisco for nine years, and also served as president of the Idaho Speech, Language and Hearing Association.

Dr. Schow, Professor of Audiology at Idaho State University, has specialized in audiological rehabilitation since earning his Doctorate from Northwestern University in 1974. He has twice been recognized at ISU with a campus-wide award as Outstanding Researcher. Dr. Schow has worked with many rehabilitation groups of hearing aid wearers, using satisfaction and other self-report questionnaires to measure successful outcomes. He's co-editor of a popular text on audiological rehabilitation now in its fourth edition.

*We both wish to acknowledge our colleague Jeff Brockett who consistently provides us with valuable input and feedback on projects like this. He has many years of experience working with hearing aid clients in a local dispensing office and in our university Veterans Administration dispensing program.

Hearing aids are electromechanical devices proven to be greatly beneficial to millions of people. Despite this fact, like any device, they are subject to breakdown. Consider that hearing aids typically are worn for long hours each day which places stress on electrical components and battery power. They exist in a relatively hostile environment of moisture, warm temperatures (especially with certain styles) and intrusive substances such as earwax, skin acids and oils. These substances may be healthy for the ear but potentially corrosive to hearing aids. Additionally, these substances can block important sound delivery pathways making the hearing aid perform poorly. For these reasons, no matter how well they're made, sooner or later they will stop working.

Hearing aid failure is almost always unpredictable and sometimes occurs at the most critical and inopportune time. Consider

Fred's plight as he headed out the door for an early meeting with upper management on his job. Fred, who had worn hearing aids for several years, was a section supervisor in a large manufacturing firm. Meetings with management occurred weekly but this one was especially important because it involved a review of company organization and possible restructuring of middle and upper management. The meeting would involve a lot of discussion which Fred needed to hear. He knew his supervisors were counting on his input. Fred was in line for a promotion and this could be a pivotal meeting for his career.

As he pulled his car out of the garage and headed down the street, he reached into his pocket for his hearing aid case, took out his hearing aids and slipped them comfortably into place. The car motor suddenly took on its normal drone as he turned the volume up. "Why is the right hearing aid sputtering?" he wondered. The aid sounded with static and seemed a bit weak. Fred arrived at work and took his place in the conference room which was already filled with 20 of his co-workers. He was just a little late that morning so he took his place in the back of the room. But he knew he would be all right as long as he could hear.

The hearing aid in his right ear continued to sputter and crackle. The company president opened the meeting and Fred's heart sank. His right hearing aid had gone dead. He hurried to throw in a fresh battery. The commotion interfered with the president's opening remarks and distracted his near-by associates; and to no avail. The hearing aid wouldn't respond. Frantically, Fred cranked up the left hearing aid to compensate. It promptly let out a wild squeal, attracting stares from his colleagues. He turned the left aid back down and sat there.

By this time, the president had finished his introductory remarks and had opened the meeting to discussion. What had the president said? Fred had caught only a small part of it and he fared no better with the other voices coming from different parts of the room. Because he was uncertain about what was being said, Fred did not feel part of the meeting. He was frustrated. He felt disappointed. He was angry.

"I hate these hearing aids!" he mumbled to himself.

It didn't help matters when his buddy George said to him on the way out, "Where were you today? I expected you to have a lot to say!"

Perhaps this episode strikes a resonate chord with you.

Hearing aid failure can be upsetting, as Fred thought it was in his case. In less critical situations, a hearing aid that quits working may only produce frustration. At the very least, hearing aid breakdown is annoying.

This chapter addresses how to keep your hearing aids performing and how to spot the cause of malfunction early when breakdowns occur. We also include tips on preventive maintenance to improve hearing instrument reliability and longevity. Remember that some hearing aid failures will be unpreventable and beyond your control. Such failure will result in "down time" on your part and may require a send-off to the factory for repair. Also addressed will be sub-par performance from hearing aids which, although working, do not function as well as they might.

But first, a few words about hearing aid styles. Some styles of hearing aids are subject to more stress and abuse than others, and the approach you should take in troubleshooting hearing aid breakdowns can vary from one style to the next. Reasons for hearing aid failure which are related to a particular hearing aid style will be noted in each section. You need to be familiar with the basic hearing aid styles of which there are five. These styles are described in terms of their location on the ear or body, and for purposes of convenience are identified by acronyms: BTE, ITE, ITC, and CIC (See Figure 6-1 in Chapter 6, page 96).

In this chapter, much of our instruction will be directed toward ITE and ITC aids because these represent the majority of styles in current use in the United States. Problems specific to CIC hearing aids will be highlighted because more and more hearing aids are being fit which are of this "deep canal" type.

As part of this introduction, a few words need to be said about hearing aid longevity. You may have asked, "How long will my hearing aids last?" Just as hearing aids will malfunction on occasion for reasons described above, it follows that they won't last indefinitely. This is true even for very expensive ones. For various reasons, cost being one of them, some wearers expect their instruments to last 10 to 15 years or more. Hearing aids that remain in useful service for this long are the exception rather than the rule. In fact, research has demonstrated that the typical hearing aid gets replaced about every five years.

Also, some hearing aids are replaced not necessarily as a result of being worn out but due to changes in a person's hearing or because individuals may desire instruments of improved technology. In any case, you're well-advised to consider five years as the average life span of most hearing aids. All things considered, proper maintenance procedures will help to extend the longevity of any given hearing aid to its optimum potential.

We present this outline of problem-solving techniques at the risk of giving you the impression that hearing aids are fragile, sensitive devices that will commonly fail and require unusual care and worry on your part. This is not at all the case. For the most part, today's hearing aids are exceptionally reliable and durable. They will serve your hearing needs day after day, year after year with rarely a breakdown.

Like your automobile, any number of problems can go wrong with a hearing aid, but for the most part, easy and relatively inexpensive remedies are available. Here are most possibilities.

## Dead and Defective Batteries

The inexperienced wearer is often disappointed by what is viewed as short battery life. After all, watch batteries of approximately the same size last a year or more before replacement is necessary. Hearing aid battery life is related to two primary factors: the size (and storage capacity) of the battery and the amount of current draw required by the hearing aid. The larger the battery, the greater the storage capacity. However, the number of hours you will get from a battery depends on the current draw.

Hearing aid amplifiers simply draw heavy current loads, much heavier, for example, than those required for simple watch circuits, or even heart pacemakers for that matter. As a useful comparison, consider the common battery-operated flashlight. Interestingly, the typical flashlight uses a standard size D battery which has 1.5 volts, almost identical to the voltage of a hearing aid battery but of vastly larger size with greatly increased storage capacity. Even so, imagine how long a flashlight would work if it were used continuously for 16 hours a day as is required for hearing aids! The fact that hearing aid batteries maintain operation for long hours at a time, day after day, is quite impressive.

Furthermore, battery efficiency has improved substantially in recent years. Today's batteries will keep a hearing aid going many days longer than the older style hearing aids (for example, BB-type) whose batteries were ten times larger! Signs of a failing battery are weak output, distortion, increased tendency of hearing aid feedback, intermittence and/or strange or unusual sounds such as static or fluttering (sometimes called "motorboating").

Weak and faulty batteries are a leading cause of hearing aid failure. In general, today's hearing aids require approximately 1.2 to 1.4 volts to operate properly. When a battery reaches 1.1 volts or less, the hearing aid will function poorly, if at all. The battery should then be replaced. In contrast to batteries of an earlier era, battery strength is sustained at a constant level until just a few hours before it dies, at which time it goes quickly. Older batteries used to lose power gradually over their life, requiring the wearer to adjust the volume at ever-increasingly higher levels to maintain proper output. This is not the case with today's batteries.

## Short Battery Life

Shortened battery life will result most likely from one of three possibilities: the battery is defective and has a weakened charge; the hearing aid is defective and draws current in excess of what it should; or the battery routinely is left in operation in the hearing aid during periods of disuse (for example, overnight). Wearers who are always careful to disconnect the battery overnight can usually assume a defective aid in the situation of poor battery life. While batteries can be faulty on occasion, as noted earlier, most commonly it will be the hearing aid itself at fault. When this happens, the likely solution is factory repair.

Before an aid is returned to your provider with this problem, it's wise to verify that your present batteries in use are in fact good. Because battery life can vary somewhat within acceptable limits, we recommend taking action with the hearing aid only when battery life is consistently one-half of what it regularly has been or should be. This would help to confirm a defective hearing aid. Otherwise, you might be dealing simply with variability in longevity among batteries.

## Anticipating the Dead Battery

So, in light of battery usage, how can you avoid hearing aid failure due to weak or dead batteries? First, you'll need to develop a replacement rhythm. Knowing the approximate time when a battery will go dead can decrease one of the sources of anxiety that may accompany hearing aid use. A replacement rhythm is most easily developed by marking a calendar each time a battery goes dead. A designation such as R-B or L-B for right aid or left aid batteries works nicely. Most hearing aids today use zinc-air batteries with a pull-tab on the back of the battery. You can just as easily stick the tab on the corresponding date on the calendar and note it as right or left replacement.

After a few weeks, you'll learn the replacement cycle required of the hearing aid and will become remarkably accurate in anticipating the impending demise of waning batteries. Calendar-marking may not be necessary after a few months, although for those with poor memory, it can be continued indefinitely.

For the technically-oriented, an inexpensive battery tester can be purchased that will read the exact voltage strength of a new or used battery. This is probably a good investment because it allows you to determine if hearing aid failure is due to the battery itself.

## Getting the most out of your batteries

Today's batteries have excellent shelf life, up to one year or more if kept in a cool, dry place. (Refrigerating batteries, a common practice years ago, is unnecessary.) Most batteries used today are of the zinc-air type which means a charge does not begin until a pull-tab is removed from the face of the battery, allowing air to enter through tiny openings. Never remove the tab until the battery is to be inserted into the hearing aid.

To optimize battery longevity, disengage it when the aid is out of use for a period of time. The most common period of regular disuse for most wearers is overnight. When the aid is removed at bedtime, the easiest thing to do is simply open the battery compartment all the way and set the aid down on a dresser top or some other safe and convenient but accessible location.

Avoid storing your hearing aids on a bed table or other similar location where children and/or dogs can get to them; otherwise they're easily lost or destroyed. It's not necessary to remove the battery from its compartment. Position the aid so that the door remains open and the battery remains in it. This will simplify hearing aid start-up the next morning. Just close the battery door and the aid is ready to go. If the aid is placed on the dresser carelessly, the battery may fall out. This isn't really a problem except that it creates an unnecessary inconvenience the next morning when the hearing aid battery must be located, oriented and reinserted. For individuals with limited vision or finger dexterity, this inconvenience can be significant. If you have an aid with the "flip up" door, you will have to remove the battery in order to prevent its discharge.

## Batteries in Backwards

The matter of inserting batteries, although not directly related to battery life, raises the question of another source of hearing aid failure. Batteries have a "negative" and "positive" polarity and therefore each side must be positioned correctly in the battery door to coincide with the electrical contact requirements of the circuit. The flashlight analogy cited earlier applies as well to battery orientation. We all know that a flashlight whose batteries are inserted incorrectly will not work. Manufacturers of hearing aids help with this problem as much as they can by marking a "+" sign on one side of the battery door to remind you that the positive side of the battery must be on that side. Because this "+" imprint is so small and for many impossible to see, the manufacturer also tailors the battery door to match the shape of the battery.

A close look at any battery will disclose that batteries are perfectly flat on one side (the positive side) and beveled on the other (the negative side). The battery door is similarly configured and should be studied by new wearers in its open position, under a magnifying lamp if necessary, to learn these identifying characteristics. Then you can position the battery appropriately in your fingers and insert it correctly with confidence.

Please note that with the battery in place, if the door doesn't close readily with only a minimum of force, this is often a sign the battery is in backwards. When this happens, reverse the battery and try again. In any case, *do not force the battery into place*. Doing so can damage the hearing aid. At this writing, some manufacturers are producing hearing aid circuits that will accept batteries placed in either position. This modification is in response to the difficulties some wearers have with battery insertion. This technological improvement may be the standard someday with all hearing aids.

Never insert the battery into its place by accidentally sliding it beneath the battery door. By-passing the battery door will usually not damage the hearing aid but may likely jam the battery in place and require a trip to your provider to have it removed.

As of this writing, probably about five percent of hearing aid manufacturers have implemented the use of a hearing aid battery compartment that allows you to install the battery regardless of its polarity. This is undoubtedly the wave of the future for all hearing aids, at a small additional cost. On your next hearing aid purchase, you may want to inquire about it.

## Spent Batteries

Naturally, every wearer likes to get the most hours possible from every battery. To do this, some people will remove batteries that show the earliest signs of weakening and save them for later use after they've recovered some of their charge. It's true that near-spent batteries will self-rejuvenate to a degree after removal from a hearing aid and may provide power for an extra day or so. This strategy of holding onto spent batteries, however, has several problems. First, it can give you a false sense of security. Hearing aid batteries with weak voltages can fail at any moment. Secondly, and of greater concern, these batteries somehow get mixed in with the fresh batteries. The result is confusion and frustration when a bad battery is picked up and inserted in the hearing aid when it's thought to be good.

Re-using worn batteries is a poor practice because the savings is not really worth the bother. Consider the following: assume a battery lasts two weeks and costs $1.00. If you get two extra days per battery by recycling spent batteries, the result would be four extra days use per month. The daily cost of batteries using two per month at a cost of $1.00 per battery is about 6 cents ($2.00 divided by 31 days). So, four extra days at 6 cents/day is 24 cents savings per month, or less than $3.00 per year. A savings of $3.00 per year is clearly not worth the hassle of keeping track of used batteries. This also holds for binaural wearers who might save approximately $6.00 per year. Our advice is, when zinc-air batteries go dead, throw them away. Also, never leave bad batteries lying around where children can get them. Batteries can do serious damage if ingested.*

## Conserving Battery Life

Some hearing aid wearers concerned with operating costs will turn their hearing aids off when they "don't need to hear." Such individuals feel they get increased longevity with this strategy, analogous to the "turn off the lights when not in use" philosophy. While there may be some justification for this practice in special

*Should this occur, call the National Button Battery Ingestion Hotline at (202) 625-3333 for assistance (collect if necessary).

circumstances (for example, while working in a noisy shop for a few hours), a habit of turning hearing aids on and off "as needed" is not recommended. You can never tell when an important auditory event will come along, such as another person's voice or a warning signal. You don't want to be inconsiderate of others by shutting off your "antenna" so you hear them only when you want to. Furthermore, it's important to be aware of the rich assortment of environmental sounds that keep us in touch with the world.

## Stockpiling Fresh Batteries

With today's batteries, is there anything wrong with storing a reasonable supply? If you see a two-for-one battery special, it's tempting to take advantage of this offer and save money but we give you this caution: such "sale batteries" are sometimes promoted to get rid of old stock and might more correctly be termed "stale batteries."

If you're inclined to store a supply of batteries, our advice is to investigate the manufacture date and then purchase no more than six months' supply at a time. Beyond this period, full storage life of the batteries might be compromised. Also, you just might decide to change hearing aids before the supply is used up, resulting in an over-supply of batteries that may no longer be of the appropriate size. People who travel are well-advised to purchase an adequate supply of batteries before taking a trip, especially if traveling overseas. Try to avoid situations where you must make a purchase of unfamiliar brands which may be of poor quality or irregular size.

## The Defective Battery

Present-day batteries are very reliable as a rule and you can usually depend on a fresh battery working as it should. Occasionally, however, a new battery or a whole pack will be defective. Your provider will gladly exchange them for a fresh package.

## Earwax Obstruction

Another leading cause of hearing aid failure is wax blockage. The technical name for common earwax is cerumen. It's produced by a gland (actually called the ceruminous gland) in the outer ear roughly one-third of the way down the ear canal. The product of this gland is a pasty substance, usually light brown or tan in color and bitter in taste. (Take our word on this one!) Cerumen is believed to exist in the ear canal to discourage flies and insects from entering this opening.

The degree of wax generated in the canal varies greatly from one person to the next. On average, men experience more wax build-up than women. Some women, however, can produce large amounts of cerumen, as can children. For reasons not clearly understood, some individuals generate little or no wax. If you're presently unaware of the wax condition in your ears, your physician or hearing health care provider can readily inform you of this after examination with an otoscope (ear light).

Hearing aid wearers must continually be on the lookout for adverse effects of earwax. When hearing aids are inserted into the ear canals, (or earmolds in the case of BTE hearing aids), they can slide alongside or directly into accumulated wax. The fresher the wax, the softer and more easily it can get pushed into the sound bore (receiver) of an aid. A thin smear of earwax over the receiver (sound) tube will shut the aid down instantly.

## Preventing Wax Build-up

The first defense against wax build-up is regular cleaning of your ear canals by a physician or audiologist, or as simply as it sounds, in a shower by direct spray into the canals. The cautions here are to be careful of the water pressure, and be certain you don't have a hole in the eardrum, or any other condition which might prevent such easy management of earwax.

Hearing instrument specialists are generally not trained to remove earwax, and while wax removal is within the scope of practice for audiologists, many prefer not to provide this service. In any case, you are well-advised to locate a person or office that will provide this service as needed. Attempting to control build-up of earwax by regular use of cotton swabs is not recommended. Aside from the possibility of doing physical damage to the ear canal or drum (the "don't put anything in your ear smaller than your elbow" concept), cotton swabs will usually only serve to pack the wax deeper with each attempt. By looking into the ear, professionals can readily discern the cotton swab users, as the wax shows a nicely formed concave surface down in the ear canal.

Some hearing aid wearers with chronic wax problems may find regular use of "ear lavage" effective. Equipment (along with instructions for home use) is available in many hearing care offices and drug stores. Wax softeners for use prior to cleaning can also be purchased. Some people may be uncomfortable squirting water into the ear canal. A discussion with your physician would be advisable before attempting it. The main problem with this type of treatment is the difficulty knowing when the wax is all out.

The second defense against wax blockage is utilization of some type of wax guard. There are a number of commercially available products which suit this purpose. Many manufacturers now provide such a device as original equipment. Directly, or under magnification, you can look into the sound opening of the hearing aid to see if a wax guard is there. These common devices include "spring," "Band-Aid" or "trap-door" style guards. All such devices should be discussed with your hearing health care provider who can explain service requirements.

## Responsibility for Wax Maintenance

This is not to say that whoever dispensed your hearing aids has primary responsibility to keep them free of earwax. You need to develop a daily habit of inspecting the end of the hearing aid where the sound comes out and looking for wax blockage. If accumulation is noticed, this wax can be readily removed in most cases.

## When and How to Remove Wax

The best time to inspect hearing aids for wax is at the close of the day. At this time, any accumulated wax will still be soft and more easily removed. If you use the Band-Aid style guard, you can wipe across it gently. After a few days if you observe the cushion separating from the adhesive backing, remove it altogether and replace. If used properly, you'll never need to clean out the receiver (loud speaker) which is the rubber housing hole at the tip of an aid.

If your hearing aids have the wire coil in them, you may use a device known as a wax loop. This is merely a wire looped around the end of a piece of plastic. Gently insert it into the receiver tube, turn it one full rotation, then remove. Avoid picking or poking. Clean any debris from the loop. Nightly cleaning has the added advantage of keeping the receiver tube open for more adequate ventilation and drying. Review this procedure carefully and thoroughly with your provider so that inadvertently you don't damage your hearing aids by cramming the wax loop into the wrong opening (such as the microphone port on the face of the hearing aid) or too deeply into the receiver port which can damage the speaker diaphragm.

Additionally, a wax tool that is a little too large to fit readily into the receiver tube can push the tube itself down into the shell of the hearing aid. This will damage the instrument, often causing it to squeal, resulting in needed repairs.

Wax should also be removed from hearing aid vents. This is the other port in the hearing aid next to the receiver (loud speaker) port. It can be identified because vents are longer, they do not have a rubber housing through the channel, and often run the length of the earpiece or earmold. This also means they're not as easily cleaned. Some people have resorted to the use of wires of various gauges to ream out vents. Wire should be used with caution as it can crack the shell. Large vents are less likely to get plugged up and much easier to clean. Pipe cleaners work extremely well for large vents, such as ITEs, and light gauge fishing line for vents in CICs. Your provider will have suggestions for obtaining these and other suitable tools for cleaning.

Sometimes, wax build-up becomes dry and flaky before it's removed. When this happens, a good brushing of the hearing aid openings can be helpful in addition to use of the wire loop. When brushing, always hold the hearing aid upside down so that wax particles fall out of, rather than down into, the hearing aid. Also, keep your brush clean so that wax particles which collect in the bristles from previous brushing aren't injected inadvertently into the openings.

## Ear Discomfort

Like pressure on the feet from a tight fitting pair of new shoes, hearing aids can occasionally be uncomfortable. Unlike feet, however, such discomfort in the ear is not tolerated well. Hearing aid-related ear pain can distract from intended amplification. Discomfort associated with hearing aid use usually has a specific anatomical site of origin but a widespread reaction. That is, a tight-fitting earmold may cause specific tenderness in one spot in the ear canal but in time the sensation can radiate. Additionally, accumulation of earwax and moisture may result in periodic ear discomfort.

## Causes of Ear Discomfort

The most common cause of ear discomfort is an ill-fitting earmold (in the case of BTE) or hearing aid shell (in the case of ITE, ITC or CIC). Earpieces are fabricated from impressions taken of your ear. Usually they'll fit precisely. They're designed to fit snugly but not uncomfortably. It should be realized, however, that your degree of hearing loss will have a bearing on the tightness. Severe hearing losses must have a tight fit to prevent feedback (whistling).

There are two causes for ear discomfort which can result from a poorly fitting hearing aid or earmold. Either the earpiece was made improperly or incorrectly positioned in the ear. Impressions can and usually do provide exact replicas of the ear canal. This is because most providers are experienced in taking ear impressions. Occasionally, however, impressions can be distorted during preparation, while in transit to the laboratory, or during fabrication.

Another factor affecting comfort has to do with jaw movement. In some cases ear pain is caused or aggravated by movement of the jaw when earpieces are in place. For many, movement of the jaw can have significant influence on the shape of the canal. This is really quite normal. The effects of jaw movement can be felt by placing the "pinkie" finger deep in the ear canal while moving the jaw. (Try it while you're reading this). This movement arises from the joint of the lower jaw called, technically, the temporomandibular joint, or simply TMJ.

Even though earmolds may have reflected accurate impressions of the canal, the resulting earpieces may not "give" when the jaw and ear canal are moving, as when talking or chewing. If you suspect a poorly fitting earmold or hearing aid due to influences of the TMJ, you may want to discuss this matter with your hearing care professional.

The second most common cause of ear discomfort is the earpiece which is placed incorrectly in the ear. Figure 9-1 shows both proper and improper insertion. Earmolds that have been accurately fabricated can cause ear pain if not inserted correctly. When placing the earmold or hearing aid in the ear, you must make certain the device is "seated" into its exact position or it can create pressure points in the canal. Difficulties with correct placement are a common problem, especially for new wearers.

Those who use BTE hearing aids, for example, must make sure the entire earmold is properly placed. A common problem here is when the earmold is inserted into the canal, the uppermost portion isn't tucked into the groove of skin at the top of the ear. This incomplete placement can shift the angle of the earmold just enough to create a tender spot down in the canal. ITE wearers can have the same problem.

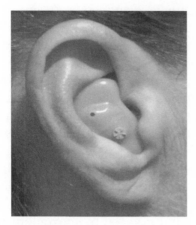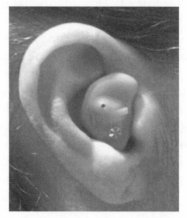

Figure 9-1 The *correct* (left) and *incorrect* (right) placement of a shell-type hearing aid in the ear.

Those who try CIC instruments may experience some fitting and placement problems initially. The deeper a hearing aid is placed in the canal, the more sensitive the canal tissue. Some wearers are simply reluctant to push an aid fully into the canal, fearful that doing so will cause pain. This is understandable. Also, there can be concern the aid can be pushed too deeply into the canal and cause damage. This also is a logical concern. However, ear canals tend to be carrot-shaped (that is, the deeper into the canal, the narrower the opening) and the aid cannot be pushed without discomfort beyond its appropriate location.

With practice, however, you will soon get a "feel" for the exact location of the aid and should be able to insert it correctly with confidence and without discomfort. If the hearing aids are difficult to insert, repeated "fiddling" can also cause discomfort. Special earmold lubricant is available to assist in the insertion. If placement difficulties aren't easily resolved, practicing proper insertion of the hearing aid in the presence and under the watchful eye of your provider is helpful and reassuring.

## Correcting a Fitting Problem

Ear discomfort associated with a new set of hearing aids can be either transitory or persistent. If you're a new wearer, you should understand that initial discomfort of a slight degree can be expected. Normally, we wear nothing inside the ear canal, so tolerating that first earpiece will require some adjustment. Such discomfort will subside substantially or be completely gone after only a few days. Again, it's like adjustment to new shoes.

Discomfort which persists after going through an initial adjustment period is another matter. Unrelenting discomfort present each time the hearing aid is worn should certainly be noted in follow-up visits with your clinical audiologist or hearing instrument specialist. During such visits your provider will either need to modify the earpiece by grinding or buffing, or remake the fitting by taking a new impression. It's helpful here to note that in most situations of poor fit, satisfactory corrections can be made right in the office. Also, please be aware that most wearers don't experience these initial difficulties at all and "hit the ground running" with new hearing aids. Often, we hear in our office, "I forget they're even in my ears!"

## Plugged Up Vents

A vent in an earmold or hearing aid is simply an open passageway or tube that extends from the front of the earpiece to the tip. It almost always exits the tip very close to the sound opening (receiver tube). Except in the case of more significant hearing loss, a vent will always be present. The diameter of the vent may be either large or small. In general, hearing aids fit to people with mild loss will have large vents while those fit to individuals with more severe losses will have smaller vents. They're usually placed in earmolds or hearing aid shells by manufacturers. They can also be placed there or modified by your provider. Vents should always be kept open to perform their intended function.

## Purposes for Vents

Vents are placed in earpieces for four rather important reasons. They allow sounds that you may hear normally to enter the ear canal directly without being amplified. You don't want to block the ear to sounds which you hear normally. Vents that serve this purpose are usually fairly large and obvious. This type of vent is very helpful if your hearing loss affects only higher pitches (technically called frequencies).

The second purpose of venting is to reduce amplification of unwanted sounds. Often these are low-pitched tones which you may already hear normally. Experienced and sometimes even new wearers will report hearing better when their provider enlarges the vent by drilling. This diminishes low-pitch bothersome background sounds. Hearing aids and earmolds fit to those with more severe loss will require smaller vents.

A third purpose of venting, perhaps the most important in some fittings, is to decrease the acoustic effects of your own voice. You'll readily identify this as the objectionable sounds of your own voice while the ears are blocked off. This is called the "occlusion effect," as described in the previous chapter. It's the "my voice sounds like I'm talking in a barrel" effect.

## Moisture Problems

Handling moisture problems will depend on what type of hearing aids you own. The use of water to remove wax or dirt from any part of the hearing aid itself is inadvisable. Moisture is a natural enemy to electronic devices. The use of a dry cloth or tissue to wipe clean the *outside* surface of the hearing aid is the only recommended cleaning practice.

With regard to BTE style hearing aids, earmolds used with these instruments must be removed from the hearing aids before cleaning. They can be soaked in a solution of soap and warm water, gently scrubbed clean, then completely dried before re-connecting to the hearing aid. Two methods we recommend for drying is a hand-held, forced-air blower which simply pumps air through the tubing, or a can of compressed air (typically used to blow dust off computer keyboards). Failure to dry earmolds will risk moisture seepage into the aid.

Another useful tool in keeping moisture from being a problem is regular use of a dehumidifier. Commercial versions are available and very reasonable. The device is simply a container for your hearing aid with a built-in, moisture-absorbing chemical. The hearing aids are placed in the container anytime they're not being worn. The device absorbs accumulated moisture and leaves the hearing aids dry. The chemical eventually becomes saturated with moisture but can be recharged by heating it in a warm oven. Be sure to follow the manufacturer's instructions.

As noted earlier, ear canals can produce a degree of moisture which can affect hearing aid performance. Like the problem of earwax, the amount of moisture present in human ear canals can vary widely from person to person. Your activity level and climatic conditions in which hearing aids are worn are two of the more common variables affecting moisture build-up. People with high levels of physical activity who perspire easily can be more prone to moisture problems than those who lead a more sedentary life.

Moreover, a moisture problem can be further aggravated by conditions of high humidity. Moisture build-up can result from either internal or external sources. Internal sources are those related to the condition of the auditory canal while the latter refers to liquids which arise from outside the ear, as those, for example, associated with rain or severe perspiration.

## The Effects of Moisture

While BTE-type hearing aids, if maintained properly, can outlast in-the-shell types, they tend to have the worst problem with moisture. Water vapors arising from the canal condense in the connecting tube. When these vapors reach a region outside the canal of slightly cooler temperature, condensation converts to small droplets of water which appear as tiny bubbles in the tube. The accumulation of enough water droplets can be sufficient to close the tube and shutdown amplification.

Externally-produced moisture surprisingly is less of a problem. Rain water, unless very severe or persistent, usually runs around the ear and off the head with little or no adverse affects. A worse condition, especially for BTE use, exists for the person who perspires a lot. With such individuals, beads of perspiration form in the hair along the top of the hearing aid. In time, this moisture can seep into the cracks and openings along the upper surface of the hearing aid and eventually affect operation. The case of the postal worker comes to mind whose daily walking route involved extreme outside weather conditions. The operation of his BTE hearing aid was little affected by rain water which was easily diverted by wearing a wide-brimmed hat. Heavy perspiration, however, caused predictable shutdowns during workdays of extreme heat and high humidity. It's worth noting here that proper care and maintenance will reduce mechanical problems associated with moisture.

Hearing aids of the type worn in the ear have less difficulty with moisture build-up. Externally produced moisture with in-the-shell-type hearing aids tends to flow around rather than into the ear as a rule. Also, the further the aid is placed inside the canal, the less the problem as moisture from the canal lining has less of an opportunity to get into the receiver tube. Therefore, CICs are the least affected by internal and external moisture.

## Resolving Moisture Problems

The point was emphasized earlier that moisture and electronic devices are a poor mix. To every extent possible, moisture in the region of the ear must be avoided. This means, to state the obvious, that hearing aids are not to be worn while showering, bathing, or swimming. They should also be removed before getting into a hot-tub, steam room, or while participating in water sports of any kind. These precautions apply equally well to moisture-related exposures such as spray paint, spray deodorant, hair sprays, and most aerosols. Chemicals in these particles are particularly destructive because they leave permanent residues which build up over time. With repeated use, they are certain to cause eventual hearing aid failure and permanent damage.

When hearing aids are unavoidably exposed to moisture, as with individuals who must work outdoors, extra precautions must be used. In the case of the postal worker cited earlier, a simple plastic sleeve slipped over each BTE instrument resolved the problem without significantly affecting performance. Some hearing aids are constructed specifically with watertight gaskets and are more weatherproof than others. Actually, most recent vintage hearing aids are surprisingly resistant to water damage and function in a variety of situations without intermittence, especially if they can thoroughly dry out overnight.

In this regard, hearing aids should be left in the open air when stored overnight with battery doors open, especially if moisture build-up is a problem. The use of dry-packs which absorb moisture can also be used to advantage during storage. These dry-packs are inexpensive and available from your hearing care professional.

Other drying techniques may also be tried. One recent BTE wearer who had a chronic problem with moisture solved it by dangling his hearing aids (overnight) *upside down* by the earmolds from a homemade wire hanger. In this position, moisture was more readily able to escape from the hearing aids than when they were stored laying flat which tended to trap the moisture.

It should be noted that hearing aid failure due to moisture is not always easy to diagnose. Except for water vapor forming in the tube of BTE hearing aids which is readily visible, moisture is difficult to observe. If hearing aid stoppage is found to be unrelated to the more obvious causes, such as faulty batteries or wax blockage, then moisture build-up should be suspected. The use of drying procedures previously described should help isolate this problem. Also, perhaps with the help of your provider, you could check your daily routine. For example, it will do little good to faithfully dry out hearing aids overnight if every morning after they're inserted you apply a healthy portion of hair spray!

# The Problems of Intermittence

We have touched upon a variety of hearing aid problems to this point, each of which can cause some degree of intermittence: a bad battery, a fleck of earwax, a little moisture. In addition, hearing aids can develop intermittence from other causes though these may be less frequent.

## Dirty Volume Control

Hearing aids that still use volume controls (some current hearing aids don't) operate on the basis of metal contact points that slide against each other in normal operation. You can almost feel movement in the contacts as you rotate the volume wheel up and down. These contact points can become corroded with dirt or other residue that will not allow current to pass. This may occur when the volume control is in certain positions where corrosion is the worst. The result is an aid that goes on and off or even produces a very audible static noise as it's being adjusted. If you experience this problem, we recommend you rotate the volume control knob in continuous movements back and forth between low and high power up to 20-30 times. If this does not resolve the problem, it will require factory cleaning and/or repair.

## Dirty Battery Contacts

Battery contact points can also become corroded and create similar problems. As with the volume control, dust, moisture, and earwax are the primary culprits. Corroded contacts in the battery compartment result in intermittent or stopped current flow which has a direct effect on hearing aid output. Corroded battery contacts are also quite difficult for you to clean and will require office or factory servicing.

## The Problem of Oily Skin

Some individuals with oily skin have battery contact problems. During routine handling and insertion of batteries, oily residue can be transferred from finger tips to the surfaces of the battery and adversely affect contact pickup. Such oily film can cause intermittence. If you suspect this problem, replace batteries with an ordinary tissue to prevent their surface "contamination," or be careful to wash your hands thoroughly before handling them.

## Overview

It should be noted in summary that during regular use, it's impossible to prevent a certain amount of contamination of hearing aids from elements in the environment. Sooner or later these elements are bound to affect instrument performance. The auto mechanic, for example, who works in a greasy, dust-laden environment is highly susceptible to hearing aid corrosion. Intermittence and frequent servicing should be expected when hearing aids are used in such unfavorable environments.

Intermittent problems can be difficult to diagnose. One strategy is to rule-out the most obvious causes. Often, when a hearing aid quits working, the first thing that comes to mind is that the battery is dead. An easy test is to take the battery from the other side (assuming it is working) and place it in the hearing aid that is not working. If the hearing aid begins working, then the problem was the battery and a new one can be activated. If it does not work, then other problems, such as wax build up, battery contacts, etc. may be to blame. Similarly, a battery in question can be placed in the working hearing aid to see if it has adequate capacity.

## Poor Telephone Reception

If hearing and understanding speech are difficult face to face, even with hearing aids, then telephone reception will be similarly difficult. Likewise, if your hearing aids allow you to function well in a face to face situation, you should converse with little difficulty on the telephone.

At the outset, it should be noted that some people have no difficulty hearing on the telephone without their hearing aid. This is because the telephone system has some built-in amplification, and a telephone held closely to the ear can provide adequate pickup while blocking out some background interference. Individuals with greater loss will need additional amplification to hear well on the telephone. On the other hand, those with severe to profound loss may be unable to converse at all on the telephone, with or without amplification. To explore what telephone amplifying devices are available to you, see Appendix I.

Whether you use hearing aids or not for the telephone, if you're in the presence of noise, cover the mouthpiece each time after you speak. This prevents undesirable room noise from traveling into your telephone receiver and being amplified into your own ear (or hearing aid), adding confusion to what you may already be finding difficult to hear.

## The Telecoil Circuit

One mechanism developed to improve telephone reception that has been available for many years is the telecoil (short for telephone coil). Not all hearing aids have them. If yours has it, you'll see some designation or switch on the case. BTE-type hearing aids with this device will have a switch position labeled "T." In-the-shell hearing aids may simply have a manual two-way switch. Because the telecoil circuit requires extra space, smaller hearing instruments such as the ITC or especially CIC will not have them.

Telecoil circuits work by processing electromagnetic waves produced by the telephone receiver (a process known in electronics as induction). When the hearing aid switch is on "T," a special wire coil is activated within the hearing aid circuit in place of the microphone. The only sounds that will come through the hearing aid in this position is what you hear through the telephone. Background noise near the telephone, for example, is not amplified which is a big advantage. Hearing aids with T-coils (as they're called) should work on nearly all currently available telephones. Telecoils can be quite satisfactory for mild to moderate hearing losses.

## Successful Use of the Telecoil Circuit

Review of your Operator's Manual will familiarize you with the telephone setting. If the hand-switch on the aid is not set to the telephone mode, only the regular microphone will pick up sound which may provide inadequate reception. To get the best reception from the telecoil, the receiver of the telephone must be positioned within the most sensitive area of the hearing aid. To find this position, simply move the telephone earpiece around the ear during conversation until the voice comes in loudest. Your provider will be more than happy to demonstrate this procedure on an office telephone.

## Other Tips for Improved Telephone Listening

Selection of the most appropriate hearing device is the first step toward successful telephone use. The clinical audiologist or hearing instrument specialist should be consulted during the selection process so that your individual needs are given full consideration. For some, telephone use is of little consequence. To others, it may be critical. For this latter group all possible telephone options need to be carefully explored.

The next most important step is <u>practice</u>. Optimum telephone pickup is often achieved only after periods of trial and error. When asked about telephone use, an occasional hearing aid wearer will say, "I tried it once but it didn't work." You'll need more patience than that. Don't expect to get your best results after only one or two attempts. Practice is especially important here and the best way to get practice is to prearrange a long telephone conversation with a friend or relative. Explain that you're experimenting over the telephone with your new hearing aids. A patient listener will allow you to try your hearing aid in a variety of telephone positions (or perhaps hearing aid settings as well) until you achieve optimum reception. Such practice will result in success with the telephone in a wide majority of cases. Also realize that poor telephone reception can be the fault of the <u>telephone</u> in isolated cases.

## Hearing Aid Squeal (Acoustic Feedback)

Feedback is the term we use for the high-pitched squeal commonly associated with amplifiers which have microphones and loudspeakers connected to them. This is the case with hearing aids (see Chapter 6, page 98). The squeal is caused by amplified sound that radiates from the speaker, is inadvertently picked up by the microphone and gets continuously re-amplified. The same thing can happen in an auditorium when the loudspeaker and microphone are too close together, or the amplifier volume is set too high. The hearing aid is said to "go into oscillation," and the squealing sound coming from the loudspeaker is the result. Feedback can be avoided when the sound coming out the loudspeaker is prevented from reaching the microphone.

In the case of hearing aids, the pathway of sound from the loudspeaker opening (receiver) to the microphone input is along the side of the hearing aid or earmold in the ear canal, or through a vent. If the earmold or shell-type hearing aid fit snugly into the ear, and the vent is not too large, sound is unable to leak out and reach the microphone located outside the ear canal, in which case the aid won't squeal. When hearing aids or earmolds fit too loosely in the canal, the opposite can result. In general, a loose-fitting hearing aid or earmold is more likely to squeal than a tight one. Also, a high-powered hearing aid will have a greater tendency to feedback than a low-powered aid and therefore will require a tighter fitting earmold. Competent hearing care professionals realize that the size and placement of hearing aid vents must be determined with the utmost regard to the potential for feedback.

## Acceptable Versus Unacceptable Feedback

We want to emphasize that acoustic feedback is a natural phenomenon of amplifiers and not of concern, in and of itself. Feedback is to be expected, for example, when a hearing aid is "on" and held in a cupped hand. It does no damage to use feedback in this way to tell if the hearing aid is working. Similarly, it's usually not a problem to purposely cup the hand to the ear and listen for the "beep" as the hand is moved toward and away from the ear. Many wearers test the hearing aid in this way to be sure it's on. Others will rotate the volume control to the position of feedback during adjustment. Here again, this is no problem. These are all examples of predictable and acceptable feedback.

Unacceptable feedback is the type that spontaneously rings without warning or provocation that happens, for example, while you're chewing, brushing your hair, scratching the side of your head, or tilting your head downward. This latter movement causes a slight shift in the position of the hearing aid, sometimes just enough to allow sound to leak out. The squeal associated with all of these activities can be vexing. Feedback of the unacceptable kind also occurs when you try to turn the volume of the hearing aid up to a more desirable level but cannot because the aid starts to squeal. At this volume position, with you attempting to extract the last decibel of sound possible, the aid is on the verge of feedback and will squeal at the least little disturbance. These are examples of feedback which you will not want to tolerate. Almost all of them can be corrected.

# Earwax and Feedback

Feedback can occur anytime sound is deflected toward the microphone. Normal eardrums tend to absorb energy so that if an earpiece is reasonably snug, leakage is minimal and feedback doesn't occur. Earwax, on the other hand, seems to absorb very little sound and will bounce the sound right back out of the canal toward the microphone. Therefore, individuals who experience unexplained feedback should have their ears checked for wax build-up.

# Solving the Feedback Problem

People with the most severe hearing loss provide the greatest challenge to their provider when it comes to feedback control. Most of it is still manageable. As noted earlier, a first consideration in dealing with feedback is to ensure that your ear canals are clear of wax. This does not usually require a medical evaluation each time the ears need to be checked. The audiologist or hearing instrument specialist can do the job just as well and usually at no cost. If the canals are obstructed, your provider may charge a fee to remove wax, or if necessary refer you to a physician. You may want to insist that examination of your ear canals be a part of regular office hearing aid check-ups.

Given clear canals, the next obvious concern in dealing with feedback is the fit of the hearing aids. The most common cause of all feedback problems is poorly fitting earpieces. Sometimes the hearing aid or earmold are ill-fitting from the very beginning. Hearing aids that have been used for several years without a feedback problem can gradually develop it as the aid "loosens up" in the ear. This results from two possibilities. If you wear BTEs with earmolds, the earmolds can shrink and change shape. Also, tissues along the wall of the canal can gradually give way to small but persistent pressure associated with the instrument—the shoe and foot analogy again. This problem of increasing tendency for feedback is pronounced in children whose bodies undergo relatively rapid changes. Therefore, more frequent remakes can be expected with this age group to control feedback, especially in cases of severe loss.

# Feedback with New Purchases

If you have purchased new hearing aids that squeal or act like they're always on the verge of squealing, or do when volume is moved up to a desired level, insist on getting the problem corrected—

the sooner the better. Correcting a feedback problem with a new fitting is most easily done during the initial issuance.

Some feedback problems can be corrected readily in the office while the more severe cases may require a remake of the fitting. This will involve, of course, taking new impressions and going without the hearing aid for a brief time. But the temporary inconvenience will be well worth it. Whatever you do, don't allow the problem to go uncorrected, thinking, "Well, in time it'll probably straighten itself out." A feedback problem will rarely go away on its own. If anything, it usually gets worse. Left unattended, a feedback problem can result in a fitting that is less than optimal.

## Feedback and Telephone Use

Feedback occurs most often when some object is placed next to the hearing aid. This object can be a telephone, your own hand or even a nearby wall or other flat surface. Feedback is not a problem with hearing aids (having a telecoil circuit) when the switch is in the "T" position. However, it is a common problem with non-digital hearing aids. Digital hearing aids have feedback managing capabilities.

With analog hearing aids, careful positioning of the telephone receiver by moving it a slight distance from the ear or tilting it at a slight angle often eliminates feedback and still allows adequate reception. Some hearing aids are less susceptible to feedback than others. CIC-type instruments, for example, are the most feedback-free. If feedback is a problem for you, a donut-shaped, sponge-like product that fits onto the receiver of the phone can be purchased from your provider or ordered directly through a catalog from one of the companies represented in Appendix I.

## Static and Other Unwanted Sounds

Be assured that unless you happen to be listening to an old radio badly tuned to the station, internally generated static of any kind is abnormal and in need of correction. Static resulting from internal causes means that the noise is created from some problem inside the hearing aid or telephone and not existing in the environment.

Recall that for the hearing aid to have clear sound, adequate battery voltage must be maintained. Likewise, current drawn from the battery must be appropriate or the hearing aid can produce strange sounds. In cases of low voltage or dirty contacts, cleaning or replacing the battery, or servicing the contact points in the battery door should correct the problem. Moisture and dirt in the volume control or other switches can also cause static. Here again, cleaning and regular servicing will help.

Sometimes strange sounds including static-type noise come through the hearing aid even though it's relatively clean and the batteries are fresh. This can be caused by defective components in the amplifier. These components can wear out in time and require replacement. Also, some hearing aids will pick up strange sounds that radiate from electrical appliances or light fixtures, especially fluorescent. Such sounds are externally generated. Hearing aids that pick up these kinds of unwanted sounds seem to be less of a problem now than with older hearing aids. Regardless, if you detect a problem that you think may be caused by such a thing, bring this to the attention of your hearing care practitioner to solve.

Another source of unexplained sound coming through a hearing aid that should be mentioned here are those sounds in the environment that you may have forgotten existed or you've not heard for a long time. New wearers often pick up on these *new noises* right away. One such person complained, "Since I bought these hearing aids, I hear a terrible noise in my kitchen I never heard before. It's mostly constant but sometimes it goes off for awhile. What's wrong with these hearing aids?" A courtesy home visit revealed that what she was hearing was the compressor of her old refrigerator! Obviously, she hadn't heard this noise for a long time. Other sounds to which you'll need to become re-acclimated are common noises associated with motion, like paper rattling, water running, utensils dropping on a plate, and wind.

## Wind Noise

If you spend a lot of time outdoors, wind noise can be especially bothersome. If so, you might want to investigate a CIC-style fitting which will eliminate or greatly reduce wind sounds. For non-CIC instruments, a "windhood" or "windscreen" can be installed that can also help the problem. Discuss these options with your provider.

## Background Noise

The single largest complaint of hearing aid wearers is difficulty hearing in the presence of background noise. Unfortunately, hearing aids, even the most expensive ones, have difficulty separating the sounds and voices you want to hear from those in which you have no interest. So you'll have to learn to put up with a certain amount of noise just as people with normal hearing do. The new programmable hearing aids do offer some relief for those who must function regularly in noisy situations.

## Preventive Hearing Aid Maintenance

Few consumer purchases have any faster rate of depreciation and limited resale value than hearing aids. Stated differently, from an economic standpoint your hearing aids are of no value to anyone but you. For this reason and because they're expensive to replace, it makes good sense to service them on a regular basis. Systematic maintenance will reduce repair costs, lessen the number of "down" times, and most importantly extend the life of your hearing instruments. What follows is a brief list of maintenance procedures that will help you to accomplish this:

- **Clean Your Hearing Aids Daily:** This is best accomplished by first wiping the hearing aids with a dry cloth or tissue to remove wax, oil and moisture from the surface. Then lightly dry-brush all components using the wax removal techniques described earlier, and remove wax from the receiver and vent tubes. This cleaning should be done daily, preferably at bedtime.
- **Proper Storage:** Place hearing aids in a safe, convenient and protected location, being certain to disengage the battery door in a manner recommended previously. Sticking hearing aids in pockets or at the bottom of purses without a protective container exposes them to dirt and dust that can eventually do damage. Dust-free carrying cases are provided with nearly all new hearing aids. You should have this case available when necessary. If moisture build-up is a concern, store the hearing aids in a closed container with an absorbent dry-pack available from your provider.
- **Schedule Regular and Periodic Checkups with Your Provider:** In-office cleaning and servicing are usually included free with your purchase of hearing aids and you should take advantage of this. We recommend servicing be done at least every three months (like servicing an expensive car). Hearing

aids should be checked for power loss, dirty contact points, plugged vents and openings, and so forth. A more comprehensive servicing should be performed at least annually. This should include electroacoustic analysis (test box evaluation to ensure maintenance of original manufacturer's performance specifications). BTE wearers should also have the tubing replaced at this time (if not needed at 6 months). There may be a modest charge for this more comprehensive servicing but it's worth it. Residents of drier climates like Arizona will need more frequent tubing changes than those living in more moist environments like Louisiana. Next to daily cleaning, regular in-office servicing is the most important maintenance you can obtain.

## Have a Spare Set of Hearing Aids

We conclude with a discussion of hearing aid spares. We hope it's clear from the information contained in this chapter that basic knowledge of hearing aid operation together with use of simple maintenance techniques can go a long way to preventing hearing aid breakdown. We hope it's also apparent that despite your best efforts, without warning, your hearing aids can fail from time to time. If you're a person who's totally dependent on your hearing aids in order to communicate, you might want to consider the purchase of backup hearing aids for use in emergencies. Maintaining two sets of hearing aids may initially cost more. It could be argued, however, that two sets used more or less alternately will last twice as long as one set used full time.

So, spare aids may not cost more in the long run. It's like the wisdom of owning two pairs of shoes versus only one pair. For some wearers, this works. Also, the availability of spare hearing aids removes the anxiety that might accompany this loss. Some dispensers provide loaner instruments which may or may not be suitable to your personal needs but is worth inquiring.

How can you judge whether you should have spare hearing aids? The best test we know is an honest answer to the following question: *Does the mere thought of even a temporary loss of the use of your hearing aids create in you the slightest tinge of anxiety?* If it does, then you probably should have a spare set.

Actually, the availability of "spares" is something we all insist upon with commonly used devices we consider vital. (Our cars have spare tires, for example, so we can avoid panicking when a tire fails.) In our experience, people with severe hearing loss will regularly maintain a backup set of hearing aids, especially when the livelihood of such individuals is dependent on good hearing. Furthermore, the federal government for decades has issued to eligible military veterans two complete sets of hearing aids so that good hearing won't be interrupted by temporary breakdowns. You may be one who would also like the extra security of backup instruments in case yours go in for repair.

Backup hearing aids can be the still-functioning old set that you just replaced with new ones, or where money is of lesser concern, they can be hearing aids of more current vintage. If you choose to purchase or otherwise have available a set of spare hearing aids, try to ensure that they take the same size battery as your regular ones. This will lend itself to far more convenience than having to store and maintain two different kinds of fresh batteries.

## Hearing Aid Disuse and Longevity

The question arises, "Will my spare hearing aids wear out faster or maybe even slower if they're not used regularly?" It's true that peak performance of electromechanical devices can decline with disuse. This need not happen with spare hearing aids, however. This is avoided by rotating them periodically with your regular instruments, for example, once each month or more. This level of activity will keep them running and assure you that they're available and working if and when needed. During extended periods of storage (30 days or longer) the batteries should be completely removed so as to prevent corrosion from possible leakage. While cost is a serious consideration, two sets of hearing aids is ideal.

## Help From Family and Friends

Sometimes you just need a little help. Your spouse, family member or friend can provide that help with problem solving. As hearing aids have gotten smaller, so have the batteries. Sometimes the batteries are difficult to insert and remove from the hearing aid. Having someone help you orient the battery so that you get it in right will avoid the consequences of getting it in wrong and possibly damaging your hearing aid.

Inserting and removing your hearing aid can be difficult and if the hearing aid is placed in your ear improperly it may not function properly or even irritate your ear. A family member or spouse can help you make sure that the hearing aid is fitting correctly and well positioned in the ear.

The openings in your hearing aid where sound is delivered to your ear are very small and when they become blocked with debris this will keep you from hearing at your best. Sometimes, the cleaning process requires small tools and it can be a frustrating process when you have difficulty seeing. A friend or family member can help with the cleaning to make sure your hearing aid is working properly.

Probably the best help you can get from a friend or family member is their help in monitoring your communication ability. You may not always be aware of communication that you are missing or problems with the hearing aid. This person can alert you that your hearing aid is making that "squealing" from feedback or an adjustment is needed in order to hear better. Friends and family can help out with just about every aspect of problem-solving and extending the life of your hearing aids.

## Conclusions

Today's hearing aids, products of an unprecedented technology, are creations of remarkable quality. Their more accommodating size, improved performance overall and generally high reliability are characteristics as impressive to most audiologists and hearing instrument specialists as they perhaps are to you. They're built to operate for long hours under adverse conditions and they do so with batteries that, while smaller, work harder and produce more energy for their size than those of an earlier era. For the most part, these hearing instruments perform their valuable service unfailingly.

# CHAPTER TEN
# Aging and Hearing Loss
## *James F. Maurer, Ph.D.*

Dr. Maurer received his Doctoral Degree in Audiology from the University of Oregon Medical School in 1968. In 1971, he developed and directed the first mobile auditory testing and rehabilitation program in the United States for low-income older persons, which carried on for more than two decades. He has written and co-authored seven books and many articles on hearing loss and aging. His efforts in Costa Rica establishing an Audiology diagnostic testing clinic, which bears his name, earned him a Governor's Commendation. He was also instrumental in the discovery of a new hereditary deafness syndrome. Dr. Maurer is a Professor Emeritus at Portland State University in Oregon.

This chapter is dedicated to you with hearing loss who have passed the fifth decade of life. It's also written for friends and family members who desire to understand the personal consequences of auditory loss in older persons. There is much within this chapter aimed at teaching rehabilitation strategies for helping yourself and others, so that both of your lives are enriched by the experience.

I don't mean to be a snob, but I'm not a great believer in growing old. Having passed the big "Seven Ohhh," I think I can now understand why some people get face lifts, dye their hair, lie about their age, fall for quick fix rejuvenation supplements and even, like my dear mother, disassociate from others of the same age because they "look even older."

Not that I have acquiesced to any of these strategies, you understand. But I did experience a secret moment of exhilaration a few days ago when the lady in the pro shop made me pull out my I.D when I asked for senior golf rates. And I admit to avoiding the kid who sacks groceries at the checkout stand because he once offered to carry them for me. In fact, if he even looks at me I quickly shove two fingers through the plastic bag loops, lift them off the counter like they're weightless, and try not to sway like a drunken sailor as I exit.

So whatever it takes to make you feel young and viable is okay. It's like one of my hearing-impaired oldsters said to me when I was a wee lad of forty-five. "You don't quit playing the game because you've grown old. You grow old because you've quit playing the game."

He wore his hearing instruments constantly.

As stated earlier in this book, among the great chronic health conditions of the sixty-five and older group, hearing impairment ranks *number three,* right after arthritis and hypertension. While it might seem we are dealing with a minor epidemic, the truth is we start losing our hearing very early in life.

Most experts now agree that age-related changes that affect our hearing are in the inner ear, the auditory nerve, the brain stem, or the auditory part of the brain. It is interesting to note that most changes due exclusively to aging don't present a whole lot of hearing problems. In fact, there are many older persons who can put up with a few misunderstood conversations and neither they nor their friends perceive loss of hearing sensitivity as a problem. These people are fortunate. Fully a third of 50-plus persons in the United States have real impairments. Over age seventy, the incidence of hearing impairment increases to nearly 50 percent. But this is not entirely due to growing old.

Many of us not only have a touch of presbycusis, but we've picked up a few other causes of hearing loss on our trek through life. We also undergo a gradual depletion of cells in the auditory processing part of our central nervous system. Once these neurons within the brain stem and brain structures are depleted, they're not replaced, although we now know that nature compensates for dead cells by establishing new connections around them. Moreover, scientists recently have discovered ways of preventing neuron destruction. In fact, some neurons have been "rescued" even after damage had already begun!

Changes due to aging at this "central" level don't show up in a conventional hearing test, yet they do account for many aging issues. There's reduced short-term memory span. There's lengthened reaction time to auditory signals. Try keeping up with your grandkids playing an arcade game! As we age, we may experience difficulty tracking a fast-paced conversation or shifting gears to a new topic.

Lucky for us Walter Winchell was doing his "rapid fire" commentary when we were kids! We now find ourselves having more difficulty understanding speech, especially in background noise and particularly the "noise" of other people talking, such as in a cafeteria.

A 61-year-old woman confided in me that she was seated in a beauty salon, trying to read a new diet book. Finally, in a moment of exasperation, she put it down. "I simply couldn't concentrate with all those people talking! I never used to be this way."

Even in a fairly quiet place there's a greater problem paying attention ("Great sermon wasn't it?"). The drone of sounds that become neural noise may be someone speaking, or the neighbor's lawnmower, or music playing. Even our thoughts at the moment can interfere with our ability to concentrate on something else, causing us to make poor judgments or creating a momentary lapse of memory, such as when driving a car ("Honey, you just missed our exit!"). We simply cannot handle as many inputs as we used to, and it's harder to focus on what we're doing when there are multiple hearing challenges.

Sometimes changes associated with aging can be misinterpreted as hearing impairment. An older couple came into my office for a second opinion. Urged by her husband, the woman had purchased two hearing aids, which she was wearing with some discomfort. Upon examining her I found that her hearing was normal for her age, sixty-four years, she had excellent word discrimination. After testing her ability to repeat sentences presented in cafeteria noise, I found she had a slight, but not clinically significant difficulty. In this instance, the husband's perception of his wife's "hearing impairment" was incorrect.

Additional testing revealed was a problem with short-term memory. Her husband would ask her to bring something from another room, and she would interrupt her activities in the kitchen to do what he asked. Then she forgot what it was that he wanted. He took this to mean that she didn't hear him, which was not so. She had simply forgotten. We older folks can identify with this short quip titled, "Enigma:" *Where did I put what I saw before it went?*

Psychologists have known for years that aging affects our ability to recall things in the immediate past more than our ability to remember the distant past with our "crystallized" intelligence. Does this mean we get dumber as we age? No. Does it mean we aging persons have trouble with a task that requires *new* learning? No, but our minds may not be as nimble as they used to be. Does it mean we're more likely to forget someone's name after just being introduced than a playmate's name recalled from childhood? Yes! Is this a new problem for us? No. We've forgotten things stored in short-term memory all our lives because we were distracted or focused on something close, or simply forgot. This is not "new" behavior. It's just that as we grow older, it increases in frequency, often because of neural noise interference.

## Living with a Hearing Loss

Even a slight hearing impairment during this time of life may occasionally affect our ability to understand others. Since the voices of people with whom we talk vary in those characteristics that contribute to understanding, we misinterpret some individuals more than others. Voices differ in pitch, loudness, quality and output (words per minute), each of which can influence the clarity and intelligibility of the speaker's voice. Words spoken are more understandable for some voices than others. The clearer speaking person utters words that are more precisely formed, or articulated.

Obviously, teenagers can keep up with the accelerated speech of their age group. But many of us cannot. We simply have to ask them to speak more slowly.

Broadcaster "hype" has turned "hyper" for many of us who remember all too well the comfortably paced, resonant and clear voices of the golden age of radio. Today, radio and television stations that still endorse clear and reasonably paced communication are not as easy to find. Since some voices are clearer than others, it pays to shop around the networks and public broadcasting for better listening experiences.

Visual cues, seeing the speaker as she or he is communicating, contribute to our getting the message. But constraints in our communication environments differ considerably. Some places are worse than others, where messages spoken reverberate from bare walls and floors and are lost in the wake of their own noise. In rooms containing carpets and drapes that are farther away from outside traffic noise, interference is minimized. Something to think about if you're apartment shopping.

Places where older people congregate should be stellar listening environments. Unfortunately, this is not always the case. I recall visiting a dozen or more senior adult centers, noting the fact that while most were clean and pleasant, many were located in high noise areas and few attempts had been made to reduce interior noise. One center was actually located under a roller skating rink!

If you're reading this because you have an older parent or grandparent with hearing problems, keep in mind that it's much easier to converse with them in a quiet room. Make sure there's good lighting and try to maintain a speaking distance of less than nine feet. You'll be pleasantly surprised at how much easier conversation becomes and how much stress is reduced.

Background sounds around us can also be a positive experience. We constantly monitor the world we live in, often unconsciously. Our hearing sense, as well as our vision, keeps tabs on what is happening in our space. There's often comfort in the constant background of sounds and sights in our environment. There's a sense of belonging.

Even a very mild hearing loss can change this monitoring behavior and affect how we feel. As one 56-year-old woman described to me before she began wearing hearing instruments, "Not being able to hear little background sounds was an experience I wouldn't like to repeat. I had entered an upstairs art gallery in an old community college building. Normally I would expect to hear hushed conversations, feet shuffling or other sounds. Except for the clack of my shoes on the old wooden floor, there was complete silence! I must have been the only one in the gallery, and I began to feel anxious. It was as if I was the last person alive on this planet. I hurriedly left the place...and I didn't even know why."

Like brush strokes on a canvas, the myriad of small sounds that we're so accustomed to hearing tell us we are a part of reality. They also contribute to our sense of security. Detection of some warning signals may be challenged by our hearing loss, sounds such as footsteps on carpet, tires on soft snow, or even fire burning in the next room, as one hapless 77-year-old apartment dweller recounted to me. He had barely escaped from the burning building.

Hearing loss dampens the enjoyment of some activities that gave us pleasure in the past: theater-going, music appreciation, church services, watching television, dining out, having a drink in places with background noise, talking to others on the telephone. Even a mild hearing loss can reduce life satisfaction for some things we once took for granted.

There is an acoustic issue that afflicts a few of us. We are all blessed with tiny tubes that extend from the back wall of the throat (behind the nose) into the middle ear cavities of each ear. The purpose of these Eustachian tubes is to ventilate the middle ears with fresh air. The tiny mouth of each tube is normally closed, but may open when we yawn, cough, or snore, thus permitting air to come in. Now comes the rub.

The mouth of the aging tube may tend to remain open in some cases. This condition is not something to get excited about, but for some persons it creates the complaint, "My voice echoes." And sometimes when they wear hearing instruments that amplify their voices, they say, "My voice echoes a bit louder." So an open Eustachian tube can cause voice echo, and wearing a hearing instrument may make this echo a little bit louder. Some people are troubled by this and some are not. Hearing care practitioners are experienced in helping those who are uncomfortable with this condition.

None of us are alike. We differ because of genetic influences, environmental effects, and luck of the draw from injuries and diseases that damage us permanently. The specific problems that we encounter with our hearing deficit also differ, as do our physical and emotional capabilities to overcome adversity, lifestyle, support system of friends and relatives, tolerance for breakdowns in communication, the severity of our hearing impairment, and whether we have successfully pursued professional help. What we have in common is that we will circumvent a lot of future problems by seeking quality professional help in getting evaluated and discovering the resources available to us.

## Other Influences that Affect Hearing

The amount of loss that we accrue in growing older can be compounded by the consequence of exposures to other events or agents that damage our hearing mechanisms from infancy onward. These include noise exposure, diseases, high fever, head injury, toxic chemicals and drugs, blood supply deficiency, lack of oxygen and genetic influences.

Some of these causes are preventable, such as further damaging our ears from noise exposure. Some are not, such as familial or genetic loss of hearing, although microbiologists are getting closer to a solution to even this problem. In any case, it's rare to find a hearing loss that is not impacted by non-aging causes, especially among men. Noise exposure is a most common cause of reduced hearing sensitivity. According to the National Institute of Deafness and Communication Disorders, more than 30 million Americans are exposed to hazardous sound levels on a regular basis. Of the 28 million Americans who have hearing loss, about one-third can attribute their hearing loss, at least in part, to noise exposure. Older persons are no exception. Because many of us pursue noisy hobbies in later years, the topic bears further discussion.

While the Occupational Safety and Health Administration (OSHA) has required noisy industries to provide ear protection since 1970, this partial solution came too late for many who are now retirement age. We live in an industrialized society where noise is seemingly omnipresent. We were endowed with eyelids to keep out most light while sleeping but no "earlids" to suppress background sounds of traffic, air conditioners, furnaces, and a host of other noise sources that are pervasive in our homes. In fact, we are indeed fortunate if we can sit in the quiet security of the living room, close our eyes, and hear nothing.

Both community and recreational noise has increased over the years with the rise in population and proliferation of noisy vehicles and gadgets. Intrusion by other people's noises in formerly quiet neighborhoods often taxes our patience and our hearing ability. Automobile boom boxes, chain saws, lawnmowers, firearms, noisy vehicles and 50-plus years of Fourths of July all have a cumulative effect.

Other places include jazzercise facilities, which often feature loud music, and where the more vulnerable ears of infants parked in strollers in the back of the room are unprotected from this clamor. Beauty salons can be very noisy, but fortunately some manufacturers of hair dryers are now building quieter machines.

Older men often spend time in home workshops, where electric drills, saws, sanders and other equipment can add to the hearing loss associated with aging. The intrusion of jet sleds, all-terrain vehicles, snowmobiles, high volume music in unwelcome places, such as parks and wilderness areas add to mental confusion and the physical demise of delicate inner ear structures. Shooting high-powered rifles, magnum pistols and shotguns is a very efficient way to lose decibels of hearing as well. In fact, conventional ear protectors do not completely protect against such firearms. And usually we don't even know our loss of hearing sensitivity is happening until it's too late for it to recover.

Women who are homemakers are not immune to this onslaught. Some years ago my graduate students did a sound level survey door-to-door, interviewing women and measuring the noise intensity of home appliances to which they were regularly exposed. Guess what took First Place honors, the loudest ruckus of the week:

an ordinary vacuum cleaner generated a whopping 105 decibels at one lady's ear. By OSHA standards, she was running the risk of permanent hearing damage by operating that machine more than one hour a day!

Neither presbycusis nor noise-induced hearing loss is medically correctable. But they can combine to produce a greater hearing impairment. We can't turn the clock back and start wearing ear protectors at an earlier age, but there's something to be said for protecting what hearing we have left. I carry an inexpensive pair of foam earplugs for use on long airplane trips and other situations where noise exposures may be loud or lengthy.

I find it interesting, having provided hearing tests on a number of rock musicians back in the early 1970s, that many who were slow in requesting advice on hearing protectors now seek advice on hearing instruments. I wonder about the hearing sensitivity of their audiences, the baby boomers, who are now joining our aging population. Our children and grandchildren seem to perpetuate the thirst for loud music, despite our warnings and presentiments.

## Adjusting to Hearing Loss

Do you remember when someone first called you "Sir" or "Madam"? Did you experience a momentary flicker of surprise, an evaporating thought that you somehow must be different from that moment on? It was as if you had suddenly arrived on some plateau in life from which there was no return.

Interestingly, our arrival may have more to do with our biological age (how old we look and feel) than our chronological age (how many birthdays we've celebrated). Some of us look our age, some of us don't. Realization of our hearing difficulties can be like that, when someone younger gives us the bad news, "Dad, you've got to do something about your hearing!" We are different from that moment on. However, for many of us there's no sudden realization. Since our loss of hearing sensitivity is usually gradual, it may take us a long time to recognize that we're having increasing difficulties associated with the loss.

An older gentleman living in a townhouse called this to my attention. "We used to hear the clock ticking," he said.

"What concerns me," his wife added, "is that we don't hear the gas jet in the fireplace anymore."

It's also interesting that some rather important sounds in our lives disappear without a whimper. A 74-year-old gentleman insisted that his new hearing instrument had a strange noise in it. He kept cocking his head and saying, "There it is again." Then he handed the aid to me. I listened to the instrument and shook my head. "I don't hear any noise, except normal background sounds."

He put the instrument back in his ear, listening, and he could hear it again. His face lit up when we both realized he was hearing his breathing for the first time in years.

Hearing old sounds again is like visiting old friends. It's a very positive experience. Some of us don't accept hearing loss so readily. And this lack of acceptance creates a quandary for the specialist trying to help us.

John was a 70-year-old longshoreman who came to my office announcing that his physician told him he had the arteries of a 30-year-old. He flexed his triceps and asked me to feel them. "Hard as steel," I responded, knowing what was coming next.

"Doc," he shouted, "I don't have any trouble hearing. I don't know why they sent me here. I can hear a pin drop."

But he couldn't. In fact, he couldn't hear a brick drop. Not only that, he couldn't understand conversational level speech. And ability to hear in noise? Forget it!

I always have great compassion for such patients. I know they want to stay young. They want to have youthful hearing skills. They don't want to wear hearing instruments because they see them as another indication that their bodies are growing older. But not tending to the needs of our ears is like letting a garden go to weeds. Tiny hair cells and nerve cells in our hearing mechanism depend on sound stimulation. Not wearing hearing aids is a poorer choice.

Another reason why denial takes place is manifested by the slope of the hearing loss on the audiogram (see Chapter 3). When we look at our hearing test, most of us see a hearing sensitivity curve that drops off—getting poorer in the high frequencies. We may still hear low-pitched sounds very well, but we don't hear higher-pitched sounds. Thus, telling this person, "You're not hearing!" is not entirely true. Some sounds may be heard quite well. Others may not be heard at all. Nevertheless, our ever-active brain fills in the blanks, sometimes correctly, sometimes not.

Grandpa and his grandson Joey were painting the shed. Joey said, "Gramps, let's go get some **thinner**."

Grandpa laughed and shook his head incredulously. "**Dinner?**

Why son, we just had lunch!"

This illustrates the difference between <u>hearing</u> and <u>understanding</u>. Joey's grandfather *thought* he heard the message. In fact, he correctly heard five out of six words spoken by his grandson. But he didn't hear one critical consonant, the soft /th/ sound, so his brain tried to fill in the blank. This small misperception changed the entire meaning of his grandson's request. When this starts happening to us frequently in conversations with others, we're overdue for help!

Many of us endure the typical high frequency hearing loss that Grandpa experiences. Such a loss allows us to hear the louder vocalized speech sounds, as the /a/ in the word ba*ll*, but we have trouble with the softer and higher frequency consonant sounds in words such as **th**igh. These voiceless consonant sounds, like /F/ in the word *F*ish and /S/ in *S*ee, contribute much more to our understanding of human communication than do voiced sounds like vowels and voiced consonants. Not hearing the voiceless sounds because of the slope of our audiogram creates errors for us in interpreting messages, even though we hear the lower frequency sounds quite well—perhaps even normally. So, we may reject the fact that we have a hearing impairment simply because we hear *some* sounds well. Such a paradigm leads to the remark, "I can hear you, but I can't understand what you're saying."

The high frequency loss may create a quandary for us when we *see* a bird singing, but don't *hear* its song, or when someone draws our attention to the chirping of crickets, the whisper of wind in the trees, or the swishing of clothing. Missing a sound also can be an unnecessary annoyance.

A gentleman in his fifties told me, "I couldn't understand why every time we went to the cabin I ended up with more mosquito bites than the rest of the family. Then one time my daughter pointed out that there was one buzzing around my ear. I realized suddenly that I hadn't even heard it!"

I used to routinely advise people with hearing instruments to take them off before going to bed. One 82-year-old woman was offended by that statement as a cardinal rule. "I've slept on my left side and worn one hearing aid in my right ear for over ten years," she admonished. "Who knows who might be knocking on my door in the middle of the night? Or what if the phone rings? I might miss something!"

A few indomitable individuals take immediate and aggressive action to counteract a recently discovered hearing difficulty. One gentleman bounced into my clinic like a bandy rooster one morning, gesturing wildly and shouting, "How do I get some hearing devices?"

When I asked him why he thought he needed them, he said that he no longer could understand his patent attorneys at board meetings. "I have to depend on what they say. Trouble is they mumble separately. If they all mumbled together," he quipped, "I think I'd understand what they were talking about." He wanted a quick solution, and he wasn't about to let a hearing impairment stand in his way. This was a man who was used to making adjustments. He was 82 years old. Did I say "old?" I mean *young!*

Others of us refuse to accept our impairments as we do our chronological age, by ignoring senior citizen discounts in restaurants and malls, because of the embarrassment in admitting the truth. Similarly, we may ignore the pleas of others by not appearing in hearing clinics willingly. Often, our late appearance is a begrudging one, something we're doing for "them," but not for ourselves. Some even deny that they want to hear. "Look, I can hear most things around me," a 57-year-old attorney said, folding his arms. "There's a whole lot going on out there that I don't want to hear. I hear just fine!"

His wife sat quietly in the corner, realizing her husband included her in what he did not want to hear.

Often our reluctance to seek help presents a barrier to those attempting to talk with us. If straining to hear is fatiguing, imagine what it must be like for another person who has to keep repeating all day.

The denial of aging is often projected as a stigma against hearing instruments that are for "older" persons. This can become an attitudinal disclaimer that hearing difficulty is not an important part of our lives. A glass of water won't suffice when we're thirsting for the Fountain of Youth. Some of us even engineer our lives to convince ourselves that we hear normally. We simply minimize our exposure to situations where the hearing deficit compromises our enjoyment of life!

I asked a woman in her late fifties, "What things did you do ten years ago that gave you a lot of satisfaction?"

She responded, "Let's see, I was very active in the church. I really enjoyed that. I taught Sunday school. I went to a symphony about once a month. Oh, and bridge club. That meant a lot to me ten years ago."

"Are you still enjoying these activities?"

She was quiet for a moment. "Well no, not really," she shrugged. "It became too much work teaching those children, and too much fussing to get ready for the symphony. I moved onto other things, I guess."

As we talked on, it became clear that she had sacrificed part of her life satisfaction because of increasing hearing difficulties. She had carefully limited her activities so that the impairment wouldn't affect her life. And she had accomplished this without ever admitting that the cause of her withdrawal was her inability to hear. Fortunately, this woman turned out to be an excellent candidate for aural rehabilitation, where she was involved in group counseling. Once she could identify with other women in the group who had similar problems, her self-esteem increased and she began to move out of her self-imposed isolation.

Because there are situations where we honestly feel we can hear normally, in front of a blasting television, for example, it becomes easy to blame others for our social inadequacy. In the hearing health care field, many of us have heard the following during an interview with an older couple.

"<u>He</u> doesn't hear what I'm saying."

"<u>She</u> doesn't speak up!"

When you think about it, we all project our problems onto other people or other things at some point in our lives. How many times have we heard statements like, "I know where I got this miserable cold—that sneezing kid in the shopping mall," or, "You forgot to remind me that I had a meeting!"

There's nothing unique about a hearing-impaired person projecting his or her problem. We all need a scapegoat at times, in order to reduce our stress. Similarly, we may find withdrawal appropriate for some situations, such as a frustrating conversation in a noisy room. These ways of avoiding or escaping from stress, denying the problem, compensating for it, projecting it, withdrawing from it actually make us feel better when our backs are against the wall. They help us maintain a positive self-image, which takes a beating when we can't hear well. But if carried too far, these bailout behaviors can interfere with getting help and reducing our life satisfaction.

Compromising our lives in order to convince ourselves that we hear normally is an all-too-common experience among those of us with impairments. Like the woman described earlier, curtailing formerly enjoyable activities can seriously reduce enjoyment of life!

If you find you're no longer showing up at holiday parties, club activities, homes of friends or other previously reinforcing events, take a good look at yourself. Maybe it's time to seek professional help.

What's also missing here is social responsibility. We hearing-impaired people owe others the right to conversations that are free of frustration. We owe our friends freedom from continually having to repeat conversations. We owe them an honest appraisal of our hearing difficulties.

What is not realized by many of us is that once we can hear better, we may discover a rebirth of more youthful participation in social activities. We become better social companions. As one wife exclaimed, "When he puts those digital instruments on, he's more like himself."

## Retiring Comfortably with a Hearing Loss

It's interesting to talk to people with auditory problems who have recently retired. Some experience a sudden loss of power, the ingratiating experience of sliding backwards down the slope that leads to non-person status in the eyes of once admiring co-workers. Normal hearing people may experience the same thing. This was the feeling that a recently retired physician related to me. His repeated returns to his beloved medical school, where he had held an office for more than thirty years, were met with disengaging smiles and chafing comments like, "What are you doing back here?"

He began questioning whether a prejudice was operating because of his new hearing instruments, his whiter-than-others' hair, and the fact that he was retired. Ultimately, he felt that his once respected opinion no longer mattered, and with some reluctance, he ended his visits.

Some years later after my own retirement, he called me. "You know," he said, "if you ever write another book or have to counsel a lonely retiree, you might remember this piece of advice: if you live alone and your world is passing you by, be grateful for what you have left. Then make yourself important to someone. You'll be pleasantly surprised how important you become to yourself."

He was embarking on his third trip to China to help children with birth defects. He had decided that nothing could get in the way of his need to help others, neither hearing aids, aging body, nor unresponsive colleagues.

We are a diverse population, we older persons. Some of us cross over to retirement more slowly, tenaciously clinging to our previous roles in life through occasional work or social and service activities. We may express joy at having left our working selves behind. We network with friends seeking a newfound freedom, finding companionship in the excitement of long-awaited travel, new recreational activities, educational pursuits, or greater involvement in hobbies. Some of us don't retire at all.

Hearing loss does not respect our differences. We find individuals with auditory difficulties in all lifestyles. What's important is that we don't let this problem curtail our pleasures in life. A pharmacist friend who had been a trap shooter since boyhood was left with a significant high frequency hearing impairment in both ears. He wears two hearing instruments in retirement, and when I visit his home I always take a handful of earplugs. He constructed a woodworking shop in his garage and now creates quality furniture both as a hobby and to supplement his pension.

He and his wife are very happy in retirement, and I was prompted to ask him, "If you had it to do over, would you give up thirty years of shooting?"

"No, I wouldn't give that up. Nor these either," he grinned, pointing to his ears.

Enjoyment is found in a quiescent lifestyle for many of us. Our activities may be limited to television viewing, reading, eating, sleeping, and occasionally making visits to friends, relatives, church, and senior adult centers. We find pleasure where we can and enjoy predictability in our lives.

One such individual, age 72, has neuropathy in his hands. Because of this lack of feeling, he can no longer operate his hearing instruments. He has been perfectly content with his adjustment to his impairment because his lifestyle does not involve a great number of social activities. He's an avid sports fan, and enjoys watching these contests vicariously.

One of his concessions to his hearing difficulty is a pair of earphones connected to an infrared television amplifying system. This "assistive listening device" is easy to manipulate. It allows him to turn up baseball games as loud as he wants without interfering with adjoining apartment tenants. He also has a telephone amplifier. Such devices (as described in Appendix I) are very useful in supplementing or substituting for traditional hearing instruments.

Regaining life satisfaction may mean letting go of some of our former attitudes about aging and hearing loss and beginning to accept the realities of a new emerging self. It helps to take stock of all the positive attributes in our lives. There are people who like us for who we are, wrinkles and all. They could care less about our need for prosthetic devices. They care about <u>us</u>. They accept our baggage. In fact, it becomes so much a part of us that the people we care about don't even see it anymore.

It also helps to look around at the place where we spend most of our waking hours. What are the positive attributes in our home environment? What things produce pleasure for us? If we close our eyes, how many of these things would no longer be pleasurable, such as a picture that is dear to us, or a good book? If you could close your ears and hear nothing, what things of enjoyment would be missed?

Now take inventory of positive activities outside the home, things we like to do with our time. This could include hobbies, meetings, entertainment, and activities that are more physical, such as walking, fishing, travel, golf. If we apply the same limitations to our activities, in turn, closing our eyes and ears, what would the effect be? What enjoyable activities would we have to give up?

What we discover from this simple exercise is that first, there are many positive things operating in each of our lives. Getting older is not a virus that takes away all our satisfaction with life. Second, recounting our pleasures with one of our senses "closed" eliminates many positive aspects of our lives that we would not give up willingly.

Now hang onto that thought, because not giving up is exactly the attitude that must persist if we are to realize our most positive potential in spite of our hearing loss. This means accepting ourselves wearing devices that will open up a part of the world's pleasures that would otherwise be forsaken. It means accepting our new selves.

Interestingly, the world will accommodate our new self-image, and we can now move forward with our lives. People began to like us better because we are *real* in projecting who we are, and we're happier for that experience. Popeye probably said it best, "I am what I am, and that's what I am!" Did he wear hearing aids? You mean you didn't notice?

During the aging process, we consciously or unconsciously make other adjustments as well. Our eyes admit less light than in former years, so we try to adjust our reading habits accordingly, or reduce some activities such as night driving. Ability to understand conversations in background noise becomes diminished, so we try to avoid the incompatible combination of noisy places and conversations.

We find quieter places to converse. Knowledge of reduced physical stability makes us move more cautiously in risky situations where we might fall, such as walking down steps, getting into the bathtub, climbing a ladder. We discover that sudden movements can produce dizziness or unsteadiness, so we avoid quick changes in position. Diets may change to cope with various health conditions after age fifty. We find ourselves getting less sleep at night because of awakenings, and may discover a decrease in the quality of sleep. So we may compensate with naps. And the list goes on.

Compensating for perceived changes is a healthy, friendly way of insuring survival and happiness. It is taking charge of one's life. It's making a positive statement about the aging years! Like the old adage that a graying dowager told me years ago, "There may be snow on the roof, but there's fire in the furnace!" And stoking that furnace, managing one's life experiences, reducing the impact of a hearing difficulty by acknowledging the problem to others, getting professional help, and arranging living places so we can hear better, are giant steps in the right direction.

## Helping Yourself

Arranging where we reside, eat, work, play or pray means getting closer to the source of sound, i.e., TV set, stereo, church pew, or the waitress in a cafe. What we're accomplishing by favorably positioning ourselves in living situations is improvement in understanding communication. The greater the distance we are from the sound source, the more distortion we'll experience, whether we realize it or not. Besides, there are those visual cues: facial expressions, mouth movements, gestures, and body language. These nuances of visual communication may not be visible from a distance but do help to actually clarify the message up close.

Stage-managing our lives also means getting away from distracting or overpowering noise or loud music. One may enjoy the power of organ music and sit close to it in a place of worship, but at what cost to hearing the message? If one ear is better than the other, favor the "good" ear. Think of places in your life where it's difficult to hear: sitting in the back seat of an automobile, sitting in a breakfast nook adjacent to the humming of appliances, standing at the cash register in a busy restaurant, or before the agent in a bus terminal. Make a list of these noisy places in your life and then think of alternatives.

Reluctance to get help actually may stem from any of several factors, many of which surfaced in a survey we once conducted among several thousand low income older persons. Cost of hearing appliances ranked number one. Fino et al,[1] reported on a general population study which indicated that older persons with hearing loss who did not buy amplification said hearing instruments were too conspicuous, too expensive, too noisy, and drew attention to the impairment, in that order.

Dr. Kochkin[2] cited admission of a hearing loss made people look old and disabled. Vanity (how we perceive our appearance) was also a prevalent reason. Many of us still find wearing eyeglasses more "fashionable" than hearing aids. Perceived geographic isolation from clinics providing hearing instruments ranked high on the survey, as well as lack of mobility. Older folks tend to view other health problems as more serious than their hearing impairment, despite the fact that it can degrade their mental health. My thought to those in the 50-plus age group who have hearing difficulties is that there are ample reasons for finding out what gains these instruments now offer. We may lose more by not helping ourselves if we fail to try them.

## Helping a Loved One in a Restricted Environment

If you know someone in a nursing home is benefiting from hearing instruments, keep tabs on their ability to use them. Does this person have the skills and dexterity to put the instruments in the ear, turn them up, and remove them before going to bed? Can the individual change the batteries when appropriate? Is the family physician checking to see that the ear canals are free of wax buildup? Does the nursing staff complain of hearing aid whistling? This "feedback" can be caused by earwax. Is someone remembering to open up the battery doors at night, saving on battery life during sleeping hours?

And while we're at it, is anybody cleaning this person's glasses once in a while? Remember, visual skills also help the hearing-impaired person. If your loved one can no longer manage prosthetic devices, ask who in the nursing staff is responsible. In many cases I've witnessed, the primary person who cares and oversees the maintenance of your loved one's prosthetic devices is you!

Strange things happen to hearing aids in nursing homes. They can be stolen, substituted for someone else's instrument down the hall, uncomfortably stuck in the wrong ear, chewed on or digested by someone's visiting dog or cat, dropped in the toilet, plugged with wax, sentenced to lifetime solitary confinement in a dresser drawer, stepped on by a 250 pound attendant, or awaiting invitation under the bed to the fraternal order of dust bunnies.

If the instrument seems to be helping the older person only by making him or her more alert, take this as a positive sign and reward the use of hearing aids. If you make a visit and find it's not being worn, check to make sure the aids are working. It's wise of you to participate in getting the hearing aids in the ears during your visit. Chances are your warm gestures of touching, smiling, talking and caring will have positive consequences on this special person. And on you, as well.

You may be reading this book to find out what you can do for a loved one who sadly can no longer understand the printed word, cannot write effectively, or may be wandering in that personal void associated with severe mental deterioration. Unfortunately, the lower the level of intellectual functioning, the poorer the prognosis for gaining much benefit from amplification. But check first to see if increasing the volume of the soothing sound of your voice seems to create a pleasant experience, or even an increase in understanding.

I took some graduate students to a nursing home to do hearing testing on some residents. One gentleman sat very quietly in a corner of the hallway not socializing with anyone. He just looked emptily at the opposite wall. One of the staff told us he had been diagnosed aphasic, which is lack of speech understanding and expression due to brain damage. We had brought with us a powerful body hearing aid with a big red volume control. We placed it in a harness on his body, hooked his right ear up to it, and slowly began turning up the volume. His mouth opened slightly, his head turned toward us, and as we watched, a wisp of a smile turned into a full-fledged grin. One student tried to subdue her excitement and quietly asked, "Can you hear me?"

He looked at her, lips moving, eyes glistening, and managed an "uh...Yes!" A few weeks later, after we had showed him how to use the aid and charge the battery each night, I returned to see how he was doing. I found him sitting on the sun porch, holding hands with an elderly woman, talking quietly. The big box with the red volume control hung like an Olympic medallion on his chest.

# References

1. Fino MS, Bess FH, Lichtenstein MJ, and Logan SA. Factors differentiating elderly hearing aid users and nonusers, <u>Hearing Instruments</u>, 43, 2.6, 8-10, 1992.

2. Kochkin S. Why 20 million in U.S don't use hearing aids for their hearing loss. <u>The Hearing Journal</u> 46(4):36-37, 1993.

# CHAPTER ELEVEN
# Improving Your Listening and Hearing Skills
## *Mark Ross, Ph.D.*

Dr. Ross received his doctorate at Stanford University. He has worked as a clinical audiologist, a director of a school for the deaf, Director of Research and Training at the League for the Hard of Hearing, and as a professor of audiology at the University of Connecticut where he's now Professor Emeritus of audiology. Currently, Dr. Ross is an associate at the Rehabilitation Engineering Resource Center (RERC) at the Lexington Center in Jackson Heights, N.Y. Among his activities for the RERC, he writes a bimonthly feature on Developments in Research and Technology for *Hearing Loss: the Journal of Self Help for Hard of Hearing People.*

I don't know any hard of hearing person who, if a magic wand could be used to wave away his or her hearing loss, would not jump at this miraculous opportunity. I know that I would like to be at the head of the line! But life is not a fairy tale and magic wands are in short supply. For most of us with hearing loss, it's simply a pain, one whose impact we're constantly trying to overcome or minimize. We don't approach the world as "hard of hearing" people, seeking acceptance as a separate social entity.

On the contrary, we're trying not to make it a defining condition of our personal identity by striving to reduce the impact of hearing loss in our lives. To realize our goal of continued engagement with the larger society—with our friends, family, jobs, and interests— we employ the modern technology of hearing aids and other assistive devices. And we use various communication strategies to reduce the inevitable consequences of hearing loss.

By "communication strategies" I mean any activities that might increase your ability to understand speech, either generally or in particular situations—not just technological solutions. Of course technology is vitally important, but the adjustment process doesn't end there. There are other things you can do to improve your ability to communicate in different situations. When you purchase hearing instruments, you depend upon the hearing healthcare provider's expertise to help in making the proper decision. When it comes to communication strategies and making the best use of all types of hearing technology, *you* have to take the major responsibility. The concept of personal responsibility for one's own action underlies the three recurring themes stressed throughout this chapter: acknowledgment, assertiveness, and communication exchanges.

I'll begin this chapter by discussing your personal responsibilities as you strive to improve your hearing capabilities, after which I'll comment on your initial experiences with hearing aids. My focus will be on how you can learn to interpret, enjoy and expand the new world of sound to which you've suddenly been exposed. I'll follow this by discussing speechreading and various exercises that can help you make the most of your residual hearing.

Finally, in the last section, I'll present some "hearing tactics," i.e., various kinds of adaptations to real-life situations aimed at improving speech comprehension. In writing this chapter, I've drawn heavily on what I've personally experienced during the many years that I've worn hearing aids (and I shudder to think what my life would be like without them).

## Acknowledgment

The first and indispensable step in practicing effective communication strategies is to accept the reality of the hearing loss. Unless and until you can acknowledge its presence, openly and in a matter of fact way, you are always going to be limited in how effectively you can deal with it. A hearing loss is not something to be ashamed of; it's not a stigma that has to be hidden. *Its presence does not diminish you as a human being.* By denying or projecting your hearing difficulties onto other people's mouths ("people don't talk as clearly as they used to!"), you fool only yourself. The point is worth emphasizing. The hearing loss is there. Magical thinking, denial, not "wanting to talk about it," will not make it go away. If you don't face up to this reality, unpleasant as it may be, you're condemning yourself into a life of unnecessary stress, anxiety and isolation.

The onset of hearing loss is typically very gradual. What makes this situation particularly difficult for older people is that at first they are truly not aware that a hearing loss may be the main reason they're having communication difficulties. They can't very well deny hearing sounds that they're not aware of. This is the point where many of the conflicts between the hard of hearing person and his/her significant others first arise. It's not so much denial as disbelief; they know there are times when they can hear well. After a while, of course, the effects of the hearing loss become apparent to everyone, including the person involved. If these are ignored, then someone can truly be said to be "in denial."

## Assertiveness

Once you've acknowledged the hearing loss to yourself and to others, you are then in a position to assert your communication needs in various kinds of situations. "Assertiveness" is a concept that underlies many of the specific steps I'll be suggesting later. As the person with a hearing loss, you must be willing to inform and educate others about what they have to do in order to make it easier for you to hear and understand. It may be as simple as asking the waiter in a restaurant to turn down the background music or to provide you with a written choice of the day's selections, or as involved as arranging the seats at a meeting or suggesting how your conversation partner can be a more effective communicator.

Being more assertive about your listening needs by asking others to modify their behavior does not come naturally for many people. It may mean changing the habits of a lifetime, but it can be done and it can be quite liberating (there's got to be <u>some</u> advantage to getting older!).

Of course, you don't have to take giant steps in the beginning. Even little ones, as long as you take enough of them, will eventually get you to your goal. You can be assertive about listening needs without being aggressive or hostile.

"Would you mind talking a little louder? I have a hearing loss and that will make it easier for me to understand you," will get better results than, "For Pete's sake, get the mud out of your mouth when you speak to me!"

When we assert our hearing needs, we're saying to somebody, "Yes, I really do want to communicate with you."

## Communication Exchange

This brings up the third recurring theme in this chapter: both you and the person with whom you are talking are equally involved in a communication exchange. Presumably, this person wants to be understood as much as you want to understand. Unlike a monologue, a conversation is a two-way street. When you suggest that a seating arrangement be modified, or you inform your conversational partners what verbal modifications to make so that you can understand them, it's as much for their benefit as it is for yours. What I'm suggesting is that when you work with and help other people communicate more effectively with you, both you and others benefit. So, acknowledge your hearing loss, be *assertive about your hearing needs, and know that you are a crucial half of any communication interchange.*

## Getting the Most Out of Your Hearing Aids

As a hard of hearing person you want to ensure that you're making the best use of your residual hearing. This means maximizing the benefit you're receiving through your hearing aids. Amplification is the only "therapy" that directly increases the actual amount of acoustic information available. All the training and practice procedures that are to be covered are predicated on you getting as much useful acoustic information as possible through your hearing aids. Although you should realize some immediate benefit from hearing aids, you should obtain even more help after you get used to them. Getting the most from your hearing aids requires us to consider both some general principles and some specific practice procedures.

### Tenacity

Foremost—don't get discouraged! Remember that while you've had a hearing loss for a number of years and experienced the frustrations of poor hearing, for you the sounds you had been receiving seemed perfectly "normal." Now with hearing aids you're suddenly exposed to sounds that are not only louder, but a different pattern. You're going to have to reeducate your brain to accept different sound patterns as "normal." As a rather simple analogy, what you now perceive with hearing aids can be likened to someone talking English with a very different accent.

Just as it takes time for an American to get used to, for example, an Australian speaking English, or for a New Englander to comprehend the speech of someone who comes from the Deep South (and vice versa), so it will take some time for you to adjust to the amplified "accent" coming through your hearing aids.

### The Adjustment Process

When you first put on your hearing aids, you're suddenly going to hear many sounds of which you previously were unaware. Many of these sounds will jog familiar memories. For others, you're going to have to consciously identify the source of the sound, either by asking someone or by honing in on it yourself. One woman in a recent hearing aid orientation group was going a little crazy with the hissing and splattering sounds she kept hearing until she realized it was coming from her frying pan. She hadn't heard the sounds of frying food for many years.

All at once you're going to be exposed to a world of sound you had forgotten, such as the whirl of the dishwasher, the whine of an electric can opener, the sounds of birds singing, or the "ting" of your microwave when the food is done. Other familiar sounds will be experienced somewhat differently and may even be disturbing, such as traffic noises in the city, the tumult in your favorite restaurant, and the screeching from your grandchildren's boombox (I'm told it's music!). It's true that it's a noisy world in which we live, and it seems to be getting noisier all the time. But it's the only world we have and it's the one in which you're going to feel more comfortable when you can more fully hear what's going on.

## Expectations

Not everybody will be able to realize the same degree of benefit from hearing aids. After resisting the notion of hearing aids for years, some people, when they finally relent, expect that hearing aids will re-create their hearing abilities of fifty years ago. It doesn't work that way. While hearing aids will help most people with hearing loss, no matter how advanced a hearing aid or how skilled the hearing aid dispenser, the ultimate benefits achievable through amplification are determined by the nature of the hearing loss. Even though just about everybody with a hearing loss can obtain some benefit from hearing aids (hopefully, quite a lot), the degree of benefit will vary among individuals. Your satisfaction with hearing aids is going to depend greatly on your expectations, which should be set neither too high nor too low.

One important way to develop realistic expectations is to educate yourself about hearing loss (which is what you're doing by reading this book). Another is by talking to other people with hearing loss. A third is by working closely with the professional who fit you with hearing aids. You'll find most of them ready and willing to help you understand what you can and cannot readily achieve with hearing aids. It is important that you identify specific situations in which you appear to have the greatest difficulty, and then work with the hearing care professional to determine if there is some hearing aid feature or other assistive device that can provide additional help. Such features as telephone coils, personal frequency modulation (FM) devices and television listening systems can often provide just the extra boost a person needs to overcome specific listening problems (see Appendix I). Developing realistic expectations does not mean acceptance of anything less than is possible for you.

## Initial Experiences

Every hearing professional seems to have a favorite "recipe" for helping a new wearer adjust to the new world of sound produced by hearing aids. The user information booklet that comes with your hearing aids undoubtedly contains such material. I really haven't seen any wrong recipes. If you persist and work with your provider, I have no doubt that you'll eventually find your hearing aids to be helpful. Some professionals suggest that you begin by wearing hearing aids an hour or so each day, gradually increasing the time; others recommend beginning with easy listening situations (such as in quiet while talking to one person) and work yourself up to more difficult listening environments. Still others suggest just jumping right into daily use. There's nothing wrong with these recipes—they'll work if you try them diligently. But remember, it's your hearing and you can modify any rule for your convenience and comfort.

## Be in Control

A key in your successful use of hearing aids is working closely with the professionals from whom you received the hearing instruments. They can't give you the full benefits of their skills unless you call upon them with your questions, comments, and experiences. For new hearing aid wearers in particular, the period right after acquiring the hearing aids is crucial. It is at this time that "Murphy's Law" (whatever can go wrong, will) seems particularly active. Most hearing aid related problems can be solved, or at least minimized, but they won't be if you don't bring them to the attention of your hearing aid practitioner. Of all the tales of woe I hear from people regarding their hearing difficulties, unsuccessful attempts to use hearing aids are surely among the most common. It really is a shame; so many people could have been greatly helped and their lives enriched if they had just persisted.

What I suggest is that you wear your hearing aids for as long each day as you feel comfortable, with the goal of wearing them all day every day. But you have to be satisfied that they're helping you hear better and they don't hurt your ears after a few hours. Sometimes, depending upon the nature of what you're hearing, you may want to remove them (e.g., at a hard rock concert, mowing the lawn on a windy day, etc.). Go ahead and take them out and don't feel guilty. Remember—you're the boss. You're in control. They're your ears!

## Reeducating the Brain

What "getting used to hearing aids" really means is that you'll be undergoing a learning process. Not only will you have to get used to the hearing aids themselves, but also you will have to get used to a new pattern of sounds. For some people with long-standing hearing loss, the process of reeducating the brain can be enhanced by specific training or fitting techniques. Because you haven't heard certain sounds for a long time, the signals amplified by the hearing aids may sound strident, artificial, or just downright unpleasant. These "unnatural" or "harsh" quality sounds that you may experience can actually improve speech comprehension in the long run, but only if you can get used to them.

What the hearing aids may be doing is amplifying high frequency speech sounds (like /s/, /sh/ and /f/), elements of which you may not have heard, or have heard differently for years. Your hearing aid dispenser has a good idea of what the final amplification target should be; he or she just can't get there sometimes in one fell swoop. So, don't get discouraged if you're asked to come back for tune-ups. In fact, this may be a mark of an especially conscientious hearing care practitioner. Each time you return, your provider may perk up the high frequencies, drop the low frequencies, or do something else to help ease your adjustment to a new auditory experience. While just actively listening to people may be enough to get you used to these new sound sensations, you may also find it helpful to engage in the kinds of "listening" practice procedures that will be presented later.

# Speechreading

Until recently, the preferred term for speechreading was lip-reading. We now use speechreading to emphasize the fact that when people talk, a great deal of nonverbal but important information is conveyed via facial and hand gestures, body stance, the intonation and rhythm of sentences, and the nature of the vocal emphasis placed on words and syllables. For example, the phrase "<u>Where</u> are you going?" conveys quite a different meaning than "Where are <u>you</u> going?" And "CONvict" has quite a different meaning than "conVICT," even though the two words look alike on the lips. Lip movements alone are insufficient to clarify the different meanings in these instances. What speechreading is, then, is lip-reading "plus." Our goal is not only to understand more of what a person is saying by looking at the lips, but also to be attuned to these other important sources of information. While much of this "tuning" may be unconscious, it is nevertheless very real. Speechreading will help you whether you have a mild or profound hearing loss.

If you can see a person's lips and you know the language, then you have already been speechreading—to some extent. I'll bet if I asked you if you can speechread, you'd say, "No!"

But you do!

Ask your significant other to silently mouth a month of the year (one of twelve choices). If you can't get it, try a day of the week (that is, seven rather than twelve choices). If you still don't get it (and assuming your partner's lips can be seen clearly—this is very important to check), ask this person to lip the movements for numbers "three" or "four." Nobody misses this. So, the chances are that to some extent you have already been speechreading as long as you can observe the lips of the speaker. But you should do even better if you know the general principles of speechreading.

## Speechreading Principles

### Visibility

The first general principle is that you must be able to see the lips of the person talking. Now this not only sounds simplistic, but positively insulting! Of course one has to see the lips in order to speechread. But you would be surprised how many people with hearing loss who need and can benefit from speechreading do not observe the lips of their conversational partners. They may look them "right in the eye" or simply stare off to one side.

The lip movements we're trying to pick up are minuscule, rapid, and very fleeting. Since our vision is most acute at the point of focus, our best chance of perceiving these cues is by looking right at the lips. For example, our peripheral vision should be sufficient to detect facial expressions, hand gestures, body stance, and so forth because they are larger movements. Try it. Look at someone's lips and note that you can also see the expression on his or her face as well as any hand movements.

Think about the implications of these simple rules. You will not be able to speechread when:

- in the dark
- a person's back is turned
- you're far from a person
- your visual acuity is poor (so, pay as much attention to your vision as to your hearing)
- a person's mouth is covered
- your conversational partner wears a full mustache and beard
- light is in your eyes
- the head of the person you're talking to is shadowed

In other words, any situation that reduces the visibility of the lips is going to interfere with speechreading. How often have you, or people you know, made an extra effort, perhaps unconsciously, to ensure that you can see the person who's talking? If you have, you've been speechreading, even though you may not have known it.

## Restricting Lip Movements

Anything that interferes with the movements of the lips is also going to interfere with speechreading. Some people seem unable to talk unless they have a pencil or the frame of eyeglasses jutting out of their mouth. Other people talk as if they were practicing to be ventriloquists—their lips hardly move at all. And some people seem to talk with a perpetual smile, making speechreading almost impossible because of the way the smile distorts lip movements. In a few of these instances, a little assertiveness may help, such as "Please take the pencil out of your mouth."

But for others it's a losing battle. (Although I've often been tempted, I have not yet said "Wipe that smile off your face!" to someone with a perennial grin.) Because of the wide variations in the size and movement of the lips while talking, there will be large individual variations in the speechreadability of someone's lips. For people with whom you have a continuing relationship, it's worth reminding them to use more lip movements while talking. Sometimes this works quite well. For the tight-lipped stranger, this may be a futile endeavor. It may be easier to change the world than the way some people talk. So, be realistic. You can't win them all.

## Familiarity with the Language

You can't speechread unless you know the language. This also sounds quite simplistic, and in a way it is. If you're trying to speechread someone talking in a foreign language, of course you won't be able to. But what this brings up is the notion of predictability. Since only about 30 percent of the sounds in the English language are clearly visible on the lips, even in the best of circumstances there are lots of gaps that have to be filled in. This is not quite as imposing a task as it may appear, as long as you and the person you're talking to share a common language. English is very redundant, with many linguistic and situational cues that can help you correctly predict some words you otherwise couldn't. For example, try filling in the blanks in the following sentences:

A. Please put the dish on the _____.
B. He hit a home _____ in the last _____.
C. Where are you _____?
D. It snowed again last _____.
E. I just heard the weather report. They are _____ a major _____ tonight.

In sentence "A," someone could be saying "floor" or "bookcase," rather than "table," but this is unlikely. Sentence "E" is an example of how a previous sentence (or sentences) can improve predictability. The words are "predicting" and "storm." Now—wasn't that easy?

Native language speakers do this kind of thing unconsciously. No matter what language you've grown up with, you can (or could prior to the onset of your hearing loss) effortlessly understand verbal messages. Don't you often fill in the last part of people's conversations before they finish? This is the kind of predictability I mean. If you're not listening to your native language, then you will have more difficulty making these predictions (as well as more difficulty understanding speech in noise or other difficult listening situations).

## Topic Restrictions

The ability to speechread improves when you can reduce the conversational possibilities. When you go to the bank, a travel agency, a municipal office, shop in a clothing store, or talk to a co-worker regarding a particular project, the topics are likely to be limited by the context. I don't suppose you talk about certificates of deposit in the clothing store, or the weather in Italy at the bank. Basically, "topic restrictions" are another way of employing linguistic predictability.

This is not something you necessarily do consciously. However, the fact that topic restrictions do enter into almost any conversation should make it easier for you to speechread and to keep from making bad guesses. If it makes no sense at all, it probably wasn't the message! Yes, a lot of guessing does take place, and sometimes, as has happened to me, I guess wrong (with occasional embarrassment but just as often, a laugh for everybody). Still, I would rather guess and keep the conversation going than give up.

## It's the Message Not the Medium

When you're engaged in a conversation, don't focus on speechreading particular sounds or words. Instead, attend to the message—the meaning of what the other person is trying to convey. If you consciously try to analyze the minuscule, rapid, and fleeting movements of the lips, you're going to be three sentences behind before you figure out the missing sounds or words—if you ever do. Many books on speechreading spend an inordinate amount of time describing how the different sounds of speech are made. Speechreading successfully, however, does not require you to identify all the sounds a person forms on his or her lips. What it means is that you're able to comprehend what the person is saying.

Listen to the message rather than focusing on how the different sounds appear on the lips. Because so many of the sounds of speech are either invisible or are formed exactly the same way as other sounds, even the most skilled speechreader cannot identify all of them. What they do, and what you must do, is use your knowledge of the language and your awareness of topic restrictions to fill in the gaps. By focusing on the message rather than specific movements, you'll find that subsequent sentences may clarify words that you may have missed.

## Hearing

One crucial principle in speechreading is the necessity for you to use your residual hearing as well as you can. Now, this seems like a contradiction! If we're talking about speechreading, why bring up hearing? Well, how often are you talking to someone while you're not wearing your hearing aids? Maybe late at night or early in the morning, but at most other times you're likely to be wearing them. And why would you not wear them if you know they help you? Normally, then, when conversing with other people, you're going to depend on both speechreading and hearing. And that's fine. Because your goal is to understand speech as well as you can, you should use whatever cues are available to help you realize this goal.

As I mentioned earlier, many of the sounds in English are completely invisible on the lips. For example, look in the mirror while saying the word "key." It can be said with no movement at all. This is the kind of word that requires context in order to understand.

For example, to the teenager in the house, "No you can't have the _____to the car!" Context is the only way the word can be understood. Now, while you're still in front of the mirror, silently say the words /pan/, /ban/, and /man/. They all look alike, don't they? This is where hearing comes in. Fortunately, it's relatively easy to hear the difference between the /b/, /p/, and /m/ sounds, since /b/ is voiced, /p/ is voiceless and /m/ is a nasal sound (also voiced).

In other words, much of what you can't see, you can hear. This is an important principle. It turns out that there are many speech sounds that are very difficult to tell apart visually, and yet are relatively easy to distinguish through hearing (i.e., while the /t/, /d/, and /n/ sounds look identical, they can be differentiated through hearing). Conversely, other sounds that are difficult to hear (like /s/, /f/, /t/, and /th/) are relatively easy to speechread. So, what we find is that vision and audition provide complementary information. What is lacking or difficult to perceive in one modality can often be picked up in the other. Therefore, depending only on speechreading, or only on hearing, limits your ability to communicate.

In real-life situations, there are always going to be variations in how well you can see and hear someone talking. Noise will tend to mask out many speech sounds and reduce the amount of information you get through hearing. This forces you to depend more on visual cues in order to understand a spoken message. But because the loudness and type of noise constantly vary, these changes will cause your ability to understand speech to vary as well. In some situations you may have to rely almost entirely on vision to understand speech, while in other situations, you may be able to understand even without looking at the speaker.

Therefore, you have to be prepared for an unpredictable

amount of hearing information due to varying noise backgrounds, as well as unpredictable visual cues. By using both vision and audition as much as possible, and any other sources of information, *most* hard of hearing people can comprehend *most* of what *most* people say in *most* situations. I'm qualifying because there will inevitably be times when you miss part or almost all of a conversation. This will happen. What I'm suggesting is that you think positively. Think of the occasions you can understand rather than the times you can't. That is, the glass is half full, not half empty!

## Practice Procedures

There have been hundreds of books and articles purporting to teach people how to speechread, often extolling some specific theory and providing lots of practice material. Personally, I find the practice material more helpful than the theories. Practice will help improve just about any skill. I personally had experienced the benefits of speechreading practice several years ago. For about a month I could not use my hearing aids because of an infection in both ear canals. All I could depend upon was speechreading (with an 85-95 dB loss in both ears, without hearing aids I'm functionally deaf).

Ordinarily, I'm a very poor speechreader. After several weeks of trying to communicate without hearing, mainly with my wife, I found my ability to speechread her noticeably improving. I still couldn't carry on an extended conversation by speechreading alone, but at least in context I was able to carry on abbreviated conversations. (We did cheat once in a while and use finger spelling to clarify difficult words!)

So, it's very possible that speechreading practice, with and without sound, wherever and with whomever you do it, is going to help you improve your understanding of spoken messages. In addition to the informal practice you get every day when you talk to people (and don't underestimate the value of these experiences!) formal training activities can also help. One creative such exercise, termed tracking procedures, is practiced "live," with a communication partner. Don't be discouraged by the professional jargon. These are basically exercises that require you to comprehend segments of speech before proceeding to subsequent segments. In other words, you're required to "track" through a conversation in a sequential manner. The tracking exercises can be structured so that they incorporate speechreading, auditory training, as well as communication repair strategies. Let me explain how this works.

You are sitting across from your conversational partner. The room is well lit and you're relaxed. (It's going to be fun!) This person has selected a paragraph as practice material; it can be from the newspaper, from a magazine article or book, or specific material related to one's vocation or interests. Whatever material is selected, it's important that the sentences follow each other in some kind of logical sequence. You should be informed of the general content or topic of the paragraph, as would be the case in real life.

Now, while using a soft voice and normal, not exaggerated lip movements (adding noise via television or radio will enhance the realism of the exercise), your partner should read the first sentence of the paragraph to you. Did you get it all? Did you get any of it? Your job is to repeat whatever you understood of the sentence, guessing when you're not sure. You probably made some errors but also got some words correct.

If you missed any part of the sentence, the first step is for your partner to repeat the whole sentence again, verbatim. You may or may not get it all this time. If not, what your partner has to do is emphasize the parts you missed, increasing the duration, exaggerating the pronunciation, and so forth.

For example, "Did you remember to shut off the WATER when you left the house?"

Your partner keeps doing this until you get the entire sentence correct. At the beginning of the paragraph, to get the process going, you may need a few more cues. If you repeatedly miss a part of the sentence, despite the extra emphasis, your partner should give you extra hints.

For example, "The word begins with an /s/ sound," or "It's the name of a country in Europe." Paraphrasing the sentence before going back to the original version also can help. In this exercise (unlike a later one), it is the partner who has to determine the correct "communication repair" strategies.

The point is for you to be able to repeat the sentence correctly, using whatever clues the partner provides, including raised voice or writing the words down as last resorts. Then your partner should repeat the sentence, even though you now know it, but this time followed by the second sentence—the one you don't yet know. The more sentences you comprehend in a paragraph, the more the internal linguistic cues will help you understand subsequent sentences. The more practice you get, the quicker you'll be going through the process. This is a wonderful exercise for teaching concentration and identifying specific sounds and words that give you the most difficulty.

## Practicing "Communication Repair" Strategies

In this exercise, <u>you</u> take the responsibility for "repairing" the broken communication during the tracking exercise. What has broken down, of course, is the communication exchange. You didn't quite get the entire intended message. When you don't understand, the person you're talking to doesn't really know why or what he or she can do to correct the situation. But you should know what aspect of a person's speech made it difficult for you to understand, and you can advise your conversational partner how to communicate more effectively with you. The rationale is simple. In real life conversation, asking "what?" or "huh?" when you don't understand doesn't often help very much. Mostly what people will do when they hear these expressions is to simply say the whole thing over and over again, maybe just as softly, quickly, or poorly articulated.

In this exercise, your task is to try to figure out why you missed what you did, and then to ask your partner to make specific modifications in his or her speech. Maybe you don't need the entire sentence repeated; maybe all you didn't get was the last word. So you ask the person to repeat only the portion you missed. Or maybe your partner looked down while talking, slurred a particular word, or talked too fast. With a creative collaborator, you can simulate many real-life situations. Your goal is to practice "communication repair" strategies enough so that you can utilize them in everyday life. Like asking a ticket agent at an airport to look at you when talking, or to talk a little louder, slower, and so forth. When you help the person you're talking with to be a more effective communicator with you, you're applying the three themes I spoke about earlier: you're acknowledging your hearing loss, being assertive about your communication needs, and placing equal responsibility for the communication exchange on the person with whom you're talking.

## Listening Practice (Auditory Training)

If we've learned anything in audiology in the past 50 years, it's that the hard of hearing person's perception of speech is not immutable. This has been dramatically illustrated to us in recent years by deaf people who have received cochlear implants (see Chapter 8 Q&A #8). People initially report some strange auditory sensations that they're unable to identify or use. After a while, however, learning takes place. The brain "links up" to the acoustic environment and strange sounds become identifiable. While new users of hearing aids may not experience anything quite so dramatic, improvements in speech perception do take place, sometimes quite rapidly and sometimes slowly. Focused listening practice can help accelerate this process as well as stimulate the maximum use of a person's residual hearing.

## With a Partner

Adaptations of the previously described tracking procedure can serve as helpful "auditory training" procedures. In the auditory version, your partner reads the material for you to repeat while his or her lips are covered (no visual cues). For most people, this is still going to be too easy.

Think about situations in which you have the most difficulty understanding the spoken word—in noise, right? Okay, then that's how you should structure the tracking procedures. Perhaps the best kind of "noise" to use is narration on audiocassettes, such as books on tape. This will make the listening task difficult, as it should be. Use these recordings as background sounds and not as training stimuli. In a later section, you'll see how the same recordings can be used for self-administered auditory training.

The first sentence is read. If you miss part or all of it, your partner should, in this order:

- repeat it verbatim;
- repeat it stressing the words you missed;
- if you still miss it, the sentence should be rephrased, but then go back to the original version for you to repeat;
- and finally, let you see and hear the sentence if you still missed it.

After you get the first sentence, your partner should then read the second one and continue the process throughout the entire paragraph. How long should you do this? I suggest no more than 15-30 minutes in the beginning (as long as you and your partner feel comfortable). As you well know, trying to listen under adverse circumstances can be very fatiguing.

## Self-Administered Auditory Training

Getting and keeping a cooperative partner can be quite a challenge. After a while, you may run out of cooperative partners! Remember, though, the purpose of the training procedure is not to endanger relationships, but to foster good listening habits! You can advance toward the same goal working by yourself, using available audiocassette materials that come with written scripts.

Years ago I used this technique to help convince severely hearing-impaired children and their parents and teachers that the children could use and benefit from their residual hearing. While we recorded our own material and wrote our own scripts, this is no longer necessary. There's a lot of this kind of material now—for example, books on tape, and audio tapes developed for second language learners that include a word-for-word written transcript. Check with your local bookstore or reference librarian. You'll find that there are recorded poems, short stories, formal lectures, and so on that include verbatim written transcripts. You could apply this technique, or a variation on this theme, in a few ways:

1) Most easily, all you do is listen to the tape while following the written script. This will get you used to hearing aid amplified sounds, and you may even enjoy the recording! But this doesn't present you with much of an auditory challenge.

2) A more difficult procedure would be to listen to a short paragraph and then read the script. What did you miss just by listening? Even though you may have missed some words, did the meaning come through? With some English as a Second Language (ESL) tapes, you're required to answer written questions to determine if you got the basic point. In addition to answering these questions, you can also check to see if you could comprehend all the words. Try to analyze the words you consistently missed—did they incorporate specific sound elements (like some high frequency consonants) of which you should be aware?

3) An even more challenging method is to make two copies of the same script, one for the exercise and one for verification. Ask someone else to randomly whiteout several words in each sentence in one of the copies, starting with just one word in the first sentence, then increasing the number of words eliminated in later sentences. Some of the words should be predictable from the context; others, like proper nouns, much less so. Stress the fact that you want both "easy to hear" and "hard to hear" words removed with whiteout. Your

task is to listen to this edited script and fill in the omitted words. After you listen to the entire page, you then check the original copy to determine how well you did. This process will help you "reeducate" your hearing (and brain) as you become a more focused listener.

## Carry-over

All training procedures are designed to prepare you to use these techniques in real life, outside of the practice sessions. If your training partner is someone you talk with all the time, these training activities can eventually carry over to your real-life verbal interchanges. There's some good research to indicate that extra effort on the part of the person talking does improve speech comprehension for hard of hearing people. It's called "clear speech" or what Grandma has been telling the kids to do for centuries (slow down a bit, pronounce words more clearly, speak just a little louder).

But even strangers and infrequent communication partners want you to understand what they are saying. You can be assertive in such situations without being aggressive. Put the burden on yourself. Say, for example, "Could you talk a little slower please. I have a hearing loss and it would make it easier for me to understand you."

*You must acknowledge your hearing loss in order to employ these communication strategies effectively.* Don't bluff and pretend you understand. You no doubt already know you can damage a relationship, misunderstand important instructions, and get into a heap of trouble. When it comes to important instructions, dates, names, and so forth, even if you think you understand, make sure you clarify just to be certain, by repeating what you think you heard. "Did you say two blue pills every three hours and three white pills every two hours?" It can make a difference!

# Hearing Tactics

"Hearing tactics" is a term used to describe environmental manipulations that make it easier for you to understand other people. I don't mean being sneaky or manipulative in the usual sense of the word. You're reading this book because you're having difficulty in many situations and you want to do something about it. While the procedures described earlier will help, they are not the only steps you can take to help yourself. Most likely, as you interact with other people in a number of situations, you're still going to have some difficulty hearing everything that's going on.

Using hearing tactics like military tactics means you plan ahead, marshal your resources, and engage the "enemy"—the difficult communication situation. Now, no hearing tactic, or any hearing device for that matter, will eliminate all of your hearing problems. But you can take a giant step toward reducing many of them by understanding how you can exert more control over the communicative situation. Several examples follow.

## Move closer

Always try to move closer to the person talking (but do respect their "personal space!") This is an underestimated but valuable technique. For example, in the average room, if you're eight feet from someone speaking and you can move to within four feet of this person, you've increased the sound pressure at the microphone of your hearing aids by 6 dB. If you can get within two feet of the speaker, then the increase is 12 dB — a rather significant boost. I really don't recommend getting much closer unless you have a "special relationship" with this individual!

While it's true that some modern hearing aids will compensate for distance by providing more amplification of weaker sounds, and less for the stronger sounds, they will also amplify strong and weak background noises in a similar fashion. Better comprehension results when the sound you want to hear is located close to the hearing aid microphone, whether this sound is a person talking, a television set, radio, or anything else. This will improve the speech to noise ratio (the intensity level of the speech relative to the noise) which is perhaps the most important factor underlying your speech perception.

## Quiet the Room

This is a principle that applies just about every place you go. When you walk into a restaurant for a relaxing meal and find that the young staff is playing loud music through the PA system, what do you do? Here's where assertiveness pays off. Many young people seem completely unaware that there is loud music in the background—this all seems very normal to them.

When it's explained that the music makes speech comprehension virtually impossible for the person with a hearing loss, more often than not they graciously comply with the request to lower the volume. Hopefully, after a few such requests, they may learn to appreciate the "sounds of silence." Wouldn't it be nice to have "noise-free" areas in the same way we now have "smoke-free" restaurants?

When you arrive, look or ask for the quietest table. The hostess usually knows. Don't sit in the middle of a room with parties all around you, although you can seat yourself in the center <u>of your group</u> where it's easy for you to see and hear everyone. Stay away from any extra noise-producing areas such as the kitchen, background piano music, an air conditioner or heating system. Better yet, look for places to eat that encourage private conversations; restaurants do differ in their sensitivity to noise.

Many people feel that they have to have the stereo turned on when entertaining people in their home. A gentle reminder to turn it down or even off usually suffices. In a family gathering, the youngsters may have the television set turned up while ignoring it; if it's your house, pull the plug and/or move the youngsters to another room. If it's not your house, try diplomacy or try to move your personal conversation to a quieter area in the house. Whatever house you happen to be in, make sure you have a good sight-line to all the guests. Don't sit at the end of a long couch. You won't be able to see or hear the person at the other end. If only a small group is involved, try to get some conversational "rules" established. If these people are friends, you can ask that only one person talk at a time. "Cross-conversation" presents one of the most difficult situations for people with hearing loss.

Senior centers and retirement homes, particularly those that serve meals, often present a challenging communication environment. In such places, the acoustical conditions can be improved by:

- acoustical treatment on ceilings and walls
- rugs, if possible, on the floor
- or rubber coasters on chair and table legs
- soft material, such as felt, on dining tables under the tablecloths to reduce  the clattering sounds of dishes and silverware
- sitting at a smaller (4-person) rather than larger (8-person) table during meals and other activities

## Advance Planning

Do some anticipatory planning for any activity. For example, before you attend any large-area listening situation (theater, lecture, house of worship, etc.) call ahead to see if an assistive listening device is available. These devices basically transmit the sound from its source to special receivers (FM radio, infra-red, or the telephone coil in your hearing aid). They enhance acoustical clarity of sounds that emanate from loudspeakers some distance from you.

Most such places are required to have such listening devices available, according to the Americans with Disabilities Act (ADA). Houses of worship are an exception, yet many provide such devices as a moral obligation. I personally would not attend any large area listening event without ensuring that such devices were available. Without one, I either don't know what's going on or I'm straining so hard to hear that I don't enjoy the activity or performance.

## Microphone Technique

Even if assistive listening devices are available in an auditorium, listening problems can still occur, particularly if the sound source comes from someone using a microphone. What I have observed over the years is an abysmal ignorance of proper microphone technique, even by people who should know better.

In any large area listening situation, the lack of good microphone technique is often the weakest link in the communication chain. What seems to happen is that talkers get so wrapped up in what they're saying, they forget that there's a microphone on the podium. Most of these are low-sensitivity microphones, requiring a talker to be within four to six inches of it for effective pick-up. Sometimes if it's a hand-held microphone, many people wave it around as if it were a baton or a pointer—everywhere but close to their mouth. So what do you do?

- You arrive a little earlier and remind the event organizer, the speaker or the minister, of the necessity for the speaker to stay close to the microphone while talking.
- During the talk, some speakers are going to walk away from the microphone still speaking. You ask loudly (but politely) for the speaker to move closer to the microphone. Other people in the audience will appreciate your assertiveness because of their own hearing difficulty.
- If a lapel instead of a podium microphone is available, ask that it be used and pinned close to the person's mouth.
- If there's a public question and answer period after the talk and you can't hear the questions, don't suffer in silence. Ask for the questions to be repeated before answers are given. Remember that you're probably not the only one in the audience who can't hear the questions.

In a recent hearing aid orientation group, I heard of an excellent example of how a bit of assertiveness can help many other people in the audience. One of the participants complained that he never heard the homilies prepared by the same two women in his church. Their voices were soft and they typically sat two feet or so away from the microphone. Every Sunday, he said he just sat there and waited for them to finish, not understanding a word.

His normal hearing wife then piped up and said, "I never understand them either and I don't think anyone else can!"

Before the next service, the husband asked the two women to talk right into the microphone as he was having difficulty understanding them. That Sunday, not only my client, but everyone heard the women loud and clear.

## Wrap up

In this church anecdote, we have an example of the three themes with which I began this chapter. The hard of hearing person had to *acknowledge* his hearing loss, had to *be assertive* in approaching speakers, and the *effort served the purposes of both parties* in the communication exchange. The lesson in this example is that you, as a hard of hearing person, must be more than a passive recipient of hearing "services." You have to take more control over your own listening needs. Work closely with your hearing healthcare professionals. They have information and skills that will help you.

No—magic wands are not available to "wave" away your hearing loss, but with the appropriate use of modern technology and the judicious use of appropriate communication strategies, you can go a long way in reducing the impact hearing loss is having in your life.

# APPENDIX I
# Assistive Listening Devices [ALDs]

*Assistive Listening Devices* (ALDs) describe equipment that amplifies sound and enhances your ability to hear. As a result, your hearing world becomes a more pleasant experience through less strain and frustration. If you have a hearing loss of even a mild degree, you can benefit substantially from many of these devices.

Many ALDs operate in conjunction with your hearing aids through a built-in telecoil switch, commonly identified on BTE hearing aids with a "T." On In-The-Ear models you may simply find a toggle switch that triggers the telecoil function. This allows activation of a small, harmless, electromagnetic field through which the external assistive listening device can operate with your hearing aid. While some hearing aids now have electromagnetic connections built into the circuit without you having to do anything, this is certainly the future trend in all such technology.

Most BTE hearing aids can accommodate what is called a Direct Audio Input (DAI). This system comes with a special manufacturer-designed boot (a coupler) that clips around your aid enabling you to plug into and listen to TV, radio, stereo, DVD, FM or conference system. In-The-Ear hearing aids can also utilize direct audio input if they have the optional "T" switch on them. The DAI is a wonderful advantage to you because it offers the cleanest, clearest sound reception. However, it does require that you have a "T" position on your hearing aid by means of which your target listening system is linked to your aid through an electromagnetic field. Ask your hearing care provider about how this option may work for you.

Some ALDs do not require that you even wear hearing aids in order to benefit from amplified sound such as television and some telephone amplifiers. You will find a wide variety of devices in this section that represent only a small sampling of what is actually available—from telephone and alerting products to television and signaling devices. These products will enhance your hearing ability, resulting in less stress, increased clarity and audibility.

Many of these devices can actually solve hearing problems. Something as simple as not blasting the television (by having your own remote amplifier) has solved many an argument and household disruption.

Your initial thought might be, "Why would I need these since I just purchased a top-of-the-line set of hearing aids!"

The answer is that hearing aids are designed to amplify human speech. You may derive some added benefits from them, such as hearing the car radio better, or the ticking of a clock, but they may not adequately amplify specific auditory needs such as television, or the doorbell or telephone ringing from another room. There are many alternative amplified systems designed that will nicely augment your hearing aids, allowing you to hear sounds other than speech.

To better understand the development of ALDS, it might be helpful to have some background. In the 1970s, most telephone amplification equipment was issued at no charge to accounts under American Telephone and Telegraph companies. However, since "Ma-Bel's" break-up, a tremendous flood of market possibilities opened up for new companies and products. This was a great boon to all who had hearing loss, as the rather fierce competition for this narrow market kept the prices of these products affordable.

Something you need to realize is that not all hearing care practitioners carry ALDs in their offices. This is largely due to the very narrow profit margins manufacturers and distributors allow. In a busy office, many practitioners may feel ALDs are a distraction to their primary clinical functions. Don't be dismayed. Ask your hearing care practitioner for names of companies you can directly contact. Many practitioners have giveaway catalogs in their office. You can also go on the Internet and search for *assistive listening devices*, locating company catalogs online and ordering.

Because wireless communication (such as cell phones) has come into being as a viable and important avenue of communication, this appendix will include some cell phone items that will enhance your ability to hear. However, it's worth mentioning here that cell phone designs have not really kept up with the personal needs of people with hearing loss.

Typically, you could find cell phones are not loud enough and there's too much interference with background noises. As of this writing in 2004, the FCC is moving slowly to mandate laws for hearing aid compatibility with cell phones. This means they are making strong suggestions for manufacturers to operate by in order to establish better compliance between digital cell phones and hearing aids.

In the final analysis, it may be up to you to discover what augmentative products will best serve your cell phone needs. You might find that your most optimal hearing is derived from "hands free" speaker-phone style cell phones whereby you have the advantage of hearing with both ears along with your hearing aids.

Something to keep in mind is there are a number of companies that manufacture or distribute very similar devices, particularly in the area of alarm clocks, television amplified equipment, and telephone ringer-amplified and receiver-amplified products. For example, for standard telephone receiver handsets, several items are available to clip over the earpiece of the receiver to allow you significant audio boost on incoming calls. Such "portability" offers you the convenience of carrying this in your pocket wherever you go and using it on any telephone when you travel (worldwide). Others are fixed units built into the receiver handset and are sold as a single device that replaces your current receiver. And still other products are manufactured that connect into your telephone line (wire) and provide amplification this way.

Naturally, there are a variety of prices, depending on which products you select from a particular company. With respect to prices, none are listed in this section because they change from year to year. Most products in this section are under $100; some are up to $300; and the more sophisticated amplified systems can run as high as $1000 or more.

The names of companies cited as having provided a photo courtesy of their organization is done to allow hearing healthcare professionals who might not be familiar with these devices and companies to have an opportunity to contact them and establish an in-house corner of their office to display some of them. You can also find ALD distributors on the Internet.

Finally, something of importance you should know is the warranty coverage you have on particular products. For example, some items carry only a one-year warranty while others have five years. Some companies have no fees for returns while others may charge you a "restocking fee." Make these inquiries *before you make the purchase*.

Good luck!

DISCLAIMER: Listing of products should in no way be construed as an endorsement of any company, product or device by the Publisher, the Editor or any contributing authors of this book. Any purchases of these devices are a responsibility between you and the company from which you make the purchase. Also, bear in mind that these products were not rated in any way. That is, it cannot be assumed that a particular product listed here is any better or worse than a comparable item available elsewhere.

# Alerting Devices

### Bed Shaker
is a device that can be connected to an alarm clock to awaken you by fitting under and vibrating your bed or pillow. It is an excellent system for especially heavy sleepers, and gives you the most assurance of waking up on time.

[Photo Courtesy of
General Technologies]

## Vibrating Wristwatch

is a multi-purpose watch that can be preset to a specific time to vibrate and remind you to take your medication, attend a meeting, make a phone call, and so forth. It comes with an audio alarm setting as well. Additional features include a

99-hour stop watch function, 99-hour countdown timer with count repeat mode, and LCD displays day of week and month. It uses a long life lithium battery, and comes with a one-year warranty.

[Photo Courtesy of LS&S, LLC]

## Sonic Alert Wireless Doorbell/Telephone Signaler

plugs into any modular telephone jack and does not draw any phone line power that could prevent some phones from ringing. It has a selectable number of flashes to alert you, works at home with all intercom systems, flash codes can be set at different rates to identify back door, front door, etc., and has built-in chimes for hearing members of the family.

[Photo Courtesy of Sound Clarity, Inc.]

## Gentex 710-CSW Smoke Detector

is a photoelectric single station smoke detector designed to give reliable early warning of the presence of smoke where both audible and visual alarms are required. (This model is hard-wired so you would need an electrician to hook it up.) Standard features include 177 candela rating (very bright strobe light); solid state 90 dB horn (very loud); full function test switch (easy for you to test that it is working); flashes 60 times per minute; quick-disconnect wiring harness; mounting hardware for wall; tandem connection up to 6 detectors per system; AC-powered also available; one year warranty.

[Photo Courtesy of Harris Communications, Inc.]

## Sonic Boom Alarm Clock

is a unique clock that can wake up even heavy sleepers. When the alarm goes off, you can select to wake up to any combination of loud pulsating audio alarm, flashing lights, or shaking bed (vibrator sold separately). The vibrator can produce steady or pulsating vibration pattern for maximum effectiveness. There is a test button on the unit to explore which combination of flashing lights, shaking bed or loud pulsating audio alarm will work best for you.

[Photo Courtesy of Sound Clarity, Inc.]

# Enhanced Listening Systems

## Sound Wizard II

is a complete communication system. It utilizes either a directional microphone (for one-to-one conversation in noise) or omni-directional microphones (for groups). Dual headset jacks allow two people simultaneous use with good clarity in noise. The powerful amplifier and tone control allows you to hear better in many situations. It can be connected to your existing telephone and is compatible with headsets, earbuds, neckloops, silhouettes, and external speakers for use in movie theaters and public facilities. Two AA batteries included (for 200 hours of life), with a five-year warranty.

[Photo Courtesy of Hitec Group International, Inc.]

## PocketTalker Pro

is an easy-to-use, portable, battery-operated amplifier that can improve your ability to communicate in difficult listening situations. It utilizes a sensitive directional microphone that can be placed close to the sound source to minimize background noise. It comes with 2 AA batteries that provide up to 100 hours of use. Included in the package is a microphone extension cord for TV listening with optional links for use with hearing aids, telephones and neckloops. It comes with a five-year warranty.

[Photo Courtesy of Adco Hearing Products, Inc.]

228

## Room Amplification System

amplifies a person's voice in a room with other hard-of-hearing people if you need more power than your hearing aids provide. It distributes sounds equally throughout the room by means of 4 speakers with hanging brackets that can be used in different speaker arrays. A wireless microphone allows for ease of movement throughout the room for the primary person speaking (such as a teacher), and the two-channel amplifier makes team teaching easy. Among a number of items, the system includes a rechargeable battery; an amplifier; wireless transmitter and receiver; and one neckloop.

[Photo Courtesy of Harris Communications, Inc.]

# FM, Infrared and Loop Systems

### Nady 351 VR Personal (Wireless) FM System

gives you clear, professional sounding high fidelity audio without distracting ambient noise from the environment and is made for commercial video sound recording. The operating range is up to 200' even in the most adverse conditions, and up to 500' line-of-sight. It is available in 5 different frequencies and can be effectively used in multiple system set-ups.

[Photo Courtesy of General Technologies]

229

## Personal FM System "Hearing Helper"

broadcasts the speaker's voice directly to the ears of individual listeners. While the person speaking wears a compact transmitter and microphone, listeners use portable receivers and earphones to hear the presentation clearly and easily,

even from the back of the room. It helps listeners overcome background noise, reverberation, and distance from the speaker in classrooms and small groups, thus maximizing their ability to hear and understand. It operates on 2 AA batteries and includes a transmitter and portable receiver.

[Photo Courtesy of Adco
Hearing Products, Inc.]

## Personal FM (PPA 375) Public Address System

features the new T35 high performance transmitter; powerful microprocessor; sleek digital display; and easy-to-use menu controls. The T35 configures itself to the appropriate setting, taking the guesswork out of complicated audio installation. Operating up to 1000 feet, the T35 is ideal for auditoriums,

theaters, or other large venues where excellent coverage area is essential. The system includes 4 impact-resistant R35 single-channel receivers. The R35 receiver will operate up to 80 hours for long-lasting performance!

[Photo Courtesy of Adco
Hearing Products, Inc.]

230

## ICON-TR60 Infrared Conference Emitter

is an advanced, wireless, self-contained infrared emitter combining portability with ease of use. Great for conference and boardroom meetings, group therapy, jury deliberation rooms, or situations around tables where it's difficult to hear.

When multiple microphones are used, the one nearest the person speaking sets the level of volume for the others, which has the effect of reducing background noise whenever anyone speaks into any microphones.

[Photo Courtesy of Harris Communications, Inc.]

# Telephone Devices

## The Teletalker

is designed to improve speech understanding over the telephone. It combines a powerful amplifier with a sophisticated signal processing circuit to enhance phone signal quality. To enhance or amplify a call, press the amplify button, then adjust the volume and enhancement controls for maximum comfort and clarity. When you hang up, it automatically returns to normal operation, protecting others from unintended amplification. The phone lets you boost high

[Photo Courtesy of Adco Hearing Products, Inc.]

frequencies as needed to emphasize speech sounds that contribute to maximum understanding. The anti-feedback circuit permits full use of amplification without problems of howling, feedback or distortion. It can be used with a telecoil–equipped hearing aid coupled with the handset speaker, and comes with a five–year warranty.

231

## Walker Clarity High Frequency Telephone Amplifier

is designed to help people with high frequency hearing loss hear words clearer, not just louder. It amplifies incoming calls up to 25+ dB when the boost button is activated. Also, it is

compatible with standard and electronic phones, single or multi-lines, and has a low battery indicator. It cannot be used with dial-in handset receivers. It requires 2 AAA batteries (not included) and comes with a one-year warranty.

[Photo Courtesy of
LS&S, LLC]

## V-Tech 2400-A Cordless Amplified Phone

utilizes 2.4 GHz digital transmission, providing outstanding operating range while maintaining clarity for people with hearing loss who need help in noisy situations. Incoming voices are amplified up to 30 dB. The phone is hearing aid compatible with a powerful t-coil built into the handset. The

phone also has a 3.5mm amplified stereo jack for an optional neckloop and a 2.5mm non-amplified jack for an optional telephone headset. It has 50 number caller ID; call waiting; multi-level volume control; time/date; hands-free belt clip; low battery and out-of-range indicators; and a one-year warranty.

[Photo Courtesy of Hitec
Group International, Inc.]

## HA-40 In-Line Telephone Amplifier

is a powerful in-line amplifier with a tone selector, allowing words to be heard loud and clear. A separate boost feature blocks out background noise and feedback for maximum amplification. To achieve the full 40 dB of amplification, you must hold down the "BOOST" button while listening and then release the button when talking. Without the "BOOST" feature

activated, the unit operates as a powerful 30 dB amplifier with the additional 10 dB of assistance available only when needed. It will not work on phones where the dial pad is in the handset, or on cordless phones. This item includes batteries, and comes with a manufacturer's one-year warranty.

[Photo Courtesy of Hitec Group International, Inc.]

## PA 25 Portable Telephone Amplifier

increases volume of incoming voices up to 25 dB, easily straps to most any telephone handset style, ideal to use with payphones, cordless or cellular telephones, lightweight and extremely portable, and hearing aid compatible. It comes with 2 AAA batteries, a carrying case, and a six-month manufacturer's warranty.

[Photo Courtesy of Sound Clarity, Inc.]

233

## Walker Clarity Extra Loud Telephone Ringer

allows you to hear the telephone ring up to 95 dB. A red light indicator also alerts you to incoming calls. It comes with a built-in surge protector, requires no batteries or AC hook-up, is compatible with all analog phone systems, and requires no special jacks. It carries a one-year warranty.

[Photo Courtesy of
LS&S, LLC]

## Ringer Audible Telephone Signaler TR100

alerts you to your telephone ringing by automatically sounding a loud adjustable horn. It can flash lights and sound horns in other rooms by use of remote receivers. It has adjustable volume and tone controls and requires no batteries (powered by the telephone line). It comes with a five-year factory warranty.

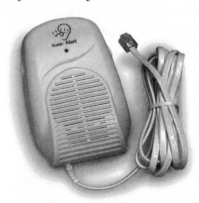

[Photo Courtesy of Adco
Hearing Products, Inc.]

## Earware Cell Phone "Hands-Free" Amplifier

plugs into the earphone jack on a cell phone and offers two selectable levels of audio boost with improved listening in background noise. It's ideal for molded earpieces or special headsets that require more volume to oversome the increased air space between the transducer and the eardrum.

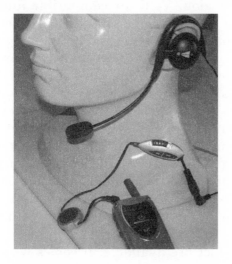

[Photo Courtesy of Harris Communications, Inc.]

## Cell-U-Hear Listening Pads

are spongy oval pads that adhere to any cell phone handset enabling improved volume and comfort between your cell phone and your hearing aid. Through its design, it directs sound into the hearing aid for an increase in volume without feedback. The set includes two different ring sizes.

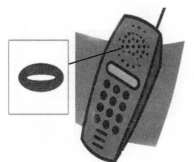

[Photo Courtesy of Harris Communications, Inc.]

# Television

## DirectEar 100 Personal Listening System

is an infrared wireless system that provides the listener with complete, private and substantial audio amplification (up to 124 dB SPL) of the television, VCR, or compatible audio source, independent of the volume on the set itself. Therefore, it doesn't interfere with other people viewing or listening in the same room. It's also compatible with many infrared amplifying systems in movie theaters and other facilities. In fact, many theaters will allow you to bring the headset with you. The system comes with one rechargeable battery. However, a second rechargeable battery is recommended so that you won't be inconvenienced from listening due to battery recharge time. Operating time is about 10 hours; recharge time is about 14 hours (typically overnight if you use only one battery). The earphone is lightweight. Among several optional accessories, an external microphone for TVs with no audio output capability, and induction neckloop systems compatible with this product are available. It comes with a two-year warranty.

## DirectEar 250 Personal Listening System

is quite similar to the system 100 but it cannot be used in movie theaters. One advantage over the 100 system is that the transmitter can charge two batteries at the same time. However, operating time is less, about 6 hours per rechargeable battery.

[Photo Courtesy of Hitec
Group International, Inc.]

# APPENDIX II
# Professional Resources

There are a number of service organizations that offer information to consumers with hearing loss. Some offer leaflets or brochures and others offer referral services. Some do not have any current consumer services but are cited here to allow you to write them regarding any questions you might have about a particular problem that you feel might best be addressed by them. Hopefully, this will give you the opportunity to expand your present search.

In the organization listings, in addition to telephone and fax, you should note that all telephone contacts are *voice* unless otherwise specified as TTY (for deaf callers). If you have access to the Internet, you can reach many groups directly through their websites or E-mails. Listings in this section without E-mails can generally be found by directly visiting an organization's website.

In the text that follows, background, company function, and their publications are included. If you're writing a request for information, you're encouraged to enclose a self-addressed, stamped (business-size) envelope, large enough to accommodate the requested literature. If you are telephoning, keep in mind that many of these offices are in the east (EST zone) and some close earlier than 5:00 p.m.

## Academy of Dispensing Audiologists

3008 Millwood Avenue, Columbia, SC 29205
Toll Free: (800) 445-8629 Fax: (803) 765-0860
E-mail: info@audiologist.org   Website: www.audiologist.org

Founded in 1977, the Academy supports audiologists who dispense hearing aids. They must have achieved a graduate degree in the field, and in the near future, the only acceptable degree for membership qualification will be a doctorate. The Academy holds an annual meeting in the fall, and during the year smaller regional meetings and seminars providing information regarding all aspects of hearing aid dispensing. *Feedback* is their quarterly magazine for professionals that addresses topics and current issues pertinent to audiologists dispensing hearing aids. As of this writing, they are not staffed for consumer outreach although they offer consumer brochures and professional referrals to a practitioner in your local area.

# Alexander Graham Bell Association for the Deaf

3417 Volta Place NW, Washington, D.C. 20007-2770
Tel: (202) 337-5220    TTY: (202) 337-5221    Fax: (202) 337-8314
Website: www.agbell.org

The Association is a nonprofit organization comprised of individuals who are hearing impaired, and their parents, professionals, and others. The organization's mission is to empower those with loss of hearing to function independently by promoting universal rights and optimal opportunities. They provide scholarships and awards to students and their families. They publish two periodicals, one research based, the other consumer oriented. There are over 20 chapters in North America, all of which provide leaflets on a range of problems affecting those suffering with hearing loss.

# American Academy of Audiology

11730 Plaza America Drive, Suite 300 Reston, VA 20190
Toll Free: (800) 222-2336    Tel: (703) 790-8466    Fax: (703) 790-8631
E-mail: info@audiology.org    Website: www.audiology.org

The Academy is a professional membership organization of audiologists. They have two primary journal publications. *Audiology Today* is a magazine format that deals with a wide variety of topics including clinical activities and hearing research. The *Journal of the American Academy of Audiology* publishes scientific papers of a scholarly nature. The Academy provide audiologists with current practice information and ongoing research knowledge. Their annual national meeting allows clinicians and scientists a forum for exchange and education in the areas of hearing science and hearing aids. They are not staffed for consumer outreach although they offer consumer brochures and professional referrals.

# American Academy of Otolaryngology— Head and Neck Surgery, Inc.

One Prince Street, Alexandria, Va 22314
Tel: (703) 836-4444    TTY: (703) 519-1585    Fax (703) 683-5100
Website: www.entnet.org

Founded in 1896 as a medical specialty society, they now have 11,000 physician members  who provide medical care and surgery for disorders of the ears, nose, throat, head and neck regions. The primary missions of the Academy are to provide continuing medical education and to represent the interests of the specialty in governmental areas. The Academy publishes about a dozen patient education leaflets on various aspects of hearing loss which are available to the public at no charge. They also will refer you to a local practitioner if you specifically request the "Physicians List."

## American Speech-Language-Hearing Association

10801 Rockville Pike, Rockville, Maryland 20852
Toll Free: (800) 638-8255  Tel: (301) 897-5700  Fax: (301) 571-0457
E-mail: actioncenterwebsite.org    Website: www.asha.org

ASHA is a national professional and scientific association for audiologists and speech-language pathologists. Their mission is to ensure that all people with speech, language or hearing disorders have access to quality services to help them communicate more effectively. They inform the public about communicative disorders through published materials available by request. They can also provide professional referrals.

## American Tinnitus Association

P.O. Box 5, Portland, OR 97207
Toll Free: (800) 634 8978  Tel: (503) 248-9985  Fax: (503) 248-0024
E-mail:tinnitus@ata.otg    Website: www.ata.org

This nonprofit organization is dedicated to the support of scientific research leading to a better understanding of tinnitus. They provide pamphlets of information on tinnitus and publish a consumer-based quarterly magazine (by subscription) discussing various issues pertaining to understanding this problem.

## The Audiology Awareness Campaign

822 Montgomery Avenue, Suite 318, Narberth, PA 19072
Toll Free: (800) 445-8629    Toll Free (for free literature): (888) 833-3277
www.audiologyawarness.com

AAC was organized by five professional audiology organizations with one goal in mind—helping people with hearing loss. At the website you can take an online "hearing test," read patient-friendly brochures on hearing loss and hearing aids, find out what an audiologist is, post a question on the "Question and Answer" board, and even find an audiologist in your area who can further answer your questions and offer you help. Their web page is one part of the informational process. AAC distributes educational information through various aspects of national media such as newspapers, magazines and television.

## Better Hearing Institute

515 King St., Suite 420, Alexandria, VA 22314
Toll Free:(888) 432-7435 Tel: (703) 684-3391 Fax: (703) 684-6048
E-mail:mail@betterhearing.org    Website: www.betterhearing.org

BHI, a nonprofit educational organization, implements public information programs on hearing loss and available hearing solutions for millions with uncorrected hearing loss. The Institute promotes awareness of hearing loss and help through television, radio, and print media public service messages that typically feature well known celebrities who themselves suffer from impaired hearing. You may contact them for literature on hearing loss or specific subjects such as tinnitus, hearing aids, children's ear conditions, lists of local hearing professionals, and assistive listening devices.

## The Deafness Research Foundation

1050 17th Street, NW, Suite 701, Washington, DC 20036
Tel: (202) 289-5850    Fax: (202) 293-1805
Website: www.drf.org

Founded in 1958, DFR is a leading source of private funding for basic and clinical research in hearing science. The DRF is committed to making lifelong hearing health a national priority by funding research and implementing education projects in both the government and private sectors. They annually award grants to promising young researchers and established researchers to explore new avenues of hearing science, having awarded over $21 million through more than 1,750 research grants. This seed money has led to dramatic innovations that increase options for those living with hearing loss, as well as protect those at risk. These innovations include the diagnosis and treatment of otitis media (middle ear infections), the cochlear implant, implantable hearing aids, breakthroughs in molecular biology and hair cell regeneration.

# Education and Auditory Research Foundation

1817 Patterson St., Nashville, TN 37203
Toll Free: (800) 545-4327 Tel: (615) 627-2724  Fax: (615) 627-2728
E-mail: ear@earfoundation.org     Website: www.earfoundation.org

One of the mission's of the EAR Foundation is to administer education about Meniere's disease through their "Meniere's Network." This is a national network of people who share coping strategies regarding this condition. EAR publishes a few in-depth management brochures which provide education on Meniere's, including dietary management. They also publish a Newsletter, *Steady*, covering many aspects of the problems with Meniere's along with coping strategies. They also publish a Newsletter, *Otoscope*, that addresses problems more associated with hearing loss. They have a *Young Ears* focus on children who suffer from hearing loss, with a helpful section on early detection (what you can expect in normal developmental sounds in the first 24 months of your infant).

# Hearing Education and Awareness for Rockers [HEAR] San Francisco Center on Deafness

P.O. Box 460847, San Francisco, CA 94146
Tel: (415) 409-3277 24 Hr Hotline: (415) 773-9590 Fax: (415) 409-5683
E-mail:hear@hearnet.com     Website: www.hearnet.com

HEAR is a nonprofit public-benefit health organization founded in 1988 by Kathy Peck and Flash Gordon, M.D. They inspired large numbers of musicians and medically concerned physicians, music lovers and other music professionals to participate with them. Their advisory board consists of some members—now hearing impaired—from a variety of the loudest 1960's Rock 'n Roll bands. The organization is dedicated to raising consumer awareness about the risks of noise, and its damaging effects on hearing. They achieve this through television and radio public service messages featuring well known artists. Also, they have outreach programs which distribute hearing information and earplugs at music concerts/ conferences, health fairs and community events. You may contact them for a free leaflet about noise risks. They've also produced a video on this subject for use in schools.

# Hearing Health Magazine

Voice International Publications, Inc.,
P.O. Drawer V, Ingleside, TX 78362-0500
Tel/TTY: (361) 776-7240   Fax: (361) 776-3278
E-mail:ears2u@hearinghealthmag.com
Website: www.hearinghealthmag.com

Owned by the Deafness Research Foundation, Hearing Health's mission is to educate (and entertain) people who are deaf and hard of hearing. Each quarterly issue includes articles ranging from technological research and development, to humor, human success stories, and philosophical discussions about topics like education, cochlear implants, modes of communication, and living without hearing. Contact them for a complimentary current magazine.

# International Hearing Society

16880 Middlebelt Rd., Suite 4, Livonia, MI 48154
Toll Free: (800) 521-5247 Tel: (734) 522-7200 Fax (734) 522-0200
Website: www.ihsinfo.org

The IHS began in 1951 as the primary organization for hearing aid dispensers. They conduct programs of competence qualification and training, and offer continuing education courses in the selection, fitting, counseling, and dispensing of hearing instruments. They also publish an industry magazine, the *Audecibel*, articles of which cover issues pertaining to hearing loss and hearing aid electronics, performance and use. A charitable subgroup of the IHS is the Hearing Aid Foundation which specifically focuses on education of the consumer. For a dispenser in your area, you may contact them.

# National Institute on Aging - Information Center

P.O. Box 8057, Gaithersburg, MD 20898-8057
Toll Free: (800) 222-2225   TTY: (800) 222-4225   Fax (301) 589-3014
E-mail: niaicjbs1.com   www.nih.gov/nia.

The NIA is responsible for the conduct and support of biomedical, social, and behavioral research, training, health information dissemination, and other programs with respect to the aging process and the diseases and other special problems and needs of the aged. They publish a number of detailed leaflets covering such broad areas as aging, grants, diseases, prevention, medical care, medications, planning for later years, and safety.

242

# National Institute on Deafness and Other Communication Disorders [NIDCD] - Information Clearinghouse

1 Communication Avenue, Bethesda, MD 20892-3456
Tel: (800) 241-1044    TTY: (800) 241-1055    Fax (301) 770-8977
E-mail:nidcdinfo@nidcd.nih.gov    Website: www.nidcd.nih.gov

This is a branch of the U.S. Government's National Institutes of Health. They are an information clearinghouse that provides information on hearing, balance, smell, taste, voice, speech and language disorders. They collect and disseminate information; maintain a computerized database; and develop and distribute publications that include fact sheets, bibliographies, information packets and directories of information resources. The Clearinghouse also publishes a biannual newsletter.

## Self Help for Hard of Hearing People, Inc.

7910 Woodmont Avenue, Suite 1200, Bethesda, MD 20814
Tel: (301) 657-2248    TTY: (301) 657-2249    Fax (301) 913-9413
E-mail:national@shhh.org    Website: www.shhh.org

SHHH seeks to provide information and educational outreach to people with hearing loss. Founded in 1979, their membership of 12,000 is the largest consumer organization in the world. Their extensive volunteer-based network includes 250 groups and chapters which reach an additional 9,500 hard of hearing people, their family members, friends, and others. They are governed by a 21-member volunteer board of trustees. SHHH provides its educational offerings in a number of ways, including written materials such as the bimonthly magazine, *Hearing Loss: The Journal of Self Help for Hard of Hearing People*, and other publications and videos; annual conventions for consumers that exceeds 1,000 attendees; encouragement and participation in research activities with the government, private sector, and other nonprofit organizations; and the provision of guidance to national, state and local policy makers and private companies on a wide range of topics affecting people with hearing loss.

# INDEX

## A

244

removing, 161-162
responsibility for, 161
**change,** 7, 12, 20
**cochlear implants,** 145-147
**communication strategies,**
200-221
acknowledgement, 201
assertiveness, 202
repair, 214
tenacity, 203

# D

**Deafness Research**
**Foundation,** 240
**diabetes,** 55
**dizziness** (see *Meniere's*
*Disease*), 140-144, 145
**drainage from ear,** 144
**dysequilibrium,** 141

# E

**ear pain,** 145
**earwax** (see *cerumen*)
**Education and Auditory**
**Research Foundation,** 241
**ego,** 5
**emotions of losing hearing,**
3-22 (also see *feelings*)
**Eustachian tubes,** 185-186
**exercise and hearing,** 132
**expectations,** 20-21

# F

**family doctor** (see *physicians*)
**feedback** (see *hearing aids*)
**feelings of,**
acceptance, 22
anger, 14, 16, 63, 74, 114

anxiety, 14-15, 71, 74-75,
112, 114
arrogance, 71
avoidance, 14
social activities, 63
confusion, 14, 71
defeat, 17-18
defense, 4
depression, 14-15, 20, 63, 70,
74-75, 112, 114
discontentment, 14, 70
discouragement, 5
disorientation, 4, 14, 71
embarrassment, 19, 63, 87
extroversion, 114
fatigue, 63
fear, 14
frustration, 14, 17-18, 74,
114
handicap, 87, 127
inadequacy, 4
inattention, 71
incompetence, 4
independence, 71
inferiority, 14
insecurity, 14, 70, 112
instability, 14, 70
intolerance to social
interaction, 13
irritability, 14, 63
isolation, 14-15, 63, 75, 112
loneliness, 63
looking older with hearing
aids, 127
negativism, 63, 70
nervousness, 14, 70, 87
paranoia, 14, 71, 74, 114
phobias, 14, 71, 74-75, 114
poor-
concentration, 14, 71

otoscopic exam, 39
ototoxic medications, 132

# P

physicians, 37, 76, 125-127, 144
pistols, 187
prejudices (see *hearing aids* and *hearing loss*)
professional help, seeking, 23-42
professional resources, 237-243

# Q

quality of life, 62-77

# R

rifles, 187

# S

Self Help for Hard of Hearing People, Inc., 243
sensory deprivation, 12-13
sensory stimulation, 13
shotguns, 187
significant others (also see *spouses*), 20-21, 31, 179-180
speechreading, 206-214
  familiarity with the language, 209
  principles of, 207-214
  restricting lip movements, 208-209
  topic restrictions, 209-210
  visibility of, 207-208
speech recognition, 14
spouses (also see *significant other*), 20-21

# T

telecoils (see *hearing aids*)
telephone use (see *hearing aids*)
television,
  assistive listening, 148
  too loud, 6
tinnitus, 123

# U

U.S. Surgeon General, 132

# V

vents (see *hearing aids*)
vertigo, 140-144
vestibular compensation, 141
vestibular neuritis, 141
Veterans Administration, 114
vitamins and hearing, 135

# Y

yellow pages, 37